Language Planning and Policy in Europe, Vol.1

LANGUAGE PLANNING AND POLICY
Series Editors: A/Professor Richard B. Baldauf Jr., *University of Queensland, Brisbane, Australia*
Professor Robert B. Kaplan, *University of Southern California, USA*

Other Books in the Series
Language Planning and Policy in Africa, Vol.1: Botswana, Malawi, Mozambique and South Africa
    Richard B. Baldauf Jr. and Robert B. Kaplan (eds)

Other Books of Interest
Identity, Insecurity and Image: France and Language
    Dennis Ager
Community and Communication: The Role of Language in Nation State Building and European Integration
    Sue Wright
Can Threatened Languages be Saved?
    Joshua Fishman (ed.)
Language and Society in a Changing Italy
    Arturo Tosi
Language Planning From Practice to Theory
    Robert B. Kaplan and Richard B. Baldauf Jr. (eds)
The Other Languages of Europe
    Guus Extra and Durk Gorter (eds)
Motivation in Language Planning and Language Policy
    Dennis Ager
Multilingualism in Spain
    M. Teresa Turell (ed.)
Beyond Boundaries: Language and Identity in Contemporary Europe
    Paul Gubbins and Mike Holt (eds)
Ideology and Image: Britain and Language
    Dennis Ager
Where East Looks West: Success in English in Goa and on the Konkan Coast
    Dennis Kurzon
English in Africa: After the Cold War
    Alamin M. Mazrui
Politeness in Europe
    Leo Hickey and Miranda Stewart (eds)
Language in Jewish Society: Towards a New Understanding
    John Myhill
Maintaining a Minority Language
    John Gibbons and Elizabeth Ramirez
Urban Multilingualism in Europe
    Guus Extra and Kutlay Yagmur (eds)
Cultural and Linguistic Policy Abroad: The Italian Experience
    Mariella Totaro-Genevois
Language Decline and Death in Africa: Causes, Consequences and Challenges
    Herman M. Batibo

For more details of these or any other of our publications, please contact:
Multilingual Matters, Frankfurt Lodge, Clevedon Hall,
Victoria Road, Clevedon, BS21 7HH, England
http://www.multilingual-matters.com

LANGUAGE PLANNING AND POLICY

Language Planning and Policy in Europe, Vol.1
Hungary, Finland and Sweden

Edited by
Robert B. Kaplan and Richard B. Baldauf Jr.

MULTILINGUAL MATTERS LTD
Clevedon • Buffalo • Toronto

Library of Congress Cataloging in Publication Data
Language Planning and Policy in Europe/Edited by Robert B. Kaplan and Richard
B. Baldauf, Jr.
Language Planning and Policy
Includes bibliographical references.
Contents: v. 1. Hungary, Finland, and Sweden.
1. Language planning–Europe. 2. Language policy–Europe. I. Kaplan, Robert B.
II. Baldauf, Richard B. III. Series.
P40.5.L352E854 2005
306.44'94–dc22   2005009432

British Library Cataloguing in Publication Data
A catalogue entry for this book is available from the British Library.

ISBN 1-85359-811-9 (hbk)
ISBN 1-85359-812-7 (electronic)

Multilingual Matters Ltd
UK: Frankfurt Lodge, Clevedon Hall, Victoria Road, Clevedon BS21 7HH.
USA: UTP, 2250 Military Road, Tonawanda, NY 14150, USA.
Canada: UTP, 5201 Dufferin Street, North York, Ontario M3H 5T8, Canada.

Material in this book has also appeared in Vol.1, No. 2 and Vol. 3, No. 2 of the
journal *Current Issues in Language Planning* and Vol. 20, Nos 4 &5 of the *Journal of
Multilingual and Multicultural Development*.

Printed and bound in the United States of America.

Contents

Series Overview

Since 1998 and 1999 when the first six polity studies on language policy and planning – addressing the language situation in particular polities – were published in the *Journal of Multilingual and Multicultural Development*, 13 studies (through the end of 2003) have been published in *Current Issues in Language Planning*. These studies have all addressed, to a greater or lesser extent, 22 common questions or issues (Appendix A), thus giving them some degree of consistency. However, we are keenly aware that these studies have been published in the order in which they were completed. While such an arrangement is reasonable for journal publication, the result does not serve the needs of area specialists nor are the various monographs easily accessible to the wider public. As the number of available polity studies has grown, we have planned to update (where necessary) and republish these studies in coherent areal volumes.

The first such volume published concerned Africa (i.e., Botswana, Malawi, Mozambique and South Africa) (Baldauf & Kaplan, 2004), both because a significant number of studies had become available and because Africa constituted an area that is significantly under-represented in the language planning literature and yet is marked by extremely interesting language policy and planning issues. This second volume – including Finland, Hungary and Sweden – focuses on Europe, again examining polities that have not been the subject of much published language planning and policy activity – at least in English. This volume will shortly be followed by a third volume, also with a focus on Europe (i.e., The Czech Republic, the European Union and Northern Ireland.)

We hope that these areal volumes will better serve the needs of specialists. It is our intent to continue to publish other areal volumes subsequently as sufficient studies are completed. We will do so in the hope that such volumes will be of interest to areal scholars and others interested in language policies and language planning in geographically coherent regions. The areas in which we are planning to produce future volumes, and some of the polities which may be included, are:

> **Africa** (2), including Algeria, Burundi and Rwanda, Côte d'Ivoire, Nigeria, Tunisia, Zimbabwe;
> **Asia**, including Bangladesh, Malaysia, Nepal, the Philippines, Singapore, Sri Lanka and Taiwan;
> **Europe** (3), including the Ireland, Italy and Malta;
> **Latin America**, including Ecuador, Mexico and Paraguay;
> **Pacific Basin**, including Fiji and Vanuatu.

In the meantime, we will continue to bring out *Current Issues in Language Planning*, adding to the list of polities available for inclusion in areal volumes. At this point, we cannot predict the intervals over which such areal volumes will appear, since those intervals will be defined by the ability of contributors to complete work on already committed polity studies.

Assumptions Relating to Polity Studies

There are a number of assumptions that we have made about the nature of language policy and planning that have influenced the nature of the studies presented. First, we do not believe that there is, yet, a broader and more coherent paradigm to address the complex questions of language policy / planning development. On the other hand, we do believe that the collection of a large body of more or less comparable data and the careful analysis of that data will give rise to a better paradigm. Therefore, in soliciting the polity studies, we have asked each of the contributors to address some two dozen questions (to the extent that such questions were pertinent to each particular polity); the questions were offered as suggestions of topics that might be covered. (See Appendix A.) Some contributors have followed the questions rather closely; others have been more independent in approaching the task. It should be obvious that, in framing those questions, we were moving from a perhaps inchoate notion of an underlying theory. The reality that our notion was inchoate becomes clear in each of the polity studies.

Second, we have sought to find authors who had an intimate involvement with the language planning and policy decisions made in the polity about which they were writing; i.e., we were looking for insider knowledge and perspectives about the polities. Furthermore, we have asked authors to locate those policies in the local socio-historical context. However, as insiders are part of the process, they may find it difficult to take the part of the 'other' – to be critical of that process. But it is not necessary or even appropriate that they should do so – this can be left to others. As Pennycook (1998: 126) argues:

> One of the lessons we need to draw from this account of colonial language policy [i.e., in Hong Kong] is that, in order to make sense of language policies we need to understand both their location historically and their location contextually. What I mean by this is that we can not assume that the promotion of local languages instead of a dominant language, or the promotion of a dominant language at the expense of a local language, are in themselves good or bad. Too often we view these things through the lenses of liberalism, pluralism or anti-imperialism, without understanding the actual location of such policies.

While some authors do take a theoretical or critical stance, or one based on a theoretical approach to the data, many of the studies are primarily descriptive, bringing together and revealing, we hope, the nature of the language development experience in the particular polity. We believe this is a valuable contribution to the theory / paradigm development of the field. As interesting and challenging as it may be to provide a priori descriptions of the nature of the field (e.g., language management; Neustupný & Nekvapil, 2003; minority language rights; May, 2003) based on partial data – nor have we been completely immune from this ourselves (e.g., Kaplan & Baldauf, 2003, Chapter 12), we believe the development of a sufficient data base is an important prerequisite for paradigm development.

An Invitation to Contribute

We welcome additional polity contributions. Our views on a number of the issues can be found in Kaplan and Baldauf (1997; 2003); sample polity monographs have appeared in the extant issues of *Current Issues in Language Planning* <http://www.cilp.net/> and in previously published volumes in this series. Interested authors should contact the editors, present a proposal for a monograph, and provide a sample list of references. It is also useful to provide a brief biographical note, indicating any personal involvement in language planning activities in the polity proposed for study as well as any relevant research/publication in LPP. All contributions should, of course, be original, unpublished works. We expect to work with contributors during the preparation of monographs. All monographs will, of course, be reviewed for quality, completeness, accuracy, and style. Experience suggests that co-authored contributions may be very successful, but we want to stress that we are seeking unified monographs on particular polities, not an edited compilation of various authors' efforts. Questions may be addressed to either of us.

Robert B. Kaplan (rkaplan@olypen.com)
Richard B. Baldauf, Jr. (rbaldauf@bigpond.com)

References

Baldauf, R. B., Jr., and Kaplan, R. B. (eds) (2004) *Language Planning and Policy in Africa, Vol. I: Botswana, Malawi, Mozambique and South Africa*. Clevedon: Multilingual Matters.

Kaplan, R. B. and Baldauf, R. B., Jr. (2003) *Language and Language-in-Education Planning in the Pacific Basin*. Dordrecht: Kluwer.

Kaplan, R. B. and Baldauf, R. B., Jr. (1997) *Language Planning From Practice to Theory*. Clevedon: Multilingual Matters.

May, S. (2003) Language planning and linguistic human rights. *Current Issues in Language Planning* 4, 95–125.

Neustupný, J. and Nekvapil, J. (2003) Language management in the Czech Republic. *Current Issues in Language Planning* 4, 181–366.

Pennycook, A. (1998) *English and the Discourses of Colonialism*. London and New York: Routledge.

Volume previously published in this series

Baldauf, R. B., Jr. and Kaplan, R. B. (eds) (2004) *Language Planning and Policy in Africa, Vol. I: Botswana, Malawi, Mozambique and South Africa*. Clevedon: Multilingual Matters.

Appendix A

Part I: The Language Profile of . . .

1. Name and briefly describe the national/official language(s) (*de jure* or *de facto*).
2. Name and describe the major minority language(s).
3. *Name and describe the lesser minority language(s) (include 'dialects', pidgins, creoles and other important aspects of language variation)*; the definition of minority language/dialect/pidgin will need to be discussed in terms of the sociolinguistic context.
4. *Name and describe the major religious language(s)*; In some polities religious languages and/or missionary policies have had a major impact on the language situation and provide *de facto* language planning. In some contexts religion has been a vehicle for introducing exogenous languages while in other cases it has served to promote indigenous languages.

5. Name and describe the major language(s) of literacy, assuming that it is/ they are not one of those described above.
6. Provide a table indicating the number of speakers of each of the above languages, what percentage of the population they constitute and whether those speakers are largely urban or rural.
7. Where appropriate, provide a map(s) showing the distribution of speakers, key cities and other features referenced in the text.

Part II: Language Spread

8. Specify which languages are taught through the educational system, to whom they are taught, when they are taught and for how long they are taught.
9. Discuss the objectives of language education and the methods of assessment to determine that the objectives are met.
10. To the extent possible, trace the historical development of the policies/ practices identified in items 8 and 9 (may be integrated with 8/9).
11. Name and discuss the major media language(s) and the distribution of media by socio-economic class, ethnic group, urban/rural distinction (including the historical context where possible). For minority language, note the extent that any literature is (has been) available in the language.
12. How has immigration effected language distribution and what measures are in place to cater for learning the national language(s) and/or to support the use of immigrant languages.

Part III: Language Policy and Planning

13. Describe any language planning legislation, policy or implementation that is currently in place.
14. Describe any literacy planning legislation, policy or implementation that is currently in place.
15. To the extent possible, trace the historical development of the policies/ practices identified in items 13 and 14 (may be integrated with these items).
16. Describe and discuss any language planning agencies/organisations operating in the polity (both formal and informal).
17. Describe and discuss any regional/international influences affecting language planning and policy in the polity (include any external language promotion efforts).
18. To the extent possible, trace the historical development of the policies/ practices identified in items 16 and 17 (may be integrated with these items).

Part IV: Language Maintenance and Prospects

19. Describe and discuss intergenerational transmission of the major language(s); (is this changing over time?).
20. Describe and discuss the probabilities of language death among any of the languages/language varieties in the polity, any language revival efforts as well as any emerging pidgins or creoles.
21. Add anything you wish to clarify about the language situation and its probable direction of change over the next generation or two.

22. Add pertinent references/bibliography and any necessary appendices (e.g., a general plan of the educational system to clarify the answers to questions 8, 9 and 14).

Language Policy and Planning in Hungary, Finland and Sweden: Some Common Issues

Robert B. Kaplan
Professor Emeritus, Applied Linguistics, University of Southern California. Postal address: PO Box 577, Port Angeles, WA 98362 USA (rkaplan@olypen.com)

Richard B. Baldauf Jr.
Associate Professor of TESOL, School of Education, University of Queensland, QLD 4072 Australia (r.baldauf@bigpond.com)

Introduction

Methodological and historical barriers to language policy and planning (LPP) research have often made generalizability of results difficult if not impossible – sometimes because comparable information has not been produced, but often because basic data is simply unavailable. In many polities, Côte d'Ivoire (Djité, 2000) for example, conditions and the state of academic research (i.e., not only the work published about the polity, but access to journals and recent books, computer facilities, time to do research, adequate salaries and working conditions, let alone funds for travel and research projects, etc.) are such that many LPP issues, such as those represented by the 22 questions suggested for these studies, simply could not be adequately addressed (Baldauf & Kaplan, 2004: 7).

Furthermore, LPP research, unlike science, does not have a rich culture of controlled experiments – nor perhaps, despite some early thinking to the contrary (see, e.g., Rubin & Jernudd, 1971), is such work possible. Instead, a wide variety of methodological perspectives have been used to examine various aspects of LPP (see, Baldauf, 2002), but central to this body of work, a descriptive culture of citing 'best practice' has evolved, which is inherently anecdotal (see, e.g., Kaplan & Baldauf, 2003). Furthermore, as Noss (1985) noted twenty years ago in relation to language-in-education planning, evaluation of language planning is relatively rare. This remains the case, and what evaluative work is done, at least at the macro level, is often poorly funded, empirical reports and experimental follow-ups that describe the 'effects' of some recent 'innovation,' often forgetting the basic tenet of science that association is not causation.

Thus, there has been a global tendancy to view LPP research as one fad (or one 'innovation') after another, each with a typical life span of five to ten years (often tied to the life of a political administration) (see, e.g., Kaplan & Tse, 1982). It is rare that anyone critically examines the evidence that validates one or another new practice. This soft approach to LPP research has led to redundancy and has inspired cynicism and existential fatigue among policy makers, journalists, and the public. In the process, LPP research has become a low-status undertaking, increasingly open to critique, although unfortunately much of the critique has focused on the way the discipline is seen to operate through its 'involvement' in issues like 'linguistic imperialism' or 'minority language rights', rather than on developing research based studies that appropriately address and try to understand the issues involved.[1]

Another recent direction taken by some scholars has been to attempt to deal with language policy activities in terms of a dichotomy of *success* and *failure*. Given that language policy activity is commonly an on-going or continuous process, it is quite impossible to dichotomise LPP outcomes in such terms, though there are other attempts at structuring order that may be more useful.

For example, Pennycook (1998) provides a critical analysis of English and the discourses of colonialism, especially the tension between views of 'the self' and 'the other', between the 'insider' and the 'outsider', the emic and the etic. His primary focus of analysis is on colonialism – both historic and in its Eurocentric neo-colonialist forms – and the positive manner in which Europeans portrayed themselves versus the way they portrayed the colonised others. Following from this, he points out that there is a need to look 'more contextually . . . at the sites and causes of the development of colonial discourses on language . . .' as there is a 'constant negotiation of colonial language policy images of the Self and the Other' where 'culture and language were always being produced, developed and redefined' (1998: 128). This dichotomy and interaction between the Self and the Other – which Pennycook illustrates with Hong Kong as an example – is also characteristic of the tension in perspectives that individual LPP authors bring to their studies (Kaplan & Baldauf, 2004: 8).

Another obstacle to dichotomising outcomes – i.e., as successes or as failures – lies in the matter of the actors. Key actors in language policy designs can warp those designs to support quite different objectives (e.g., Kaplan & Baldauf 2003, the discussion of the role of Kim Il Sung in North Korea). In some polities, language policy activity has had a quite specific political objective, often without reference to the realities of language use in the polity, and sometimes to the detriment of the speaker population. As Kayambazinthu points out (Baldauf & Kaplan, 2004: 79), in her study of language planning in Malawi, ' . . . language planning practices (past and present) present an interesting case study of pervasive ad hoc and reactive planning, based more on self-interest and political whim than research.' In such cases, dichotomising outcomes becomes futile.

Furthermore, policy efforts may show some successes and some failures simultaneously. But, as we have pointed out earlier, ' . . . there is a great deal of language planning that occurs in other societal contexts [not necessarily at governmental level] at more modest levels for other purposes' (Kaplan & Baldauf, 1997: 3). At these more micro levels, it is virtually impossible meaningfully to discuss *success* and *failure*. In short, dichotomising outcomes on a two-part scale seems not to constitute a useful activity – the world is not 'black and white'; rather it consists of many shades of grey. Indeed, there is a variety of policy and planning that occurs without planning (e.g., Baldauf, 1994; Eggington, 2002) – i.e., a situation in which some language planning occurs as fall-out from some other planning activity; e.g., the multi-polity accords of the International Postal Union on the required mode for addressing envelopes to assure international delivery.

A purpose of this series is to work with authors, involved in LPP in their polities, to bring together the available research in its socio-historical context, exploring with them what has happened, and the extent to which this has been documented in their particular polity. Hopefully this will help us to understand the language planning process better.

In particular, this volume brings together three language policy and planning studies related to Northern and Eastern Europe.[2] (See the 'Series Overview' in this volume for a more general discussion of the nature of the series, Appendix A for the 22 questions each study set out to address, and Kaplan *et al.* (2000) for a discussion of our underlying concepts for the studies themselves.) In this introductory paper, rather than trying to provide an introductory summary of the material covered in these studies, we have tried to draw out and discuss some of the more general issues raised by these studies in light of the debates which have been going on in the field.

Polity Planning Characteristics

Except that all three of these polities fall within the broad definition of *Europe* (and that all three are included within the European Union), the three studies included in this volume do not represent any sort of geographic or linguistic coherence. Hungarian and Finnish are languages belonging to the same language family – the Uralic family; however, the relationship between these two languages can only be established on historical linguistic grounds. Sweden and Finland are part of the Nordic region – together with Denmark, Iceland and Norway. In addition, Finland was part of the Swedish empire for nearly five centuries from 1323 to 1809 and the Swedish language as well as the legal and social structures left their mark on the country. Indeed, Finnish and Swedish are the Constitutional national languages of Finland, and some 300,000 Swedish speakers reside in Finland (out of a total population of about five million, thus just under six per cent of the population). Sweden, on the other hand, has two distinct Finnish speaking populations; those more recent 'economic' migrants speaking standard Finnish and those speaking Meänkieli (Tornedalen Finnish), distinguished by the relative amount of 'Swedisation'. Finnish is not officially recognised as a national language in the Swedish Constitution.

It is important to recall that Hungarian and Swedish have long histories and especially that they were at one time 'imperial' languages which have now been reduced essentially to minor roles in the context of contemporary Europe and in the context of the European Union (EU). At the same time, virtually hundreds of new 'minority' languages have appeared in Europe, in part as the result of the political rearrangements occurring within Europe over the past two centuries, and in part as the result of significant immigration from non-European areas echoing the movement of populations toward seemingly better economic conditions and relative political stability. These population movements, combined with current concerns for minority language rights within the EU, raise language policy and planning concerns in each of the polities.

Minority populations in all three polities are, nevertheless, quite small, but of course in some respects this makes the problem of language provision and support even more difficult. Varietal variation in some groups (e.g. the Roma) increases the problem.

- Finland's minority populations include: Russian 28,205, Estonian 10,176, English 6.919, Somali 6,454, Arabic 4,892, Vietnamese 3,588, German 3,298,

Albanian 3,293, Kurdish 3,115, Chinese 2,907 (out of a total population of five million). None of these groups approaches 1% of the total population.

- Hungary's minority populations are also more fully defined: Roma 142,683, German 30,824, Croatian 13,570, Romanian 10,740, Slovak 10,459, Serbian 2,905, Slovenian 1,930 (out of a total population of ten million). None of these groups approaches 1% of the population.
- Sweden's minority populations are only available as estimates: Saami 5,000 to 10,000; Tornedalians 25,000 to 70,000; Swedish Finns 200,000 to 250,000; Roma 5,000 to 15,000, and Jews about 3,000 (out of a total population of about nine million). The largest of these groups represents only about 2% of the population. The small Jewish population is attributable to some extent to antisemitism over the past 300 years.

While the numbers of speakers of languages other than the respective national languages are really quite small, it is apparent that all of these polities are multilingual and multicultural.

As Figure 1 indicates, while these polities differ in a number of ways, they are all smaller states within the European context in population size, in area, and in GDP (as compared with, e. g., France [population = 59,329,691; area = 547,030 sq. km.; GDP = $1.32 trillion; 5th republic] or Germany [population = 82,797,408; area = 356,910 sq. km.; GDP = $1.813 trillion; parliamentary democracy]).

Country Name	Population	Area in sq. km.	GDP* in US$ (billions)	Type of Government
Finland	c. 5,000,000	337,000	$103.6	Republic
Hungary	c. 10,000,000	93,000	$75.4	Republic
Sweden	c. 9,000,000	449,000	$175.0	Constitutional Monarchy

Figure 1 Basic facts pertaining to Finland, Hungary and Sweden
* Gross Domestic Product

Finland and Sweden also share some minority languages – Saami (see, e.g., Bull, 2002), Yiddish (and to some extent Hebrew as a language of religion) and Romani; Finland also includes communities of Tatar and Russian speakers. After World War II, and especially after 1980, groups of immigrants migrated to the Nordic Countries – speakers of Arabic, Chinese (various regionalect varieties), English, Farsi, French, German, Greek, Japanese, Polish, Spanish, Turkish, and Vietnamese – though the population numbers of these communities are quite small. Hungary, like much of the rest of Europe, also has communities of speakers of these languages. All three of these polities have reported special problems with respect to speakers of Romani.

It is interesting to note the extent to which the respective Ministries of Education are basically responsible for language policy. In all three polities, it is the Ministry of Education that is responsible for first language education – Swedish in Sweden, Hungarian in Hungary and both Finnish and Swedish in Finland. It is also of interest that the minority languages are defined by the Ministries of Education. While all three polities have problems with respect to the Romanispeaking populations, and while Finland and Sweden have special problems with respect to the Saami people, the other minority languages are essentially consigned to community responsibility; that is, the polities do not assume much responsibility for education in the minority languages, and such education in those languages as is provided is often provided largely through 'Saturday Schools,' basically funded by the respective communities. It is apparent that smaller communities (basically those of 'new' immigrant populations) do not have the resources for extensive language education. Thus, there is a need to provide language support for both traditional minorities and recent immigrant communities (particularly in accord with the provisions of various recent EU treaties) and the difficulties this need poses for all members of the EU, for the three polities under discussion here, and for the increasing membership of the EU.

All three polities essentially endorse a state religion, and communities espousing other religions are left essentially to their own devices. In Finland, some 85% of the population is Lutheran, despite the existence of the 1922 Religious Freedom Law granting religious freedom of choice to all citizens. In Sweden, the Church of Sweden (Lutheran) is dominant, though other sects are permitted to conduct services. In Hungary, the Austro-Hungarian Compromise of 1867 allowed the 'churches' to select the languages used in their rites, but the Roman Catholic Church has played a significant role. The Church is credit with an important part in the spread of Hungarian. In this instance, duration of residence in the polity is a factor. Thus, Jewish communities which have been in place for at least two centuries have more fully developed language and culture programs than do most of the more recent arrivals; indeed, recent arrivals have very few options in terms of language and culture preservation. The issues pertaining to the Roma appear to be impervious to national solutions and probably will require EU-wide attention.

All three polities report extremely high rates of literacy. However, the meaning of literacy is not uniform. The expansion of the EU has had some impact on language education/preservation, but these developments are too recent to have had any measurable effect. In sum, in all three polities, basic long-term policies have been directed toward assimilation. While these polities share a number of common educational, social and economic problems, the approach to problem solution tends to be largely restricted within the polity; there is relatively little evidence of broader – European-wide – solutions. But the development of the EU holds great promise for more effective recognition of multilingualism and multiculturalism and for the development of more effective remedies in first and second language education and literacy. Indeed, the EU seeks to expand language ability beyond the national language. While Finland has relatively broadly held bilingualism and trilingualism within the base population, Hungary is struggling to increase bilingual and multilingual fluency in its population.

At the same time, the expansion of the EU has exacerbated problems relating to the role and reach of English as a language of wider communication within the European context. The language situation in the operations of the EU is extremely complex (see, e.g., van Els, 2001; van Els & Extra, 1987), but there is no question that English has assumed an important role. Not only has the role of English changed, but the operations of the EU have created a significant terminological issue, since it is desirable that terminology should be consistent across all the members of the EU. These matters have placed great pressure of language policy practitioners with respect to language maintenance in the context of both inter-polity and intra-polity use. Many of what are now perceived as minor languages (including national language now reduced to minority status) may have had significant histories, in some cases may have a standard variety, indeed, may be national languages in other parts of the world, and may have extensive oral and written literatures (see, e.g., Trim, 1999).

Finland and Hungary recognize the existence of relatively large overseas populations and pay some attention to the maintenance of the national languages in the expatriat populations. Sweden also has a significant expatriat population, but there seem to be no efforts to facilitate language maintenance in those populations.

Concluding Remark

We hope that by bringing these studies together in this second areal volume they will be more accessible and will better serve the needs of specialists. It is our intent to publish other areal volumes subsequently. We will do so in the hope that such volumes will be of interest to areal scholars and others concerned with language policies and language planning in geographically coherent regions. (See the Series Overview elsewhere in this volume for more detail on our future plans.)

Notes

1. The literature on this topic is large and expanding, and has been drawn together in a number of studies (e.g., May, 2003) and contexts (e.g., the EU, van Els, 2001). The highly charged tenor of aspects of the debate also can be seen in exchanges such as those that have occurred in 'the Forum' between Skutnabb-Kangas, Bruitt-Griffler, Canajarajah, Pennycook, and Tollefson in the journal *Language, Identity and Education* (2004, 3(2), 127–160).
2. The studies in this volume were previously published as follows: **Hungary** *Current Issues in Language Planning* (2000) 1, 148–242; **Finland** *Current Issues in Language Planning* (2002) 3, 95–202 and **Sweden** *Journal of Multilingual and Multicultural Development* (1999) 19, 376–473. Authors' updates to the Hungarian study – taking into account major changes in the language planning and policy situations in that polity – follow as an addendum to the original article.

References

Bull, T. (2002) The Sámi language(s), maintenance and intellectualisation. *Current Issues in Language Planning* 3, 28–39.

Baldauf, R. B. Jr. (1994) Unplanned language policy and planning. In W. Grabe *et al.* (eds) *Annual Review of Applied Linguistics, 14: Language Policy and Planning* (pp. 82–89). Cambridge: Cambridge University Press.

Baldauf, R. B., Jr. (2002) Methodologies for policy and planning. In R.B. Kaplan (ed.) *Handbook of Applied Linguistics* (pp. 391–403). Oxford: Oxford University Press.

Baldauf, R. B., Jr. and Kaplan, R. B. (2004) *Language Planning and Policy: Africa, Vol. 1: Botswana, Malawi, Mozambique and South Africa* (pp. 5–20). Clevedon: Multilingual Matters.

Djité, P. (2000) Language planning in Côte d'Ivoire. *Current Issues in Language Planning* 1, 11–46.

Eggington, W. G. (2002) Unplanned language planning. In R. B. Kaplan (ed.) *The Oxford Handbook of Applied Linguistics* (pp. 404–415). New York: Oxford University Press.

Kaplan, R. B.and Baldauf, Jr., R. B. (2003) *Language and Language-in-Education Planning in the Pacific Basin.* Dordrecht: Kluwer.
Kaplan, R. B., Baldauf, Jr., R. B., Liddicoat, A. J., Bryant, P., Barbaux, M.-T. and Pütz, M. (2000) Current issues in language planning. *Current Issues in Language Planning* 1, 135–144.
Kaplan, R. B. and Tse, J. K.-p. (1982) The Taiwan English language survey revisited. *English Around the World* 27: 6–8.
May, S. (2003) Rearticulating the case for minority language rights. *Current Issues in Language Planning* 4, 95–125.
Noss, R. B. (1985) The evaluation of language planning in education. *South East Asian Journal of Social Science* 13, 82–105.
Pennycook, A. (1998) *English and the Discourses of Colonialism.* London and New York: Routledge.
Rubin, J. and Jernudd, B. H. (1971) *Can Language be Planned?* Honolulu: The University Press of Hawai'i.
Trim, J. L. M. (1999) Language education policy: Europe. In B. Spolsky (ed.) *Concise Encyclopedia of Educational Linguistics* (pp. 122–127). Amsterdam: Elsevier.
van Els, T. J. M. (2001) The European Union, its institutions and its languages: Some language political observations. *Current Issues in Language Planning* 2, 311–360.
van Els, T. J. M. and Extra, G. (1987) Foreign and second language teaching in Western Europe: A comparative overview of needs, objectives and policies. *Sociolinguistica* 1, 100–125.

Further Reading

Hungary

Ágoston, M. (1980) For the unity of our orthography [Nyelvművelés: Írásunk egységéért]. *Magyar Nyelv* 76(2), 218–220.
Angyal, E. (1987) Hungary: Exemplary lessons [Ungarn: Exemplarische Lektionen]. *Deutschunterricht* 39(2), 82–90.
Beller, B. (1988) On the history of Hungarian Germans [Zur Geschichte der Ungarndeutschen]. *Germanistische Mitteilungen* 28, 87–108.
Beregszászi, A. (1995) Language planning issues of Hungarian place-names in Subcarpathia. *Acta Linguistica Hungarica: an International Journal of Linguistics* 43(3–4), 373–380.
Bradean Ebinger, N. (1988) Language loss-language abandonment by Hungarian Germans? [Sprachverlust-Sprachverzicht bei den Ungarndeutschen]. *Grazer Linguistische Studien* 29 (spring), 7–22.
Csiszár, N. (1998) TEJO en la internacia junulara politiko. In T. Gecso and Z. Varga-Haszonits (eds) *Memorlibro: Kolekto de la prelegoj dum la solena internacia konferenco, eldonita okaze de la tridekjarigo de la universitata fako Esperantologio* (pp. 378–382). Budapest, Hungary: Eötvös Loránd University.
Drescher, J. A. (1999) Foundations and practice contrasted [Grundsatze und Praxis im Gegensatz zueinander]. In A. Raasch (ed.) *Deutsch und Andere Fremdsprachen-International LanderBerichte-Sprachenpolitische Analysen-Anregungen [German and Other Foreign Languages-International State Reports-Language Policy Analyses-Suggestions]* (pp. 139–144). Amsterdam: Rodopi.
Fábián, P. (1974) Foundations of Hungarian orthography [Helyesírásunk alapelvei]. *Magyar Nyelv* 70(2), 212–222.
Fenyvesi, A. (1998) Linguistic minorities in Hungary. In C. B. Paulston and D. Peckham (eds) *Linguistic Minorities in Central and Eastern Europe* (pp. 135–159). Clevedon: Multilingual Matters.
Fodor, F. and Peluau, S. (2003) Language geostrategies in eastern and central Europe: Assessment and perspectives. In J. Maurais and M. A. Morris (eds) *Languages in a Globalising World* (pp. 85–98). Cambridge: Cambridge University Press.
Fodor, I. (1983) Hungarian: Evolution – Stagnation – Reform – Further development. In I.

Fodor and C. Hagège (eds) *Language Reform: History and Future* Vol. II (pp. 49–84). Hamburg: Buske.

Gal, S. (1993) Diversity and contestation in linguistic ideologies: German speakers in Hungary. *Language in Society* 22(3), 337–359.

Gerner, Z. (1991) Schlaf, Kindlein Schlaf . . . On the 'Exemplary' minority policy and its consequences for the German language in Hungary ['Schlaf, Kindlein schlaf . . . '. Uber die 'vorbildliche' Minderheitenpolitik und ihre Folgen fur die deutsche Sprache in Ungarn]. *Germanistische Mitteilungen* 34, 43–69.

Győri Nagy, S. (1984) Problems of the ontogeny of bilingualism of Germans in Hungary [Probleme der Zweisprachigkeitsontogenese von Ungarndeutschen]. *Germanistische Mitteilungen* 20, 61–70.

Heltai, P. (1994) Hungary's nationwide needs analysis. In W. Scott, S. Muhlhaus, M. Loschmann, C. Wilks and L. Csizmadia (eds) *Languages for Specific Purposes* (pp. 84–89). Kingston upon Thames: CILT with Kingston University School of Languages.

Hinderdael, M. and Nelde, P. H. (1988) A plea for a contact-linguistic treatment of the Hungarian German minority [Pladoyer fur eine kontaktlinguistische Betrachtungsweise der ungarndeutschen Minderheit.] *Germanistische Mitteilungen* 28, 109–114.

Imre, S. (1977) A few syntheses of contemporary Hungarian linguistics [A mai magyar nyelvtudomany nehany szintezise]. *Magyar Nyelv* 73(3), 279–287.

Kálmán, L. (ed.) (2001) *Descriptive Hungarian Grammar. Syntax I. [Magyar Leíró Nyelvtan. Mondattan I].* Budapest: Tinta Könyvkiadó.

Kern, R. (1987) Reflections on the consolidation of German as a mother tongue in Hungary [Uberlegungen zur Konsolidierung der deutschen Muttersprache in Ungarn]. *Germanistische Mitteilungen* 26, 85–98.

Kontra, M. (1992a) Class over nation–Linguistic hierarchies eliminated: The case of Hungary. *Multilingua* 11(2), 217–221.

Kontra, M. (1992b) Language cultivation in Hungary: An overview. *New Language Planning Newsletter* 7(2), 1–3.

Kontra, M. and Székely, A. B. (1993) Multilingual concepts in the schools of Europe. *Sociolinguistica*, 135–142.

Luk, A. N. (1993) Language education for intercultural communication in Slovenia. In D. Ager, G. Muskens and S. Wright (eds) *Language Education for Intercultural Communication* (pp. 181–191). Clevedon: Multilingual Matters.

Martin, D. S. (2001) The English-Only movement and sign language for deaf learners: An instructive parallel. *Sign Language Studies* 1 (2), 115–124.

Mathuna, L. M. (ed.) (1987) The Less Widely Taught Languages of Europe Proceedings of the Joint United Nations Éducational, Scientific, and Cultural Organization, International Association of Applied Linguistics, and Irish Association of Applied Linguistics Symposium (St Patrick's College, Dublin, Ireland, April 23–25, 1987). ERIC Document Reproduction Service, ED344420

Nelde, P. H. (1986) German as a minority language: The comparability of linguistic contacts [Deutsch als Minderheitssprache-Vergleichbarkeit von Sprachkontakten]. *Deutsche Sprache in Europa und Ubersee* 11, 251–273.

Nelde, P.H., Vandermeeren, S. and Wolek, W. (1991) The German language in Hungary: Results of a contact-linguistic survey. *Germanistische Mitteilungen* 33, 79–90.

Priestly, T. (1999) Linguistic propaganda against perceived irredentism. *International Journal of Applied Linguistics* 9(1), 37–75.

Rácz, E. (1978) On the question of historical linguistics [A történeti nyelvtudomány kérdéseihez]. *Magyar Nyelv* 74(1), 66–68.

Radnai, Z. (1994) The educational effects of language policy. *Current Issues in Language and Society* 1(1), 65–92.

Szemere, G. (1975) The legitimacy of the principles of traditional writing in our orthography [A hagyományos írás elvének érvényesülése helyesírásunkban]. *Magyar Nyelv* 71(2), 211–220.

Szende, T. (1973) About the theoretical bases of the spoken standard [A beszédnorma elméleti alapjairól]. *Magyar Nyelvőr* 97(3), 315–324.

Szépe, G. (1984) Mother tongue, language policy and education. *Prospects* 14(1), 63–73.

Szépe, G. (1994a) Central and Eastern European language policies in transition (With special reference to Hungary). *Current Issues in Language and Society* 1(1), 41–64.

Szépe, G. (1994b) Recent changes in language policy in Hungary. In W. Scott, S. Muhlhaus, M. Loschmann, C. Wilks and L. Csizmadia (eds) *Languages for Specific Purposes* (pp. 24–29). Kingston upon Thames: CILT with Kingston University School of Languages.

Terestyéni, T. (1985) The knowledge of foreign languages in Hungary [Helyzetkép a hazai idegennyelv-tudásról]. *Nyelvtudományi Közlemények* 87(1), 197–208.

Thomas, G. (1996) Some remarks on the role of purism in the literary languages of the Habsburg Empire in the nineteenth century [Neskol'ko zamechaniy o roli purizma v literaturnykh yazykakh gabsburgskoy imperii v devyatnadtsatom stoletii]. *Studia Slavica Savariensia* 1–2, 170–179.

Weisgerber, B. (1986) Hungarian-German impressions and information [Ungarndeutsche Impressionen und Informationen]. *Germanistische Mitteilungen* 24, 95–105.

Finland

Aikio, M. (1984) The position and use of the same language: Historical, contemporary and future perspectives. *Journal of Multilingual and Multicultural Development* 5(3–4), 277–291.

Aikio, M. (1991) The Sami language: Pressure of change and reification. *Journal of Multilingual and Multicultural Development* 12(1–2), 93–103.

Alapuro, R. (2000) Language socialization and standardization [Kieli sosiaalisena taistelukenttana]. *Franco British Studies* 30 (autumn), 13–18.

Allardt, E. (1985) Bilingualism in Finland: The position of Swedish as a minority language. In W. R. Beer and J. E. Jacob (eds) *Language Policy and National Unity* (pp. 79–96). Totowa, NJ: Rowman & Allanheld.

Andersson, H. and Herberts, K. (1996) The case of the Swedish-Speaking Finns. *International Review of Education* 42(4), 384–388.

Boyd, S. and Huss, L. (eds) (2000) *Managing Multilingualism in a European Nation-State: Challenges for Sweden*. Clevedon: Multilingual Matters.

Bradean Ebinger, N. (1984) The sociolinguistic aspects of bilingualism in the Scandinavian area. [Soziolinguistische Aspekte der Zweisprachigkeit im nordlichen Areal]. *Nyelvtudományi Kozlemenyek* 87(2), 320–325.

Brunstad, E. (1998) Purism towards English: A comparative analysis of language planning in the Nordic language communities. In J. Niemi, T. Odlin, J. Heikkinen and J. Niemi (eds) *Language Contact, Variation, and Change* (pp. 1–14). Joensuu, Finland: Faculty of Humanities University of Joensuu.

Collis, D. R. F. (ed.) (1990) *Arctic Languages: An Awakening*. Paris: UNESCO.

Dressler, G. (1984) The teaching and learning situation at German Institutes in Finland–Remarks from a West German perspective [Zur Lehr- und Lernsituation an germanistischen Instituten in Finnland-Anmerkungen aus bundesrepublikanischer Sicht]. *Bielefelder Beitrage zur Sprachlehrforschung* 13(1), 83–92.

Fernandez Vest, M. M. J. (1987) From bilingualism [Swedish] to semilingualism [Sami]: What is the future of the languages of Finland? [Du bilinguisme (suedois) au semi-linguisme (same): quel avenir pour les langues de Finlande?] *Etudes de Linguistique Appliquee* 65(Jan-Mar), 37–57.

Finnas, F. (1998) The role of bilingual families in population development [Die Rolle der zweisprachigen Familien in der Bevolkerungsentwicklung]. *Europa Ethnica* 55(3–4), 122–129.

Fix, U. (1983) Wer seine Muttersprache redet wie ein Pferd, der ist der Verachtung wert: Sprachpflege in Finnland und das Forschungszentrum fur die Landessprachen Finnlands. *Sprachpflege: Zeitschrift fur Gutes Deutsch* 32(5), 68–71.

Gambier, Y. (1987) Institutional bilingualism in Finland: Law and reality [Le Bilinguisme institutionnel en Finlande: droit et realites]. *Etudes de Linguistique Appliquee* 65 (Jan-Mar), 58–68.

Garant, M. (2000) EFL testing and university admission in Finland and Japan. *Asian Journal of English Language Teaching* 10, 115–135.

Haarmann, H. and Holman, E. (2001) The impact of English as a language of science in Finland and its role for the transition to network society. In U. Ammon (ed.) *The Dominance of English as a Language of Science: Effect on other Languages and Language Communities* (pp. 229–260), Berlin: Mouton de Gruyter.

Hansen, S. E. (1987) Mother-tongue teaching and identity: The case of Finland-Swedes. *Journal of Multilingual and Multicultural Development* 8, 75–82.

Hansen, S.-E. (1991) Word and world in mother tongue teaching in Finland: Curriculum policy in a bilingual society. *Language, Culture and Curriculum* 4, 107–117.

Hilmola, V. and Ruotonen, L. (1994) Toward a multicultural school [Kohti monikulttuurista koulua]. *Kasvatus* 25(5), 501–509.

Holma Kokkonen, H. (1997) How do native speakers decide on language change? [Miten aidinkielen paattokoetta voisi uudistaa?] *Virittaja* 101(4), 597–598.

Hube, H.-J. (1981) Zur Sprachsituation in Skandinavien. *Sprachpflege: Zeitschrift fur Gutes Deutsch* 30(10), 148–151.

Huss, L. (1999) Reversing language shift in the far north: Linguistic revitalization in Northern Scandinavia and Finland. *Acta Universitatis Upsaliensis: Studia Uralica Upsaliensia* 31, 9–212.

Karppinen, M.-L. (1992) Problems in the implementation of foreign language policy in Finland. In K. Sajavaara (ed.) *National Foreign Language Planning: Practices and Prospects.* Jyväskylä, Finland: Institute for Educational Research, University of Jyväskylä.

Kauppinen, S. (1987) Finland: Changing orientations in literature instruction [Finnland: Wechselnden Betonungen des Literaturunterrichts]. *Deutschunterricht* 39(2), 13–17.

Koivusalo, E. (1978) Standard Language-Language Upkeep-Society; Yleiskieli-kielenhuolto-yhteiskunta. *Virittaja* 82(3), 316–318.

Koivusalo, E. (1979) What is standard language?; Mita on yleiskieli? *Virittaja* 83(3), 216–222.

Koivusalo, E. and Haarala, R. (1981) Sprachpflege in Finnland. *Der Sprachdienst* 25(11–12), 169–172.

Lainio, J. (1997) Swedish minority language treatment and language policy: Positive public rhetoric vs. grassroot struggle. *Sociolinguistica* 11, 29–42.

Laitinen, L. (1997) Popular language-National language; Kansankieli-kansallinen kieli. *Virittaja* 101(2), 279–288.

Laporte, P.-E. and Maurais, J. (1991) Some aspects of language planning in Quebec and in Finland. Discussion Papers in Geolinguistics, 17. ERIC Document Reproduction Service, ED332531.

Latomaa, S. (1995) On bilingualism and education of language minority children in Finland. *Finlance* 16, 5–18.

Latomaa, S. (2002) Immigrants' language rights. *AFinLAn vuosikirja* 60, 61–81.

Lauren, C. (1998a) Language supervision, terminological work and language planning. *UNESCO ALSED LSP Newsletter* 21(1(45)), 26–33.

Lauren, C. (1998b) The Project 'Languages in the Nordic Countries as Languages of Science'. *UNESCO ALSED LSP Newsletter* 21(1(45)), 34–39.

Lindgren, A. R. (1998) Revitalization of minority languages–Language emancipation [Kielten Revitalisaatio–Kielten emansipaatio]. *Nordlyd* 26, 36–47.

Lindgren, A. R. (2001) Language rights [Oikeus omaan kieleen]. *Virittaja* 105(2), 239–255.

Lyytikainen, E. (2000) Language standardization [Kieli taistelukenttana]. *Franco British Studies* 30 (autumn), 56–64.

Maamies, S. and Raikkala, A. (1997) A return to *Virittaja* language norms [Virittaja kielenhuollon kimpussa]. *Virittaja* 101(2), 272–276.

McRae, K. D. (1978) Bilingual language districts in Finland and Canada: Adventures in the transplanting of an institution. *Canadian Public Policy/Analyse de Politiques* 4(3), 331–351.

McRae, K. D. (1988) Finland: Marginal case of bicommunalism? *Publius* 18(2), 91–100.

McRae, K. D., Helander, M. and Luoma, S. (1999) Conflict and compromise in multilingual societies: Finland. *Annales Academiae Scientiarum Fennicae/Suomalaisen Tiedeakatemian Toimituksia, Series B* 306, 1–429.

Modeen, T. (1991) Thoughts on the problem: Security through law: The example of

Finland [Gedanken zum Problem: Sicherheit durch Recht-Beispiel Finnland]. *Europa Ethnica* 48(4), 198–203.

Modeen, T. (1997) Population groups in Finland in the 1920s and 1930s [Die Lage der Volksgruppen in Finnland in den 1920er und 1930er Jahren]. *Europa Ethnica* 54(1–2), 57–63.

Modeen, T. (1999a) The cultural rights of the Swedish ethnic group in Finland. *Europa Ethnica* 56(3–4), 135–145.

Modeen, T. (1999b) The legal situation of the Lapp (Sami) ethnic group in Finland, compared to the position of other national, religious and ethnic groups. *Europa Ethnica* 56(3–4), 150–155.

Moore, D. (1992) Testing oral competence in a second language: An account of the Finnish project [Tester les competences orales en langues etrangeres: echos de la reflexion finlandaise]. *Bulletin CILA* 55(Apr), 35–39.

Nikki, M. L. (1994) The implementation of the Finnish national plan for foreign language teaching. *Dissertation Abstracts International, C: Worldwide* 55(1), 8-C.

Nordberg, B. (1976) Sociolinguistic research in Sweden and Finland: Introduction. *International Journal of the Sociology of Language* 10, 5–15.

Nuolijarvi, P. (1999) The Finnish mother tongue [Suomen aidinkielet]. *Virittaja* 103(3), 402–410.

Oinonen, T. (1997) From language battle to language planning–The Finnish Language Bureau. *ATA Chronicle* 26(2), 31–32.

Oksanen, L. (1972) The further training of foreign language teachers [Kielten opettajien taydennyskoulutus]. *Kasvatus* 3(5), 279–282.

Packer, J. and Myntti, K. (eds) (1993) *The Protection of Persons Belonging to National Minorities in Finland* (3rd edn). Turko, Finland: Abo Academi University, Finland Institute for Human Rights.

Palmgren, S. (1996) Legal language in a multilingual society [Lakikieli monikielisessa yhteisossa]. *Virittaja* 100(4), 570–573.

Piehl, A. (1996) Language standardization and guidance on correct usage in *Virittaja* [Oikeakielisyytta ja kielen kaytantoa virittajassa]. *Virittaja* 100(4), 490–503.

Piri, R. (2002) Foreign language teaching policy in Finland: National and international contexts. *Dissertation Abstracts International, C: Worldwide* 63, 4, 623-C.

Pyoli, R. (1997) The danger of language death–Whose responsibility? [Kieli kuolemanvaarassa-kenen vastuu?] *Virittaja* 101(1), 66–70.

Raino, P. and Savolainen, L. (1999) The Finnish Sign Language Board [Suomalaisen viittomakielen lautakunta]. *Virittaja* 103(2), 241–245.

Reuter, M. (1979) Swedish in Finland: Minority language and regional variety. *Word* 30(1–2), 171–185.

Reuter, M. (1981) The status of Swedish in Finland in theory and practice. In E. Haugen, J. McClure, Derrick, D. Thomson and A. J. Aitken (eds) *Minority Languages Today* (pp. 130–137). Edinburgh: Edinburgh University Press.

Reuter, M. (1996) Finnish Swedish language normativization: Linguistics, sociology, or politics? [Finlandssvensk spraknormering-lingvistik, sociologi eller politik?] *Virittaja* 100(4), 555–562.

Saari, M. (1978) On the linguistic relations in the Aland Islands [Uber die sprachlichen Verhaltnisse der Aland-Inseln]. *Language Problems & Language Planning* 2(1), 27–34.

Sajavaara, K. (1997) Implementation of foreign-language policy in Finland. In T. Bongaerts and K. de Bot (eds) *Perspectives on Foreign-Language Policy* (pp. 113–128). Amsterdam: Benjamins.

Sajavaara, K. (1992) Communication, foreign languages, and foreign language policy. In K. Sajavaara (ed.) *National Foreign Language Planning: Practices and Prospects*. Jyväskylä, Finland: Institute for Educational Research, University of Jyväskylä.

Savijarvi, M. and Varteva, A. (1997) What sort of monument? The fate of the 1915 language planning committee [Mika hautasi mietinnon?-vuoden 1915 kielioppikomitean mietinnon kohtalosta]. *Virittaja* 101(1), 96–103.

Skutnabb-Kangas, T. (1996) The colonial legacy in educational language planning in

Scandinavia: From migrant labor to a national ethnic minority? *International Journal of the Sociology of Language* 118, 81–106.

Slotte, P. (1994) Dialectology and research on the Swedish spoken in Finland [Dialettologia e ricerca sullo svedese parlato in Finland]. *Rivista Italiana di Dialettologia* 18, 353–393.

Sutton, G. (1979) Cultural and socio-economic factors in the formation of foreign language education policy in Sweden – with a comparison with the Finnish case. *Language Problems & Language Planning* 3(1), 9–24.

Sysiharju, A. L. (1980) On the role and dilemma of Swedish-medium pedagogy in Finland [Den svensksprakiga pedagogikens betydelse och dilemma i Finland]. *Kasvatus* 11(2), 90–94.

Takala, S. (1983) English in the socio-linguistic context of Finland. ERIC Document Reproduction Service, ED231187.

Takala, S. (1980) New orientations in foreign language syllabus construction and language planning: A case study of Finland. Institute for Educational Research. Bulletin 155.

Takala, S. (1992) Language policy and language teaching in Finland. In K. Sajavaara (ed.) *National Foreign Language Planning: Practices and Prospects*. Jyväskylä, Finland: Institute for Educational Research, University of Jyväskylä.

Takala, S. (1998) Language teaching policy effects – A case study of Finland. *Studia Anglica Posnaniensia* 33, 421–430.

Tandefelt, M. (1992) Some linguistic consequences of the shift from Swedish to Finnish in Finland. In W. Fase, K. Jaspaert and S. Kroon (eds) *Maintenance and Loss of Minority Languages* (pp. 149–168). Amsterdam: John Benjamins.

Trosterud, T. (1998) One Finnish and four Scandinavian written languages: Or the other way round? [Yksi suomi ja nelja skandinaaviskaa-vai painvastoin?] *Nordlyd* 26, 27–35.

Ureland, S. (1987) Language contact research in northern Scandinavia. *Journal of Multilingual and Multicultural Development* 8(1–2), 43–73.

Vihonen, I. (1996) Multinational Euro-language norms [Monikansalliset eurokielen normit]. *Virittaja* 100(4), 573–577.

Vilkuna, M., Barnes, D., Britton, J. and Rosen, H. (1972) Language, the learner and the school. *Virittaja* 3, 348–350.

Wester, H. (1984) Sprakgransen: Ett matproblem. In M. Engman and H. Stenius (eds) *Svenskt i Finland, II: Demografiska och socialhistoriska studier* (pp. 281–287). Helsinki: Svenska Litteratursallskapet i Finland.

Sweden

Andersen, J. K. (1998) A general survey of the linguistic stuation in Scandinavia [Apercu de la situation linguistique en Scandinavie] *Europe Plurilingue* 7(15), 29–34.

Anonymous. (1980) Bilingualism policy in Sweden. *Integrateducation* 18(1–4), 42–51.

Anonymous. (1995) TNC Swedish Centre for Technical Terminology. *New Language Planning Newsletter* 9(4), 2–4.

Berg, C., Hult, F. and King, K. (2001) Shaping the climate for language shift? English in Sweden's elite domains. *World Englishes* 20(3), 305–319.

Boyd, S. (1999) Sweden: Immigrant languages. In B. Spolsky (ed.) *Concise Encyclopedia of Educational Linguistics* (pp. 73–74). Amsterdam: Elsevier.

Boyd, S. and Huss, L. (eds) (2000) *Managing Multilingualism in a European Nation-State: Challenges for Sweden*. Clevedon: Multilingual Matters.

Bradean Ebinger, N. (1984) The sociolinguistic aspects of bilingualism in the Scandinavian area. [Soziolinguistische Aspekte der Zweisprachigkeit im nordlichen Areal]. *Nyelvtudomanyi Kozlemenyek* 87(2), 320–325.

Bron, A. 2003 From an immigrant to a citizen: Language as a hindrance or a key to citizenship. *International Journal of Lifelong Education* 22, 6, 606–619.

Bucher, A. L. (1981) The Swedish Center for Technical Terminology–40 Years Old. *Language Planning Newsletter* 7(2), 1–2.

Cabau Lampa, B. (1999) Decisive factors for language teaching in Sweden. *Educational Studies* 25(2), 175–186.

Cabau Lampa, B. (2000) Swedish language and culture education for immigrants [L'Experience suedoise en matiere d'enseignement des langues-cultures d'origine]. *Language Problems & Language Planning* 24, 149–165.

Cedillo, P. (1993) Bilingualism in some countries of the European Community [Il bilinguismo in alcuni paesi della CEE]. *Effeta* 86(5), 115–116.

Clausen, U. (1986) Principles in Swedish language cultivation. *Språbruk* 2, 9–14.

Clyne, M. G. (1992) *Pluricentric Languages: Differing Norms in Differing Nations.* Berlin: Mouton de Gruyter.

Collis, D. R. F. (ed.) (1990) *Arctic Languages: An Awakening.* Paris: UNESCO.

Dahlstedt, K. H. (1976) Societal ideology and language cultivation: The case of Swedish. *International Journal of the Sociology of Language* 10, 17–50.

Dahlstedt, K.-H. (1976) Societal ideology and language cultivation: The case of Swedish. *Linguistics* 183, 17–50.

Dahlstedt, K.-H. (1972) Mother tongue and the second language: A Swedish viewpoint. *International Review of Applied Linguistics in Language Teaching* 10(4), 333–350.

Elenins, L. O. (2002) Both Finnish and Swedish: Modernization, nationalism and language change in the Torne Valley, 1850–1939 [Bade finsk och svensk: modernisering, nationalism och sprakforandring i Tornedalen, 1850–1939]. *Dissertation Abstracts International, C: Worldwide* 63(1), 29 -C.

Fris, A.-M. (1982) Policies for minority education: A comparative study of Britain and Sweden. Studies in Comparative and International Education, No 7. ERIC Document Reproduction Service, ED257891, 198 pp.

Gunnarsson, B.-L. (2001) Swedish, English, French or German: The language situation in Swedish universities. In U. Ammon (ed.) *The Dominance of English as a Language of Science: Effect on other Languages and Language Communities* (pp. 287–316). Berlin: Mouton de Gruyter.

Gunnarsson, B.-L. (2000) Swedish tomorrow: A product of the linguistic dominance of English? *Current Issues in Language and Society* 7(1), 51–69.

Gunnarsson, B-L. and Öhman, K. (1997) *Det internationaliserade universitetet: En studie av bruket av engelska och andra främmande språk vid Uppsala universitet.* Uppsala: Uppsala University.

Hamalian, A. and Bhatnagar, J. (1984) The education of children of immigrant groups: A comparative perspective of Britain, France, the Netherlands, the Federal Republic of Germany, and Sweden. In G. K. Verma and C. Bagley (eds) *Race Relations and Cultural Differences: Educational and Interpersonal Perspectives* (pp. 99–142). New York: St Martin's Press.

Haugen, E. (1976) *The Scandinavian Languages: An Introduction to their History.* London: Faber and Faber.

Hill, H. L. (1988) The language education of adult immigrants in Sweden: The reification, codification and actualization of an educational problem. *Dissertation Abstracts International, A: The Humanities and Social Sciences* 48(7), 1624-A.

Hollqvist, H. (1984) The use of English in three large Swedish companies. *Studia Anglistica Upsaliensia* 55.

Hube, H. J. (1978) On the position of current Swedish in relation to other Scandinavian Languages [Zur Position des Gegenwartsschwedischen im Vergleich zu anderen nordischen Sprachen]. *Wissenschaftliche Zeitschrift der Humboldt Universitat zu Berlin Gesellschafts/Sprachwissenschaftliche Reihe* 27(5), 559–562.

Hult, F.M. (2003) English on the streets of Sweden: An ecolinguistic view of two cities and a language policy. *Working Papers in Educational Linguistics* 19 (1), 43–63.

Huss, L. (1999) Reversing language shift in the far north: Linguistic revitalization in northern Scandinavia and Finland. *Acta Universitatis Upsaliensis: Studia Uralica Upsaliensia* 31, 9–212.

Hyltenstam, K. (1999) Svenska i minoritetsspråkperspektiv. In K. Hyltenstam (ed.) *Sveriges sju inhemska språk: Ett minoritetssprakperspektiv* (pp. 205–240). Lund: Studentlitteratur.

Impara, M. M. (1987) A comparative study of educational programs for linguistic minorities in three pluralistic nations: Canada, Peru, and Sweden. *Dissertation Abstracts International, A: The Humanities and Social Sciences* 47(8), 2928-A.

Karker, A. (1983) Language reforming efforts in Denmark and Sweden. In I. Fodor and C. Hagege (eds) *Language Reform: History and Future, Vol. 2* (pp. 285–299). Hamburg: Buske.

Kentta, M. (1998) The Swedish Torne Valley [Ruottin Tornionlaakso]. *Nordlyd* 26, 70–83.

Kerr, A. (1979) Language and the education of immigrants' children in Sweden. *Polyglot* 1(fiche 3), F1-F14.

Kommittén för svenska språket (2002a) *Mal i mun: Förslag till handlingsprogram för svenska språket* (SOU 2002:27). Stockholm: Statens Offentiliga Utredningar.

Kommittén för svenska språket (2002b) *Speech: Draft Action Programme for the Swedish Language: Summary*. Stockholm: Statens Offentiliga Utredningar.

Korhonen, O. (1976) Linguistic and cultural diversity among the Saamis and the development of Standard Saamish. *International Journal of the Sociology of Language* 10, 51–66.

Kristensen, K. and Thelander, M. (1984) On dialect levelling in Denmark and Sweden. *Folia Linguistica* 18(1–2), 223–246.

Lainio, J. (1997) Swedish minority language treatment and language policy–Positive public rhetoric vs. grassroot struggle. *Sociolinguistica* 11, 29–42.

Lainio, J. (2000) The protection and rejection of minority languages in the Swedish school system. *Current Issues in Language and Society* 7(1), 32–50.

Lauren, C. (1998) The Project 'Languages in the Nordic Countries as Languages of Science'. *UNESCO ALSED LSP Newsletter* 21(1(45)), 34–39.

Linde, S. G. and Lofgren, H. (1988) The relationship between medium of instruction and school achievement for Finnish-speaking students in Sweden. *Language, Culture and Curriculum* 1(2), 131–145.

Lindgren, A. R. (1998) Revitalization of minority languages: Language emancipation [Kielten Revitalisaatio–Kielten emansipaatio]. *Nordlyd* 26, 36–47.

Loman, B. (1988) Sprachliche Standardisierungsprozesse in Skandinavien. *Sociolinguistica* 2, 209–231.

Mannberg, G-A. (1986) Engelskan–inkräktare eller befriare? *Språkvård* 1, 18–22.

Melander, B. (2001) Swedish, English and the European Union. In S. Boyd and L. Huss (eds) *Managing Multilingualism in a European Nation-state: Challenges for Sweden* (pp. 13–31). Clevedon: Multilingual Matters. [Reprinted from *Current Issues in Language and Society* 7(1), 13–31.]

Molde, B. (1975) Language planning in Sweden. *Language Planning Newsletter* 1(3), 1, 3–4.

Municio, I. (1986) The home language reform [Hemspraksreformens genomforande]. *Forskning om Utbildning* 13(2), 15–24.

Nordberg, B. (1976) Sociolinguistic research in Sweden and Finland: Introduction. *International Journal of the Sociology of Language* 10, 5–15.

Nordberg, B. (1999) Sociolinguistic Research in Europe: Sweden Part I. *Sociolinguistica* 13, 261–271.

Nordberg, B. (2003) Sociolinguistic Research in Europe: Sweden Part II. *Sociolinguistica* 17, 141–167

Olsson, M. (1995) Aspects of language preservation. A typology and critique with Swedish examples [Aspekter pa sprakvard. En typologi och kritik med svenska exempel]. *Sprak och Stil* 5, 49–77.

Paulston, C. B. (1982) Swedish Research and Debate About Bilingualism: A Critical Review of the Swedish Research and Debate about Bilingualism and Bilingual Education in Sweden from an International Perspective. ERIC Document Reproduction Service, ED228843.

Paulston, C. B. (1992) Linguistic minorities and language policies: Four case studies. In W. Fase, K. Jaspaert and S. Kroon (eds) *Maintenance and Loss of Minority Languages* (pp. 55–79). Amsterdam: John Benjamins.

Paulston, C. B. (1994) *Linguistic Minorities in Multilingual Settings: Implications for Language Policies*. Amsterdam: John Benjamins.

Pupini, G. (2002) The promotion of bilingualism in Sweden [Die Zweitsprachforderung in Schweden]. *Deutsch als Zweitsprache* 2, 24–26.

Reich, H. H. (1997) How do schools deal with [immigration-related] multilingualism? European Approaches [Wie geht das Bildungswesen mit der (auch migrationsbedingten]. Veilsprachigkeit um? Verschiedene Ansatze in Europa). *Deutsch lernen* 22(1), 48–59.

Sandelin, B. (1999) Lingvoj en nelingva doktoriga edukado: Sveda ekzemplo. *Internacia Pedagogia Revuo* 29(1), 8–14.

Santesson, L. (2000) Leopold's 1801 List of Foreign Words: A diachronic study of word selection and spelling [Leopolds forteckning over frammande ord 1801-En diakronisk studie av ordurval och stavning]. *Sprak och Stil* 10, 87–128.

Selander, E. (1980) Language for professional use from the Swedish point of view. *International Journal of the Sociology of Language* 23, 17–28.

Seppanen, A. (1981) On the notion of correct usage. *Moderna Sprak* 75(3), 225–233.

Siren, U. (1995) Minority language transmission in early childhood. *International Journal of Early Years Education* 3(2), 75–84.

Skutnabb-Kangas, T. (1983) Research and its implications for the Swedish setting: An immigrant's point of view. In T. Husen and S. Opper (eds) *Multicultural and Multilingual Education in Immigrant Countries* (pp. 127–140). Oxford: Pergamon.

Skutnabb-Kangas, T. (1984) Children of guest workers and immigrants: Linguistic and educational issues. In J. Edwards (ed.) *Linguistic Minorities, Policies and Pluralism* (pp. 17–48). London: Academic.

Skutnabb-Kangas, T. (1988) Resource power and autonomy through discourse in conflict – A Finnish migrant school strike in Sweden. In T. Skutnabb-Kangas and J. Cummins (eds) *Minority Education: From Shame to Struggle* (pp. 251–277). Clevedon: Multilingual Matters.

Skutnabb-Kangas, T. (1991) Swedish strategies to prevent integration and national ethnic minorities. In O. Garcia (ed.) *Bilingual Education: Focusschrift in Honor of Joshua A. Fishman* (pp. 25–40). Amsterdam: Benjamins.

Skutnabb-Kangas, T. (1996) The colonial legacy in educational language planning in Scandinavia: From migrant labor to a national ethnic minority? *International Journal of the Sociology of Language* 118, 81–106.

Skutnabb-Kangas, T. and Phillipson, R. (2000) The world came to Sweden – But did language rights? *Current Issues in Language and Society* 7, 70–86.

Stockfelt Hoatson, B. I. (1977) The teaching of bilingual infant immigrants in a Swedish town. *Linguistics* 198 (Oct 15), 119–125.

Sutton, G. (1979) Cultural and socio-economic factors in the formation of foreign language education policy in Sweden – With a comparison with the Finnish case. *Language Problems & Language Planning* 3, 9–24.

Teleman, U. (1992) Det svenska riksspråkets utsikter i ett integrerat Europa. *Språkvård* 4, 7–16.

Teleman, U. and Westman, M. (1997a) Behöver Sverige en nationell språkpolitik? *Språk i Norden 1997*, 5–22.

Teleman, U. and Westman, M. (1997b) Behover vi en nationell sprakpolitik? *Sprakvard: Tidskrift Utgiven AV Svenska Spraknamnden* 33(2), 5–16.

Torp, A. (1989) On the central common Scandinavian vocabulary and on the purism in Nynorsk [Zum zentralen gemeinskandinavischen Wortschatz und zum Purismus im Nynorsk]. *Zeitschrift fur Deutsche Philologie* supplement 5, 220–240.

Toukomaa, P. (1980) Education through the medium of the mother tongue of Finnish immigrant children in Sweden. In L. K. Boey (ed.) *Bilingual Education* (pp. 136–161). Singapore: Singapore University Press.

Trosterud, T. (1998) One Finnish and four Scandinavian written Languages: Or the other way round? [Yksi suomi ja nelja skandinaaviskaa-vai painvastoin?] *Nordlyd* 26, 27–35.

Ureland, S. (1987) Language contact research in northern Scandinavia. *Journal of Multilingual and Multicultural Development* 8(1–2), 43–73.

van Els, T. and Extra, G. (1987) Foreign and second language teaching in Western Europe: A comparative overview of needs, objectives and policies. *Sociolinguistica* 1, 100–125.

Westin, C. (1983) Migrant children and language: Comments on a hot report [Invandrarbarnens sprak-kommentar till en het rapport]. *Forskning om Utbildning* 10(3), 31–38.

Westman, M. (1996) Har svenska språket en framtid? In L. Moberg and M. Westman (eds) *Svenska i tusen år: Glimtar ur svenska språkets utveckling* (pp. 182–194). Stockholm: Norstedts.

Wingstedt, M. (1998) *Language Ideologies and Minority Language Policies in Sweden: Historical and Contemporary Perspectives.* Stockholm: Stockholm University.

The Language Situation in Hungary

Péter Medgyes and Katalin Miklósy
Centre for English Teacher Training, Eötvös Loránd University, Ajtosi Durer, sor 19,
1146 Budapest, Hungary

This monograph reports on the language situation in Hungary, a largely monolingual country, where nearly 98% of the population speak Hungarian as their first language. Therefore, the *primary focus* of the study is on the Hungarian language as used by some 10 million people within the national borders of Hungary, and less attention is paid to either Hungarian as a minority language spoken mostly in the neighbouring countries, or the language of ethnic minorities living in Hungary. At the same time, conscious of the fact that the Hungarian language is of limited use outside Hungary, Hungarians have always attached great importance to foreign language learning. The *secondary focus* of this monograph, therefore, is placed on issues concerning foreign language instruction. While the language situation of Hungary is examined from a historical perspective, the main emphasis is placed on the presentation of recent developments, especially those occurring since the fall of communism in 1989.

Part I: The Language Profile of Hungary

The Native Language Profile

It is a truism to state that every country is multilingual – the concept of monolingual nationhood is a myth. However, it is also true that countries differ in the degree of their multilingualism: certain countries are less multilingual than others. Hungary, for example, where nearly 98% of the population speaks Hungarian as a first language (Statistical Yearbook, 1998), is certainly less multilingual than most of its neighbours. Moreover, Hungarian is a language belonging to the Finno-Ugric family of languages, while all the surrounding countries use a language of Indo-European origin as their first language: in five of them a Slavic language is spoken (Slovak, Ukrainian, Serbian, Croatian and Slovenian), whereas Romanian is a Neo-Latin language, and German, the official language of Austria, is a Germanic language. Thus Hungarians are not able to communicate with their non-Hungarian neighbours unless they have learnt to speak foreign languages. In view of this, it is small wonder that the knowledge of foreign languages has always been held in high esteem in Hungary – as a Hungarian proverb puts it: 'You are as many persons as many languages you can speak.'

In this monograph, the space allotted to the discussion of foreign languages will be commensurate to their importance: the issues related to foreign language knowledge, instruction and study will be dealt with in greater length than those concerning Hungarian. As for minorities in Hungary, since they represent a mere three per cent of the total population, their language situation will receive less attention.

As the words 'Hungary' and 'Hungarians' can be interpreted in several ways, depending on which historical period is being discussed, it seems important to make clear how these terms will be used in this monograph. 'Hungary' will refer to the area presently covered by the Republic of Hungary. 'Hungarians' will denote Hungarian citizens whose first language is Hungarian. Hungarian minority groups who live in neighbouring countries will be referred to as 'ethnic Hungarians', whereas Hungarians living in non-neighbouring countries will be termed 'emigrant Hungarians'.

A brief history

Hungary is a landlocked country, occupying almost the whole of the Carpathian Basin in central Europe. The area of Hungary is 35,920 square miles (93,033 km^2) and its population is slightly more than 10 million. The territory of present-day Hungary has always been a busy crossroads and, consequently, was attacked and occupied repeatedly by foreign invaders. Wedged among several peoples, Slavs, Germans and Romanians, Hungarians have been exposed to a variety of influences. Two major influences were the Turks, who invaded and occupied Hungary for 150 years in the 16th and 17th centuries and, in their wake, the Austrian Hapsburgs with their strong Germanising impact. National feeling, however, could not be suppressed: Hungarians have a history of heroic but tragic uprisings, including the Revo-lution and War of Independence in 1848–49. Hungary received autonomy in 1867 after the Austro-Hungarian Monarchy was established, and full inde-pendence when the monarchy was defeated after World War I. As a conse-quence of the war, in 1920 some two thirds of the former territory of Hungary was annexed to Austria, Czechoslovakia, Romania and Yugoslavia.[1] Thus large Hungarian minority groups were created in the neighbouring countries. Hoping to recover its lost territories, Hungary sided with Nazi Germany in World War II. After the defeat of the Axis powers in 1945, 'Soviet liberation forces' remained in the country ostensibly to ensure the implementation of a peace treaty reaffirming the 1920 frontiers. Following a communist take-over in 1949, the Hungarian People's Republic was proclaimed under Stalinist rule. A revolution broke out against this regime in 1956, only to be crushed by the Soviet Union with military force. Between 1956 and 1988, Hungary gradu-ally adopted more and more liberal policies in the economic and cultural spheres, with the result that it was considered to be the most tolerant country behind the 'Iron Curtain'. In 1989, Hungary's communist leaders voluntarily abandoned their monopoly of power, thus facilitating a peaceful shift to a multi-party democracy and free-market economy. Since 1990, three consecu-tive free elections have been held – an exceptionally long democratic period in the history of Hungary.

The origins of the Hungarian language

Hungarian is a unique and isolated language of central Europe, because it is not Indo-European in origin; rather it belongs to the Finno-Ugric branch of the Uralic family of languages (Figure 1). According to estimates, the total number of speakers of Uralic languages all over the world is about 25 million, the majority of whom (approximately 15 million) speak Hungarian. The beginnings of the development of an independent Hungarian language date back to about 1000 BC, and the oldest written records of the language can be traced back to the 11th

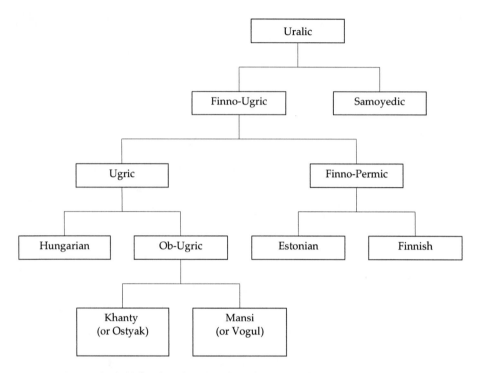

Figure 1 An outline of the family tree of Uralic languages

century AD. Its closest relatives are Mansi (or Vogul) and Khanty (or Ostyak), spoken together by a total of 10,000 people in Western Siberia. More distant relatives are Finnish and Estonian.

Although there have been several theories concerning the origins of the Hungarian language, it is now generally accepted that Hungarian belongs to the Uralic family of languages. Are any of these languages mutually intelligible? Mansi and Khanty are as closely related to each other as Serbian is to Croatian but in neither case would a speaker understand Hungarian. Hungarian and Finnish are as comprehensible to each other as, for example, English is to Greek. In other words, their kinship is based merely on linguistic evidence, revealed in regular and systematic differences and similarities between the two languages – peculiarities that would not be noticed by speakers of either Finnish or Hungarian.

Hungarian Grammar in a Nutshell

Spelling and pronunciation

Orthography

Hungarian uses the Roman alphabet. It contains 44 graphemes, including digraphs, i.e. combinations of single letters which represent one consonant. Among the 30 consonant letters, *q, w, x, y* are not 'native' in the sense that they only appear in foreign or archaic words such as *tequila*, *Wekerle* (family name), *taxi*, or *papaya*.

There are eight digraphs, e.g. *cs* (like English *ch* in church) and *ny* (like British English *n* in new). There is one consonant which is spelled with three letters (a trigraph): *dzs* (like English *j* in jam). Consonant letters can be doubled to denote phonetically long consonants, e.g. *ott* [ot:] 'there'. In the case of digraphs only the first character is doubled to express length, e.g. *busszal* [bus:al] 'by bus' (and not *'buszszal'*).

Hungarian has 14 vowels, many of which appear with diacritical marks. They form seven short/long pairs, e.g. *a–á, i–í, ö–ő, ü–ű*. Those without an accent or with umlauts are short, those with accents or double accents are long. Length is a distinctive feature of Hungarian vowels since it may affect the meaning of the word, e.g. *tör* [tør] '(s/he) breaks' and *tőr* [tø:r] 'dagger'.

Hungarian vowels are either front (*i–í, ü–ű, e–é, ö–ő*) or back (*u–ú, o–ó, a–á*), either rounded (*ü–ű, ö–ő, u–ú, o–ó, a*) or unrounded (*i–í, e–é, á*).

Vowel harmony

One of the most important regularities of the sound pattern of Hungarian is that most endings harmonise with the stems they are attached to. This means that most endings have two or three alternative forms differing only in the vowel, e.g. *-nál, -nél* 'at', *-hoz, -hez, -höz* 'to'.

As a rule, two-form suffixes have one form with a back vowel and one with a front vowel, e.g. *-ban, -ben* 'in'. The selection of the ending depends on the vowel(s) of the word stem. Back vowel words take the suffix with the back alternant, front vowel words take the front alternants: *ház – házban* 'house – in the house', *kert – kertben* 'garden – in the garden'. Some suffixes have three alternative forms, one with the back vowel *o*, one with the unrounded front vowel *e*, and a third with the rounded front vowel *ö*: *-on, -en, -ön* 'on'. Words with a rounded front vowel in the final syllable take the rounded front (*ö*) alternant of the three-form suffixes: *föld – földön* 'ground – on the ground'.

Mixed vowel stems usually harmonise according to the vowel of the last syllable, e.g. *virág – virággal* 'flower – with flower'. If the last syllable contains one of the so-called neutral vowels: *i–í, é*, the mixed vowel stem harmonises with the vowel of the second last syllable, e.g. *kávé – kávéba* 'coffee – into coffee' (Polgárdi, 1998; Vago, 1976).

Sound-letter correspondence

In Hungarian, letters tend to have constant phonetic values: it is generally true that a given letter always corresponds to the same sound.

There are no diphthongs in standard Hungarian, so adjacent vowels are pronounced as separate syllables: *mai* [mai] 'of today'.

Word stress

In Hungarian, stress always falls on the first syllable of the word, even in loan words: Amerika ['amerika] 'America' (Kontra, 1995).

Morphology and syntax

An agglutinative language

As there are no prepositions in Hungarian, words are built up in a sequence of units, with each unit expressing a particular grammatical meaning. For example, 'for my pictures' in Hungarian is *képeimnek*, which can be analysed as:

   kép/eim/nek

picture + plural possessive (i.e. the 1st person singular possessor has more than one possession: 'my pictures') + for. So the direct equivalent of the Hungarian sequence is 'pictures my for'.

Verb conjugation

Verbs are conjugated in Hungarian by putting endings after the basic form of the verb. The basic form is the present tense 3rd person singular, the 's/he' form. Thus the 'dictionary' form means: 'he/she . . . s' (e.g. *fut* 'he/she runs'). This is the stem to conjugate when a different person/number is to be described (Törkenczy, 1997).

There are two 'slots' after the Hungarian verb stem; each slot gives only certain kinds of information. The first slot provides information about tense/mood, the second one about person/number.

   sétál/t/unk   sétál/ná/tok   walk/-ed/we   walk/would/you (plural)

As the verb ending indicates which person is meant, personal pronouns are not usually used except for emphasis.

There are two sets of person/number suffixes and, consequently, two verb conjugations in each tense: definite and indefinite. This distinction is based on the definiteness or the indefiniteness of the object. The object is definite when it is uniquely identifiable, either absolutely (e.g. the name of a person or a place) or through context (e.g. the object is preceded by the definite article). Therefore, there is an important grammatical difference between 'I'm watching *a* film' and 'I'm watching *the* film': the Hungarian verb takes an indefinite suffix in the first sentence and a definite suffix in the second one. This distinction does not exist in English: compare the Hungarian equivalent of the two sample sentences:

   Nézek egy filmet.   I'm watching a film. (indef.)
   Nézem a filmet.   I'm watching the film. (def.)

Tri-directionalism

When expressing location and direction, the most important suffixes can be considered as belonging to three sets: one indicating movement towards a position, one indicating a state of rest in a certain position, and one indicating movement away from the position. Hence the name 'tri-directionalism'. The three 'directions' correspond to the question words *hová?* 'where to?', *hol?* 'where?' and *honnan?* 'where from?' (see Table 1).

A peculiarity of the Hungarian language is that while all towns and countries in the world are associated with a closed space, e.g. *Oxfordban* 'in Oxford', the word '*Hungary*' and most Hungarian place names are regarded as a surface, e.g. *Budapesten* 'in Budapest' (literally 'on Budapest').

'Reverse order'

When endings are attached to some verbal and nominal forms, they are also extended 'to the right', and suffixes express the meanings indicated by preposi-

Table 1 The tri-directionalism of Hungarian nominal suffixes. After Payne (1987, p.72)

	hová? [where to?]	*hol? [where?]*	*honnan? [where from?]*
closed place (e.g. a shop)	-ba/-be (into)	-ban/-ben (in)	-ból/-ből (from)
surface (e.g. a table)	-ra/-re (on to)	-on/-en/-ön (on)	-ról/-ről (from)
point in space (e.g. my friend)	-hoz/-hez/-höz (to)	-nál/-nél (at)	-tól/-től (from)

tions in English. In these cases the order of units is reversed compared to English. Thus *barátomtól* 'from my friend' can be analysed as

> *barát/om/tól*   friend / my / from

The order of personal names is reversed as well; the given name follows the family name, e.g. *Bartók Béla*. The same rule applies to addresses and dates. The sequence goes from general to specific, i.e. town → street → number of block; and year → month → day. However, there are lots of cases when the 'reverse order' rule does not apply: adjectives precede nouns; articles precede nouns and noun phrases just as in English: *a fehér kutya* 'the white dog'.

What Hungarian does not have

There is the absence of gender. In the third person singular, *ő* is the equivalent of both 'he' and 'she' in English.

There is no equivalent of the English continuous tense in the Hungarian conjugation system: *futok* 'I run / I am running'. There is no perfect aspect either; thus a single Hungarian past verb form can have four English equivalents: *olvastam a könyvet* 'I read the book (yesterday), I have read the book, I was reading the book, I have been reading the book'.

There is no direct equivalent of the possessive 'to have' in present-day Hungarian. It is expressed by using a construction which involves the possessive forms. *Van egy álmom* 'I have a dream' would translate literally as 'Is a dream my' (Kiefer, 1985).

A numeral is followed by a singular noun, e.g. *hét könyv* 'seven books', literally 'seven book' (cf. 'three quid' in British English.)

Further exploration of Hungarian phonology and morphology in English may be found in the following sources: Abondolo, 1988; Benkő & Imre, 1972; Kenesei *et al.*, 1998; Nádasdy, 1985.

Vocabulary

Finno-Ugric lexis

In current Hungarian there are approximately 700 base words of Finno-Ugric origin. They include:

> Pronouns: *én* 'I', *te* 'you', *ő* 'he/she'
> Parts of the body: *fej* 'head', *fül* 'ear', *szem* 'eye'

Kinship: *atya* 'father', *anya* 'mother'
Nature: *ég* 'sky', *csillag* 'star', *víz* 'water'
Plants: *gyökér* 'root', *tő* 'stem', *fa* 'tree'
Animals: *lúd* 'goose', *hal* 'fish', *fecske* 'swallow'
Activities: *alszik* 'sleep', *áll* 'stand', *mond* 'say'
Existence: *lesz* 'will be', *él* 'lives', *hal* 'dies'
The words for 'yes' (*igen*) and 'Hungarian' (*magyar*) are also Finno-Ugric.

The Ugric language community broke up when Hungarian tribes started migrating to the west. The migrations were caused by the attacks of various nomadic peoples from the east and by overpopulation within the local tribes. To reach the Carpathian Basin from the southern foothills of the Ural mountains took about 2000 years; in this period Hungarians settled among other tribes (they lived as part of the Kazar Empire in Levedia, for example). This intermingling had a number of consequences. Among others, it left its mark on the Hungarian vocabulary:

Early Iranian loan words are: *tíz* 'ten'
Persian loan words (probably from traders) include: *vásár* 'market'
Iranian-Alan loan words are: *híd* 'bridge'.

However, it was ancient Turkish that exerted the strongest impact on Hungarian during the period of migrations. The approximately 300 ancient Turkish loan words include:

Parts of the body: *boka* 'ankle', *kar* 'arm'
Colours: *kék* 'blue', *sárga* 'yellow'
Animal husbandry: *bika* 'bull', *disznó* 'pig'
Agriculture: *alma* 'apple', *búza* 'wheat'
Religious beliefs: *boszorkány* 'witch'
Domestic life: *kapu* 'gate', *bölcső* 'cradle', *szék* 'chair'

Slavic loan words

When the Hungarians arrived in the Carpathian Basin, the area had been dotted with Slavic settlements. Slavic loan words appeared between the conquest of Hungarian tribes (around 900 AD) and the battle of Mohács (1526).[2] They emerged in many economic, administrative, religious and everyday contexts. Some examples are:

Manufacture and trade: *kovács* 'smith'
Administrative and legal: *király* 'king', *pénz* 'money'
Church and religion: *keresztény* 'Christian'
Family: *cseléd* 'servant', *család* 'family'

Between the 10th and 18th centuries three other languages had a considerable impact on the Hungarian vocabulary: German, Latin and Turkish.

German, Latin and Turkish loan words

The appearance of German loan words can be dated to two different historical periods. The first coincides with the foundation of the Hungarian kingdom (1000 AD) when, at the Bavarian-born Hungarian queen's invitation, missionary priests and knights appeared in the country, followed by German-speaking settlers. Then, after the end of the Turkish occupation, another wave of Germans settled in Hungary. As German was used mostly in Hungarian cities, well-to-do parents would send their children there to study German.

A few German loan words are:

Court: *herceg* 'prince'
City: *borbély* 'barber'
Rural life: *csűr* 'barn'
Dressing: *gallér* 'collar'

Latin, as the lingua franca in Europe, had a dominant role in Hungarian governmental, economic and cultural life. Moreover, during the Middle Ages and centuries thereafter, Latin also served as the *lingua patriae*. It was only in 1844 that Hungarian became the official national language. From the 10th century on, Latin was used in official communication: the earliest charters and laws were all written in Latin. The first significant Hungarian poet, Janus Pannonius, who lived in the 15th century, wrote all his poems in Latin. Some of the commonly used 200 words of Latin origin are in connection with the following:

Church: *templom* 'church', *oltár* 'altar', *próféta* 'prophet'
School: *iskola* 'school', *professzor* 'professor'
Administration and law: *prókátor* 'lawyer', *voks* 'vote', *paktum* 'pact, contract'
Animals: *tigris* 'tiger', *vipera* 'viper'
Plants: *cédrus* 'cedar', *pálma* 'palm'
House: *porta* 'house, home', *kamra* 'chamber' (some of these words are archaic now)
Months: *január* 'January', *február* 'February', etc.

There are Ottoman-Turkish loan words in Hungarian owing to the 150-year-long Turkish occupation in the 16th–17th centuries. These include words related to

Eating: *findzsa* 'pot', *pite* 'pie'
Smoking: *burnót* 'snuff', *csibuk* 'pipe'
Weapons: *handzsár* 'sword', *korbács* 'whip'

A movement to renew Hungarian

Until the late 18th century, Hungarian was often considered the 'inferior' language of peasants, not suitable for sciences, law or literature, even though outstanding literary works had been written in Hungarian since the 16th century. However, when Joseph II of Hapsburg (1780–1790) introduced German as the official language of the empire, the decree elicited stiff national resistance and drew special attention to linguistic matters. A campaign was launched by writer and poet Ferenc Kazinczy to modernise and beautify the language. This movement of 'language renewal' lasted for several decades and sparked off fierce debates between 'neologists' and 'orthologists'.

Language reformers used several methods. They shortened words, e.g. *gépely* → *gép* 'machine', combined and shortened words, e.g. *rovátkolt + barom = rovar* 'grooved + animal = insect' and created several new ones which had had no native Hungarian equivalent. These innovators even tried to replace existing words of unmistakable Latin origin with 'true' Hungarian ones, e.g. *masina* 'machine', which resembled the original Latin word *machina* was superseded by the Hungarian-sounding word *gép*. *Matéria* 'material' was almost identical with the Latin *materia* and thus was 'Hungarianised' as *anyag*.

The language reformers managed to expand and alter the vocabulary of Hungarian to a great extent. Approximately 10,000 of the words introduced or created at that time are still in regular use. In a sense, more was gained than was bargained for: had neologists been less successful, Hungarian vocabulary would be closer to the lexis of Indo-European languages.

English as the major source of recent loan words

The present trend in vocabulary change demonstrates a continuous influx of foreign (mostly English) words. The spread of English words in ads, street signs and shop-windows is a global phenomenon and Hungary is no exception (Medgyes, 1992).

Most of the English loan words refer to the world of entertainment, business, mass media, computers and politics. Here are a few examples: *diszkó* 'disco', *menedzser* 'manager', *marketing*, *CD-játszó* 'CD player', *talk show, winchester* 'hard disk', *diszk* 'disc/disquette', *lobbi* 'pressure group', *lobbizik* 's/he is lobbying'. Spelling varies: the older the loan word, the more likely it is to follow the rules of Hungarian spelling. Words of English origin have to take on Hungarian suffixes, e.g. *diszkózik* 'goes to the disco', *szörföl* 'does surfing'.

Purists, language educators and several pressure groups have voiced their reservations about this trend. In the mid-1990s there was even a proposal for a language law (following the French example) to combat the expansion of English. In response to this suggestion, a group of academics and linguists published a letter in the Hungarian newspapers, arguing against the necessity and feasibility of such a law.

Dialects

Dialectal variants do not cause significant problems in comprehension, partly due to the relatively small size of the country. Figure 2 shows the main dialects and their spread. Differences are phonological, morphological or lexical. The major Hungarian dialects are:

(1) Western. In this area the vowels *í* and *ú* are represented by their short counterparts, e.g. *viz* (for *víz*) 'water', *kut* (for *kút*) 'well'.
(2) Transdanubian. The vowel *a* is frequently pronounced like *ó*, e.g. *házbó* (for *házba*) 'into the house'.
(3) Southern. *Ö* is used instead of *e* in certain positions, e.g. *Szöged* (for *Szeged*) (city name).
(4) Tisza. Compared to standard Hungarian, certain vowels are represented by their long counterparts, e.g. *tanúlt* (for *tanult*) 's/he learned'; *í* replaces *é*: *szíp* (for *szép*) 'beautiful'.
(5) Palóc. It can be identified by the illabial *a* sound. Diphthongs are used, e.g. *voult* or *vuolt* (for *volt*) 'was'.
(6) North-eastern. The literary language has stemmed from this dialect. The

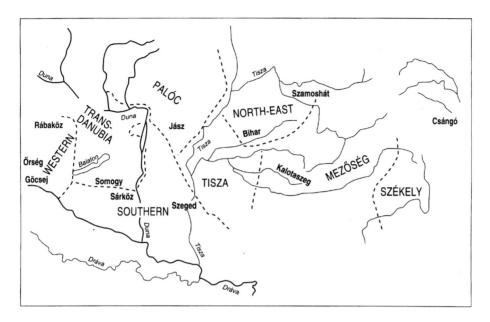

Figure 2 Hungarian dialects (Balázs, 1997)

consonant *j* is pronounced instead of *l*, e.g. *pájinka* (for *pálinka*) 'brandy', *jány* (for *lány*) 'girl'.

(7) Mezőség. The central part of the Hungarian area in Romania. The vowel *e* is pronounced instead of *é*, e.g. *tehen* (for *tehén*) 'cow', *nehez* (for *nehéz*) 'heavy'.

(8) Székely. Also in Romania. The archaic past tenses are still used. Special suffixes are used with family names, e.g. *Sándorni* (for *Sándorékhoz*) 'to the Sándor (family)', *Sándornul* (for *Sándoréktól*) 'from the Sándor (family)'.

There are two language enclaves separated from the Hungarian core language area for historic reasons.

(1) Csángó. In Moldavia, Romania. They still use an archaic version of Hungarian. *Várt lenne* (for *várt volna*) 's/he would have waited', *tyukmon* (for *tojás*) 'egg'.

(2) Slavonian. Four villages in Croatia.

Standard Hungarian and the Budapest slang

When in 1873 Budapest became one city with the unification of Buda, Pest and Óbuda, it played a decisive role in the standardisation of Hungarian. Originally, the movement to reform the language started in the north-east of Hungary, but soon after the process was transferred to Budapest during the second half of the 19th century. At that time, for example, there were still two variants of the *j* sound in Hungarian, but it disappeared from 'Budapest Hungarian' and, subsequently, from Hungarian altogether. However, it has been preserved in spelling in the dual form of *ly* and *j*, which indicates the same sound. Budapest still exerts a strong homogenising influence on the language. In the mass media (located mainly in Budapest) only standard Hungarian is used, and dialects are rarely if ever heard in public communication. Moreover, in comic sketches, if a writer wants to present a person as ignorant, backward, or uncouth, the character invariably talks in a (usually fake) dialect.

The most characteristic feature of 'Budapest Hungarian' is its slang which radiates wit, irony and humour, and it is often vulgar. Budapest slang frequently borrowed from German, Yiddish[3] and Romani, in particular.

German:	*smaci*	'kiss',	*pejsli*	'lung'
Yiddish:	*meló*	'work',	*jatt*	'handshake/tip'
Romani:	*lóvé*	'money',	*csaj*	'girl'. (Balázs, 1997).

The Minority Language Profile

Demographic figures

Language polities may be numerically represented by two criteria: (1) by nationality, and (2) by first language. On both counts Hungary may be called a homogeneous country. According to the latest national census in 1990, 97.8% of the population claimed to be ethnic Hungarian and 98.5% marked Hungarian as their first language (Statistical Yearbook, 1995). In a statistical sense, then, minorities play an insignificant role in the present-day life of Hungary. Table 2 shows the distribution of the population by nationality. If this is compared to the distribution by first language, virtually the same rank order results. The only striking difference is that the number of those who speak Gypsy as their first language is 48,072 – one third of those who identify themselves as ethnic Gypsies. In addition to the languages indicated above, the National Census of 1990 specifies five languages spoken in Hungary (in this order): Polish, Greek, Bulgarian, Ukranian and Armenian, ranging from a few thousand speakers to a few dozen. It is important to note, however, that, with the exception of foreign nationals residing in Hungary, Hungarian is understood and spoken by the entire population of Hungary (Fenyvesi, 1998).

Hungary was not always such a homogeneous country, and in fact was once one of the least monolingual countries in Europe. According to the data of the 1851 census, for example, merely 40.5% of the total population of around 11 million claimed to be Hungarian, followed by Romanian, Slovak and German

Table 2 The distribution of the Hungarian population by nationality

Hungarian	10,142,072
Gypsy	142,683
German	30,824
Croatian	13,570
Romanian	10,740
Slovak	10,459
Serbian	2,905
Slovenian	1,930
Other	19,640
Total	10,374,823

with 19.5, 15.2 and 12.3%, respectively. The last census before the Treaty of Trianon (1910) shows that the population of Hungary grew rapidly (18.25 million), and so did the proportion of ethnic Hungarians (54%) at the expense of other ethnic groups: the proportion of Romanians fell to 16.1, and Germans to 10.4%, whereas the proportion of Slovaks increased to 19.7% (Fenyvesi, 1998). The decline of minorities can mainly be attributed to a swift process of assimilation occurring in the second half of the 19th century.

The Treaty of Trianon (1920) dramatically changed the demographic picture of Hungary once and for all. Together with a loss of over two thirds of its territory, Hungary lost 90% of its minorities and one third of its ethnically Hungarian population. Out of a population of less than 8 million, the proportion of ethnic Hungarians rose to 90%, while the proportion of the major ethnicities dropped to fragments of their pre-Trianon size: the most conspicuous decrease may be registered for the Romanian minority which was reduced to a mere 0.3% of the total population of Hungary in 1920; the figures for ethnic Slovaks and Germans were 1.8 and 6.9%, respectively. During these turbulent years, the number of Hungarians fleeing from the neighbouring countries was estimated at 350,000 (Fenyvesi, 1998).

In the 80 years since Trianon, every ethnic minority has shrunk, except for the Gypsy population, while the proportion of the Hungarian majority has steadily grown. Rather than examining the development of the ethnic minorities one by one, only the two largest groups will be described briefly.

The Gypsy minority

'Gypsy' is used as an umbrella term for a large ethnic group that exhibits a high degree of variation in traditions, language use and occupation. The first Gypsies are recorded to have arrived in Hungary in the 15th century, followed by other tribes coming from Serbia in the 16th and 17th, and by Romanian speaking Gypsies in the 17th and 18th centuries. Empress Maria Theresa of Habsburg was the first to attempt to intergrate wandering Gypsies into Hungarian society, by forcing Gypsy children into schools and foster homes; all children are said to have fled back to their families (Crowe, 1991).

Nevertheless, for centuries Gypsies played a marginal role in the history of Hungary, traditionally working as blacksmiths, locksmiths, tinkers, horse traders and musicians. In 1851 they were registered as a minority with only 0.7% of the total population (83,800). Although growing in number (148,000), Gypsies still made up only 0.8% of the population by 1910. According to the figures of the National Census in 1930, there were 14,000 Gypsies living in Hungary, but other sources put their number at 100,000. At the end of World War II, the Gypsy population was estimated to stand between 30,000 and 40,000, a major reason for this sharp decrease being that 31,000 Gypsies from Hungary were exterminated in concentration camps (Crowe, 1991).

During the communist era, the process of industrialisation and urbanisation affected Gypsies as well: losing their traditional trades, they joined the workforce of industry as unskilled or semi-skilled workers. At the same time, an enormous increase in the Gypsy population was registered, in sharp contrast to the population decline of all other ethnic groups, including Hungarians. While according to the National Census of 1990 only 1.4% of the population identified themselves as Gypsies, Kemény *et al.* put their number at 3% in 1971, 5% in 1994 and at a predicted 8% by 2000 (cited in Póczik, 1996). Despite these contradictory figures, it is a well-known fact that the Gypsy population of Hungary is very young; 49% is below the age of 24, and every tenth child under seven years of age is of Gypsy descent (Halász & Lannert, 1998).

The German minority

In the aftermath of Turkish occupation, vast areas of Hungary were left depopulated and some of its most fertile lands lay fallow in the late 17th century. In line with the subordination policies of the Hapsburgs, masses of Swabian Germans from the south-western region of present-day Germany were lured to settle in Hungary. They were granted by the imperial administration not only free land, construction materials, livestock and tax exemption, but were also permitted to erect their own churches and schools. In comparison to other minorities, the German settlers enjoyed much higher social and economic prestige and living standards than Hungarians or any other ethnic group. This privileged status may partly explain why it was the German population in Hungary who were the most ardent promoters of assimilation among ethnic groups. In any case, Hungarian arts and culture were enriched by hundreds of Germans, tracing their heritage to Swabian smallholder families (Manherz, 1993).

During World War II, pan-German nationalism did not leave Hungarian Germans unaffected. The younger generation especially flocked to join the Volksbund, an organisation that gradually came to be associated with Nazi Germany. By the end of the war, 120,000 ethnic Germans from Hungary served in Nazi units recruited in Hungary. In late 1944, 50,000 ethnic Germans decided to leave Hungary to be repatriated in Germany. Those who remained loyal to Hungary had a much less auspicious fate awaiting them. Some 60,000 ethnic Germans were deported to the Soviet Union – many would perish in prisoner-of-war camps. Another 225,000 people of German descent were forcibly repatriated to the two parts of Germany. Finally, those who stayed in Hungary were stripped of Hungarian citizenship. Although their citizenship was returned to them in 1949 and 1950, thousands of them were relocated to remote parts of the country, and had their homes and lands confiscated and given over to Hungarians (Fenyvesi, 1998).

As the darkest period of communist rule ended, hostile feelings towards the German ethnicity gradually eased. This tendency of reconciliation was facilitated by the 'comradely' relations between Hungary and East Germany, and subsequently also by the economic ties that brought Hungary nearer and nearer to Austria and West Germany (Szablyár, 1998).

According to a survey conducted by the Central Statistical Office in 1990 (cited in Szántó, 1995), only 27.5% of those who claimed to speak German as their first language identified themselves as Hungarians of German nationality – theirs was the lowest ratio among the nationalities of Hungary. In investigating the national identity of adolescents of German origin in Hungary, Szántó (1995) was confronted with a similarly ambivalent situation. One of his questions was as follows: 'How would you introduce yourself at an international youth camp?' Of the young respondents, 46.6% said that they would claim to be Hungarian, and a further 21.2% were reported to say that they came from a place in Hungary with a German population. Less than one third of the respondents admitted to their

German descent in a more or less open fashion. The reasons for the ambivalent feelings of ethnic Germans in Hungary appear to be too complex for the authors of this monograph to attempt to interpret.

The Foreign Language Profile

How many people speak foreign languages in Hungary?

Before Hungary had shrunk to one third of its original territory in 1920, out of the ten million native speakers of Hungarian, roughly 1.3 million could speak German as a foreign language (Statistical Report 1910, cited in Huszár, 1998) – the existence of the Austro-Hungarian Monarchy explains the high proportion of German speakers. Disregarding the languages of ethnic minorities, German was followed by French and English with 82,000 and 37,000 speakers, respectively.[5]

Twenty years later, while the number of those who spoke Hungarian as their first language in Hungary dropped to about eight million, in absolute numbers the foreign language palette remained stable: while German was the leader with nearly 840,000 speakers, the number of French and English speakers was 87,000 and 52,000, respectively (Statistical Report 1930, cited in Huszár, 1998). Incidentally, these were the first statistics that registered Russian as well, with 23,000 speakers.

The forty years of communist rule made an indelible mark on the foreign language situation in Hungary. According to the National Census of 1990 (Statistical Yearbook, 1995), out of the nearly 10.4 million native speakers of Hungarian 453,000 claimed to speak German, followed by 229,000 English, 157,000 Russian and 53,000 French speakers. However, these data can be misleading, because they fail to distinguish between high- and low-proficiency speakers.

The changes of 1989 hugely increased language learning motivation. In this age of globalisation, the importance of foreign language competence needs hardly any justification anywhere in the world, but the pressure on the Hungarian population has been particularly acute. It is no exaggeration to suggest that the career prospects of Hungarian citizens are greatly enhanced by a good command of English and/or German. In present-day Hungary, stating the vital importance of foreign language proficiency is stating the obvious.

Nevertheless, the foreign language competence of Hungarians leaves a lot to be desired. Few people can speak foreign languages and very few can speak at least one foreign language well. In the light of recent statistical data, foreign languages are spoken by a relatively small minority of the population. Although such data may be indicative of the real situation, they should be treated with caution, because they draw on survey results largely based on questionnaire-elicited self-reports which reflect stated behaviour rather than actual behaviour – and there may be a wide gap between the two (Csepeli, 1987; Marton, 1981).

The most comprehensive survey, conducted by Terestyéni (1995), comprises a representative sample of 2000 respondents, who were asked to rate their foreign language proficiency on a five-point scale, from 5 ('very good') to 1 ('almost zero'). On the basis of the results including proficiency level 3 and above, 11.2% of the population (aged 18 or above) claimed at least to 'get by' in one foreign language, 3.3% in two languages and 0.8% in three or more languages.[6] Another questionnaire-type survey, which included 2998 respondents aged 18 and above, demonstrated a slightly higher proportion (15.7%), but the validity of this enquiry was weakened by the lack of fine-tuning with respect to proficiency levels (Imre, 1995). In a third survey, 50% of respondents admitted to having no foreign language competence and a mere 6% claimed to speak one language fluently (Manherz, 1995). Viewed in a European context, this meant that Hungary was followed only by Albania in terms of foreign language competence.

Terestyéni's report (1995) also revealed that foreign language competence is closely related to social, geographical and age factors: better educated, young urban people were found more likely to speak foreign languages. The validity of these trends was confirmed by Imre's survey (1995). Terestyéni further established that 90% of secondary school graduates and 59% of university and college graduates could not manage in any foreign language, a clear indication of the ineffectiveness of foreign language education at school. In terms of school instruction, the age group which scored the lowest in terms of their foreign language proficiency was that between 51 and 60. This generation went to school between 1945 and the early 1960s, a period when foreign languages other than Russian were expunged from the curriculum.[7]

The picture becomes even bleaker if the data from 1994 are compared to those obtained from a similar survey conducted fifteen years earlier (Terestyéni, 1981, 1985): the proportion of those who claimed to speak at least one language at an adequate level was 9.2%, a mere 2% increase by 1994.

According to a more recent survey (Sík, 1998), 18% of the population claims to speak a foreign language. As opposed to Terestyéni's report (1995), this percentage includes Romani, German and other ethnic languages, which are spoken as first language by members of these ethnic groups but perceived as foreign languages by the overwhelming majority of the Hungarian population. Sík argues, however, that the representation of ethnic language use was too small to alter the general picture in significant measure. This being the case, the foreign language competence of the Hungarian population seems to have accelerated faster in the past four or five years than in the previous fifteen years.

Which languages do Hungarians prefer?

The distribution of foreign languages spoken in Hungary, is presented in Table 3 (Terestyéni, 1995).By 1994, German had retained its leading position, but the gap between German and English had significantly narrowed. The same trend was perceived by a comparative survey which included five Central Euro-

Table 3 The distribution of foreign language speakers per language

Language	1979–1982	1994
German	5.4	6.1
English	1.9	5.1
Russian	2.9	2.0
French	0.8	0.9
Italian	0.5	0.5

pean countries (Croatia, Czechoslovakia, Hungary, Poland and Slovenia): German was the most widely spoken language in all the countries except in Croatia (Petneki, 1993). Although the survey was conducted in 1991/92, and since then the situation might have changed in favour of English, the relative popularity of German is likely to have remained.

Furthermore, Terestyéni (1995) found that while German was typically spoken by less educated and older people who lived in smaller towns and villages, English was favoured by the better educated and the young from metropolitan areas. Russian, which used to be the compulsory foreign language at all levels of school education for forty years, was reported spoken by 2.9 of the population in 1979–82 as opposed to 2.0 in 1994; this downward trend is likely to continue for the foreseeable future. The fourth foreign language, French, was lagging behind with no significant change registered in the number of its speakers. Albeit with somewhat different proportions, the same rank order of foreign languages was established by two more recent surveys (Marián, cited in Udvardi, 1999a; Sík, 1998).

While Sík (1998) acknowledges the rapid progress of English, especially among the younger generation, he adds that this trend does not take place at the expense of German – indeed, the number of German speakers is also on the increase. It is patently wrong, Sík contends, to talk of a 'cultural shift of paradigm' between English and German. Figure 3 shows the relationship between age and language choice.

Respondents were also queried about areas of activity where they needed to use foreign languages (Terestyéni, 1995). In comparing German and English, English was more widely exploited for occupational purposes and for reading books and magazines, while German was the most frequently used language of TV viewing, possibly owing to better access to German speaking TV channels. In

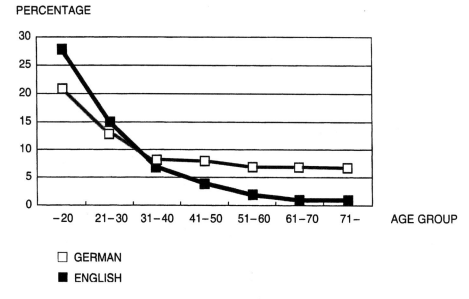

Figure 3 The ratio of speakers of English and German by age

Table 4 The distribution of favourite foreign languages (in percentages)

Language	1979–1982	1994
English	29.8	46.1
German	43.1	45.5
French	5.1	2.6
Russian	17.4	0.8
Italian	n/a	2.4

Table 5 The order of language preferences

Language	Score	Mean
English	11,352	2.38
German	8,466	1.78
French	3,921	0.82
Italian	2,485	0.52
Russian	684	0.14

addition, German proved to be the most useful language in tourism and interpersonal communication. All the other foreign languages played a significantly lesser role in all areas of interaction.

Terestyéni's survey (1995) included a few questions relating to attitudes towards language learning; 84% of respondents expressed their intention to learn foreign languages. As Table 4 indicates, English had caught up with German in popularity by 1994. When asked about their motives to learn English or German, most respondents referred to the role both languages were playing in various forms of international communication, whereas those who preferred French and Italian were primarily motivated by the intrinsic 'beauty' of these languages. Although the big loser on the preference list was Russian, obviously due to the radical changes taking place in Hungary, French had also lost a good deal of its erstwhile appeal.

In the 1992/93 school year, a large-scale survey was conducted by Dörnyei *et al.* (1996), which included 4765 eighth-graders (aged 13–14) in 77 schools across Hungary. The purpose of the investigation was to gather data on students' language learning motivation and foreign language preferences. They were asked to give three points to their first choice, two points to their second choice and one point to their third choice. After the scores had been tabulated, the rank order presented in Table 5 resulted. The data in Tables 4 and 5 clearly reveal that the popularity of English increases in inverse proportion to age.

How many people take language examinations?

It is a common experience that many proficient foreign language users have no language certificates, and many who have passed a language examination cannot use the language at all. Although an examination certificate is often an unreliable indicator of language proficiency, the existence of a casual relationship between actual and certified language proficiency cannot be denied. It is

Table 6 The number of exams and the percentages of pass rates in different languages (1997)

	No. of exams	*Pass rate (percentage)*
English	55,601	46
German	36,552	54
French	3,116	44
Russian	1,824	66
Italian	1,580	63

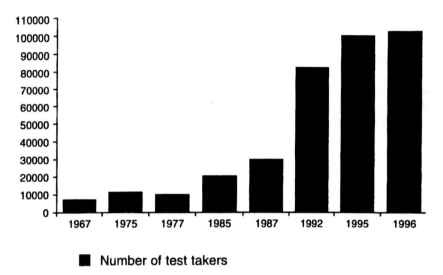

■ **Number of test takers**

Figure 4 The number of exams between 1967 and 1996 at all levels

further assumed that both of these parameters are interrelated with perceived competence.[8]

Hungarian citizens have been taking the state language examination for decades. A certificate of language proficiency entitles the holder to be the beneficiary of various kinds of bonuses, and although the nature of incentives has changed over time, it is as attractive today as ever. To illustrate some of those benefits, students with such a certificate are exempt from foreign language classes and examination at school, secondary school graduates may be awarded bonus points at university or college entrance examinations, students in tertiary education are not allowed to graduate without a certificate of language proficiency, civil servants are entitled to language allowances, etc.

By far the largest provider of language examinations in Hungary is the State Foreign Language Examination Board. This organisation administers exams in 52 languages, out of which English and German together account for some 91% of all the examinations (Nikolov, 1999) (Table 6). The rise of interest in foreign language learning and, in turn, taking language examinations, may be illustrated by the number of test takers between 1967 and 1996 (Figure 4). What these tables and figures do not reveal is the fact that, at Intermediate Level,[9] 80% of all the test takers are secondary school students and a further 10% are university or college students. These data clearly indicate the extent to which the younger generation is conscious of the importance of foreign language proficiency, and of *certified* knowledge.

What is the foreign language profile of teachers and university students?

In a large-scale survey comprising 4419 respondents, roughly half of whom were teachers and university/college students respectively, Székelyi *et al.* (1998) investigated, among other things, the respondents' foreign language competence. Since the inquiry was based on self-reports, its findings do not necessarily reflect the respondents' actual language competence; nor do the responses shed light on the level of proficiency.

In the sample of teachers, 96% in tertiary education claimed to speak one or several foreign languages, while the respective data for secondary and primary teachers were 65 and 51%. Whereas among school teachers German and English were similar in numbers of speakers, in the population of university/college teachers English had a significant edge over German (82 vs. 65%). It is no surprise that within each group under investigation the probability of language proficiency increased in direct proportion to higher qualifications and employment in more prestigious types of institution. In contrast, language proficiency and age were in inverse proportion to each other: the older the group, the fewer members could speak languages other than Hungarian. Significantly more women than men were found to speak foreign languages.

The student population consisted of first year and final year students. About 87% of first year students reported speaking at least one foreign language; while 66% claimed to speak English, only 44% claimed to speak German. The same three data points for final year students were 91, 78, and 50%, respectively. Although the overall results appear to be impressive, it is disconcerting that 9% graduate with no foreign language competence at all.

What is the foreign language profile of Hungarian scholars?

While there is ample evidence that students at all levels of education are highly enthusiastic language learners, less data are available about those at the top of the social pyramid, namely about the language proficiency of leading Hungarian scholars. The most recent data on this cohort were compiled in the last year of communist rule (Medgyes & Kaplan, 1992).

Hungarian scholars participating in this survey were aware that, as native speakers of a language spoken by few, they were at a distinct disadvantage unless they spoke the dominant language of a disciplinary community, which for the majority of these scholars was English. The results indicated that the average Hungarian scholar was a polyglot, but relatively few scholars claimed to speak English well. Table 7 demonstrates the frequency distribution of their perceived command of English.

The knowledge of English distributed across the population is in inverse proportion to age (i.e. the older the scholar, the less likely it is that s/he will have mastered English). Furthermore, while scholars from the social sciences tended to speak far more languages more fluently than their colleagues from the natural sciences, their English proficiency occupied a disproportionately

Table 7 The frequency distribution of perceived English language competence (N = 342)

Level	N	Percentage
Zero	37	10.8
Low	34	9.9
Medium	97	28.4
High	155	45.3
Near-native/native	19	5.6

small segment of their language volume. By way of illustration, while 'hard scientists' published more than half of their work in English, humanists and social scientists published two thirds of their work in Hungarian.[10] The next highest frequency was achieved by German, with Russian and French lagging behind.

Part II: The Language Spread

The Spread of Hungarian

The education system

The 'old' system until 1989

School education in Hungary was centralised and monolithic until 1990. Nearly 90% of the age group 3–6 attended kindergarten (*óvoda*) for one or more years before starting their formal education in primary school at the age of six. Basic education was provided almost exclusively by the eight-year primary school (*általános iskola*), which was divided into lower grades (grades 1–4) and upper grades (grades 5–8).

There were three main types of secondary education: the four-year general secondary school (*gimnázium*), the four-year technical secondary school (*szakközépiskola*) and the three-year vocational school (*szakmunkásképző*). Students of the former two took a secondary school-leaving examination (*érettségi*) at the end of the fourth year, which enabled them to apply for a place in higher education. Students of three-year vocational schools were able to get a skilled-worker qualification upon graduation.

Higher education institutions were divided into colleges (*főiskola*) and universities (*egyetem*). College studies took 3–4 years, granting a diploma, which is the equivalent of a Bachelor's Degree. The duration of university studies was from 4 to 6 years, which led to a degree, considered to be equivalent to a Master's Degree.

The present structure of the Hungarian education system

Since 1990, the Hungarian education system has undergone radical changes along with the transformation of the wider political, social and economic environment. These changes may be summarised as follows:

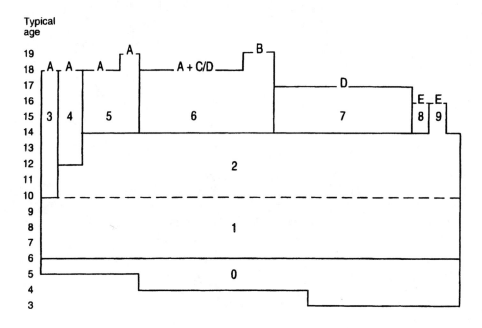

Figure 5 The Hungarian education system

Education levels
0.   Kindergarten
1.   'General' basic school, lower section (primary)
2.   'General' basic school, upper section (lower secondary)
3–4–5. Secondary grammar school
6.   Professional school
7.   Technical school
8–9.   Special apprenticeship school
Output channels, exams
A   Maturity exam
B   Technician's exam
C   Combined maturity and professional exam
D   Skilled worker's exam
E   Lower level training qualifications

(1) The old monolithic education system gave way to a new decentralised
     structure: elements of the 'old' and the 'new' now coexist in such a way that
     they are difficult to disentangle.
(2) Following the 1990 Self-government Act, the right and obligation to main-
     tain schools were transferred from the state to local authorities. Today,
     schools may also be maintained by churches and the private sector.
(3) The duration of compulsory education was lengthened from 8 to 10 years.

This heterogeneity is revealed in Figure 5.

Enrolment and qualification of the student population
     The number of children and older students enrolled in various schools is
presented in Table 8. The number of full-time graduates from different types of

Table 8 Full-time enrolment in different types of schools, 1997/98 (Statistical Yearbook of Hungary, 1998)

Kindergartens	383,486
Primary schools	963,997
Secondary schools	368,645
Universities / colleges	152,889
Total	1,869,017

schools (in thousands) is given in Figure 6. In 1998, 96.2% of the population finished primary school (grades 1–8) by school-leaving age. Moreover, 95.8% of all primary graduates enrolled in different types of secondary schools. Universities and colleges were attended by 18.8% of the population between 20 and 24 years of age (Statistical Yearbook of Hungary, 1998).

As mentioned in Part I, over 97% of the population speak Hungarian as their first language. When considering the spread of Hungarian, two periods should be distinguished: the first lasts until 1920 when Hungary was a polyglot country; the second continues up to the present when Hungary has had an almost exclusively Hungarian population. During the first period, school instruction played an important role in the spread of Hungarian. According to the 1910 census, 65% of the population spoke Hungarian, but only 54.5% spoke it as their first language (Huszár, 1998). However, after 1920 the promotion of Hungarian through education lost its *raison d'être* but the importance attributed to it remained unchanged. Throughout the history of Hungary, the first language has often been regarded as a symbol of national identity, and language maintenance has been identified with the preservation of the nation, instrumental in the strug-

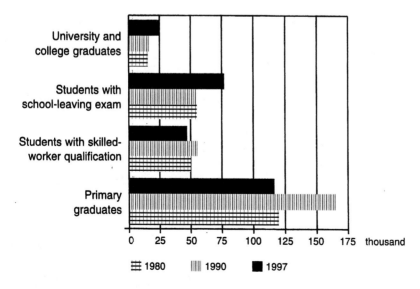

Figure 6 Full-time graduates from different types of schools, 1997/98 (Statistical Yearbook of Hungary, 1997 [1998])

gle for independence. Thus Hungarian as a school subject has carried more significance than any other subjects.

To understand the present situation, the historical development of Hungarian as a school subject is worth tracing from the 18th century to the late 20th century.

The development of Hungarian language and literature

In his thought-provoking paper, Margócsy (1996) states that Hungarian language and literature has always been regarded as the most important subject. In fact, 'Hungarian language and literature' have been the *two* most important subjects throughout Hungary's education history. At any Hungarian university, majoring in Hungarian implies taking courses in two schools: the School of Hungarian Literature and the School of Hungarian Linguistics. How did this situation arise? Explaining the history of the development of the subject, Margócsy divides it into two periods, the 'rhetoric' period and the 'historical'.

From the Middle Ages up to the early 19th century, Latin was the language of instruction in Hungary. In schools during the mid-18th century, the Hungarian language was used only in Hungarian lessons, and taught only if Hungarian was one of the subjects. In 1790, Diet passed a law that Hungarian Departments should be established in every university. Soon after, the first Hungarian Language and Literature Department was established at the University of Pest in 1791. Since 1806, Hungarian has been a compulsory subject in every secondary school, college and university. This occurred at a time when Hungary was a multi-ethnic society. Since a mere 40.5% of the population spoke Hungarian as their first language (1851 census), teaching Hungarian meant to teach it as a second language to Hungarian citizens with a different first language. For native speakers, the main objective of teaching Hungarian was to enable them to use the 'educated, literary register' of the language in science and literature as a replacement for Latin. The goals of teaching Hungarian as a second language and as a native tongue did not overlap, nor did they exclude each other.

Among the goals of teaching the Hungarian language, the primary goal was set in response to a patriotic urge to spread Hungarian among the other nationalities of the Hungarian Kingdom (within the Hapsburg Empire). The rationale behind this concept was that by teaching Hungarian to non-Hungarian minorities you would assimilate them into the Hungarian nation. In an attempt to describe the situation in 1810, the Chair of the Hungarian Department of the University of Pest started his inaugural lecture with the following words: 'Too few of us speak Hungarian', and asserted that every university student should be taught Hungarian (Czinke, 1810, cited in Margócsy, 1996).

In the 19th century, the concept of teaching a language included the teaching of its culture as well. Culture was considered the foundation of 'national education' as well as the tool through which to comprehend science and poetry. Thus grammar, poetics, rhetoric and literature were all integrated into language teaching, with Latin being the model for teaching Hungarian. The method of the day was the Grammar Translation Method, which laid a strong emphasis on the correct use of the written language.

Although the limitations of the Grammar Translation Method are all too obvious today, an approach that regarded poetry as the pinnacle of language use proved beneficial for the teaching of Hungarian literature. The first anthology for secondary school students, edited by István Tatay, was published in 1847. It quotes exclusively contemporary authors, including modern poets and outstanding orators of the time (e.g. Mihály Vörösmarty, Sándor Petőfi, Lajos Kossuth).

The 'historical' period can be dated from the second half of the 19th century. In the aftermath of the 1848–1849 Revolution and War of Independence, Hungarian as a school subject underwent two major transformations. One concerned the separation of the teaching of the language from the teaching of its literature. By identifying the learning of the Hungarian language exclusively with the study of grammar, literature was ousted from language lessons, and was dealt with separately in literature classes. The other change was due to a concept, widespread in the early 19th century, which brought the historical development of literature and linguistics into focus. This historical approach implied that literature equalled the *history* of literature whereas in linguistics the main emphasis fell on Finno-Ugrian comparative linguistics and language history. The two disciplines (literature and linguistics) became too divergent to be contained within the confines of a single department. At the University of Pest, the Hungarian Department split into two: the Department of Linguistics and the Department of Literature. Paradoxically, in teacher training a different approach to Hungarian was taking shape around the same time. In 1875, the Hungarian Royal Teacher Training School (*Magyar Királyi Tanárképezde*) designed the structure of Hungarian as a subject; this structure is considered valid to this day. It aimed at 'unity in duality' by training teachers-to-be both in Hungarian Grammar and in the History of Literature, without paying proper heed to the interrelation of the two components.

Teaching Hungarian as a means of ideological manipulation up to the 1970s

During the 20th century, two consecutive anti-democratic social systems exploited the teaching of Hungarian for their own purposes. From the 1920s until World War II, the central curriculum for secondary schools stipulated that the main objective of teaching Hungarian language and literature was to convey and inculcate strict morals, national pride and patriotic feelings. Hungarian literary works were shown to present a model to children, while language teaching focused on basic grammar rules and emphasised the idea that good patriots ought to use 'appropriate' Hungarian.

During the harshest years of Stalinism (1950s), the method of direct ideological manipulation remained, but its contents altered significantly with the compulsory reading list drastically curtailed: Only authors professing 'progressive' ideas were included in the curriculum. Hungarian language instruction was largely neglected, its only concern being that the traditional standards of grammatical correctness were to be preserved, and that the native language was to be protected from inimical foreign influences.

Up to the mid-1960s, 'Hungarian language and literature' in schools meant separate lessons in literature and language but one grade in the school report books. To increase the weight of language classes, linguists suggested that students receive separate marks in the two subjects. The idea was implemented –

and unwittingly it dealt a final blow to the erstwhile unity of 'Hungarian language and literature'.

The 'aesthetic' period from the 1970s

As a reaction to the political manipulations of the preceding decades, new teaching concepts were formulated from the mid-seventies that changed the focus of both literature and language teaching.

In literature, literary works were no longer analysed by the place they were assigned in the history of Hungarian literature but by their aesthetic functions and literary merits, while in Hungarian language teaching the communicative function of the language was given top priority.

These changes precipitated heated debates between the supporters of a more traditional way of teaching language and literature and teachers who preferred the aesthetic approach to the historical approach. Poetry and rhetoric returned to the curriculum but within the framework of literature classes. In both subjects, considerable effort has been made to bring them closer to the state-of-the-art literature and up-to-date linguistic research and achievements. Nonetheless, little has been attained in relating Hungarian language and literature to each other.

Teaching materials

Literature textbooks

Traditional Hungarian education has always preferred coursebooks of a positivist approach, based on the lives of the authors rather than on their work. The new textbooks published after World War II were ideologically biased and served the purposes of the monolithic, centrally planned curriculum.

The year 1979 was a turning point in the teaching of literature in Hungary: the first volume of a radically new set of secondary school coursebooks was published during this year. The authors, literary scholars of international renown, focused on the aesthetic merits and the in-depth analyses of literary works (Ritoók *et al.*, 1979).

From 1980 on, new curricula and coursebooks to supplement the centrally issued textbooks were written. The most significant of these, developed by Zsolnai (1982), has been an optional curriculum with the accompanying coursebooks. Zsolnai's 'language-literature-communication' programme lays a special emphasis on developing skills of verbal communication through drama techniques. In addition, to stimulate children's interest in reading, the programme provides them with works of top quality literature from the age of six.

The political changes of 1989 brought about a boom in coursebook writing and publishing; as a result, teachers have a free choice to select the book they think serves their goals best. A new concept concentrating on skills development and creativity in the teaching of literature has been elaborated.

Hungarian Language textbooks

The structure of the Hungarian Language textbooks used at school after 1945 was as follows: phonetics, parts of speech (including morphology) and syntax. To facilitate students' improvement in spelling, it was considered logical to teach morphology prior to dealing with syntax. Stylistics, rhetoric and poetics were omitted. As a result of a proposal to include language cultivation and stylistics in the curriculum, a coursebook of stylistics was published in 1964.

The 1980s witnessed a change in first language education. Morphology and spelling lost priority to the new approach based on communication theory. Based on Zsolnai's 'language–literature–communication' programme, new coursebooks were introduced. The grammar books were inspired by the transformational-generative approach and applied grammar discovery techniques. Bánréti's alternative programme (1991), *'Nyelvtan–kommunikáció–irodalom tizenéveseknek'* (Grammar – Communication – Literature for Teenagers), is also based on the transformational–generative approach and includes the study of pragmatics. Szende's book (1993), *'A magyar nyelv tankönyve'* (A Textbook of Hungarian Language), deals with the history of the language, the language family of Hungarian, stylistics, rhetoric and the issue of minority language use. Furthermore, a new programme for first language education (1988–1995) was developed for students of teacher-training colleges, specialising in the education of 6- to 12-year-olds. The five volumes skilfully combine traditional grammar with the latest theories of modern linguistics.

The effectiveness of instruction

Although Hungarian Language and Literature is one of the compulsory subjects in the school-leaving examination (*érettségi*), no extensive research has been done yet to evaluate and compare students' level of proficiency in the four language skills. In a remarkable study, Horváth (1998) carried out a validity survey in the domain of first language use among three different groups of society: young adults with school-leaving examination, school teachers and business managers.[11] First, the author examined the content, task types and assessment methods of the school-leaving examination and their validity in present-day society. After mapping both the informants' performance and deficiencies in first language use, she concluded that the most problematic areas for all three groups were public speech and formal writing. Lacking the necessary skills in these fields, informants often expressed frustration and a desire to obtain knowledge and skills through formal training. The results, the author argued, may be due to the fact that in central and east europe two principal paradigms have been identified in the first language and literary education: the 'tradition oriented' and the 'pragmatic' approach. For historical reasons, the former was more dominant until as late as 1989. Along with the rapid and basic social changes, there has been a pressing need for a more pragmatic oriented way of teaching Hungarian language and literature. Its goal would be to strike a balance between traditional and pragmatic approaches, thus meeting a social demand.

Teaching Hungarian to ethnic Hungarians

The present situation

Demographics

As described in Part I, there is a significant number of ethnic Hungarians living in all the countries surrounding Hungary. Table 9 shows their approxi-

Table 9 Ethnic Hungarians in the neighbouring countries

Country	Number of Hungarians	Census
Romania	1,620,199	1992
Slovakia	569,628	1991
Yugoslavia	340,946	1991
Ukraine	163,000	1991
Croatia	22,355	1991
Slovenia	9,000	1991
Austria	4,937	1991

Source: Government Office for Hungarian Minorities Abroad

mate numbers. Overall, the number of ethnic Hungarians is decreasing. It can be assumed that the decline is mainly caused by a very low birth rate (a similar situation is occurring in Hungary) and by emigration. This has a negative impact on the age demographics and, consequently, strengthens the process of decline.

The present situation of ethnic Hungarians living around Hungary displays general as well as individual features. First, the common characteristics of their situation will be described. This will be followed by a brief description of how Hungarian is taught, what is taught and to whom it is taught through the education systems in these countries.

The language situation for ethnic Hungarians

Bilingualism

The most significant factor in the life of ethnic Hungarians is that they live in a bilingual environment. Even if early childhood socialisation proceeds in the first language, the language competence of a monolingual minority child is not the same as that of a child living in Hungary as minority children usually acquire a language variety influenced by the majority language. If not earlier, on entering school the minority child acquires the majority language and becomes bilingual. However, there are significant differences in the degree of bilingualism in these countries even between 'compact' residential areas. To cite a couple of examples, in Romania almost every ethnic Hungarian speaks Romanian as a second language, whereas in Ukraine ethnic Hungarian children are able to learn Ukrainian as a 'foreign language' at school.

There are several motivating factors to learn the majority language, but the two most effective ones are economic advancement and social prestige. In order to succeed in these societies, it is imperative that ethnic Hungarians master the language of the dominant group.

Domains

The use of Hungarian is limited in all spheres of life in these neighbouring countries, but the extent of the restrictions varies from country to country. Hungarian is generally used at home, within the community, and possibly at church and at school. In regions where ethnic Hungarians represent the majority of the population, it is also used in public domains: at work, in shops and – especially in Romania – in the field of arts such as literature, theatre and publications. The official use of Hungarian, even if guaranteed by law, is restricted in practice, owing to the fact that authorities and other influential people in the community, such as priests or policemen, often belong to the dominant group and communicate with ethnic Hungarians in the majority language. Thus the majority (national) language and the minority (Hungarian) language exist in some form of functional distribution, with each language assigned its own role and domain.

Language shift and language maintenance

Language situations, as Crystal (1995) has pointed out, are rarely stable or balanced when languages are in contact with each other. The influence of the majority language, often backed by government policy, attenuates the use of the minority language and thus accelerates the shift in its favour. Another factor that facilitates the assimilation to the dominant culture has to do with living within a nation-state and learning the majority language. Exogamy, i.e. the practice of marriage outside one's own group, also results in language shift; the rate of exogamy varies greatly in individual countries. In Slovakia, for example, approximately a third of all married ethnic Hungarians have a Slovak spouse (Votruba, 1998). Surprisingly, in Slovak-Hungarian mixed marriages there is a reverse tendency of language shift: in areas with an ethnic Hungarian majority Hungarian is more likely to be used at home. The explanation of this phenomenon may be that mixed marriages more likely involve Hungarian women and Slovak men than the other way round.

In the fluid situation where bilingualism occurs, the minority language may be 'holding its own despite the influence of powerful neighbours' (Crystal, 1995: 360). In the case of ethnic Hungarians, successful language maintenance is attributable to several factors. Owing to the former dominant political and social role of ethnic Hungarians, Hungarian culture may still maintain a considerable degree of prestige and a strong cultural tradition. Some ethnic Hungarians live in compact settlements and are consequently less exposed to the majority language. The proximity of Hungary is also a determining factor that enables ethnic Hungarians to maintain their first language. These two opposing phenomena – language maintenance and language shift – can often be observed simultaneously. Although language shift seems unavoidable and inexorable for more and more people, ethnic Hungarians, especially those living in compact ethnic regions, are experiencing varying degrees of success in maintaining their first language.

Hungarian minority education

Following World War I, the Treaty of Trianon (1920) redrew the national borders, and almost overnight turned the once dominant Hungarians into ethnic minorities. Owing to their former political and social dominance, Hungarians had had a well-established education network from pre-school to university level, especially in Transylvania (in Romania), Slovakia and the Vojvodina (in Yugoslavia). Generally speaking, the complex system of Hungarian education has been subject to restrictions, and the number of schools has been continuously decreasing since Trianon. As education is regarded as the key factor for the retention of national identity through language maintenance, Hungarian minority groups have endeavoured to slow down or even reverse the language erosion process by ensuring that Hungarian instruction was available at every level of education. A special emphasis has been given to tertiary education and teacher training in Hungarian; these appear to be indispensable for continuing Hungarian instruction in schools and, consequently, for language maintenance.

Language education goals and coursebooks

The most important objectives in minority education are those concerning the protection of first language use. On the other hand, in order for minorities to become part of mainstream society, the majority language has to be taught as well. The final goal for the students is to become functionally bilingual. In comparison to these aims, the teaching of a world language such as English or German seems to be an issue of lesser importance.

Simon (1996) states that coursebooks used by minority students generally present the standard variety of Hungarian currently used in Hungary. Although in theory present-day colloquial Hungarian is advocated, most of the examples supplied are from written prose, regarded as the more prestigious variety. By teaching a 'pure' language variety, coursebook authors ignore two important factors: first, that the students are bilingual, and, second, that their language use differs from that of monolingual speakers. As a consequence, students do not become aware of the differences between standard Hungarian and its varieties. Every reference to whether something is grammatically correct or stylistically appropriate comes from sources written in Hungary and appropriate for the Hungarian context. To give an example, standard Hungarian is compared to standard Slovak, instead of the Hungarian language varieties spoken in Slovakia. The situation is similar in Sub-Carpathia (Ukraine): one of the coursebooks compared Hungarian to Russian in 1983, only to compare it to Ukrainian in 1995, due to the political changes occurring in the former Soviet Union. However, neither edition used the Sub-Carpathian variety of Hungarian as a reference point. If examples *are* given for the minority Hungarian usage, they are treated as cases of 'environmental harm' to be prevented. The goal is to eradicate the students' own linguistic variety and replace it with standard Hungarian as used in Hungary.

Some linguists and teachers carrying out research in this field propose a double goal in teaching Hungarian to Hungarian minorities (Lanstyák, 1996; Sándor, 1996b). They contend that students should maintain their own language variety while acquiring standard Hungarian as well. In order to achieve this, as Lanstyák explains, a distinction ought to be made between language *mistakes* versus *features* of the language variety in question. Mistakes stem from the incomplete or improper acquisition of the language, and as such they need to be corrected. On the other hand, features of ethnic Hungarians' linguistic variety require a different treatment: students should be aware of them, but should not regard them as signs of 'language decay'.

There is a shortage of coursebooks in almost all neighbouring countries. The ones that are available either come from Hungary or are translations from the majority language. In some cases, coursebooks have been written by ethnic Hungarian teachers and professors (most of these have been published in Romania) – experts seem to agree that this is the best solution. In Vojvodina, the writing and printing of coursebooks has proved unfeasible lately, and only educational booklets (*Ismeretterjesztő Füzetek*) have been issued as supplements to weekly magazines. Paradoxically, the coursebooks sent from Hungary thwart the efforts of ethnic Hungarian coursebook writers, as they are unable to compete with market oriented publishers and distributors from Hungary.

Hungarian Language education in Romania

After a short period of liberal educational state policy following the revolution of 1989, Romanian policy has become laden with restrictions (Ring, 1998a). While the Constitution of 1991 granted all Romanian citizens the right to study in their first languages at all levels of education, a government decree of 1993 exempted from this law two subjects, Geography and history, and the Education Act of 1995 imposed further restrictions on first language schooling. In 1991, although Hungarian kindergartens were available for ethnic children, half of the Hungarian teachers did not have sufficient qualifications. The number of schools which provide instruction in Hungarian, or Hungarian sections within Romanian schools, rose from 2145 in 1989/90 to 2428 in 1990/91. At present there are eight teacher training colleges in operation (Jordan, 1998). The Babes-Bolyai University in Cluj-Napoca (*Kolozsvár*) offers 35 different majors in Hungarian. Since the 1996 parliamentary elections, the Hungarian Democratic Association in Romania (RMDSZ) has been a junior party in the coalition government. Although the demand for establishing an autonomous Hungarian university has become stronger, the chances of establishing such an institution in the short run appear to be slim (Jordan, 1998).

Hungarian Language education in Slovakia

While approximately 73% of ethnic Hungarian children of school age attend Hungarian schools in Slovakia, in 130 settlements where Hungarians are in majority there are no schools offering Hungarian instruction (Votruba, 1998). As a general trend, the number of Hungarian schools has been decreasing over the past decades (Table 10). Table 11 shows the number of schools and the number of ethnic Hungarian students in 1994/95.

With respect to tertiary education, ethnic Hungarians may study Hungarian

Table 10 Hungarian primary schools in Slovakia between 1960 and 1996 (Ring, 1998b)

School year	No. of schools	No. of classes	No. of students	Percentage of Slovaks
1960–61	555	2,490	72,144	10.2
1964–65	472	2,863	79,206	9.8
1970–71	490	2,854	68,902	9.1
1976–77	414	2,479	57,903	8.4
1979–80	309	2,216	51,379	7.9
1983–84	277	1,996	47,917	6.9
1989–90	245	2,008	48,756	6.7
1994–95	268 (31)*	2,081	45,467	7.0
1995–96	267 (31)*	2,078	44,655	7.0

*In parentheses the number of schools under mixed directorate

Table 11 Number of schools and ethnic Hungarian students in Slovakia

Type of school	Hungarian school	Mixed school	Number of students
Pre-school	297	106	12,350
Primary schools	268	31	4,467
Church schools	9	–	890
Grammar schools	11	8	4,622
Technical schools	4	18	4,186
Vocational schools	2	22	10,500
Total	591	185	37,015

Source: Report on the Situation of Hungarians in Slovakia, 1998

language and literature at the Comenius University in Bratislava (*Pozsony*). Also, the university of Nitra (*Nyitra*) trains teachers for both Hungarian and Slovak-Hungarian schools, but there is no institute exclusively for Hungarian teacher training at present.

Hungarian Language education in Yugoslavia

The 1990 Education Law and the 1992 amendments significantly restricted ethnic Hungarian education by stipulating that the language of instruction should be in Serbian, with the token allowance of the minority language as a subject as well. Consequently, the number of students being taught in Hungarian has dropped dramatically. In 1978, the number of ethnic Hungarian students attending primary schools with Hungarian instruction was 30,564. In 1993 the total number of students receiving Hungarian education at all levels was about 26,000. At present, education in Hungarian is offered in 110 primary and 27 secondary schools (eight of them are secondary grammar schools, called *gimnázium*). There are no Hungarian institutions in tertiary education except for the Technical College in Subotica (*Szabadka*) where – depending on the availability of Hungarian teachers – first and second year courses are also offered in Hungarian. Teacher trainees can attend the Hungarian Department of the University of Novi Sad (*Újvidék*) or teacher training colleges in Novi Sad and Subotica (Poulton, 1998).

Hungarian Language education in Ukraine

Since the establishment of the independent Ukraine in 1991, Hungarian pre-school education as well as primary and secondary schooling have flourished. In 1994/95 there were 90 kindergartens where Hungarian was employed, 68 of which were exclusively Hungarian, 21 Ukrainian-Hungarian and 1 Ukrainian-Hungarian-Russian. Instruction is conducted in Hungarian in ten elementary schools only (for grades 1–4), 36 primary schools and 17 secondary schools (Ring, 1998c). As for higher education, ethnic Hungarian students can attend the Hungarian Department at the State University of Uzhorod (*Ungvár*) or can enrol in the Beregovo Hungarian Teacher-Training College (*Beregszászi Magyar Tanárképző Főiskola*) in Beregovo (*Beregszász*). In addition, since 1990 approximately 350 students from Ukraine have studied at universities and colleges in

Hungary, with the support of the Hungarian government (Bagu, 1996; Ring, 1998c).

Hungarian Language education in Croatia

Prior to the Yugoslav War of 1991, 2502 ethnic Hungarian students studied at 41 educational institutions from kindergarten to secondary school. During the war, the entire Hungarian education system ceased to exist. At present, there are two exclusively Hungarian eight-grade elementary schools in Croatia, attended by 232 students. Another 150 students take part in bilingual education in the only bilingual secondary school offering Hungarian instruction. In 1994, a Department for Hungarian Studies was set up at the University of Zagreb (*Zágráb*) (Tóth, 1992).

Hungarian Language education in Slovenia

In the 1960s, the government introduced bilingual education for ethnic Hungarian children; these students learn in mixed ethnic groups from kindergarten to secondary school. In the 22 kindergartens each group is taught by two teachers, a Hungarian and a Slovenian. Bilingual education is conducted in the 42 elementary schools in a rather peculiar way: both languages are used in each lesson; the proportion is 70 to 30% to the advantage of the majority language (Arday *et al.*, 1987; Vörös, 1996). There is one bilingual vocational secondary school in Lendava (*Lendva*). Teachers for bilingual kindergartens and schools are trained at the Hungarian Department of the University of Maribor. Hungarian is also taught at the University of Ljubljana.

Hungarian Language education in Austria

The 1976 Minority Law recognised ethnic Hungarians as a minority and guaranteed them language rights. In bilingual pre-schools children receive a minimum of six hours of Hungarian instruction per week. There are two types of primary schools: in the first Hungarian is the only medium of instruction if a minimum of seven students want it; in the second education is purely bilingual. In secondary schools a minimum of nine registrants is necessary for setting up a new Hungarian class. With a minimum of five registrants, Hungarian is taught as a compulsory subject. In the secondary grammar schools in Oberwart (*Felsőőr*) and Oberpullendorf (*Felsőpulya*), Hungarian and Croatian are taught five lessons per week for a total of eight years. At present, there is no schooling at tertiary level for ethnic Hungarians.

Hungarian as a Second and Foreign Language

Hungarian as a second and foreign language in Hungary (HSL/HFL)

Hungarian as a second language (HSL) is taught both within and outside Hungary. In Hungary, it is taught to a special group: to ethnic Hungarians who come to Hungary to attend universities and need to be prepared for their studies by learning the technical jargon of their fields in Hungarian, or to bridge the gap between their own and their fellow Hungarian students' language competence. For ethnic Hungarians, Hungarian is neither a second nor a foreign language but the native language, and their occasional language deficiencies are caused by their bilingual language background. The other major group of learners of

Hungarian are foreigners: students participating in 'education abroad' pro-grammes, employees and their families, spouses married to Hungarians and settled in Hungary, most of them being young adults (Nádor & Giay, 1988).

In 1927, a summer university was set up in Debrecen (a town in eastern Hungary). Since then, courses have been offered in different fields related to Hungarian language and culture. Teachers of the Summer University of Debrecen worked out their own method of teaching HFL and published a teach-ing package in the 1980s, complete with audio and video cassettes.

In 1952, HFL was introduced at Eötvös Loránd University, Budapest.[12] Its primary aim was to teach HFL to foreign students from Third World countries, who were granted scholarships to study in Hungary. In 1957, an international preparatory institute with the aim of offering one-year intensive language train-ing to mainly African and Asian students was set up (*Nemzetközi Előkészítő Intézet*). Between its foundation and 1989, approximately 16,000 students attended the institute. Along with the political changes in the early 1990s, the Institute lost its original aim and clientele, but it managed to survive under a new name and to attract a different student population. Called the Hungarian Language Institute (*Magyar Nyelvi Intézet*), it prepares mostly Hungarian minor-ity students to attend universities in Hungary. In addition, graduate training in HFL was implemented at the Eötvös Loránd University, Budapest, in 1982 (Éder, 1981, 1993; Éder *et al.*, 1984, 1989; Giay, 1986).

In the 1990s, several language schools, following British-American models have been set up to cater for the increasing demand for HFL. As their students mostly consist of foreign business people and their families, apart from teaching conversational Hungarian, the schools have also experimented with introducing Business Hungarian.

Hungarian in the neighbouring and non-neighbouring countries

Hungarian is also taught abroad as a foreign language and as a second language. The latter is the concern of the second and third generation Hungari-ans in the neighbouring countries and beyond. Emigrants run Saturday and Sunday schools, and organise summer camps for young people from the age of three to twenty, with the purpose of transmitting Hungarian language and culture.

The two main venues for teaching HFL abroad are universities and language courses. Currently, Hungarian can be studied as a major, a minor or as part of independent studies at more than 100 universities in 30 countries. The Interna-tional Center of Hungarian Studies (*Nemzetközi Hungarológiai Központ*) in Buda-pest co-ordinates the Hungarian instructors' academic and scholarly activities related to Hungarian society, history, culture and language (Giay, 1987; Giay & Nádor, 1989; Szépe, 1969, 1983; Várdy, 1973; Várdy Huszár, 1978).

The role of the Church in the spreading of Hungarian

Although the language of Catholic religious activities was Latin, the Church was instrumental in spreading the Hungarian language. Thirteenth century Franciscan and Dominican nunneries, emerging from communities of Beguines, were the first to use Hungarian as the language of worship since nuns did not speak Latin. As the heretic Hussite movement had reached Hungary in the 15th century, it gave a further boost to the expansion of Hungarian, for Hussism considered Latin as the language of the privileged and insisted on celebrating Mass in the mother tongue of the congregation. This led to the first Hungarian translation of the Bible, the so-called 'Hussite Bible' by two Hussite priests, Tamás and Bálint, in the first half of the 15th century. The translation, of which only fragments have survived, was a turning point in Hungarian literacy: Tamás and Bálint reformed the orthography of the language and created new words. A further major improvement owes much to the Reformation of the Church: from 1530 on, Calvinist Hungarian literature outweighed Latin. Similarly, in Slovak- and German speaking towns, Slovak and German, the language of the ordinary people, gradually replaced Latin. The educational policies of Calvinism further enhanced the spread of Hungarian: many of schools were founded and literacy was a top priority to enable everyone to read the Bible. These decades saw the spread of printing in Hungary and Gáspár Károli's unabridged translation of the Bible, published in 1590, has been republished more than a hundred times since then. It is still in use, albeit in a slightly modernised form. Counter-reformation maintained the use of Hungarian as a powerful tool against Calvinist heresy.

The Church also played an important role in maintaining the minority languages in Hungary. The Austro-Hungarian Compromise of 1867 laid down the right of choice of language for churches. This enabled the Romanian Greek Catholic and the Romanian and Serbian Orthodox Churches with minority congregations to preserve their language (Paikert, 1967: 44, cited in Fenyvesi, 1998: 141).

Sándor (1996a) describes a reverse tendency when scrutinising the relationship of religion and language shift among the Csángós. A Hungarian-speaking community in Romania for centuries, the Catholic Csángós do not use Hungarian in church. Owing to a shortage of Catholic priests after the Reformation in the 16th century, the formation of the Romanian state in 1920, and Romania's assimilating tendencies, Romanian is used in religious activities, slowly but surely bringing about a complete language shift in other domains as well.

The media

The first newspaper published in Hungary was written in Latin (*Mercurius Hungaricus*, 1705). From the 1730s onwards, German-language newspapers began to appear. It was in 1780 that the first Hungarian language newspaper was printed in Bratislava (*Pozsony*). Edited and published by Mátyás Rát, the *Magyar Hírmondó* (Hungarian Courier) could boast of 320 subscribers, and was published twice a week.

Although the number of Hungarian-language newspapers gradually increased, it was not until the mid-19th century that they became a majority of all newspapers printed in the country. After World War II, the printed media, radio and television broadcasting (the history of which goes back to 1924 and 1957 respectively) were controlled and censored by the state; it was only in 1989 that the state finally relinquished control. Having regained the freedom of the press, the early 1990s experienced a boom in newspaper publishing. Since the passing of the Media Act[13] (in effect from 1996), commercial radio stations and television channels have mushroomed all over the country.

In accordance with the proportion Hungarians represent in the whole population, the language of the media (printed as well as electronic) is almost exclusively Hungarian.

The Spread of Minority Languages

A brief history

In the era of liberal educational policy following the Compromise of 1867,[14] scores of minority schools were set up in the Hungarian Kingdom, in which the minority language was the exclusive medium of instruction. From 1879, however, Hungarian was decreed to be a compulsory language in all schools of the country, and the role of Hungarian in the curriculum gradually became more pronounced at the expense of minority languages. After the turn of the century, nationalistic zeal and intolerance towards national minorities had negative consequences in education, too. To illustrate the situation, whereas in 1901 minority primary schools made up 40% of all the schools in Hungary, this ratio dropped to 20% by 1910 (Vámos, 1998). Another characteristic figure from 1910 shows the literacy rate across the major nationalities in Hungary (Table 12).[15]

Following the shock of Trianon, in 1925 three categories of minority education were set up: (1) in *minority-language schools* all the subjects were taught in the language of the ethnic group and Hungarian was just one compulsory subject; (2) in *bilingual schools* certain subjects were taught in the minority language while others were taught in Hungarian; and (3) in *Hungarian-language schools* all the subjects were taught in Hungarian with the minority language being but one ordinary subject. As for the proportion of these three types of minority schools, in the 1932/33 school year, for example, 63% were Hungarian-language schools, 27% were bilingual schools and only 9% were minority-language schools (Báthory & Falus, 1997). In conformity with the historical changes, the proportions within this system kept changing, but the basic three-prong structure has remained the norm to the present day.

The first three years of the post-war period brought several laws and decrees which aimed at improving the situation of minorities in Hungary in the field of education too. The ensuing communist system, on the other hand, weakened minority education, most blatantly when in 1960 by decree it turned minority-language schools into bilingual schools.[16] In the 70s and especially in the 1980s, several measures were taken to widen the scope for bilingual education (Drahos & Kovács, 1991).

Table 12 The literacy rate by nationality

German	70.7
Hungarian	67.1
Croatian	62.5
Slovak	58.1
Serbian	51.3
Romanian	28.2
Ruthenian	22.2

The present situation

The issue of minorities has gained momentum since 1989. Educational authorities have been led by the principle of positive discrimination and affirmative action, although they have grappled with numerous difficulties at the level of implementation. Due to historical circumstances, minorities in Hungary live in small communities scattered around the country, which makes the running and financing of minority schools a daunting task.[17] At a more abstract level, educational policy-makers have been confronted with a dilemma: how can education contribute to the process of integrating minorities into the social fabric of the majority and simultaneously help reinforce the linguistic and cultural traditions of the given minority group? How can these two contradictory objectives of minority education be reconciled (Halász & Lannert, 1998)?

After a short period of growth, the second half of the 1990s has recorded a slow decrease in the number of students attending minority schools. This is due to several factors such as a decline in the student population of the whole country, lack of resources, administrative difficulties, shortage of teachers, poor quality teaching materials, etc. (Halász & Lannert, 1998). In addition, minority education is losing its importance for representatives of the ethnic groups themselves, evident in indifference to minority education, children's low level of competence in the minority language when they first enter school, the inefficiency of pressure groups and minority representations, etc. (Csipka, 1995).

With respect to primary schools, in the 1997/98 school year the number of students participating in some form of minority education was 53,021, which constituted 5.5% of all primary school students in Hungary. Of this group, 83.6% of the student population attended German-language schools, the respective percentage of Slovak students and Croat students being 8.3 and 4.7; the remaining 3.4% was distributed among all the other minorities (Statistical Report, 1998). As for the ratio of primary students in the three major types of school, the overwhelming majority went to Hungarian-language schools (83.8%); bilingual schools catered for 11.8% and minority-language schools 4.4% of the population.[18]

Since minority educational programmes in Hungary typically end in the primary school, most students of ethnic origin are deprived of the opportunity to continue their studies in minority schools at secondary level. According to the data for the 1997/98 school year, out of 368,645 secondary school students, a mere 0.6% went to one of 22 secondary schools offering minority education. While half of these schools are minority-language schools, the other half are Hungarian-language schools which provide the instruction in a minority language. Of these, 11 schools specialise in German, five in Slovak, two in Croatian and one each in Romanian, Serbian, Slovenian and Gypsy.

The media

Publishing books in minority languages has become more widespread since 1989. There are both publishing houses which specialise in minority language books only, and others which tend to supplement their list of Hungarian publications with books written in minority languages. Occasionally, local educational authorities and research institutes also undertake to issue books for ethnic minorities in Hungary. Since books written in minority languages can never break even on their sales, their publication possibilities largely hinge on the availability of funds. The annual number of books published in minority languages has been between 40 and 50 in recent years.

There are around 400 libraries catering for minority language books. They gain regular information about new publications through the National Foreign Language Library, but it is up to the libraries themselves to place orders and distribute books. Although thus far all the libraries have managed to stay in business, their financial situation may be described as shaky. The National Foreign Language Library has also been instrumental in creating the basis for a collection in Gypsy languages and on Gypsy folk art and literature.

In accordance with the Media Act of 1996, both the National Radio Company and the National Television Company are obliged to broadcast programmes in the language of national minorities. On TV, there are programmes for the major nationalities twice a week, each with a duration of about 30 minutes, but smaller minorities are also given their due at regular intervals. The distribution of minority language broadcasts is similar on national radio.

The Spread of Foreign Languages

Even though the notion that language-in-education planning is sufficient to spread language learning and language use throughout society has been questioned, the importance of school instruction cannot be dismissed (Kaplan & Baldauf, 1997). In order to clarify some of the problems encountered in Hungary, a retrospective look at the changing role assigned to foreign languages in that polity over the past 120 years is presented.

Throughout its history, the teaching and learning of foreign languages in Hungary, like anywhere else in the world, has been deeply rooted in and determined by the political and economic structure of the country. Although Hungary has never had a well-designed national foreign language planning programme, foreign languages have been invariably offered at school, in accordance with overarching national interests – for better or for worse. As Hungary came under the influence, and indeed domination, of German speaking countries in the 18th and 19th centuries, so German featured as a school subject in the curriculum. After the country had been forced to join the community of Soviet-style dictatorships in 1948, Russian became the compulsory foreign language at school, ensuring little room for the instruction of other foreign languages. Today, when the only superpower left in the world is the United States, with the English language monopolising more and more spheres of life, English is on its way to becoming the leading foreign language in the Hungarian school system.

Foreign languages in the curriculum (1879–1948)

Education systems rarely change overnight – nor did foreign language education in Hungary for 70 years. A comparison of the foreign language spread featuring in the successive curricula for secondary grammar schools (*gimnázium*) reveals little mobility (Báti, n.d.). The recalcitrant attitude to change may be demonstrated by the pride of place the two classical languages were granted in all three curricula (Table 13): Latin and Ancient Greek accounted for 25–30% of

Table 13 The distribution of foreign languages in three curricula between 1879 and 1938

Language	Year	Grades	Average number of lessons/week
Latin	1879	1–8	6.1
	1924	1–8	5.6
	1938	1–8	4.2
Greek	1879	5–8	4.7
	1924	5–8	5.5
	1938	5–8	3.7
German	1879	3–8	3.0
	1924	2–8	2.8
	1938	3–8	3.3
French/English/Italian	1938	5–8	3.7

all lessons (Ballér, 1996). Compared to this, German, let alone other foreign languages, could play only a modest role. By 1938, however, the share of foreign languages, classical and modern together, reached its peak: they accounted for more than 34% of the total number of lessons in the curriculum (Kontra *et al.*, 1989)!

While grammar schools were attended by students with academic interests, technical schools (*reáliskola*) served practice-oriented students, who did not intend to study in higher education. In such schools, Latin and Greek were superseded by modern languages. While German remained the first foreign language throughout this period, the second foreign language in 1879 was French; later the choice was enriched with English or Italian depending upon availability (Ballér, 1996; Báti, n.d.).

The objectives of language teaching (1879–1948)

For several decades, the objectives of German and other modern language instruction were the same as those of Latin and Greek: to develop students' ability in reading the classics of literature in the original on the basis of solid grammatical knowledge, and in translating Hungarian texts into the foreign language. The ruling dogma was the Grammar Translation Method, which insisted on rote learning, deductive grammar study and consistent error correction. Towards the end of the century, advocates of the Direct Method with its emphasis on the spoken language, the use of the target language and inductive learning also succeeded in making their voices heard. Simultaneously, the focus on literature shifted towards a more comprehensive interpretation of culture, formalised by the German concept of *Kulturkunde* (Lux, 1932). A more practice-oriented approach which implicitly called for the enhancement of modern languages at the expense of classical languages was supported even in some conservative quarters. In 1922, Minister of Education Kunó Klebelsberg himself argued that 'In our new situation the teaching of modern foreign languages is of utmost importance. It is not only our diplomats who need modern languages, but also businessmen […] and everyone who wishes to understand foreign affairs' (cited in Báti, n.d., p.110). Judged by the 1924 curriculum, his message seems to have fallen on deaf ears, yet it paved the way for the 1936 curriculum. This pre-war curriculum diminished, however tentatively, the proportion of Latin and Greek while widening the scope for German and, to a greater extent, for French, English and Italian.

In summarising the objectives and methods of foreign language instruction in the first half of the century, it may be said that this period was spent on battles between conservatives and modernists, with the latter party gaining ground. Latin and Greek were gradually losing out to modern languages, and the Grammar Translation Method was in slow retreat. However, since neither group of policy makers was strong enough to gain the upper hand, every curriculum designed in this era was the result of a more or less principled compromise.

The effectiveness of instruction (1879–1948)

With regard to the effectiveness of instruction, there is only indirect evidence available, which indicates that students in higher education had a fair level of language proficiency. According to self-reported data from 1930/31, 46.4% of the student population in universities and colleges spoke at least one foreign language. While almost all of them identified German as the language they spoke, the number of French, English and Italian speakers was much smaller. The data further reveal that fewer male students had competence in modern languages than female students (43.5% vs. 64.5%) (Statistical Office, 1932, cited in Báti, n.d.). This discrepancy may be due to the fact that modern languages were usually offered in a higher number of contact hours in girls' schools than in boys' schools; the opposite was true of classical languages.[19]

It should be noted, however, that this relatively high percentage describes the foreign language competence of only the top of the student population – average secondary school students would not go into higher education, and their command of languages as a rule must have been far lower than that of their more ambitious peers. Indeed, if teachers' reports are to be believed, the foreign language proficiency of secondary students was low. As one practising teacher admitted, 'Only those can speak more or less fluently who have had the opportunity to study this language outside school' (Rakitovszky, cited in Báti, n.d., p.157). This comment also rings true in the present.

Foreign languages in the curriculum (1949–1989)

Although the 1946 national curriculum already included Russian in the choice of foreign languages, major educational change occurred in 1950, when – in the wake of the communist takeover – Russian was decreed to be the compulsory 'first' foreign language in all types of school (Ballér, 1996; Medgyes, 1993).[20, 21] This coincided with the virtual expulsion of all the other modern languages from schools while classical languages were pushed to the periphery: Ancient Greek became extinct educationally as well as historically, and Latin suffered heavy losses, with its instruction being tolerated only in secondary grammar schools (Table 14).[22]

However, the darkest years of communist dictatorship were not to last long. After the revolution of 1956 had been crushed by Soviet tanks, a brief period of

Table 14 The distribution of foreign languages in three curricula between 1949 and 1989

Language	Year	Grades	Average number of lessons/week
Russian	1950	prim. 5–8	3.0
		sec. 1–4	4.5
	1963/65[23]	prim. 5–8	3.0
		sec. 1–4	3.0
	1978	prim. 5–8	3.0
		sec. 1–4	3.0
Latin	1950	sec. 2–4	3.0
'Second' foreign languages[24]	1965	sec. 1–4	2.0
	1978	sec. 1–2	2.5

reprisal was followed by a protracted process of liberalisation. As a result, foreign languages gradually crept back into the curriculum, even though they were overshadowed by Russian until 1989. The curricula of 1963/1965 and 1978 clearly demonstrate the limited scope of instruction allotted to 'second' foreign languages (Ballér, 1996; Bánó & Szoboszlay, 1972).

As the cracks in the wall of communism became increasingly visible, so foreign language experts became bolder in their disapproval. In the 1980s, for example, a major educational journal gave voice to their long-suppressed concerns. Most contributors called for fundamental reforms in language education, and some went as far as to suggest, albeit between the lines, that most of the problems afflicting foreign language education were caused by the privileged place occupied by Russian (Bárdos, 1984a, 1984b; Fülöp, 1984; Medgyes, 1984). Paradoxically, it was a teacher of Russian who expressed the most devastating critique: Köllő (1978) called Hungary a country of foreign language illiterates, which had not yet decided to remedy the situation.

Despite such criticisms, the number of students learning 'second' foreign languages in public schools showed no sign of rapid increase[25]: even in the last year of communist rule in Hungary less than 3% of primary and 16.5% of secondary school students had access to instruction in English, for example, in spite of the upsurge of interest in this language (Medgyes, 1993). From the beginning of the 1980s, in an effort to offset the shortcomings of state-sector education, private and cooperative language schools were allowed to admit adult (and teenage) learners, who attempted by the thousand to make up for what had been lost during their formal schooling. Not surprisingly, the most sought-after languages were English and German (Dörnyei & Medgyes, 1987).

The objectives of language teaching (1949–1989)

The curriculum of 1950 placed the main emphasis on developing students' speaking skills in Russian and familiarising them with the greatest figures of Russian and Soviet literature. The teaching method being advocated was the

'Combined Method', an amalgamation of the Grammar Translation Method and the Direct Method. There may be legitimate arguments for the adoption of such principles, but the way they were turned into practice was ineffective. To begin with, there were hardly any qualified Russian teachers available in schools. Most of them were self-taught retrainees of abolished foreign languages, who were often only a few lessons ahead of their pupils. As a consequence, the majority of students did not even know how to ask for a glass of water after eight years of study. To be fair, since very few of them would ever meet Russian speakers, there was little genuine need to acquire communicative abilities. The textbooks were rife with the biographies of Russian, mostly Soviet, writers and poets, sprinkled with extracts from their works, descriptions extolling the virtues of Lenin, Stalin and other communist heroes, accounts of happy encounters between Hungarian and Soviet communist pioneers, etc. As for language exercises, they were of the most traditional type, demanding the rote learning of uncontextualised grammatical forms. Although the textbooks written in the 1960s and 1970s conveyed less dogmatic messages, they remained insipid and mechanical, lacking in authentic language use. It was only in the 1980s that Russian textbooks, under the influence of the new wave of imported English and German coursebooks, showed considerable improvement.

The main objective of 'second' foreign languages, reinstated by the secondary school curriculum of 1965, was to serve practical aims. The focus of attention shifted from the teaching of reading skills to the development of speaking skills. As subsidiary objectives, the 'second' foreign language was obliged '(a) to introduce the motherland, life and culture of the target language nations in an authentic fashion; (b) to develop the virtues of true communists, particularly their love for their socialist homeland and proletarian internationalism' (Bencédy, 1965: 3). To fulfil the practical aim, the methods described in the curriculum document were suggestive of the Audio-Lingual Method although the epithet itself was not actually used. While textbook writers were expected to follow slavishly the directives of the curriculum in terms of its lexical and grammatical content, only a few exploited the major innovative feature of the Audio-Lingual Method: pattern practice for habit formation. As for the ideological objectives of the 1965 curriculum, since they were far too general to pinpoint, textbooks writers had a lot of leeway. While providing lots of information about the civilisation of the target language countries, most textbooks only paid lip service to the promulgation of communist ideals.

The curriculum of 1978 for secondary grammar schools (Szabolcs, 1978) coincided with the advent of the Functional-Notional Approach and, concomitantly, with what is generally called 'communicative language teaching'. In contrast with its counterparts for other foreign languages, the English curriculum was modelled on the Threshold Level (Van Ek, 1975). While introducing new concepts and a novel specification of language forms, including language functions and topics,[26] the curriculum identified fairly detailed indicators of language competence. Anticipating the spirit of *perestroika* and *glasnost*, as it were, it was rid of ideology. In spelling out the objectives of teaching English, the English curriculum stated: 'The foreign language is a skills subject, therefore – especially at elementary level – there is no need to refer to ideological objectives except in the broadest sense' (Horváth, 1980: 4). Other signs of 'loosening up' in curricular terms were the far less prescriptive distribution of teaching content, the adoption of a more balanced approach to skills development and trust in the teacher's creative contribution to the fine-tuning of the curriculum. The most successful coursebooks written during this period reflected this freer atmosphere and made the best of communicative principles.

The effectiveness of instruction (1949–1989)

It is a sorry fact that over a period of 50 years the share of foreign languages in the secondary school curriculum fell from 34% in 1938 to 13% by 1978, reaching an all-time low (Kontra *et al.*, 1989). This in itself explains the low standards of foreign language education. However, there is more to this than meets the eye. Especially in the 1950s and 1960s, Hungary was a country cloaked behind the 'Iron Curtain'. Since people had only limited opportunities to use foreign languages owing to drastic restrictions on travel and access to the mass media, there was a lack of genuine learner motivation. In relation to Czechoslovakia, Healey pointed out that 'until 1989, the learning of English and other "western languages" was treated as an intellectual and social accomplishment [. . .] comparable with playing a musical instrument, dancing the waltz and polka, or reading poetry' (1993: 13). Speaking about the same polity, Gill said that the status of English 'was low bordering on subversive' (1993: 15). Although Hungary was rightly called the 'happiest barracks' in the Eastern bloc and, especially from the 1970s, an increasing number of citizens had the chance to indulge in the favours offered by 'Goulash communism', including travel,[27] communication and business, foreign language learning was slow to become an issue of priority for the majority of the population.

Despite the disproportionately huge investments in terms of instructional time and energy, Russian was the worst off. Even though it was apparent for teachers, parents and students alike that, for a variety of reasons, Russian instruction in Hungary was doomed to failure, political motives kept it alive.[28] In a typical gesture of hypocrisy, in 1982 the authorities pushed back the starting age for the study of Russian to nine, thereby adding a year to the length of study. It is small wonder that the extra year yielded no improvements.

With respect to English, the International Association for the Evaluation of Education Achievement (IEA) conducted a survey in the early 1970s, with the purpose of investigating the teaching and learning of English in ten countries, including Hungary. Results of this study revealed that Hungarian 17–18 year-olds occupied the bottom part of the European scale (Dörnyei, 1992; Kádár-Fülöp, 1979; Kontra, 1981). Although these data illustrate the plight of English, it is assumed that the results would have been no less inadequate for other foreign languages – after all, 'second' foreign languages suffered in equal measure.

Foreign languages in the curriculum (since 1989)

By the mid-1980s, it had become obvious that the situation was not going to improve until the entire political and economic system underwent change. As a herald of an imminent cataclysm, the Education Act of 1985 undermined the communist educational system while the 1990 Amendment, passed by the last communist government, gave it the *coup de grace*. By reducing heavy administrative and political control over education, these two acts allowed more autonomy to individual schools, cancelled the prescriptive control of curricula and restored teachers' pedagogical sovereignty, offering them a free choice of teaching materials (Halász, 1987, 1990; Kelemen, 1992).

Communism collapsed in 1989. In the same year, consonant with the historic changes occurring in Hungary and, in quick succession, over the whole of central and eastern Europe, the Russian language was officially stripped of its privileged status. Since then, it has been possible for Hungarian school children to learn any foreign language they wished (as long as it is available), and thus the distribution of foreign languages at every level of education in Hungary has changed irrevocably. The magnitude of these changes is illustrated in Figure 7 and Figure 8 (Statistical Report, 1989–1998).

For almost two decades now, primary school children have been required to study one foreign language from Grade 4.[29] As can be seen in Figure 7, after Russian ceased to be the compulsory foreign language, its share in the curriculum dramatically dropped from 100% in 1988/89 to 1.1% by 1997/98. The downward curve is likely to have been even steeper had it not been for the acute shortage of foreign language teachers other than Russian: because the study of one foreign language remained obligatory, Russian instruction had to be retained in many places until teachers of other foreign languages had become available. In any case, German and English were quickly filling the vacuum left by Russian.

Figures show that German is the most popular language in primary schools. This is mainly due to the long-standing good relations in all spheres of life between Hungary and the two major German speaking countries, Germany and Austria. At a national level, the sizeable ethnic German minority still plays an important role; the popularity of German in counties and towns with sizeable German speaking communities is significantly greater. The proportion of German in the distribution of foreign languages exceeded 50% for the first time in 1993/94, and since then it has been stagnating around that figure. The second favourite language in the primary curriculum is English, which reached its plateau at 40–45% by 1994/95. The steady progress of English seems to have stopped and a slight decline was experienced in 1997/98. German and English together leave a margin of merely 3–4% for all the other foreign languages to share among them. Interestingly enough, the popularity of French, which was modestly but steadily rising until 1992/93, went on a downward trend thereafter. This explains why French, with one per cent of the primary school population studying it, still has not caught up with Russian.

In secondary grammar schools,[30] the study of two foreign languages has been compulsory for about three decades – hence the presence of foreign languages other than Russian in the 1988/89 school year and, compared to its nose-diving in primary schools, the gently sloping curve of Russian instruction. Nevertheless, the number of students studying Russian in 1997/98 had declined to 2.4%. It would be naïve to think that the predicament of Russian is still mainly attributable to bitter feelings against the erstwhile oppressor – rather, it has to do with the recognition that the Russian language plays only a negligible role in present-day international communication. As for the English-German rivalry, the rank order is the reverse of that in the primary school, but the distance between

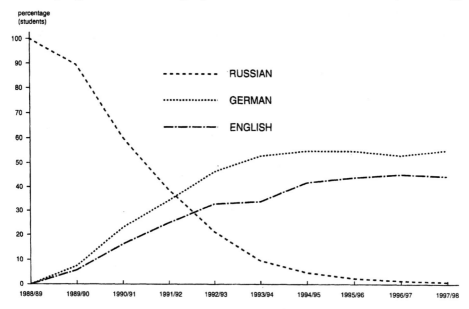

Figure 7 The distribution of foreign languages in the primary school

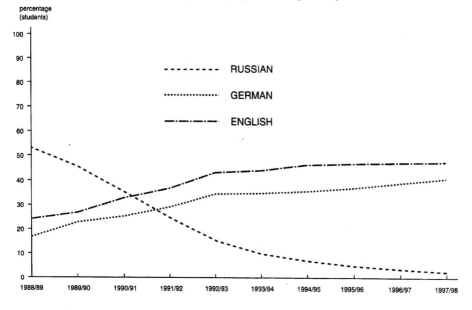

Figure 8 The distribution of foreign languages in the secondary grammar school

them is similar (respectively 49.4% and 40.2% in 1997/98). While both languages exhibit steady progress on the popularity index, the rate of their climb is slowing down. The total share of English and German being somewhat less than 90%, there is some room left for the French language. Although some 8% of secondary grammar school students studied it in 1997/98, French had been losing ground since its peak of 9.2% in 1992/93.[31]

The objectives of language teaching (since 1989)

Since 1989, Hungary has taken bold steps to get into the mainstream of inter-national communication; there is every reason to believe that Hungary will be admitted to the European Union in the first decade of the 21st century. Thus, alongside with informatics, foreign language education has become a buzz word. There is an abundance of news coverage in the mass media concerned with the lack of the average Hungarian's foreign language competence, the duties of educational authorities and schools to grapple with the situation, the causes of language teacher shortages, etc. There is an increasing number of job advertise-ments which not only require the candidate to have a good command of English and/or German, but also are written in English or German to filter out the linguistically deficient. The streets of major Hungarian towns are adorned with large posters advertising language schools with the promise of 'Learn English Fast and Easy' (Medgyes, 1992). In the shop window of bookstores the centre stage is usually taken by language books. Since 1990, Hungary has had three democratically elected governments: while disagreeing on most issues, they have been equally vociferous in support of issues concerning foreign language education.

In the past ten years, the assumption that the main objective of foreign language instruction at school should be the development of communicative abilities has passed unchallenged (Medgyes, 1995). Some utilitarians have gone so far as to suggest that the teaching of foreign languages at school should aim at nothing less than the mastery of the language. In the area of foreign language teaching, too, this may be characterised as a transitional period: the 1978 curricu-lum, for understandable reasons, was declared defunct in 1993, whereas the National Core Curriculum began to be gradually implemented as late as 1998.[32] Speaking of the past decade, positive thinkers might have welcomed the advent of educational freedom; realists would be more inclined to perceive it as anarchy.

Teaching materials (since 1989)

The 'textbook boom' may be a typical example of the ambivalence of the pres-ent situation. While nobody would query that a free choice of teaching materials, sanctioned by the Public Education Act of 1993, has greatly enhanced teachers' autonomy, it has also led to a kind of chaos. Many teachers complain that they can no longer see the forest for the trees.

This applies with particular force to teaching materials for the English class-room. As soon as the ban on using imported books in public education was lifted in the late 1980s, the market was inundated with materials, nearly all of them based on communicative principles (Medgyes, 1999b). As they were a whiff of fresh air and had a very attractive appearance, they were an instant success, thus pushing under-capitalised and inefficient local publishers to the periphery or out of business. The onslaught of foreign books was facilitated by the shrewd marketing policies of the local agencies of large publishing companies, which were running regular promotional seminars under the guise of in-service train-ing. To illustrate the growth of the market, while in 1989/90 the official book list licensed by the Ministry of Education contained six English titles, by 1997/98 this number had gron to 353. In the same year, the aggregate list for foreign languages carried 645 titles, so the share of English was nearly 55%. German was the second with 175 titles (27%), leaving a narrow margin for all the other languages (Halász & Lannert, 1998).

Incidentally, although books that are not on the official list may also be used in schools, those on the list are sold VAT-free; needless to say, this has intensified the fight to get a licence. At the same time, the Government decided to give short-term credit guarantees to small Hungarian textbook publishers to boost their competitive edge. This measure is all the more welcome since teaching materials produced in Hungary, involving local authors, are more likely to be able to satisfy local needs and expectations than imported books with their 'to whom it may concern' character (Bálits, 1998; Benedek, 1996; Enyedi & Medgyes, 1998; Herold, 1998; Miszlai, 1998; Petneki & Szablyár, 1997a; Poros, 1998).

The effectiveness of instruction (since 1989)

In the first half of the 1990s, certain sectors of foreign language education were given considerable financial assistance. Nevertheless, much less was achieved than had been hoped for: the average Hungarian youth still does not speak foreign languages. The government is beginning to realise that 'it was easier to pull down the barbed wire on the border than it has been to cross the [. . .] language barrier' (Hartinger, 1993: 33).

While it is common experience that there is something woefully inadequate in language instruction at school, this assumption is hard to corroborate with figures. Although out of the five compulsory subjects at the school-leaving examination (*érettségi*), one has to be a foreign language, this exam fails to provide feedback on students' proficiency level. It is not only an unreliable instrument, but it aims to assess formal knowledge rather than practical skills which are given a priority in the curriculum. Thus teachers are thrown in a schizophrenic situation: after they have been teaching from communicative course materials for several years, a few months before the school-leaving examination they switch into traditional 'testing mode' (Einhorn, 1998; Nagy & Krolopp, 1997). To make matters worse, a good proportion of students are exempt from having to take the foreign language part of the school-leaving examination: those who have passed the state language exam are granted a waiver. It can only be hoped that the examination reform currently under way will not only be capable of giving a true picture of language competence, but will exert a beneficial back-wash effect on the teaching process as well.

Part III: Language Policy and Planning

Hungarian Language Policy and Planning

The public education act and the national core curriculum

In Hungary, the use of the first language as well as language teaching and learning are regulated by several laws, the most significant being the Public Education Act.[33] The Public Education Act stipulates that the language of instruction should be Hungarian or a minority language, but education may also be provided partly or wholly in any foreign language. Based on the tenets of the Public Education Act, the Ministry of Education, together with specialised advisory and decision-making bodies including teaching experts, developed the key component of the Hungarian educational reform, the National Core Curriculum (NCC) (*Nemzeti alaptanterv*). The two most important consultative bodies of the Ministry of Education are the National Council for Public Education (*Országos Köznevelési Tanács*) and the Council for Public Education Policy (*Közoktatáspolitikai Tanács*). The former has consultative rights on subjects linked to the development of educational programmes, recommends coursebooks to be used in schools and deals with issues connected to in-service teacher training. Under the auspices of the National Council for Public Education, permanent and temporary expert committees are set up. The Council for Public Education Policy is primarily charged with the reconciliation of the interests of state organisations, school operators, and professional and parent organisations.

The contents and objectives of the NCC

Among the general objectives of the NCC, the emphasis is laid on democratic values, basic human rights, children's rights, and the freedom of conscience and religion. As a national document, the NCC gives considerable weight to national values and traditions, including those of ethnic minorities living in Hungary. In addition, the NCC promotes humanistic European values as well as openness towards global issues.

The NCC formulates contents and objectives according to cultural domains, instead of traditional subjects. The domains and their proportions across grades are as set in Table 15.

The NCC broke with the traditional central European approach of detailed central planning and overregulation of the curriculum. Instead, it advocates a *two-tier system*, with NCC representing the higher level whereas local curricula represent the lower. As its name suggests, it is a 'core curriculum', a foundation upon which local curricula and local education programmes can be developed. Consequently, it defines objectives, contents and requirements for up to 50–70% of the time available. The remaining 30–50% of the time frame gives teachers, parents and students the scope for pursuing their own interests and caters for individual needs. Following the guidelines of the NCC, teachers are free to develop their schools' own curricula, which may follow a thematic, a chronological or any other feasible order or concept.

Ever since the NCC was introduced by a government decree and issued by the Minister of Education in 1995, it has triggered heated debates and caused lively controversy between the parties concerned.[34] On the one hand, the concept of autonomy that makes it possible for teachers to develop their local education programmes has been judged favourably by those teachers who are willing to undertake the task and regard it as a means of professional development. On the other hand, antagonists argue that most teachers are not qualified as curriculum writers and may lack the necessary skills or inclination to design their own local curricula. Many teachers add that under the present circumstances, being overburdened and underpaid as they are, it is unfair to expect them to perform such duties.

Table 15 The cultural domains in NCC and their proportional distribution

Grades 1–6	Proportional distribution in grades	
Cultural domain	*1–4 (%)*	*5–6 (%)*
First language and literature (Hungarian or minority language and literature)	32–40	16–20
Modern foreign language	–	11–15
Mathematics	19–23	16–20
Man and society	4–7	5–9
Man and nature	5–9	8–12
Our Earth and environment	–	–
Arts	12–16	12–16
Computer science	–	2–4
Technical and household skills	4–7	5–9
Physical education and sports	10–14	9–13
Grades 7–10	*Proportional distribution in grades*	
Cultural domain	*7–8 (%)*	*9–10 (%)*
First language and literature (Hungarian or minority language and literature)	11–13	11–13
Modern foreign language	9–12	9–13
Mathematics	10–14	10–14
Man and society	10–14	10–14
Man and nature	16–22	15–20
Our Earth and environment	4–7	4–7
Arts	9–12	9–12
Computer science	4–7	4–7
Technical and household skills	6–10	5–9
Physical education and sports	6–10	6–10

Therefore, the present Ministry of Education, under the auspices of the new government formed in 1998, decided to launch a *three-tier system* by interposing frame curricula between the NCC and local curricula.[35] According to this concept, the cultural domains of the NCC are subdivided into subjects, and a limited number of frame curricula are developed for each subject by education experts and curriculum writers. Schools are obliged to choose one of the frame curricula for each school subject and adjust it to their local teaching context. Upon the implementation of such a three-tier system, it is hoped that teachers' work will become easier by having at their disposal these frame curricula. On the other hand, this policy may be regarded as a return to a centralised education system.

At present, students take a complex school-leaving examination (*érettségi*) at the end of the twelfth year of secondary education. This examination includes compulsory and optional subjects; the compulsory subjects are Hungarian language and literature, history, mathematics and a foreign language; for minority students Hungarian language and literature is replaced by native language, and the foreign language by Hungarian as a foreign language. Success in the secondary school-leaving examination represents the completion of secondary education and allows students to apply to colleges or universities.

Hungarian language and literature

The importance of 'Hungarian language and literature' is demonstrated by its pre-eminent position and highest proportion among the cultural domains. As the NCC document (1995) states, studying the first language has a key role to play in developing students' personalities, hence it is a crucial component of the curriculum.

The study of Hungarian language and literature is closely interrelated with all the other domains – the quality of instruction is claimed to have a direct impact upon the standard of teaching and learning in the rest of the domains (Table 15). Conversely, a higher level of instruction attained in other domains causes a positive backwash effect on the students' language development.

The NCC document also declares that the study of Hungarian and the national literature is inseparable (1995: 28): they are 'indispensable prerequisites' in forming the national identity of the individual. The general aim of first language education is to enable students to apply their L1 skills (especially those of speaking, reading and writing) as vehicles of communication as well as a means to ensure autonomous learning and self-development.

The objectives of teaching literature are manifold and interrelated. They can be classified as: to arouse children's interest in reading; to enhance a more profound understanding of texts and to develop an ability to analyse texts; to form the students' views about the world, strengthening their ties to the national culture; to make them absorb moral and aesthetic values as well as to enrich their emotional lives. To ensure that the objectives are fulfilled, a list of set readings is provided. While teachers generally agree with these objectives, they often complain that this list ties their hands too much.

Although the NCC emphasises the unity of the two components, language and literature are treated as two different subjects, as has been discussed in Part II. In primary and secondary education the only link between the two is that they are generally taught by the same teacher.

Teacher training

Hungarian language and literature teachers are trained at colleges and universities. With a study period of three years, pre-school teachers receive their training at Pre-school Teacher Training Colleges (*óvóképző főiskolák*). Primary school teachers may get their basic training at Junior Primary School Teacher Training Colleges (*tanítóképző főiskolák*), which train teachers for pupils between 6–12 years of age and which takes four years to complete. Those who will be qualified to teach children aged 10 to 14 go to Teacher Training Colleges (*tanárképző főiskolák*). Future secondary school teachers, on the other hand, are required to study at universities for a period of five years.

Literacy

A brief history
Tracing back the spread of literacy to medieval Hungary, it is obvious that
very few people could read or write. Between the 16th and 18th centuries a gradual but inexorable expansion of literacy can be observed. While 16% of both Catholic and Protestant schoolmasters were able to read but not write at the end of the
17th century, semi-illiterate schoolmasters became the exception rather than the
rule by the mid-18th century (Tóth, 1996). In the 16th and 17th centuries, the
Reformation played an important role in spreading literacy by founding schools
and setting up print shops to publish religious as well as other kinds of literature.
With regard to literacy, up until the 18th century Hungary represented the
borderline between West and East. Compared with England or the Netherlands,
Hungary fell behind in this area but proved well ahead of the less developed
parts of eastern and southern Europe. However, with the introduction of
compulsory education in 1868, literacy became more and more prevalent, and
the rapid increase of this trend between 1880–1910 can be observed in Table 16.
During the Austro-Hungarian Monarchy, according to a turn-of-the-century
census, 77% of the population could read or write, compared to the 68.7%
surveyed in Hungary (excluding Austria).

The present situation
In the 20th century, up to the 1980s, illiteracy was practically eliminated in
Hungary. An international literacy survey put Hungary into the top third of
European countries (Gereben *et al.*, 1993). However, the appearance of functional
illiteracy is a worldwide phenomenon and Hungary is no exception to the rule. In
1985, according to a national survey representing the adult population of
Hungary, approximately 25% were found more or less functionally illiterate. The
survey was replicated ten years later, and the preliminary results published by
Terestyéni (1996) indicated that the percentage of the functionally illiterate
remained virtually unchanged. Alarmed by such a high rate of functionally illiterate people, a conference was held under the auspices of the Hungarian Academy of Sciences in 1996 to discuss this predicament and to work out suggestions
for a possible 'action plan' (Csoma & Lada, 1997).

Among the reasons for functional illiteracy cited were the lack of equal opportunity in society and the concomitant failure of the education system. Moreover,
participants in the conference pointed out the negative tendency in consecutive
authorised curricula to reduce the number of Hungarian language and literature
lessons per week[36] and the use of unsuitable methods in the teaching of reading.
The overall reading comprehension of approximately 30% of eight graders
(14-year-olds) was found to be unsatisfactory.

Table 16 Percentage of literacy in Hungary between 1880–1910 (Tóth, 1996)

1880	1890	1900	1910
43.5	53.2	61.4	68.7

Language policy and language planning agencies

The status of Hungarian

Three periods can be distinguished in the status of Hungarian: it was a *minority* language up to 1844, when it became officially recognised as the national language of Hungary, or rather, until 1867, the year of the 'Compromise' that led to the establishment of the Austro-Hungarian Monarchy. Between 1867 and 1920, Hungarian was a majority language in the area of present-day Hungary, but not in the Austro-Hungarian Monarchy and not even in its Hungarian 'component', the Hungarian Kingdom. It is only since 1920 (The Treaty of Trianon) that Hungarian has been the *majority* as well as the *official* language of Hungary.

As mentioned in Part I, Hungary used to be a polyglot country with Latin as the official language until 1844. In the Middle Ages and thereafter, Hungarian was primarily used in rural towns and villages. However, in 1784, when Joseph II of Habsburg replaced Latin with German as the official language of the Hapsburg Empire, it fomented a fierce resistance, and the use of Hungarian became an issue of national identity and rights. In 1790, the decree was withdrawn, but the movement to elevate Hungarian to the status of an official language instead of Latin continued into the 19th century. The cause was supported by a cross section of socio-economic classes including the minor nobility, the gentry, the intellectuals of non-noble origin and the newly burgeoning class of the bourgeoisie.

The movement to renew Hungarian was a combined issue of corpus and status planning; that is, by renewing and expanding its lexis, the leading figures of the movement wanted to elevate Hungarian to the status of an official national language. With the foundation of the Hungarian Academy of Sciences (*Magyar Tudományos Akadémia*) in 1827, the founding aristocrats (with Count István Széchenyi as the primary leader) created the most influential and august body in charge of Hungarian. As a result of the endeavours of fifty years, Hungarian became the official language in 1844. After a period of forceful Germanisation, following the defeat of the 1848–49 Revolution and War of Independence, Hungarian was once again declared the national language in 1867. Afterwards, Hungarian as a majority language ceased to need any special support to ensure its maintenance.

Between 1867 and 1918, the national minorities living in Hungary started their own struggle to be granted the same language rights that Hungarians had achieved, and to have their own national languages officially recognised. The Hungarian national language policy often proved insensitive and narrow-minded when treating the minority language issue, ironically very much as *their* issue had been treated earlier by the dominant Austrians. These unresolved national language policy issues were one reason for the dismantling of the Austro-Hungarian Monarchy following World War I.

As mentioned in Part I, large numbers of Hungarians became minorities after the war, which had significant repercussions for national language policy. Since 1920, language policy and planning issues have been fundamentally altered in Hungary and in the neighbouring countries, owing to the different status of Hungarian in Hungary and beyond the national borders.

The Hungarian Academy of Sciences and the Linguistics Institute

The 1994 Hungarian Academy of Sciences Act (*Törvény a Magyar Tudományos Akadémiáról*) states that the academy was founded by the nation in order to foster the Hungarian language and to promote sciences. The main body in charge of the Hungarian language within the Academy is the Linguistics Institute (*Nyelvtudományi Intézet*). Among its ten departments, the Structural Linguistic Department (*Strukturális Osztály*) is concerned with synchronic and descriptive linguistic matters. The department has prepared a Hungarian structural grammar, the first two volumes of which, Syntax and Phonology, have already been published; the forthcoming third volume will cover Morphology. The Language History Department (*Nyelvtörténeti Osztály*) conducts diachronic research. There are two bodies with a more prescriptive agenda: the Hungarian Language Committee (*Magyar Nyelvi Bizottság*) and the Language Cultivation Department (*Nyelvművelő Osztály*). The task of the Hungarian Language Committee is to standardise Hungarian spelling and to periodically publish the authorised Hungarian Spelling Dictionary. The Language Cultivation Department publishes Hungarian grammars and various monolingual dictionaries including a Language Cultivation Handbook (*Nyelvművelő Kézikönyv*) with the aim of providing advice on language use. Furthermore, it runs a phone-in service to offer advice to the general public on language use and language appropriateness. Although financial support from the Academy has been decreasing since the 1990s, language cultivation is still regarded by many as a cause of national importance.

Informal organisations

Several societies and organisations deal with language awareness raising. For example, a series of events called Hungarian Language Week (*A Magyar Nyelv Hete*) is held each year; an annual conference on Hungarian (*Anyanyelvi Konferencia*) is organised by the World Association of Hungarians (*Magyarok Világszövetsége*); school students may enter the Contest of Correct Diction (*Kazinczy Szépkiejtési Verseny*) each year. In addition, there are various television and radio programmes that inculcate language use considered to be proper by purists and seek answers to questions such as: what is the standard pronunciation? how to avoid foreign words? how to speak and write in an appropriate style? – to name but a few.

Language policy for ethnic Hungarians in the neighbouring countries

Language policy and the situation of ethnic Hungarians are inextricably intertwined. In neighbouring countries, following the social and economic changes of 1989, the issue of minority rights was judged more favourably than before. Owing to the transition to democracy, the neighbouring countries' admission to the Council of Europe, and their overt endeavour to seek accession to the EU, the new governments were willing to consider the recommendations promulgated by the European Charter of Regional or Minority Languages (1992), which supports the use of regional and minority languages (Romsics, 1998).

Nevertheless, the situation is ambivalent. As far as minority rights legislation is concerned, laws have been passed to guarantee the right to use the first language in both private and public domains. The trouble is that in the new democracies (including Hungary) minority rights often exist on paper but have not yet been sufficiently implemented. Be that as it may, the issue of language rights is so volatile and so deeply rooted in politics that it is very hard for the authors of this monograph to provide a reliable and authentic description of recent developments.

Language policy in Romania

Although individual minority rights were granted by the 1991 Romanian Constitution, its implementation was occasionally overruled by specific laws. Among these, the Public Administration Act passed in 1994 restricted the constitutional rights by instituting the exclusive use of Romanian in offices (Jordan, 1998). Having attained membership of the Council of Europe in 1993, Romania undertook to pass a new education and minority law in accordance with the recommendations of the Council. When, after heated debates, the Education Act was passed in 1995, it precipitated heavy protests from both ethnic Hungarians' organisations and the Hungarian government, as it restricted the language use of ethnic minorities at every level of schooling. In 1996, Romania and Hungary signed a bilateral treaty ratified by the Romanian parliament, and soon after, following the 1996 parliamentary elections, the Democratic Association of Hungarians in Romania (*Romániai Magyarok Demokratikus Szövetsége*) joined the coalition government. This led to several concessions for ethnic Hungarians; for example, the Romanian parliament passed an amendment to the Public Administration Act in 1999, which allows the official use of Hungarian in offices wherever the proportion of the minority exceeds 20% of the staff.

Language policy in Slovakia

The Constitution of the Slovak Republic ensures equal rights to all ethnic minorities in the country, including the right of education in their first language. Although Slovakia and Hungary signed a bilateral treaty in which they declared the acceptance of international documents for the protection of ethnic minorities, minority rights, including the use of the first language has not been consistently adhered to. The situation is likely to improve now that, following the 1998 general elections, an alliance of ethnic Hungarian parties has joined the newly formed coalition government.

Language policy in Yugoslavia

In 1990, a new Education Act was passed for the ethnic minorities in Vojvodina (*Vajdaság*), Serbia, replacing the old 1976 law, which aimed to make the education system more uniform, thus severely restricting Hungarian instruction in schools. More recently, the 1992 amendments to the law on education state that the language of instruction must be Serbian with the possibility of using minority languages only if all the parties concerned were able to reach an agreement. Not surprisingly, as a result of this legislation, the number of ethnic Hungarian students has dropped dramatically in the 1990s (Poulton, 1998).

Language policy in Ukraine

In 1991, Ukraine and Hungary signed a declaration that guarantees ethnic minority rights in both countries. The principles of this declaration were reinforced by the adoption of a law on national minorities in 1992, which ensures the use of the first language in public domains and education in the first language. When Ukraine joined the Council of Europe in 1995, it undertook to study the European Charter of Regional or Minority Languages with a prospect of ratification. Although minority laws may be considered satisfactory, their implementation is often blocked at local levels.

Language policy in Croatia

Although Croatia and Hungary signed a bilateral treaty and Croatian laws guarantee the use of minority languages, Hungarian instruction is severely restricted in schools. The use of Hungarian is limited even in settlements where ethnic Hungarians are in the majority.

Language policy in Slovenia

As a full member of the Council of Europe, Slovenia guarantees several rights to ethnic Hungarians, including the right to education in the first language, albeit not at every level.

Language policy in Austria

Hungarians have been officially recognised as a minority since the 1976 Minority Act. The law enforces protection and support only if a minority group makes up 25% of the population. As the general political climate is not especially favourable for ethnic minorities, the number of people claiming minority status is rather low.

In 1994, the new Burgenland Education Act came into effect, regulating minority language education and bilingual education for Hungarians and Croats in primary and secondary schools. Austria's minority policies may be characterised by an observation of de Cillia *et al.*: ' . . . [After a] promising start immediately after World War II, [they] have been characterised by increasing restrictiveness . . . ' (1998: 29).

Minority Language Policy and Planning

Local and national agencies of minority education

The Act on the Rights of National and Ethnic Minorities stipulated that minority language education be provided at the request of a minimum of eight students who belong to the same ethnic group. The same law enjoined the establishment of local minority councils whose responsibility entails issues relating to minority education.[37]

Local minority councils have the right to establish and maintain schools and any other institution catering for education. They may initiate action, make recommendations and lodge an appeal against any decision considered to offend minority rights. More importantly, no decision concerning ethnic minorities may be made without the prior endorsement of the local minority government, including budgetary plans, the appointment of minority school principals and the implementation of pedagogic programmes. Despite their strong legal position, local minority councils have played only an insignificant role in the life of minorities. This is due to their financial dependence on the local government, as much as to their inexperience in dealing with educational matters (Halász & Lannert, 1998). Their scope of activity is further constrained by the diminishing number of students who wish to participate in minority education, especially at secondary level.

At a national level, while large-scale programmes aimed at the modernisation of education have given minority education the chance for development, minority education has seldom availed itself of this opportunity. To give an example, it is increasingly true that minority children start their school education with limited proficiency in the minority language. To alleviate this problem, minority schools may respond in one of two ways: either by applying more effective methods of language education, or by lowering requirements. More often than not, with the connivance of local minority councils, they resort to the latter option. Concomitantly, the number of lessons at the disposal of language education is often devoted to the teaching of foreign languages at the expense of minority languages. To be fair, this decision is often taken at the express wish of parents (Vámos, 1998).

To counterbalance these inauspicious tendencies, the Ministry of Education has set up its own Department of National and Ethnic Minorities whose responsibility includes the provision of inservice teacher education. At the same time, it has taken steps to guarantee a more efficient way of allocating supplementary funds for minority education.

Minority education in the national core curriculum

In harmony with the Hungarian Constitution, the Act on the Rights of National and Ethnic Minorities and the Public Education Act, the objectives of the National Core Curriculum (NCC) also apply to the education of national and ethnic minorities, with the additional and unique goal of preserving and strengthening minority identity. To accomplish this goal, the NCC 'strives to:

- promote the acquisition of the given minority language on an erudite standard level, through developing the ability to understand and use the language in writing and speech;
- acquaint students with folk poetry, music, fine art, customs and traditions, and encourage them to cultivate these;
- teach students the historic traditions, culture in first language and the knowledge of their people and country;
- help students to accept and appreciate other cultures by underlining their values;
- familiarise students with the culture, history and everyday life of their motherland;
- promote the upward mobility and social integration of Gypsies' (National Core Curriculum 1995: 18).

The NCC further stipulates that any of Hungary's 13 minority languages may be taught as a foreign language or used as a medium of instruction. In addition to the traditional types of minority education (minority-language, bilingual and Hungarian-language), the NCC creates scope for two further programmes: *intercultural education* and *upgrading education for Gypsy children*. Intercultural education aims at the integration of minority and majority students by ensuring that they are together introduced to the minority culture and, if parents so wish, to the minority language.[38] Upgrading education is supposed to help Gypsy children fulfil the educational objectives set for other students in the given age group, within or apart from normal daily lessons. Such programmes may also offer the teaching of the varieties of the Romani language.

The plight of Gypsy students

It is generally accepted that the primary victims of the cataclysmic changes of 1989 were the Gypsies. They were the first to lose their jobs and the last to find work, due to their lack of skills as well as social discrimination. By the end of the 1990s, the rate of unemployment is eight times as high for Gypsies as for non-Gypsy Hungarians. As a result, the Gypsy population has become greatly impoverished: some 70% of Gypsy school children have been found living in indigent circumstances (Halász & Lannert, 1998).

At the same time, prejudice against Gypsies is rampant (Szabó & Örkény, 1998). One such prejudice holds that the rate of criminals among the Gypsy population is much higher than among non-Gypsy Hungarians, and a perfunctory glance at the statistics confirms this assumption: the percentage of Gypsy criminals is double the percentage of non-Gypsy criminals. At closer inspection, however, it turns out that criminal behaviour has a lot more to do with poverty than with ethnicity (Póczik, 1996); that is to say, between Gypsies and non-Gypsies who are at a similar level of poverty there is no significant difference in crime rates.

Prejudice extends to Gypsy children, and damage is often done despite the best of intentions. Classes specially reserved for Gypsy children is a case in point. While advocates assert that such 'Gypsy classes' give Gypsy children the opportunity to participate in 'tailor-made' instruction and thus catch up with children studying in ordinary classes, opponents assert that this aggravates their segregation. Worse still, 'problem children' of Gypsy nationality are often sent to remedial classes or even to schools for the mentally handicapped, even if there is nothing wrong with their intellectual capacity (Póczik, 1996).

In Halász and Lannert's (1998) view, the Hungarian educational system is unprepared to tackle an issue of such magnitude. The standard creed and practice of Hungarian education is that of facilitating assimilation and integration; little concession is granted to those who come from a different background. Derdák & Varga (1996) are right in asserting that 'children are not selected according to their intellectual capability. Those in possession of tacitly assumed linguistic skills are perceived as bright, whereas those who have not been not been prepared to meet these expectations are considered dumb' (1996: 22–3). Since Gypsy culture is deeply rooted in oral traditions, Gypsy children often have grave difficulties in learning to read and write (Bognár & Gordos, 1995). Derdák & Varga (1996) suggest that Hungarian and Gypsy cultures also differ in terms of their oral traditions, so much so that 'it looks as if the Hungarian brought by Gypsy children from home and the Hungarian required at school were *two different languages*''(1996: 29, original emphasis). As a consequence, Gypsy children are doomed to failure at school.

With respect to the 'Gypsy problem' in Hungary, there is little cause for optimism. As opposed to all the other minorities, Gypsies are still officially treated as an ethnic and not as a national minority, under the false pretext that they have no real language, traditions and religion of their own. This explains, for example, why there are no Romani language programmes, why there is an acute shortage of Gypsy teachers, and why providing statistics on Gypsy children has been banned since 1993. Between the 1960s and the 1980s, Gypsies were given a great deal of support, albeit often in an unsystematic manner. Today, when 'there is growing awareness that the "Gypsy problem" can only be addressed in its entirety, as a complex issue with demographic, medical, economic, social, ethno-cultural, political and municipal implications, the resources have dried up' (Póczik 1996: 91).

Foreign Language Policy and Planning

Foreign languages in the Public Education Act and the National Core Curriculum

The Public Education Act (*Közoktatási Törvény*) includes no clauses relating to foreign language education as such. However, by stipulating the conception and implementation of the National Core Curriculum (NCC) (*Nemzeti Alaptanterv*) and determining the basic principles therein, the Public Education Act does exert an indirect influence on the development of language teaching and learning in Hungary. Although the NCC was approved by the Government in 1995, its implementation only began in the last school year, and through a gradual process of introduction the system will have reached all levels of education by the 2003/04 school year.

Introduction

Out of the ten cultural domains (*műveltségi terület*) articulated in the basic NCC document, the discussion of the domain called 'Modern Foreign Languages' takes up merely 14 pages of the whole publication. As stated in the introduction to this chapter, the NCC addresses language issues only in general terms, without specifying the languages being taught in Hungary.[39] The tasks of identification and, in accordance with local characteristics and needs, the definition of ' . . . the system of requirements for each foreign language based on their unique characteristics . . . ' (1995: 56), is left to the discretion of local educational authorities, schools and teaching staff.

The preamble to the document opens by asserting that 'The main objective of teaching foreign languages is to provide learners with practical language skills', and this principle is reiterated a little while later: 'It is a requirement that students [. . .] be taught at least one modern foreign language at a level which *enables them to use the language* in everyday situations' (1995: 64, original italics). Apart from passing references to secondary objectives, such as familiarity with the values of different cultures, personality enhancement and the development of co-operation skills, the whole document is predicated on a pragmatic concept of foreign language education.

Although the NCC does not take sides in the methodology debate, it implicitly advocates the principles of communicative language teaching in the broadest sense of the term. Furthermore, it remarks that ' . . . when establishing the general requirements in relation to foreign languages, the proposals of the Council of Europe were adhered to . . . ', with the rationale that ' . . . all member states of the European Union use these guidelines for developing foreign language curricula . . . ' (1995: 64).

The essential uniqueness of the NCC lies in its flexibility – never before has a national curriculum in Hungary professed such liberal pedagogical views. Its guiding principles are trust in teacher's integrity, student involvement and local initiatives. On the other hand, it prescribes that:

- students must start studying the first foreign language by Grade 5 at the latest;
- they must learn this language for at least six years;
- language learning may begin one or more years earlier; and
- a second foreign language (including Latin) may be studied as well.

Requirements

The preamble is followed by two main sections which identify 'general development objectives' as minimum requirements to be fulfilled by the end of Grade 6 and Grade 10, respectively. Both lists of general objectives are divided into 'detailed objectives' with specifications referring to 'knowledge' (functions, notions, topics) and 'skills' (listening, speaking, reading, writing). Detailed objectives are set for Grade 6, Grade 8, and Grade 10.

Critique

The final version of the NCC document is the product of a team of experts who have had many years of teaching experience. They had circulated their preliminary ideas among colleagues and had taken many observations and suggestions into account before finalising the document (Horváth, 1996). As a result, apart from a few critical remarks (Petneki, 1998a), the professional content of the document has met with the approval of the language teaching community.

In language policy terms, however, the NCC has come under vicious attack (Fónagy, 1997; Petneki, 1998a; Szűr & Parrott, 1998; Vágó, 1997). Firstly, it has been attacked because it allows foreign language instruction to begin as late as Grade 5. Critics assert that this is a step back compared to the present situation, when children normally start their language studies in Grade 4 and over a hundred thousand pupils even earlier (Vágó, 1997). Pushing up the starting age runs in the face of the trend featured in all documents of the European Union and the Council of Europe, which argue for an early start of foreign language instruction, fully supported by evidence from psycholinguistic research (Szépe, 1997). Under parental pressure, school principals may decide to launch fee-paying afternoon courses and, failing that, parents may hire private teachers.[40] Needless to say, this defies the 'equal opportunity policy' reaffirmed by successive Hungarian governments. In justification of a late start, educational authorities often complain about the shortage of language teachers and, in turn, the high percentage of unqualified teachers operating in schools. However, the legitimacy of this argument is weakened by recent statistics which show that the percentage of unqualified teachers in Grade 4 is only slightly higher than in Grades 5–8 (Vágó, 1997). (Teacher supply and demand will be dealt with later.) In addition, there is a fear that once they are not obliged by law to run language classes in Grade 4, budget conscious school principals may choose to economise by merging smaller classes or not dividing larger ones (Morvai, 1998).[41] Worse still, some may decide to close down their junior language classes and dismiss language teachers, including qualified teachers (Vágó, 1997).

Secondly, the main target of criticism is aimed at the low number of lessons

Table 17 Comparative data on the number of foreign language lessons

	Total number of lessons
Before NCC	448
NCC minimum	542
NCC maximum	748
EU average	670

allocated for foreign language instruction. In view of the NCC suggestions, the proportion available to the 'Modern Foreign Language' domain is 11–15%. Since the maximum number of hours per week has been stipulated by the Public Education Act, an average of 2.5–3.0 lessons per week is available for the study of foreign languages across the six grades of compulsory education. This is less than what most schools currently provide, and it will become wishful thinking for most learners to achieve communicative proficiency in one language, let alone two. Moreover, one cannot fail to note the contradiction between the virtual exclusion of the possibility to master a second foreign language and the inclusion of two languages among the requirements of the school-leaving examination. It is unrealistic to expect students to devote most of their energy to learning a second foreign language from scratch in Grades 11 and 12, when they are busy preparing for the demanding school-leaving and entrance examinations. In conclusion, Petneki says: 'In principle the NCC gives the teacher a good deal of freedom – the freedom to dance with shackles' (Petneki, 1998a: 6).

All these criticisms have to be treated with caution. After all, it is only too natural for foreign language teachers to fight for creating and maintaining the best possible circumstances for the teaching of their subjects. But this self-assertive attitude is no less characteristic of teachers of other subjects, especially at volatile and uncertain times of curriculum reform. Teachers tend to lock horns with each other over issues that concern time allocation in the curriculum, each group fervently promoting its cause – and of course all the arguments are true. This is exactly what happened in the first half of the 1990s, when the terms of reference of the NCC were being negotiated. Modern foreign languages got as much as their lobbyists managed to force out of decision makers – quite successfully, as revealed in Table 17 which shows the total number of lessons available for the study of the first foreign language. In the light of these figures, the concerns of foreign language teachers are only partially justified. Whereas the position of the first foreign language will improve with the implementation of the NCC and approximate EU averages, the weight of the second foreign language will decrease.[42] Considering the fact that the Government continually reiterates the vital importance of foreign language competence and, in principle, assigns language education high priority, there is little reason to be jubilant. Decision makers either insincerely 'go through the motions' or, worse still, have no consistent language policy to pursue.

The examination reform in foreign language education

In conjunction with the creation of the NCC, a new system of school examinations was envisaged, which is currently in the process of elaboration. The principal aim of this system is to modernise the school-leaving examination and to re-establish its prestige (Nikolov, 1999). Since this system includes a foreign language component, it is worth subjecting it to a detailed analysis.

The reform introduces two kinds of examinations: the Basic Examination (BE) (*alapműveltségi vizsga*) and the School-leaving Examination (SLE) (*érettségi*). The BE is to be taken at the age of 16, with the aim of establishing the extent to which the student has fulfilled the requirements of the NCC. It is an optional examination in the sense that all students may continue their studies in Grades 11 and 12, regardless of whether or not they have a BE certificate. The SLE, on the other hand, is mandatory: it simultaneously serves as a multifunctional 'closing act' of general schooling and an 'initiation ritual' for young people to start their career in a modern society (Halász & Lannert, 1998: 201). The SLE may be taken at two levels: intermediate level and advanced level. The elements of this three-prong examination system (BE + two levels of SLE) are built upon each other.

The Basic Examination

The BE certificate may be issued to those who have taken BE successfully in at least six subjects. In addition to the three compulsory subjects (Hungarian language and literature, mathematics and history), students may choose one subject from each of three blocks; in one of the blocks the choice is between a foreign language and informatics. Finally, there is a block with an unspecified menu of subjects; students who have gone for Informatics may still wish to take a foreign language exam. In other words, a foreign language is not a compulsory subject in the BE, and the first results concerning its popularity will be accessible only at the end of the 2002/03 school year, when the examination is administered to the first cohort of students who have completed their Grade 10 studies according to the NCC. In a more general framework, too, the future of the BE is unpredictable at this present stage.

Nevertheless, curriculum experts are busy setting the requirements for all the subjects. With respect to foreign languages, the general requirements have already been made public (Nikolov, 1997), and the detailed requirements are under review at the time of writing of this monograph. Aimed at assessing learners' communicative competence, the examination will consist of a written and an oral part with a duration of 90 and 15 minutes, respectively, with the two parts carrying equal weight during the evaluation process.

As for the written part of the examination, candidates have to carry out tasks on a worksheet. All the tasks are centrally selected from a test bank. Special measures are taken to ensure that all the tasks are standardised and based on authentic materials, which can be evaluated in a reliable, valid and objective fashion. The worksheet contains tasks that assess the candidates' listening, reading and writing skills. The candidates' production is subjected to criterion-referenced evaluation to be performed by their teacher, who has been specially trained for this job and is helped with centrally issued keys and guidelines. The teacher's evaluation is checked by an external assessor. The oral examination is aimed at assessing the candidates' speaking and listening skills by means of free conversation and role play. The students' production is jointly evaluated by their teacher and a specially trained examiner, who is present throughout the oral exam.

Compared to examinations traditionally administered in Hungary, the BE adopts a radically new approach to assessment, and employs modern examination instruments. Interestingly enough, the results of a recent survey show that the overwhelming majority of responding teachers are in favour of the way the BE is being planned. On the other hand, the responses reveal that teachers in Hungary have not been trained to be able to apply up-to-date evaluation methods (Nikolov, 1997).

The School-leaving Examination

The government decree determining the SLE (The School-leaving Examination Decree, 1997) is a unique document in the sense that it is not only concerned with the school-leaving examination itself, but it also determines the curriculum for Grade 11 and Grade 12, and is thus a follow-up curriculum to the NCC. In its capacity *as an examination document*, it

- identifies the school subjects, both compulsory and optional;
- controls the administration of the examination;
- determines evaluation procedures (Halász & Lannert, 1998).

In its capacity *as a curriculum*, it

- specifies the subjects to be taught in the last two grades of secondary education; and
- sets the general requirements thereof.

The standards and detailed requirements for Grades 11 and 12 will be determined by a special document, still in preparation; interim documents have already been circulated in relation to foreign languages. Although the new type of SLE will be administered in the 2003/04 school year for the first time, instruction according to the reformed curriculum in Grades 11 and 12 will start as of 2001/02 and 2002/03, respectively.

Foreign languages play a central role in the SLE: one of the four compulsory subjects is a foreign language.[43] Examination in a fifth subject is mandatory, but candidates are free to choose this subject – it may well be a second foreign language. This kind of output control has a backwash effect on the foreign language component of the curriculum and, in turn, on the teaching of foreign languages. The general requirements for foreign languages as expressed in the Examination Rules prescribe that students in secondary grammar schools study for four years at least two foreign languages[44] whereas in vocational schools they study one or two languages depending on their specialisation. This regulation is in clear conflict with the limited scope assigned by the NCC for Grades 9 and 10 (Ábrahám & Jilly, 1999; Horváth *et al.*, 1996; West, 1997).

The objectives of foreign language education specified in the Examination Decree echo those formulated in the NCC. The primary objective is the development of communicative competence through the provision of authentic materials and communicative tasks, in compliance with students' interests and age. Besides the realisation of such pragmatic objectives, however, the development of cognitive knowledge (information about the target language and target culture) as well as the development of personality traits (openness, tolerance, learner independence, teamwork) are given due attention. The general requirements set for the SLE list ten topics, four skills, a variety of cultural and intercultural skills, and communicative strategies.

In foreign languages, too, the SLE may be taken at two levels: intermediate (*középszint*) or advanced (*emelt szint*). An intermediate level exam will be used to test everyone graduating from secondary school, whereas an advanced level exam tests mostly those students who wish to enter universities or colleges. In contrast with the present system, it is planned that universities should refrain from setting written entrance examinations for foreign language majors, but rather should screen candidates on the basis of their advanced level SLE results. Another important change concerns the relationship between the SLE and the State Foreign Language Examination. On the one hand, a certificate at the State Foreign Language Examination will no longer exempt anyone from having to study that foreign language in Grades 11 and 12, nor will it ensure a waiver at the SLE. On the other hand, high scores at the advanced level SLE will allow the candidate to qualify for an advanced level certificate at the State Foreign Language Examination. Although the situation is more complicated than is presented here, all these changes aim at granting more prestige to the SLE in comparison with the State Foreign Language Examination (Halász & Lannert, 1998).

It must be admitted that there are several contradictory and nebulous clauses in the Examination Decree (Nikolov, 1999). It is more than desirable, therefore, that before the first SLE is administered, amendments to the present document be added. Such an amended version should also consider including the findings of various surveys carried out among teachers, school principals, school leavers, university students and employers (Bárány *et al.*, 1999; Vámos, 1996; Vándor, 1998). In view of the huge investment into reforming the present examination system, it is reassuring that the overwhelming majority of English teachers asked in the survey conducted by Bárány *et al.* (1999) approved of the undertaking. When requested to specify what exactly was necessary, most of the respondents mentioned that the new SLE should cover all the language skills, evaluation should be objective, standards should be higher, the level of difficulty should be consistent from year to year, tasks should be more varied and natural, and so on. Many of them added that if the SLE was to be a real proficiency test, it should be both administered and assessed externally,[45] a view which, for obvious reasons, is not shared by the majority of school leavers. At the same time, employers insist that the new examination should include more job-related tasks such as writing documents and reports, filling in forms, taking messages.

Relatively speaking, the clauses referring to foreign languages in the Examination Decree seem to be better designed than those referring to the other three compulsory subjects. A question based on a survey of 2353 teachers ran like this: 'Do you agree that students will sit for the examination in your subject as they are set in the Examination Decree?' While the percentage of those who agreed were 75, 85 and 50 in Hungarian language and literature, mathematics and history, respectively, it was 89 in foreign language (Halász & Lannert, 1998). This bodes well for the foreign language teaching in Hungary in the 21st century.

The State Foreign Language Examination

The system of state foreign language examination (SFLE) (*államilag elismert nyelvvizsga*) was first devised and legally regulated in 1967 (Vágó, 1997). Since then, the examinations have been organised and administered by the State

Foreign Language Examination Board (*Állami Nyelvvizsga Bizottság*), a semi-governmental body. As described earlier, a SFLE certificate grants the holder various privileges; therefore, it is a high-stake examination, the popularity of which has grown rapidly in the past decade, especially among the young.

Ever since it was established, the work of the SFLE Board has been the target of harsh criticism formulated by both stakeholders and language teaching experts (Crighton & West, 1993; Dörnyei, 1992; Dörnyei & Tóth, 1987; Manherz, 1995). Partly because of this, the system has undergone several changes over the decades. The latest major reform in 1991 introduced quality control procedures aimed at modernising the SFLE. At the same time, the Board has expanded its scope by setting up six provincial examination centres and appointed 17 towns where examinations can be provided, thereby partly relinquishing its exclusive right to issue SFLE certificates. Most recently, the Board has launched a public relations campaign in an effort to dispel its bad image due to insufficient security measures, and supply the public with a range of badly missed information materials (Fekete & Katona 1999; Fonyódi, 1996).

Nevertheless, a government decree (The State Foreign Language Examination Decree) broke the monopoly of the Board, by granting the right of running examinations and issuing SFLE certificates to any institution which has submitted a viable examination proposal and has been found suitable by a newly established Foreign Language Accreditation Committee (*Nyelvvizsgát Akkreditáló Testület*). Thus this decree provides the opportunity for both private language schools and the foreign language departments of universities and colleges to seek accreditation, as well as to enable international examination centres (which have thus far been setting only their own type of examinations in Hungary) to run the SFLE and issue certificates with all the bonuses attached to them (Fazekas, 1998). The contribution of international examination centres is facilitated by a clause in the government decree which endorses the administration of monolingual exams, in addition to the traditional bilingual exams which include translation and interpretation tasks at Intermediate and Proficiency levels (Bárdos, 1994).

The new government decree has not been met with unanimous approval. Some fear that profit-oriented smaller centres will not take the trouble to offer examinations for less popular languages, which in the long run may lead to a further reduction in the teaching and learning of those languages – 'an alarming case of linguicism,' says Kontra (1997: 10). Another quibble raised by Kontra concerns the authorisation of a monolingual form of the SFLE: such examinations promote the unattainable ideal of the near-native speaker, instead of the more realistic goal of the competent bilingual.

Dual-language schools

On the eve of the fall of communism in Hungary, there was increasing pressure on educational authorities to give foreign language education a boost. As the Russian language was still completely protected, the curriculum left little space for speeding up the development of the teaching of other foreign languages on a national scale. For want of a more comprehensive solution, the Ministry of Education resuscitated dual-language (DL) education (i.e. bilingual education) in a few selected schools.

The idea of this form of foreign language education was anything but new.

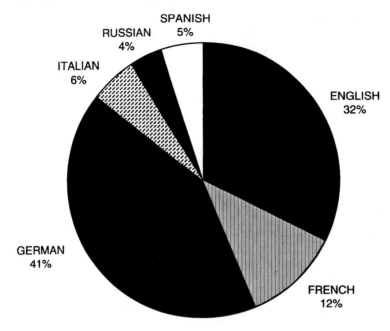

SPANISH
5%

RUSSIAN
4%

ITALIAN
6%

ENGLISH
32%

GERMAN
41%

FRENCH
12%

Figure 9 The breakdown of students in secondary schools per purpose-language

Despite their cherished tradition (or because of it), DL schools were closed down in 1948 and, apart from a few half-hearted attempts at setting up DL schools in Russian, they were only allowed to be reintroduced in the 1986/87 school year. As the pioneering DL schools became an instant success, they were quickly followed by others, and so the number of DL schools rose to 58 by the 1996/97 school year. This set comprises 31 secondary grammar, 20 secondary vocational and seven primary schools, whereas the number of students attending DL schools accounts for slightly more than four per cent of the total number of students in this age cohort. Figure 9 shows the distribution of languages in the 51 secondary schools: German and English together constitute 73% of all the languages available (Vámos, 1998).

The rationale of DL education in Hungary, not unlike the rationale of immersion programmes elsewhere, is that through content-based instruction students can learn a foreign language not simply as a school subject but rather as a tool for obtaining relevant information about certain segments of the world, hence communication in the foreign language has an element of authenticity. In a typical Hungarian DL school, the number of subjects taught in the foreign language ranges between three and five, and the length of study is five years, instead of four years for students in ordinary secondary schools (Vámos, 1998). In the preparatory 'zero' year, students in DL schools receive 20 language lessons a week so that they can cope with the subjects they are obliged to study in the foreign language by the time they begin their first 'normal' year.

Dual-language schools are admittedly élitist places of education. This assumption is evidenced by the fact that out of the 51 DL schools 18 are situated in the capital city of Budapest. Another indication of their privileged status is that they require *and* receive additional state subsidies as stipulated by a Ministry of Education order issued in 1997 (The Dual-language Schools Order). DL schools are better equipped, teachers are better paid, and students have greater educational opportunities to visit the target language country. As a result, students do far better on entrance examination scores than their peers graduating from ordinary schools. Students in the best English-language school are even eligible to take the International Baccalaureate, a school-leaving examination which has been accredited by over 800 universities, including such eminent places as Harvard, Oxford and The Sorbonne (Bognár, 1997; Bognár *et al.*, 1998).

DL schools have also attracted large amounts of funding from various international agencies. A good deal of this support has been spent on contracting native speaker teachers. In relation to English-language schools, Duff (1991) agreed with such a policy, because native speaker teachers were assumed to (1) ensure face validity to the endeavour, and (2) provide expertise in target language literature and essay writing. However, as less qualified native EFL applicants began to seek employment, these arguments carried less and less weight. In a more recent article, Duff (1995) asserted that highly qualified, proficient and experienced Hungarian teachers are more appropriate for teaching the content areas by virtue of their more thorough familiarity with the curricular and other requirements. Her conclusions echo the findings of recent literature on the comparative analysis of native and non-native speaking foreign language teachers (Braine, 1999; Medgyes, 1999a; Reves & Medgyes, 1994).[46]

In spite of the high acclaim they enjoy, DL schools often face insurmountable difficulties. Many are not equipped with suitable teaching materials, their native teachers are often underqualified while their non-native (i.e. Hungarian) colleagues are less than proficient speakers of the target language, local educational authorities cannot cover the extra costs incurred by DL education, etc. (Szablyár, 1998). To be sure, this form of education has produced remarkable achievements, Hungary cannot afford to expand the network of DL schools. A more realistic solution might be to offer only one subject in a foreign language within the framework of ordinary schools to as many students as possible.

Foreign languages in higher education

In the spirit of the Higher Education Act (*Felsőoktatási Törvény*) of 1993 and its amendments of 1996, tertiary education institutions attach great importance to the knowledge of foreign languages. As mentioned earlier, most universities and colleges acknowledge certified foreign language competence by awarding bonus points, which are added to the score achieved at the entrance examination (Halápi & Király, 1999).[47] Hence the relatively high percentage of students (87%) who claim to speak at least one foreign language on entering an institution of higher education.

By the time of graduation, the number of students with perceived foreign language proficiency is reported to have grown by four per cent (Székelyi *et al.*, 1998). Although no data are available as to what triggers this growth, it must be partly attributable to language instruction provided by the universities and colleges. In the 1997/98 academic year, well over one third of the student population were studying in the foreign language service departments (*idegen nyelvi lektorátus*) of the tertiary institutions (Statistical Report, 1998).[48] The rest do not avail themselves of this free service, probably because they already have certified knowledge of one foreign language competence at minimum intermediate level and another one at basic level, as required by the Higher Education Act.[49]

The leading language of instruction offered in the foreign language service departments is English (51.4%) followed by German (27.7%), the two languages accounting for nearly 80% of the student population. Surprisingly, Latin is ranked third (7%), being especially widely studied in colleges of theology, medical universities and certain majors in the humanities.

In the early 1990s, the Hungarian government recognised the need to lend extra support to institutions of tertiary education involved with foreign language instruction. This led to a decision to set up a special foreign language programme within the framework of a long-term World Bank loan called 'Catching Up with European Higher Education' Fund ('*Felzárkózás az európai felsőoktatáshoz*' *Alap*). The programme budget had $10.5 million and a similar volume of government contribution available for the implementation of various projects (Abosi, 1998). Run between 1991 and 1997, four consecutive rounds of competition were advertised with the aim of instituting reforms in foreign language education. The priority areas included:

- development and introduction of innovative forms of pre-service teacher training;
- restructuring of the Hungarian language examination system;
- provision of more up-to-date service courses;
- implementation of modular systems of in-service training;
- production of communicative syllabuses and materials for both teaching and testing purposes;
- organisation of language and pedagogical retraining for Russian teachers.

Out of the 201 proposals, 93 were given financial support by the National Council of Foreign Languages (*Országos Idegennyelv-oktatási Tanács*), an independent body consisting of representatives from the government, professional organisations, institutions of higher educations and stakeholders. The complex programme was designed and implemented in collaboration with external bodies such as the British Council, the Goethe Institut, the Soros Foundation and the US Peace Corps, which contributed to the success of the programme both professionally and financially.

As a result of concerted efforts in gaining access to sizeable funds, tertiary institutions concerned with foreign language education were able to acquire up-to-date computers and audio-visual facilities, set up resources and self-access centres, as well as buy large stocks of books and other teaching materials. External funds also gave impetus to an exchange of 'human flesh'; hundreds of local experts were granted the opportunity to attend conferences, workshops and training courses, and to pursue further studies abroad. At the same time, resident and visiting consultants from the west came in droves to lend support to the launching and running of various projects.

As a landmark of the attitudinal change that accompanied all these developments, when the word 'project' became a buzz-word in the early 1990s, most institutions of higher education were in for a shock as they were completely unaccustomed to the notion of institutional planning. Throughout long decades of communist rule, all educational decisions had been made by top-level authorities and then passed down for implementation. Suddenly, foreign language institutions were forced to learn to comply with the strict rules of application set by donor agencies, to gain skills in project design, costing, development plans and job descriptions – in a word, to adopt a business-like professional attitude (Enyedi & Medgyes, 1998; Medgyes 1997b).

However, the external funds that came pouring in during the early 1990s have gradually dried up.[50] As a consequence, local experts are obliged to make the best of the professional and financial resources they have hoarded thus far. Sustainability is yet another key-word with which they are trying to come to grips. Unfortunately, this situation is exacerbated by the cyclical change of policy makers in the government and other top organisations: new people tend to make new decisions which are seldom in harmony with previous decisions.

Private language schools

As mentioned in Part II, the first private language schools were allowed to be founded in the early 1980s, in response to the huge demand for foreign language instruction and the incapability of state education to cope with a problem of such magnitude. Most of the schools established before the 'big bang' provided high-quality instruction, which was ensured by a host of factors such as:

(1)   teaching was conducted in small groups.
(2)   teachers were carefully screened.
(3)   they received higher wages than their colleagues working in state education.
(4)   schools organised successful in-service training courses.
(5)   they used up-to-date teaching materials (Dörnyei, 1992).

After 1989, the number of schools skyrocketed – Bonifert (1997) may well be right that Hungary today has the highest number of private language schools in the region and not all of them are good. In the hope of quick profit, some entrepreneurs go out of their way to deceive customers: 'Perfect English in Three Months' and similar gimmicks are rife in the media. In an effort to dissociate themselves from such practices, better schools decided to set up a system modelled on ARELS (The Association of Recognised English Language Services) and similar British accreditation systems (Enyedi & Medgyes, 1998). With support lent by the British Council and USIS, the Association of Language Schools – Hungary (*Nyelviskolák Szakmai Egyesülete*) was founded in 1992. At a time when competition is stiff, the association believes that only those schools can regain public trust and keep afloat in the long term which operate with the combined aim of setting high standards, maintaining quality control, attracting the best teachers and giving potential customers reliable information. Schools which have passed a stringent accreditation procedure, involving external assessors, may wear the logo of the association for two years, after which they have to solicit re-accreditation. The association is member of EAQUALS (European Association for Quality Language Services) (Babai, 1998).

Pre-service teacher education

Traditionally, secondary school teachers in Hungary have been trained in a five-year degree course and primary school teachers in a four-year college curriculum. Both types of training have an academic rather than a practical bent. Students are required to obtain a thorough knowledge of literature, linguistics and a fair command of the target language. Methodology courses, which are regarded as add-ons, are followed by only a brief spell of actual teaching practice. The philosophy underlying this pattern of teacher training posits that teachers should be, first and foremost, highly erudite in the humanities, and should gradually acquire the necessary teaching skills while on the job.

A major recent change in teacher education resulted when Russian ceased to be the compulsory first foreign language in 1989. From that point on, some 15,000 English and German teachers were immediately required to supplement the existing supply of approximately 5000 teachers (Vágó, 1997). The situation was aggravated by the fact that, due to the low salaries of teachers, there was a steady drain from state education into the private sector, and thousands of qualified teachers of English and German were syphoned off to more lucrative jobs in business, commerce, banking and tourism (Medgyes, 1993).

To alleviate the shortfall, it became standard practice for school principals to hire *under*qualified and even *un*qualified teachers. The most obvious candidate was the Russian teacher whose work had suddenly become superfluous,[51] but teachers of other subjects, retired teachers, student teachers and even secondary school graduates were commonly used in schools. Almost anyone who claimed to have a smattering of the target language was welcome, let alone young native-speaking backpackers, whose native command of the target language was sometimes thought to make up for their incompetence as teachers (Medgyes, 1999b).

As the available universities and colleges reached their saturation point and were unable (and indeed unwilling) to provide an appropriate accelerated form of training, a new system of teacher training had to be devised. In an effort to tackle this problem, the Hungarian government decided to launch two ambitious programmes. The retraining programme for Russian teachers (*orosztanárok átképzési programja*) gave these teachers the opportunity to become fully qualified teachers of another foreign language, most commonly English or German. The other programme provides an innovative fast-track form of pre-service teacher education (*nyelvtanárképző központok*) for secondary school leavers.

The retraining programme for Russian teachers

This programme was first run in 1990/91 and the last cohort graduated in 1997/98. Lying between pre-service and in-service education, it had no forerunners or established traditions in teacher education, and therefore a curriculum which would meet the retrainees' special needs had to be designed from scratch by the host universities and teacher training colleges.

The training programme itself consisted of two stages. In the first stage, the volunteering Russian teachers enrolled in commercial language schools that prepared them for the State Foreign Language Examination in their chosen language. The low cost-effectiveness of the two-year language training programme may be demonstrated by the fact that only 25% of the participants eventually passed the exam at intermediate level and thus became eligible for continuing their studies (Vágó, 1997).

The second stage consisted of a three-year training course offered by the host insitutions. In spite of the fact that the costs were fully covered by the government for the whole duration of the training programme, there were invariably fewer volunteers than places available. To fill up these vacancies, in 1993/94 the government made the programme accessible to teachers of any school subject.[52] By the end of the project period, out of the 4900 teachers who completed the programme, less than two thirds were Russian teachers (Vágó, 1997).

Interviews with teacher trainers involved in the retraining programme as well as with the retrainees themselves indicate that the participants were an unhappy lot (Enyedi & Medgyes, 1998). Firstly, they had to get over the shock of having to learn a foreign language in mid-career and reach a level of competence high enough to teach it well for the rest of their professional career. Secondly, the teaching methodology of the new language was different from that of Russian, usually requiring the adoption of an entirely new teaching attitude (Enyedi, 1997). Finally, most of the participants were obliged to pursue their studies while remaining full-time teachers to make ends meet, often as teachers of the language they were studying.

The fast-track programme

A less formidable but more comprehensive task undertaken by the Hungarian government has been the establishment of a network of new teacher training centres within existing universities and colleges. The main brief of these centres has been to offer fast-track training programmes, mostly in German and English. Their profile is different from traditional pre-service training programmes in two major respects. On the one hand, they provide a shorter duration of training: their duration is three years. On the other hand, and more importantly, practical methodology and teaching practice are granted a much larger scope than is customary in philology tracks. In this regard, Szépe went as far as to suggest that 'the three-year training system is the first in the history of Hungary, whose primary aim is to prepare students for teaching a language' (1997: 12). According to some estimates, fast-track graduates are superior to their university counterparts in terms of practical teaching skills and are comparable in terms of language competence (Bárdos & Medgyes, 1997; Petneki & Szablyár, 1997b).

One such programme, The Centre for English Teacher Training (*Angol Tanárképző Központ*) in Budapest, has gained international acclaim for several aspects of its work (Medgyes & Malderez, 1996), including its teaching practice component. Under this scheme, trainee teachers take over the responsibility for the teaching of one class in an ordinary primary or secondary school. Throughout this period, they are supported by a school-based mentor, their trainee partner, and a university-based tutor. This system displays at least three innovative features. The first concerns the length of the internship period. Instead of a few weeks, which is the standard length in most training systems, the Centre requires its trainees for a full school year. Secondly, trainees are obliged to teach in pairs (Medgyes & Nyilasi, 1997), with the rationale that working in close partnership with a peer not only provides additional support and fosters the idea of teacher cooperation, but also helps trainees guard against 'isolation stress' in their future career. Finally, the school-based mentors receive special training before they are commissioned to look after their trainees. This mentor course is designed to develop an understanding of reflective practice and the necessary skills for its implementation (Malderez & Bodóczky, 1999).

The success of fast-track programmes has exerted a positive backwash effect on certain traditional university and college departments, urging them to give more weight to the teacher training components in their own curriculum (Medgyes, 1997b). Nevertheless, there is general apprehension that fast-track programmes will be disbanded once the teacher shortage problem has been solved. It is the university centres that are especially under threat; indeed, several of them have already been 'swallowed up' by traditional university programmes.

The predicament of fast-track programmes is mainly caused by the low prestige of language pedagogy in university hierarchies. Petneki & Szablyár (1997b) argue, for example, that language pedagogy is moving in a vicious cycle: short of qualified experts in the field, relevant PhD programmes get turned down by the National Accreditation Board, whereas until such programmes have been established, the shortage of experts is bound to remain. The picture is perhaps less gloomy: at the time of writing this monograph there are three PhD programmes in Applied Linguistics and/or Language Pedagogy in operation, and a fourth one stands a good chance of being accredited next year.[53]

In-service teacher education

Before 1989, in-service training for foreign language teachers usually meant having to attend sessions 4–6 times a year hosted by regional pedagogical institutes. These sessions consisted of listening to invited lecturers, who often spoke about issues not directly relevant to language teachers, and observing 'model' lessons held by school-based teacher trainers. By far the most interactive form of in-service training was offered during the summer holiday, when volunteers retreated for two or three weeks to participate in intensive language-cum-methodology update courses; such courses would normally be run by native speaking teachers under the auspices of educational agreements between the Hungarian and the target language governments.

After 1989, the activity of these traditional networks was eclipsed by more genuine patterns of further education such as the retraining programme of Russian and other-subject teachers, the mentor training programme and various other university and college programmes, which were specially designed for teachers who wished to upgrade their qualifications. A corollary of these undertakings was that they enhanced the role of higher education in the implementation of in-service training activities, thus bridging the gap between schools and tertiary education (Halápi et al., 1999). At the same time, publishers and foreign agencies such as the British Council and the Goethe Institut also stepped up their efforts in the provision of in-service training courses. In the 1990s, new professional journals and teachers' associations contributed to invigorating the professional development of foreign language teachers.

On the debit side, it has to be admitted that the majority of teachers were reluctant participants in this national campaign or refused to join in altogether. Few teachers could afford the luxury of long-term commitment if it meant having to give up extra jobs, especially since the majority of school teachers were women, who traditionally bear the brunt of household and child rearing duties. Another general problem that militated against widening the scope for teacher development schemes was the lack of enhanced career prospects.

Realising the need for a more proactive educational policy, the Government issued a decree in 1997 for the implementation of a new system of in-service training. This stipulates that every school teacher should engage in further education once in seven years, with a training period of 120 contact hours. The costs of participation are covered largely by the government[54] and the local educational authorities, apart from a token tuition fee borne by the participants themselves.

This government decree gave further education a tremendous boost; in 1997 nearly 5000 programmes were advertised by 627 institutions, more than half of which were units of higher education. In order to ensure quality control, a National In-service Accreditation Board has been set up, but it may take years before it can filter out low-quality programmes.

In 1997, the number of programmes with a language pedagogy profile was 178, including 71 programmes in English and 40 in German (Poór & Rádai, 1999). One of the most comprehensive programmes is a two-year course for teachers of English, which consists of successive once-a-week seminars followed by intensive one-week blocks. Teachers may take one module per semester, each with a duration of 120 hours. After completing a core methodology update module, they may choose three from a menu of seven modules (Rádai, 1996).

Foreign language teachers

As indicated earlier, the foreign language policy of Hungary quickly responded to political and economic changes after 1989. New forms of pre-service training were launched and simultaneously the distribution of languages altered. Between 1990/91 and 1998/98 the number of students admitted to the foreign language departments of universities and colleges almost quadrupled. Since 1997, more than 3000 students have graduated annually with foreign language teacher's certificates (Halász & Lannert, 1998).

Due to the greatly increased intake in pre-service training, schools are far better supplied with English and German teachers today than they were in 1989. In secondary schools, it was in the 1996/97 school year that the number of qualified English teachers first exceeded the number of qualified Russian teachers. At present, 31% of all qualified foreign language teachers are teachers of English, whereas the percentage of Russian and German teachers is 27% each. An even more revealing trend is that while 92% of qualified English and German teachers are harnessed to teach their respective language, this proportion does not even reach 13% in the case of qualified Russian teachers (Statistical Report, 1998). Another figure shows that while the student/teacher ratio for both English and German is 71 students per teacher, for French it is 41 and for Russian it is merely four. By the 1997/98 school year, the shortage of English, German and French teachers had all but disappeared in secondary schools, in spite of the fact that over 50% of qualified foreign language teachers do not seek employment in public education (Halász & Lannert, 1998).

Needless to say, the situation in primary education is far less satisfactory, especially with respect to small towns and villages, where the demand for foreign language teachers other than Russian is still excessive. Even in the 1997/98 school year, 54% of all qualified foreign language teachers were Russian teachers, but only slightly more than 4% of them were actually teaching Russian, while these proportions for English and German were in the above-90% range (Statistical Report, 1998). In the same school year, 83% of English and 75% of German instruction was provided by qualified teachers of that foreign language, which indicates significant progress in comparison to the respective data of 75 and 66% in 1992/93. The disadvantaged position of primary schools may also be demonstrated with figures on the student/teacher ratio: for English and German the ratio is 144 and 135 respectively, for French it is 41, whereas there are less than an average of two pupils for each Russian teacher (Vágó, 1997).

Obviously, quantitative data such as those on teacher supply are not sufficient to understand the state of foreign language education. It is equally important – albeit far more difficult – to examine qualitative variables. In this regard, language teaching experts have little reason to be jubilant at the results of a public opinion survey conducted in 1997 to find out the extent to which the respondents said they were satisfied with the teaching of various school subjects. On this rank order, foreign languages lag behind Hungarian language and literature, mathematics, informatics, science and social science subjects (Marián, 1997).

There must be several factors to account for the relatively low quality of foreign language instruction at school, but one certainly has to do with salaries. Whereas in 1990 a school teacher's average salary was 106% of the national average, by 1999 it was a mere 88% (Udvardi, 1999b). In other words, the relative status of teachers has dramatically deteriorated in the past decade. As a consequence, only 5.5% of teachers can afford to make a living on their salaries while the rest are forced to take on extra work. Although foreign language teachers' salaries are the same as any other teacher's, their opportunities to moonlight are probably better. Most commonly, they supplement their salaries by running special afternoon classes in the school, for which they are paid well above the fees other subject teachers receive. Many teachers teach in private language schools in the evening or do private tutoring at home.

Enyedi & Ryan (1998) conducted a questionnaire survey of graduates who had received their English teacher's qualifications at Eötvös Loránd University, the largest university in Budapest, between 1993 and 1997. Out of the 1600 graduates, 760 returned the completed questionnaire. While 38% reported working in primary or secondary education, 23% in private language schools and 5% in both, the remaining 34% were employed outside the language teaching profession. One respondent tersely said: 'I haven't taught anything to anyone at any level.' While such a non-committal attitude appears to be extreme, the fact that more than one third of young graduates decided to opt out of the profession is more than disconcerting.

In a recent study, the life stories of nine Hungarian teachers of English were examined in order to gain insight into their attitudes, perceived social status and career paths. The authors' conclusion is that, although these 'stories reflect idiosyncratic career paths and views of the profession', they all suggest that 'well-being and altruism are the keys to quality control in education' (Elekes *et al.*, 1998: 19).

Hungary in an international context

Although comparative data on education are seldom reliable, the following two sets of figures shed light on the relationship between foreign language and other school subjects in an international context.

Table 18 is based on data which were designed to compare one aspect of education in Hungary and the OECD countries in 1996, the year Hungary became an OECD member country (Halász & Lannert, 1998: 438). The relevant question asked: 'Young people learn or may learn these subjects at secondary school. How important do you find these subjects?' On a 100-point scale, the rank order shown in Table 18 was produced. According to these data, the Hungarian population attaches a lot more importance to school instruction than its OECD counterparts. This applies to all the subjects, including foreign languages.

The two sets of data in Figures 10 and 11 refer to countries of the European Union (EU), the European Free Trade Association/European Economic Area (EFTA/EEA) and Central and Eastern Europe (CEEC) (Key data, 1997: 51 & 71). They show the distribution of the annual hours of teaching of compulsory subjects for two cohorts: 10-year-olds (Figure 10) and 16-year-olds (Figure 11). In the light of these data, Hungary does not do particularly well from an international perspective, as if confirming the legitimacy of teachers' and parents' concern over the relatively small role assigned to foreign languages in the primary curriculum. The results for the 16-year-old cohort demonstrate that the teaching of foreign languages usually retains a fairly important relative position in most countries which do not work according to flexible timetables. Again, Hungarian students do not seem to be well off in terms of opportunities to learn foreign languages at school.

Since the 1960s, Hungary has been building up an ever-growing network of

Table 18 The importance of school subjects in Hungary compared to the average rating in OECD countries

	Hungary	OECD average
Hungarian	98	86.9
Foreign language	96	79.0
Mathematics	96	84.6
Computer science	94	71.5
Social science	93	59.5
Natural science	92	64.1
Physical education	89	56.0
Civil studies	86	59.0
Practical skills	81	50.3
Art	75	38.4

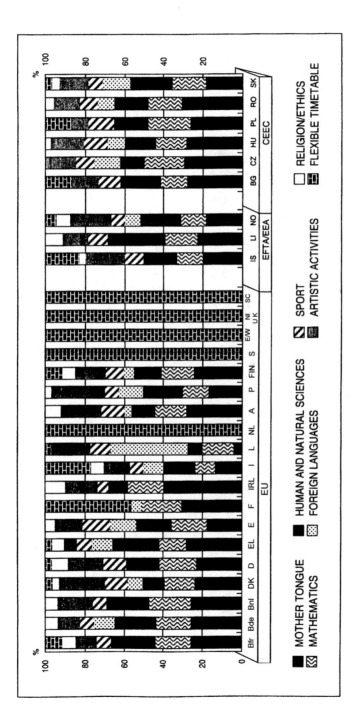

Figure 10 The distribution of annual hours of teaching of compulsory subjects at around age 10, 1995/96

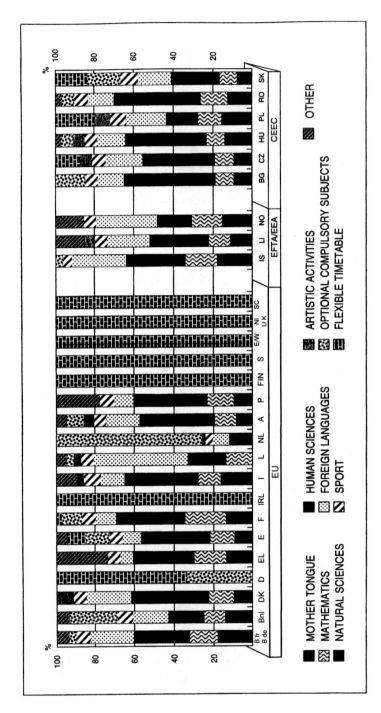

Figure 11 The distribution of annual hours of teaching of compulsory subjects at around age 16, 1995/96

educational relationships with western European countries. Initially, contacts were limited to those under the auspices of UNESCO. The fact that Hungary was admitted to the Council of Europe in 1990 and OECD in 1996 greatly enhanced opportunities in the area of foreign language education. However, it was the Tempus programme, launched in 1990, which enabled central and eastern European countries to get into the mainstream of student and teacher mobility in Europe. While this programme is in its final stage, several other EU programmes have been made available for Hungarian participants. The most comprehensive of them is the Socrates programme; its subcomponent, the Lingua programme, has been designed to give support to a plethora of projects in the field of language education (Bognár, 1997). Albeit not yet a full fledged member state, Hungary has accepted the main document of the European Community (White Paper, 1996), in which it has been proclaimed that Europe is proud to be a multingual continent and the average European citizen should be plurilingual, capable of speaking at least two foreign languages. To achieve this goal, the member states have expressed their commitment to creating the conditions both in the form of school education and life-long learning. Hungary is planning to celebrate the Year of Languages in 2001, initiated by the Council of Europe, by attending and hosting various national and international events.

As a result of the opportunity to become the beneficiary of EU resources, schools have become more active in developing international relations (Krolopp, 1996). While at present over two thirds of the international contacts are maintained with German speaking countries, most schools indicated that their priority country in the future would be the UK, which suggests their intention to learn English. This assumption was confirmed by the project plans submitted by schools in the 1996/97 school year, with language learning being the primary area specified (Kovács, 1997). On the other hand, the scope of planned activities was rather narrowed; this may be attributable to the lack of foreign language competence of teachers who teach subjects other than foreign languages. Although foreign language teachers should, as a matter of course, be involved in international networking, they cannot be expected to bear the brunt of this responsibility.

For Hungary, accession to the European Union is a matter of vital importance. Far more controversial is the country's attitude to its erstwhile 'comrades', i.e. countries of central and eastern Europe. *Comradeship*, which before 1989 consisted in little more than maintaining formal ties between respective ministry, university and trade union leaders, has been replaced by genuine *partnership*. Even at times when at government levels friction is observed between Hungary and its neighbours, at grass-roots levels there is growing realisation that in fact we have a lot to learn from each other. Numerous opportunities for language teachers to network have been created over the past ten years. National conferences are becoming international venues. While native speaker teachers have remained priority guests, an increasing number of central and eastern European colleagues are also represented at such gatherings. Professional journals adopt a similar policy: partners from the region not only get on their mailing list, but are welcome contributors as well (Medgyes, 1997b).

Part IV: Language Maintenance and Prospects

The Future of Hungarian in Neighbouring Countries

As mentioned in Part II, language maintenance or shift largely depends on the economic gain and social prestige of the language in question. More specifically, the future of Hungarian is determined by the attitude of governments of countries with an ethnic Hungarian population. In this respect, there are reassuring signs: membership of the Council of Europe as well as a drive towards European integration may be sufficient reason for cautious optimism. Other factors could militate against this trend: political, social and economic instability may give impetus to nationalistic attitudes, which in turn may exacerbate distrust between nations speaking other languages in the majority and ethnic Hungarians.

Considering the chances of language maintenance, it seems that in Romania and Slovakia ethnic Hungarians will maintain their strong cultural position and language, but may lose ground demographically due to lower birth rates. The same applies to Vojvodina, with the reservation that the political situation in Yugoslavia is more unstable and its future more unpredictable than in the other neighbouring countries. As for the smaller ethnic Hungarian groups, language shifts have been recently discerned in all of them. In Austria, for example, frequent code-switching has been observed, that is, switching from Hungarian to German even within the same sentence (Gal, 1979).[55]

The Future of Minority Languages in Hungary

In an article on language rights, Phillipson & Skutnabb-Kangas (1995) argue that language is one of the most important cultural assets in the life of minorities. Therefore, if their language use is restricted, the survival of the entire group comes under threat. The authors add that minorities cannot hope to achieve equal status in education, economy and politics, unless their language rights are guaranteed by law.

The Act on the Rights of National and Ethnic Minorities secures the idea that members of any ethnic group in Hungary may use their first language at any time and in all spheres of life, whether in local government offices, court trials, prison or military service. This law ' . . . for the first time in the legislation of Hungary, and, in fact, of the countries of the region, guarantees collective rights in addition to the individual rights to ethnic and national minorities' (Fenyvesi, 1998: 155). The protection of their interests was reinforced by the nomination of a minority rights ombudsman in 1995.

Whereas *de jure* Hungary may well be set as a model in its treatment of minorities, *de facto* the situation calls for improvement. Apart from deficiencies in the implementation of the minority law, there are two issues that deserve special mention.

One concerns prejudice. While resentment against Gypsies has been traditionally deep-seated, often tainted with racist overtones, other minorities have also suffered maltreatment. Investigating prejudices among various age groups in Hungary, Szabó & Örkény (1998) conclude that negative attitudes towards otherness correlate with age: school-aged youngsters have been found far more tolerant than adults. Otherness in language use is often rejected on grounds of nationalistic conviction. Challenging the idea of 'cosmopolitan multilingualism' which is supposed to bring nations closer together, Ankerl contends, for example, that peoples living in the same region or country hardly ever learn each other's languages. But then, in contradiction with his own line of reasoning, he complacently asserts that 'despite the forcible partitioning of our homeland more than a half-century ago, Hungarian is still the most widely spoken language in the Carpathian Basin, therefore the most useful regional language of communication' (1998: 28–9).

The other problem is related to the internal development of minorities. On the basis of survey results gained from ethnic German respondents, Szántó maintains that 'feelings of national allegiance to ethnic culture are more intense in the elderly population. The younger the population is, the weaker such feelings become' (1995: 21–2). What can schools do to raise the minorities' awareness of ethnic belonging and language use? On the basis of pedagogic experience and educational research, it must be admitted that school education is fighting a losing battle unless children are made susceptible to such issues within the family and among peers. In relation to the Slovak minority in Hungary, Garami points out that the overwhelming majority of parents do little in the way of 'spontaneous socialisation' (1995: 42), i.e. they do not speak Slovak with their children. As this finding is likely to apply to the other minorities of Hungary as well, there is little cause for optimism.[56]

Garami (1995) concludes her article by suggesting that ethnic consciousness is bound to rise in two contradictory situations: (1) in situations where the maintenance of the minority is secured in every possible way, including direct state intervention; (2) in situations where its survival is seriously threatened, or attempts are made to forcefully assimilate the minority. Minority policies in present-day Hungary offer no radical solutions in either direction. If Garami's argument is correct, such moderate policies may, paradoxically, lead to a dampened sense of ethnic allegiance and a gradual retreat in minority language use.

The Future of Foreign Language Teaching

The use of foreign languages in any country is determined by a number of circumstances. While direct political and economic factors play a decisive role in the spread, or in the recession, of a foreign language, individual preferences may also be important. What no responsible government could afford is to let such issues run their own course. It is vital that each country should adopt and pursue some kind of language policy (Kaplan & Baldauf, 1997; Labrie, 1999).

As shown in previous sections, foreign language needs and hence the provision of foreign languages in Hungary have dramatically changed in the past ten years. Although not all these changes have been unanimously welcome, it looks as if those in charge of language-in-education planning have conducted a fairly consistent policy.

A comparative analysis of two major foreign language documents, one conceived by the previous socialist-liberal government (1994–98) and the other one by the present conservative government, shows that there is full consensus over most issues relating to foreign language instruction. Both documents emphasise that young people should graduate from secondary schools, universities and colleges with a command of foreign language which can be used for effective communication in the field of science, economy or culture alike. The foreign language competence of young graduates should enable them to understand different peoples and cultures, as well as to convey information about the achievements of Hungarian culture. The foundation of foreign language competence should be laid in public education and subsequently improved and specialised in higher education. The provision of high standards of foreign language instruction in public education is a prerequisite for ensuring equal opportunities in education. Hungarian foreign language policy has adopted the aims set by the Council of Europe, namely that every citizen should be able to speak three languages: their first language plus two foreign languages. More specifically, every Hungarian school leaver is expected to speak one foreign language at intermediate and another one at basic level.[57]

Within the framework of a general review of the National Core Curriculum, it has been decided by the present Ministry of Education that obligatory foreign language instruction should begin one year earlier, in the fourth grade. Another decision concerns the allocation of contact hours: between Grade 4 and Grade 8 the first foreign language will be taught for a minimum of four contact hours per week, whereas between Grade 9 and Grade 12 a total of seven hours will be assigned for the study of two foreign languages; group size for the foreign language class will be limited to 16. In addition to maintaining a free choice of foreign languages, special measures will be taken to prevent the regression of foreign languages other than English and German. Particular emphasis will be laid on widening the scope for content-based teaching and, in connection with this, on improving the foreign language competence of non-language teachers. Further steps include the rationalisation of the examination system, the implementation of projects with the aim of ensuring a better supply of qualified school teachers and, above all, the establishment of a national foreign language institute to provide better coordination and services.

With the advent of the 21st century, interaction between stakeholders and decision makers is likely to intensify. In view of the present trend, there is every reason to believe that the pressure on decision makers involved in language planning and language-in-education planning will only increase. This in turn is hoped to result in a growing number of Hungarian citizens who are capable of using foreign languages for effective communication in all spheres of activity. In sum, the present state of Hungary bodes well for the teaching and learning of foreign languages.

The Effect of English on Hungarian

For a range of reasons, today the English language is viewed as the *lingua franca* in most parts of the world. To give just one illustration, some 85% of international organisations now use English as one of their working languages, but in a European context the hegemony of English is even stronger: 99% of European organisations cite English as a working language (Crystal, 1995). Similar data could be supplied in the area of scientific publications, international banking, economic affairs and trade, advertising, international tourism, technology transfer, the Internet, etc. Although it is clear that the irresistible spread of English is due to historical factors rather than to its superiority to any other fully-fledged language (Kaplan, 1993), its huge impact in the 20th century cannot be denied.

Inevitably, the cultural sphere has not been left untouched. Just as sand in the Sahara penetrates even the most hermetically sealed niches, English worms its way into the local culture of almost every country in the world. The English language does not only extirpate or bar the native language from certain areas of discourse, but it makes an indelible imprint on the lexis of the native language itself.

·In the past decade, as already mentioned in Part I, English has been increasing in popularity in Hungary at a breathtaking pace. As a concomitant of its perva-sive effect, it has both enriched and contaminated the Hungarian language itself. Most of the English words that have crept into the vocabulary are neologisms with no suitable equivalents in Hungarian. Here is a short list of loan words: *marketing, holding, joint venture, dealer, broker, leasing, discount, brainstorming, performance, zoom, talk-show, underground, team, baby-sitter, hamburger, popcorn, public relations, tuning, high-tech, hi-fi, playback, winchester, hard-disk, drive, floppy, desktop, scanner, microchip, thriller, disco, topless, outfit, x-large, teenager, yuppie, punk, styling, jogging* – and the list could be expanded *ad infinitum.*

However, there is a great deal of insecurity in Hungarian usage about the pronunciation and spelling of borrowings. The pronunciation of *know-how*, fran-chise or *licence* varies from person to person, but the orthography of *computer, image* or *discount* has several variants, too. Hybrid constructions which apply Hungarian morphological rules to English words are similarly bewildering: *Becsekkeltél már?* ('Have you checked in yet?'), *Dilítold az utolsó bekezdést!* ('Delete the last paragraph.') and so on.

Currently, all forms of mass media are crammed with English words and phrases. Advertisements and commercials often harness English to enhance effect: *Mire a milk, mire a lotion?* ('What's the milk for, what's the lotion for?') or *Crocky chips, csípj fel!* ('Crocky chips, pick us up!'). Many job advertisements are published either in Hungarian with the insertion of English terms or directly in English. Furthermore, it appears that newly formed companies stand a better chance of selling their products if they use an English logo. Posters and graffiti in English are rife in the streets of Budapest and other larger towns; pop songs have a flair for embellishing the lyrics with English words.

One cannot fail to notice that a growing number of people feel irritated by such incursions of English usage, and many give voice to their frustration. In govern-ment circles, too, decision makers have mixed feelings about the spread of English or openly resent it. Educators, purists and politicians with less tolerant views go as far as to suggest that the onslaught of the English language in Hungary should be contained. They argue that too much English is detrimental to the development of the Hungarian language and impairs first language competence. For example, 48.5% of the schools in a survey conducted at the beginning of the 1990s were of the opinion that those students who had difficulty in coping with their first language should not be obliged to learn a foreign language (Szebenyi, 1991). With far more English around these days, this proportion is likely to have risen. People with a streak of nationalist zeal go even further by claiming that students' awareness of national identity is threatened by

Americomania, Americanisation (Kontra, 1997), cultural and linguistic imperial-ism, the diffusion-of-English paradigm (Phillipson & Skutnabb-Kangas, 1996) and so-called linguicism (Phillipson, 1992). Ankerl says that globalisation, the magic word of the last quarter of the 20th century, is 'tacitly the concubine of English-language cultures' (1997: 2), while 'cyberspace and especially the internet act as rams' to ensure the privileges of the English language (1997: 8). Doomsayers predict that the full-scale invasion of English will lead to the death of the Hungarian language.

Liberal-minded language educators, on the other hand, argue that it would be irresponsible to run in the face of a worldwide tendency. As Hungary is intent on catching the 'eurotrain', it is imperative that the learning of English be promoted. Concerning the issue of language death, moderates assert that the Hungarian language needs no salvaging. Thousands of vigorous local languages have weathered through the siege of previous world languages – Hungarian has been one of them. And just like other survivors, the Hungarian language has always crawled from under the ruins not only unharmed but in fact enriched. Another reassuring argument is that although English is the unrivalled world language at present, its pride of place should not be regarded as eternal. Graddol points out that 'The "rush" for English around the world may . . . prove to be a temporary phenomenon which cannot be sustained indefinitely . . . The ELT industry may also find itself vulnerable to shifts in public opinion, like other global business enterprises now experiencing "nasty surprises" in their world markets' (1997: 55). To be sure, there are rival languages on the horizon – in Hungary German is a close runner-up, as has been pointed out repeatedly in earlier sections. Considering the proximity and economic strength of Germany and Austria, these languages may well gain further popularity in the future (Petneki, 1993).

Although foreign-language experts have limited leg room, their share of liability should not be disregarded, either. While they are primarily responsible for the effectiveness of the language teaching operation, they are also faced with a moral dilemma. In the midst of an unprecedented boom of English language instruction, the question arises: should English teachers rejoice in their good fortune or develop a guilty conscience? In a 1992 issue of The Budapest Post, an English-language weekly, Hughes meditated over the paradox of English teach-ing in Hungary. She asked, 'Does that mean we're accomplices in the blanketing over of an erstwhile *super culture* by a *superculture*?' Her answer was a resonant yes! Rejecting this attitude as liberal nonsense, Cheng (1992) argued that English, like any other *lingua franca* from earlier times, enriched rather than obliterated local tongues and local cultures. Therefore, his suggestion to fellow American teachers in Hungary was that they should count their blessings instead of flagel-lating themselves.

The odds are that English will enjoy a special position in the 21st century. However, this is not to say that it will achieve absolute dominance, let alone make vernacular languages extinct. The ideal of multilingual societies and plurilingual citizens is being advocated at the highest fora of decision makers. At a recent Council of Europe conference (1999) entitled 'Linguistic diversity for democratic citizenship in Europe', Peter Leuprecht, the keynote speaker, finished his lecture with these words:

The Europe we are trying to build and of which we want to be responsible citizens must be a Europe that achieves unity in diversity; a Europe that appreciates, nurtures and celebrates its diversity as a fabulous treasure; a Europe in which meeting the other's face is a challenging and enriching every day reality; a Europe of citizens aware of their rights and, even more importantly, the rights of others and of their ensuing responsibilities; Europe as a marvellous symphony in which a multitude of different voices produces harmony – harmony through mutual respect.

This message is sure to apply to Hungary as much as to countries beyond the geographical boundaries of Europe.

Acknowledgements

The authors would like to thank *András Barabás, Litza Juhász, James Leavey* and *Ádám Nádasdy* for their comments and suggestions.

Correspondence

Any correspondence should be directed to Katalin Miklósy, Centre for English Teacher Training, Eötvös Loránd University, Ajtosi Durer, sor 19, 1146 Budapest, Hungary.

Notes

1. The treaty enforced by the allied powers is called the Treaty of Trianon (1920). Apart from territorial loss, Hungary also lost one third of its ethnically Hungarian population and 90% of its minorities. While the stated intent of the allied powers was to apply national self-determination, the actual implementation ignored the interests of Hungarians and caused lasting grievances in post-Trianon Hungary.
2. In 1526, the Ottoman sultan, Süleyman the Magnificent advanced into Hungary. The Hungarian king, Louis II, with a force of 16,000 men, attacked the Turks at Mohács. Heavily outnumbered, the Hungarian army was almost annihilated and the king himself drowned. In the wake of the 'disaster of Mohács', the Turks occupied large parts of central and southern Hungary.
3. There has been a Jewish population in Hungary since medieval times. Their number had increased to 4% of the whole population by the mid-19th century. They spoke Yiddish or German (McCragg, 1990: 64, cited in Fenyvesi, 1998: 139). After the 1840 Diet granted the Jews free settlement and the 1867 Compromise conveyed them equal political and civil rights, a swift process of assimilation occurred and, by the turn of the 20th century, the Hungarian Jewry became almost completely Hungarian speaking. In World War II, approximately 564,000 of Hungary's 825,000 Jews were deported and exterminated in concentration camps.
   The Hungarian Jewish population refused to accept official nationality status and accepted the status of a religious minority in 1920 (the Treaty of Trianon). Their status has not changed since then.
4. When dealing with minority issues, we are only concerned with traditional minorities as opposed to non-traditional minorities, and, in turn, indigenous languages as opposed to immigrant languages (Candelier *et al.*, 1999). Thus issues concerning recent immigrants to Hungary, such as the Chinese, will not be discussed in this report. Those interested in learning about such developments should consult Nyíri, 1999.
5. While French was spoken mostly by women, English was preferred by men.
6. In comparison, 34% of the equivalent Austrian population was reported to speak at least one foreign language at an adequate level in 1990.
7. By the way, the data obtained from countries of the European Union are no less dispir-

iting. Nearly 40% of the age group between 40 and 54, and over 50% of people above 55 have learnt no foreign languages at all (Bognár, 1997).

8. In a recent survey, also based on questionnaire data (Marián, cited in Udvardi, 1999a), it was found that while 24% of the respondents claimed to speak at least one foreign language, only 7% had a state language certificate at intermediate level and 2% at advanced level.

9. Tests can be taken at three levels: Basic, Intermediate, and Proficiency Level.

10. The authors predict that 'the situation is likely to change more in the next four years than it has in the past 40' (Medgyes & Kaplan, 1992: 86). With the purpose of establishing the direction of changes in the foreign language competence of Hungarian scholars, the study is being replicated, but its findings are not available at the time of writing.

11. The surveys were carried out within the frame of a joint Dutch-Hungarian project with the following participants: CITO (National Institute for Curriculum Development and Examinations, Arnhem), Department of Educational Sociology of University Amsterdam and OKI ÉK (National Institute for Public Education, Centre for Educational Evaluation, Budapest).

12. Founded in 1635, Eötvös Loránd University (ELTE) in Budapest is the oldest university in Hungary. With approximately 14,000 students studying at its faculties, it is also the largest and one of the most prestigious universities in the country.

13. The 1996 Media Act (Act 1/96) carried out three major reforms in order to establish the independence of the media from the government in power. The reforms (1) transformed the state controlled media to public media; (2) allocated half of the available broadcasting frequencies to privately owned commercial channels; (3) established the National Radio and Television Authority (*Országos Rádió és Televízió Testület*) which has been authorised to issue licences and to exercise control.

14. The Compromise of 1867, reached by the Hapsburg Emperor Francis Joseph and the Hungarian Diet, restored Hungary's territorial integrity and ensured Hungary's independence in internal affairs within the Austro-Hungarian Monarchy.

15. While there is a striking difference between nationalities in terms of literacy rate, it has to be pointed out that, despite their relative backwardness, Romanians and Ruthenians exhibited by far the fastest growth.

16. Apart from the educational damage it did in Hungary, this decree had a serious backwash effect in Hungarian minority schools in Slovakia. Following the Hungarian pattern, the Czechoslovak educational authorities resolved to teach science subjects in Slovak instead of Hungarian. As a result of large-scale protests from Hungarian minority quarters, the authorities never implemented this plan (Drahos & Kovács, 1991).

17. About 75% of the minorities live in villages, and there are only about two dozen villages where the local minority population is in majority (Fenyvesi, 1998).

18. Csipka (1995) mentions that even minority-language schools are bilingual, because the science subjects are usually provided in Hungarian.

19. It is worth noting that even in 1938 the number of girls attending secondary school was insignificant in comparison with boys.

20. Communist authorities granted curriculum designers little more than six months to prepare and implement the new curriculum (Ballér, 1996).

21. The introduction of Russian was all-encompassing: in addition to four years in primary schools and four years in secondary schools, students had to learn Russian even in the first two years of their college or university studies.

22. Note that the pre-war school structure, which comprised four years of primary and eight years of secondary education, was reshaped after the war. Primary education was extended to eight years (age 6–14), and it was followed by four years of secondary education (age 15–18). From our point of view, however, this structural change makes little difference: foreign language education was offered to the 11–18-year-old age cohort in both systems.

23. The curriculum for primary schools was introduced in 1963, the one for secondary schools in 1965.

24. The category of 'second' foreign languages included English, French, German, Italian, and Spanish. In grammar schools, the menu contained Latin, too.
25. As of 1963, certain secondary schools were allowed to run specialised classes in 'second' foreign languages, which meant that students had five to eight lessons a week, instead of two or three. In 1967, this privilege was also granted to primary schools. Towards the late 1980s, the number of specialised classes increased year by year.
26. By the mid-80s, the Threshold Level had permeated the whole language teaching scene and set the tone for the curricular development of all the foreign languages being taught in Hungary.
27. Petneki (1998b) refers to revealing statistics concerning travel:

Year	Number of Hungarians travelling abroad (in thousands)
1951	19
1960	300
1964	1500
1973	2000
1976	4700
1984	5400

28. A joke from 1989: Crossing a bridge in Budapest, a man spots somebody drowning in the Danube. He yells down from the bridge: 'Can you speak Russian?' 'Da,' the man in the water yells back. 'Idiot! Why didn't you learn to swim instead?'
29. Although in many primary schools it is possible to learn a second foreign language as well, the number of students taking this opportunity is small; Figure 7 only shows the trend for the study of the first foreign language.
30. With respect to the other two major types of secondary schools, in vocational schools one foreign language is compulsory whereas trade schools seldom provide opportunities for language learning.
31. The same tendency can be observed in secondary vocational schools: English is the leader followed closely by German, while Russian and French lag well behind.
32. As mentioned earlier, the introduction of the National Core Curriculum began in 1998. Each year it is implemented for two grades; the first two grades affected are Grade 1 and Grade 7, but since most schools do not provide foreign languages in Grade 1, only the foreign language teaching of Grade 7 has been hitherto regulated by the requirements of the NCC.
33. Regulations concerning Hungarian, minority and foreign language use and education are enacted at three levels: laws are created by Parliament, decrees by Government and orders by the Minister of Education. The following list contains the ones referred to throughout the report (No. of Act/year).
- The Public Education Act (*Közoktatási Törvény*) 79/1993; Amendments 85/1995; 62/1996; 68/1999
- The Higher Education Act (*Felsőoktatási Törvény*) 80/1993; Amendment 61/1996
- Act on the Rights of National and Ethnic *Minorities* (*Törvény a nemzeti és etnikai kisebbségekről*) 77/1993
- Act on the Hungarian Academy of Sciences (*Törvény a Magyar Tudományos Akadémiáról*) 60/1994
- The National Core Curriculum Decree (*Kormányrendelet a Nemzeti Alaptanterv kiadásáról*) 130/1995
- The School-leaving Examination Decree (*Kormányrendelet az érettségi vizsgáról*) 100/1997
- The State Foreign Language Examination Decree (*Kormányrendelet az Állami Nyelvvizsgáról*) 71/1998
- In-service Teacher Education Decree (*Kormányrendelet a pedagógus továbbképzésről*) 277/1997

- The Basic Examination Order (*Minisztériumi rendelet az Alapműveltségi vizsgáról*) 24 / 1997
- The Dual-language Schools Order (*Minisztériumi rendelet a Két tannyelvű iskolákról*) 26 / 1997
- Minority Education Order (*Minisztériumi rendelet a kisebbségek oktatásáról*) 32 / 1997

34. Before the final version was approved by Parliament, the proposals for the NCC were opened up for public debate. These proposals were also hotly debated nationwide.
35. The latest amendments of the Public Education Act were passed at the time of writing this monograph, in June 1999.
36. In 1950, in Junior Primary Schools there were 12 Hungarian language and literature lessons per week, compared to the seven lessons per week ratio in the 1990s.
37. The election of a minority council can be initiated by any five people of voting age from any of Hungary's 13 officially recognised minorities. In 1997, the total number of local minority councils was 760, rising to 1135 by 1998. The two nationalities with the highest number of local minority councils are the Gypsies and the Germans with 673 and 211 councils, respectively.
38. In spite of its humanistic appeal, intercultural education has not taken root in Hungarian schools yet: nowhere has it been recorded to operate (Halász & Lannert, 1998).
39. Examples are supplied in all four major languages being taught in Hungarian schools: English, German, French, and Russian.
40. As a matter of fact, this is already the case. Many teachers teach for their salary in the morning, and then for a fee in the afternoon – often in the same school.
41. It is worth noting that classes in Hungary have been halved for the language lessons, with the two groups learning different languages in the same slot. Now that the student population is steadily decreasing, class sizes have become so small that many schools have abolished this custom. In primary schools the average class size is 21.2, in secondary schools 29.1 at present (Statistical Report, 1998).
42. As outlined in previous chapters, due to the domination of German and English, there is less room for the study of other languages. Last year, four ambassadors representing countries where these languages are spoken submitted a formal petition to the Hungarian Minister of Education, demanding immediate action to prevent the continued decline of these languages.
43. The other compulsory subjects are Hungarian language and literature, history and mathematics.
44. In a survey on a population of 862 school principals and teachers' staff, one question inquired: 'Schools have to provide the opportunity for students – based on their choice – to prepare at intermediate and advanced levels for the compulsory subjects and two foreign languages. Do you agree with this measure?' While 81% of the respondents agreed, only 17% expressed disagreement (Halász & Lannert, 1998).
45. Einhorn (1997) draws attention to the ambivalence of the new SLE: it is both an achievement test in that it is destined to assess knowledge gained after several years of language study (retrospective), and a proficiency test in that it intends to assess general capabilities (perspective). The dual nature of the SLE is likely to be conducive to problems.
46. There is a surprisingly large number of native speaking language teachers working in Hungary. A survey of a representative sample of school principals, conducted in 1997, showed that 27% employed native speaking teachers (Vágó, 1997). The figures do not reveal what proportion of these native speakers were qualified teachers of the language they were teaching.
47. 'Certified' competence means that the candidate has a certificate issued by the State Foreign Language Examination Board. While certificates from various international English examinations are usually accepted, the school-leaving examination is no basis for bonus points.
48. This excludes foreign language majors, who will be discussed in the next section.
49. Due to the austerity measures of 1995, universities and colleges were compelled to dismiss thousands of teaching staff. Many institutions decided to take the line of least resistance by closing down their foreign language service departments.

50. Legend has it that when the last director of the United States Information Agency in Hungary was asked at his farewell party why USIS had chosen to pull out, the director curtly answered: 'Hungary is no longer sexy, you know.'
51. According to statistics, the number of Russian teachers in 1989 was around 15,000 (Vágó, 1997).
52. Strangely enough, in the last two years of the retraining programme junior primary school teachers, who had lost their job due to a decrease in the student population, exceeded the number of Russian teachers.
53. In the past twelve years, several methodology books have been published; notably Bárdos, 1988; Holló et al., 1996; Medgyes, 1997a; Zerkowitz, 1988.
54. According to the 1996 Amendment of the Public Education Act, 3% of the annual budget of public education is earmarked for in-service training projects.
55. Although this monograph focuses on Hungarians living in Hungary and in the neighbouring countries, there are expatriate Hungarian communities in a number of other countries as well. Among these, the largest population lives in the US, where 1.6 million people claimed to have Hungarian ancestry, 600,000 of whom said that their first language was Hungarian, whereas approximately 180,000 people reported that they spoke Hungarian at home (1980 census). The issue of their language preservation and language shift has been explored, among others, by Kontra (1990), Várdi & Várdy Huszár (1985) and Vázsonyi & Kontra (1995).
56. For a discussion of intergenerational transmission see Fishman (1991) and Kaplan & Baldauf (1997).
57. Unfortunately, no provision is made for an important aspect of EU policy, namely that member states ' . . . are requested to give particular attention to the learning of minority languages'(Baetens Beardsmore, 1994: 94).

References

Abondolo, D. (1988) *Hungarian Inflectional Morphology*. Budapest: Akadémiai Kiadó.
Abosi, I. (1998) *Report on the Implementation of the 3313-HU Human Resources Development Program, Higher Education Component*. Budapest: Office of Higher Education Development Programmes. Manuscript.
Ábrahám, K. and Jilly, V. (1999) The school-leaving examination in Hungary. In M. Nikolov (ed.) *English Language Education in Hungary: A Baseline Study* (pp. 21–53). Budapest: The British Council, Hungary.
Ankerl, G. (1997) A globalizmus, az angol és a többi nyelv [Globalisation, English and the other languages]. *Valóság* 40 (1), 1–11.
Ankerl, G. (1998) Anyanyelv és kultúrközösség, írás és civilizáció [Native language and cultural community, writing and civilisation]. *Valóság* 40 (10), 22–31.
Arday, L., Joó, R. and Tarján, G.G. (eds) (1987) *Magyarok és szlovének [Hungarians and Slovenians]*. Budapest: Állami Gorkij Könyvtár.
Babai, É. (1998) A Nyelviskolák Szakmai Egyesülete [The Association of Language Schools]. *Nyelv*Infó* 6 (3), 9–11.
Baetens Beardsmore, H. (1994) Language policy and planning in Western European countries. In W. Grabe *et al.* (eds) *Annual Review of Applied Linguistics* 14 (pp. 93–110). Cambridge: Cambridge University Press.
Bagu, B. (1996) Anyanyelvi oktatás Kárpátalján [Hungarian language education in Ukraine]. In I. Csermicskó and T. Váradi (eds) *Kisebbségi magyar iskolai nyelvhasználat [Use of Language in Ethnic Hungarian Schools]* (pp. 47–51). Budapest: Tinta Kiadó.
Balázs, G. (1997) *The Story of Hungarian*. Budapest: Corvina Könyvkiadó.
Bálits, É. (1998) Melyik könyvből érdemes olaszul tanulni? [Which book is it worth learning Italian from?]. *Tandem* 3 (4), 12–16.
Ballér, E. (1996) *Tantervelméletek Magyarországon a XIX-XX. Században [Curriculum Theories in Hungary in the 19th and 20th Centuries]*. Budapest: Országos Közoktatási Intézet.
Banó, I. and Szoboszlay, M. (eds) (1972) *Általános Metodika az Angol, Francia, Német, Olasz, Spanyol Nyelv Iskolai Tanításához [General Methodology for the School Instruction of the English, French, German, Italian and Spanish Languages]*. Budapest: Tankönyvkiadó.
Bánréti, Z. (1991) *Nyelvtan – Kommunikáció – Irodalom Tizenéveseknek [Grammar –*

108   *Language Planning and Policy in Europe*

Communication – Literature for Teenagers]. Veszprém: Országos Továbbképző, Tantervfejlesztő és Értékesítő Vállalat.

Bárány, F., Major, É., Martsa, S., Nagy, I., Nemes, A., Szabó, T. and Vándor, J. (1999) Stakeholders' attitudes. In M. Nikolov (ed.) *English Language Education in Hungary: A Baseline Study* (pp. 137–204). Budapest: The British Council.

Bárdos, J. (1984a) Az idegen nyelvek tanítása a 80-as években [Foreign-language teaching in the 80s]. *Pedagógiai Szemle* 34, 105–18.

Bárdos, J. (1984b) Nyelvek és elvek [Languages and principles]. *Pedagógiai Szemle* 34, 471–5.

Bárdos, J. (1988) *Nyelvtanítás: Múlt és Jelen* [*Language Teaching: Past and Present*]. Budapest: Magvető Kiadó.

Bárdos, J. (1994) Egynyelvűség és többnyelvűség a nyelvvizsgák rendszerében [Monolingualism and multilingualism in the language examination system]. *Folia Practico-Linguistica* 34, 344–54.

Bárdos, J. and Medgyes, P. (1997) A hároméves angol nyelvtanárképzés továbbfejlesztésének lehetőségei: 1994/96 [Options for the development of the three-year English teacher training programme]. *Modern Nyelvoktatás* 3 (1–2), 3–19.

Báthory, Z. and Falus, I. (eds) (1997) *Pedagógiai Lexikon I–III.* [*Encyclopedia of Pedagogy I–III*]. Budapest: Keraban Könyvkiadó.

Báti, L. (n.d.) A modern nyelvoktatás kérdései a múlt század második felétől a felszabadulásig [Issues of modern foreign language instruction from the second half of the 19th century to 1945]. Budapest: Eötvös Loránd Tudományegyetem. Manuscript.

Bencédy, J. (ed.) (1965) *Tanterv és Utasítás a Gimnáziumok Számára: Angol, Francia, Latin, Német, Olasz és Spanyol* [*Curriculum and Directives for Secondary Grammar Schools: English, French, Latin, German, Italian and Spanish*]. Budapest: Tankönyvkiadó.

Benedek, M. (1996) English/Hunglish avagy szükség van-e Magyarországon írt angol tankönyvre? [English/Hunglish or is there a need for English coursebooks written in Hungary?]. *Tandem* 1 (1), 49–51.

Benkő, L. and Imre, S. (eds) (1972) *The Hungarian Language.* The Hague: Mouton.

Bognár, A. (1997) Az idegen nyelvek oktatásának helye és szerepe az Európai Unióhoz való csatlakozásban [The place and role of teaching foreign languages in joining the European Union]. *Új Pedagógiai Szemle* 47 (10), 60–73.

Bognár, A., Frank, G., Gergely, Z. and Vukovics, M. (1998) Az idegen nyelvek a nemzetközi érettségi rendszerében [Foreign languages in the International Baccalaureate system]. *Modern Nyelvoktatás* 4 (2–3), 82–8.

Bognár, M. and Gordos, G. (1995) A nyolcadik osztályos roma tanulók pályaválasztási szándékai [The career prospects of gypsy eight-graders]. *Új Pedagógiai Szemle* 45 (6), 3–20.

Bonifert, M. (1997) Új nyelvoktatási stratégia kell: Kelet-Európában nálunk van a legtöbb magániskola [New language teaching strategies needed: We have the most private schools in Eastern Europe]. *Népszabadság* 12 December.

Braine, G. (ed.) (1999) *Non-native Educators in English Language Teaching.* New Jersey: Lawrence Erlbaum Associates.

Candelier, M., Dumoulin, B. and Koishi, A. (1999) *Language Diversity in the Education Systems of the Member States of the Council for Cultural Co-operation.* Strasbourg: Council of Europe.

Cheng, D. (1992) Are teachers accomplices in imperialism? *The Budapest Post* 3–9 December.

Cillia, R. de, Menz, F., Dressler, W.U. and Cech, P. (1998) Linguistic minorities in Austria. In C.B. Paulston and D. Peckham (eds) *Linguistic Minorities in Central and Eastern Europe* (pp. 18–37). Clevedon: Multilingual Matters.

Crighton, J. and West, R. (1993) World Bank foreign language examinations consultancy – Hungary. Budapest: Office of Higher Education Development Programmes. Manuscript.

Crowe, D. (1991) The gypsies in Hungary. In D. Crowe and J. Kolsti (eds) *The Gypsies in Eastern Europe* (pp. 117–31). Armonk, New York: M.E. Sharpe.

Crystal, D. (1995) *The Cambridge Encyclopedia of the English Language.* Cambridge: Cambridge University Press.

Csepeli, G. (1987) *Csoporttudat – nemzettudat [Group Awareness – National Awareness].* Budapest: Magvető Kiadó.

Csipka, R. (1995) A nemzetiségi oktatás néhány kérdése Magyarországon [Questions of minority education in Hungary]. *Új Pedagógiai Szemle* 45 (6), 45–50.

Csoma, G. and Lada, L. (1997) Tételek a funkcionális analfabetizmusról [On functional illiteracy]. *Magyar Pedagógia* 97, 167–80.

Derdák, T. and Varga, A. (1996) Az iskola nyelvezete – idegen nyelv [School language – foreign language]. *Új Pedagógiai Szemle* 46 (12), 21–36.

Dörnyei, Z. (1992) English teaching in Hungary: How far behind? *Studies in Educational Evaluation* 18, 47–56.

Dörnyei, Z. and Medgyes, P. (1987) Nyelvoktatás kisvállalkozásban [Language teaching in private language schools]. *Kritika* 87 (12), 31–5.

Dörnyei, Z., Nyilasi, E. and Clément, R. (1996) Hungarian school children's motivation to learn foreign language: A comparison of target languages. *NovELTy* 3 (2), 6–16.

Dörnyei, Z. and Tóth, Z. (1987) Megmérettetett – a magyar állami nyelvvizsgarendszer áttekintése [Language state examination in Hungary: A critical analysis]. *Pedagógiai Szemle* 37, 1119–32.

Drahos, Á. and Kovács, P. (1991) A magyarországi nemzeti kisebbségek oktatásügye 1945–1990 [The educational system of ethnic minorities in Hungary 1945–1990]. *Regio* 91, 167–92.

Duff, P.A. (1991) The efficacy of dual-language education in Hungary: An investigation of three Hungarian-English programs. Los Angeles: UCLA. Manuscript.

Duff, P.A. (1995) An ethnography of communication in immersion classrooms in Hungary. *TESOL Quarterly* 29, 505–36.

Éder, Z. (1981) A magyar mint idegen nyelv oktatásának elvi és módszertani kérdései a magyar egyetemeken [Theoretical and methodological issues of Hungarian as a foreign language instruction at Hungarian universities]. In B. Giay and M. Ruszinyák (eds) *Magyar nyelv külföldieknek [Hungarian Language Instruction for Foreigners]* (pp. 29–35). Budapest: Eötvös Loránd Tudományegyetem Központi Magyar Nyelvi Lektorátus.

Éder, Z. (1993) A magyar mint idegen nyelv a felsőoktatásban [Hungarian as a foreign language in higher education]. *Magyar Nyelvőr* 117, 311–20.

Éder, Z., Hegedűs, R., Horváth, J. and Szili, K. (1989) A magyar mint idegen nyelv tanári szak [Hungarian as a foreign language major]. In Z. Éder (ed.) *Dolgozatok a magyar mint idegen nyelv és a hungarológia köréből* 17 [*Papers in Hungarian as a Foreign Language and Hungarian Studies* 17]. Budapest: Eötvös Loránd Tudományegyetem Központi Magyar Nyelvi Lektorátus.

Éder, Z., Kálmán, P. and Szili, K. (1984) Sajátos rendezőelvek a magyar mint idegen nyelv leírásában és oktatásában [Special principles in the description and instruction of the Hungarian language]. *Nyelvünk és kultúránk* 56 (9), 7–15.

Einhorn, Á. (1997) Az érettségi vizsga reformja – például a német nyelv [The reform of the school-leaving examination – the case of German]. *Nyelv*Infó* 5 (5), 5–9.

Einhorn, Á. (1998) Az 1997. évi német nyelvi érettségi áttekintése [Reviewing the German school-leaving examination of 1997]. In Á. Einhorn (ed.) *Vizsgatárgyak, vizsgamodellek I, Német nyelv [Examination Subjects, Examination Models I, German]* (pp. 99–124). Budapest: Országos Közoktatási Intézet.

Elekes, K., Magnuczné Godó, Á., Szabó, P. and Tóth, I. (1998) A view of teaching careers in Hungary in the late 1990s. *NovELTy* 5 (4), 6–22.

Enyedi, Á. (1997) Just another language or a new vocation? How teachers of Russian experience career change. *NovELTy* 4 (3), 31–47.

Enyedi, Á. and Medgyes P. (1998) ELT in Central and Eastern Europe. *Language Teaching* 31, 1–12.

Enyedi, Á. and Ryan, C. (1998) Where have all the teachers gone? Budapest: Centre for English Teacher Training. Manuscript.

Fazekas, M. (1998) Az államilag (végre) elismert új nyelvvizsga [The new state foreign languages examination – accredited at last]. *Nyelv*Infó* 6 (3), 3–6.

Fekete, H. and Katona, L. (1999) Public examinations available in Hungary. In M. Nikolov (ed.) *English Language Education in Hungary: A Baseline Study* (pp. 63–92). Budapest: The British Council.

Fenyvesi, A. (1998) Linguistic minorities in Hungary. In C.B. Paulston and D. Peckham (eds) *Linguistic Minorities in Central and Eastern Europe* (pp. 135–59). Clevedon: Multilingual Matters.

Fishman, J.A. (1991) *Reversing Language Shift.* Clevedon: Multilingual Matters.

Fónagy, E. (1997) A NAT és az idegennyelv-oktatás [NCC and foreign language education]. *Nyelv*Infó* 5 (5), 3–5.

Fonyódi, J. (1996) What is the future of the Hungarian language exams? *NovELTy* 3 (3), 46–51.

Fülöp, K. (1984) Idegen nyelvek a mai iskolában 1–2 [Foreign languages in present-day schools]. *Pedagógiai Szemle* 34, 249–255; 291–298.

Gal, S. (1979) *Language Shift: Social Determinants of Linguistic Change in Bilingual Austria.* New York: Academic Press.

Garami, E. (1995) A magyarországi szlovákok nemzetiségi identitása [The national identity of Slovaks in Hungary]. *Új Pedagógiai Szemle* 45 (6), 32–44.

Gereben, F., Lőrincz, J., Nagy, A. and Vidra Szabó, F. (1993) *Magyar olvasáskultúra határon innen és túl [Hungarian Reading Customs in Hungary and Beyond].* Budapest: Közép-Európa Intézet.

Giay, B. (1986) Differenciálódási tendenciák a magyar mint idegen nyelv leírásában és oktatásában [Different trends in the description and instruction of HFL]. *Folia Practico-Linguistica* 16, 65–83.

Giay, B. (1987) Magyar vendégoktatók külföldi egyetemeken [Hungarian visiting professors at foreign universities]. *Felsőoktatási Szemle* 36, 180–86.

Giay, B. and Nádor, O. (eds) (1989) A magyar mint idegen nyelv kutatása és oktatása a NEI-ben [Research and instruction of Hungarian as a foreign language in the International Preparatory Institute]. *A hungarológiai oktatás elmélete és gyakorlata, 2 [The Theory and Practice of Teaching Hungarian Studies]* (pp. 47–60). Budapest: Nemzetközi Hungarológiai Központ.

Gill, S. (1993) Insett in Slovakia: past simple, present tense, future perfect? *Perspectives* 2, 15–21.

Graddol, D. (1997) *The Future of English?* London: The British Council.

Halápi, M., Jilly, V., Király Z. and Nagy, I. (1999) Testing issues in teacher education. In M. Nikolov (ed.) *English Language Education in Hungary: A Baseline Study* (pp. 205–20). Budapest: The British Council.

Halápi, M. and Király, Z. (1999) University and college entrance requirements. In M. Nikolov (ed.) *English Language Education in Hungary: A Baseline Study* (pp. 55–62). Budapest: The British Council.

Halász, G. (1987) A new education act. *The New Hungarian Quarterly* 23, 49–56.

Halász, G. (1990) School autonomy and the reform of educational administration in Hungary. *Prospects* 20, 387–94.

Halász, G. and Lannert, J. (1998) *Jelentés a Magyar Közoktatásról: 1997 [Report on Hungarian Public Education: 1997].* Budapest: Országos Közoktatási Intézet.

Hartinger, K. (1993) Why language learning difficulties are not always linguistic. *Perspectives* 1 (1), 33–5.

Healey, R. (1993) The international working language of engineers: A new challenge for teachers of English in Czechoslovakia. *Perspectives* 1 (1), 13–18.

Herold, Á. (1998) Hogyan kezdjünk spanyolul tanulni? [How shall we start learning Spanish?] *Tandem* 3 (2), 17–19.

Holló, D., Kontráné Hegybíró, E. and Tímár, E. (1996) *A Krétától a Videóig [From Chalk to Video].* Budapest: Nemzeti Tankönyvkiadó.

Horváth, A. (1996) Az 'élő idegen nyelv' a Nemzeti Alaptantervben [The 'modern foreign language' in the National Core Curriculum]. *Nyelv*Infó* 4 (1), 3–6.

Horváth, A., Jilly, V. and Szálka Gyapay, M. (1996) *Tájékoztatók a NAT Műveltségi*

Területeiről – Élő Idegen Nyelv [*Information on the Cultural Domains of NCC – Modern Foreign Language*]. Budapest: Korona Kiadó.

Horváth, J. (1980) *A Gimnáziumi Nevelés és Oktatás Terve: Tantervi Útmutató, Angol Nyelv* [*Curriculum for Education and Instruction in Secondary Grammar Schools: Curriculum Guidelines, English*]. Budapest: Tankönyvkiadó.

Horváth, Z. (1998) *Középiskolai Tantárgyi Feladatbankok III. Anyanyelvi Tudástérkép* [*Subject Data Banks for Secondary Schools III. First Language Knowledge-map*]. Budapest: Országos Közoktatási Intézet.

Hughes, F. (1992) Cultural imperialism? Nonsense. *The Budapest Post* 29 October – 4 November.

Huszár, Á. (1998) A magyar népesség nyelvtudása a XX. században [The foreign language competence of the Hungarian population in the 20th century]. *Modern Nyelvoktatás* 4 (2–3), 45–56.

Imre, A. (1995) A nyelvtudás társadalmi háttere [The social background of foreign language competence]. *Iskolakultúra* 95 (1–2), 62–6.

Jordan, P. (1998) Romania. In C.B. Paulston and D. Peckham (eds) *Linguistic Minorities in Central and Eastern Europe* (pp. 184–224). Clevedon: Multilingual Matters.

Kádár-Fülöp, J. (1979) Az anyol nyelv tanításának eredményei [The Hungarian report on the IEA English Study]. In Á. Kiss, S. Nagy and J. Szarka (eds) *Tanulmányok a Neveléstudomány Köréből* [*Studies from Educational Science*] (pp. 276–341). Budapest: Akadémiai Kiadó.

Kaplan, R.B. (1993) The hegemony of English in science and technology. *Journal of Multilingual and Multicultural Development* 14, 151–72.

Kaplan, R.B. and Baldauf, R.B. (1997) *Language Planning: From Practice to Theory.* Clevedon: Multilingual Matters.

Kelemen, E. (1992) Törvények nélkül – törvényen kívül [Without laws – beyond law]. *Új Pedagógiai Szemle* 42 (3), 3–11.

Kenesei, I., Vago, M.R. and Fenyvesi, A. (1998) *Hungarian Descriptive Grammar Series.* London: Routledge.

Key data on education in the European Union (1997) Brussels: European Commission.

Kiefer, F. (1985) The possessive in Hungarian: A problem for natural morphology. *Acta Linguistica Academiae Scientiarum* 35, 65–116.

Köllő, M. (1978) *Az Orosz Nyelv Oktatásának Néhány Kérdése* [*Issues Concerning the Teaching of Russian*]. Budapest: Tankönyvkiadó.

Kontra, G., Franyó, I. and Victor, A. (1989) *Az Iskolai Műveltség Belső Arányai* [*The Internal Proportions of School Curricula*]. Budapest: Magyar Tudományos Akadémia.

Kontra, M. (1981) On teaching English in Hungary in the 1970s. *ELT Journal* 35, 186–91.

Kontra, M. (1990) *Fejezetek a South Bend-i Magyar Nyelvhasználatról* [*The Hungarian Language as Spoken in South Bend, Indiana*]. Budapest: MTA Nyelvtudományi Intézet.

Kontra, M. (1995) On current research into spoken Hungarian. *International Journal of the Sociology of Language* 111, 9–20.

Kontra, M. (1997) English linguistic and cultural imperialism and teacher training in Hungary. Second conference on 'Teacher training in the Carpathian Euro-region', Debrecen, 24–26 April. Debrecen: Kossuth Lajos Tudományegyetem. Manuscript.

Kovács, I. V. (1997) A magyar közoktatás felkészülése az Európai Unió közösségi programjaiban való részvételre [The preparation of Hungarian public education for participating in the community programmes of the European Union]. Budapest: Országos Közoktatási Intézet. Manuscript.

Krolopp, J. (1996) Hungary. In P. Dickson and A. Cumming (eds) *Profiles of Language Education in 25 Countries* (pp. 47–50). Slough: National Foundation for Educational Research.

Labrie, N. (1999) Nyelvpolitika [Language politics]. In G. Szépe and A. Derényi (eds) *Nyelv, Hatalom, Egyenlőség* [*Language, Power, Equality*] (pp. 15–24). Budapest: Corvina Könyvkiadó.

Lanstyák, I. (1996) Anyanyelvi nevelés a határon innen és túl [Hungarian language education in Hungary and beyond]. In I. Csermicskó and T. Váradi (eds) *Kisebbségi*

Magyar Iskolai Nyelvhasználat [*Language Use in Ethnic Hungarian Schools*] (pp. 11–17) Budapest: Tinta Kiadó.

Leuprecht, P. (1999) Language, diversity and democratic citizenship. Council of Europe conference on 'Linguistic diversity for democratic citizenship' Innsbruck, 10–12. Strasbourg: Council of Europe. Manuscript.

Lux, G. (1932) *Modern Nyelvoktatás* [*Modern Language Instruction*]. Budapest: Magyar Királyi Egyetemi Nyomda.

Malderez, A. and Bodóczky, C. (1999) *Mentor Courses: A Resource Book for Trainer-trainers.* Cambridge: Cambridge University Press.

Manherz, K. (1993) *A Magyarországi Németek Néprajza* [*The Ethnography of Ethnic Germans in Hungary*]. Budapest: Tankönyvkiadó.

Manherz, K. (1995) Nyelvvizsga-rendszerünk vizsgája [A test of our language examination system]. *Modern Nyelvoktatás* 1 (1), 21–2.

Margócsy, I. (1996) Magyar nyelv és/vagy irodalom. Egy tantárgy kialakulása és változásai. [Hungarian language and/or literature. The formation and alterations of a school subject]. *Budapesti Könyvszemle* 8 (1), 45–53.

Marián, B. (1997) Az iskolák feladatai – közvélemény-kutatás közoktatással kapcsolatos kérdésekről [The tasks of school – public opinion survey on questions concerning public education]. Budapest: Országos Közoktatási Intézet. Manuscript.

Marton, F. (1981) Phenomenography: Describing conceptions of the world around us. *Instructional Science* 10, 177–200.

McCragg, W.O. Jr. (1990) The Jewish position in interwar Central Europe: A structural study of Jewry at Vienna, Budapest and Prague. In D. Yehuda and V. Karady (eds) *A Social and Economic History of Central European Jewry* (pp. 47–81). New Brunswick: Transaction Publishers.

Medgyes, P. (1984) Angoltanításunk fő gondjai [Major problems afflicting the teaching of English in Hungary]. *Pedagógiai Szemle* 34, 566–71.

Medgyes, P. (1992) Angol – a kommunikáció pótnyelve: körkép az angol nyelv magyarországi oktatásáról és terjedéséről [English – the ersatz language of communication: An overview of the teaching and spread of English in Hungary]. *Magyar Pedagógia* 92, 263–83.

Medgyes, P. (1993) The national L2 curriculum in Hungary. In W. Grabe *et al.* (eds) *Annual Review of Applied Linguistics* 13 (pp. 24–36). Cambridge: Cambridge University Press.

Medgyes, P. (1995) *A Kommunikatív Nyelvoktatás* [*Communicative Language Teaching*]. Budapest: Eötvös József Könyvkiadó.

Medgyes, P. (1997a) *A Nyelvtanár* [*The Language Teacher*]. Budapest: Corvina Könyvkiadó.

Medgyes, P. (1997b) Innovative second language education in Central and Eastern Europe. In G.R. Tucker and D. Corson (eds) *Encyclopedia of Language and Education, Vol. 4, Second Language Education* (pp. 187–96). Dordrecht/Boston/London: Kluwer Academic Publishers.

Medgyes, P. (1999a) *The Non-native Teacher* (2nd edn). Ismaning: Hueber Verlag.

Medgyes, P. (1999b) Language training: A neglected area in teacher education. In G. Braine (ed.) *Non-native Educators in English Language Teaching* (pp. 117–95). New Jersey: Lawrence Erlbaum Associates.

Medgyes, P. and Kaplan, R.B. (1992) Discourse in a foreign language: An empirical survey of the foreign language competence of leading Hungarian scholars. *International Journal of the Sociology of Language* 98, 67–100.

Medgyes, P. and Malderez, A. (eds) (1996) *Changing Perspectives in Teacher Education.* Oxford: Heinemann Educational Books.

Medgyes, P. and Nyilasi, E. (1997) Pair-teaching in pre-service teacher education. *Foreign Language Annals* 30, 352–68.

Miszlai, G. (1998) 'A jó tankönyv mindennél fontosabb' – avagy mikor használható jól egy francia nyelvkönyv? ['The good coursebook is above all' – or how can a French coursebook be used well?] *Tandem* 3 (3), 29–33.

Morvai, E. (1998) Az általános iskolai nyelvoktatás [Language teaching in primary schools]. In Á. Einhorn (ed.) *Vizsgatárgyak, Vizsgamodellek I, Német nyelv* [*Examination*

Subjects, Examination Models I, German] (pp. 41–55). Budapest: Országos Közoktatási Intézet.

Nádasdy, Á. (1985) Segmental phonology and morphophonology. In I. Kenesei (ed.) *Approaches to Hungarian I: Data and Descriptions* (pp. 225–246). Szeged: József Attila Tudományegyetem.

Nádor, O. and Giay, B. (eds) (1988) *Ajánló bibliográfia a magyar mint idegennyelv tanulmányozásához 1945–1988*. [*Selected Bibliography for Hungarian as a Foreign Language 1945–1988*]. Budapest: Nemzetközi Hungarológiai Központ.

Nagy, E. and Krolopp, J. (1997) Angol nyelv. In Z. Mátrai (ed.) *Középiskolai Tantárgyi Feladatbankok I*. [*Subject Data Banks for Secondary Schools I*] (pp. 161–207). Budapest: Országos Közoktatási Intézet.

Nemzeti alaptanterv [*National Core Curriculum*] (1995) Budapest: Művelődési és Közoktatási Minisztérium.

Nikolov, M. (1997) Vélemények az idegen nyelvi alapműveltségi vizsga általános követelményeiről [Views on the general requirements of the foreign language basic examination]. *Új Pedagógiai Szemle* 47 (5), 42–6.

Nikolov, M. (ed.) (1999) *English Language Education in Hungary: A Baseline Study*. Budapest: The British Council.

Nyíri, P.D. (1999) *The Hong Kong of Europe: Hungary in Writings, Talks, and Films by Hungarian Chinese*. Budapest: Eötvös Loránd Tudományegyetem. Manuscript.

Paikert, G.C. (1967) Hungary's national minority policies, 1920–1945. *American Slavic and East European Review* 12, 201–18.

Payne, J. (1987) *Colloquial Hungarian*. London: Routledge.

Petneki, K. (1993) Mit ér az idegen nyelv, ha német? [How much is the foreign language worth if it is German?] *Magyar Pedagógia* 93, 135–47.

Petneki, K. (1998a) A NAT és ellentmondásai – alkalmazás előtt [NCC and its contradictions – before introduced]. *Nyelv*Infó* 6 (4), 3–6.

Petneki, K. (1998b) A tantervek és az érettségi vizsga [Curricula and the school-leaving examination]. In Á. Einhorn (ed.) *Vizsgatárgyak, Vizsgamodellek I, Német nyelv* [*Examination Subjects, Examination Models I, German*] (pp. 57–85). Budapest: Országos Közoktatási Intézet.

Petneki, K. and Szablyár, A. (1997a) Német nyelvkönyvek tesztje [Testing German coursebooks]. *Tandem* 2 (1), 23–5.

Petneki, K. and Szablyár, A. (1997b) A hároméves némettanár-képzés eredményei és kérdőjelei [Achievements and questions concerning the three-year German teacher training programme]. *Modern Nyelvoktatás* 3 (3), 15–24.

Phillipson, R. (1992) *Linguistic Imperialism*. Oxford: Oxford University Press.

Phillipson, R. and Skutnabb-Kangas, T. (1995) Linguistic rights and wrongs. *Applied Linguistics* 16, 483–504.

Phillipson, R. and Skutnabb-Kangas, T. (1996) English only world wide or language ecology? *TESOL Quarterly* 30, 429–52.

Póczik, S. (1996) Rendszerváltás és kriminalitás: külföldiek és cigányok a bűnpiacon [Change of regime and criminality: Foreigners and gypsies on the crime market]. *Valóság* 39 (6), 73–102.

Polgárdi, K. (1998) Vowel harmony: An account in terms of government and optimality. PhD dissertation, HIL/Leiden University.

Poór, Z. and Rádai, P. (1999) Gondolatok a nyelvpedagógus-képzésről, -továbbképzésről [Thoughts about preservice and inservice teacher education]. *Nyelv*Infó* 7 (2), 12–15.

Poros, A. (1998) Régi és új franciakönyvekről [On old and new French coursebooks]. *Tandem* 3 (1), 13–15.

Poulton, H. (1998) Linguistic minorities in the Balkans (Albania, Greece and the successor states of former Yugoslavia). In C.B. Paulston and D. Peckham (eds) *Linguistic Minorities in Central and Eastern Europe* (pp. 37–80). Clevedon: Multilingual Matters.

Rádai, P. (1996) The Hungarian inservice training programme for teachers of English. Budapest: Centre for English Teacher Training. Manuscript.

Reves, T. and Medgyes, P. (1994) The non-native English speaking EFL/ESL teacher's self-image: An international survey. *System* 22, 353–67.

114   *Language Planning and Policy in Europe*

Ring, É. (ed.) (1998a) *Report on the Situation of Hungarians in Romania*. Budapest: Government Office for Hungarian Minorities Abroad.
Ring, É. (ed.) (1998b) *Report on the Situation of Hungarians in Slovakia*. Budapest: Government Office for Hungarian Minorities Abroad.
Ring, É. (ed.) (1998c) *Report on the Situation of Hungarians in Ukraine*. Budapest: Government Office for Hungarian Minorities Abroad.
Ritoók, Z., Szegedy-Maszák, M. and Veres, A. (1979) *Irodalom a Gimnázium I. Osztálya Számára* [*Literature Textbook for Secondary School Students, Grade 1*]. Budapest: Tankönyvkiadó.
Romsics, I. (1998) *Nemzet, Nemzetiség és állam Kelet-, Közép- és Délkelet-Európában a 19. és 20. században* [*Nation, Nationality and State in Eastern, Central and South Eastern Europe in the 19th and 20th Centuries*]. Budapest: Napvilág Kiadó.
Sándor, K. (1996a) A nyelvcsere és a vallás összefüggése a csángóknál [The relationship between language shift and religion with the Csángós]. *Korunk* 11, 60–75.
Sándor, K. (1996b) Apró ábécé – apró esély: a csángók 'nyelvélesztésének' lehetőségei és esélyei [A slim spelling-book – a slim chance: The possibilities and chances of the Csángó language revival]. In I. Csermicskó and T. Váradi (eds) *Kisebbségi magyar iskolai nyelvhasználat* [*Language Use in Ethnic Hungarian Schools*] (pp. 51–69). Budapest: Tinta Kiadó.
Sík, E. (1998) Minden ötödik magyar beszél idegen nyelvet [Every fifth Hungarian speaks a foreign language]. *Magyar Hírlap* 28 December.
Simon, S. (1996) Nyelvváltozatok a szlovákiai magyar tannyelvű középiskolák számára írt magyarnyelv-könyvekben [Language varieties in Hungarian Language textbooks written for secondary schools with Hungarian instruction in Slovakia]. In I. Csermicskó and T. Váradi (eds) *Kisebbségi Magyar Iskolai Nyelvhasználat* [*Language Use in Ethnic Hungarian Schools*] (pp. 17–29). Budapest: Tinta Kiadó.
Statistical Yearbook of Hungary 1994 (1995) Budapest: Központi Statisztikai Hivatal.
Statistical Yearbook of Hungary 1997 (1998) Budapest: Központi Statisztikai Hivatal.
Statisztikai tájékoztató 1989–1998 [*Statistical Report 1989–1998*]. Budapest: Művelődési és Közoktatási Minisztérium.
Szablyár, A. (1998) Az idegen nyelvek tanításának néhány kulcskérdése a németnyelv-oktatás tükrében [Key questions in foreign language instruction: The case of German]. In Á. Einhorn (ed.) *Vizsgatárgyak, Vizsgamodellek I, Német Nyelv* [*Examination Subjects, Examination Models I, German*] (pp. 13–40). Budapest: Országos Közoktatási Intézet.
Szabó, I. and Örkény, A. (1998) *Tizenévesek Állampolgári Kultúrája* [*The Civic Culture of Teenagers*]. Budapest: Minoritás Alapítvány.
Szabolcs, O. (1978) *A Gimnáziumi Nevelés és Oktatás Terve* [*Curriculum for Education and Instruction in Secondary Grammar Schools*]. Budapest: Tankönyvkiadó.
Szántó, J. (1995) A magyarországi serdülőkorú németek nemzetiségi identitása [The national identity of adolescent Germans in Hungary]. *Új Pedagógiai Szemle* 45 (6), 21–31.
Szebenyi, P. (1991) Az iskolák véleménye a Nemzeti alaptantervről [The opinion of schools about the National Core Curriculum]. *Új Pedagógiai Szemle* 41 (10), 3–13.
Székelyi, M., Csepeli, G., Örkény, A. and Szabados, T. (1998) *Válaszúton a Magyar Oktatási Rendszer* [*The Hungarian Education System at Crossroads*]. Budapest: Új Mandátum Könyvkiadó.
Szende, A. (1993) *A Magyar Nyelv Tankönyve* [*A Textbook of the Hungarian Language*]. Budapest: Tankönyvkiadó.
Szépe, G. (1969) A magyar mint idegen nyelv tanítása és az alkalmazott nyelvészet. [Hungarian as a foreign language and applied linguistics]. In K. Ginter (ed.) *Magyartanítás külföldön* [*Hungarian Instruction Abroad*] (pp. 63–67). Budapest: Művelődésügyi Minisztérium Nemzetközi Előkészítő Intézet 1.
Szépe, G. (1983) A magyar tanulmányok tartalmáról és szerkezetéről a Magyarországon kívüli felsőoktatásban [The content and structure of Hungarian Studies in foreign higher education]. In M.J. Róna (ed.) *Hungarológiai Oktatás Régen és ma* [*Hungarian Studies in the Past and Present*] (pp. 201–8). Budapest: Tankönyvkiadó.

Szépe, G. (1997) Modernizálási törekvések a legújabbkori magyarországi idegennyelv-oktatásban [Attempts to modernise foreign language education in present-day Hungary]. In P. Deák and G. Máté (eds) *A Nyelvtanulás Folyamata és Mérése* [*The Process and Assessment of Language Learning*] (pp. 7–24). Pécs: Lingua Franca Csoport.

Szűr, K. and Parrott, J. (1998) A NATtitudinal survey of English teachers in Szeged. *NovELTy* 5 (1), 7–19.

Terestyéni, T. (1981) The knowledge of foreign languages in Hungary. *Acta Linguistica Academiae Scientiarum* 31, 229–331.

Terestyéni, T. (1985) Helyzetkép a hazai idegennyelv-tudásról [State of the art in foreign language knowledge in Hungary]. *Nyelvtudományi Közlemények* 1, 197–208.

Terestyéni, T. (1995) Helyzetkép az idegennyelv-tudásról [State of the art in foreign language knowledge]. *Jel-kép* 1 (2), 47–60.

Terestyéni, T. (1996) Írás- és olvasásnélküliség Magyarországon [Without reading or writing in Hungary]. In I. Terts (ed.) *Nyelv, Nyelvész, Társadalom I.* [*Language, Linguists, Society I*] (pp. 289–99). Budapest: Keraban Könyvkiadó.

Törkenczy, M. (1997) *Hungarian Verbs and Essentials of Grammar.* Budapest: Corvina Könyvkiadó.

Tóth, J.G. (1996) *Mivelhogy Magad Írást nem Tudsz . . .* [*Since You Yourself Cannot Write*]. Budapest: Magyar Tudományos Akadémia Történettudományi Intézete.

Tóth, L. (1992) Jugoszláviai helyzetkép I. Az anyanyelvű oktatás a nemzeti kisebbségek fennmaradásának és fejlődésének alappillére [A state-of-the-art report on Yugoslavia I. Hungarian language instruction as a pillar of the survival and development of ethnic minorities]. *Iskolakultúra* 2 (11–12), 104–13.

Udvardi, J. (1999a) Megszólalni mások nyelvén [To speak in the language of others] *Népszabadság* 18 February.

Udvardi, J. (1999b) Olvasnak, de nem nyaralnak a pedagógusok [Teachers read but do not go on holiday]. *Népszabadság* 5 June.

Vágó, I. (1997) Az élő idegen nyelvek oktatása – egy modernizációs sikertörténet [Teaching modern foreign languages – a success story of modernisation]. Budapest: Országos Közoktatási Intézet. Manuscript.

Vago, M. R. (1976) Theoretical implications of Hungarian vowel harmony. *Linguistic Inquiry* 7, 243–63.

Vámos, Á. (1996) A kétszintű, standardizált, középiskolai érettségi koncepciójának fogadtatása a középiskolákban [Reception of the concept of the two-level, standardized secondary school leaving examination]. *Új Pedagógiai Szemle* 46(9), 32–37.

Vámos, Á. (1998) *Magyarország Tannyelvi Atlasza* [*Atlas of Languages of Instruction in Hungary*]. Budapest: Keraban Kiadó.

Vándor, J. (1998) Vélemények az érettségi vizsga általános követelményeiről és a vizsgaszabályzatról [Opinions about the general requirements and rules of the school-leaving examination]. In Á. Einhorn (ed.) *Vizsgatárgyak, Vizsgamodellek I, Német Nyelv* [*Examination Subjects, Examination Models I, German*] (pp. 87–95). Budapest: Országos Közoktatási Intézet.

Van Ek, J.A. (1975) *Systems Development in Adult Language Learning: The Threshold Level.* Strasbourg: Council of Europe.

Várdy, B. (1973) *Magyarságtudomány az Észak-amerikai Egyetemeken és Főiskolákon* [*Hungarian Studies at North-American Universities and Colleges*]. Cleveland: Árpád Kiadó.

Várdy, B. and Várdy Huszár, Á. (1985) Historical, literary, linguistic and ethnographic research on Hungarian-Americans. *Hungarian Studies* 1, 77–122.

Várdy Huszár, Á. (1978) A magyar irodalomtanítás lehetőségei az amerikai egyetemeken és főiskolákon [Chances of teaching Hungarian Literature at universities and colleges in the US]. *Nyelvünk és kultúránk* 30 (1), 56–61.

Vázsonyi, A. (collected and compiled) and Kontra, M. (ed.) (1995) *Túl a Kecegárdán. Calumet-vidéki Magyar Szótár* [*Beyond Castle Garden. American Hungarian Dictionary of the Calumet Region*]. Budapest: MTA Nyelvtudományi Intézet.

Vörös, O. (1996) A szlovéniai kétnyelvű oktatás és tankönyvei [Bilingual education and textbooks in Slovenia]. In I. Csermicskó and T. Váradi (eds) *Kisebbségi Magyar Iskolai Nyelvhasználat* [*Language Use in Ethnic Hungarian Schools*] (pp. 79–85). Budapest: Tinta Kiadó.

Votruba, M. (1998) Linguistic minorities in Slovakia. In C.B. Paulston and D. Peckham (eds) *Linguistic Minorities in Central and Eastern Europe* (pp. 255–79). Clevedon: Multilingual Matters.

West, R. (1997) School-leaving examinations and university entrance examinations in Central and Eastern Europe. *Testing Matters* 2 (3), 5–14.

White Paper on Education and Training: Teaching and Learning Towards the Learning Society (1996) Brussels: European Community.

Zerkowitz, J. (1988) *Tanítsunk Nyelveket!* [*Let's Teach Languages!*]. Budapest: Tankönyvkiadó.

Zsolnai, J. (1982) *Nyelvi-irodalmi-kommunikációs nevelési kísérlet* Vols. 1–2 [*Language-Literature-Communication: A Pedagogical Experiment*]. Veszprém: Országos Oktatástechnikai Központ.

The Language Situation in Hungary: An Update

Péter Medgyes
Hungarian Ministry of Education, 10–14 Szalay utca, Budapest H-1055 Hungary

Katalin Miklósy
Centre for English Teacher Training, Eötvös Loránd University, 19–21 Ajtósi Dürer sor, Budapest, H-1146 Hungary

Hungarian Language Policy and Planning

This brief addendum updates the proceeding monograph, examining key language planning related changes that have occurred in Hungary and changes that have occurred more generally related to the use of the Hungarian language. It should be read and cross referenced in conjunction with the original study.

The latest amendments of the Public Education Act and those of the National Core Curriculum Decree [NCC] were passed in 2003 (Hajdú, 2000). As the NCC is the key component of the Hungarian educational reform, the latest changes play an important role in formulating the general objectives of education as well as the contents and objectives of language education.

Among the general objectives – owing to Hungary's accession to the European Union on 1 May 2004 – stress is laid upon promoting a 'European identity' together with providing knowledge about the European Union itself.

In accordance with a strong social demand supported by teaching experts, the renewed NCC places emphasis on the importance of skills development instead of the requirement of acquiring a wide range of factual knowledge. Skills development includes study skills, the skill for social adjustment by communication and co-operation, as well as preparation for life-long learning.

While consolidating the three-tier system in curriculum planning launched in 1998, the amended Public Education Act implements a major change in the system. Up to 2003, schools were obliged to choose one of the frame curricula, i.e. the second tier, interposed between the national 'core' curriculum and the local curricula. From 2003 on, the frame curricula together with education programmes and packages are only intended to orient teachers; their use is optional (Kerber, 2000; Halász, 2002).

Within the framework of the NCC, Hungarian Language and Literature has preserved its crucial position. However, the 'renewed' objectives and contents of Hungarian Language and Literature instruction have triggered heated debates ever since the Ministry of Education initiated the supervision of the NCC in 2002 (Kojanitz, 2001; Kerber, 2002; Vass, 2003).

In his thought-provoking contribution, Arató (2003) outlines the objectives of Hungarian Language and Literature instruction in light of the general goals of the NCC: skills development and acquiring communicative competence should replace rote learning; students' comprehension deficit should be reduced by means of text interpretation. Text interpretation will also be instrumental in allowing students to reach a better understanding of themselves and of the world around them (Jászó, 2002; Kelemen, 2003).

Arguing for a radical change of approach, Arató suggests selecting a limited number of literary works for thorough analysis rather than giving students an exhaustive overview in chronological order. By taking students' preferences into consideration, teachers may motivate them to become regular readers and help them to comprehend the classics of Hungarian literature. At the same time, Arató points out that the requirements of the new, two-level school-leaving examination, to be introduced in 2005, are not compatible with the principal aims of the NCC because the enormous amount of material required by the school-leaving examination may have a backwash effect on the guiding principle of skills development advocated by the NCC.

The Situation of Ethnic Hungarians

Regarding the number of ethnic Hungarians, the dwindling of the population has continued in the majority of the neighbouring countries. Slovenia and Austria are the exceptions with a slight increase (the growth between 1991 and 2003 is approximately 1,000 people in both countries). Interestingly enough, in the Ukraine the figures indicate 200,000 ethnic Hungarians in 2003 as compared to 163,000 in 1991. This increase in number, however, may well be due to the changing political atmosphere, with people now being more willing to admit that they belong to a minority group rather than to an actual increase of the ethnic population.

While it is true that the ethnic Hungarian population is decreasing, language policy for ethnic Hungarians has taken a positive turn in most neighbouring countries since 2000, owing to favourable international circumstances. In Croatia, Romania, Serbia and Slovakia, laws were passed to guarantee the rights to use the first language in public domains where at least 20% of the population belong to the minority group. At the same time, the implementation of the right to use the first language (L1) in education is still ambivalent in most neighbouring countries (Beke, 2000; Juhos-Kiss, 2000; Novák, 2000a, 2003). The number of schools providing education in Hungarian dropped between 1999–2003, in accordance with the decrease in the number of ethnic Hungarian students. Contradicting the general trend, the number of Hungarian language primary schools and bilingual secondary schools has grown in Slovakia, and Hungarian schools have reopened in Vojvodina, Serbia. In Romania, a private Hungarian university was founded in 2000 (*Sapientia Erdélyi Magyar Magánegyetem*), while at the Babes-Bolyai University 58 majors are offered in Hungarian in 2002/2003 compared to the 45 in 1999/2000 (Source: Government Office for Hungarian Minorities Abroad).

The minority language situation

As regards the minority language situation within Hungary, the most substantial changes concern the Gypsy minority, that being not only the largest minority group in Hungary but also representing the community facing the most pressing problems (Babusik, 2003). The general objectives of facilitating the assimilation and integration of the Gypsy minority on the one hand, and the preservation of their minority identity on the other have not changed. However, an about- face took place in 2002 concerning the accomplishment of these goals. As the NCC (1995) created scope, from 1997 on, for special, upgrading education for Gypsy children, programmes were offered to help them successfully fulfil their school objectives within or apart from regular daily classes (Novák, 2000b). Based on the experience that upgrading education strengthens segregation rather than integration, in 2002 the Ministry of Education decided to stop the programme and put forward the concepts of skills development and integration in its stead. At the same time, in order to preserve minority identity and culture, schools may offer the teaching of any Romani language in two classes per week apart from the daily schedule. Up to the present time, no Romani languages have been taught in Hungarian schools with the exception of two secondary schools (Babusik, 2001). The new opportunity has attracted 30 schools to volunteer to launch this programme from 2003/2004.

Foreign languages policy and planning

Hungary, along with nine other countries, gained entry into the European Union as of 1 May 2004. While the importance of foreign language competence had long been recognised in Hungary, this historic event placed a premium on the knowledge of foreign languages and accelerated the process of effective language teaching and learning.

Although significant progress has been recorded since the change of regime (the number of foreign language speakers has doubled in fifteen years), there is little reason for jubilation. According to recent statistical data (A 2001. évi . . . , 2002), merely 19.2 percent of the Hungarian population claimed to speak at least one foreign language at some level. This translates into 25 percent for the population above age 18, while the corresponding average for the 15 original EU member states was 53 percent (Europeans and Languages, 2001). But even in the context of the new member states, Hungary turned out to be way behind any other country in terms of its citizens' foreign language competence (Euro-barometer, 2002).

Both statistical evidence and everyday experience made it imperative for the new government taking office in 2002 to face up to this problem and quickly to impose measures for improvement. The Minister of Education passed a resolution for the prompt design of a language-in-education policy document and the introduction of a range of concomitant measures to put this policy into practice. The resulting document and the programme itself came to be called 'World–Language' (W-L). Approved by the Government a year later, this became the official foreign language strategy of Hungary. To generate wide publicity, the 2003/04 school-year was declared 'The year of foreign language learning', and a simultaneous campaign was launched with an array of slogans, such as 'Speaking foreign languages is cool', 'We shouldn't join Europe mute', and 'Speak up', which shows a young woman speaking to a fish.

The principal aims and guiding principles of the document which underlie the W-L programme are:

- The foundations of foreign language competence should be laid in primary and secondary education, the most formative periods of human development.
- To ensure equal opportunities, W-L should lend increased support to learners who come from socially disadvantaged families and/or have learning disabilities.
- Rather than imposing obligatory measures, W-L should offer a framework for teachers and learners to exploit their creative potential freely.
- While acknowledging the importance of quantitative parameters, W-L should reward initiatives fostering quality and innovation in language education.
- W-L should contribute to establishing a stimulating learning environment not only within the classroom, but also outside the classroom and the school.
- W-L should facilitate the integration of ICT and language teaching, most directly within the framework of the National Schoolnet Express programme.
- Espousing the ideal of life-long learning, W-L should also provide opportunities for the adult population.

Having outlined the current situation and a vision for action, the document presents the ten-item W-L programme package designed to achieve the aims defined above. The package for 2003 was made accessible through an open application system, with clearly stated and self-explanatory bidding criteria, such as easy access to information, transparency, motivating objectives, innovation, financial reward and professional recognition for participants, measurable achievements, sustainable development, and integration with other projects. With the programme period nearly over now, it is no exaggeration to claim that the package, albeit in varying degrees, was highly successful: half of the one thousand applicants were given financial aid to implement their ideas.

However, the W-L programme would have had only limited scope if it had not been accompanied by a host of legislative measures aimed at effecting radical improvements in language education. Here are just three key elements:

(1) A clause in the new Public Education Act (2003) concerns the provision of a year of intensive language training for 9th graders in grammar schools and vocational secondary schools. Namely, as of 2004 one such class per school may be launched, with one additional class each year thereafter. Introducing the programme is optional, but once established, a minimum 40 per cent of the total curricular time (11 contact hours per week or more) should be allocated for foreign language study. As a follow-up, volunteering schools are obliged to assign a sufficient number of lessons in grades 10 through 13 for students who participated in the intensive training programme to take the advanced-level school-leaving examination in their first foreign language and possibly in one additional language. The students who have followed this program will leave school after grade 13, that is a year later than their peers. Incidentally, the law does not specify

the number of languages to be taught during this intensive year, and schools are also free to determine the languages to be offered.

The rationale for this dramatic increase of contact hours is not simply a matter of quantity. Arriving at Grade 9, students have been learning a first foreign language in three lessons per week on average for at least five years. It is hoped that the introduction of a highly intensive form of language study will boost students' flagging interest and enable them to make a qualitative leap forward. Moreover, this regulation is intended to create an opportunity for students who come from socially disadvantaged backgrounds. It should be noted that in Hungary financially better-off students have eight times as good an opportunity to learn foreign languages in and outside school as their less fortunate peers (Család változóban, 2002).

According to a preliminary survey, 43 per cent of all concerned schools plan to launch such a class. This seems to be an extremely high proportion, especially in view of the following constraints: (a) this will be a pilot year for this kind of language study; (b) many schools are still short of qualified foreign language teachers; (c) local educational authorities will have to contribute to the expenses incurred. What seems to account primarily for this keen interest is parental pressure exerted on local authorities and school principals to participate (Világ–Nyelv, 2003); this pressure demonstrates, incidentally, a high degree of citizens' awareness of the importance of foreign language knowledge in contemporary Hungary.

The survey shows a decided preference for two languages: English (61%) and German (36%). While the outstanding representation of English needs hardly any explanation (Medgyes, 2002; Medgyes and László, 2001), the good position of German is largely due to the historically close links between Hungary and the German-speaking countries. Hence, despite the fact that, in 2001, German was spoken by a slightly higher percentage of the population than English (9.87 versus 9.79%) it is a safe bet that English will have overtaken German by the time this paper is published. Nevertheless, the rapid spread of English did not take place at the expense of German or any other foreign language – the absolute number of foreign language speakers, including Russian speakers, was also on the increase (Vámos, 2000; A 2001. évi . . . , 2002).

At the time of writing this report (January 2004), preparatory work on the intensive year and its follow-up in subsequent grades is well under way, encompassing the development of suitable syllabi and teaching materials, as well as the in-service training of teachers to be involved in the project.

(2) The new Public Education Act, in harmony with the amended Higher Education Act (2003), abolished entrance examinations, rendering the school-leaving examination the only eligibility criterion for entry into higher education as of 2005. A language examination will be administered to measure communicative proficiency, and the level of competence will be expected to correspond to A2/B1 for the intermediate and B2 for advanced level as specified in the Common European Framework of Reference (2001). By passing the examination at advanced level (which is obviously free of

charge), school graduates will automatically be granted the state foreign language examination certificate as well (for which they would otherwise have had to pay).

The measure outlined in the previous paragraph is expected to contribute to the development of foreign language education in several ways: (1) By ensuring that advanced level language certificates are worth bonus points for entry at any institution of higher education, foreign language learning will yield short-term benefits. (2) The emphasis on communicative competence will create an incentive for teachers gradually to change their conservative teaching style (Nikolov, 2003). (3) The correspondence with common European measures will help Hungary enter the mainstream on a European scale. (4) Increasing the value of school-leaving language examinations is also intended to reduce inequalities among students.

(3) Pursuant to the Adult Training Act (2001), an amendment of the Act on Personal Income Tax (2003) allows all adult citizens who have participated in an accredited language course to deduct from their personal income tax 30 percent of the tuition fee, up to a limit of 60,000 Hungarian forints (US$260) per year.

This scheme functions as a modest incentive to promote the life-long learning of foreign languages in Hungary.

As for the W-L budget, the 1.3 billion forints (US$6.2 million) earmarked for 2003 was increased to 1.8 billion forints (US$8.2 million) for each of the following years – 2004 and 2005. At the same time, the National Development Plan of Hungary includes a sub-measure having the aim of enhancing the foreign language competence of Hungarian citizens. This is meant to supplement national support from possible EU resources.

On the whole, it may be argued that the first years of the 21st century have brought about substantial language-in-education reforms in Hungary. These positive developments are in large measure due to the determination of the government to improve foreign language competence through innovation. In addition to the favourable external circumstances, the remarkable success of the pilot year of W-L hinged on establishing adequate internal conditions, such as the use of expert advice, before policy decision had been made (Medgyes & Nikolov, 2002). It can only be hoped that the language policy outlined in this paper will carry over consecutive governments, with appropriate modifications if need be. Following this course of action, there is a fair chance that Hungary will be able to break out of its linguistic isolation.

Acknowledgement

We would like to thank Enikő Oveges for her dedication and massive support extended in the first year of the World–Language programme.

References

A 2001. évi népszámlálás adatai, Összefoglaló adatok, 1. kötet [National census 2001, Summary data, Volume 1] (2002) Budapest: Központi Statisztikai Hivatal.
Arató, L. (2003) Állóvíz vagy reformkáosz? [Dead Water or the Chaos of Reforms?]. Népszabadság 15 December.

Babusik, F. (2001) Az iskolai hatékonyság kulcstényezői a roma fiatalok oktatásában [Key factors of school efficiency in the education of Romany children]. *Új Pedagógiai Szemle* 51 (7–8), 157–171.

Babusik, F. (2003) Késői kezdés, lemorzsolódás – cigány fiatalok az általános iskolában [Late school-starters and dropouts – Roma children in the primary school]. *Új Pedagógiai Szemle* 53 (10), 3–19.

Beke, G. (2000) Erdélyi iskolák [Transylvanian schools]. *Köznevelés* 56 (12), 4–5.

Common European Framework of Reference for Languages: Learning, Teaching, Assessment (2001) Strasbourg: Council of Europe / Cambridge: Cambridge University Press.

Család változóban 2001 [*Changing Families* 2001] (2002) Budapest: Központi Statisztikai Hivatal.

Eurobarometer 2001, Candidate Countries (2002) Brussels: European Commission, Directorate-General Press and Communication – Online document: http://europa.eu.int/comm/public_opinion

Europeans and Languages: A Eurobarometer Special Survey (2001) Brussels: European Commission, Directorate-General for Education and Culture – Online document: http://europa.eu.int/comm/dgs/education_culture/index_en.htm

Hajdú, E. (2000) A Nemzeti Alaptanterv bevezetésének hatása a tantárgy- és tanórarendszer alakulására [The introduction of the NCC and its impact on the system of school subjects and weekly timetables]. *Új Pedagógiai Szemle* 50 (3), 22–38.

Halász, T. (2002) A kerettanterv céljai és a valóság [Frame curriculum – aims and reality]. *Új Pedagógiai Szemle* 52 (6), 14–21.

Jászó, A. (2002) A szövegértő olvasásról [About reading comprehension]. *Magyartanítás* 43 (4), 4–15.

Juhos-Kiss, J. (2000) Csángók Magyarfaluban [The Csángós of Magyarfalu]. *Köznevelés* 56 (12), 5.

Kelemen, E. (2003) A PISA-vizsgálat eredményeinek közoktatás-politikai konzekvenciái [Consequences in public education of the PISA test results]. *Új Pedagógiai Szemle* 53 (3), 21–34.

Kerber, Z. (2000) A kerettanterv hatása a NAT-ra és a helyi tantervre [The impact of the frame curriculum on the NCC and on local curricula]. *Új Pedagógiai Szemle* 50 (4), 23–32.

Kerber, Z. (2002) A magyar nyelv és irodalom tantárgy helyzete az ezredfordulón [The state of Hungarian language and literature as a school subject in the new millennium]. *Új Pedagógiai Szemle* 52 (10), 45–62.

Key Data on Education in Europe 2002 (2002) Brussels / Luxembourg: European Commission.

Kojanitz, L. (2001) Hány tantárgy a magyar nyelv és irodalom? [Hungarian language and literature – How many subjects?]. *Köznevelés* 57 (20), 2.

Medgyes, P. (2002) 'Very English, very good!' – Gondolatok az angol nyelv magyarországi térhódításáról ['Very English, very good!' – On the spread of English in Hungary]. In J. M. Kovács (ed.) *A zárva várt Nyugat – Kulturális globalizáció Magyarországon* [*The West Closed Shut – Cultural Globalisation in Hungary*] (pp. 263–283) Budapest: 2000/Sík Kiadó.

Medgyes, P. and László, M. (2001) The foreign language competence of Hungarian scholars: Ten years later. In U. Ammon (Ed.) *The Dominance of English as a Language of Science* (pp. 261–286). Berlin/New York: Walter de Gruyter Publishers

Medgyes, P. and Nikolov, M. (2002) Curriculum development in foreign language education: The interface between political and professional decisions. In R. B. Kaplan (ed.) *The Oxford Handbook of Applied Linguistics* (pp. 195–206). New York: Oxford University Press.

Nikolov, M. (2003) Angolul és németül tanuló diákok nyelvtanulási attitűdje és motivációja [The language learning attitudes and motivation of students studying English and German]. *Iskolakultúra* 103 (8), 61–73.

Novák, G. (2000a) Kárpátaljai magyar iskolák [Sub-Carpathian Hungarian Schools]. *Köznevelés* 56 (4), 8.

Novák, G. (2000b) Roma oktatási programok [Roma education programmes]. *Köznevelés* 56 (26), 6.
Novák, G. (2003) Konferencia a nemzetiségi és etnikai oktatásról [Conference on National Minority and Ethnic Education]. *Köznevelés* 59 (36), 4–5.
Statisztikai tájékoztató 2002 [Statistical Report 2002] (2003) Budapest: Oktatási Minisztérium.
Vámos, Á. (2000) A tanítási nyelvek helyzete a kilencvenes évek második felében [The situation of the languages of instruction in the second half of 90s]. *Új Pedagógiai Szemle* 50 (7–8), 56–66.
Vass, V. (2003) 'Tartalmi és pedagógiai paradigmaváltás' [Shift of the paradigm in pedagogy and content]. *Köznevelés* 59 (29), 8–9.
Világ – Nyelv: Kutatások a nyelvtanulásról [World – Language: Research on Language Learning]. (2003) Budapest: Marketing Centrum.

The Language Situation in Finland

Sirkku Latomaa
School of Modern Languages and Translation Studies, University of Tampere,
Finland

Pirkko Nuolijärvi
Research Institute for the Languages of Finland, Helsinki, Finland

This monograph provides an overview of the language situation in Finland, an officially bilingual country in northern Europe. The national languages, Finnish and
Swedish, have equal status, guaranteed in language legislation since 1922. During the
19th century, however, Swedish was still the language of the élite, while Finnish was
the language of the common people. Therefore, the main accomplishment during the
19th century was the rapid development of the Finnish language into a language of
education and administration, after Finnish was accorded official status in 1863. The
beginning of independence (1917–) witnessed a number of language conflicts that
gradually subsided and led to a long stable period between the languages. In the
1980s, the linguistic situation changed again in many ways. The former emigrant
country became an immigrant country. Even though immigrant minorities in
Finland are still small compared with, for example, other Nordic countries, immigration has created a situation where there are several established linguistic minorities. In the 1990s, the status of linguistic minorities was improved through a number
of legislative and educational reforms, and in 2001, proposals for the new Language
Act and the Saami Language Act were written. Simultaneously, the status of Finnish
has changed somewhat. In 1995, Finland joined the European Union. Internationalisation and globalisation have become a part of Finnish society, and the role of English
in business, education, media and science has become more accentuated than ever
before. In this new situation, the future of Finnish as well as the other national
language, Swedish, is discussed from the viewpoint of less widely used languages in
a globalising world.

Introduction

The outline of the monograph

The monograph consists of four parts. Part I presents the language profile of
Finland: the national languages, the major minority languages, religious
languages, foreign languages, and literacy in Finland. Part II gives a detailed
overview of the spread of all the languages used in the country. The main emphasis is placed on the position of languages in the Finnish school system as well as
on language-in-education policy. Special emphasis has also been given to immigrant minorities, as a relatively new phenomenon in Finnish society. In addition,
the languages used in the national and other churches and in the media are
described. Part III focuses on language planning and language policy legislation,
as well as on the major activities carried out by language planning agencies. The
description of status planning covers, in addition to the national languages, the
minority languages mentioned in the Constitution (2000) – the Saami languages,
Finnish Romani, and Finnish sign language. Finally, Part IV discusses the current
status of the languages spoken in Finland and attempts to outline the trends visible in present-day society.

Map 1 The map of Finland (www.lib.ntexax.edu)

A brief history of Finland[1]

Finland belongs to the Nordic region, together with Sweden, Norway, Denmark and Iceland. Altogether, these five countries cover approximately a quarter of the territory of Europe, but their share of the total population of the continent is only 3–4%. The countries neighbouring Finland are Sweden, Norway, Russia and Estonia (see Map 1).

Prior to the Crusades in the mid-12th century, Finland had remained politically intact between Russia and Sweden. Two centuries later the peace treaty of 1323 divided the country: the eastern parts of Finland were assigned to Novgorod (Russia) with its Greek Orthodox Church, while the western sections of the country were tied to Sweden and the prevailing Roman Catholic Church. The Swedish influence over most of the country during the following five centuries implanted not only the Swedish language but also the legal and social structures of Sweden deeply into Finnish soil. In the 14th century Finns were given the right to participate in the election of the King of Sweden and in the 16th century the right to representation in the Swedish Diet. The religious Reformation in the early 16th century reached Sweden and Finland, initiating the rise of the Finnish-language culture. The New Testament was translated into Finnish in 1548.

While under Swedish rule, Finland was legally a set of provinces governed from Stockholm rather than a national entity. This strengthened Swedish influence and the position of the Swedish language in Finland throughout the period. After Sweden lost its war with Russia, Finland became an autonomous Grand Duchy of Russia in 1809. The Russian Czar was the Grand Duke with the Governor General as Russia's representative, and Finland's highest governing body was the Finnish Senate.

During the first two decades under Russian rule, Finland enjoyed extensive autonomy that laid the foundation for the Finnish state. Despite Russian rule, the Lutheran Church retained its position in Finland, as did Swedish as the official language of the country. The capital seat was moved from Turku to Helsinki in 1812. Furthermore, during the 19th century, the national movement came into being. The Finnish national epic, the Kalevala, was compiled by Elias Lönnrot and published in 1835. J.V. Snellman promoted the Finnish language, and his work finally led to the Language Decree issued in 1863. This started the process through which Finnish became an official language in the country while, from the beginning of the 20th century, Swedish gradually lost its dominant position.

As nationalists gained influence in Russia, the autonomous position of Finland with its own legal, financial (including postal) and military structures came under increased domestic political pressure in Russia. This was manifested in Finland in the policy known as Russification during two eras of oppression (1899–1905 and 1909–1917). After the 1905 Revolution in Russia, Finland, too, changed from a four-estate parliament to a unicameral one. In addition, universal suffrage was realised in 1906, and Finnish women were the first in Europe to obtain the right to vote in parliamentary elections.

On 6 December 1917, the Finnish Parliament approved the declaration of independence of the nation. After a short but intense Civil War during the first half of 1918, Finland became a republic in 1919. The independent republic developed briskly during the 1920s with major legal work conducted in the parliament, including the Finnish Language Act of 1922.

As a consequence of the Soviet–German non-aggression pact and its implementation, Finland was drawn into World War II as the Soviet Union attacked Finland on 30 November 1939. The conflict ended 105 days later, and Finland lost its south-eastern part to the Soviet Union. After some 15 months of peace, Finland attacked the Soviet Union as a German co-belligerent in the summer of 1941. As a result of the Paris Peace Treaty of 1947, further Finnish losses to their territory were confirmed. In 1948, Finland concluded a Treaty of Friendship, Co-operation and Mutual Assistance with the Soviet Union.

In 1955, Finland joined both the United Nations and the Nordic Council. Finland's international position was further established by the work of the late President Urho Kekkonen who, over two decades, worked actively to increase Finland's latitude in foreign policy by pursuing a policy of neutrality. Finland became a full member of

European Free Trade Association (EFTA) in 1986 and a member of the Council of Europe in 1989. After a referendum held in October 1994, the Finnish Parliament approved European Union (EU) membership as of the beginning of 1995. In 2002, Finland changed over to the EU common currency, the Euro.

PART I: The Language Profile of Finland

The National Languages

There are about 5.2 million inhabitants in Finland (*Suomen asukasluku*, 2001–2002). In fact, 92.3% of Finns have Finnish as their first language; the share of Swedish-speaking people is about 5.7%, and the rest of the people speak other languages as their first language. Currently, Finns make up 35% of the world's population north of latitude 60° (Peltonen, 1999).

According to the Constitution, Finland's national languages are Finnish and

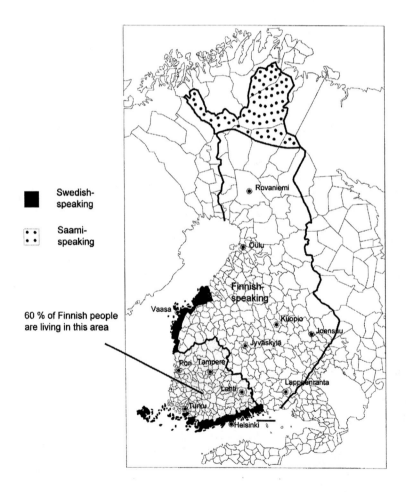

Map 2 Finnish, Swedish and Saami areas in Finland

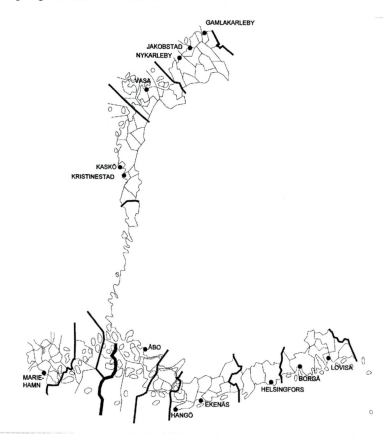

Map 3 The division of the Swedish dialects

Swedish, and the public administration must provide for the cultural and societal needs of the country's Finnish-language and Swedish-language population on equal terms. The Language Act states that a Finnish citizen is entitled to use either Finnish or Swedish in courts of law and in dealings with other national authorities. What the law requires concerning language is based on local circumstances, that is, through monolingual or bilingual municipalities. In a bilingual municipality, people are entitled to use either Finnish or Swedish with local authorities, while in a monolingual one only one language may be used. In 2002, there were 385 monolingual Finnish-speaking municipalities, 21 monolingual Swedish-speaking municipalities, 22 bilingual municipalities with Swedish as the predominant language, and 20 bilingual municipalities with Finnish as the predominant language (see also Part III).

Today, the majority of Finns (over 60%) live in the south-western urbanised areas of Finland and in larger cities (Map 2). Historically, these areas have also been the core of Finland. The speakers of Swedish live in the southern and western coasts of Finland and in Åland (Map 3). It is especially the southern coast that is largely bilingual.

Finnish, the majority language

Finnish in its language family

The oldest traces of human habitation in Finland date from about 7000 BCE. Little is known about the language of the early settlers, but in the middle of the 12th century CE, the country had a Finnish-speaking population (Kulonen, 1998).

Finnish belongs to the Uralic family of languages, which has two main branches: the Finno-Ugrian and the Samoyed languages. Finnish and its closely cognate languages are jointly called Baltic-Finnic languages. Besides Finnish, these languages include Karelian, Ludian, Vepsian, Votian, Ingrian, Estonian and Livonian. Given some practice, Finns can understand other Baltic-Finnic languages fairly well, but not automatically. The Saami languages are remotely cognate languages of Finnish. Hungarian is distant from Finnish, and the relation between these two languages can only be established on historical linguistic grounds. It has been said that Finnish is as far from Hungarian as English or German is from Persian (Karlsson, 1999).

Finnish is the largest of the Baltic-Finnic languages, and even in its Finno-Ugrian language family it is the second largest; only Hungarian has more speakers than Finnish (see e.g. Medgyes & Miklósy, 2000). Finnish is spoken by 4.8 million people in Finland. In addition, there are Finnish-speaking people in Sweden (*c.* 300,000) (see Winsa, 1999), Northern Norway (probably some 12,000), Eastern Karelia and Ingria (50,000–100,000), and as emigrants in, *inter alia,* the United States and Australia.

It is typical of Finnish – like the other Uralic languages – that grammatical relationships are expressed by adding suffixes and affixes to the body of the words. Other elements added to the word body, i.e. morphemes, are the personal suffixes (*tule+n* 'I come', *tule+mme* 'we come'), possessive suffixes (*kirja+si* 'your book', *talo+mme* 'our house'), enclitic particles (*tulet+han* 'you come, don't you', *sinä+kin* 'you, too', *on+pa+s* 'but it is!'), as well as derivatives. The word structure and the morphology are rather similar in Uralic languages, but the syntax of Baltic-Finnic languages has been influenced by Germanic languages (see e.g. Salminen, 1993: 29–30).[2]

Briefly described, the phonological, morphological and syntactic features of Finnish (and Finno-Ugrian languages) are presented on the following page (see e.g. Karlsson, 1999; cf. Medgyes & Miklósy, 2000).

The majority of the Baltic-Finnic vocabulary is of Finno-Ugrian origin. In Finnish, about 80% of the undivided stem words are of old Finnic origin, and only 20% are loans. The oldest words in Finnish date back to the Uralic (Finno-Ugrian) proto-language, spoken at least 6000 years ago, e.g. Fi. *elää* 'live', *uida* 'swim', *kala* 'fish', *nuoli* 'arrow', *suksi* 'ski', the numbers from 1 to 6: *yksi, kaksi, kolme, neljä, viisi, kuusi.* Some of these could be ancient loans from the Indo-European proto-language, e.g., *nimi* 'name' or *tehdä* 'do, make' (Häkkinen, 1990, 1996).

The earliest loans were taken from Indo-European languages. Finnish, as well as other Finnic languages, has been deeply impregnated by Indo-European (especially Baltic and Germanic, also Slavic) influences, both in vocabulary and grammar. Finnish has even preserved some Indo-European loanwords in a nearly original form: Fi. *kuningas* is closer to Old Germanic *kuningaz* than its modern descendants, English *king*, German *König* or Swedish *k(on)ung*.

The structure of Finnish in a nutshell

(1) There are fewer phonemes in Finnish than in many other languages: 8 vowels and 13 consonants.

(2) Vowel harmony: if the stem contains one or more of the vowels *u, o, a,* the ending also has to have a back vowel (*talo* 'house': *talo+ssa* 'in the house'). If the stem contains one or more of the vowels *y, ö, ä,* the ending also has to have a front vowel (*kylä* 'village': *kylä+ssä* 'in the village').

(3) Each letter corresponds to one and the same phoneme, and each phoneme corresponds to one and the same letter.

(4) The difference between short and long sounds is used in Finnish to distinguish different words (*tulee* '(s/he) comes' cf. *tuulee* 'it is windy', *takka* 'fireplace ' cf. *taakka* 'burden', *kansa* 'people' cf. *kanssa* 'with ').

(5) Word stress falls on the first syllable of the word.

(6) Words are inflected by adding grammatical affixes, instead of using prepositions (*talo+ssa* 'in the house', *talo+sta* 'from the house'). Finnish has 15 cases (the number may vary according to the counting principle).

(7) Verb conjugation: verbs are also inflected by person, as in *sano+n* 'I say', *sano+t* 'you say'. These basic elements also generate the possessive suffixes attached to nouns, as in *kirja+ni* 'my book', *kirja+si* 'your book', *auto+ssa+ni* 'in my car'.

(8) Derivation is a common method of word formation (e.g. *kirja,* 'book' > *kirjoittaa* 'write', *kirje* 'letter', *kirjailija* 'author', *kirjasto* 'library', *kirjallisuus* 'literature').

(9) There is no grammatical gender in Finnish.

(10) There are no articles, the word order often marks the indefinite and the definite: *Kadulla on auto.* 'There is a car in the street.' *Auto on kadulla.* 'The car is in the street.'

(11) Concord: When adjectives occur as premodifiers, they agree in number and case with the headword, i.e., they have the same ending: *iso auto* 'the big car': *iso+ssa auto+ssa* 'in the big car'.

At present, English is an important source of loan words, e.g. *meikki* 'make up', *rokki* 'rock', even if the tradition to create indigenous equivalents is still strong in Finnish (e.g. *tulostin* 'printer', *tietokone* 'computer', *levyke* 'disc').

The background of Modern Standard Finnish

The Finnish written language is some 500 years old. The New Testament (*Se Wsi Testamenti*) was translated into Finnish in 1548 by the Bishop of Turku, Mikael Agricola (1510–1557), who brought the Reformation to Finland. The entire Bible appeared in Finnish in 1642. However, the oldest book published in Finnish is Mikael Agricola's 1543 ABC-book *Abckiria*. Even before this, there were texts written in Finnish for the purposes of, e.g., teaching Christianity, but they have not survived. The age of Agricola and his successors is called the period of Old Finnish. It was during this period that the bases for written Finnish and its orthography were established. The period of Old Finnish ended in the early 19th century. The period after that, from 1820 to 1870, is called the Early Modern Finnish period, after which one may speak of Modern Finnish (see e.g. Ikola, 1984).

Old Finnish was largely based on western and south-western dialects, as during the Swedish reign Turku was the capital. As the process of establishing a cultural language suitable for all branches of society was begun in the 19th century, the rich expressions of the other dialects were taken into account, as well. The literary language was thus enriched with the vocabulary and structures from the eastern dialects. In the 19th century, young educated Finns created new words for various scientific and professional fields and practical purposes in everyday life (see e.g. Hakulinen, 1979; Häkkinen, 1994). Finally, at the beginning of the 20th century, Finnish was used in all fields of society.[3]

The major Finnish varieties

The Finnish spoken in Finland is divided into many dialects. The main dialect groups are the eastern and western dialects: the eastern dialects include the Savo dialects and the south-eastern dialects, whereas the western dialects are the south-western, mid-south-western dialects, Häme dialects, Southern Ostrobothnian dialects, Northern and Central Ostrobothnian dialects and Far Northern dialects (the places that are referred to in the text are marked on Map 4).

The Finnish dialects are not distant from each other. They are mostly intelligible to all Finnish-speaking people. As described in the previous section, Standard Finnish is mainly based on western dialects, but it also has phonological and lexical items from the eastern dialects.

The main differences with regard to Standard Finnish in the eastern and western dialects are presented in Table 1 (Itkonen, 1964; Kettunen, 1940; Rapola, 1962). In the fifth section of the table, the common variants in the densely populated southern and western area in Finland, especially in the urban areas, are described.

The Finnish language variation has been studied by many scholars and students (e.g. Makkonen & Mantila, 1997; Mielikäinen, 1982; Nuolijärvi, 1986, 1994b; Paunonen, 1995 [1982]). Variation has been analysed in cities, as well as in the countryside. The differences in the Finnish dialects have merged during the past few decades, especially in vocabulary. However, as Table 1 shows, there are still clear phonological and morphological differences between the various dialects.

Especially during the second half of the 20th century, urbanisation has changed the linguistic map of Finland. People moved from the countryside to the cities, especially to the Helsinki region and other southern parts of Finland. The linguistic profiles of migrants and other Finns differ greatly from the profiles of earlier generations. There are speakers who to some extent maintain their regional variety in all circumstances, even after moving, even if their significant dialectal variants had disappeared; there are speakers who adopt the new common southern variety; there are speakers who adopt a variety close to Standard Finnish, and there are speakers with strong urban varieties, e.g. Helsinki colloquial. The variation is very rich. However, the morphological and phonological variants are so similar that it is still easy to understand other varieties in spite of regional and social differences (Nuolijärvi, 1986, 1994b).

It has been said that the differences between written and spoken varieties have increased in the 1990s. At the same time, spoken variants have been adopted in certain written texts, e.g. in afternoon newspapers and texts for youth. Thus, in fact, there are now different written varieties. However, the differences are quite

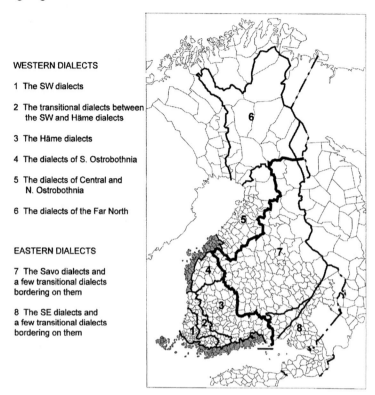

Map 4 The division of the Finnish dialects. The Swedish-speaking areas are marked with diagonal lines

small. Normative Standard Finnish is still the predominant written variety, and it does not change rapidly.

It has often been predicted that the traditional dialects would gradually merge and disappear, but this has not occurred. In the 1990s, the dialects have gained even greater standing, which has given rise to the concept of the 'dialect boom'. There are translations from Standard Finnish to dialects, like the *Kalevala* into the Savo dialect, and the Catechism and parts of the Bible, as well as Donald Duck and Asterix, into various other dialects. Dialects are popular ways of speaking not only in Finland but also in many other European countries.

There are also varieties of Finnish spoken outside of Finland, especially in Sweden (Huss, 1991; Lainio, 1989; Winsa, 1999), Norway (Lindgren, 1990), Ingria, Russia, North America (Virtaranta *et al.*, 1993) and Australia (Kovács, 2001). These varieties have been influenced by the respective majority languages, but they are still to a great extent intelligible to Finns in Finland. Differences can be found especially in vocabulary.

Swedish spoken in Finland

Swedish in the Finnish society

Swedish is an Indo-European language belonging to the Nordic branch of the Germanic language group. Swedish is spoken by nine million people in the

Table 1 The main differences between standard Finnish and the eastern and western dialects

Feature	Standard Finnish	Western dialects	Eastern dialects	Southern city varieties	Gloss
Apocope of A	talossa	talosa, talos	talossa	talos	in the house
Opening of diphthongs	nuori	nuari, nuori	nuori	nuori, nuari	young
Forms corresponding to standard d	vuoden, meidän	vuaren (vuoren), meirän	vuojen, mei(j)än	vuoden, mei(j)än	year's, our
Forms corresponding to standard ts	metsä	mettä	mehtä	metsä	forest
Primary gemination	makaa	makaa, makkaa	makkaa	makaa	lies, rests
Reduction of diphthongs	sauna	sauna	sa:una, saana	sauna	sauna
Past particle active	ollut	ollu	ollu, ollunna	ollu	been
Labialisation	tulee	tuloo, tulee	tullee, tulloo	tulee	comes
Epenthetic vowel	kylmä	kylmä, kylymä	kylymä	kylmä	cold
First person singular pronoun	minä	mä(ä), mnä(ä), minä	minä	mä	I
First person plural pronoun	me	me, met	myö	me	we

Source: Nuolijärvi (1994b: 155)

world, approximately 291,000 in Finland (2002). There is also a small Swedish minority in Estonia, but it has diminished considerably (Sarv, 1999). A small number of the descendants of the Swedish and Finland-Swedish immigrants in, e.g. the United States and Canada also understand or speak Swedish.

From the 12th century onwards there was an influx of colonists from central Sweden to Finland. This immigration appears to have been entirely spontaneous, although it was encouraged by the Roman Catholic Church and, later, by the Swedish Crown, both of which wanted to extend their influence eastwards. The Swedish immigrants settled in the Åland Islands and along the Gulf of Finland and the Gulf of Bothnia, which had been uninhabited until then. This wave of largely peaceful colonisation ebbed at the beginning of the 14th century. Since then, Finnish and Swedish speakers have lived side by side in Finland (Beijar *et al.*, 1997; McRae, 1997).

In 1815, there were an estimated 160,000 speakers of Swedish in Finland, about 15% of the population. After 1880, the Swedish-speaking population continued to increase until 1900. Then it remained roughly stable for half a century, after which it started to decline, especially during the emigration to Sweden between 1950 and 1970. The evidence since 1970 suggests a partial stabilisation of the decline (Finnäs, 2001; McRae, 1997; Table 2).

It has been suggested that there are three reasons for the decrease of the Finland-Swedish population (Allardt & Starck, 1981; Tandefelt, 1988, 1992): (1) a lower birth rate than that of the later urbanised Finnish-speaking Finns, (2) emigration, especially from rural areas like Ostrobothnia in the 1960s and at the beginning of the 1970s, and (3) the Fennification of the previously monolingual Swedish or bilingual Swedish-dominated environments resulting from the large influx of Finnish-speaking people and Fennification resulting from marriages across the language border.

The pressure of the Finnish-speaking majority can be felt in various ways, and despite well-planned legislation (see Part III), the everyday-life of the speakers of Swedish is not as unproblematic as one would hope. The largest practical problems are probably found in bilingual municipalities where the majority of the population is Finnish-speaking. Carrying out everyday activities in Swedish has become more difficult. It has become increasingly difficult to find Swedish-speaking officials, experts or neighbours who could help the speakers of Swedish in their own language. Even well-designed laws cannot help in this situation, nor guarantee that the practical activities can be carried out without problems; e.g. they do not increase the number of Swedish-speaking nurses or tax authorities. Also, there are situations where Swedish-speaking Finns are not understood. According to Allardt (1997), a decrease in the use of Swedish brings the speakers of Swedish in Finland into a situation where their intellectual, cultural and linguistic resources are impaired – today there is a risk that the Swedish spoken in Finland may become nothing more than a home language.

However, the idea of a nation with two languages is a self-evident fact in Finland, and it is only rarely questioned in modern Finland. The attitudes of the Finnish-speaking population are mostly very positive, and the interest in the Swedish language even seems to have increased in the 1990s (Allardt, 1997). This

Table 2 Swedish speakers and total population in Finland 1880–2000

Year	Total population	Swedish speakers	Percentage of total population
1880	2,061,000	295,000	14.3
1890	2,380,000	323,000	13.6
1900	2,713,000	350,000	12.9
1910	2,921,000	339,000	11.6
1920	3,105,000	341,000	11.0
1930	3,381,000	343,000	10.1
1940	3,696,000	354,000	9.6
1950	4,030,000	348,000	8.6
1960	4,446,000	331,000	7.4
1970	4,598,000	303,000	6.6
1980	4,788,000	300,000	6.3
1990	4,998,000	297,000	5.9
2000	5,181,000	292,000	5.7

Source: McRae (1997: 86); *Statistical Yearbook of Finland* (2001: 114)

positive attitude can be seen, among other things, in the widespread interest in Swedish-language immersion both in day-care centres and in comprehensive school (Buss & Mård, 2001), as well as in the interest among Finnish-speaking students in acquiring a better knowledge of Swedish. These facts are not as frequently discussed in the press when compared to the individual negative attitudes towards Swedish.

Swedish varieties in Finland

Finland-Swedish is not an independent language, but rather a regional variety, that is, Swedish spoken and written by Finland-Swedes. Finland-Swedish differs from Swedish partly in pronunciation, partly through certain differences in vocabulary (af Hällström & Reuter, 2000), expressions and syntax and, to some extent, morphology. Some of the differences are noticeable, but they apply only to a very small part of the vocabulary. In most cases, it is possible to replace the Finland-Swedish special features by Sweden-Swedish ones.

Swedish spoken in Finland had earlier been divided into two main groups: Standard Swedish and dialects (Ahlbäck, 1971). There are two main groups of Finland-Swedish dialects: northern and southern (see Map 3). The northern dialects are spoken in Ostrobothnia and Åland and the southern ones in Åboland and Nyland. The northern dialects have borrowed a lot of features from Sweden-Swedish. The main differences are described in Table 3.

Nearly half of the Finland-Swedes, particularly in Ostrobothnia, have a dialect as their first language. The Finland-Swedish dialects, which are regarded as eastern dialects of Swedish, have preserved many features that are found in Sweden only in peripheral, especially northern, dialects (Reuter, 1992). The main phonological differences between Sweden-Swedish and Finland-Swedish are noted in Table 4.

The syntactic and morphological differences between Sweden-Swedish and Finland-Swedish are relatively small, especially in written language and formal speech. Some features frequent in Finland-Swedish are unknown in Sweden, e.g. the use of certain prepositions and the inflection of a number of verbs and nouns. On the syntactic level, there is an obvious Finnish influence in Finland-Swedish (Reuter, 1992).

Differences in vocabulary are to be found both in spoken and written language. Words that are used somewhat regularly in Finland-Swedish but not in Sweden-Swedish are referred to as *finlandisms*. Some of them can be considered as well established even in formal Finland-Swedish, e.g. *ministerium* 'ministry' in Finland and *departementet* in Sweden, *skyddsväg* 'zebra crossing' in Finland

Table 3 Examples of phonological differences between northern and southern Finland-Swedish dialects

Feature	Northern dialects	Southern dialects
Short a in short syllables	släji 'hit'	slaji 'hit'
Overlong syllable	–	blå:tt 'blue', fö:dd 'born'
Vowels in definite forms	bå:ten 'the boat'	bå:tn 'the boat'
R before l after long vowels	fa:li 'dangerous'	fa:rli 'dangerous'

Source: Ahlbäck (1971)

Table 4 Main phonological differences between spoken Sweden-Swedish and Finland-Swedish

Feature	Spoken Swedish in Sweden	Spoken Swedish in Finland
Accent	Opposition between acute and grave accent	No tonemes
Phonetic quantity	Stressed syllables contain a long vowel or a short vowel followed by a long consonant; ka:mera	Stressed syllables contain a short vowel followed by a short consonant: kamera
Consonant quality	Voiceless stops are aspirated	Voiceless stops are unaspirated
Apocope in certain words	None: inte 'not', måste 'must', skulle 'should'	Apocope: int 'not', måst 'must', sku 'should'

Source: Reuter (1992)

and *övergångsställe* in Sweden, *förena* 'connect a call' in Finland and *koppla ett samtal* in Sweden (af Hällström & Reuter, 2000; Reuter, 1992).

In the late 20th century, urbanisation in Finland has affected the Swedish variation. At present, Finland-Swedish can be divided into Standard Swedish, homogenised dialects (urban varieties), and rural dialects. There are, of course, differences between usage in various towns (Ivars, 1996).

The Minority Languages

In this section, we will describe the situation of the language groups and languages besides Finnish and Swedish mentioned in the Constitution of Finland. Furthermore, we will briefly describe a couple of other established language groups living in Finland, namely the Jewish group, the Tatar group and the Russian group. In the last section of this part, we will discuss the situation with regard to several new languages in Finland in the 1990s.

Saami languages

The Saami (*sápmelaš* in Saami)[4] are one of the indigenous peoples of Europe, just as the Inuit are in Greenland. They have their own history, language, culture, livelihood, way of life, and identity. The Saamiland (*Sápmi* in Saami) reaches from Central Norway and Sweden through the northernmost part of Finland and into the Kola Peninsula in Russia (Map 5). There are over 75,000 Saami in the area.

The Saami languages are the most closely cognate languages of the Baltic-Finnic languages. There are a total of 10 Saami languages: The western Saami languages include South, Ume, Pite, Lule and North Saami, while the eastern Saami languages are Inari, Skolt, Akkala, Kildin and Ter Saami. The Saami languages are spoken in Finland, Sweden, Norway and Russia.

In Finland, there are 6500 Saami of whom 4000 live within the Saami Homeland in northern Finland, consisting of the municipalities of Enontekiö (*Eanodat*), Inari (*Anár*) and Utsjoki (*Ohcejohka*) and the northern part of the municipality of Sodankylä (*Soađegilli*). The area includes a special region reserved for the Skolt Saami, who came to Finland after World War II from the Russian Saami area. At present, the Saami constitute a third of the total popula-

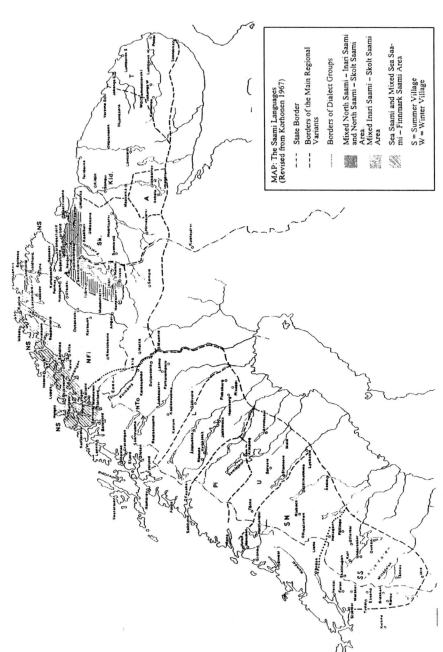

Map 5 The Saami languages and their main dialect areas (Sammallahti, 1998: 5)

tion living in the Saami Homeland. Saami are a majority in the municipality of Utsjoki, but a minority elsewhere. The Skolt and Inari Saami live mostly in the municipality of Inari, which is the only four-language municipality in Finland: official communications are issued in Finnish, Inari Saami, Skolt Saami and North Saami. Besides the Arctic area, there are Saami people living all over Finland: the largest 'Saami colony' in Finland is in Helsinki, where there are 400–500 Saami (Lindgren, 2000).

Three Saami languages are spoken in Finland: Inari, North and Skolt Saami. The language most commonly spoken among the Saami in Finland is North Saami (1800). There are about 400 speakers of Inari Saami, and about 400 speakers of Skolt Saami (Seurujärvi-Kari *et al.*, 1995). Each language has its own literary language and orthography. Although there are no strong linguistic boundaries between the Saami languages, they differ from each other to some extent (Sammallahti, 1998).

Even though multilingualism has always been part of the Saami culture, many Saami people have lost their own language because of the pressure from Finnish (Aikio, 1988; Olthuis, 2000). Only half of the Saami people living in Finland speak Saami as their first language. Consequently, the revival and support of the Saami languages is one of the most important missions in the Nordic countries. Since 1992, the Saami languages in Finland have had an official status in the Saami Homeland (see Part III). In practice, this means that Saami people are entitled to use their first language when dealing with authorities and in hospitals.

The Saami and the Finns originally shared a common proto-language. Saami differs from the Finnic languages in a number of features. With regard to phonology, the vowel system has undergone a radical reorganisation, whereas the consonant system has retained many old features. In morphology, Saami has retained the dual number in personal pronouns, personal endings and possessive suffixes. Furthermore, Saami lacks the external local cases. The Saamic and Finnic languages have both developed consonant gradation, but it is stronger in Saami than in Finnish: the Saami gradation comprises all the consonants, whereas in Finnic, only the stops are graded (Sammallahti, 1998). There are a number of words with the same etymology in Saami and Finnish.

The oral tradition of Saami has always been and is still very strong. The first written texts in Saami appeared in the early 17th century. For almost three hundred years, the only works in Saami were religious texts written by clergymen. At present, there is some literature in all three Saami languages (Olthuis, 2000; Seurujärvi-Kari *et al.*, 1995: 120–4).

Romani in Finland

Romani belongs to the Indo-Aryan group of the family of Indo-European languages. Together with its sister languages, Hindi, Urdu and Marathi, it is one of the cognate languages of Sanskrit, the old Indian language. The Romani languages in Europe have borrowed words from various European languages. The estimated number of speakers of Romani has varied considerably. According to one estimation, there would be as many as 40 million speakers of Romani in the world.

There have been Romani-speaking people in Finland for some 450 years.[5] The Roma in Finland belong to the Kaale group. At present, it is estimated that their total number is approximately 13,000 (10,000 in Finland and 3,000 in Sweden). It is not known how many of them speak Romani. The Roma live all over the country, although they have also been affected by urbanisation, and most of them now live in the southern urbanised area of Finland.

The Roma arrived in Finland via Sweden and the Baltic provinces (currently the Baltic States) in the 16th century. The attitude towards the Roma among the authorities was distinctly negative. For example, a law relating to the Roma was introduced in 1637, legalising the killing of any Roma discovered in the kingdom of Sweden. During the period of Finnish autonomy, some effort was made to integrate the Roma into Finnish society.

Until the 1970s, there were prejudices against the Roma among the majority of the population and especially among authorities. Since then, the status of the Roma has improved in Finnish society. There are still problems, one of which is the question of how to maintain the Roma culture and the Romani language in urbanised society. Many of the Roma have Finnish as their first language, and one of the main tasks is to preserve Romani among the younger generations, as well as to maintain Roma cultural features and customs.

The Romani spoken in Finland has been studied for over 200 years. The earliest research was a writing competition entry from the 1780s (Ganander, 1780). The first printed study material in Finland was Viljo Koivisto's ABC-book *Drabibosko ta rannibosko byrjiba* (1982). Later on, more advanced study books and dictionaries were published (Hedman, 1996; Koivisto, 1994, 2001; Vuolasranta, 1995). Finnish Romani has borrowed many words from Finnish, and especially from Swedish.

Finnish sign language

Finnish sign language[6] is the first language of about 5000 deaf people. In addition to the deaf, about 10,000 hearing people use it as their first language, as a second language or as a foreign language. The users of Finnish sign language live throughout the country.

The Finnish sign language community was established in the mid-19th century, when Oscar Malm (1826–1863), who had gone to school in Sweden for 11 years and was deaf himself, returned to Finland and founded Finland's first school for the deaf. Malm brought with him the language – Swedish sign language – which was gradually adopted by the Finnish deaf (Jantunen, 2001: 6–12; Rainò, 2000). The Finnish and Swedish sign languages have developed in their own directions over the course of the years, and now they cannot be easily mutually understood (see Malm, 2000).

Even though the Finnish sign language has regional dialects and there are differences in the signing, e.g. different age groups, those who use the sign language as their first language can understand each other very well (Malm, 2000). The sign language of the Finland-Swedish deaf can, however, be considered a separate language, and the Finland-Swedish deaf normally change their way of signing considerably when communicating with a person using the main variant of the Finnish sign language (Hoyer, 2000).

At present, many universities, the Research Institute for the Languages of Finland and the Finnish Association of the Deaf, conduct active research into sign language (see e.g. Takkinen, 2002). The first basic dictionary of Finnish sign language, *Suomalaisen viittomakielen perussanakirja*, was published in 1998 (Malm, 1998) and the first dictionary of Finland-Swedish sign language in 2002 (Hoyer, 2002).

Russian

One of the oldest minorities in Finland is the Russian-speaking population. The Russians with the oldest ties with Finland are the descendants of the serfs who were transferred from Russia to eastern Finland – to the area Sweden-Finland had to cede to Russia in the 18th century. The area was administratively organised under the Russian Government of Wyborg (Viipuri). During the period of autonomy, there were various groups of Russian-speaking people in Finland, especially merchants. In 1870, speakers of Russian constituted 12.1% of the population in Helsinki, in 1880 around 9.6%, and in 1900 only 4.7%. In 1920 there were about 5000 Russians in Finland. Their number decreased slightly, partly as a result of assimilation into the Swedish-speaking population, and partly through remigration to the Soviet Union. Since the 1960s, Russians or speakers of Russian have immigrated to Finland in increasing numbers (Baschmakoff & Leinonen, 2001; Nylund-Oja *et al.*, 1995). That immigration was extensive, especially during the 1990s. One reason for this was that the Finnish government gave the status of re-migrants to people with Finnish roots in Ingria. In 2002, the number of speakers of Russian in Finland was about 32,000. The Russian-speaking population lives all over the country.

The small group of Russians, therefore, has a long history in Finland. As the third largest language group in Finland, Russian-speaking people have a better opportunity to maintain and develop their language and culture in their new homeland than smaller groups. However, the Russians do not have the status of a ratified minority in Finland (see Part III).

Tatar

Another old minority without official status in Finland is the Tatars. Their language, Tatar, belongs to the Altaic family, Turkic group (North Western). The first Tatars came to Finland from the Kazan area in Russia in the late 19th century as merchants, trading furs and textiles. Most Tatars immigrated in the first quarter of the 20th century, and settled initially in Helsinki and its surroundings. In the 1930s, immigration stopped because of a stricter Soviet emigration policy (Horn, 1999).

At present, the Tatars are a well-established minority. Most of the Tatars live in Helsinki, or in the neighbouring areas, with a few smaller groups also living in other parts of Finland (Halikov, 1991). The number of Tatars has remained fairly constant at slightly under 1000 over the years. While having integrated well into Finnish society, they have been able to maintain their traditions and language (Halén, 1999).

Jewish people and their languages

The ancestors of the Jewish people in Finland came to Finland at the end of the 18th century. During the period of Finnish autonomy, more Jewish people from Russia established themselves as tradesmen or craftsmen or were retired officers

142   *Language Planning and Policy in Europe*

from the Czarist army. It was only after 1917, however, that Jewish people were granted full rights as Finnish citizens.

The first Jewish people who moved to Finland during the 19th century spoke Yiddish as their first language. Some of the Jewish people who arrived later had Russian as their first language. When settling in Finland, Jewish people chose Swedish as their first language. Until 1930, all of the Jewish people in Finland had registered Swedish as their first language. The language of instruction at the Jewish School was Swedish. In 1932, however, Finnish replaced it (Harviainen, 1998).[7]

Other minority languages

For a long time, Finland was not a migration destination, but rather an emigration country. At the turn of the 20th century, there were large groups that emigrated from Finland primarily to North America. From the 1950s through to the 1970s, there was another wave of emigration. Tens of thousands of Finns emigrated, notably to Sweden. Since the 1860s, a total of 1.1 million Finns have emigrated to other countries.

After World War II, Finland practised an extremely restrictive refugee and immigration policy for several decades. The smallest number of foreign citizens was recorded at the end of the 1950s: in 1957, there were only approximately 4500 foreigners living in Finland. The number of foreigners started to rise gradually in the 1960s. It was not until the 1980s, however, that the number of immigrants increased and exceeded the number of emigrants. In other words, Finland experienced a change from an emigrant country to an immigrant country relatively late in comparison with, for example, other Nordic countries. Since the beginning of the 1990s, the number of foreign citizens in Finland has increased rapidly (Latomaa, 1996).

The migration histories of the Nordic countries are similar in many respects. On the one hand, the Nordic countries were isolated culturally and linguistically for a very long time, and their inhabitants therefore have had little experience with foreigners. On the other hand, it meant that people immigrating to the Nordic countries have little prior knowledge of the area, compared, for example, with Indians or Jamaicans coming to Britain (Latomaa, 1995). However, there are many differences between the migration histories of the various Nordic countries as well. Sweden has hosted the largest number of immigrants, both in terms of absolute numbers and in terms of percentages, while Finland has had a restrictive immigration and refugee policy, thus resembling Eastern rather than Western Europe. The number of immigrants living in Finland is still low, compared to that in the other Nordic countries (Nuolijärvi, 1994a). At the end of 2001, the number of foreign citizens (98,577), permanently resident in Finland amounted to approximately 1.9% of the total population of Finland.

The linguistic map of Finland has undergone interesting changes during the last two decades of the 20th century. Slowly but steadily, the number of speakers of different languages has grown. According to the statistics, more than 120 languages were spoken in Finland at the end of the 1990s, and in 2000 there were over 20 languages spoken by more than 1000 people (Table 5)[8]. In 2000, 10 of the most widely used languages (according to the number of speakers) were Finnish, Swedish, Russian, Estonian, English, Somali, Arabic, Vietnamese, German and

Table 5 Twenty of the largest languages[1] by number of speakers in Finland 1990 and 2000

Language	1 Jan 1990	Language	1 Jan 2000
Finnish	4,656,325	Finnish	4,788,497
Swedish	296,840	Swedish	291,657
Russian	3,072	Russian	28,205
English	3,053	Estonian	10,176
German	2,302	English	6,919
Saami	1,730	Somali	6,454
Vietnamese	1,206	Arabic	4,892
Arabic	866	Vietnamese	3,588
Spanish	788	German	3,298
Estonian	740	Albanian	3,293
Turkish	703	Kurdish	3,115
Polish	702	Chinese	2,907
French	614	Turkish	2,435
Chinese	517	Serbo-Croatian	2,166
Hungarian	448	Spanish	1,946
Italian	372	Saami	1,734
Norwegian	345	French	1,585
Danish	259	Thai	1,458
Japanese	249	Persian (Farsi)	1,205
Greek	242	Polish	1,157

Source: Nuolijärvi (1991: 25); *Statistical Yearbook of Finland* (2001: 112–3)
[1] The language categories used in the statistics are broad: the number of speakers given for some languages (e.g. Saami, Chinese, Serbo-Croatian) may, in fact, consist of several languages.

Albanian. The situation of Finnish and Swedish has remained more or less stable, and Russian and Estonian seem to have gained a permanent position on the linguistic map of Finland. There are also a few new language groups in Finland, like the speakers of Somali and the speakers of Albanian. For example, Somali was not represented at all in the linguistic statistics of Finland in 1990. The greatest changes are, in fact, connected to political developments in certain European, Asian and African regions, as the slight increase in the proportions of Russian, Estonian, Somali, Vietnamese, and Arabic speakers shows. The statistics are not unproblematic; there are bilingual people who have difficulties in determining which one of their languages is their first language.[9] However, Table 5 reveals the main lines of the linguistic diversity in Finland at the beginning of the 21st century.

In addition, the statistics of those born abroad is of relevance when describing the migration situation. In 1980, there were only 39,153 people born abroad, in 1990 the number was 64,922, and in 2000 136,203 (*Statistical Yearbook of Finland*, 2001: 110).

Immigrants have come to Finland for various reasons. Many come to Finland as migrants with family ties: a great number of foreign citizens in Finland are married to Finns. Moreover, there are returnees, mostly from Scandinavia and the former Soviet Union (Finnish-speaking people from Ingria). In addition, refugees and asylum seekers constitute a visible group of immigrants (Nieminen, M., 2000). At the beginning of the 1990s, the annual number of asylum seekers grew quickly, from less than 100 to more than 3000. The number of asylum seekers has now decreased, however, due to a shift towards a more restrictive migration policy. From 1986 on, Finland has accepted refugees on a quota basis. The quota has varied between 500 and 1000. By the end of 2001, Finland had received approximately 20,000 refugees in total. Even so, in comparison with other European countries, the number of refugees and asylum seekers in Finland is still very small.[10] In addition to the groups mentioned above, some of the newcomers have come to Finland to study at various educational institutions. Unlike many other European countries, however, Finland has never had a large influx of labour migrants ('guest workers').

The Foreign Language Profile

Foreign language education has a long tradition in the Finnish school system. The geopolitical location of the country, the official bilingualism of Finnish society, and the limited possibilities to use the national languages in an international context have made the learning of foreign languages vital for the Finnish people. Internationally speaking, Finns study a large number of languages.

The popularity of various foreign languages has varied over time. Towards the end of the 20th century, English has gained ground from other languages, primarily from German and Russian. However, even if the variety of languages chosen at school has become narrower, skills in foreign languages have in general become more common in Finland. Since the comprehensive school reform in the 1970s, entire school generations have studied at least two languages other than their native language, one being the second national language, Swedish or Finnish. The leading goal of the Finnish language teaching policy has been diversification of the language teaching provision (see Part II).

Literacy in Finland

Finland has enjoyed 100% literacy for a long time. This is a result of the long tradition of education in the Lutheran Church and the comprehensive coverage of the elementary schools in the country. Literacy today means that every Finn, irrespective of her or his first language, can read Finnish or Swedish.

The roots of the literacy among Finnish and Swedish-speaking Finns date from the beginning of the Lutheran Reformation in the 16th century. In the late 17th century and at the beginning of the 18th century, the bishop of the capital city, Turku, Johan Gezelius the elder, especially stressed the education of children and youth. His ABC-book was very popular among the people. The Catechetical meetings,[11] where each citizen's level of literacy was recorded in the parish register, were decisive in the work for greater literacy. Even in those days, it was essential for young men and women to know how to read, because otherwise they were not allowed to marry. During the time of the following bishop, Johan Gezelius the

Table 6 The development of reading and writing from 1880 to 1930 in Finland

Finnish Lutheran people				
		No reading or writing skills	Can only read	Can both read and write
Year	N	%	%	%
1880	1,592 593	1.3	86.3	12.4
1890	1,866 442	0.1	78.0	21.9
1900	2,177 633	0.8	60.6	38.6
1910	1,840 270	0.6	44.1	55.3
1920	2,018 270	0.6	29.3	70.1
1930	2,285 915	0.7	15.2	84.1
Orthodox people				
		No reading or writing skills	Can only read	Can both read and write
Year	N	%	%	%
1880	30,865	54.4	21.7	23.9
1890	35,781	44.8	21.7	33.5
1900	39,710	39.3	14.7	46.0
1910	30,605	33.7	13.1	53.1
1920	33,314	23.2	18.0	58.8
1930	43,309	15.7	8.0	76.3

Source: Lehmuskallio (1983)

younger, literacy became common. In the 18th century, the Church focused on the development of literacy. The amount of published literature increased, which increased people's interest in reading (Lehmuskallio, 1983).

Thus, elementary school had, in fact, already been developed by the Church. Yet, the decree on elementary schools (1896) did not become effective until 1921. According to the law, every child at seven years of age had the right to go to elementary school for six years. Reading and writing skills were available to everybody in Finland. Table 6 illustrates this development during the last years of the Russian era and at the beginning of the period of independence.

Today, in international comparisons of first language reading skills, Finnish pupils succeed quite well (see Part II). Finland took part in *the Second International Adult Literacy Survey* (SIALS) (Linnakylä *et al.*, 2000). The Finnish data for the survey were collected in 1998. In the SIALS, literacy was examined as an adult skill using printed and written information for acting in society, achieving one's goals, and developing one's knowledge and potential. Adult literacy was assessed in three domains: prose literacy, document literacy, and quantitative literacy. The results were based on a representative sample of the Finnish adult population between the ages of 16 and 65.

According to that survey, the majority of the Finnish adult population, about two thirds, were proficient readers across the three different domains. Approximately 20% of them were even able to reach the highest performance level, necessary for carrying out expert tasks in an information society. However, a third of adult Finns belonged to the group that was literate in the traditional sense but showed a relatively low performance level. In the international comparison among 20 participating countries, Finland reached a level of literacy of a Nordic standard. All of the Nordic countries were clearly above the international average in the three domains. The extent of initial formal education proved to be the most important predicting factor in the level of adult literacy both nationally and internationally. Age was also important: the younger the respondents, the better their literacy scores. While gender-based differences in literacy levels were fairly small in Finland, there was regional variation: people living in urban regions proved to be more literate than people in rural areas. However, this difference could be explained mostly by differences in the level of education. Furthermore, the educational delivery in rural areas is sometimes more constrained than in urban areas.

Two thirds of the Finnish adults had literacy skills that fulfilled the requirements for an information society with regard to working and learning. One third of the adults, however, should have better literacy skills if they are to take up self-regulated studies. The statistics did not measure differences among first languages.

Among the adult immigrants who have come to Finland there are some illiterates. It is also important that these people have an opportunity to develop their skills in their first language, not only in Finland's national languages, Finnish and Swedish (see Part II).

The Major Religions

After the Protestant Reformation in the early 16th century, the Lutheran Church was the only official religion in Finland. During the Russian autonomy period (1809–1917), the status of the Orthodox Church became stronger, as the immigrating Russians brought their religions with them into the main parts of the country; among people who moved to Finland from Russia in the 19th century, there were people from other religious traditions, i.e. Roman Catholics, Jews and Muslims. However, religions other than Lutheran and Orthodox and some protestant churches (Methodists, Baptists) were not tolerated until the 20th century. The Religious Freedom Law in 1922 granted citizens the right to found religious denominations freely or to remain entirely outside of them (Heino, 1997; Martikainen, 2000a, 2000c).

Table 7 Religious affiliation in Finland in 1920–2000 by percentage of population

Year	Lutheran	Orthodox	Other religious communities	No religious affiliation
1920	98.1	1.6	0.3	0.0
1940	95.9	1.8	0.3	2.0
1960	92.4	1.4	0.7	5.5
1980	90.3	1.1	0.7	7.8
2000	85.1	1.1	1.1	12.7

Source: Salonen *et al.* (2000: 22); SF (2001)

Currently, a clear majority of the population belongs to the Finnish Evangelical Lutheran Church, and 1% of the population are members of the other national church, the Finnish Orthodox Church (see Table 7). Those belonging to other religious communities additionally comprise 1% of the total population. According to the latest statistics (SF, 2001), there are, for example, 18,492 Jehovah's Witnesses, 13,474 members of the Free church in Finland, 7227 Roman Catholics and 1157 Jews in Finland. In the national statistics, the total number of members in Muslim communities is 1199 but this constitutes only a fraction of the actual number of practising Muslims in Finland. Martikainen (2000b) estimates that there are actually between 10,000 and 15,000 Muslims in Finland.[12]

The Finnish Evangelical Lutheran Church functions mainly in Finnish and Swedish, while most congregations of the Finnish Orthodox Church use only Finnish for services. Since the 1990s, however, both national churches have increasingly paid attention to minority languages (see Part II).

PART II: Language Spread

The Spread of National Languages

In this section, the status of the national languages of Finland is examined from a number of perspectives. First, the national education system is described briefly. Second, Finnish and Swedish are examined in the various roles they have in the educational system. The objectives of language education as well as the effectiveness of instruction are discussed. Furthermore, the use of the national languages is described in religious life and in the media.

The national education system

A brief history

During the Swedish era (12th century to 1809), education was governed by the Church, having been provided in monastic schools and in the cathedral school in Turku. Instruction was given in Latin, and it aimed primarily at an ecclesiastical career. The Lutheran reformation introduced the idea of vernacular education (in Swedish), but Latin remained the main language of instruction for a long time. The first Finnish university was established in Turku in 1640. In the 19th century, vocational education was introduced in Finland to meet the needs of rapidly growing industry. A decree issued in 1898 included an obligation for the local authorities to provide all school-aged children with an opportunity for schooling (NBE, 2001).

During the period of autonomy (1809–1917), the legislation and the social system from the Swedish era were preserved. Russian educational statutes were not applied to Finland, and efforts to strengthen the position of Russian as a language of instruction were not successful. Swedish was the main language of instruction for most of the 19th century. However, growing nationalism affected the school system. At the beginning of the 1870s, there were only four Finnish-language state schools for boys and no Finnish-language schools for girls. As the idea of Fennomanism became more widespread, new Finnish-language secondary schools were gradually founded. The situation changed rapidly. At the end of Russian rule, two-thirds of secondary schools were Finnish. Two decades later, only 20% of secondary schools had Swedish as the medium of instruction (Mustaparta & Tella, 1999; Paunonen, 1997).

Extension of education to all citizens and to all parts of the country and the continuous efforts to raise the level of education constituted a policy for the young nation from the very beginning. In the 1919 Constitution, an obligation was laid down to provide for general free compulsory education. Moreover, the public authorities were required to maintain or support general education, vocational education, applied art and scientific higher education, as well as university education. General compulsory education was prescribed by law in 1921. Up until the 1970s, compulsory education was provided in the six-year elementary school. After four years of elementary school, a part of each age group moved up to the secondary school – the remainder completing the final two years of primary schooling. The secondary school was divided into the five-year lower secondary school and the three-year upper secondary school. In the 1970s, the comprehensive school common to the entire age class was introduced (NBE, 2001). A further streamlining occurred at the end of the 1990s. The comprehensive school used to be divided into lower (1–6) and upper stages (7–9). This administrative division was abolished at the beginning of 1999. Currently, the Finnish school system consists of pre-school education, basic education,[13] upper secondary education, and higher education. Since Finland became independent, the national school system has been divided into Finnish-speaking and Swedish-speaking sections. This has ensured the educational rights of the Swedish-speaking minority, as instruction is given in Swedish at all levels. The aims of educational policy and the curriculum content are similar for both the Finnish-speaking and the Swedish-speaking sections (SF, 1999).

The current educational system

Compulsory education in Finland consists of pre-school education for six-year-old children and nine years of basic education (grades 1–9) for children between the ages of seven and 16 (see Figure 1). Pupils can also take a voluntary 10th grade. There are two types of upper secondary education in Finland: general upper secondary schools and vocational schools. Upper secondary schools provide general education. When the pupils complete their upper secondary schooling, they take the national matriculation examination, i.e. the Year 12 school leaving examination (see http://www.minedu.fi/yo-tutkinto/ for further information). The examination consists of nation-wide tests on various subjects, and it provides a general university entrance qualification. About 60% of the cohort completes the matriculation examination.

In the early 1990s, a new type of educational institution, the polytechnic, was created. Currently, there are 31 polytechnics in Finland. The polytechnic degrees are at the same level as lower university degrees but have a vocational orientation. There are 21 universities in Finland, all of which are state-run and engage in both education and research. The higher university degree is designed to take 5–6 years to complete after the matriculation examination. Admission to Finnish universities is highly selective: universities offer openings for about one-third of

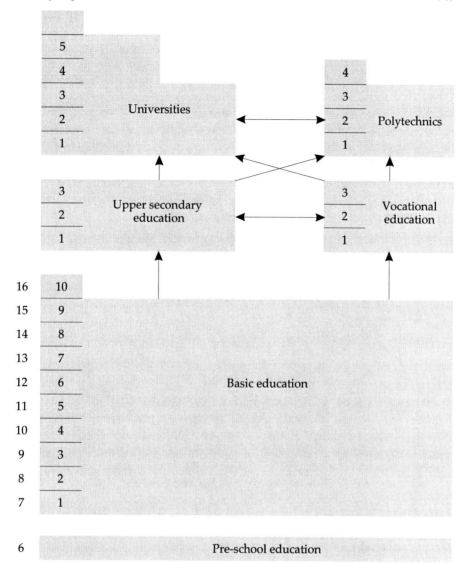

Figure 1 The education system of Finland
Source: NBE (2001)

the cohort. All fields apply *numerus clausus*, in which entrance examinations are a key element (SF, 1999).

The regulations governing the education system have been extensively revised during the 1990s. Decision-making has been significantly decentralised, and schools have been given greater autonomy than before. The government decides the broad national objectives and the distribution of teaching time for instruction in different subjects and subject groups. The National Board of Education (NBE) decides on the objectives and central contents of instruction by confirming the core curriculum. Based on the national objectives and core contents of instruction, each municipality prepares a local curriculum. Each school draws up a school-based curriculum that expresses the school's function, special character and educational assumptions. It also determines the allocation of time between subjects, based on the guidelines prescribed by the government, and at what level instruction in the various subjects is commenced. Further, the government decides whether teaching is given in groups independent of the class, what optional languages and what elective subjects are offered, how hours are divided among the compulsory subjects and the elective subjects, etc.

The most recent national core curricula date from 1994. The reform of the national core curricula for both basic education and upper secondary education is currently under way. The new curricula will be phased in for basic education in 2004–2006 and for upper secondary education in 2005.

Finnish/Swedish language and literature

This section aims to give an overview of mother-tongue education[14] in the national languages. First, the objectives set in the national core curriculum are described briefly. Second, the development of the field is examined from the viewpoint of Finnish language and literature. In addition, the challenges that the teaching of Swedish language and literature have recently met are described briefly. Thereafter, the effectiveness of instruction is examined in the light of some national and international studies. Finally, recent discussion on mother-tongue education is described.

Objectives and content

In the national core curriculum for basic education, the general aims of teaching Finnish language and literature include the following: 'the student's self-esteem, desire to express him/herself and courage are reinforced, and s/he develops into a skilful communicator' (NBE, 1994: 47). As for the aim of teaching Swedish, the first objective mentioned is 'to give the student such linguistic sureness that s/he dares and wants and knows how to express him/herself neutrally, understandably and according to each situation, both orally and in writing' (NBE, 1994: 52).

The field of mother-tongue education has always been sensitive to educational trends and continuously has broadened to include new tasks. Moreover, there has always been competition between the two parts making up the subject, with emphasis being laid either on language or on literature, depending on the prevailing view. In the 1960s, the focus gradually shifted from knowledge to skills, and literature became the content for practising various language skills. This change in focus was included in the first national core curriculum for comprehensive schools that was drawn up in the 1970s. It was criticised harshly because of the large amount of required but unrelated content that was prescribed, especially when considering the small number of hours allotted to the subject. The national curriculum was later adjusted in order to give more detailed guidance for teachers. The reforms of the 1970s made a substantial impact on the work done in schools for several decades. In the 1990s, the modest status of literature in mother-tongue education was brought up for discussion again. In 1999, the subject was renamed: instead of *Language* (*äidinkieli*, lit. 'mother tongue') it is now called *Language and literature* (*äidinkieli ja kirjallisuus*, lit. 'mother tongue and literature'). Both areas are included in teaching more equally than before, not as separate courses but integrated in the same study units (Buchberger, 2002; Lonka, 1998).

As far as Swedish is concerned, the need for differentiated instruction has grown stronger, since the language situation in Swedish-medium schools has changed rapidly. Currently, classes are much more mixed linguistically than, for example, in the 1980s. The number of bilingual pupils has grown mainly as a result of two factors: the number of mixed marriages has increased considerably, and bilingual parents have started to pay attention to school choice and bilingual issues in education in general. Currently, bilingual families choose Swedish-medium instead of Finnish-medium schools more often than had been the practice earlier. The new situation has created a major challenge for teachers. How can one determine the actual skills of pupils who seem to speak the language quite fluently but may still lack a number of concepts and some points of grammar in Swedish? More importantly, how can one develop these skills? Earlier, there was no need to take bilingual pupils into consideration in either curricula or teacher training, and, consequently, schools and teachers are now encountering a situation for which they were not prepared (Sundman, 1998).

Consequently, several campaigns and development projects have been carried out in Swedish-medium schools to create a learning environment that would develop the Swedish skills of bilingual pupils (Sommardahl, 2002; Sundman, 1998). In schools, there is a syllabus called *förstärkt modersmål* (lit. 'reinforced mother tongue') for pupils from bilingual homes, where Finnish is the dominant language. The purpose of this special syllabus is to give bilingual pupils an opportunity to achieve the same level of proficiency as their monolingual classmates. Instruction in reinforced Swedish can be given throughout basic education (NBE, 1994).

The effectiveness of instruction

In upper secondary schools, the effectiveness of instruction in language and literature has been evaluated annually in the matriculation examination. Evaluations at the stage of completion of grade 6 and grade 9, initiated by the NBE, have been undertaken only recently.

The first nation-wide study of the learning results of 6th graders ($N = 4251$) was based on written use tests (Korkeakoski, 2001), whereas learning performance of 9th graders ($N = 5050$) was evaluated using a variety of individual tests in reading skills, language competence and writing, as well as a verbal communication test carried out by a smaller sample (Lappalainen, 2000). Both studies revealed that there are major differences between girls' and boys' learning results at both grade levels: girls scored better in all subtests. This result was explained by differences in attitudes and leisure-time activities: girls' attitudes towards their first language were more positive, and they read twice the number of books that boys read (Korkeakoski, 2001). In Swedish-medium sample schools, 6th graders' scores for writing were slightly better than those achieved by Finnish-speaking pupils. In international comparison, this result is exceptional, since the achievement level of a linguistic minority is, in general, lower than that of the linguistic majority (Hannén, 2001). As for the study among 9th graders, no statistically significant differences between Finnish-medium and Swedish-medium schools were found. In contrast to the study among 6th graders, the learning results of 9th graders demonstrated some regional differences (Lappalainen, 2000). At the stage of completion of basic education, pupils achieved high scores for reading skills, especially in tests evaluating the ability to search for information and to find facts from a given text. However, the most difficult skill areas for 9th graders included written expression and language competence (Lappalainen, 2000).

Lappalainen's (2000) results were viewed with some scepticism by language and literature teachers. Criticism was targeted, among other things, at the validity of the test (Mustonen *et al.*, 1999). However, despite potential flaws in the first national test, its impact on the teaching of language and literature was useful: it opened a discussion about the state of education, and the poor results obtained in northern Finland were examined carefully. New campaigns for the promotion of reading were launched (*Kirjaseikkailu* ['Reading Adventure'] and *Lukuhaaste* ['Challenge to Read']), as part of a new priority project (*Luku-Suomi* ['Reading Finland']) of the NBE for the years 2001–2004, in order to awaken interest in reading, especially in boys, and to support less successful pupils in their language development.

Even though the results of the national tests have caused many people to worry, little attention has been given to the fact that Finnish pupils have succeeded well in international surveys concerning one part of language competence, reading literacy. In contrast to some previous international assessments that more or less concentrated on 'school' knowledge, the PISA (Programme for International Student Assessment) assessment of reading literacy aimed at measuring how well students perform beyond the school curriculum. In the study, 15-year-old Finnish pupils were found to achieve the best[15] results when compared with their peers in 28 OECD countries and in four countries outside the OECD. Canada was second, and then came New Zealand, Australia, Ireland, Korea, England, Japan and Sweden: 50% of Finnish pupils were rated as excellent readers (the mean value being 32%), and they were found to be especially skilful in searching for information, as well as in understanding and interpreting the material used (OECD, 2001).

Coincident with PISA, a second nation-wide NBE evaluation among ninth-graders' learning performance was published (Lappalainen, 2001). Altogether 3891 pupils took the test, which incorporated a variety of tasks, different from the evaluation done two years earlier. This time competence and skills were found to be similar throughout the country; regional differences were small. As in the earlier studies, the general level of reading literacy was found to be at a high level (68% of the maximum score). However, both studies conducted with 9th graders as well as the one conducted with 6th graders have revealed that writing skills of Finnish pupils are, on average, only satisfactory. For example, in Lappalainen's most recent study (2001), the average score for written expression was less than 60% (boys 50%, girls 68%) of the maximum score. Writing skills were evaluated over two texts (informative, expressive) to be written on the basis of material provided. The third task consisted of correcting a short text. The majority of pupils were found to be unaccustomed to drafting and editing their texts as a regular procedure. The level of writing skills varied considerably from school to school.

The situation of upper secondary education is no different from that of basic education. In the public debate, the weakening skills of students have been under extensive scrutiny. It has been argued that, among other things, spelling and grammatical mistakes have increased recently (Maamies, 2002). Lyytikäinen (2000) collected results of a number of studies in which errors made by students in their matriculation examination over several decades had been analysed. On the basis of these studies, he concluded that the number of errors has, in fact, increased somewhat over the past few decades. However, Lyytikäinen points out that this is only to be expected as the proportion of the population taking the exam has grown. Currently, about 60% of the cohort takes the matriculation examination, as compared to the situation three decades ago, when only 20% took the exam.

The committee report of the Ministry of Education (OPM, 2000) stated that the results of the matriculation examination had suddenly declined in 1996 and continued to decline throughout the rest of the decade (see also Leino, 2002). As the test type, assessment criteria and evaluators were the same, the committee of the Ministry of Education (OPM, 2000) stated that explanations for the growing diversity of the results in the matriculation examination would have to be found elsewhere, among other things, in teaching arrangements, national core curricula, hourly allotment and changes in the cultural situation in general. In fact, the number of obligatory courses in language and literature decreased from eight to six in the mid-1990s, and, not surprisingly, since then more than half of the students have taken only the required number of courses. In addition, the students' leisure-time reading activity has decreased from what it used to be. Leino (2002) points out that the present situation is to a high degree a result of the political decisions made at the beginning of the 1990s and thus it reflects the attitudinal climate of current Finnish society: economic growth and internationalism are valued more than anything else.

Traditionally, the test for the matriculation examination consisted of two compositions to be written about given topics (e.g. 'Us and them', 'Humour in literature', 'What is evilness?'). Since 1992, one of the compositions has been written on the basis of the samples of material provided (newspaper articles, literature, etc.). Taking both exams into consideration, the final grade has been assigned on the basis of the student's higher score, the lower score being discarded. Leino (2002) remarks that this test type is too narrow, and that the 'wash-back' effect of setting it has not helped to focus the instruction in language and literature towards the objectives mentioned in the national core curriculum. Therefore, in the coming years, one of the compositions will be replaced by a test of reading comprehension, testing especially critical and analytical reading skills. Both parts of the test will be included in the final grade.[16]

The weakening language skills of students in Swedish-medium upper secondary schools have also been under extensive scrutiny. For example, Leinonen and Tandefelt (2000) studied beginning university students from this perspective. Their test (a test of idioms and a cloze-test) results were compared with those of university students in Sweden. On average, Sweden Swedes scored better than Finland Swedes in both tests. Not surprisingly, regional differences between students from various parts of Finland were considerable: e.g. students from Ostrobothnia achieved better results than those from bilingual southern Finland.

Language-in-education planning

Since the 1990s, there has been extensive discussion of mother-tongue education in schools (Buchberger, 2002). This discussion has mainly concerned the amount of teaching of these languages. It has been suggested that the number of hours allotted to language and literature is 'a national shame'. On several occasions, the lesson per week quota in language and literature in Finnish schools has been compared with that of other European countries. Also the content of education has been discussed: How much and in what ways should grammar and writing be taught? What is the role of communication education, media education and literature?

Besides the amount and content of teaching, the status of the subject in general has been discussed. In 1993, a suggestion made by the working group for the reform of the matriculation examination gave rise to a heated debate. The group suggested that students should choose the subjects in which they wanted to be tested. Traditionally, there had been four compulsory subjects in the matriculation examination: language and literature, the second national language, a foreign language, and either mathematics or general studies (biology, chemistry, ethics, geography, history, philosophy, psychology, physics, religion and social studies). The debate gradually resulted in another suggestion: that language and literature would be the only compulsory subject and all the other subjects would be optional. This suggestion was not accepted, and the regulations were retained. Since the beginning of the 1990s, however, the practice of having language and literature as the only compulsory subject has been tried out experimentally in about 30 schools. At the beginning of 2002, the results of the experiment were published, and the proposal to restructure the matriculation examination was raised again in public and parliamentary discussions.

Referring to the results of the nation-wide tests in basic education and the most recent results of the matriculation examination, among other measures, the working group for the reform of basic education stated in its memorandum (OPM, 2001) that skills in Finnish are, in fact, in decline in Finland. According to the working group, the overall impression given by the results is fair, but the group was especially concerned about regional and gender-based differences. The working group considered that the situation is critical, since the status of Finnish, Swedish and Saami as small languages is weakening in the globalising culture. They also pointed out that the lesson-per-week quota is relatively small in Finland – the smallest allocation among the Nordic countries. Also in comparison with other EU countries, the lesson-per-week quota in primary education (at around age seven) is clearly smaller (24%) in Finland than in many other countries, e.g. Austria (33%), Denmark (45%), France (35%) and Greece (36%). In lower secondary education, native language is taught least in Finland. The time devoted to mother-tongue education in Finland represents only 9%, while in, e.g. Denmark and Italy the compulsory minimum amount of time allocated to this subject represents 20% of the total timetable (EC, 2000).

On the basis of international comparisons, of analyses of curricula and of evaluation results, the working group proposed in its memorandum (OPM, 2001) that two lessons per week across the entire school year (76 lessons) be added to the teaching of language and literature in basic education. Of this time, at least 45 minutes per (one-hour) lesson should be dedicated to instruction. In December 2001, the government decided on the aims and time allocation of basic education, and accepted, among other things, the proposal of the working group, thus decreasing the time allotted to optional studies (e.g. music, arts, craft, and home economics). The time allocation will be implemented when the NBE gradually adopts the new national core curriculum in 2004–2006.

Interestingly enough, this decision to add resources to the teaching of language and literature was made in the same month that the first results of PISA were published. In general, the results that Finnish pupils achieved in the PISA study did not get much publicity in Finland, until a large number of reporters from other European countries, especially Germany, had shown an overwhelming interest in the 'secret' of the Finnish school system. Only then was there more extensive coverage in the newspapers. Typically, the Finnish experts interviewed were not ready to celebrate the results; rather, they emphasised their concerns about the least successful pupils. They were also pondering whether the same education for all is stimulating enough for the most gifted pupils.

Finnish and Swedish as second national languages

Objectives and content

Learning Swedish is compulsory for all Finnish-speaking pupils, and learning Finnish is compulsory for all Swedish-speaking pupils, except on the Åland Islands, where pupils may choose Finnish on a voluntary basis. In general, teaching of Finnish starts in grade 3, whereas teaching of Swedish starts a few years later, in grade 7.

The objectives of teaching second national languages in Finland seem strikingly different: whereas the aims of teaching Finnish are described in quite neutral terms, the aims of teaching Swedish include several points that have to do with attitudes. Not surprisingly, the central problem of teaching Swedish is the negative attitudes of pupils and, thus, their lack of motivation for studying it. In the national tests of Swedish, girls seem to achieve better results than boys, and pupils living in towns achieve slightly better results than do those living in the rural areas. Research on attitudes has resulted in a similar kind of distribution (OPH, 1999a).

The central problem of teaching Finnish as a second national language (*finska*) has to do with the very heterogeneous linguistic background of pupils (OPH, 1999a). More than one-third of the pupils in the Swedish-medium schools come from bilingual homes. In addition, approximately 20% of the pupils regularly hear and speak Finnish in their surroundings. However, 45% do not have any contact with Finnish outside of school. The majority of bilingual families and pupils live in towns, especially in the capital region, Turku and other larger coastal towns. Monolingualism is concentrated in the rural areas of Ostrobothnia and Uusimaa, and in the archipelago of Turku and the Åland Islands (see Map 3).

Pupils who come from bilingual homes may choose the so-called mother-tongue-like syllabus of Finnish (*modersmålsinriktad finska*) instead of regular instruction in Finnish as a second language. In 1994, for the first time, the aims and description of this kind of instruction were included in the national core curricula. The purpose of mother-tongue-like Finnish is 'to grant bilingual students a chance to improve and further their language skills which they have acquired at home or in their surroundings through natural means, to make them aware of this language and thus to reinforce their identity' (NBE, 1994: 70). In principle, it has been possible to choose this option since 1988, but, in practice, the availability of instruction has largely depended on the resources of municipalities and schools. Moreover, the situation is problematic in other ways as well, as there are not enough teaching materials and teachers trained especially for this kind of instruction (Sundman, 1998). At present, there is no separate test for mother-tongue-like Finnish in the matriculation examination, and that is why most bilingual students still choose the traditional test in Finnish as a second national language (OPH, 1999a).

Language-in-education planning

In the question of second languages in the curriculum, Finland faces difficult problems of choice, since both of its national languages have a relatively limited international outreach. The problem for educational planning is to find an appropriate balance between the mother tongue, the other national language, and the most needed international languages.

The field of Finnish as a second language was, in fact, initiated early in the 17th and 18th centuries, when the first grammars and dictionaries of Finnish were written. They were meant for Swedish-speaking learners of Finnish. The need for learning Finnish became even more acute in the 19th century, when Finnish became an official language in the autonomous Grand Duchy. As early as the 1860s, Finnish as a second national language appeared in the curricula of Swedish-medium secondary schools, and also teacher training for this field was initiated (Geber, 1982).

Prior to the educational reform in the 1970s, the curriculum for the elementary school did not call for study of any language other than the language of the school. In contrast with the elementary system, secondary schools prior to reform emphasised languages extensively. Both the mother tongue and the second national language were required subjects through all eight years of the secondary curriculum. By the mid-1920s, some Finnish nationalists were questioning the continuing role of Swedish in Finnish-medium schools and calling for greater emphasis on international languages, but their attempts to reduce Swedish to the status of an optional language were unsuccessful. In the mid-1930s, some Finnish nationalists urged that Finnish be taught in Swedish-medium elementary schools to give pupils a better preparation for working in an increasingly Finnish-speaking environment. However, the Swedish-speaking political leadership strongly opposed the proposal (McRae, 1997).

The wide discrepancy between the elementary and the secondary systems made the language question one of the more difficult issues of the educational reform in the 1970s. By this time speakers of Swedish had generally accepted the need for all Swedish-speaking elementary pupils to learn Finnish, but they sought a solution in which Finnish schools would teach Swedish on a reciprocal basis. However, Finnish-speaking educators were more concerned with bridging the gulf between Finnish and various international languages. The issue provoked a long, hard-fought parliamentary struggle, which ended in a compromise: a new nine-year curriculum would require all pupils to take a seven-year course in a second language beginning in the third year, plus a less demanding three-year course in a third language beginning in the seventh year. One of these two languages would be the second national language (Swedish or Finnish) and the other a modern international language, but the choice of which to introduce first was left to local education authorities (McRae, 1997). Even after the adoption of the comprehensive school in the 1970s, opposition to the compromise has regularly surfaced, primarily from the Finnish side (see e.g. Herberts & Landgärds, 1992). Most recently, these views were expressed in connection with public and parliamentary discussions about the restructuring of the matriculation examination. But, no decision has yet been made about the proposal to have language and literature as the only compulsory subject and all the other subjects – including the second national language – as optional subjects.

Immersion in national languages

During the late 1970s and early 1980s, the unsatisfactory state of traditional language education led to the initiation of several bilingual education projects. The first programmes were aimed at attending to the needs of Swedish-speaking bilingual pupils. Although these first programmes were restricted to two or three hours a week, the second language of the pupils was introduced as the main medium of instruction during these hours and thus a new way of teaching a second language was introduced. In 1991, a change in Finnish education legislation enabled schools to use a language other than a pupil's native language as the language of instruction. Since this change, numerous bilingual education programmes have been initiated (Björklund, 1997). They range from minimal bilingual instruction (see also the section on CLIL – content and language integrated learning) to Canadian-like immersion programmes (for the concept, see Swain & Johnson, 1997).

In the 1998–1999 school year, a nation-wide survey was undertaken on the extent of language immersion (Buss & Mård, 2001). According to the survey, Swedish immersion was offered in 22 schools, Finnish immersion in 2 schools, and immersion in other languages was offered in 15 schools. In addition, 28 schools planned to start offering immersion education. Furthermore, there were about 250 schools that offered some form of bilingual instruction.[17]

Immersion in Swedish

The first Canadian-like immersion programme in Swedish for Finnish-speaking pupils was started in 1987. After a couple of years of experience, the status of the immersion programme was improved and instead of being an experimental programme it became a regular alternative education form for Finnish-speaking pupils who opted for it. Since its beginning in Vaasa, Swedish immersion has been introduced in linguistically very different environments. Many variations also occur as to the starting age (from 3 to 7 years). Most of the programmes are carried out in state kindergartens and schools, but some private immersion kindergartens have also been established. In almost all cases, parents have been the main promoters of immersion programmes. All programmes are quite new, and many of them have only recently been continued at the primary school level. A large number of teachers of immersion classes have participated in the in-service training programmes arranged at the Continuing Education Centre of the University of Vaasa (Björklund, 1997, forthcoming).

The overall Swedish immersion situation in Finland has developed and expanded rapidly. In the 1998–99 school year, 1883 pupils were involved in Swedish immersion at school level. This number constituted about 0.3% of the entire school population in Finland. Thus, even though immersion was one of the most discussed school reforms in Finland in the 1990s, it can still be considered only a small-scale project when compared with immersion in Canada where 7% of the school population is involved with immersion (Buss & Mård, 2001; Mustaparta & Tella, 1999).

Several factors have shaped Swedish immersion programmes in Finland giving them a particular character. The two languages are structurally very different from each other, and since they are internationally minor languages, other languages form an essential and necessary part of the education programme. Thus, two major changes have been made to the original Canadian-like early total immersion programmes. First, subject teaching in the pupils' first language starts in Finland as early as grade 1. Second, the immersion programme is multi-lingual: teaching of the third (in general, English) and the fourth language (e.g. German or French) begins as early as primary education.

The evaluation of immersion programmes has been going on since they were introduced. The research has included various aspects of immersion, with a clear focus on language development and language teaching. Although important, the academic mastery of pupils has not been under scrutiny in many research reports so far. However, it is evident that immersion students are not disadvantaged on national tests, and survey results show that immersion teachers are confident of the academic mastery of the pupils (Björklund, forthcoming). The results of the studies on the linguistic outcome of immersion indicate that the development of the immersion pupils' first and second language is comparable with the results obtained in Canadian immersion research. In addition, the results show that immersion is an efficient way to motivate majority students to learn languages. Even if not all immersion students reach native-like competence in their second language, they feel confident using the language whenever needed. Further, the results of the studies on first language development have been very favourable: at the end of the immersion programme, pupils develop first language skills comparable to those of mono-lingual pupils of the same age. Research on the third and the fourth language of the pupils has also been included in the evaluation of the programmes (Björklund, 1997, forthcoming).

According to Buss and Mård's survey (2001), the schools offering Swedish immersion in Finland are satisfied with the design of their immersion programmes and with student achievement. Still, immersion researchers in Finland are worried about the variation in the implementation of the programmes and especially about those modifications that have been made that are not based on research. Buss and Mård (2001) conclude that a detailed national immersion curriculum for all grade levels is needed: a national curriculum and a national model for immersion programmes would make it impossible to set up new immersion programmes with-out taking into account previous experiences and background research. The new national curricula will, for the first time, include a section on immersion education.

Immersion in Finnish

In general, immersion programmes provide minority language instruction for majority language children. In 1992, Swedish-speaking minority children began immersion education in the majority language, Finnish, in Pietarsaari. As Pietarsaari, located in Ostrobothnia, is very strongly Swedish-speaking – 55% of the population speaks Swedish as their first language – the language situation was not considered to be a threat to the children in immersion. The children to be immersed from completely Swedish-speaking homes had not previously learned Finnish. Immersion in Finnish, realised in accordance with the Canadian early total immersion model (see Swain & Johnson, 1997), is a small-scale project that involves about 100 children.

So far, immersion in Finnish has not been extensively studied. The Finnish skills of children have been studied by Grönholm (2000), and their skills in Swedish have been studied by Østern (2000). On the basis of tests in several skill areas and of questionnaires, Grönholm concluded that language immersion has provided children with better skills in Finnish, when compared to language learners who have been taught by conventional methods. In Grönholm's view, this creates an adequate basis for managing a variety of school subjects in the immersion language. According to Østern's studies, Finnish immersion has had no negative influence on the children's first language development.

National languages in religious life

After the Reformation, the vernaculars, Finnish and Swedish, became the languages of the people's church in accordance with Martin Luther's doctrines. Gradually, services were conducted in the vernacular language and texts indispensable for religious life were translated into vernaculars. After Finland became independent, the linkages between church and state were also extended to language arrangements in the Evangelical Lutheran Church of Finland. The 1922 Language Law applies to the Church of Finland in the same way as to other state bodies. All congregations with Swedish-speaking majorities, regardless of their geographic location, are grouped together into the Swedish-speaking diocese of Borgå (McRae, 1997). Currently, 505 of the 586 congregations belong to Finnish-speaking dioceses and 81 belong to the Swedish-speaking diocese.

During the period of autonomy, the Orthodox Church spread over the main parts of Finland along with immigrants from Russia. In the late 19th century, some attempts were made to use the Orthodox Church as a vehicle for Russification. However, the early years of independence saw an increasing tendency towards Finnicisation in the Orthodox Church, which was accelerated with the help of the Cabinet decree of 1923, according to which the official language of the Orthodox Church in Finland was to be Finnish, and church records must be kept in that language. The bishops, the clergy, and officials of the church administration had to have a 'full mastery' of Finnish, to be demonstrated before state boards of language examiners. A natural consequence of the new language requirements was that clergy educated in Finland gradually replaced Russian-speaking clergy, and the control of the church was firmly established in the hands of Finnish citizens. According to the decree, Swedish may be used in church assemblies to the extent allowed by the 1922 Language Law. The decree also provides a carefully circumscribed right to use Russian, but this is limited to persons formally exempt from knowing Finnish or to meetings in which the majority of members are Russian-speaking. The urban Orthodox congregations became more Finnicised after World War II, after the evacuation and dispersion of the Orthodox population in the Karelian Isthmus to other provinces (Heino, 1997; McRae, 1997).

National languages and the media

The press

The first Swedish-language newspaper to be published in Finland was founded in 1771 by the learned Aurora Society in Turku, under the title *Tidningar utgifne av et Sällskap i Åbo* ('The Åbo Swedish-language Newspaper'). The first Finnish-language newspaper in Finland was the educational *Suomenkieliset Tieto-Sanomat* ('The Finnish Newspaper') in 1775. However, prior to 1820 the press developed sporadically and almost exclusively in Swedish. Even after this date the few fragile publications in Finnish were weeklies, while their Swedish counterparts became stronger and more frequent in publication. From the 1850s to the 1890s newspapers began to grow steadily in numbers and strength. Finnish-language papers became as numerous as Swedish-language ones by the 1860s and, from 1889, they assumed a clear and growing lead (McRae, 1997; Tommila & Salokangas, 1998).

During the 20th century, the number of dailies appearing in Swedish remained relatively stable. The Swedish-language dailies included one large Helsinki daily of national significance and circulation (*Hufvudstadsbladet*), one medium-sized regional paper (*Vasabladet*) and several smaller papers. The number of daily newspapers (nine) for the Swedish minority is probably higher in Swedish-speaking Finland than that for any other language minority in the world. The combined circulation of Swedish dailies has increased modestly, but Swedish-language circulation has declined as a proportion of total circulation, more or less in parallel with the decline in the Swedish-speaking proportion of the population. Like the Swedish-language press, the Finnish-language papers range in size from small thrice-weekly 'dailies' to large metropolitan papers, *Helsingin Sanomat* having the largest share (27.9%) of the total circulation of dailies (seven issues a week) (McRae, 1997; Tilastokeskus, 2000).

Finland's per capita consumption of print media has long been one of the highest in the world. Although newspapers saw their circulation decline quite rapidly with the severe economic recession in the early 1990s, Finland still has one of the world's greatest newspaper circulations as well as the greatest circulation of book titles relative to its population of 5.2 million. In terms of total circulation related to population, Finland ranks first in Europe and third in the world. In 2000, a total of 220 newspaper titles were published in the country, 56 of them being 'dailies' with four to seven issues per week and 164 with one to three issues per week. The dailies comprised about 70% of the total circulation of newspapers. Most newspapers are bought on subscription rather than from newsstands (Tilastokeskus, 2000).

The importance of electronic media is growing fast in Finland. In fact, Finland became saturated with Internet hosts much earlier in the history of Internet growth than, for example, the United States. In 2001, there were 148 Internet hosts per thousand inhabitants in Finland. Currently, a total of 170 journalistic publications are available on the web in Finland. Of the traditional printed newspapers, a total of 100 have a journalistic net publication on the web.

Broadcasting

Broadcasting in both official languages has been well established since the development of radio in the 1920s. By the 1990s, the radio stations included three countrywide FM networks operating in Finnish. One Swedish-language radio network provided countrywide programming while a second broadcast a mixture of Swedish-language regional programmes and the national programmes to the coastal regions (McRae, 1997). From the 1930s to the 1980s, public radio broadcasting in Finland had been a monopoly of the Finnish Broadcasting Company, *Yleisradio* (YLE). After the first licences for local commercial radio stations were issued in 1985, new stations mushroomed all over the country. In March 2000, there were 9 nation-wide public radio stations in Finland, two of which were in Swedish. There were also 26 regional public channels (20 Finnish, 5 Swedish, and 1 Saami). In addition, there were 59 private seminational or regional radio stations (Tilastokeskus, 2000).

The history of Finnish television started in 1955. Even though YLE was required by its licence to broadcast in both Finnish and Swedish, TV-programming in Swedish was confined to only a few hours a week. From the 1960s onward, the underdevelopment of this important communications medium became one of the most serious sources of language dissatisfaction for the Swedish-speaking population. The solution to the problem was found in the late 1980s, when an agreement was made with Sweden to rebroadcast a selection of programmes from Sweden's two television channels as a fourth Swedish-language network, beginning in the capital region and extending over time to cover the rest of the south coast. This agreement was reciprocal, providing in return for YLE telecasts in Finnish to be rebroadcast in the Stockholm region (McRae, 1997).

In 1992, the first operating licences were granted for private local television stations. At the end of the 1990s, there were four nation-wide TV channels, two of which were public (YLE TV1 and YLE TV2) and two were commercial (MTV3, Channel Four Finland). In addition, there was a channel for programmes produced by SVT (*Sveriges Television* in Swedish) available in the coastal areas of Finland.

The first satellite television signals became available in Finland in the early 1980. At the end of the 1990s, approximately 50% of households received programmes via cable or satellite connections. However, the role of cable and satellite connections has been much less significant than it has been in the other Nordic countries because of the scarce supply of programming in the Finnish language. Cable networks have largely served as distribution networks for pan-European channels such as MTV Europe, Eurosport, and TV5 Europe. Currently, about 40 foreign satellite TV channels are available in Finland (Tilastokeskus, 2000).

More than 50% of the programmes shown on national TV channels are made in Finland. Foreign programmes on YLE channels are mostly European, whereas foreign programmes shown on the commercial channels come mainly from North America (Tilastokeskus, 2000). All foreign programmes, except some programmes for children, are subtitled in Finnish.

The most recent development in broadcasting includes three terrestrial digital television multiplexes. Licence holders must ensure that 70% of the Finnish population will be covered by digital networks by the end of 2006. Among the new digital channels there is a full-service channel in Swedish (FST-D), available throughout Finland. As compared to the situation some decades ago, this change considerably improves the possibilities for Swedish-speaking Finns to receive information and entertainment in their first language. The programming of

FST-D comprises new domestic and Nordic programmes, and in addition, it features programmes that have been shown on other channels, with Swedish subtitles, and societal services in Swedish (Tilastokeskus, 2000; YLE Annual Report, 2001).

Finnish as a second language

Most immigrants in Finland study Finnish as their second language. In the following section, the development of language education for immigrants is described from the viewpoint of Finnish as a second language (FSL). Since the history of teaching Swedish to immigrants is in many ways similar – except for the fact that it is much more marginal – and since it is governed by the same regulations as the teaching of Finnish, Swedish as a second language is described more briefly in a later section.

Immigration and educational policy

The general principle underlying Finnish immigration policy is that immigrants are entitled to the same rights and the same treatment as the rest of the population. At the same time, Finland has adopted the principle of reciprocity: that immigrants can be expected to contribute willingly to their successful integration into Finnish society (ML, 1999). The educational policy designed for immigrants follows the general design of immigrant policy. The current ideology comprises the following main principles for the education of immigrants: equality, functional bilingualism and multiculturalism. *Equality* in education implies that education aims to provide immigrants with the skills and knowledge they need in order to be able to function fully as equal members of Finnish society. *Functional bilingualism* means that immigrants are to be given an opportunity to study either Finnish or Swedish as well as to maintain and develop their own language and culture. *Multiculturalism* in Finnish education policy is a term which broadly implies that the meeting of cultures is to be understood as an experience that enriches both parties, dissolves prejudices, and increases tolerance in society (Matinheikki-Kokko & Pitkänen, 2002).[18]

FSL for immigrant pupils

Although there certainly were foreign-born children in Finland before the 1970s, it seems that it was after the first handful of refugees from Chile came to Finland in 1973 that the existence of such a group of pupils in schools was first acknowledged. However, the differentiated instruction given them was still minimal during the 1970s. In general, immigrant pupils were integrated into mainstream classes right away, being given only some remedial instruction in Finnish. The 1980s led to more changes in Finnish schools, as Finland started gradually to accept refugees on an annual quota basis and more permanent arrangements had to be developed. The solution was that refugee children were entitled to a period of preparatory instruction lasting for 12 months before attending an ordinary mainstream class. However, this arrangement was not available for other immigrant children who were not refugees. During the 1990s, the number of immigrants grew rapidly, and the educational needs of immigrant pupils started to play a greater role in more and more schools all over Finland. The pressure for more systematic planning and goal setting led gradually to several improvements. Since 1994, Finnish as a second language (FSL) has been included in the national core curriculum for the comprehensive school. Another significant step forward was taken in 1996, when FSL became an alternative for a test in language and literature (meant for native speakers) in the matriculation exam.[19] In the same year, FSL was added to the national core curriculum for the upper secondary school. In 1997, the right to preparatory instruction was extended to all immigrant pupils (not just refugees). In 1999, criteria for the final assessment at the end of basic education were drawn up for FSL. Currently, FSL can be studied at all levels of education, from pre-school to university education.[20]

According to current educational legislation (1999), municipalities may arrange preparatory classes for children who are of school age or pre-school age, but they are under no obligation to do so. During the preparatory phase, pupils receive instruction in their second language, in their first language, and also in other school subjects. The forms of preparatory instruction vary greatly from municipality to municipality and even within any given municipality. The duration also varies but, according to the legislation, the pupils are entitled to receive preparatory instruction for at least six months. Some municipalities have extended the period to 12 or even to 18 months.

Municipalities can arrange instruction in a second language as part of normal tuition, using their regular hourly resources. Alternatively, they may finance it with special resources, either from their own resources or through resources offered by the state. Immigrant pupils can receive state-funded FSL instruction during their first three years in the Finnish school system. As Savolainen (1998) and Suni (1996) have shown, the possibilities of receiving instruction in FSL vary greatly across different parts of the country. It is evident that immigrant pupils currently receive education unequally in various parts of Finland. On the one hand, some municipalities have created very detailed local curricula for the instruction of immigrant pupils. On the other hand, local curricula are still rare, and it is obvious that in many municipalities the level of awareness of the educational needs of immigrant pupils is in general relatively low. Furthermore, some municipalities offer instruction in the second language for the entire time immigrant pupils go to school, while other municipalities hardly offer it for the full three years funded by the state.

Despite the fact that FSL is included in the national core curricula, it is not mentioned as an official subject in the educational legislation. Consequently, its status in schools and the qualification criteria for teachers are still somewhat unclear. This general state of affairs leaves much responsibility to municipalities: it is up to them to finance any extra second language instruction, and they may also define the qualification criteria for teachers. The new national core curricula will probably change this situation to some extent. The current draft of the new curriculum for basic education mentions that pupils may be taught FSL in case their skills in Finnish are judged not to be at the level of native speakers of Finnish. In addition, the criteria for student evaluation from 1999 include the same idea: pupils' skills in Finnish will have to be evaluated according to a FSL syllabus, if Finnish is not their first language. Thus, in practice, municipalities will probably have to arrange more instruction in FSL in the future.

As for teacher training, in-service training for teachers working with immigrants was started in 1992 at, for example, the continuing education centres of universities. During the 1990s, FSL teacher training programmes were developed at several universities (see e.g. Nieminen, T., 2000), and professorships in FSL were founded at the universities of Jyväskylä and Helsinki. However, the growing multiculturalism of Finnish schools is still a challenge for teacher training. According to Koponen (2000), the educational content preparing for immigrant education, for example teaching Finnish, differs notably among the educational units responsible for teacher training. In some institutions, this content forms part of several different study modules, whereas other institutions are only in the process of planning these studies. Also Matinheikki-Kokko and Pitkänen (2002) consider that much work needs to be done since current institutional arrangements offer only a weak support for teachers and teacher educators in their attempts to integrate multicultural ideology and practice in their teaching.

The effectiveness of instruction

The first actual, and to date the only, study on the effectiveness of immigrant education in schools was done by Suni (1996). She examined the command of Finnish among immigrant pupils in the 9th grade. The data consisted of language tests and background information on 90 pupils as well as interviews with the pupils and their teachers of Finnish. The degree of proficiency was evaluated using the intermediate level test of the National Certificate of Language Proficiency[21], compiled on the basis of the content and goals expressed in the national core curriculum for Finnish as a second language. Test results were compared with several background variables such as length of residence, first language and amount of teaching in Finnish.

The study revealed that about two-thirds of the pupils had managed to acquire enough language so that they were able to follow and participate in instruction, to comprehend the content of textbooks and to convey their own views and ideas both orally and in writing. Characteristically, the ones who succeeded to this degree in the test belonged to three distinct groups. The first group had done their primary education in Finland. Many of them came from countries far away from Finland, and they had received a lot of differentiated teaching in Finnish. The other successful group consisted of speakers of Russian who had lived in Finland for at least three years. The majority of those students had heard some Finnish in their early childhood. In addition, all Estonian-speaking pupils reached this level, despite the fact that they had lived in Finland only for a year or so. This result shows that linguistic kinship will speed up learning Finnish at least in the early stages.

However, about one-third of the immigrant pupils had such difficulties in comprehending and producing Finnish that, according to Suni (1996), their limited skills would constitute a serious barrier to school attendance and further studies. Most of these pupils had come to Finland at the end of primary education or at the beginning of lower secondary education. Despite extensive differentiated teaching in Finnish, their linguistic skills had not developed to a point sufficiently advanced to permit communication other than in simple everyday situations or face-to-face dialogues with acquaintances. Therefore, Suni estimates that these pupils are in need of extensive supportive measures beyond basic education. Suni concludes that it is important to increase the flexibility of teaching arrangements, as the needs of the pupils vary greatly due to, for example, the differences in their educational background.

In the light of Suni's results, it is not surprising that currently only 15% of immigrant pupils continue their studies in upper secondary schools (as compared to 60% of the whole cohort).

FSL for adult immigrants

The basic idea of immigrant education has not changed much since the 1970s, when it was designed for the first refugees coming to Finland. The objectives and the form of education have, however, gradually become clearer. Since the end of the 1980s, quite a few committees set up by, e.g. the Ministry of Education have written memoranda in which a number of improvements have been suggested for immigrant education. At the beginning of the 1990s, the first curricula for adult immigrant education were drawn up (OPH, 1993). The objectives were defined anew in a document from 1997 (OPH, 1997), which was replaced by a recommendation given in 2001 (OPH, 2001). The purpose of the recommendation was to provide nation-wide objectives for the integration training of adult immigrants as well as to ensure the uniform structure of education in various parts of the country. The recommended programme consists of training in language skills and social skills, as well as educational and vocational readiness. Altogether, it consists of six study units, totalling 40 credits, and lasting for about one year. One Finnish credit corresponds to an average input of about 40 hours of work by the student.

- Studies of Finnish/Swedish   26–36
- Routines of everyday life and life management   1– 3
- Social studies   3– 4
- Cultural studies   1– 3
- Educational and vocational readiness   6– 7
- Optional studies   0– 3

Total =   37–56 credits

The extent of each study unit varies according to the individual's educational background, skills and aims. In addition to the study units mentioned above, integration training may include literacy training, the extent of which varies individually.

Until the end of the 1990s, adult immigrants were in an unequal situation with regard to the right to free instruction in Finnish. To begin with, only refugees were entitled to second language instruction free-of-charge. At the beginning of the 1990s, Ingrian returnees from the former Soviet Union were given the same right. Other groups of newcomers were obliged to obtain their studies largely at their own expense. Currently, all immigrant groups are, in principle, entitled to instruction in Finnish. However, only courses that are part of employment training are free-of-charge. A fee is charged for most other second language courses.

The unequal position of various immigrant groups is a consequence of the fact that the immigration policy was not defined until 1997, in *the Government Decision-In-Principle on Immigration and Refugee Policy Programme* (MI, 1997). The policy programme was followed by a law, which made some central changes possible in educational policy. The purpose of *the Act on the Integration of Immigrants and Reception of Asylum Seekers,* effective since 1999, is to promote equal opportunities for all immigrants in Finland. It applies to those immigrants whose residence in Finland is considered to be so permanent that they have been entered in the population register. The law states that, during their first three years in the country, newcomers have the possibility to concentrate on studying Finnish or Swedish, to complement their professional skills and to acquire the forms of knowledge and abilities needed in Finland. In exchange, immigrants have an obligation to play an active role in trying to obtain employment and training. To this end, an integration plan is drawn up for them. As long as an individual follows the agreed plan, his/her livelihood is guaranteed by means of an integration allowance (ML, 1999).

The purpose of the Integration Act was to make integration more efficient and to give all immigrant groups equal opportunities. While the Act has modified the situation in principle, practical implementation has been slow. There are not enough language courses for immigrants that are arranged as employment training, and the queues for courses are very long (Latomaa, 2002). As Matinheikki-Kokko and Pitkänen (2002) point out, the new law focuses on changes and co-operation at the administrative level rather than on actual changes in the educational practices. Moreover, they point out that the current situation in immigrant education is a result of the market-based arrangements developed in the 1990s that have produced high variability in educational practices rather than a coherent training system.

In May 2002, the Ministry of Labour issued a proposal for a government report on the implementation of the Integration Act. According to the proposal, the central problem with the law is the insufficiency of training. The waiting periods for training have been inappropriately long. Furthermore, when purchasing training services, the 40 credits required under the NBE recommendations have been compromised. In the proposal, it is pointed out that special attention should be given to the teaching of illiterate persons, immigrant children and women as well as ageing immigrants. Further, attention should be given to making vocational training more efficient, upgrading the facilities of basic education, and increasing the effectiveness of the teaching for highly educated immigrants. The creation and development of practices as well as the clarification of co-operation partners is still unfinished in many municipalities and labour administration and, for this reason, the proposed amendments of the Integration Act will only go to Parliament in 2003.

The effectiveness of instruction

Few studies deal with the effectiveness of instruction in Finnish as a second language for adult immigrants. Pälli and Latomaa (1997) studied what proficiency level immigrants ($N = 90$) had attained after a year of language training. The proficiency level was evaluated by means of the National Certificate of Language Proficiency as well as on the basis of the learners' own estimate of their proficiency and the assessment made by their teachers. The average grade of the test taker's performance in the various test areas was used to indicate the overall proficiency level that had been attained.

A little less than half of the participants in the study attained the set skill level that is deemed sufficient to make it possible to study and work in Finnish, and defined in general terms as follows:

> Manages familiar oral and written tasks and situations related to work and free-time adequately. Interference from other languages can be intrusive. Vocabulary, grammar and fluency generally adequate but variable. A dictionary may sometimes be needed for understanding main points of ordinary text, for instance, a newspaper article.

This skill level has been set by the NBE as the target proficiency level for immigrants after one year of study. For more than half of the participants, however, studies of one year's duration had not been enough. The study showed that the desired level of proficiency was attained best by those immigrants who also used Finnish outside the classroom, who had prior experience of learning languages, and who had been active in academic or similar professions, which require a high level of education.

According to their teachers, the greatest problems to be resolved in teaching included the difference between the students' study and learning cultures, the very minimal contacts of the immigrants with the native population, and the all too heterogeneous background of the teaching groups. According to Pälli and Latomaa (1997), the results obtained reveal that listening and reading comprehension need additional attention so that the proficiency level essential for continuing education could be attained. By the same token, teaching arrangements ought to be made more flexible, in order to make teaching correspond more to the needs of immigrants with varying backgrounds and a varying capacity for learning.

Swedish as a second language

Since the end of the 1980s, refugees have been placed all over the country, including in Swedish-speaking municipalities. To begin with, Vietnamese refugees and Kurdish people were placed in the Swedish-speaking municipalities in Ostrobothnia, and later in the region of Länsi-Uusimaa in southern Finland (see Map 3). The municipality can decide which of the languages newcomers will study. In unilingually Swedish-speaking municipalities, the language to be studied is naturally Swedish. In officially bilingual municipalities, however, the situation is not as self-evident. In general, the majority language of the municipality becomes the language to be studied, but there are also municipalities that offer both languages.

There is no survey of the amount of teaching of Swedish as a second language; however, the amount of such teaching can be estimated on the basis of population statistics (SF, 2001). At the beginning of 2001, only 0.6% of those who had some language other than Finnish or Swedish as their first language ($N=100,961$) lived in unilingually Swedish-speaking municipalities, and 1.6% lived in bilingual municipalities with a Swedish majority. As many as 58% lived in bilingual municipalities with a Finnish majority. However, as the three largest municipalities – Helsinki, Espoo and Vantaa – have such a large Finnish majority, the instruction in Swedish as a second language in these municipalities is not very extensive. Thus, it is realistic to estimate that instruction in Swedish as a second language is relatively marginal: it involves mainly the 2.2% of immigrants living in Swedish-dominant surroundings.

The question of placing refugees in Swedish-speaking areas has been debated from the outset (Haapamäki, 1995; Nyholm & Aziz, 1996; Söderman, 1997). On the one hand, the consequences of learning Swedish have been questioned. Will Swedish-speaking immigrants become a minority inside a minority? Will they survive in Finland with the help of Swedish, or do they have to study Finnish as well? It is well known that some refugees have moved away from the original municipality to the capital region (Hellman, 1996), and Finnish is an essential language there, for example, at work. On the other hand, the Nordic dimension argues for the Swedish language: the distance to other Nordic countries is short, and many refugees have relatives elsewhere in the Nordic region.

The effectiveness of instruction in Swedish as a second language has not been studied as such. Haapamäki (1995) investigated the proficiency in Swedish among 20 Kurdish refugees, 10 adults and 10 children, one year after immigration. The adults had participated in language courses, and the children had studied in preparatory classes for six months. Haapamäki collected material with the help of structured interviews, and on the basis of those data she discovered that there were large differences between adults, while children formed a relatively homogeneous group as far as learning results were concerned. Not surprisingly, the best adult learners had more education, and used more Swedish in their daily lives (had more contacts with Swedish-speaking people, read Swedish newspapers, etc.) than those who had not come as far in their learning process.

Another study by Söderman (1997) concerned the effects of language choice in a bilingual setting in the region of Länsi-Uusimaa. Söderman interviewed 14 Kurdish refugees from Iran and Iraq who had lived in Finland for three to six years. Half of the interviewees had studied Finnish, and half had studied Swedish. According to the results of the study, all but one of the subjects were satisfied with their language choice. All of the subjects stressed the importance of the right to choose a second language. The Swedish-speaking subjects considered moving from their region to the capital region less probable than did the Finnish-speaking group, the reason being the language barrier they feared they would encounter. According to Söderman, refugees in bilingual or unilingual Swedish- speaking municipalities can learn Swedish, if they have had the opportunity to choose their target language themselves, and if placement involves larger ethnic groups and families of several generations. She points out, however, that Finnish might be a better choice, if it is probable that learning two languages would be too demanding for refugees with little or no education and for refugees who are determined to move to a Finnish-speaking environment. In comparison with Söderman's viewpoints, Nyholm and Aziz (1996) sound very optimistic when they point out that many Kurdish refugees who first learned Swedish have continued their language studies with Finnish and thus become 'bilingual Finland Swedes'. Apparently, the language situation of immigrants living in Swedish-speaking surroundings calls for more research.

Finnish abroad

Some 90 universities in about 30 countries have Finnish language and culture in their curricula. In about 20 universities, Finnish can be studied as a major or a minor, in other universities as elective courses. In a few universities Finnish language and culture has a department of its own, but most often a programme of Finnish is a part of the department of Finno-Ugric, Uralic or Ural-Altaic languages (Raanamo, 1998).

Since the 1990s, studies of Finnish have been strengthened especially in proximate geographic areas: interest in Finnish has been increasing rapidly in the Baltic countries and in Russia, and as the result of the reawakening of Finno-Ugric nations. Since Finnish is one of the official languages of the EU, Finnish is currently considered more interesting and useful than before, not only in the EU but even outside Europe, in Asia and Australia. Finland's image as a country of high education and high technology has been sharpened by the worldwide success of companies like Nokia. One indication of the growing interest in Finnish is the fact that the number of foreign students at Finnish universities and polytechnics has been steadily increasing.

In addition to universities, Finnish is taught in primary and secondary schools in several countries, e.g. in Sweden, Norway, Russia, Estonia, Latvia, Hungary, and Canada. Teaching Finnish at this level of education is most common in proximate geographic areas and in countries where there are large numbers of Finnish emigrants.

Finnish is studied as an extracurricular activity in so called Suomi Schools. These schools have usually been initiated by Finnish immigrant women. Currently, there are about 170 Suomi schools in 40 countries, and the number is on the increase. The majority of the schools receive financial support for their activities from the Finnish NBE. Most schools are situated in Europe and North America, but there are also a few schools in Asia, Africa, Australia and South America (Seppälä, 2000).

The Spread of Minority Languages

This section focuses on the status and use of minority languages in Finnish society. Recent changes in the legislation concerning minority education are described briefly. Thereafter, the possibilities that established and new linguistic minorities have for the promotion of their native language are examined in several domains: in the educational system, in religious life, and in the media.

Education

Educational legislation

Several reforms of educational legislation enacted in the 1990s sought to ensure equality of education in different parts of the country and to strengthen the status and rights of minorities. In 1995, educational legislation was amended to allow the teaching of minority languages in schools as a subject and their use as a medium of instruction. The comprehensive reform of educational legislation, which came into force in 1999, continues in the same vein. In accordance with the pupil's language of instruction, Finnish, Swedish or Saami may be taught as his or her native language. In addition, Romani, sign language or some other first language of the pupil may be taught as a native language, at the discretion of the guardian. The current legislation gives a relatively free hand to schools to choose the language of instruction. In addition to Finnish and Swedish, the language of instruction may be Saami, Romani and sign language. Also, part of the instruction may be given in a language other than the pupil's own language 'provided it does not jeopardise the pupil's ability to cope with the instruction'. Furthermore, the law allows the provision of instruction to some special group or school mainly or entirely in a language other than those mentioned above. Consequently, all pupils can – in principle – receive instruction in and about their first language.

Prior to the adoption of the current Education Act, immigrant pupils had the right but not the obligation to follow basic education. Since then, compulsory education has been extended to all children who are permanent residents in Finland.

The importance of linguistic and cultural background of pre-school age children was emphasised in an amendment added in 1995 to the Act on Children's Day Care. In the original 1973 Act, the requirements for pre-school education did not mention children's linguistic background at all. In 1982, the Act was amended by adding a sentence stating that the municipality had to ensure that day care is given in the following native languages: Finnish, Swedish, and Saami. Before this recognition was provided, the Act treated linguistic minority children in the same way as majority children. The current version of the Act emphasises the linguistic and cultural background of the child to an even greater degree. Each local authority must provide day care in Finnish and Swedish, and the Saami languages are to be used in the Saami Homeland. In addition, day care should also support the language and culture of Romani children and of children with immigrant backgrounds, in co-operation with representatives of the culture in question.

Saami

Until the 1950s, most of the tuition provided to Saami-speaking pupils was given at itinerant schools: the teacher travelled from one village to another. The official language of instruction was Finnish, but the teacher also communicated with the pupils in Saami. Since the 1950s, children have had to leave their homes and go to elementary school, often in distant locations, and they were only able to come home for major holidays. The new system required that pupils be educated in Finnish (Olthuis, 2002). According to the law on comprehensive schools passed in the 1970s, Saami-speaking pupils should be taught, as far as possible, in their first language, along with Finnish. Instruction in Saami languages was first provided during the 1975–76 school year to the lowest grades in the schools of Utsjoki municipality. Even before that, Saami languages had been taught in some schools, but neither systematically nor continuously. During the 1980s, instruction was developed extensively, and when the legislation on primary and secondary education was enacted in 1985, Saami was established as a statutory language of school instruction. Currently, Saami may function as a medium of instruction, and it can be taught as a subject. In the Saami Homeland, Saami-speaking pupils must be provided with basic education primarily in their first language, if their parents so desire. The state has provided financing for the maintenance of the Saami culture by allocating special funds from the budget to support education in and about the Saami languages (Aikio-Puoskari & Pentikäinen, 2001).

In the 1990s, the number of schools providing instruction in and about Saami languages grew remarkably, as did the number of students. In 1994, the first students took the matriculation examination in North Saami, and in 1998 the first student took the examination in Inari Saami (Vuolab, 2000). To safeguard the survival of these languages, in 1997 language nests – i.e. immersion pre-schools – were started in both Skolt Saami (in Sevettijärvi) and Inari Saami (in Ivalo), funded in part by a grant from the Finnish Cultural Foundation. These language nests where all children and teachers speak only Saami during the classes were set up in order to provide children with surroundings in which they can learn to use their native language in their daily activities. The outcome of the language nests has been very positive so far (Olthuis, 2002).

Currently, there are approximately 400 pupils studying Saami as a subject and some 100 pupils have Saami as a language of instruction (Aikio-Puoskari & Pentikäinen, 2001). There are 12 schools that use Saami as the language of instruction, and in a total of 29 schools Saami can be studied as a subject. In spite of obvious progress towards equal opportunity, there are still many problems. The Saami language programmes in schools do not seem to be fully established yet. Providing the necessary service in the child's own language at pre-primary level is the responsibility of the local authority, but official day-care centres using Saami are still few and far between. In grades 1–6, Saami can be the only language of instruction but, as the child moves through grades 7–9, the number of subjects taught through the language decreases (Vuolab, 2000).

Since the early stages of Saami instruction, the most significant obstacles, apart from attitudes, have been the shortage of Saami-speaking teachers and the lack of teaching materials. The situation of North Saami has improved most rapidly. In addition to those materials produced in Finland, teaching materials in North Saami are produced in Sweden and Norway. At present, instruction about and in North Saami is available in nearly all schools in the Saami Homeland as well as in five schools outside that area. There are qualified teachers and textbooks for each grade level in mathematics and Saami. For other subjects, however, textbooks are only occasionally available. The situation of Inari Saami and especially Skolt Saami is much worse (Olthuis, 2002).

Saami-speaking teachers are educated at the Universities of Lapland and Oulu as well as in the Saami College in Koutokeino, Norway. To alleviate the shortage of subject teachers, a programme has been started to educate Saami-speaking classroom teachers for subject teacher qualifications (Vuolab, 2000). Currently, North Saami can be studied at the universities of Helsinki, Oulu and Lapland but as a major subject only at the University of Oulu. Earlier, only occasional short courses in Inari Saami were offered at the university level. However, a major step was taken in 2001, when the Educational Centre of the Saami Homeland, together with the University of Oulu, organised the first extensive study programme (15 credits) in Inari Saami (Olthuis, 2002).

Romani

The assimilation policy that was put in place at the beginning of the 20th century was very effective. The aim was to assimilate the Roma into the majority population as soon as possible (Kortteinen, 1997). The Roma were not allowed to speak Romani publicly, neither was there any room for the Romani language and culture in schools. By the 1950s, 80% of the Finnish Roma used only or mostly Finnish as their everyday language. In the 1980s, special government funding began to be channelled into the teaching of Romani language and culture, and instruction about the Romani language was started, initially in study circles. Since 1989, the Romani language and culture has been taught more broadly in comprehensive schools. At the end of the 1990s, Romani was included in the national core curricula. Children can currently get instruction in Romani at school for two hours a week, and, in principle, Romani can also be used as the medium of instruction for all subjects (MSAH, 2000).

The Roma have traditionally been suspicious of education, as the schools have aimed at assimilating them into the majority population. Various reports show that the education received by older people remains inadequate. During the 1990s, however, the Roma have begun to demonstrate a more positive attitude towards education, a development undoubtedly influenced by the growing strength of their language and culture. Thus, the educational level of the Roma has improved considerably, but compared to the majority population it remains low. The problem for Romani children continues to be failure to complete basic education, which makes it difficult for them to enter further education (Majaniemi & Lillberg, 2000; MSAH, 2000).

In spite of children's right to instruction in Romani, the municipalities are under no obligation to provide it, and no separate educational or cultural allocations have been assigned for the purpose, contrary to the case with the Saami languages. In practice, instruction has been provided to small groups of Romani children for two hours a week with the help of the same state funding that is meant for the teaching of immigrant minority languages. Out of the approximately 1700 Romani children in basic education, instruction in the Romani language is annually received in about 10 municipalities by an average of 250 children, i.e. less than 15% of pupils entitled to it (Majaniemi & Lillberg, 2000). Furthermore, the commendable inclusion of the support of the Romani language and culture as one of the educational objectives of the Act on Children's Day Care has not had any real impact on the relevant practice at the local level.

There are a number of reasons for the scarcity of instruction in Romani. The major obstacles include, among other things, the lack of qualified teachers and suitable teaching materials. Currently, university level studies in the Romani language are not available anywhere, and there are not enough people who are able to prepare teaching materials.

In 1994, the NBE established the Romani Education Unit, assigned to develop and implement nation-wide training and education for the Romani population, to promote the Romani language and culture, and to engage in information and publicity activity on Romani culture and education. The permanent activity of the Unit includes further training arranged annually for teachers of the Romani language, training of contact persons, and summer schools in Romani (Majaniemi & Lillberg, 2000).

Teaching material has been, and is being, drawn up to meet the needs of both the majority and Romani populations. Material for the majority population is designed to improve knowledge of Romani culture and thereby to reduce prejudice and to foster tolerance. Material for the Romani population is designed to increase their knowledge of their own roots, to strengthen their own identity, and to bolster and develop the Romani language. In addition to national funding, support for producing teaching materials has also been obtained from the EU's Comenius Programme[22]. The teaching materials include, among other things, cassettes, an alphabet book, a children's songbook, a grammar and handbook for teachers of Romani and a Romani-English-Finnish dictionary. The NBE and the Romani Education Unit are also currently working on a three-year package of teaching materials for basic and upper secondary education (Majaniemi & Lillberg, 2000).

Finnish sign language

Deaf education in Finland was initiated with the needs of the deaf as a starting point. For several decades, sign language[23] was used as a language of instruction, and it was also studied as a school subject. In 1892, deaf education became part of public school administration and, as a consequence, the approach to the educational needs and learning skills of the deaf changed radically. From this point on, education planning was reoriented to take the point of view of hearing people, and thus the oral method started gradually to dominate in deaf education.[24] The period of oralism continued for almost a century (Jokinen, 2000a; Kuurojen Liitto, 1994).

Legislation concerning deaf education dates back to the 1950s. At that time signing was allowed only as support for teaching. In the 1980s, sign language was defined as a language in school legislation, but it was to be used only 'if needed' or to support teaching. At the beginning of the 1990s, sign language was mentioned for the first time in the list of first languages. The latest school legislation (1999) included sign language as a school subject and as a medium of instruction (Lappi, 2000).

Currently, there are 16 schools providing basic education for deaf[25] pupils in Finland, three of which are state schools. The network of municipal schools was founded at the beginning of the 1970s. Before that all deaf children went to state-owned boarding schools, where sign language and the culture of signers developed and was transmitted from one student generation to another. Today, more than half of the children who use sign language go to regular schools. Most of them are hard-of-hearing, but there are also a few deaf pupils who go to school with the help of an interpreter (Kuurojen Liitto, 1994; Lappi, 2000).

The current school legislation does not obligate the municipality to provide instruction in sign language. Furthermore, the right to get instruction in sign language is still based on classifying the degrees of hearing impairment, i.e. on medical instead of linguistic or cultural grounds. In practice, only a few children using sign language have a real possibility of getting instruction in their first language. Since the number of children using sign language is relatively small, and since they are dispersed throughout the country, it is difficult to form separate groups for signers. In most schools, users of sign language are taught in the same groups with Finnish-speaking and dysphasic pupils. Thus, the teacher faces an impossible task: instruction should be given simultaneously in sign language, signed Finnish and spoken Finnish. The situation is complicated in other ways as well: there are only a few teachers who have sign language as their first language, and teaching material is still scarce (Jokinen, 2000b; Lappi, 2000).

However, the attitudinal climate has clearly changed, and deaf education and sign language are now regarded in their own right more often than before. As an example of typical attitudes present earlier, Hakkarainen claimed that 'mastery of written language has been considered the primary goal in the teaching of deaf children' (1988: xi). In her study of deaf pupils' mastery of written Finnish, Hakkarainen (1988) compared the reading comprehension skills of deaf and hearing pupils. She found that the proficiency of 15-year old deaf pupils corresponded to that of 8-year old hearing pupils. As pointed out in the Education Policy Programme for the Deaf (Kuurojen Liitto, 1994), the result of the study can actually be considered good. After all, Finnish is the second language of the pupils Hakkarainen studied, and, in fact, they had acquired the language in most cases through education that in those days did not have any trace of second language pedagogy. For deaf pupils, it is important to achieve bilingualism, to be fully competent in their first language and to be literate in Finnish (or Swedish). However, it makes a difference where and how literacy is taught. As Baker (2001) points out, literacy is likely to be broadening and empowering, if it is taught by, for example, deaf teachers in pro-signing schools. If it is taught by those keen on the assimilation of deaf people, then such literacy may work against the ethnic awakening of deaf people and may result in lower academic achievement.

Furthermore, the Education Policy Programme for the Deaf notes that deaf children entering school currently have a better prognosis for school success than, for example, they did 30 years ago, when parents' and special education instructors' skills in sign language were not as common as they are today. One of the most important recent reforms has been the first course for classroom teachers of sign language users that began in 1998 at the University of Jyväskylä; a second group started their education in 2001. The aim of the new teacher-training programme is (1) to arrange education for the deaf in their own language, not integrated into groups of hearing students, and (2) to arrange it as part of general education, instead of having it as part of special education. Teacher training has recently been more focused in other ways as well. Jokinen's (2000b) survey charted the number of children and their teachers who use sign language in the schools and day-care centres for the deaf in Finland. The results of Jokinen's survey showed a particular need for classroom teachers and subject teachers as well as for continuing education in sign language. Currently, sign language can be studied at the universities of Jyväskylä and Turku.

Other established minority languages

Some of the established minorities have had schools of their own since the 19th century. Among the numerous primary and secondary schools to meet the needs of the Russian-speaking population in Finland, the most important school was the Russian Secondary School in Helsinki (*Gel'singfórskiy rússkiy litséy*). In 1955, it was replaced by the present Finnish-Russian school (*Fínsko-Rússkaya Shkóla*). In connection with the comprehensive school reform, the school became a public school subsidised through the national budget. Finnish gradually became its language of instruction, and Russian was taught only as a subject. In the 1990s, as a result of the growing movement of people out of the Soviet Union, and later from the CIS countries, the need for instruction in the Russian language increased. Currently, instruction is given in both Finnish and Russian (Horn, 1999).

The first Jewish school functioned in Helsinki from 1893 to 1900. In 1918, the present Jewish Co-Educational School was founded. To begin with, the language of instruction at the Jewish Co-Educational School was Swedish, but in 1932 Finnish replaced it. At the school, Hebrew and the history of the Jewish people have been taught as additional courses. Yiddish, however, has never been part of the curriculum (Harviainen, 1998; Horn, 1999).

From 1948 to 1969 there was a Tatar primary school (*Türk Halk Mektebi*) in Helsinki. It was partly subsidised by the Islamic Congregation and partly by the City of Helsinki. About half of the teaching was given in Finnish and half in Tatar. In the 1970s, with the comprehensive school reform, it was no longer possible to run the Tatar school, due to the small number of pupils and the conditions governing state subsidies. Currently, the Islamic Congregation provides teaching in Tatar in the afternoon or evening, in language and culture, religion and history. The congregation also offers summer courses in Tatar. A Tatar kindergarten has existed since the 1950s (Horn, 1999).

Immigrant minority languages

In the 1990s, regulations concerning immigrant education changed profoundly, as described in the section on FSL for immigrant pupils. As far as immigrant minority language instruction (IMLI) is concerned, it was first given only to Chilean (Spanish-speaking) refugees who came to Finland in 1973. With the arrival of Vietnamese refugees at the end of the 1970s the need for IMLI became stronger. The subject was initially called *home language instruction*. On the basis of a decision made by the Ministry of Education (OPM, 1987), regular IMLI was started in 1987, and since that time all immigrant pupils have been entitled to it for the entire time they go to school. In 1987, the name of the subject was changed to *native language instruction.*[26] The term placed the subject on a more equal footing with the rest of the language programme in schools and symbolised the significance of the subject for immigrant pupils. In 1994, IMLI was included in the national core curriculum for the comprehensive school, and in 1996 it was added to the national core curriculum for the upper secondary school. Criteria for the final assessment at the end of basic education were drawn up in 2001. Currently, it is also possible to receive IMLI in day care and vocational education (Matinheikki-Kokko & Pitkänen, 2002).

Immigrant pupils study IMLI on a voluntary basis. The municipality decides how IMLI is to be arranged and can receive state funding for groups of (at least) four pupils. Groups can be formed of pupils from several schools and even from several municipalities. While IMLI is most often organised by municipalities, there are also a few associations that arrange it, e.g. the Association for Spanish-speaking Parents and the Japanese Society in Helsinki.

According to the most recently available statistics (2000), which are based on municipalities' reports on the use of state funding, as many as 10,227 pupils were given instruction in a total of 49 native languages (Table 8). This number includes Saami-speaking and Romani-speaking pupils. In addition, it includes Finnish- and Swedish-speaking pupils who have acquired the language skill in question while abroad. Pupils who participated in instruction in preparatory classes (1537) are not included in the statistics, as there is no information about how many of them also received IMLI.

Table 8 Immigrant minority language instruction for the 10 largest language groups[1] in basic and upper secondary education in 2000 and 1990

Language 2000	Pupils 2000	Municipalities 2000	Language 1990	Pupils 1990	Municipalities 1990
Russian	2,848	58	English	272	8
Somali	1,178	15	Vietnamese	162	15
English	900	9	Spanish	75	5
Arabic	700	20	German	60	4
Albanian	673	27	Chinese	53	3
Vietnamese	614	18	French	38	3
Estonian	528	12	Arabic	36	1
Kurdish	415	16	Polish	29	2
Chinese	244	8	Russian	27	2
Spanish	211	9	Italian	22	1
Total	10,227	101	Total	911	22

Source: National Board of Education
[1]Since the table contains only the ten largest languages, the numbers given in the pupil column do not add up to the total given. The numbers given in the municipality column cannot be totalled since they indicate the number of municipalities where a particular minority language is taught. Some municipalities in southern Finland teach several languages.

As Table 8 shows, the field of IMLI increased tenfold in the 1990s. In 2000, IMLI was provided in 101 municipalities, i.e. approximately one out of every four municipalities. However, as the majority of immigrants are concentrated in certain parts of the country, the coverage of instruction is better represented if the actual number of pupils entitled to IMLI (about 15,000) is compared with the total number of pupils studying IMLI. In 2000, as many as two-thirds of immigrant pupils received instruction in their native language.

As is the case among other linguistic minorities, the implementation of immigrant educational policy faces several problems. Especially during the 1980s it was common in schools for immigrant languages to be regarded as some kind of auxiliary language functioning for a transition period on the way to Finnicisation: it was assumed that IMLI would not be needed after the child had learned enough Finnish. This attitude, although not as common today, is still alive. Moreover, since immigrants live dispersed throughout the country, it is often hard to form groups of four, even with the possibility of gathering pupils from neighbouring municipalities. This is a problem especially for those minority languages that have few speakers and especially for those outside the capital region. It is also hard to hire teachers if the number of hours is small and the distance between schools is great. Furthermore, even though most immigrant parents consider IMLI to be important, there are also parents who do not want their children to participate in it. Another problem is the choice of language: who can decide which language the child should study as a native language. Sometimes parents choose a language which they for some reason or other consider more valuable or useful than their own native language. This phenomenon has been observed particularly among families who have experienced minority status before coming to Finland; for example, some Kurdish parents have wanted their children to study Persian as a native language instead of Kurdish (Nyholm & Aziz, 1996).

The educational background of IMLI teachers varies extensively. Only among the largest minority groups is it more common for individuals who work as IMLI teachers actually to have the qualifications needed for the work. Therefore, the level of teaching also varies extensively, and the objectives mentioned in the curriculum may not always be achieved. Since 1992 the NBE has arranged training programmes for teachers. The goal of these programmes has been to improve the quality of teaching. The training, comprising 19 credits, is spread over two years (Koponen, 2000).

Naturally, the problems of teaching do not arise solely from the varying backgrounds of the teachers. The work of teachers is quite challenging, since the groups are in practice very heterogeneous. In the same teaching group, the ages of the pupils may vary from 7 to 15 years, and the level of their skills in their native language may be quite varied, depending on, among other things, the pupil's age on arrival in Finland (Häyrinen, 2000). The situation of immigrant pupils in schools can be challenging in many ways and, as IMLI is very often arranged after regular school hours, the teacher's task is not an enviable one.

The legislation allows using immigrant languages as languages of instruction, but bilingual education for immigrants is still minimal in Finland, as compared to the scope of bilingual instruction offered, for example, in Sweden, Norway and Denmark. In practice, there are only a few classes in which the pupils' native language is used as one of the languages of instruction. The first bilingual classes were founded in 1992 at Männistö elementary school in Kuopio, a town in eastern Finland. At Männistö school, most education in the preliminary phase is given in the native language of the pupils. About 20 schools in the capital region and a few in other parts of the country have later adopted this model. The languages used most often as languages of instruction are Russian, Somali, Arabic, Vietnamese and Estonian.

Language-in-education planning

The minority language policy of a country is manifested most clearly in its educational policy. The status of minority languages in Finnish schools has improved considerably. Native language is not any longer commonly seen as an auxiliary language, and its value *per se* for individual pupils has been acknowledged. The objectives stated in the educational policy witness an awareness of cultural pluralism: instead of passive acceptance of linguistic diversity, multiculturalism is supported actively. Having these objectives in place, Finland moves to the same category as, for example, Holland and Sweden in policy planning for minority education (see Extra & Gorter, 2001).

However, the implementation of multicultural educational policy faces several problems in practice, as has been described previously in detail. In part, the problems have to do with the fact that multiculturalism and linguistic diversity are new phenomena in Finnish schools. Also the development of minority education shows that even the use of established minority languages like Saami and Romani in Finnish schools has been relatively rare until very recently. In the current decentralised educational system, significant responsibility is given to municipalities: they decide whether to arrange any second language, IMLI and preparatory instruction at all. The growth of multiculturalism is, however, only one of the challenges facing schools at present. In times of economic recession, municipalities are dependent on all the extra funding they get from the state; they seldom choose to invest their own funding in minority education. Therefore, the form and volume of implementation vary according to the number of minority children living in the municipality. In larger municipalities, it is easier to offer at least the bare minimum of IMLI in a large number of languages than it is in small municipalities. On the other hand, the example of Kuopio has demonstrated to the municipalities in the capital region that a wider use of minority languages as languages of instruction can succeed.

According to Jaakkola's (1999) longitudinal studies, Finnish attitudes to immigrant languages and cultures have not changed much since the 1980s. A large majority of Finns are of the opinion that it is good that immigrants maintain their native languages and teach them to their children as well. Approximately two-thirds of the respondents think that Finnish schools should arrange instruction in immigrant minority languages, if immigrants wished to have it. Compared with, for example, the attitudinal climate in Sweden (Winsa, 1999), similar negative attitudes towards immigrant minority languages can hardly be detected in Finland. Another example of the general attitudinal climate in this matter is the proposal made in *the Government Decision-In-Principle on Immigration and Refugee Policy Programme* (MI, 1997): IMLI should be increased from the present two hours a week to three to four hours a week. Furthermore, the President of Finland has taken up the importance of maintaining immigrant languages on several occasions, most recently in the main event of the European Year of Languages (2001). In the current situation, where less than 2% of Finnish society consists of immigrants, the positive – or at least neutral – attitudinal climate of that society towards minority languages forms the basis on which future initiatives to promote maintenance of minority languages can be built.

However, it is evident that positive attitudinal climate is not enough. Despite the progress made in the 1990s, the EC Committee of Ministers finds that the implementation of the Framework Convention for the Protection of National Minorities has not been fully successful for the Roma and the Russian-speaking population of Finland (see Part III). The committee has concluded in its first set of recommendations concerning country reports (2001) that there is scope for improvement in the status of the languages and cultures of these two minorities, *inter alia*, in the educational system and the media (Reinboth, 2001).

Religion

National churches

After the Reformation, the clergy of the Evangelical Lutheran Church taught Christianity to common people, and at the same time taught them to read in Finnish. The religious texts available were written in Finnish and Swedish, and thus the missionary work done among other language groups also led to Finnicisation. During several centuries, the Evangelical Lutheran Church took a half-hearted or even a negative attitude in regard to languages other than Finnish and Swedish.[27] In the 18th and 19th centuries, some religious texts, for example the Catechism, were initially translated into Saami. Other minority groups had to wait till the second half of the 20th century before their native languages were considered worthy of attention in ecclesiastical activities.

Throughout the recent history of the Saami, the church has been the only institution that has aspired to use Saami in its activities (Aikio-Puoskari & Pentikäinen, 2001). According to Aikio (1988), the Lutheran Church aimed at assimilation in teaching Christianity to the Saami in the 18th and 19th century, when religious literature was translated into Saami. Kähkönen (1990) states, however, that some efforts of the church undertaken during those centuries promoted the maintenance of Saami. For example, the catechists were often native Saamis, and they used, in part, Saami in their teaching. He also points out that ministers in Saami congregations made a remarkable contribution to the writing of Saami languages. Nevertheless, Kähkönen admits that it has taken an astonishingly long time for the church to recognise Saami in ecclesiastical legislation. As recently as 1989, the proposal for a new church law did not make any mention of Saami, even though the Utsjoki congregation proposed a motion to make the Saami languages official in the Saami area (Kähkönen, 1990). However, the final version of the current Church Law (1994) states that it is possible to found a bilingual Finnish-Saami congregation in the Saami Homeland. In addition, the law ordains that, in the Saami Homeland, Lutheran ceremonies and services such as baptisms, weddings and funerals shall be conducted in Saami whenever participants wish (Heino *et al.*, 1997).

The status of Saami has become stronger in the Evangelical Lutheran Church in many other ways as well. Since 2000, the Saami have their own representative, appointed by the Saami Parliament, in the General Synod, the highest administrative body of the church. Bilingual sermons are now preached in most congregations within the Saami Homeland. However, there is still no bilingual Finnish-Saami congregation. A common phenomenon for all the Saami languages is the shortage of religious literature in Saami. The Bible has been translated into North Saami, but only a few gospel texts exist in Inari and Skolt Saami. A new translation of the Bible into North Saami is under way through Nordic co-operation at the University of Tromsø. The translation of the New Testament was published in 1998; the translation of the Old Testament will be finished in the near future. Hymnbooks in North and Inari Saami were published in 1992 and accompanying verse books in 1993. In December 2000, a new version of the service book of the Evangelical Lutheran Church was introduced that uses three languages (Finnish, Swedish and Saami) at the same time. The Gospel of St Matthew has been translated into Inari Saami, and the Gospel of St John has appeared in Skolt Saami (Aikio-Puoskari & Pentikäinen, 2001).

For several hundred years, the Roma were not allowed to participate in any church services. For example, Lutheran priests were not allowed to baptise or bury members of the Roma community. Soon after the Roma achieved equal status with other citizens in the law (1883), they were officially recognised by church authorities and clergy. In practice, however, attitudes have changed very slowly. The policy adopted in the 19th century and practised until recently could be described as assimilationist; religion has been used as a vehicle for assimilating the Roma culturally into the mainstream population (Kortteinen, 1997). It took until the 1970s before the Gospels of St Mark (1970) and St John (1971) were translated into Romani, and a Romani version of the Gospel of St Luke was published in 2001. Romano Missio is the oldest national association of the Romanies in Finland. To begin with, it practised a similar kind of assimilationist policy as the church, but at the present time it organises services in Romani together with the Evangelical Lutheran Church, although not regularly (MSAH, 2000).

During the past few centuries, the church has worked actively among its deaf members. In the 18th century, the deaf were taught orally, with the help of signs and pictures. In 1858, they were officially given the right to participate in the confirmation school. Later in the 19th century, the clergy were active in founding deaf schools. At the turn of the 20th century, deaf associations pressured the state to get ministers of their own. Currently, there are seven ministers dedicated to this work (Honkkila, 2000). The latest step towards the recognition of sign language in the church has been the translation project for the service book. Up to the present time, the language used in churches has mostly been signed Finnish and signed Swedish. The translation of the service book was accepted by the General Synod in November 2001 (Lapintie, 2001).

At the end of the 20th century, the Evangelical Lutheran Church showed more interest in the growing multilingualism of its congregations. Since 1976, the International Evangelical Church in Finland, together with the Evangelical Lutheran Church, has organised services in a number of languages. According to Yrjölä (1998), the activities currently called 'international work' are based on the work done among the first Vietnamese refugees at the end of the 1970s. Currently, sermons are conducted regularly in 10 languages (Amharic, Arabic, Chinese, English, Estonian, French, German, Hungarian, Lingala and Russian) in the capital region.[28] A new version of the Catechism is available in Finnish, Swedish and English, and there are also plans to translate the Catechism as well as the service book of the Evangelical Lutheran Church into several other languages (Kirkkohallitus, 1999). In addition, the church supports activities in other languages by lending congregation facilities to various language groups. Compared with the earlier policy practised by the church, its current approach to linguistic minorities can be described as multicultural.

The Finnish Orthodox Church has a significant following in Finland and the provision of the Saami Language Act applies to the Office of the Orthodox Diocese of Oulu and to the Orthodox Parish of Lapland. The Skolt have the right to use their native language and receive services in that language from these institutions. However, the use of Skolt Saami in Orthodox Church ceremonies and administration is more limited than the services provided in North Saami for the Evangelical-Lutheran Saami. Despite the fact that the Orthodox Church uses the Skolt Saami language only a little in its ecclesiastical activities, the church and religion play a significant role in the identity of the Skolt Saami (Aikio-Puoskari & Pentikäinen, 2001).

During the 20th century, Church Slavonic and Russian have been used in the Finnish Orthodox Church, in addition to Finnish and Swedish. As with the Evangelical Lutheran Church, the same kind of development towards multiculturalism can be found in the recent approach adopted by the Finnish Orthodox Church (Repo, 1999). As early as the 1990s, the International Orthodox Community in Helsinki began to organise liturgies in English. Currently, services are conducted in English and Romanian approximately once a month. Occasionally, services (or parts of them) are also conducted in Amharic, Arabic, Armenian, Coptic, Estonian, German, Greek, and Syriac.

Other churches and religious communities

After the Reformation, the Roman Catholic Church disappeared from Finland for centuries. During the period of Finnish autonomy, the Roman Catholic Church started to function again in Finland, this time as a church for immigrants. In addition, small groups of Jews and Muslims settled in Finland during the Russian era. At the beginning of the 20th century, and especially after the independence of Finland in 1917, communities of Roman Catholics, Jews and Muslims grew considerably.

The linguistic situation of the Jewish community has changed in the 1990s: among the approximately 1400 members there are 200 Jewish people who have emigrated from the countries of the Commonwealth of Independent States (Horn, 1999). There are two Jewish congregations in Finland, one in Helsinki and one in Turku. They function mostly in Finnish. In addition to the main language of religious services, Hebrew, Yiddish is also used to some extent.

Recent immigration has effected the Catholic Church in Finland in several ways. On the one hand, it has increased the number of members (approximately 7000 at present) and this has revived the church's activities. On the other hand, the new linguistic and cultural diversity has also brought challenges. For example, the Roman Catholic congregation in Turku now has over twice as many members as it did 10 years ago, thus becoming the most multinational congregation in Turku (Martikainen, 2000b). In the Roman Catholic congregations in Finland, services are presently offered in at least nine other languages besides Finnish and Swedish: English, French, German, Italian, Latin, Polish, Russian, Spanish, and Vietnamese. The other languages are used once a week or even less often, for example, twice a month.[29]

The most notable change, however, has been the sudden increase in the Muslim population. The old Muslim community in Finland consists of Tatars. The Finnish Islamic Congregation was founded in 1925, and thus it became the first Muslim community in the Nordic region. Since the 1960s there has been a trickle of Muslims into Finland, but the situation changed very rapidly at the beginning of the 1990s when immigration into Finland increased. Currently, the estimated number of Muslims in Finland lies between 10,000 and 15,000. The new Muslims in Finland come mainly from the Middle East, North Africa, Somalia, and the former Yugoslavia. The Tatar Muslims have not been willing to integrate Muslims from other countries into their community, as the new migrants neither have the Tatar ethnic background nor know the Tatar language. Martikainen (2000a) points out that, for understanding the position of Tatar Muslims in relation to new Muslims, it is important to note that Tatars see themselves in the first place as a religious, linguistic and cultural minority. New Tatar immigrants will be accepted as members of the Tatar community provided they master the Tatar language. While the Tatar religious services are open to all Muslims, many of the new Muslims in Finland have chosen to found religious organisations and associations of their own. New Muslim communities are often based on ethnic and linguistic background. The languages used in the communities include, e.g. Arabic, Bosnian, French, Somali and Turkish (Heino, 1997; Martikainen, 2000b, 2000c).

According to Martikainen (2000b), immigrants have had two ways of adapting to religious life in Finland. They have become part of established religious communities that have later adopted some activities meant especially for immigrants, most often in languages other than Finnish or Swedish. Immigrants have also founded new religious communities, among others, a Buddhist community. The Buddhists in Finland are mainly Vietnamese.

The media

The Finnish Broadcasting Company (Yleisradio Oy, YLE) was established in 1926. To begin with, it transmitted programmes in the two official languages of the country – Finnish and Swedish. The licence for the company was amended in 1984 to include, for the first time, a mention of the Saami languages. According to the Act for Yleisradio Oy (1999), the duties of YLE currently include, among other things, to broadcast to Finnish and Swedish-speaking citizens on an equal basis and to produce services in the Saami and Romani languages and in sign language, as well as in other languages spoken in the country, where applicable.

In 2001, of 198,784 hours of radio broadcasts, Finnish broadcasts accounted for 69.6% of programme output, Swedish for 20.1%, Saami for 1.8% and foreign languages (i.e. English, French, German and Russian) for 8.5% (YLE Annual Report, 2001: 41). For other immigrant languages, only private radio stations provide media services.

Production of newspapers and magazines in minority languages in Finland is still minimal. However, newspapers and magazines imported from abroad (approximately 50) are available at shops, especially in southern Finland.

Saami

Among the language minorities in Finland, the Saami are the most adequately served by the media. The most important form of Saami mass media in Finland is radio. Radio broadcasts in Saami were started as early as 1947 as a result of the efforts of active individuals. News and religious programmes were the foundation on which Saami programme production was based for several years. Since 1991, it has been possible to listen to YLE's Saami programmes on a separate channel in the Saami Homeland. In 2002, YLESAAME broadcast eight hours of programmes in Saami on weekdays, and two hours on Saturday and Sunday nights. Radio programmes are broadcast in three Saami languages, most in North Saami. The national broadcasting companies of Finland, Sweden and Norway co-operate in their provision of Saami-language programmes. The Saami Radio stations in the three countries are planning to start their own digital radio channel. The digital channel would provide an opportunity to increase broadcasting and to extend the present reception area. Trial digital broadcasts began in 2000, and the new channel is expected to be in use by 2005 (Aikio-Puoskari & Pentikäinen, 2001; Horn, 1999).

Regular TV news broadcasts in Saami were started in August 2001 in Norway and Sweden and in January 2002 in Finland. Currently, the nine-minute daily news is the only TV programme broadcast regularly on national TV channels in Finland. In addition, a teletext service, Saami Info, offers news and different types of service information. For example, the Saami Parliament, organisations, municipalities and educational institutions have their own pages on the service. Teletext service Saami Info was an EU project, financed by the Finnish Broadcasting Company YLE, the Regional Council of Lapland and the Ministry of Education (Aikio-Puoskari & Pentikäinen, 2001).

The oldest cultural journal published in North Saami, *Sápmelaš*, was founded in 1934 and has been distributed ever since free to each Saami-speaking family. *Sápmelaš* used to be published once a month, but in recent years it has appeared less frequently. The North Saami weekly newspapers, *Min Áigi* and *Aššu*, are published in Norway and are also read by the Saami in Finland. From 1987 on, a quarterly paper written in Inari Saami, *Anârâš*, has also been published. It is distributed by Anârâškielâ servi, the Society for Inari Saami, to all households where Inari Saami is spoken (Aikio-Puoskari & Pentikäinen, 2001; Olthuis, 2002).

Romani

As far as other language minorities are concerned, there is even less of a media presence. In Romani a noticeable, even if only symbolic, change took place in 1995 when one of the national radio channels started broadcasting weekly news in Romani (*Romano Mirits*). Romani associations publish their own newspapers (*Romano Boodos, Latšo Diives*) containing articles both in Finnish and in Romani (MSAH, 2000). Although there are no specific TV programmes in Romani, change has taken place in other ways. At present there are more TV programmes about the Roma or programmes where the Roma play an important part than there were in the past. Still, as Marjakangas (2000) points out, the image of Romani on Finnish TV has not changed much from the stereotype of previous decades.

Finnish sign language

The only TV programme broadcast in Finnish sign language is the five-minute daily news. Other regular services produced by the national broadcasting company consist of YLE teletext that provides the deaf community with programme subtitles and other services. In 2000, approximately 15% of the programmes were subtitled in Finnish.[30] In addition to regular news and teletext services, there have been some short-lived or irregular broadcasts in sign language. In 1995, MTV3 had its morning news interpreted in sign language for a short period. Since 1996, TV1 has shown a few children's programmes and educational programmes, produced by the Finnish Association of the Deaf, in sign language (Kääpä, 2000; Kuurojen Liitto, 1997). In addition to Finnish production, some programmes in sign language, broadcast by SVT (Sweden) can be seen in the coastal areas of Finland (Kuurojen Liitto, 1997).

The Communication Policy Programme compiled by The Finnish Association of the Deaf (Kuurojen Liitto, 1997) notes that many signers lack good skills in Finnish, since sign language has been neglected or even discriminated against in school. That also explains why the media which do not require hearing ability (newspapers, books) do not necessarily reach the whole deaf community. Neither the ideas of the fundamental rights reform nor the act on YLE have been put into practice, as the deaf are provided services mostly in a foreign language (subtitles and other services in Finnish). Thus, the wishes of this group in their need for visual communication so far have not been realised. What new service digital TV will bring for the deaf community remains to be seen.

Kuurojen lehti (The Magazine of the Deaf), founded in 1894, is published eight times a year by the Finnish Association of the Deaf.

Immigrant minority languages

In the spirit of the Integration Act (1999), YLE also produces some services 'for other language groups in the country'. Before the 1999 law came into effect, *the Government Decision-In-Principle on Immigration and Refugee Policy Programme* had already been supporting immigrants' native languages and cultures in the following way:

> A sum in the State budget will annually be allocated to the activities of immigrants' own associations, spontaneous instruction of their native language and culture, production of newspapers/magazines and radio programmes in their own language and presentation of their own culture to the majority population. The Finnish broadcasting corporation will develop programme activities in immigrants' own languages making use of international co-operation. (MI, 1997: 14)

Since October 2000, there have been daily news bulletins in Russian (*Novosti po-russki*) on a nation-wide radio channel. Radio Finland, the external service of YLE, broadcasts in southern Finland in English, French, German, and Russian in addition to Finnish and Swedish. On Fridays, YLE R1 airs *Nuntii Latini*, the weekly news review in Classical Latin. In addition, there are other programme services in foreign languages: YLE World is an English-language domestic service compiled from the material of other broadcasters, and YLE Mondo offers programmes in languages other than English 24 hours a day. Capital FM is a channel compiled from Radio World's and Mondo's programming in the capital region, and to some extent in Turku, Lahti and Kuopio (in south-western, southern and eastern Finland, respectively) (YLE Annual Report, 2001).

At the end of the 1980s, the possibility for using local commercial radio stations was noticed among the Vietnamese, the largest new linguistic minority at that time. Radio City started broadcasting weekly news in Vietnamese in 1987. This service, however, ceased at the beginning of the 1990s. During the 1990s, local radio stations in various parts of Finland have started to produce news and other programmes in the largest immigrant languages. An example of a community radio, *Radio Robin Hood* in Turku, in the south-western corner of Finland, broadcasts in about 10 different languages (e.g. Albanian, Arabic, Farsi, French, Kurdish, Romani, Russian, Somali, Turkish and Vietnamese). Another community radio station, *Radio Moreeni* in Tampere, produces a multilingual news hour once a week. The languages concerned are English, Farsi, French, Kurdish, Pashtu and Russian. Another example of a community radio station is *Lähiradio* in the capital region broadcasting programmes made by immigrants. Currently, it broadcasts news regularly in, e.g. Amharic, Arabic, English, Estonian, French, German, Kurdish, Russian, Somali and Spanish (Nevala, 2001). In addition to community radio, there is a commercial Russian radio station, *Radio Sputnik Finlandia,* that has operated since September 1999.

Its programmes in Russian can be heard along the southern coastal area of Finland.

YLE's services in immigrant languages are limited to radio. However, an example of change brought about by new policy is a multicultural programme called *Basaari* that has been broadcast regularly since 1998. The programme tells Finns about the lives of immigrants, and it also informs immigrants about the lives of Finns and of other immigrants. The programmes are produced by immigrants, trained as programmers by YLE, and by the Ministry of Labour (Sandell, 2001).

When minorities are small and dispersed, it is hard to build infrastructure to support them that will last. One example of such a pattern can be seen in the Vietnamese community in Finland where, besides radio news, the community used to have a magazine of its own at the beginning of the 1990s. Currently, the Vietnamese community does not have either. Towards the end of the 1990s, the support from the Ministry of Education for the activities of immigrant associations, including the production of newspapers and magazines, increased. Currently, several minority communities have magazines of their own, for example, the Ingrian Finnish (*Inkeri*), the Somali (*Koor*), and the Kurdish (*Hangwai*) communities. The largest immigrant minority in Finland at present, the Russians, has several publications: *Rubezh, Spektr,* and *Kurjer Suomi,* all published in Russian (Markkanen, 1999).

As McRae (1997: 310) remarks, the ongoing media revolution works in two directions – spreading larger languages globally, but also enabling new support and linkages for smaller, more fragile linguistic minorities. Even if the production of newspapers or radio programmes, let alone TV programmes, in minority languages may be marginal in the new surroundings, members of some language groups can receive TV programmes in their native language by satellite. The Internet has also added the possibility of receiving information (radio news, newspapers) in one's native language, irrespective of one's location in the world.

The Spread of Foreign Languages

This section begins with an overview of foreign languages in the curriculum: what the language programme in Finnish schools is like, and what the objectives and the results of the foreign language teaching are. Thereafter, the rapidly growing field of content and language integrated learning is described in the Finnish context. Finally, the central issues in Finnish language teaching policy are examined.

In general, the national languages are included in the statistics of foreign languages in the curriculum in Finland, and that is why they are included in this section, in addition to the section on national languages as second languages.[31]

The overview given here will be limited to basic and upper secondary education. Foreign languages are taught extensively in vocational education, at universities and polytechnics, in adult education and in continuing education. See e.g. Sajavaara and Takala (2000) and Sajavaara (1995), for further information on these aspects on foreign language education in Finland.

Foreign languages in the curriculum

A brief history

Before comprehensive schooling was introduced, foreign language skills were considered a privilege of academically educated citizens, and consequently, foreign languages were taught almost exclusively in secondary schools. In the 19th century, it was thought that foreign languages were the most challenging subject group, and, therefore, foreign language education had a central role in schools' curricula. The time devoted to foreign languages could be up to 50% of the total teaching time, depending on the type of school (Piri, 2001). Even if the proportion for languages in the study programme declined in the 20th century, the upper secondary school largely retained its reputation as a demanding language environment, in contrast with elementary schools. In lower secondary schools, all pupils studied, in addition to the second national language, one foreign language. In upper secondary schools, many pupils added one or two foreign languages to their programme.

The progress of internationalisation as well as changes in the labour market set new requirements on language skills. At the same time, an increased emphasis was given to oral language proficiency. Since childhood was seen as the best time to acquire fluency in speaking, the starting age of language instruction was modified. During the 1960s, the typical starting age dropped from 11 to 9 years, as language teaching gradually became more general (Eurydice, 2001).

The comprehensive school of the 1970s continued the tradition of several foreign languages in the curriculum, but it also caused an important change in the distribution of language education. For the first time, the whole school population was required to acquire languages other than their first language. To begin with, ability grouping was used in the teaching of foreign languages, as it was not considered possible to set the same learning requirements for all pupils. However, different syllabi led to a number of problems with eligibility for further studies, and the legislative reform of 1984 ended the period of so-called level courses (Eurydice, 2001).

The language programme in Finnish schools

The national core curriculum of pre-school education for six-year-old children, adopted in 2000, does not include foreign languages. There are, however, day-care centres and pre-school classes in schools that specialise in foreign languages.

In the current educational system, pupils usually begin studying their first compulsory foreign languages (A1-language) in grade 3 (see Figure 2). Pupils in grades 1–6 may also choose to study an optional language (A2-language). The second compulsory language (B1) starts in grade 7, and it has to be one of the national languages or English. In addition, pupils in grades 7–9 can take an optional language (B2-language). In the upper secondary school, all students study at least two foreign languages, one of which is the other national language (Swedish or Finnish). Students can also take an optional language (B3-language). In addition, schools may offer short courses (less than B-language level) in foreign languages. Thus, if all the options for studying foreign languages are taken, the student may end up having as many as five or six foreign languages by the end of upper secondary school. In general, however, the number of

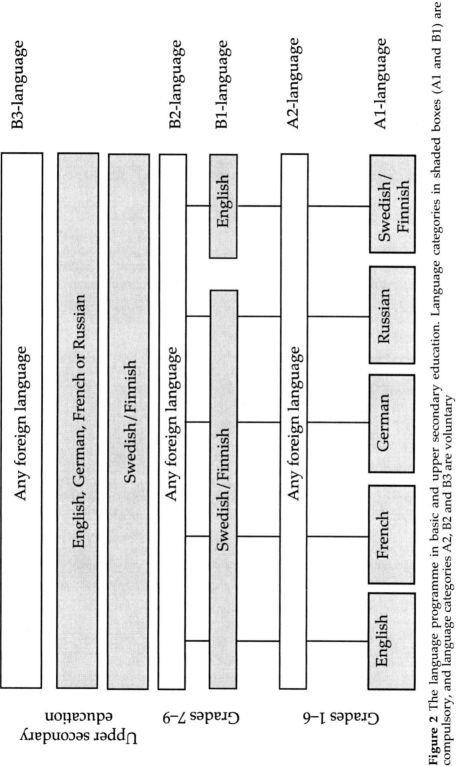

Figure 2 The language programme in basic and upper secondary education. Language categories in shaded boxes (A1 and B1) are compulsory, and language categories A2, B2 and B3 are voluntary

Table 9 Choices of first foreign language, excluding national languages, in the 1960s and 1970s, by percentage of the total number of pupils in secondary schools

Year	N	English	German	French	Latin	Russian	Total %
1962	194,098	56.9	42.6	0.1	0.3	0.1	100
1966	224,038	63.6	35.5	0.2	0.6	0.1	100
1970	267,956	78.9	20.2	0.2	0.5	0.2	100
1974[1]	218,406	90.7	8.4	0.2	0.4	0.3	100

Source: Piri (2001: 308)
[1] In the 1970s, the comprehensive school reform was gradually phased in, and therefore the number given in the statistics for secondary school pupils decreases.

languages studied is far less. In the 1998–99 school year, for example, a third of the upper secondary school students studied only the two compulsory foreign languages. About half of the students studied three languages, and less than a fifth studied four languages. Only about 3% of the students chose five or more languages in their study programme (SF, 1999). In Finland, the average number of foreign languages studied per pupil during the course of general secondary education is 2.5, whereas the average number for the whole of the EU is 1.4 (EC, 2000).

Language choices in Finnish schools

The popularity of foreign languages has varied over time. Classical languages dominated language teaching until the mid-19th century. Before the period of Russian oppression, the language programme of secondary schools offered, besides Latin and Greek, 'modern' languages. For example, the 1883 curriculum of Finnish-medium secondary schools included the following languages: English, French, German, Russian and Swedish. Willingness to study Russian diminished at the turn of the century. During the first decades of independence, German was usually the first foreign language at schools. After World War II, the language programme was re-evaluated. The NBE suggested to the Ministry of Education that the status of English and Russian had to be improved. The Ministry of Education gave instructions concerning the arrangements of language teaching. The languages to be studied depended, in part, on school type. In all school types, however, the first foreign language would be the second national language, and instruction in it started in the first year of secondary school (Piri, 2001).

In the 1960s and the 1970s, a considerable change took place in language choices made in Finnish schools (see Table 9). Until the late 1950s, the most popular foreign language was German, but English gained in popularity very rapidly. Still at the beginning of the 1960s, German was studied as the first foreign language by 43% of the cohort. By 1974, the share of German had diminished to 8% (Piri, 2001).

Except for the obligation to organise instruction in both national languages, current legislation does not prescribe which languages should be taught in schools. The local curriculum indicates which languages can be studied. Even if, in theory, any language could be taught, English is by far the most popular foreign language (see Tables 10 and 11). In 2000, as many as 91% of pupils in

Table 10 Languages chosen in basic education in 2000, by percentage of the total number of pupils

Language	Grades 1–6 (N = 392,150)	Grades 7–9 (N = 188,417)
English	64.5	98.0
Swedish	3.7	90.6
German	7.0	21.0
French	2.0	7.4
Finnish	4.0	5.4
Russian	0.3	1.0
Other[1]	0.1	0.6

Source: Tilastokeskus (2001: 45–6)
[1] Other languages include, for example, Hebrew, Italian, Saami, and Spanish.

Table 11 Languages chosen by students finishing their upper secondary education in 2000 (N = 34,744)

Language	% of pupils
English	99.4
Swedish	93.4
German	44.5
French	22.4
Finnish	5.7
Russian	5.8
Spanish	4.5
Italian	1.9
Latin	1.3
Other[1]	0.2

Source: Tilastokeskus (2001: 46)
[1] Other languages include, for example, Chinese, Estonian, Greek, Hungarian, Japanese, Portuguese and Saami.

general secondary education in the entire EU were learning English, 34% studied French, 15% German, and 10% Spanish. The pattern found in Finland is, thus, in one respect very similar to the European average: English dominates strongly. On the other hand, Finland belongs to those European countries where French, the second most taught language in the EU as a whole, is studied least (EC, 2000).

The objectives of foreign language teaching

The Finnish foreign language teaching programme has been criticised for its heaviness. Takala (2000) points out, however, that the total number of lessons reserved for foreign language study is not large in comparison to most European countries. In Finland, foreign languages have 16% of the minimum annual time-table allocated to compulsory subjects in basic education, which is average in the EU, as compared to Austria's 9% and Germany's 24% (EC, 2000). The criticism of the heavy language programme has probably been based, in part, on the objectives of language education.[32] For a long time, the importance of flawless production was emphasised, and this emphasis resulted in studying grammar and vocabulary as well as producing translations to demonstrate language learning. Due to the grammar-translation approach, foreign language study did not usually lead to the ability to use foreign languages actively. As of the 1970s, practical use of foreign languages were given priority in the objectives (Sajavaara & Takala, 2000).

Although mastery of oral skills is mentioned as an objective in the national core curriculum for the upper secondary school, the teaching of it is, in fact, to a great extent neglected. The foreign language test in the matriculation examination consists of listening and reading comprehension and sections demonstrating the student's skill in producing written work in the language. It has been argued that, as long as oral skills are not tested in the matriculation examination, the true objectives of foreign language teaching will remain the same as before, as the school-leaving examination has a considerable wash-back effect on the contents of teaching (Saleva, 1997).

In contrast to the school-leaving examination, the testing system for adults, the National Certificate of Language Proficiency, operational since 1994, seems progressive. The tasks measure language skills in practical situations, and the test consists of five subtests: speaking, listening comprehension, writing, reading comprehension, and structures and vocabulary. So far, the test has proved to have a considerable effect on adult foreign language education. The skill level descriptors of the test are widely used in many educational institutions and programmes (Härkönen *et al.*, 2000).

The effectiveness of instruction

Currently, language education constitutes an important development target in the Development Plan for Education and University Research, confirmed by the government (NBE, 2001). At the end of the 1990s, the evaluation of educational outcomes became one tool for quality assurance in language education.

At the beginning of the 1970s, the English skills of 14-year-old Finnish pupils were evaluated to be relatively weak in comparison with their peers in several other countries. However, evaluations undertaken at the end of the 20th century show that language skills have continuously improved, and the general nature of foreign language proficiency has changed radically. The ability to cope with natural situations of language use in a foreign language is much better than it was in the past (Sajavaara & Takala, 2000).[33] In a nation-wide evaluation undertaken among 9th graders in 1999, learning results in English were evaluated through a variety of tests designed to cover the aims and content laid down in the 1994 national core curriculum. Altogether 14% of the pupils ($N = 5641$) achieved a very good score, i.e., getting 85% of the test right, while a poor result (performance level below 45%) was recorded for 19% of the pupils. The best results were attained in reading comprehension and speaking, while listening comprehension proved to be the most difficult part. Girls obtained better overall scores than boys in all language skills, and their attitudes towards studying English were more positive than those of boys. On average, Swedish-speaking pupils (74%) scored better than did Finnish-speaking pupils (63%). There were also some regional differences: the top achievers came from the Åland Islands, with pupils

Table 12 Percentages of population aged 18–64 speaking foreign (or second) languages according to level of proficiency in 1995 (N = 4,107)

Level of proficiency	English	Swedish	German	French	Russian
Can speak almost natively	2	2	0	0	0
Can use the language fluently in public situations	11	3	1	0	0
Can cope well in practical uses of language	19	12	3	1	0
Can cope fairly well in ordinary spoken situations	20	21	9	2	1
Can cope in familiar routine situations	14	17	16	5	3
Cannot speak the language at all	34	45	71	92	95
Total	100	100	100	100	100

Source: SF (1999)

in southern Finland ranking second. The overall results were somewhat better in cities than in the rural areas (Tuokko, 2000).

The effectiveness of Finnish foreign language education has also been evaluated in several surveys undertaken among the adult population. In 1995, for example, a large survey was carried out on the subject of participation in adult education. The Adult Education Survey (AES) questions, administered orally in interviews, covered, among other things, the current foreign language skills of the respondents and their need for further education. The population of the survey comprised all persons aged 18–64 and registered as permanently resident in Finland. Another survey (Eurobarometer) on foreign language education was carried out in 2000 in all EU member states. In all countries, a representative sample of the population aged 15 years or older (approximately 1000 persons per member state) was interviewed.

According to the results of AES, 72% of Finns claimed that they are able to speak at least one foreign language. English is the foreign language most frequently spoken in Finland: 66% of Finns said they could speak at least some English. As many as 55% claimed they can speak some Swedish. A third of the respondents were able to speak some German, 8% said they were able to speak some French, and 4% were able to speak some Russian. The persons interviewed (N = 4107) for the survey were also asked to assess their language proficiency on a scale of 1 to 5 where 1 meant they could handle familiar routine situations, and 5 implied that they spoke the language almost natively (see Table 12). According to the results, English is also the foreign language Finns think they know best (SF, 1999).

Viewed in the European context, Finns' foreign language skills seem to be, on the one hand, similar to, and, on the other hand, different from the skills reported by other Europeans. According to the results of the Eurobarometer survey (INRA, 2001), 53% of Europeans say that they can speak at least one European language in addition to their native language. In the same study, the corresponding figure for Finns is 68%. Besides their native language, people in Europe tend to know English (41%), French (19%), German (10%), Spanish (7%), and Italian (3%). In comparison with these figures, Finns differ from the EU-average by showing much greater ability to use of English (62%). The languages Finns know best after English are Swedish (52%) and German (24%), whereas other languages have a more marginal position. Thus, the foreign language profile in Finland is connected with the official bilingualism of the country: the second national language occupies a central role in Finns' language skills.

In the Eurobarometer survey, the interviewees were asked to self-evaluate their level of knowledge of the foreign language in question by choosing between three alternatives: very good, good and elementary. In evaluating their foreign language skills, Finns seem to be close to the European average. For example, 14% of Finns evaluated their skills in English as very good, 33.7% as good, the EU average being 14% and 32.5%. All in all, the results of the INRA survey seem to support the findings of the AES survey which had been compiled five years earlier.

In addition to surveys based on self-report, the skills of the adult population have been assessed with the help of other methods. The purpose of Sajavaara's (2000) study was, in part, to evaluate the effectiveness of language training given by Finnish ministries for the purposes of Finland's 1999 EU Presidency. The subjects of the study were 1500 Finnish civil servants who were trained for Finland's Presidency. The data were collected by means of questionnaires, interviews, testing, and observation. The results showed, among other things, that while Finnish civil servants' language skills have improved in the languages they know, they master fewer languages than before: i.e. they can use only one or two languages effectively. There are fewer civil servants who know German, and a good command of Swedish, which is the language that has traditionally been used in Nordic collaboration, is much less common than before (Sajavaara, 2000).

Content and language integrated learning

The large number of foreign languages studied in Finnish schools has not ensured that there are enough people who have high level skills in all languages needed in the country. One of the earliest attempts to remedy this problem was to found schools in which the foreign language functions as the medium of instruction. Many of these schools have a long history: *Deutsche Schule Helsinki* (Helsingin Saksalainen koulu, 1881–), *The English School* (Englantilainen koulu, 1945–), *Lycée franco-finlandais d'Helsinki* (Helsingin ranskalais-suomalainen koulu, 1947–), *The Finnish-Russian School* (Suomalais-venäläinen koulu, 1955–), and *The International School of Helsinki* (Helsingin kansainvälinen koulu, 1963–). The latest foreign-language school is *the Finnish Russian School of Eastern Finland (Itä-Suomen suomalais-venäläinen koulu,* 1997–). In addition, there are currently eight upper secondary schools that provide the possibility to study towards the International Baccalaureate (IB) in English instead of the national matriculation examination. Furthermore, the Ministry of Education may exempt a school from the national time allocation and thus allow it to focus on a group of subjects, such as foreign languages. At present, there are several schools scattered across the country that specialise in foreign languages (Eurydice, 2001; NBE, 2001).

A central problem in foreign language education has been the fact that the large number of subjects to be studied results in the number of hours for languages being too low. As in many other European countries (e.g. Austria, France, Germany, the Netherlands, Sweden), a solution to this problem has been sought in the integration of content and language teaching (CLIL). The suggestion that some of the positive features of the foreign-language schools could be incorporated into mainstream education was an increasingly discussed topic through the 1980s. Immersion education in Swedish for Finnish-speaking pupils was started in 1987, and thus paved way to the integration of content and language teaching in other languages as well. The discussion of CLIL culminated in a working committee set up by the Ministry of Education, which recommended that it should be possible to teach through a foreign language in Finland (OPM, 1989). In 1991, a change made in Finnish education legislation enabled schools to use a language other than the pupil's native language in teaching when it was deemed appropriate. In 1993, the NBE produced a memorandum in which it recommended an increase in the amount of teaching through a foreign language (Nikula & Marsh, 1997, 1999).

In the mid-1990s, the NBE launched a project which examined the scale of CLIL activities nation-wide (Nikula & Marsh, 1996). In 1997 it published a complementary report (Nikula & Marsh, 1997) that provided more information on the objectives and implementation of CLIL. The first study by Nikula and Marsh was based on a questionnaire sent to all 'ordinary' primary and secondary level schools. In the second part of their study, Nikula and Marsh observed instruction given in English in nine schools during the 1996–97 school year. Of the primary schools, 8% offered CLIL. At lower secondary level the proportion of schools offering CLIL was 14%, and at upper secondary level 24%. A large proportion of the schools had plans to set up CLIL programmes in the near future. The survey findings indicated clearly that CLIL had become increasingly popular, and that its popularity was likely to continue.

During 1996–1997, CLIL was offered in a total of 252 schools. It was implemented at all school levels and in all provinces. At all school levels, CLIL was more common in the larger municipalities and larger schools respectively. CLIL was most often (80 to 90%) carried out in English at all levels. Other languages mentioned included the second national language[34], French, German, and Russian. The findings revealed that the types of CLIL introduced in Finnish schools varied extensively according to context and goals. CLIL often depended on the interest of individual teachers and was seldom a conscious school policy. The diversity of CLIL was evident in the names used for this kind of teaching: 'bilingual education', 'international classes', 'language shower'. Reasons for starting CLIL ranged from development of foreign language skills to facilitation of internationalisation and strengthening of school image. Scope and scale of operation, short-term or long-term exposure, subject choice, use of first language and foreign language, choice of students, teacher profiles as well as materials varied greatly (Nikula & Marsh, 1996, 1997).

The effectiveness of instruction

At the beginning of the 1990s, no strong opinions about the effects of CLIL had been expressed. It did not take long, however, before several groups (for example, language and literature teachers[35]) expressed their concerns about the effects of CLIL on the first language development of pupils participating in CLIL programmes. Towards the end of 1990s, even more critical attitudes to CLIL surfaced (Virtala, 2002).

To date there are not many studies on CLIL and its effectiveness in Finland. In the 1996 survey (Nikula & Marsh, 1996), teachers were asked to evaluate the effects of CLIL. CLIL was regarded as having developed students' language skills in general, in particular in relation to the building of self-confidence in actually using the language. The findings of the more detailed study (1997) suggested that CLIL had, in general, had a positive effect on students' target language skills. Receptive skills, however, appeared to have developed more rapidly than productive skills. Some students who had been taught extensively through a foreign language had considerable defects in formal language mastery. According to Nikula and Marsh, this is due to the fact that CLIL teachers rarely paid attention to formal aspects of the target language.

Nikula and Marsh (1997) pointed out that there were problems with CLIL that have to do with the lack of a national curriculum: many schools operate with unfocused aims, which often lead to equally vague approaches to CLIL. Therefore, the new national core curricula of 2004 will, for the first time, include a section on CLIL. Critical voices have also been raised about teachers' inadequate knowledge of the instructional language. At the end of the 1990s, several projects were undertaken to develop teachers' abilities to teach according to the principles of CLIL. For example, in-service training programmes were offered at continuing education centres of several universities. In addition, the NBE published a report concerning possible ways of implementing CLIL in Finnish schools in which several recommendations are provided. Moreover, it issued a decree that specifies the required language proficiency of teachers who use as the medium of instruction some language other than the pupil's native language.

The main argument raised against CLIL has to do with the possible impact it has on first language development (Virtala, 2002). On several occasions, the NBE has shown signs of concern about the impact of CLIL (and immersion) programmes on the learners' ability in Finnish as well as on overall learning results (Mustaparta & Tella, 1999). Nikula and Marsh (1997) conclude that the effects of CLIL on first language mastery depend upon how extensively, and in what ways, the target language is used. Furthermore, they point out that

> there is little research upon which we can rely which would give us the evidence necessary to find answers to questions raised . . . But most of the CLIL found in Finnish schools is so small-scale that it can be assumed that any chance of negative impact on the mother tongue is minimal. (Nikula & Marsh, 1999: 70)

When compared with immersion education, it is evident that research on CLIL programmes is still very limited. The arguments raised in the reports published so far as well as in the public debate (Virtala, 2002) call for more studies on the effects of CLIL on foreign language learning, first language development and content mastery.

Language-in-education planning

As Takala (1993) points out, states may choose to promote a policy of a unilingual, bilingual, or multilingual society. The general language policy may have explicit statutory legitimation or implicit social legitimation by tradition. The general language policy is one of the determinants of a nation's foreign language teaching policy. Finland's official language policy is embodied in a constitutional law that makes Finnish and Swedish the national languages of the republic. Other laws stipulate the linguistic status of municipalities and the language proficiency required of civil servants. Another major determinant of a nation's foreign language policy is its political and economic orientation toward other nations. For a small nation like Finland, it is of particular importance to care for the language proficiency of future generations. This interest is shown, among other things, by the fact that since the 1960s there have been several national commissions, set up by either the government or the Ministry of Education, whose specific mission has been to draw up proposals for national language policy and language teaching policy. Furthermore, this interest is shown by the fact that a considerable proportion of all educational resources is spent on foreign language teaching.

Sajavaara (1993) remarks that it takes a great many resources and a great deal of effort to raise the productivity of the entire educational system. Educational goals, societal needs, and various learner-related prerequisites are not the only criteria for implementation. Decision-making is often largely political. Political decisions that affect the outcome of foreign language teaching in Finland include, among other things, the total quota of foreign language education in Finnish schools, the number of languages to be taught, the specific languages included in the foreign language plan, the starting age, and the existence and composition of the school-leaving examination.

Since the early 1970s, entire school generations in Finland have studied at least two non-native languages. As compared with the pan-European recommendation on foreign languages (EC, 1995), according to which people living in the member states should be able to speak two official EU languages in addition to their own, foreign language teaching policy in Finland has been ahead of the times.[36] As was seen earlier, the pan-European recommendation has already been achieved by about half of the adult population in Finland (SF, 1999). By comparison, according to the Eurobarometer study (INRA, 2001), 26% of Europeans say they can speak two European languages in addition to their native language.

There has been a great deal of debate about the languages that should be included in the curriculum. Since Finland is officially bilingual, it has been considered necessary to make the study of the second national language obligatory for all students. At the same time, it has been considered necessary to offer a relatively large variety of major foreign languages. However, it has also been suggested that, since Swedish is always the second language in the compulsory programme, there is no room for other languages. For example, the preparatory work for the 1994 national core curriculum aroused debate about the status of non-native languages in the curriculum, especially whether Swedish should be compulsory for Finnish speakers. The Swedish People's party was opposed to the idea of making Swedish optional along with the other non-native languages. The only outcome of the very heated discussion was that the number of hours devoted to Swedish was reduced (Karppinen, 1993).

Since the 1970s, the leading goal of the Finnish foreign language teaching policy has been diversification of the language teaching provision and language study. The national language programme (OPM, 1978) was based on the principle of lifelong learning. The programme defined the overall language teaching policy, set the qualitative and quantitative targets for language proficiency in both national languages and in English, French, German and Russian, and outlined the process for implementing and developing the planning for language teaching policy. As a consequence of this planning, diversification of the language programme in comprehensive schools and upper secondary schools became an important development target (Eurydice, 2001; Piri, 2001).

Initially, the first foreign language for pupils was either English or the second national language. The development target outlined in the national language programme of the 1970s was instantiated in developing language legislation in the 1980s. All municipalities with more than 30,000 inhabitants were required to offer pupils a possibility to study French, German and Russian, in addition to English and the second national language, as their first foreign language. The aim was also to encourage the learning of optional foreign languages both in comprehensive schools and in upper secondary schools. The curricular reform of 1985 encouraged the studying of an optional foreign language at the lower stage of comprehensive school. By offering the possibility to study an optional foreign language (English) from the 5th grade on (A2-language), the authorities tried to encourage pupils to choose languages other than English as their first foreign language (Eurydice, 2001).

In the 1990s, when centralised language planning had come to an end, the educational authorities started a five-year project (KIMMOKE) to diversify the modern language teaching programme. The aims of KIMMOKE included, among other things, the introduction of the optional A2-language to all municipalities if possible. In addition, it aimed to increase the choice of languages available, to triple the number of pupils studying Russian (without affecting the number choosing Swedish and English) and to increase the number of pupils studying French, German and Spanish by 10 to 20% (Eurydice, 2001; OPH, 1999b).

So far, the KIMMOKE project has resulted in several reports and the development of teaching materials. Obviously, the long-term effects on pupils' language choices remain to be seen, but some changes in the 1990s can already be noted. In general, choices of an A2-language in the fifth grade have increased across the country. Swedish has been chosen more often as an A1-language. Choices of German as an A1- or A2-language have increased, and, consequently, its share as a B2-language has diminished a little. French has been chosen somewhat more often than before both as an A2-language and as a B2-language. Russian has been chosen as a B2-language more often than before. Also the number of students of Russian as a B3-language has doubled in the five-year period under study. In addition, A1-languages have lately been introduced in some schools as early as the first and second grade (OPH, 1999b). In the school year 2000–2001, as many as 6% of the first graders and 10% of the second graders started studying a foreign language. However, the aim of having an A2-language in every municipality has not been achieved. In the school year 2000–2001, there were 297 municipalities (out of 448) that offered teaching in an A2 language. Thus, opportunities for studying foreign languages depend substantially on local possibilities.

PART III: Language Policy and Planning

Status Planning and Language Planning Agencies

As in many other countries, there are three main types of language policy in Finland: status planning, corpus planning and language-in-education planning. Naturally, the three fields are connected with each other. In Part II, in the section on language-in-education policy, we have already dealt with education planning of the languages as first and second languages in the Finnish context. In the following sections, we will describe the status and corpus planning of various languages in Finland, as well as the language planning agencies.

Status planning concerns every language used in Finland at any level. The status of each language is defined and specified in legislation as well as in regulations on linguistic rights in Finland, issued, e.g. by state and municipal authorities for social welfare and the educational system. The decision-making body is Parliament, and the authorities are the Ministries, various institutions, councils and organisations. Furthermore, there are agreements that Finland has signed and directives issued by the Council of Europe with which Finland must comply although, in fact, membership in the European Union has not had a great effect on the contents of Finnish laws and decrees with regard to linguistic rights and language use as bilingual language legislation has had a long tradition in Finland. However, in the 1990s, status planning for minority language groups has increased, because of the large number of new immigrants.

As indicated in the following sections, the national languages, Finnish and Swedish, are equal according to the Language Act and other laws and decrees (Language Act, 1922), and the Saami languages have official status in the Saami Homeland and with the state authorities (Saami Language Act, 1991). Furthermore, there are two languages mentioned in the Constitution Act: Finnish Romani and Finnish sign language. They do not have the position of official languages, but they have ratified minority status.

Moreover, there are several other Acts and decrees, as well as directives that supplement the Constitution, with regard to the rights of individuals in Finland. In this context, we will provide only a few examples:

- Government officials are governed by the Act on the Linguistic Proficiency required of State Officials (149/1922);
- The Administrative Procedure Act (592/1982) stipulates, among other things, that all parties have the right to translation in their own language;
- The legislation on health care (e.g. 1062/1989) stipulates the rights of patients to use their own language and to have access to translation services;
- The Children's Day-care Act (36/1973) obliges municipalities to arrange day-care for children speaking Finnish, Swedish and the Saami languages as their first language;

- The Act on the Procedures Concerning Stipulations and Directions by the Authorities requires that all texts must be published simultaneously in Finnish and in Swedish.

Furthermore, Finland is bound by many international and Nordic agreements: e.g. the Nordic Language Agreement (1987), the general agreement between Finland and Russia (1992) and the agreements and obligations of the Council of Europe on human rights (1990) and minority languages (1998), as well as the agreements of the United Nations (see *Kielilainsäädäntö*, 2001; *Uusi kielilaki*, 2001). Since 1995, Finnish and Swedish have been official languages of the European Union.

Thus, the language legislation is not limited to the Language Act. In addition to the above-mentioned laws, several other regulations, such as, e.g. the Basic Education Act, The University Act and the Municipality Act, include regulations on the national languages and other languages, as well.

Legislative work and better interpretation of laws, decrees and orders is a continuous task. In 2002–3, the parliament of Finland will discuss and make decisions concerning a new Language Act and a new Saami Act.

The second language policy area is related to corpus planning. In Finland, this concerns particularly the languages mentioned in the Constitution: Finnish, Swedish, the Saami languages, Finnish Romani and Finnish sign language. The corpus planning of Finnish and Swedish as well as Saami and Romani involves the planning of common standard language in question (new terms for special purposes, the borders of written language variety, recommendations for users of written variety). The corpus planning of sign language involves the work for a common standard variety for Finnish sign language.

Status Planning: Language Legislation and Linguistic Rights in Finland

Finnish and Swedish: The national languages

The development of the status of Finnish and Swedish
As noted in the introductory section, during the Swedish period the language used for administrative purposes was Swedish. Despite the separation from Sweden in 1809, the language situation remained unchanged: Russian was only used in the offices of the Governor General and Secretary of State in St Petersburg; all the rest of the administrative and judicial affairs of the country were conducted in Swedish. During the 19th century, Finnish gradually developed as a literary and administrative language through a national awakening and a series of decisions made by the Russian Czar. The development was not painless. Nationalistic views on linguistic matters were expressed within several political and cultural movements in the second half of the 19th century. For a very long time, both Swedish and Russian were considered as enemies of the emerging Finnish language (Paunonen, 1997). However, during this period, the younger Swedish-speaking educated generation developed the idea of working to have two languages, Finnish and Swedish, used in the country (Beijar *et al.*, 1997: 21), thereby supporting the process of Finnish language development.

In 1863, Czar Alexander II issued a decree to the effect that, after a 20-year transitional period, Finnish was to be accepted alongside Swedish as an official language in matters pertaining to Finns. It was decided that the change should take place gradually, partly because of the resistance among the pro-Swedish officials, partly because the linguistic level of the formal varieties of Finnish did not allow for faster progress. Some decades later, there was a heated debate in the Diet as to the relative position of Finnish and Swedish among authorities and in bilingual municipalities. The Diet was unable to reach a decision, and the matter was laid before Czar Nicolai II, who in 1900 issued a decree according to which Russian was to be the language of higher authorities. Finnish and Swedish were thus demoted to the position of local languages. This period was one of great uncertainty in Finland. In 1899, Jean Sibelius composed *Historiallisia kuvia I* (Historical Pictures I) which culminated in a widely popular patriotic finale, 'Finland awakes', later to be called the Finlandia Hymn that became a symbol of Finnish nationalism. In 1905, the General Strike compelled the Czar to relent on a number of matters, including language. The 1906 statute on language restored the situation to what it had been prior to the 1900 decree (Paunonen, 1997; see Tommila, 1989).

The status of Finnish as a national official language was strongly developed in the 19th century and at the beginning of the 20th century. Thus, after the declaration of independence in 1917, speakers of Swedish felt that their position and future were threatened. The language issue was resolved in the Constitution established in 1919. The actual legislation, which still (in 2002) governs the position and relation of Finnish and Swedish, is the Language Act of 1922 (Paunonen, 1997; Reuter, forthcoming).

Following Finland's independence in 1917, attitudes to the language issue sharpened, and it was a prominent feature of internal politics during the 1920s and 1930s. It should be pointed out, however, that the language conflict between Finnish and Swedish in Finland never claimed any lives; the battle was almost entirely at the verbal level (McRae, 1997).

After 1945, the period of language conflict passed, and the situation has been equitable throughout the post-war period, although there are still people who see bilingualism as a burden rather than a resource. While it was the leading circles who attacked Finland's use of Swedish in the 1930s, the negative views since then have come from the lower socio-economic classes. In any case, 70% of Finland's Finnish-speaking population feel that Swedish is an essential part of Finnish society, and 73% would regard it as regrettable if the Swedish language and culture in Finland were to die out completely (Allardt, 1997).

Finnish and Swedish and the Language Act

The new Finnish Constitution (PL 731/1999) became effective on 1 March 2000. The law defines the basic freedoms and the rights of the individual. One of the most important rights is the right to one's own language and culture. According to the constitution (§ 6) everyone is equal before the law. Furthermore:

> No one shall, without an acceptable reason, be treated differently from other persons on the grounds of sex, age, origin, language, religion, conviction, opinion, health, disability or other reason that concerns his or her person.

In this respect the new Constitution resembles the former Constitution of 1919 (94/1919) (albeit it is somewhat more detailed) and the Language Act of 1922 (148/1922). Moreover, the Constitution includes stipulations concerning some of the established language minorities in Finland (see below).

Finnish bilingualism has a long tradition in legislation, and the new regulations are based on international conventions on the rights of minorities (Scheinin, 1999: 533). This is reflected in the Constitution (§ 17) as follows:

> The national languages of Finland are Finnish and Swedish.
> The right of everyone to use his or her own language, either Finnish or Swedish, before courts of law and other authorities, and to receive official documents in that language, shall be guaranteed by an Act. The public authorities shall provide for the cultural and societal needs of the Finnish-speaking and Swedish-speaking populations of the country on an equal basis.

The Language Act of 1922 states that a Finnish citizen is entitled to use either Finnish or Swedish before courts of law and when dealing with other national authorities. The right to use one's first language with government agencies applies to the entire country and the authorities are required to provide information in the citizens' first language. The juridical requirements for language are based on local circumstances. Every 10 years, the government decides, on the basis of official statistics, whether the local authorities should be classified as monolingual (Finnish or Swedish) or bilingual. A municipality is classified as bilingual if a minority of at least 8% of the population, or a minimum of 3000 people, speak the other language. In order for a municipality to be considered monolingual, if it used to be bilingual, the number of minority language speakers must go down to 6% of the population or less. The next classification of the municipalities will take place in 2003.

Most of the municipalities (385) are Finnish-speaking. The Swedish-speaking (21) and the bilingual municipalities with Swedish as the predominant language (22) are situated mainly in Åland and Ostrobothnia. The bilingual municipalities with Finnish as the predominant language (20) are mostly larger cities, such as the cities of the capital region, Helsinki, Espoo and Vantaa, or smaller municipalities located in southern Finland.

In a bilingual municipality, people are entitled to use either Finnish or Swedish with local authorities, while in a monolingual municipality only one language can be used. About half of all Swedish-speaking Finns live in municipalities which are entirely Swedish-speaking or where Swedish is the majority language in a bilingual municipality. The other half of the Swedish-speaking Finns live in regions which are dominated by Finnish.

The island of Åland has its own legislation, the objective of which is to protect the Swedish language and the special culture of the province. The islands are a monolingual Swedish part of Finland, with the right of its citizens to organise their internal affairs themselves at their Provincial Assembly, the Åland Parliament. The legislation is based on international conventions (The Act on the Autonomy of Åland, 1144/1991).

Towards a new Language Act in 2002

The Council of State established a Committee on the Language Act on 26 August 1999 to draft a proposal for the Language Act on the national languages, Finnish and Swedish, and related regulations. The committee consisted of specialists from the fields of politics, legislation and language.

Why does Finnish society need a new Language Act for the national languages?

When the present Language Act was drafted in 1922, the economic and social situation of Finland was different from that at the end of the century. Indeed, the Language Act was amended six times during the 20th century, with the most important amendments having been written in 1935, 1975 and 1996. The amendments were mainly technical additions or changes resulting from the consequences arising in other legislation; amendments to the principles and rights of the citizens were not made.

In spite of the intent of the old Language Act and other regulations of language legislation, the authorities' insufficient capacity to serve the citizens in both languages has caused problems. This is the case in both the mono- and the bilingual areas, but especially in the municipalities with Finnish as a majority language. The deficiencies in practice create inequality between the language groups and impair the citizens' view of bilingualism. In the past few years, this problem has gained considerable attention, and language legislation, as well as the need for its reform, has been widely discussed among the citizens, the press, in various studies and at the official level.

Thus, the core objectives of the reform of the Language Act include the securing of the linguistic equality provided for in the Constitution, the clarification of language legislation and the elimination of the failures in practical implementation. The Language Act aims to realise the requirements of the Constitution by assuring the linguistic needs and equality of the speakers of both languages.

The proposal for the new Language Act was submitted to the Council of State in June 2001. The report of the committee *Uusi kielilaki/Ny språklag 2001* (New Language Act, 2001) was published as well, and parliamentary proceedings started at the beginning of 2002.[37] The Act will become effective in January 2004.

The proposal for the new language law is clearer and more intelligible than the old law. The essence of the proposal in brief is: the act serves individuals; it is the needs of individual people that count. On the other hand, the authorities need a law that is easy to interpret. Public administration must provide for the cultural and social needs of nation's Finnish- and Swedish-speaking population on equal terms. Even though the proposal concerns only the national languages, there are also many links to decrees and orders pertaining to other language groups. As a result, the new Language Act will be a common law which will support other language groups by awarding them a more distinct position on the linguistic map of Finland.

Furthermore, in evaluating the present Language Act and the related legislation, the language proficiency levels required of state officials have been revised as a part of the reform. The working group outlined a proposal for a new language testing system planned for state officials in 2002. According to the proposal, the testing system will be in close connection with the National Certificates of Language Proficiency in Finnish and Swedish (OPM, 2002; see also Part II).

Saami languages

Finland is known for its early development of progressive language policy: the Language Act of 1922 has been a model for many countries dealing with questions concerning language policy. However, until very recently the linguistic rights of established minorities have been largely ignored. The first reform in minority language rights occurred in the Saami Language Act, enacted in 1992 though it had been under preparation for a long time. The law gives Saami-speaking people the right to use Saami in the Saami Homeland.[38]

The Saami[39] have traditionally been united by their family, language, religion, dwelling system and livelihoods. During the last decades of the 20th century, co-operation among the Saami has extended to the whole of Finland as well as to neighbouring countries. The Saami of Finland, Norway, Sweden and Russia have a co-operative body called the Saami Council. In addition, the Saami participate in the work of the World Council of Indigenous Peoples (WCIP). As an indigenous people, they also take part in the co-operation among states and autonomies within the Nordic Council, the co-operation on the Euro-Arctic Region of Barents and the work of the United Nations Human Rights Committee.

The 1970s brought the first signs of a change in Finnish social policy with the enactment of the first piece of anti-discrimination legislation. The assimilation policy of the early part of the century was abandoned, and special measures were taken to improve the economic, educational and social position of the Saami as well as other established minorities. The general change in attitudes towards minorities in the 1990s was reflected in the 1995 reform of the constitutional provision on fundamental rights, which has been included in the new Constitution of Finland (2000). According to the Constitution (2000, § 17) the Saami, as an indigenous people, have the right to maintain and develop their own language and culture.

In addition to the reform of the Constitution, two treaties of the Council of Europe that came into force at the beginning of 1998 and have subsequently been confirmed through national legislation, represent milestones on the path of strengthening the position of minorities in Finland. When ratifying the European Charter for Regional or Minority Languages, Finland named Swedish, Saami, and Romani. In 1998 Finland ratified the Application of the European Charter for Regional or Minority languages and thus declared that it will apply 59 of the provisions to the Saami languages as regional languages and 65 of the provisions to Swedish as a less widely used official language (*Kielilainsäädäntö*, 2001).

Since 1973, the Saami in Finland have elected a representative body, the Saami Parliament, to represent them. The purpose of the Saami Parliament is to attend to the rights and interests of the Saami by presenting initiatives and proposals and by preparing opinions to be presented to the authorities. Since 1991 the Saami, as Finland's indigenous inhabitants, have had the right to be heard in the Finnish Parliament on matters directly concerning them.

As noted earlier, since 1992, the Saami have had the right to use the Saami language both in speaking and writing when dealing with the authorities and to receive answers in their own language (*Asetus saamen kielen käyttämisestä viranomaisissa*, 1201/1991). The three Saami languages, North Saami, Inari Saami and Skolt Saami, are specifically included in the Act, but are not accorded legal status equal to that of Finnish and Swedish. Official government employees are not obliged to know the language, but translation or interpretation must be offered in the event that the officials in question do not speak Saami. The Saami also have the right to receive documents and information in their language and to use it with authorities. It can also be included as a native language in the official census.

In 1993 the Finnish Parliament required that the future of the Saami language and culture be secured through cultural autonomy. Here, the term *culture* also includes the traditional usage of land and of particular areas.

The proposal for the new Saami Act was approved in the Saami Parliament in December 2001. The proposal will be discussed in Finland's Parliament in 2002–3, as a proposal to be included in the new Language Act on the national languages, Finnish and Swedish.

The main reform proposed in the new Saami Act is that the authorities would now have to provide Saami-language services. Thus, the authorities in the Saami Homeland should speak Saami. This means that the authorities would need employees with good Saami language skills and that Saami languages would be studied more in the future if the proposal is approved by the Parliament.

Romani

As previously noted, the Constitution (2000, § 17) stipulates that the Roma have the right to maintain and develop their own language and culture.

Status for the Roma has long been denied in Finland, as in many other countries. It took many centuries for the Roma to be accepted in Finnish society. From 1750 to 1850, there was an interlude of greater tolerance of the Roma in Finland. Since then, discrimination has increased, including a vagrancy law affecting the Roma. The first report on a policy on the Roma was produced in 1901: that was a policy of assimilation. Until the middle of the century, assimilation continued to be the main aim of the official policy. From 1970 to 1990, the status of the Roma was improved: the first law prohibiting discrimination was enacted, and social awareness increased among the Roma. These 20 years constituted a period of social, educational and cultural policy development leading to improvements in housing conditions, the beginnings of adult education, the development of the Romani language for education and a start to teaching it in the comprehensive schools. In the 1990s, international co-operation concerning the human rights of minorities was promoted, the majority population re-evaluated the status of the Roma, while the Roma's sense of their own identity strengthened. In 1995, a constitutional amendment was confirmed, prohibiting discrimination on the grounds of ethnic origin; the Roma's rights to their own language and culture were guaranteed, e.g. educational policy was amended to allow the teaching of Romani in schools as a subject and its use as a language of instruction; the legislation on children's day care was amended to include the goal of supporting Romani-speaking children's own language and culture in co-operation with the Romani people. In 1997, the law governing the Research Institute for the Languages of Finland was amended to extend the Institute's brief to cover research into Romani and its standards (Grönfors, 1995; Ollikainen, 1995; Suonoja & Lindberg, 1999; http://www.vn.fi/stm).

As noted previously, in 1998 Finland signed both the European Charter for Regional or Minority Languages, in the context of which Finland identified Romani as a non-territorial minority language of Finland, and the Framework Convention for the Protection of National Minorities, in the context of which Finland identified the Romani people as a traditional national minority. Finland has, *mutatis mutandis*, declared that it shall apply the targets and principles of the convention to Romani and other non-regional languages used in Finland.

A programme of action for the prevention of ethnic discrimination and racism was adopted by the Finnish government in 2001. Under the programme of action, the authorities shall ensure that issues pertaining to ethnic relations, cultural diversity, religion and ethics are addressed in teaching materials and at all levels of education. The programme is important for the Roma as well as other minorities.

The Finnish Roma have a dual identity: as Finnish citizens they feel themselves to be both Finns and Roma, and consider themselves primarily a national minority. They justify this view on the basis that they have lived in Finland since the 16th century and are therefore every bit as much Finnish as everyone else. As previously described, at the end of the 1900s there had been efforts to revive the Romani language, which was on the verge of disappearing altogether at one point.

Finnish sign language

The Constitution (2000, § 17) stipulates that the rights of people using sign language and of persons in need of interpretation or translation aid owing to disability shall be guaranteed by an Act.

Thus, Finland became one of the seven countries in which the national sign language is protected by the Constitution. The other countries are Ecuador, Portugal, South Africa, Switzerland, Venezuela and Uganda (Jokinen, 2000a). For the first time in Finland, sign language users were considered to be a linguistic and cultural group at a constitutional level. For the deaf community, the reform was a major step towards linguistic equality.

The status of sign language in Finland was poor for a long time. Sign language was allowed neither at school nor in many other contexts, and it was not considered a language at all as late as the 1960s. However, the situation has changed considerably, and the status of sign language has improved during the 1990s in Finland (see Lappi, 2000). In accordance with the European Charter for Regional or Minority Languages, Finland declares that it undertakes to apply, *mutatis mutandis*, the goals and the principles of the charter to sign language and to other non-territorial languages in Finland. In 1997, the law governing the Research Institute for the Languages of Finland was amended to extend the Institute's brief to cover research into Finnish sign language and its standards: The Sign Language Board was appointed at the Institute in co-operation with The Finnish Association of the Deaf.

However, more important than declarations and institutional solutions are practical activities. Even though there are still many problems regarding the use of sign language and in having interpretation in sign language available at, e.g.

social or health care offices in Finland, the situation has improved considerably. The most important improvements are, perhaps, the right to study sign language at some universities, better teaching material for pupils and students, and dictionaries, courses, etc. for deaf people and their family members. Sign language is more visible and natural in Finnish society than ever before.

Other established minority language groups

When ratifying the Framework Convention for the Protection of National Minorities, Finland did not take an exclusive position as to which minorities in Finland should or should not fall within the scope of application of the Framework Convention. In reports submitted to United Nations treaty bodies, Finland has included information on the Saami, the Roma, the Jews, the Tatars, the 'old' Russians, and the Swedish-speaking Finns.

The agreement between Russia and Finland in 1992 involves a clause wherein both states guarantee to support the preservation of the identity of people belonging to the Russian minority in Finland and the Finnish minority in Russia. The Russian minority in Finland has been very active, both in Finland and in European Bureau for Less Used Languages (EBLUL). The Russian association, *Foorumi*, was founded in Finland in 1994, and a new organisation, *Suomen Venäjänkielisten Yhdistysten Liitto ry* (The Union of the Associations of speakers of Russian in Finland), was set up in 1999. The main task of the Russian associations is to achieve the status of a ratified minority for the whole Russian group, not just for the Russian people with old roots in Finland.

In contrast to some other countries, like Germany and Hungary, the Jewish people in Finland have had no objection to being considered a national minority. To what extent the European Framework Convention for the Protection of National Minorities will be considered relevant to the Jewish people and to what extent the European Charter on Regional or Minority Languages will be considered relevant to Yiddish is still under discussion within the Jewish community of Finland (Horn, 1999).

Corpus Planning Authorities

People speaking the so-called less frequently used languages are often very active in maintaining and planning for their own languages. Finland is no exception in this regard. There are many institutions and associations working not only with the national languages, Finnish and Swedish, but also with the minority languages in the country. In this section, some of the main actors in the field are examined briefly.

The Research Institute for the Languages of Finland

In Finland, the official language planning authority is The Research Institute for the Languages of Finland (RILF). It serves to research, plan and maintain Finnish, Swedish, Saami, Finnish Sign Language and Romani. The Finnish Language Planning Department (*Kielitoimisto*) is responsible for the planning of Finnish, and the Swedish Language Department (*Svenska språkbyrån*) is responsible for the planning of Swedish used in Finland. The Institute also has on staff a researcher on Saami, two researchers on Romani and a researcher on Finnish sign language. All of them have close contacts with other institutional actors in the field, as will be seen in the following sections.

The expert bodies for language planning are the Language Boards that make in principal decisions as well as concrete recommendations. The objective of language planning is to establish, maintain and develop a common, publicly standardised written language for Finnish, Swedish, Saami and Romani as well as a common standard variety for Finnish sign language (The language policy programme of the RILF, 1998). The roles of the Romani Board and the Sign Language Board are emphasised in present corpus planning activities.

In the following sections, the historical development and present corpus planning of various languages in Finland by RILF is briefly described.

Finnish

A hundred years ago, the work of every Finn writing in Finnish served as the basis for Standard Finnish. The bishops (e.g. Mikael Agricola) and the priests also helped to develop the written variety of Finnish in their translations of religious texts. Furthermore, the writers of grammars established the standard syntactic forms and lexicon of Finnish. In the 19th century, scientific societies (e.g. the Finnish Literature Society [*Suomalaisen Kirjallisuuden Seura*, founded in 1831] and the Society for the Study of Finnish [*Kotikielen Seura*, founded in 1876]) played an important role in establishing the standard for Finnish (Häkkinen, 1994; Paunonen, 1976; Räikkälä, 1995). During the 19th century, the orthography and the grammatical structure as well as the vocabulary was actively developed and established by many scholars – not only by linguists, but also by other scientists, priests and journalists (Hakulinen, 1979; Rintala, 2001).

By the 1870s, Finnish was used in many levels of administration, education and literature. The vocabulary had been diversified, the various dialects had been used as sources of grammatical features and new words for new concepts in various fields in society, and the orthography and the grammatical structure had been developed – often after long debates (Rintala, 2001); in other words, intellectualisation and modernisation had taken place.

In 1928, the Finnish Literature Society founded a standing language committee. The task of the committee was to discuss questions related to linguistic correctness. In 1945, the language office of the Finnish Literature Society opened its doors with the support of two private publishing companies, Otava and Werner Söderström Oy. The purpose was, on the one hand, to give advice concerning Finnish language use free of charge, and on the other to consult researchers and other authors about variation in and the history of Finnish. A further task of the office was to investigate grammatical questions (e.g. the use of the partitive subject in different types of sentences, the use of possessive suffixes, comparative forms of adjectives) (Räikkälä, 1995).

Subsequently, it was suggested that the state should support language planning. Many European countries had founded offices for language planning purposes (e.g. *Deutsches Sprachpflegeamt* in Germany, *Office de la langue Française* in France and *Centro Consultivo* in Italy). In 1949, the language office of the Academy of Finland was founded. Unlike many European nations, which also had recognised language academies (e.g. Italy – *Academia della Crusca*, 1582; France – *Académie Français*, 1635; Spain – *Real Academia Española*, 1713; Portugal – *Instituto de Alta Cultura*), the activities in Finland were not intended to constitute a language academy at that time, even though the language office was a part of the Academy of Finland. Consequently, the work for planning standard Finnish was funded by the government. In 1968, the first issue of the journal *Kielikello* (*Language Bell*) appeared. In 1976, the language office, as well as the Institute for Modern Finnish, were incorporated into the RILF which at present has tasks corresponding to those of the language academies in other countries (Räikkälä, 1995).

The Language Planning Department and its predecessors have had close contacts with the Broadcasting Company (YLE) since 1946. Hundreds of programmes offering language advice have been broadcast on the radio. *Kielikorva* (*Language Ear*), a regular programme, has been popular for 30 years.

In 1982, the Finnish government issued the so-called official language decree (*virkakielipäätös*). The purpose of the decree was to call attention to the language used by the authorities and to require its correctness and transparency. The decree has now been overruled, but the proposal for a new administrative law (which the parliament will discuss in 2002–3) includes a paragraph with the same contents as the 1982 decree. Thus, the rights of the individual to be presented with understandable texts written by officials will be established in law. This work was intended to emphasise that it is important to write laws, decrees and orders used by everyone in a society in plain language.

There has been close cooperation between the Nordic language boards since 1954. Even though Finnish belongs to a different language group than the Scandinavian languages (i.e. Swedish, Norwegian, Danish, and Icelandic), there are many common tasks in language policy and planning. In this respect, the cultural neighbourhood and the similarity of Nordic societies are more important than the kinship of the languages. Furthermore, the researchers in the field have close contacts with the European Commission. Co-operation with translators and interpreters in the Commission and in the European Parliament is an important part of planning Finnish, one of the official languages of the European Union. There is also a special researcher in the Institute for Finnish in the European Union.

The Institute for the Languages of Finland includes a Finnish Language Board (*Suomen kielen lautakunta*) that includes external experts. The committee discusses topics related to Finnish, organises seminars, and makes recommendations.

The tasks of language planning in Finnish (and also Swedish used in Finland) in the RILF are:

- the description and guidance of literary and standard language, its structures and vocabulary (structural language planning);
- the analysis of language in different contexts and the improvement of texts (text planning);
- the analysis of the scope of usage of language and its function in society, as well as the attitudes of the linguistic community (language policy) (http://www.kotus.fi).

Language planning aims take into account the decision-making and the functions of various organisations, thereby causing them to consider language and the possibilities of its usage from as wide a perspective as possible. The current topics include, *inter alia*, whether the national languages are losing ground to English and what the position of the Finnish language is in education and in working life.

The official language planning conducted in the Institute concerns only written, not spoken, Finnish in Finland. The Language Planning Department studies and follows the development of language (including personal and place names), issues recommendations and guidelines in principle, publishes an informative magazine *Kielikello*, gives presentations and lectures and offers education and other services. The recommendations are also provided, to a great extent, in an electronic form, and by phone, free of charge. The questions and discussions deal with many levels of the Finnish language, the most popular ones involving the coining of new words (e.g. the Finnish word for *portfolio* or *hands-free*) and the orthography of loanwords (*tutor* ~ *tuutori, meili* ~ *maili*), as well as the spoken varieties used currently in written texts.

Swedish

The Swedish Language Board in Finland was founded with private funds in 1942. As was the case for Finnish, language planning as well as the other private activities for Modern Swedish in Finland was transferred and incorporated into the RILF in 1976. The Institute includes a Swedish Department and a Swedish Language Board (*Svenska språknämnden i Finland*) including external experts. At the beginning of the 21st century, the main task of the board is to produce a plan for the future development of the Swedish language in Finland.

The Swedish department provides advice and recommendations in matters relating to Swedish usage in Finland; it has published a quarterly journal *Språkbruk* (*Language Usage*) since 1981. It also assists in terminological work, provides lectures on Swedish usage, sends circular letters to journalists and keeps in touch particularly with translators and authorities. The main tasks of Swedish planning in Finland resemble the tasks for Finnish mentioned previously. The goal is to look after that variety of Swedish used in Finland and to ensure that it does not drift too far away from the variety of Swedish used in Sweden, even if the regional differences are obvious and natural.

The Swedish Department has close and concrete contacts with Swedish schools (Sommardahl, 2002), publishers, radio and television channels, and newspapers. The co-operation between the Nordic language boards and agencies is close, especially the co-operation with those in Sweden.

Saami languages

Since 1976, the RILF has included the Saami Language Board (*Sámegiela lávdegott*) which involves Saami-speaking experts. The Saami researcher of the Institute, living in the Saami area in northern Finland, provides advice and recommendations on matters relating to the usage of the Saami languages in Finland. The researcher's tasks are similar to the tasks relating to Finnish and Swedish.

The Institute researcher has close contacts with the Saami Language Office, set up by the Saami Parliament and its Saami Language Board (see below). Furthermore the researcher has contacts with the Saami Institute (*Sámi Instituhtta*) in Kautokeino, Norway, and with many other bodies in the field of the Saami languages and cultures.

Finnish Romani

Since 1997, the RILF has included the Romani Language Board (*Romanikielen lautakunta*) which involves four Romani-speaking members. The committee discusses and makes decisions in matters relating to Romani standardisation in Finland (Leiwo, 2001). The Romani researchers in the Institute write reports regarding contemporary Finnish Romani usage. They also analyse details of variation and produce research for grammar work by the Board.

The RILF has supported and published the Finnish-Romani dictionary (Koivisto, 2001) and also publishes other material in Romani. The electronic Romani corpus (including, e.g. ordinary spoken Romani and Romani news from the Broadcasting Company) is used by researchers with permission granted by the Romani Language Board. The vocabulary of the language is quite well-documented (see e.g. Koivisto, 2001; Thesleff, 1901; Valtonen, 1972), but there are only a few publications on grammatical structure. The structure and variation of Romani are consequently the primary focus of current research.

The co-operation with other Romani boards concerning language and culture has been intense. The researchers and the Board also have many contacts with Romani researchers and boards all over Europe and across the world.

Finnish sign language

Since 1997, the RILF has included the Finnish Sign Language Board (*Viittomakielen lautakunta*) which involves both deaf and hearing members. The committee discusses and makes decisions in matters relating to Finnish sign language. The Institute researcher, as well as the committee, has close contacts with the Finnish Association of the Deaf, and all of the work has been carried out together with the Centre for Sign Language (*Viittomakielen keskus*) in Helsinki (see below). The RILF has, together with the Finnish Association of the Deaf, produced dictionaries[40] (Hoyer, 2002; Malm, 1998), and also provided electronic material.

The co-operation with other actors working for Sign Language has been close. The researcher and the committee also have many contacts with researchers and boards all over Europe and the rest of the world.

The Finnish Centre for Technical Terminology

The Finnish Centre for Technical Terminology (in Finnish *TSK – Tekniikan Sanastokeskus*) is a private agency for terminology development, especially for technical fields. The agency was founded in 1974. From the beginning, it has been closely connected with the RILF.

TSK is the only language service in Finland specialising in the terminology of specialist fields. The service is free of charge for the member companies and institutions of TSK. All legally compliant corporations can become TSK's members if they wish to support and develop TSK's activities, need TSK's services or are interested in terminology work and its results. Other users pay for the service. TSK's participation in different types of terminology projects varies from giving advice or comments to the management of larger vocabulary projects.

When conducting searches, TSK uses the information available in its own library, as well as using online and CD-ROM terminology banks. The most typical users of the term service are language for special purposes (LSP) translators, information and documentation specialists, technical writers and secretaries both from the public and the private sectors. Since 1995, the terminology service has also been available to translators from the European Commission.

TSK's online termbank, TEPA, is a multilingual database: in addition to Finnish terms and definitions, it contains equivalents in several languages of which Swedish and English are the most common. TSK is also a partner in a project called Nordterm-Net. The purpose of this project is to set up a Nordic terminology bank on the Web. The project constitutes part of the Multilingual Information Society programme of the European Commission.

TSK publishes a quarterly newsletter, called *Terminfo*, specialising in terminological issues. Most of the terms compiled in TSK's projects are published in the TSK vocabulary series. In addition to vocabularies, TSK publishes guides and handbooks concerning the tools and methods used in terminology work.

TSK participates actively in international co-operation in the field of terminology work and science. One of the most important forums is Nordterm (http://www.uwasa.fi/termino/nordterm), the forum for professional co-operation by the terminology centres in the Nordic countries. Another partner of major importance to TSK is the Terminology Unit of the European Commission. Since 1995, TSK has provided more than 100,000 Finnish terms to Eurodicautom (http://www.echo.lu/edic), the multilingual termbank of the Commission.

The Government Translation Unit

The Government Translation Unit (*Valtioneuvoston kielipalvelu*) provides terminology service for the administration. It offers advice on the basis of its terminology bank to officials in many fields both in Finnish and in Swedish. Furthermore, it publishes various vocabularies (e.g. the vocabulary of taxation and the vocabulary of agriculture and forestry) to serve the needs of the European Union.

Language planning in the European Union

Finnish and Swedish are two of the eleven official languages of the European Union. In the Union, multilingualism takes on an aspect which is at the very basis of democracy, namely the right of every citizen to be informed and to be heard in his or her own language. Thus, translation is necessary at all of the stages in the preparation of Community legislation: preparing working papers, examining draft versions, putting together the final text, and preparing the written information of the Commission. The Commission's Translation Service is, therefore, called upon to deal with a considerable volume of language work. In order to satisfy an ever-increasing demand for its services, it has developed its own tools (terminology and documentation databases, computer-assisted translation, dedicated software, electronic archiving, etc.). Furthermore, translators working in the Union have close contacts with the national corpus planning agencies (see e.g. van Els, 2001).

The Lexical Committee of the Finnish Medical Society, Duodecim

The old Finnish medical society, *Duodecim*, was founded at the end of the 19th century. From the very beginning, the members of the society discussed the status of Finnish in their own professional field. During the past century, the lexical committee has created Finnish equivalents for medical terms from other languages as well as put existing Finnish words into new use. The committee is still very active and provides advice and recommendations concerning new terms in many of the medical areas. The society publishes the journal *Duodecim* that disseminates the newly coined Finnish terms to doctors. Another important task of the committee is to update and reissue the dictionary *Medical Terms* [*Lääketieteen sanakirja*].

The Saami Language Office of Saami Parliament

The Saami Language Office, established by Saami Parliament (in Saami *Sámediggi*), ensures that public buildings and road signs are bilingual in Finnish and Saami; in addition it insures that various announcements by the authorities and notices in newspapers are bilingual in Finnish and Saami.

The Saami Parliament also has its own Language Board. It maintains and develops Saami languages, provides advice and recommendations on Saami language planning, names, and terminology in Finland, and takes part in Nordic Saami co-operation. Furthermore, every year, the Saami Parliament submits a report on the status and development of the Saami languages and their uses to the government of Finland.

The Consulting Advisory Committee for Romani affairs

During the past 30 years, the consulting advisory committee for Romani affairs (*Romaniasiain neuvottelukunta*) in the Ministry of Social Affairs and Health has contributed to the status of the Roma in Finland. One of the tasks of the committee is to promote the Romani language and culture in Finland. The committee has close contacts with many Roma organisations in Finland as well as in the European Union and worldwide. Furthermore, one of the important partners of the committee is the Roma Education Unit of the National Board of Education.

The Centre for Sign Language

The Finnish Association of the Deaf includes the Centre for Sign Language (*Viittomakielen keskus*). The Centre conducts many tasks, e.g. interpretation services and research in sign language. Furthermore, it compiles dictionaries and electronic corpora. It has close connections with the RILF and other Nordic organisations and societies. The Centre, as well as The Finnish Association of the Deaf, is active on the Nordic level (KPN) on the European level (EUD) and world-wide (WFD).

PART IV: The Future of the Languages in Finland

The language situation in Finland is not unique: similar trends are visible in many other polities, as migration and globalisation change the linguistic situation all over the world. However, there are some factors that make the situation in Finland special. The role and tradition of bilingualism in Finland has been and is still strong. In addition, the importance of foreign language education has always been self-evident in Finland, due to the nature of Finnish and Swedish as less frequently used languages in the world.

In conclusion, this section provides a review of the present linguistic situation in the light of recent developments in Finland. Firstly, we discuss the situation of the national languages, Finnish and Swedish. Secondly, we review the status and the future of minority languages in Finland, and thirdly, we consider the foreign language programme.

National Languages – Finnish and Swedish

Even though Finnish belongs to the 200 most frequently used languages in the world, its use in Europe and in the world is decreasing. Thus, Finnish society has important tasks to attend to in the future if it wishes to maintain and develop its own language in all domains of society. A core area in that respect is the area of scientific life. Even though the tradition of using Finnish is still strong in scientific writing, young researchers in science and technology often write their reports and articles only in English, no longer using Finnish. At the same time, researchers in humanities and social sciences use both their first language and English. This could be a good model for all academic fields in the future. However, such a development would imply that higher education in all academic fields would have to be taught in Finnish (Häkkinen, 2001; Kangas, 2001; Kauppi, 2001). Furthermore, this suggests that the status of Finnish and Swedish in the comprehensive school language programme has to be evaluated continuously.

Another current topic in Finland and in Europe is the future status of Finnish and Swedish in the European Union. The EU will face a new situation in the near future when new countries will join the Union, bringing their languages with them. It has been suggested that only three languages, English, French and German, should remain the official languages of the European Union. If this were agreed to, Finnish, Swedish and many other languages would lose their status at the European level. Thus, how the language situation in the EU is resolved will be very significant for Finnish-speaking and Swedish-speaking society (van Els, 2001).

There are many laws and decrees, which guarantee the rights of Swedish-speaking Finns in Finnish society, and the proposal for the new Language Act (2002) will maintain and develop the status of Swedish in Finland. However, the pressure of Finnish as the majority language is obvious, especially in the bilingual cities where Finnish is the majority language. The use of their language by Swedish-speaking Finns is sometimes problematic; e.g. there are not enough health-care personnel or service personnel with Swedish skills. This makes daily life difficult for many Swedish-speaking people.

However, the attitudes towards Swedish are generally positive among the Finnish-speaking majority (Allardt, 1997). Many Finnish families are interested in Swedish immersion, and their children grow up to be bilingual, with Finnish as their first language and near-native skills in Swedish. Second, bilingual families use Swedish at home and send their children to Swedish-language schools. In addition, Finnish-speaking students understand that it is important to have good skills in Swedish, and they are interested in learning Swedish to a high level.

In the next few decades, the threat for Swedish in Finland is a loss of domain usage mainly to Finnish but also to English. Finnish-Swedish official bilingualism is in many spheres replaced by Finnish and English. Many people, among them researchers, believe that Swedish will gradually become a language spoken only in the home in bilingual areas of Finland. It has been argued that Swedish-speaking persons have to decide to use Swedish in every register outside home as well and thus to strengthen the role of Swedish (Allardt, 2000). On the other hand Swedish in Finland is a part of a greater Swedish region. The contacts with Sweden have always been, and still are, abundant, and the co-operation with Sweden-Swedish in the European Union is of great importance for the Swedish-language community in Finland.

Minority Languages

Saami, Romani and Finnish sign language

During the past few decades, Saami language groups have strengthened their status in Finland, as well as in Sweden and Norway. The law for using Saami with the authorities and in the Saami Homeland in northern Finland had great importance for the Saami people in the 1990s. The opportunity to learn Saami and to be taught in Saami at school and at universities has marked a giant step forward in the lives of the Saami-speaking people. Furthermore, the proposal for the new Saami Act will strengthen the status of Saami even further, because the authorities will be required to have Saami-language skills, and not just to provide interpretation when necessary. The Saami-language organisations are active, and they have direct contact with Parliament and with the Saami people in the neighbouring countries.

The three Saami languages in Finland are not, however, equal. North Saami, also used in Sweden and Norway, has better status than the other Saami languages – Inari Saami and Skolt Saami. Yet, there are many activities also available in these languages, especially among people speaking Inari Saami. In language nests, i.e. in immersion programmes in Inari and Skolt Saami, many children are learning Saami, and the Saami languages have strengthened their position in schools (Olthuis, 2000). Thus, the future of Saami depends on the young Saami people and their choices in the near future, as well as on the attitudes of the majority population and society at large (Olthuis, 2002). Furthermore, it is important that the state supports the Saami population and, especially, the learning of the Saami languages more than before.

During the past decades, the conditions for learning Romani and for maintaining the Roma culture have improved considerably. There is now literature available in Romani, and Romani organisations, as well as the state and the municipalities, have become more aware of the Roma culture.

Within the European Union, Finland has raised human rights issues related to the Roma and influenced, for instance, the drafting in 1999 of *Guiding principles for improving the situation of the Roma.* Yet, the EC Committee of Ministers concluded in their state report (2001) that even though Finland has done much to improve the status of the speakers of Swedish and Saami, the implementation of the Framework Convention has not been entirely successful. The Committee expressed concern especially about the discrimination suffered by the Roma and about their socio-economic status. The Committee also pointed out that Finland has to improve the educational system for the Roma. Furthermore, the Committee stressed the importance of the media and the way it treats the Roma and other minorities.

At present and in the near future, the most important task with regard to Romani in Finland is to try to revitalise it. This depends significantly on the possibilities for learning Romani, on the choice to teach Romani on many levels, and on the attitudes of the authorities and the majority population as well as the Roma. Linguistically, the standardisation of Romani is important for the written culture of the Roma in Finland. This continuing work may support the Roma in using their language and maintaining their culture.

What we have said about the Roma applies, to a great extent, to the situation of sign language and of its users in Finnish society. In the 1990s, the organisations of the deaf, as well as the state, have achieved much in several areas. Currently, sign language can even be studied at the university level, and teacher training is available. According to the Education Policy Programme for the Deaf, the needs of the new minorities have also enhanced the status of the older ones, e.g. the status of the deaf people in Finland. There is, of course, still much to develop in interpretation, language teaching, and creating new material. However, the future of Finnish sign language users seems hopeful because of the active work for sign language in Finnish society.

Other minority languages

Finland, formerly an emigrant country, has become an immigrant country. Finland has gradually adopted a policy similar to that of the other Nordic countries: provisions have been made for the education of immigrants and their children on virtually all levels. In the 1980s, however, the provisions were still marginal. In addition, the official policy was, it seemed, to scatter the few refugees as far from each other as possible, in order to 'integrate' them into Finnish society. A study of language maintenance in immigrant families, conducted in the early 1990s, showed that language shift had already proceeded rapidly among the Vietnamese in Finland, more rapidly than in a comparison group in Norway (see Berggreen & Latomaa, 1994).

Since the beginning of the 1990s, the number of immigrants in Finland has increased rapidly. The changes in immigration policy made in the 1990s were partly a consequence of this trend, and partly connected with Finland's accession to various European organisations, particularly the European Union and the European Council (Lepola, 2000). The purpose of the Integration Act (1999) was to make integration more efficient and to give all immigrant groups equal opportunities. Thus, immigrants have been granted more rights, reaching an increasingly equal status with Finnish citizens. Many of the recently obtained rights have accrued at the educational level.

Consequently, when compared with the situation of the immigrants who came to Finland in the 1980s, the current opportunities to use their native languages and to maintain their languages in the family seem, in principle, much improved. Now, the immigrant minority languages have more support in the educational system, and many of the languages may also be used in the media and in religious life, at least to some extent. In addition, the possibilities among immigrant minorities to study either of the national languages as a second language are greater today than they were in the 1980s. However, while the changes in legislation have improved the situation in principle, it is obvious that practical implementation still lags, as previously noted. For example, in order to avoid additional risks for marginalisation, the acute need for a more coherent language training system for adult immigrants is evident. Furthermore, the decentralised educational system in which the municipalities have the bulk of the power is clearly problematic from the point of view of immigrant minorities, especially in times of economic recession, as occurred at the beginning of the 1990s.

The illusion of a homogeneous people is problematic at a time when society must change from being exclusive to being inclusive, i.e. becoming capable of including as members people who were not born and bred in the country. Forsander and Trux (2002) point out that the transition will be more dramatic in Finland compared with most other western nations as Finland has not experienced the same steady stream of new immigration characteristic of many other countries. Currently, the linguistic diversity in Finland is growing rapidly and, as a new phenomenon, it will challenge Finnish society in many ways in the future. The growing multiculturalism will inevitably affect the identity of Finns. The term *Finn* has been used to refer either to any Finnish citizen, or to someone who can be ethnically and culturally defined as Finnish (see also Laari, 1998). As a result, immigrants have so far been left completely outside the notion of Finnish identity, with the possible exception of Ingrian Finns. Immigrants, or people with immigrant backgrounds, are most often called *ulkomaalainen* (foreigner). It is also typical that newcomers' backgrounds are either ignored or seen from a very ethnocentric perspective. Notions such as *kielitaidottomat lapset* (lit. children without any language skills) or *vierasta kieltä äidinkielenään puhuvat lapset* (lit. children who speak a foreign language as their native language) – both referring to immigrant children – were used for a long time, not only in everyday discussion but also in many official documents. Furthermore, the recent discussion of the deficient or non-existent Finnish skills among Ingrian Finns (and especially among their descendants) as well as the demands for a higher skill level as a condition for allowing Ingrian Finns to immigrate to Finland shows that the discussion of what constitutes Finnishness has barely begun.

Foreign Languages

In Finland, the schools have an exceptionally broad language programme. In addition to the national languages and English, it is assumed that Finnish pupils should also know other European languages: French, German, Italian, Russian or Spanish. Even though the objectives set for foreign language teaching in Finland are high, there are still several problems in the implementation of the language programme. The further one moves away from densely populated areas, the more there is a lack of resources that limit the languages available for study. The more frequent selection of English is not based on media culture or fashion alone, but also on the very few language 'choices' that are available in smaller municipalities. Therefore, the current challenge for Finnish language-teaching policy involves making a wide choice of languages available in all parts of the country.

Content and language integrated learning (CLIL) has increased rapidly in Finland, as it has in many other European countries. In addition to the level of general education, CLIL has been adopted in higher education as well. The number of programmes and study modules offered in foreign languages is increasing at universities and polytechnics. Thus, CLIL can certainly be considered a growing trend throughout Finnish education. With the help of various bilingual programmes, Finland will, in the future, produce a growing number of young people whose fluency in foreign languages they have learned in school will be greater than is that of students who have participated in regular foreign language classes. The language of instruction most often used in CLIL is English. In immersion education, the language of instruction is commonly Swedish. Thus, in fact, the current trends in bilingual programmes will not increase the multilingualism of the Finnish population on the national level. On the individual level, however, fluency in English or Swedish will be an advantage for students in their future working lives. Consequently, bilingual programmes may generate bilingual elitism in Finland, thus increasing linguistic inequality within the population. In a school system that aims to create equal opportunities for all citizens, this possibility should create a moral problem.

The need for skills in foreign languages is self-evident in a small country like Finland. Foreign-language teaching has been a priority area of Finnish educational policy for a long time and, in international comparison, this policy has yielded very positive results. The increasing number of foreign languages in the Finns' normal repertoire can be considered a result of growing internalisation and globalisation. The need for foreign languages, and especially for English, is more evident than it was, for example, a few decades ago. On the other hand, English is gradually occupying a greater range of language domains in Finland: i.e. the media, economics, science, and education. English as a working language finds its way into more and more companies. The number of study programmes offered in English is increasing throughout the Finnish educational system.

Concern about the maintenance of Finnish has been mentioned especially in connection with the criticism of the rapidly growing field of CLIL. It has been claimed that the liberation of the language of instruction in basic education at the beginning of the 1990s was the starting point for a gradual language shift. Considering the public debate that had been going on in Finland about the status of Finnish during the 1990s, the result of the Eurobarometer survey (INRA, 2001) that showed that as many as 90% (as compared with the EU-average of 63%) of Finns shared the view that it is increasingly necessary to protect one's own language as the EU expands, is not surprising. Is Finnish then truly endangered? Several Finnish scholars have addressed the question of the future of languages in Finland. The darkest visions (Tommola, forthcoming) predict the death of Finnish – or the birth of Finglish – thus aiming to provoke language awareness among Finns. Leiwo (2000), however, questions the usefulness of the discourse of threat, as there is actually no evidence for a language shift taking place in Finnish-speaking families, and calls for more positive visions of the linguistic development in Finland. He points out that a very important factor with an impact on language maintenance, besides the 'objective' factors affecting the vitality of the language, is the subjective perception of the speakers of the language: if they perceive it as vital, it has a better chance to survive. Nuolijärvi (1999), Saukkonen (2000) and Mantila (2002) suggest a number of measures in order to combat 'the enemy' – i.e. systematic language policy and language planning, and most importantly, the use of Finnish in everyday life in all domains.

Acknowledgements

We wish to express our sincere gratitude to Professors Robert B. Kaplan and Richard B. Baldauf, Jr, the series editors, whose enthusiasm, commitment and carefully considered feedback have helped us to improve our drafts of the manuscript considerably. We would also like to thank the following people for their valuable comments and suggestions: Language Rights Secretary Kristina Beijar (The Swedish Assembly of Finland), Professor Maisa Martin (University of Jyväskylä), Researcher Karita Mård (University of Vaasa) and Researcher Tuomas Martikainen (Åbo Akademi University).

Correspondence

Any correspondence should be directed to Sirkku Latomaa, School of Modern Languages and Translation Studies, University of Tampere, Finland (sirkku.latomaa@uta.fi).

Notes

1. This brief history of Finland is based mainly on three sources, Klinge (1999), McRae (1997), Zetterberg (1999), and the literature mentioned in those sources.
2. For discussion of the structure of the Baltic-Finnic languages see also Turunen (1988).
3. See Paunonen (1997) for a detailed description of the changes in the position of Finnish in different periods.
4. The description of the Saami people and Saami languages is based on the following sources: Aikio (1988), Kulonen *et al.* (1994), and the literature mentioned in those sources. See also the websites http://www.samediggi.fi, http://www.ethnologue. com, http://www.eurolang.net, and http://www.kotus.fi. Additional sources have been mentioned in the text.
5. The description of the Roma and Romani is based on the following sources: Grönfors (1995), Ollikainen (1995), Suonoja and Lindberg (1999) and the literature mentioned in those sources. See also the websites http://www.vn.fi/stm, http://www.eurolang. net, and http://www.kotus.fi. The status of Romani and the Roma in Europe has been described in Bakker (2001).
6. The description of Finnish sign language is based on the following sources: Malm (2000) and the literature mentioned there. See also the websites http:// www.kl-deaf.fi, and http://www.kotus.fi.
7. Why did the Jewish people choose Swedish and later Finnish as their first language? One reason that has been given is that at the beginning of the 19th century, Swedish had an influential position, and later on Finnish became more important in the public life in Finland (Torvinen, 1989).
8. The numbers on Romani speakers and Finnish sign language users are not given in the official statistics.
9. In the 1990s, the problematics of interpreting statistics has been discussed in Finland. The registration according to first language concerning Finnish and Swedish has been successful for many centuries in Finland, but the information about binguality (i.e. about the possibility of two first languages) has never been collected in the official statistics. See e.g. Forsander (2000).
10. In 1999, the number of refugees was 159,500 in Sweden, 69,000 in Denmark, and 975,500 in Germany. Even if the criteria for defining refugee status differ in various

countries, the difference between Finland and, for example, other Nordic countries, is obvious.

11. A special itinerant teaching system, the catechist system, was developed in the mid-1700s. The catechists were itinerant elementary school teachers working under the auspices of the church. Catechistic teaching continued for about 200 years until the first decade of compulsory elementary education, with the catechists travelling from home to home and from village to village.

12. In order to be registered as a practitioner of a religion one has to belong to a registered religious community. Therefore, the official statistics do not include Pentacostals and Muslims living in Finland. The Pentacostal congregations have not been organised as religious communities but rather as registered associations, which means that they are not apparent in national religious statistics. Most Muslims in Finland are not members of official religious communities either. Altogether, there are approximately 45,000–50,000 Pentacostals and 10,000–15,000 Muslims in Finland. Thus, in reality, the other religious communities in Finland constitute at least 2.5% of population aside from those mentioned in the official statistics (Heino, 1997; Martikainen, 2000b).

13. However, the core curriculum for the comprehensive school of 1994 is still in use, and therefore, the terms *primary education* and *lower secondary education* appear in the text together with the current term *basic education*.

14. By the term *mother-tongue education* we refer to subject teaching in the pupils' first language. In the Finnish educational context, the term *äidinkieli* (lit. mother tongue) is widely used, e.g. in educational legislation and in the national core curricula. The school subject is called *Äidinkieli ja kirjallisuus* (lit. mother tongue and literature). The names of various syllabi of *Äidinkieli ja kirjallisuus* follow the same pattern: *saame äidinkielenä* (lit. Saami as a mother tongue), *romani äidinkielenä* (lit. Romani as a mother tongue), *viittomakieli äidinkielenä* (lit. sign language as a mother tongue), *maahanmuuttajien äidinkieli* (lit. mother tongue of immigrants). We have chosen to use *(Finnish/Swedish) language and literature* as the translation of the name of the subject. See Extra and Gorter (2001: 5) and Kaplan and Baldauf (1997: 14–27) for the varying nomenclature used in the field.

15. In fact, in the earlier IEA Studies of Reading Literacy (Linnakylä, 1995) both 9-year-old and 14-year-old Finnish pupils had attained the highest level in the test. Furthermore, the results of this study were compared with some international studies undertaken at the beginning of the 1970s, and it was found that reading literacy among Finnish school children had clearly improved in 20 years, especially among younger school children.

16. In the matriculation examination, there is no oral test, but students may receive separate diplomas in, for example, communication education, media education and literature.

17. Immersion teaching has been kept separate from teaching in a foreign language, since immersion is by definition a very intensive language programme where at least 50% of the time is spent with a foreign language as the language of instruction. Immersion is also defined by certain linguistic and didactic criteria.

18. A detailed analysis of the development of immigration policy, and, in particular, the educational response to increased cultural and ethnic diversity in Finland can be found in e.g. Matinheikki-Kokko and Pitkänen (2002).

19. In 1996, 40 students took the examination in FSL. In 2001, the number of students had grown by a factor of about 8; i.e. to 309.

20. At the University of Helsinki, students may major in Finnish Language and Culture. At several other universities, Finnish Language and Culture can be chosen as a minor.

21. The development of the National Certificate of Language Proficiency was started in 1992 as a joint project between the NBE and the University of Jyväskylä. The tasks measure language skills in practical situations. Currently, the test can be taken in English, Finnish, French, German, Italian, Russian, Saami, Spanish and Swedish.

22. COMENIUS is part of the SOCRATES programme, which supports European co-operation in all areas of education. COMENIUS focuses on the first phases of

education, emphasising, among other things, learning in a multicultural framework, support for disadvantaged groups, countering underachievement at school and preventing exclusion.

23. *Sign language* is used in this context to cover both the variety used in the Finnish-medium deaf schools and the one used in the Swedish-medium deaf schools.

24. Jokinen (2000a) explains the period of acceptance in the 19th century by the fact that speakers of Finnish were eager to fight for their own linguistic rights, and thus the position of the deaf was better understood at the time.

25. The term used in the names of these schools is actually *hearing-impaired* in Finnish.

26. As compared with Sweden, where IMLI was labelled *home language* instruction until 1997.

27. There was one exception to this general practice. In the 1850s, a German congregation was founded in Helsinki, and it is still active today. The current *Deutsche ev. luth. Gemeinde in Finnland* is its successor. The German congregation is part of the Swedish-speaking diocese.

28. This information was received through personal communication with Marja-Liisa Laihia (The Evangelical Lutheran Church).

29. This information was received through personal communication with Father Peter Gebara (The Parish of the Holy Cross, Tampere).

30. This information was received through personal communication with Jorma Lampinen (The Finnish Broadcasting Company).

31. In addition, learning the second national language, be it Finnish or Swedish, is for many pupils learning a language that is as foreign as any other non-native language. Finnish-speaking Finns do not use Swedish as a means of regular communication outside some areas along the coasts, and Swedish-speaking Finns in strongly Swedish-speaking areas in Ostrobothnia do not use Finnish in their daily lives.

32. Another factor may be the fact that, in most other European countries, students study languages that belong to the Indo-European family of languages and sometimes the languages are quite closely related. Thus, the learning situation differs from that of a Finnish-speaking pupil.

33. It has often been noted that during the past decades television has given extensive input in a number of foreign languages, as all foreign programmes shown on national TV channels are subtitled and not dubbed.

34. In their letter to the schools, the researchers had made a clear distinction between CLIL and early total immersion. However, they received some answers from schools that offered immersion. These answers were not included in the analysis. The instruction given in Swedish or Finnish and reported in Nikula and Marsh (1996) does not refer to immersion programmes.

35. In some schools where CLIL programmes were adopted, the number of hours allotted to language and literature was decreased.

36. However, as Takala and Sajavaara (2000) point out, the language policy decision of the 1970s was not derived from language planning considerations but was an outcome from a purely political compromise between representatives of the Finnish government and representatives of the Swedish People's Party in Finland.

37. An English summary of the proposed Language Act is available on the web-sites of the Ministry of Justice (http://www.om.fi).

38. The Saami Language Law was enacted earlier (in 1990).

39. The main sources here are Aikio-Puoskari & Pentikäinen (2001), http://www.eurolang.net, and http://www.samediggi.fi.

40. Since signs are not static, it has often been asked, how to describe sign language in a book. The signs of *The Basic Dictionary of Finnish Sign Language* are so-called frozen signs: they have basic forms, and their meanings are limited. The pictures of the signs are taken from a video. Movements of the hand are shown with the help of piles. Currently, the Centre for Sign Language is working on a multimedia dictionary that will make the video material of the published dictionary available for everybody.

References

Ahlbäck, O. (1971) *Svenskan i Finland* [*Swedish in Finland*]. Stockholm: Läro medels förlagen.

Aikio, M. (1988) *Saamelaiset kielenvaihdon kierteessä. Kielisosiologinen tutkimus viiden saamelaiskylän kielenvaihdosta 1910–1980* [*The Cycle of Language Shift: A Sociolinguistic Study of Language Shift in Five Saami Villages 1910–1980*]. Helsinki: Suomalaisen Kirjallisuuden Seura [Finnish Literature Society].

Aikio-Puoskari, U. and Pentikäinen, M. (2001) The language rights of the indigenous Saami in Finland – under domestic and international law. *Juridica Lapponica* 26. University of Lapland, Rovaniemi: University of Lapland Press.

Allardt, E. (1997) *Vårt land, vårt språk. Tvåspråkigheten, finnarnas attityder samt svenskans och finlandssvenskarnas framtid i Finland / Kahden kielen kansa. Kaksikielisyys, Suomalaisten asenteet sekä ruotsin kielen asema ja tulevaisuus Suomessa* [*Our Country, Our Language: Bilingualism, the Attitudes of Finns, and the Status and Future of Swedish in Finland*]. Finlandssvensk rapport nr 35 [Finland Swedish Report 35]. Helsingfors: Yliopistopaino [Helsinki University Press].

Allardt, E. (2000) *Svenska på stan. En attitydundersökning / Stadin ruotsi. Asennetutkimus* [*Swedish in the City: A Study of Attitudes*]. Finlandssvensk rapport nr 39 [Finland Swedish Report 39]. Helsingfors: Yliopistopaino [Helsinki University Press].

Allardt, E. and Starck, C. (1981) *Språkgränser och samhällsstruktur. Finlandssvenskarna i ett jämförande perspektiv* [*Language Boundaries and Social Structure: Finland-Swedes in Comparison*]. Stockholm: AWE/Gebers.

Baker, C. (2001) Sign language and the deaf community. In J.A. Fishman (ed.) *Handbook of Language and Ethnic Identity* (pp. 122–39). Oxford: Oxford University Press.

Bakker, P. (2001) Romani in Europe. In G. Extra and D. Gorter (eds) *The Other Languages of Europe. Demographic, Sociolinguistic and Educational Perspectives* (pp. 293–313). Clevedon: Multilingual Matters.

Baschmakoff, N. and Leinonen, M. (2001) *Russian Life in Finland 1917–1939: A Local and Oral History*. Studia Slavica Finlandensia XVIII. Helsinki: Institute for Russian and East European Studies.

Beijar, K., Ekberg, H., Eriksson, S. and Tandefelt, M. (1997) *Life in Two Languages – the Finnish Experience*. Espoo: Schildts.

Berggreen, H. and Latomaa, S. (1994) Språkbytte och språkbevaring blant vietnamesere i Bergen og Helsinki [Language shift and language maintenance among the Vietnamese in Bergen and Helsinki]. In S. Boyd, A. Holmen and J. N. Jørgensen (eds) *Sprogbrug og sprogvalg blandt indvandrere i Norden* [*Language Use and Language Choice among Immigrants in the Nordic Region*] (pp. 137–82). Københavnerstudier i tosprogethed 22 [Copenhagen Studies in Bilingualism 22]. København: Danmarks Lærerhøjskole [Royal Danish School of Educational Studies].

Björklund, S. (1997) Immersion in Finland in the 1990s: A state of development and expansion. In R.K. Johnson and M. Swain (eds) *Immersion Education: International Perspectives* (pp. 85–101). Cambridge: Cambridge University Press.

Björklund, S. (forthcoming) A trilingual school in Vaasa, Finland. In *Proceedings of the Symposium on Trilingual Primary Education in Europe*. Leeuwarden: Fryske Akademy.

Buchberger, I. (2002) Äidinkielen opetuksesta on tullut globaali projekti [Mother-tongue education has become a global project]. In I. Herlin, J. Kalliokoski, L. Kotilainen and T. Onikki-Rantajääskö (eds) *Äidinkielen merkitykset* [*The Meanings of Mother Tongue*] (pp. 370–87). Helsinki: Suomalaisen Kirjallisuuden Seura [Finnish Literature Society].

Buss, M. and Mård, K. (2001) Swedish immersion in Finland – facts and figures. In S. Björklund (ed.) *Language as a Tool: Immersion Research and Practices* (pp. 157–75). Proceedings of the University of Vaasa. Reports 83. Vaasa: University of Vaasa.

European Commission (EC) (1995) *White Paper on Education and Training: Teaching and Learning – Towards the Learning Society*. Luxembourg: Office for Official Publications of the European Communities.

European Commission (EC) (2000) *Key Data on Education in Europe*. Luxembourg: Office for Official Publications of the European Communities.

Eurydice (2001) *Foreign Language Teaching in Schools in Europe*. Brussels: Eurydice.

Extra, G. and Gorter, D. (2001) Comparative perspectives on regional and immigrant minority languages in multicultural Europe. In G. Extra and D. Gorter (eds) *The Other Languages of Europe: Demographic, Sociolinguistic and Educational Perspectives* (pp. 1–41). Clevedon: Multilingual Matters.

Finnäs, F. (2001) *Finlandssvenskarna inför 2000-talet – en statistisk översikt* [*The Finland-Swedes in the 2000s – A Statistical Overview*]. Finlandssvensk rapport 40 [Finland Swedish Report 40]. Helsingfors: Yliopistopaino [Helsinki University Press].

Forsander, A. (2000) Tilastot maahanmuuttajien kuvaajana [Statistics describing the immigrants]. In M-L. Trux (ed.) *Aukeavat ovet – Kulttuurien moninaisuus Suomen elinkeinoelämässä* [*Opening Doors – Cultural Diversity in Finnish Business Life*] (pp. 335–41). Helsinki: WSOY [Werner Söderström Oy].

Forsander, A. and Trux, M-L. (2002) Conclusion: Toward new immigration strategies? In A. Forsander (ed.) *Immigration and Economy in the Globalization Process: The Case of Finland* (pp. 226–34). Sitra Reports series 20. Vantaa: Sitra.

Ganander, K. (1780) Undersökning om de så kallade TATTERE eller Zigeuner, Cingari, Bohemiens, Deras härkomst, Lefnadssätt, språk m.m. Samt om, när och hwarest några satt sig ner i Swerige? [A Study on so called TATARS or gipsies, e.g., their origin, their habits, their language, and when and from where they moved to Sweden?]. Manuscript. Tukholman kuninkaallisen kaunokirjallisuusakatemian arkisto [Archive of the Royal Literature Academy in Stockholm].

Geber, E. (1982) Suomenruotsalaisten koulujen suomen kielen ('finskan') opetuksen ongelmia [Problems in teaching Finnish ('finskan') in Swedish-medium schools]. In F. Karlsson (ed.) *Suomi vieraana kielenä* [*Finnish as a Foreign Language*] (pp. 115–38). Helsinki: WSOY [Werner Söderström Oy].

Grönfors, M. (1981) *Suomen mustalaiskansa* [*The Roma People in Finland*]. Helsinki: WSOY [Werner Söderström Oy].

Grönfors, M. (1995) Finnish Rom: A forgotten cultural group. In J. Pentikäinen and M. Hiltunen (eds) *Cultural Minorities in Finland. An Overview towards Cultural Policy* (pp. 149–60). Publications of the Finnish National Commission for Unesco 66, Helsinki: Finnish National Commission for Unesco.

Grönholm, M. (2000) Sentence comprehension by language-immersed children. *SKY Journal of Linguistics* 13, 29–46.

Haapamäki, S. (1995) '*Språk de e som snöre'. En studie av tjugo kurders svenska språkfärdighet* ['*Language; It is Like a Rope'. A Study on Twenty Kurds' Language Proficiency in Swedish*]. Skrifter från svenska institutionen vid Åbo Akademi nr 2 [Reports from the Swedish Department at Åbo Akademi University]. Åbo: Åbo Akademi.

Hakkarainen, L. (1988) *Kuurojen yläasteen oppilaiden kirjoitetun kielen hallinta* [*Mastery of Written Language by Deaf Pupils at the Upper Level of Comprehensive School*]. Jyväskylä Studies in Education, Psychology and Social Research 67. Jyväskylä: University of Jyväskylä.

Hakulinen, L. (1979) *Suomen kielen rakenne ja kehitys* [*The Structure and Development of Finnish*]. Helsinki: Otava.

Halén, H. (1999) Suomen tataarit [Tatars in Finland]. In M. Löytönen and L. Kolbe (eds) *Suomi: Maa, kansa, kulttuurit* [*Finland: The Country, the People, the Cultures*] (pp. 315–32). Helsinki: Suomalaisen Kirjallisuuden Seura [Finnish Literature Society].

Halikov, A. (1991) *Tataarit, keitä te olette?* [*Tatars, Who Are You?*]. Vammala: Abdulla Tukain Kulttuuriseura r.y. [The Cultural Society of Abdulla Tukai].

Hannén, K. (2000) *Nationell utvärdering av inlärningsresultat i modersmålet i åk 9, 1999* [*National Evaluation of the Learning Results in Mother Tongue in the 9th Grade, 1999*]. Helsinki: Opetushallitus [National Board of Education].

Hannén, K. (2001) *Utvärdering av Inlärningsresultat i modersmål i åk 6 i den grundläggande utbildningen våren 2000* [*Evaluation of the Learning Results in Mother Tongue in the 6th Grade, Spring 2000*]. Helsinki: Opetushallitus [National Board of Education].

Harviainen, T. (1998) Juutalaiset Suomessa [Jews in Finland]. In T. Harviainen and K-J. Illman (eds) *Juutalainen kulttuuri* [*Jewish Culture*] (pp. 291–304). Helsinki: Otava.

Hedman, H. (1996) *Sar me sikjavaa romanes. Romanikielen kielioppiopas* [*A Grammar of the Romani Language*]. Jyväskylä: Opetushallitus [National Board of Education].

Heino, H. (1997) *Mihin Suomi tänään uskoo* [*What does Finland Believe in Today*]. Helsinki: WSOY [Werner Söderstöm Oy].

Heino, H., Salonen, K., Rusama, J. and Ahonen, R. (1997) *Suomen evankelis-luterilainen kirkko vuosina 1992–1995* [*The Evangelical Lutheran Church of Finland from 1992 to 1995*]. Tampere: Kirkon tutkimuskeskus [Research Institute of the Evangelical Lutheran Church of Finland].

Hellman, S. (1996) De talar svenska bättre än finska [They speak Swedish better than Finnish]. *Hufvudstadsbladet* (18 March). Finland's leading Swedish language newspaper – based in Helsinki.

Herberts, K. and Landgärds, A-S. (1992) *Tvång eller privilegium? Debatten om Obligatorisk svenskundervisning i den finska grundskolan* [*Compulsion or Privilege? The Debate about Compulsory Swedish in the Finnish Comprehensive School*]. Institutet för finlandssvensk samhällsforskning [Social Science Research Unit]. Forskningsrapporter 17 [Research Reports 17]. Vasa: Åbo Akademi.

Honkkila, H. (2000) Kohti viittomakielistä seurakuntaa [Towards a parish of native signers]. In A. Malm (ed.) *Viittomakieliset Suomessa* [*Sign Language Users in Finland*] (pp. 61–70). Helsinki: Finn Lectura.

Horn, F. (1999) National minorities in Finland. On WWW at http://virtual.finland.fi. Accessed 29.2.2000.

Hoyer, K. (2000) Vähemmistö vähemmistössä: Suomenruotsalaiset kuurot ja heidän viittomakielensä [A minority in a minority: Deaf Fenno-Swedes and their sign language]. In A. Malm (ed.) *Viittomakieliset Suomessa* [*Sign Language Users in Finland*] (pp. 205–15). Helsinki: Finn Lectura.

Hoyer, K. (ed.) (2002) *Se vårt språk! = Näe kielemme!: Finlandssvenskt teckenspråk. 38 ordboksartiklar. Suomenruotsalainen viittomakieli. 38 sanakirja-artikkelia* [*See our language! Finland-Swedish sign language. 38 lexical entries*]. Helsinki: Kuurojen Liitto [Finnish Association of the Deaf].

Huss, L.M. (1991) *Simultan tvåspråkighet i svensk-finsk kontext* [*Simultaneous Bilingualism in a Swedish-Finnish Context*]. Studia Uralica Upsaliensia 21. Acta Universitatis Upsaliensis.

Häkkinen, K. (1990) *Mistä sanat tulevat? Suomalaista etymologiaa* [*Where do Words Come from? Finnish Etymology*]. Helsinki: Suomalaisen Kirjallisuuden Seura [Finnish Literature Society].

Häkkinen, K. (1994) *Agricolasta nykykieleen. Suomen kirjakielen historia* [*From Agricola to Modern Finnish: The History of Written Finnish*]. Helsinki: WSOY [Werner Söderström Oy].

Häkkinen, K. (1996) *Suomalaisten esihistoria kielitieteen valossa* [*The Prehistory of the Finns in the Light of Linguistics*]. Helsinki: Suomalaisen Kirjallisuuden Seura [Finnish Literature Society].

Häkkinen, K. (2001) Kymmenen teesiä tieteen kielestä [Ten theses on scientific language]. *Virittäjä* [Journal of the Society for the Study of Finnish] 105 (2), 272–4.

af Hällström, C. and Reuter, M. (2000) *Finlandssvensk ordbok* [*Dictionary of Finland-Swedish*]. Esbo: Schildts.

Härkönen, R., Immonen, H., Kärkkäinen, A., Kärkkäinen, K. and Takala, S. (2000) *Yleisten kielitutkintojen satoa – Tietoa ja tilastoja suorituksista ja suorittajista 1994–2000* [*Results of the National Certificate of Language Proficiency – Statistical Facts about the Tests and Test Takers 1994–2000*]. Helsinki: Opetushallitus [National Board of Education].

Häyrinen, M-L. (2000) *Maahanmuuttajanuoret ja suomalainen koulu. Kokemuksia pääkaupunkiseudun kunnista* [*Immigrant Adolescents and the Finnish School: Experiences of the Municipalities in the Metropolitan Area*]. Ulkomaalaisvaltuutetun toimiston moniste 1 [Report from the Office of the Ombudsman for Foreigners 1]. Helsinki.

Ikola, O. (1984) Suomen kielen historia [The history of the Finnish language]. In H. Paunonen and P. Rintala (eds) *Nykysuomen rakenne ja kehitys* 2 [*The Structure and Development of Modern Finnish*] (pp. 111–38). Helsinki: Suomalaisen Kirjallisuuden Seura [Finnish Literature Society].

International Research Associates (INRA) (2001) *Europeans and Languages*. Eurobarometer Report 54. Brussels: European Commission.

Itkonen, T. (1964) *Proto-Finnic Final Consonants. Their History in the Finnic Languages with Particular Reference to the Finnish Dialects* (vol. I:1). Helsinki: Suomalaisen Kirjallisuuden Seura [Finnish Literature Society].

Ivars, A-M. (1996) *Stad och bygd. Finlandssvenska stadsmål i ett regionalt och socialt perspektiv* [*City and Country: Finland-Swedish Urban Varieties from the Regional and Social Perspective*]. Folkmålsstudier 37 [Dialect Studies 37]. Meddelanden från Föreningen för nordisk filologi [Publications of the Society for Nordic Philology]. Helsingfors.

Jaakkola, M. (1999) *Maahanmuutto ja etniset asenteet. Suomalaisten suhtautuminen maahanmuuttajiin 1987–1999* [*Immigration and Ethnic Attitudes: Finns' Attitudes towards Immigrants in 1987–1999*]. Helsinki: Edita.

Jantunen, T. (2001) *Suomalaisen viittomakielen synnystä, vakiintumisesta ja kuvaamisen periaatteista* [*The Origin, the Standardisation and the Principles of the Description of the Finnish Sign Language*]. Helsinki: Kuurojen Liitto [The Finnish Association of the Deaf].

Jokinen, M. (2000a) Kuurojen oma maailma – kuurous kielenä ja kulttuurina [The world of the deaf – deafness as a language and a culture]. In A. Malm (ed.) *Viittomakieliset Suomessa* [*Sign Language Users in Finland*] (pp. 79–101). Helsinki: Finn Lectura.

Jokinen, M. (2000b) *Viittomakielinen opettajankoulutus. Opettajien perus- ja täydennyskoulutuksen ennakointihanke (OPEPRO) selvitys 7* [*Sign Language Teacher Training. Anticipatory Project to Investigate Teachers' Initial and Continuing Training Needs, Report 7*]. Helsinki: Opetushallitus [National Board of Education].

Kangas, U. (2001) Suomen kieli oikeustieteen kielenä [Finnish as a legal language]. *Virittäjä* [Journal of the Society for the Study of Finnish] 105 (2), 274–6.

Kaplan, R.B. and Baldauf, R.B., Jr (1997) *Language Planning From Practice to Theory*. Clevedon: Multilingual Matters.

Karlsson, F. (1999) *Finnish: An Essential Grammar*. London and New York: Routledge.

Karppinen, M-L. (1993) Problems in the implementation of foreign language policy in Finland. In K. Sajavaara, R.D. Lambert, S. Takala and C.A. Morfit (eds) *National Foreign Language Planning: Practices and Prospects* (pp. 72–6). Institute for Educational Research, University of Jyväskylä.

Kauppi, L. (2001) Ei joko – tai, vaan sekä – että [Not either – or, but both – and]. *Virittäjä* [Journal of the Society for the Study of Finnish] 105 (2), 271–2.

Kettunen, L. (1940) *Suomen murteet II. Murrealueet* [*The Finnish Dialects II. The Dialect Areas*]. Helsinki: Suomalaisen Kirjallisuuden Seura [Finnish Literature Society].

Kiele yhteiskunnassa – yhteiskunta kielessä [Language in Society – Society in Language] (pp. 61–81).

Kielilainsäädäntö. Kansainvälisoikeudelliset velvoitteet ja kansainvälinen vertailu. / *Språklagstiftning. Internationella förpliktelser och internationell jämförelse* [*Language Legislation. International Obligations and International Comparison*]. Oikeusministeriö. Lainvalmisteluosaston julkaisu / Justitieministeriet. Lagberedningsavdelningens publikation [Ministry of Justice. Publication of the Law Drafting Department] 1/2001. Helsinki: Hakapaino [Hakapress].

Kirkkohallitus (1999) *Kansan kirkosta kansojen kirkoksi: Suomi matkalla monikulttuurisuuteen* [*From the National Church to the Church of Nations: Finland on the Way to Multiculturalism*]. Suomen ev.lut. kirkon kirkkohallituksen julkaisuja 2 [Publications of the Council of the Finnish Evangelical Lutheran Church 2] Helsinki: Kirkkohallitus [Church Council].

Klinge, M. (1999) *A Brief History of Finland*. Helsinki: Otava.

Koivisto, V. (1982) *Drabibosko ta rannibosko byrjiba* [*Beginnings of Reading and Writing*]. Helsinki: Ammattikasvatushallitus – Kouluhallitus [National Board of Vocational Education – National Board of Education].

Koivisto, V. (1994) *Romano-finitiko-angliko laavesko liin* / *Romani–suomi–englanti sanakirja* [*Romani–Finnish–English Dictionary*]. Helsinki: Painatuskeskus [State Printing Office].

Koivisto, V. (2001) *Suomi–romani-sanakirja. Finitiko–romano laavesko liin* [*Finnish–Romani Dictionary*]. Helsinki: Suomalaisen Kirjallisuuden Seura [Finnish Literature Society].

Koponen, H. (2000) *Maahanmuuttajaopetukseen valmentavat sisällöt Opettajankoulutuksessa. Opettajien perus- ja täydennyskoulutuksen ennakointihankkeen (OPEPRO) selvitys 8* [*Educational Contents Preparing for Immigrant Education in Teacher Training. Anticipatory*

Project to Investigate Teachers' Initial and Continuing Training Needs, Report 8]. Helsinki: Opetushallitus [National Board of Education].

Korhonen, M. (1967) *Die Konjugation im Lappischen: Morphologisch-historische Untersuchung* [*The Conjugation in Saami: A Morphological-Historical Study*]. Helsinki: Suomalais-Ugrilainen Seura [The Finno-Ugrian Society].

Korkeakoski, E. (2001) *Perusopetuksen äidinkielen oppimistulosten kansallinen arviointi 6. Vuosiluokalla keväällä 2000* [*National Evaluation of the Learning Results in Mother Tongue in the 6th Grade, Spring 2000*]. Helsinki: Opetushallitus [National Board of Education].

Kortteinen, J. (1997) Romanit ja muut perinteiset vähemmistömme [The Roma and other traditional minorities in Finland]. In T. Dahlgren, J. Kortteinen, K.J. Lång, M. Pentikäinen and M. Scheinin (eds.) *Vähemmistöt ja niiden syrjintä Suomessa* [*Minorities and Discrimination in Finland*] (pp. 75–108). Second edition. Helsinki: Yliopistopaino [Helsinki University Press].

Kovács, M. (2001) *Code-Switching and Language Shift in Australian Finnish in Comparison with Australian Hungarian*. Åbo: Åbo Akademi University Press.

Kulonen, U-M. (1998) The origin of Finnish and related languages. *Finfo* 13, 1–12. Helsinki: Ministry of Foreign Affairs of Finland.

Kulonen, U-M., Seurujärvi-Kari, I. and Pentikäinen, J. (1994) *Johdatus saamentutkimukseen* [*An Introduction to the Study of Saami*]. Helsinki: Suomalaisen Kirjallisuuden Seura [Finnish Literature Society].

Kuurojen Liitto (1994) *Kuurojen koulutuspoliittinen ohjelma* [*The Educational Policy Programme for the Deaf*]. Helsinki: Kuurojen Liitto [The Finnish Association of the Deaf].

Kuurojen Liitto (1997) *Kuurot ja viestintä. Kuurojen liiton viestintäpoliittinen ohjelma* [*The Deaf and Communication: The Communication Policy Programme of the Association of the Deaf*]. Helsinki: Kuurojen Liitto [The Finnish Association of the Deaf].

Kähkönen, A. (1990) *Kirkko ja saamelaisvähemmistö* [*Church and the Saami Minority*]. Historian laitos [Department of History]. Oulu: Oulun yliopisto [University of Oulu].

Kääpä, K. (2000) Tavoitteena tunti viikossa viittomakielistä tv-ohjelmaa [The aim: Signed TV-programmes for an hour a week]. *Kuurojen lehti* [*The Magazine of the Deaf*] 7, 24–5.

Laari, O. (1998) Immigrants in Finland: Finnish-to-be or foreigners forever – Conceptions of nation-state in debate on immigration policy. In I. Söderling (ed.) *A Changing Pattern of Migration in Finland and its Surroundings* (pp. 29–50). Helsinki: Population Research Institute.

Lainio, J. (1989) *Spoken Finnish in Urban Sweden*. Uppsala Multiethnic Papers 15. Uppsala: Centre for Multiethnic Research.

Lapintie, P. (2001) Uskon perustekstien käännökset videoitu viittomakielelle [The central religious texts have been translated into Finnish sign language]. *Helsingin Sanomat* (6 November). Finland's largest circulation newspaper – based in Helsinki.

Lappalainen, H-P. (2000) *Peruskoulun äidinkielen oppimistulosten kansallinen arviointi 9. Vuosiluokalla* [*National Evaluation of Learning Results in Mother Tongue in the 9th Grade*]. Helsinki: Opetushallitus [National Board of Education].

Lappalainen, H-P. (2001) *Perusopetuksen äidinkielen ja kirjallisuuden oppimistulosten kansallinen arviointi 9. vuosiluokalla 2001* [*National Evaluation of Learning Results in Mother Tongue and Literature in the 9th grade in 2001*]. Helsinki: Opetushallitus [National Board of Education].

Lappi, P. (2000) Viittomakielen lainsäädännöllinen asema [The legal status of Finnish sign language]. In A. Malm (ed.) *Viittomakieliset Suomessa* [*Sign Language Users in Finland*] (pp. 71–7). Helsinki: Finn Lectura.

Latomaa, S. (1995) Finland as a multilingual society yesterday, today – and tomorrow? In H. Haarmann (ed.) *European Identity and Language Diversity* (pp. 113–35). Tübingen: Max Niemeyer Verlag.

Latomaa, S. (1996) Finnish as a second and foreign language: Perspectives on teaching and research. In M. Martin and P. Muikku-Werner (eds) *Finnish and Estonian – New Target Languages* (pp. 10–30). Proceedings of the Fenno-Ugric Languages as Second and Foreign Languages Symposium. Centre for Applied Language Studies. Jyväskylä: University of Jyväskylä.

Latomaa, S. (2002) Maahanmuuttajien kielelliset oikeudet [The linguistic rights of immigrants]. In A. Mauranen and L. Tiittula (eds) Kieli yhteiskunnassa – yhteiskunta kielessä [Language in Society – Society in Language] (pp. 61–81). Jyväskylä: AFinLA.

Lehmuskallio, K. (1983) *Mitä lukeminen sisältää? [What is Reading?]* Helsinki: WSOY [Werner Söderström Oy].

Leino, P. (2002) Ylioppilasaine – äidinkielen taitojen mittari [Matriculation exam – the measure of native language skills]. *Kielikello [Language Bell]* 2, 4–10.

Leinonen, T. and Tandefelt, M. (2000) *Svenskan i Finland – ett språk i kläm [Swedish in Finland – a Language under Pressure]*. Helsingfors: Swedish School of Economics and Business Administration.

Leiwo, M. (2000) Suomen kieli 2000-luvulla: Voiko kielen kehitystä ennustaa? [The Finnish language in the 21st century: Is it possible to predict the development of a language?] In P. Kalaja and L. Nieminen (eds) *Kielikoulussa – Kieli koulussa [In the Language School – Language in School]* (pp. 387–404). Publications de l'Association Finlandaise de Linguistique Appliqueé 58 [Publications of the Finnish Applied Linguistics Association 58]. Jyväskylä: AFinLA.

Leiwo, M. (2001) Suomen romanikielen asemasta ja huollosta [The status and cultivation of Finnish Romani]. *Virittäjä* [Journal of the Society for the Study of Finnish] 105 (2), 281–90.

Lepola, O. (2000) *Ulkomaalaisesta suomenmaalaiseksi. Monikulttuurisuus, kansalaisuus ja suomalaisuus 1990-luvun maahanmuuttopoliittisessa keskustelussa [From Foreigner to Finlander: Multiculturalism, Nationality and the Finnish Identity in the Political Debate on Immigration during the 1990s]*. Helsinki: Suomalaisen Kirjallisuuden Seura [Finnish Literature Society].

Lindgren, A-R. (1990) *Miten muodot muuttuvat: Ruijan murteiden verbintaivutus Raisin, Pyssyjoen ja Annijoen kveeniyhteisöissä [How Forms Change: The Verb Conjugation of the Dialects in Raisi, Pyssyjoki and Annijoki Kven Communities in Finnmark]*. Institutt for språk og litteratur [Department of Language and Literature]. Tromsø: Universitetet i Tromsø [University of Tromsø].

Lindgren, A-R. (2000) *Helsingin saamelaiset ja oma kieli [The Saami People in Helsinki and their Own Language]*. Helsinki: Suomalaisen Kirjallisuuden Seura [Finnish Literature Society].

Linnakylä, P. (1995) *Lukutaidolla maailmankartalle: Kansainvälinen lukutaitotutkimus Suomessa [The IEA Study of Reading Literacy in Finland]*. Kasvatustieteiden tutkimuslaitos [Department of Education], Jyväskylä: Jyväskylän yliopisto [University of Jyväskylä].

Linnakylä, P., Malin, A., Blomqvist, I. and Sulkunen, S. (2000) *Lukutaito työssä ja arjessa. Aikuisten kansainvälinen lukutaitotutkimus Suomessa [Literacy in Work and Everyday Life: An International Study of Literacy among the Adult Population in Finland]*. Jyväskylä: Koulutuksen tutkimuslaitos, Jyväskylän yliopisto [Institute for Educational Research, University of Jyväskylä].

Lonka, I. (1998) ÄOL ja opetussuunnitelmien kehittäminen [ÄOL and the development of curricula]. In R. Kaipainen, I. Lonka and J. Rikama (eds) *Siitäpä nyt tie menevi. Äidinkielen opettajain liiton viisi vuosikymmentä 1948–1998 [There Goes the Way Now: The Five Decades of the Association for Mother Tongue Teachers 1948–1998]* (pp. 125–57). Helsinki: Äidinkielen opettajain liitto [Association for Mother Tongue Teachers].

Lyytikäinen, E. (2000) Ylioppilasaineiden kielivirheet – lisääntymään päin? [Grammatical errors made in the matriculation examination essays – increasing or not?] *Virittäjä* [Journal of the Society for the Study of Finnish] 104 (4), 602–9.

Maamies, S. (2002) Ylioppilasaine ja ajan henki – sensorien ajatuksia aineista [Matriculation examination and the spirit of the times – evaluators' thoughts on the essays]. *Kielikello [Language Bell]* 2, 11–21.

Majaniemi, P. and Lillberg, E. (2000) *Romanikielinen opettajankoulutustarve Suomessa. Opettajien perus- ja täydennyskoulutuksen ennakointihanke (OPEPRO) 6 [The Need for Teacher Training in the Romani language in Finland: Anticipatory Project to Investigate Teachers' Initial and Continuing Training Needs 6]*. Helsinki: Opetushallitus [National Board of Education].

Makkonen, S. and Mantila H. (eds) (1997) *Pohjoissuomalaisen puhekielen sosiolingvistinen variaatio [The Sociolinguistic Variation of Spoken Northern Finnish]*. Suomen ja saamen kielen ja logopedian laitoksen julkaisuja 8 [Publications of the Department of Finnish, Saami and Logepedics 8]. Oulu: Oulun yliopisto [University of Oulu].

Malm, A. (ed.) (1998) *Suomalaisen viittomakielen perussanakirja [Basic Dictionary of Finnish Sign Language]*. Kotimaisten kielten tutkimuskeskuksen julkaisuja 104 [Publications of the Research Institute for the Languages of Finland 104]. Helsinki: Kuurojen Liitto [Finnish Association of the Deaf].

Malm, A. (ed.) (2000) *Viittomakieliset Suomessa [Sign Language Users in Finland]*. Helsinki: Finn Lectura.

Mantila, H. (2002) Language situation in Finland. In K. Matsumura (ed.) *Lectures on Language Situation: Russia, Estonia, Finland* (pp. 49–64). ICHEL Linguistics Studies Vol. 6. Tokyo: University of Tokyo.

Marjakangas, K. (2000) Mira ja me. Romanin kuva ja vähemmistön asema televisiossa tapauksessa 'Tumma ja hehkuva veri' [Mira and us: The image of Romani and the status of minorities on TV in the case of the programme 'Dark and glowing blood']. Unpublished MA thesis. Tiedotusopin laitos, Tampereen yliopisto [Department of Journalism and Mass Communication, University of Tampere], Tampere.

Markkanen, K. (1999) Tietoa ja uutisia uudesta maasta [Information and news about the new country]. *Helsingin Sanomat* (5 May). Finland's largest circulation newspaper – based in Helsinki.

Martikainen, T. (2000a) Muslims in Finland: Facts and reflections. In N. G. Holm (ed.) *Islam and Christianity in School Religious Education* (pp. 203–47). Åbo: Åbo Akademi.

Martikainen, T. (2000b) Globalization and the religious field in Turku. In J. Kaplan (ed.) *Beyond the Mainstream: The Emergence of Religious Pluralism in Finland* (pp. 201–22). Helsinki: Suomalaisen Kirjallisuuden Seura [Finnish Literature Society].

Martikainen, T. (2000c) Muslim groups in Turku. *Journal of Muslim Minority Affairs* 20 (2), 329–45.

Matinheikki-Kokko, K. and Pitkänen, P. (2002) Immigrant policies and the education of immigrants in Finland. In P. Pitkänen, D. Kalekin-Fishman and G. Verma (eds) *Education and Immigration: Settlement Policies and Current Challenges* (pp. 48–73). London: Routledge Falmer.

McRae, K.D. (1997) *Conflict and Compromise in Multilingual Societies: Finland*. Waterloo, Ontario: Wilfried Laurier University Press.

Medgyes, P. and Miklósy, K. (2000) The language situation in Hungary. *Current Issues in Language Planning* 1, 148–242.

Mielikäinen, A. (1982) Nykypuhesuomen alueellista taustaa [The regional background of modern spoken Finnish]. *Virittäjä* [Journal of the Society for the Study of Finnish] 86 (3), 277–94.

Ministry of the Interior (MI) (1997) Government decision-in-principle immigration and refugee policy programme. On WWW at http://www.intermin.fi/eng/refuge.html.

Ministry of Labour (ML) (1999) Act on the integration of immigrants and reception of asylum seekers. On WWW at http://www.mol.fi/migration/act.pdf.

Ministry of Social Affairs and Health (MSAH) (2000) *Finland's Romani People*. Ministry of Social Affairs and Health Brochures 1999, no. 14. Helsinki: Ministry of Social Affairs and Health.

Mustaparta, A-K. and Tella, A. (1999) *Vieraskielisen opetuksen järjestäminen peruskoulussa ja lukiossa [How to Arrange Content and Language Integrated Learning in Primary and Secondary Schools]*. Helsinki: Opetushallitus [National Board of Education].

Mustonen, R., Oksanen, I., Saure, A. and Suova, L. (1999) Kansallinen koe on pidetty – tekijät esiin [The national test has been given – let's see the authors]. *Virke* [*Sentence*] 2, 36–7.

National Board of Education (NBE) (1994) *Framework Curriculum for the Comprehensive School 1994*. Helsinki: National Board of Education.

National Board of Education (NBE) (2001) The education system in Finland. On WWW at http://www.edu.fi/info/system/english.

Nevala, L. (2001) Kaikkien kanava [Everybody's channel]. *MoniTori* [*Monitor*] 3, 18–9.

Nieminen, M. (2000) Maahanmuutto [Immigration]. In K. Andreasson and V. Helin (eds) *Suomen vuosisata [The Century of Finland]* (pp. 34–5). Jyväskylä: Gummerus.

Nieminen, T. (2000) *Suomi toisena kielenä -opettajien koulutuksen kehittäminen Helsingin yliopistossa* [*Developing the Education of Teachers of Finnish as a Second Language at the University of Helsinki*]. Helsinki: Helsingin yliopiston suomen kielen laitos [Department of Finnish, University of Helsinki].

Nikula, T. and Marsh, D. (1996) *Kartoitus vieraskielisen opetuksen tarjonnasta peruskouluissa ja lukioissa* [*Availability of Content and Language Integrated Learning in Finnish Primary and Secondary Schools*]. Helsinki: Opetushallitus [National Board of Education].

Nikula, T. and Marsh, D. (1997) *Vieraskielisen opetuksen tavoitteet ja toteuttaminen* [*Aims and Implementation of Content and Language Integrated Learning*]. Helsinki: Opetushallitus [National Board of Education].

Nikula, T. and Marsh, D. (1999) Case Study: Finland. In D. Marsh and G. Langé (eds) *Implementing Content and Language Integrated Learning* (pp. 17–72). Jyväskylä: Continuing Education Centre, University of Jyväskylä.

Nuolijärvi, P. (1986) *Kolmannen sukupolven kieli. Helsinkiin muuttaneiden suurten ikäluokkien pohjoissavolaisten ja eteläpohjalaisten kielellinen sopeutuminen* [*The Language of the Third Generation: The Linguistic Adaptation of Representatives of Large Age Groups who have Moved to Helsinki from Southern Ostrobothnia and Northern Savo*]. Helsinki: Suomalaisen Kirjallisuuden Seura [Finnish Literature Society].

Nuolijärvi, P. (1991) Monikielinen Suomi [Multilingual Finland]. In T. Lehtinen and S. Shore (eds) *Kieli, valta ja eriarvoisuus. Kieli 6* [*Language, Power, and Inequality. Language 6*] (pp. 11–32). Helsinki: Helsingin yliopiston suomen kielen laitos [Department of Finnish, University of Helsinki].

Nuolijärvi, P. (1994a) Migrationen inom och till Norden [Migration in and into the Nordic region]. In S. Boyd, A. Holmen and J. N. Jørgensen (eds) *Sprogbrug og sprogvalg blandt indvandrere i Norden* [*Language Use and Language Choice among Immigrants in the Nordic Region*] (pp. 5–25). Københavnerstudier i tosprogethed 23 [Copenhagen Studies in Bilingualism 23]. København: Danmarks Lærerhøjskole [Royal Danish School of Educational Studies].

Nuolijärvi, P. (1994b) On the interlinkage of sociolinguistic background variables. In B. Nordberg (ed.) *The Sociolinguistics of Urbanization: The Case of the Nordic Countries* (pp. 149–70). Berlin and New York: Walter de Gruyter.

Nuolijärvi, P. (1999) Suomen kielitilanne 2000-luvulla [The language situation in Finland in the 21st century]. *Tieteessä tapahtuu* [*It happens in science*] 17 (1), 22–9.

Nyholm, L. and Aziz, A. (1996) Kurdiska som invandrarspråk i Svenskfinland. Språksituationen för flyktingar med varieteten sorani [Kurdish as an immigrant language in the Swedish-speaking areas in Finland: The language situation of refugees with the Sorani variety]. *Multiethnica* 16/17, 30–35.

Nylund-Oja, M., Pentikäinen, J., Horn, F., Jaakkola, M. and Yli-Vakkuri, L. (1995) Finnish emigrants and immigration. In J. Pentikäinen and M. Hiltunen (eds) *Cultural Minorities in Finland: An Overview Towards Cultural Policy* (pp. 173–228). Publications of the Finnish National Commission for UNESCO 66. Helsinki: Finnish National Commission for UNESCO.

OECD (2001) *Knowledge and Skills for Life: First Results from the OECD Programme for International Student Assessment (PISA)*. Paris: Organisation for Economic Co-operation and Development.

Ollikainen, M. (1995) *Vankkurikansan perilliset. Romanit, Euroopan unohdettu vähemmistö* [*The Successors of the Wagon People: The Roma, the Forgotten Minority in Europe*]. Helsinki: Yliopistopaino [Helsinki University Press].

Olthuis, M-L. (2000) Inarinsaamen kielen vuosisadat [Centuries of the Inari Saami language]. *Virittäjä* [Journal of the Society for the Study of Finnish] 104 (4), 568–75.

Olthuis, M-L. (2002) Inarisaami – a minority in a minority. In *Samiska i ett nytt årtusende* [*Saami in the New Millennium*] (pp. 97–102). Köpenhamn: Nordiska Ministerrådet [Nordic Council of Ministers].

Opetushallitus (OPH) (1993) *Suositus aikuisten maahanmuuttajien opetussuunnitelman perusteiksi* [*Recommendation for the Education of Adult Immigrants*]. Helsinki: Opetushallitus [National Board of Education].

Opetushallitus (OPH) (1994) *Lukion opetussuunnitelman perusteet 1994* [*Framework Curriculum for the Upper Secondary School 1994*]. Helsinki: Edita.
Opetushallitus (OPH) (1997) *Aikuisten maahanmuuttajakoulutuksen tavoitteet ja periaatteet* [*The Aims and Principles for the Education of Adult Immigrants*]. Helsinki: Edita.
Opetushallitus (OPH) (1999a) *Toisen kotimaisen kielen opetuksen kehittämisen suuntaviivoja. Kieltenopetuksen monipuolistamis- ja kehittämishanke 1996–2000* [*Directions for Developing the Teaching of the Second National Language: Diversification of Language Teaching Programme 1996–2000*]. Helsinki: Edita.
Opetushallitus (OPH) (1999b) *Kimmoke-indikaattorit. Tilastoja kieltenopetuksesta perusopetuksessa ja lukioissa* [*Kimmoke Indicators: Statistics of Language Education in Comprehensive and Upper Secondary Schools*]. Helsinki: Opetushallitus [National Board of Education].
Opetushallitus (OPH) (2000) *Peruskoulun opetussuunnitelman perusteet 1994* [*Framework Curriculum for the Comprehensive School 1994*] (4th edn). Helsinki: Edita.
Opetushallitus (OPH) (2001) *Suositus aikuisten maahanmuuttajien kotoutumiskoulutuksesta* [*Recommendation for the Integration Training of Adult Immigrants*]. Helsinki: Opetushallitus [National Board of Education].
Opetusministeriö (OPM) (1978) *Kieliohjelmakomitean mietintö* [*Memorandum of the Committee on Language Teaching Policy in Finland*]. Helsinki: Opetusministeriö [Ministry of Education].
Opetusministeriö (OPM) (1987) *Vieraskielisten lasten äidinkielen opetuksen työryhmän muistio* [*Memorandum of the Working Group on Mother Tongue Instruction for Immigrant Pupils*]. Helsinki: Opetusministeriö [Ministry of Education].
Opetusministeriö (OPM) (1989) *Kieliohjelman monipuolistamista ja oppilaalle vieraalla kielellä annettavaa opetusta selvittäneen työryhmän muistio* [*Memorandum of the Working Group on Diversification of the Language Programme and Content and Language Integrated Learning*]. Helsinki: Opetusministeriö [Ministry of Education].
Opetusministeriö (OPM) (2000) *Suomi (o)saa lukea. Tietoyhteiskunnan lukutaidot -työryhmän linjaukset* [*Finland Can/May Read: Guidelines of the Working Group on Literacy in the Information Society*]. Helsinki: Yliopistopaino [Helsinki University Press].
Opetusministeriö (OPM) (2001) *Perusopetuksen uudistamistyöryhmän muistio* [*Memorandum of the Working Group on the Reform of Basic Education*]. Helsinki: Yliopistopaino [Helsinki University Press].
Opetusministeriö (OPM) (2002) *Valtionhallinnon kielitutkintojärjestelmän uudistaminen* [*Revising the Language Testing System for State Officials*]. Helsinki: Yliopistopaino [Helsinki University Press].
Paunonen, H. (1976) Kotikielen Seura 1876–1976 [The Society for the Study of Finnish in 1876–1976]. *Virittäjä* [Journal of the Society for the Study of Finnish] 80 (3–4), 568–75.
Paunonen, H. (1995 [1982]) *Suomen kieli Helsingissä. Huomioita Helsingin puhekielen historiallisesta taustasta ja nykyvariaatiosta* [*The Finnish Language in Helsinki: Observations on the Historical Background and Present Variation of Spoken Finnish in Helsinki*]. Helsinki: Helsingin yliopiston suomen kielen laitos [Department of Finnish, University of Helsinki].
Paunonen, H. (1997) Finland. In H. Goebl, P.H. Nelde, Z. Starý and W. Wölck (eds) *Kontaktlinguistik / Contact Linguistics / Linquistique de contact* (pp. 993–1007). Berlin and New York: Walter de Gruyter.
Peltonen, A. (1999) Finnish population. On WWW at http://virtual.finland.fi. Accessed, 4/12/01.
Piri, R. (2001) *Suomen kieliohjelmapolitiikka. Kansallinen ja kansainvälinen toimintaympäristö* [*Foreign Language Teaching Policy in Finland: National and International Context*]. Jyväskylä: Soveltavan kielentutkimuksen keskus, Jyväskylän yliopisto [Centre for Applied Language Studies, University of Jyväskylä].
Pälli, P. and Latomaa, S. (1997) *Aikuisten maahanmuuttajien suomen kielen taito. Maahanmuuttajakoulutuksen arviointia* [*Proficiency Level in Finnish among Adult Immigrants: Evaluation of Immigrant Education*]. Helsinki: Opetushallitus [National Board of Education].

Raanamo, A-M. (1998) Suomi-buumia maailmalla. Ulkomaisten yliopistojen Suomen kielen ja kulttuurin opinnot ['Finland boom' in the world. Finnish studies at universities abroad]. *Campus* 1, 4–7.

Rainò, P. (2000) Carl Oscar Malm – suomalaisen viittomakielen isä [Carl Oscar Malm – the father of Finnish sign language]. In A. Malm (ed.) *Viittomakieliset Suomessa* [*Sign Language Users in Finland*] (pp. 35–47). Helsinki: Finn Lectura.

Rapola, M. (1962) *Johdatus suomen murteisiin* [*An Introduction to Finnish Dialects*]. Helsinki: Suomalaisen Kirjallisuuden Seura [Finnish Literature Society].

Reinboth, S. (2001) EN:n ministerikomitea moittii Suomea romanien kohtelusta [The EC Committee of Ministers criticizes Finland about the discrimination suffered by the Roma] *Helsingin Sanomat* (10 November). Finland's largest circulation newspaper – based in Helsinki.

Repo, M. (1999) Ortodoksinen Suomi [Orthodox Finland]. In M. Löytönen and L. Kolbe (eds) *Suomi: Maa, kansa, kulttuurit* [*Finland: the Country, the People, the Cultures*] (pp. 290–302). Helsinki: Suomalaisen Kirjallisuuden Seura [Finnish Literature Society].

Reuter, M. (1992) Swedish as a pluricentric language. In M. Clyne (ed.) *Pluricentric Languages. Differing Norms in Different Nations* (pp. 101–15). Berlin and New York: Mouton de Gryuter.

Reuter, M. (forthcoming) Swedish in Finland in the 20th century. In O. Bandle, K. Braunmüller, E-H. Jahr, A. Karker, H-P. Naumann and U. Teleman (eds) in cooperation with G. Widmark and L. Elmevik. *The Nordic Languages: An International Handbook on the History of the North Germanic Languages, I-II.* Handbücher zur Sprach- und Kommunikationswissenschaft [Handbooks on Linguistics and Communication Studies]. Berlin and New York: Mouton de Gruyter.

Rintala, P. (2000) Oikeakielisyydestä kielenhuoltoon [From linguistic correctness to language cultivation]. *Kielikello* [*Language Bell*] 1, 19–23.

Räikkälä, A. (1995) Menneiltä vuosilta [From the years gone by]. *Kielikello* [*Language Bell*] 1, 3–17.

Sajavaara, A. (2000) *Virkamies ja vieraat kielet. Virkamiesten kielikoulutuksen arviointihankkeen loppuraportti* [*Civil Servants and Foreign Languages: An Evaluation of Language Training in Finnish State Administration*]. Jyväskylä: Soveltavan kielentutkimuksen keskus, Jyväskylän yliopisto [Centre for Applied Language Studies, University of Jyväskylä].

Sajavaara, K. (1993) Communication, foreign languages, and foreign language policy. In K. Sajavaara, R.D. Lambert, S. Takala and C.A. Morfit (eds) *National Foreign Language Planning: Practices and Prospects* (pp. 31–53). Institute for Educational Research. Jyväskylä: University of Jyväskylä.

Sajavaara, K. (1995) Language studies in higher education in Finland. In *Language Studies in Higher Education in Europe: National Reports* (pp. 123–43). Stockholm: Sigma Scientific Committee on Languages. On WWW at http://www.fu-berlin.de/elc/natreps/natr-fin.htm.

Sajavaara, K. and Takala, S. (2000) Kielikoulutuksen vaikutus ja tulokset Suomessa [Effectiveness and results of languages education in Finland]. In K. Sajavaara and A. Piirainen-Marsh (eds) *Näkökulmia soveltavaan kielentutkimukseen* [*Approaches to Applied Language Studies*] (pp. 155–230). Jyväskylä: Soveltavan kielentutkimuksen keskus, Jyväskylän yliopisto [Centre for Applied Language Studies, University of Jyväskylä].

Saleva, M. (1997) *Now They're Talking: Testing Oral Proficiency in a Language Laboratory.* Studia Philologica Jyväskyläensia 43. Jyväskylä: University of Jyväskylä.

Salminen, T. (1993) Uralilaiset kielet maailman kielten joukossa [The Uralic languages among the languages of the world]. In T. Salminen (ed.) *Uralilaiset kielet tänään* [*Uralic Languages Today*] (pp. 24–30). Kuopion Snellman-instituutin julkaisuja A 13 [Publications of the Snellman Institute of Kuopio A 13]. Kuopio: Snellman-Instituutti.

Salonen, K., Kääriäinen, K. and Niemelä, K. (2000) *Kirkko uudelle vuosituhannelle. Suomen evankelis-luterilainen kirkko vuosina 1996–1999* [*The Church at the Turn of the Millennium. The Evangelical Lutheran Church of Finland from 1996 to 1999*]. Tampere: Kirkon tutkimuskeskus [The Research Institute of the Finnish Evangelical Lutheran Church].

Sammallahti, P. (1998) *The Saami Languages. An Introduction.* Kárášjohka: Davvi Girji.

230

Language Planning and Policy in Europe

Sandell, M. (2001) Basaari koulutti uusia tekijöitä televisioon [Bazaar trained news reporters for television]. *MoniTori [Monitor]* 3, 14–15.

Sarv, A. (1999) Eestirootslased [Swedish people in Estonia]. In J. Viikberg (ed.) *Eesti rahvaste raamat. Rahvusvähemused, -rühmad ja -killud [The Ethnic Groups in Estonia]* (pp. 147–56). Tallinn: Eesti Entsüklopeediakirjastus [Estonian Encyclopedia Publishing Company].

Saukkonen, P. (2000) Suomen kieli, suomalaiset ja Eurooppa [The Finnish language, Finns and Europe]. *Kielikuvia [Metaphors]* 2, 19–27.

Savolainen, A. (1998) Suomi toisena kielenä -opetussuunnitelmat. Selvitys opetussuunnitelmatilanteesta kesällä 1998 [Local curricula for Finnish as a second language: A report on the situation in the summer of 1998]. Unpublished report, Opetushallitus [National Board of Education], Helsinki.

Scheinin, M. (1999) Oikeus omaan kieleen ja kulttuuriin [The right to one's own language and culture]. In P. Hallberg (ed.) *Perusoikeudet [Basic Rights]* (pp. 533–59). Helsinki: WSOY [Werner Söderström Oy].

Seppälä, A-M. (2000) Suomi-koulut vaalivat suomalaisuutta maailmalla [Finland-schools cherish Finnishness abroad]. *Opettaja [Teacher]* 10, 26–8.

Seurujärvi-Kari, I., Aikio-Puoskari, U., Morottaja, M., Saressalo, L, Pentikäinen, J. and Hirvonen, V. (1995) The Sami people in Finland. In J. Pentikäinen and M. Hiltunen (eds) *Cultural Minorities in Finland: An Overview towards Cultural Policy* (pp. 101–45). Publications of the Finnish National Commission for UNESCO 66. Helsinki: Finnish National Commission for UNESCO.

Sommardahl, E. (2002) *På god grund. Idébok för skolan [On Good Grounds: A Book of Ideas for the School]*. Helsinki: Svenska kulturfonden & Forskningscentralen för de inhemska språken [The Finland Swedish Cultural Foundation & The Research Institute for the Languages of Finland].

Statistical Yearbook of Finland (2001) – *Suomen tilastollinen vuosikirja 2001 – Statistisk årsbok för Finland 2001*. Helsinki: Tilastokeskus [Statistics Finland].

Statistics Finland (SF) (1999) *Education in Finland 1999: Statistics and Indicators*. Education 1999 (4). Helsinki: Statistics Finland.

Statistics Finland (SF) (2001) *Population Structure 2000*. Population 2001 (6). Helsinki: Statistics Finland.

Sundman, M. (1998) *Barnet, skolan och tvåspråkigheten [The Child, the School and Bilingualism]*. Helsinki: Yliopistopaino [Helsinki University Press].

Suni, M. (1996) *Maahanmuuttajaoppilaiden suomen kielen taito peruskoulun päättövaiheessa [Proficiency in Finnish among Immigrant Pupils at the End of Comprehensive School]*. Helsinki: Opetushallitus [National Board of Education].

Suomen asukasluku 2001–2002 [Population in Finland 2001–2002]. Helsinki: Väestörekisterikeskus [Population Register Centre].

Suonoja, V. and Lindberg, V. (1999) *Romanipolitiikan strategiat [Strategies of the Policy on Roma]*. Selvityksiä 9 [Reports 9] . Helsinki: Sosiaali- ja terveysministeriö [Ministry of Social Affairs and Health].

Swain, M. and Johnson, R.K. (1997) Immersion education: A category within bilingual education. In R.K. Johnson and M. Swain (eds) *Immersion Education: International Perspectives* (pp. 1–16). Cambridge: Cambridge University Press.

Söderman, T. (1997) *Flykting i ett tvåspråkigt land. Effekter av svenska och finska som andraspråk – en studie bland kurder i Västra Nyland [Refugees in a Bilingual Country: The Effects of Swedish and Finnish as a Second Language among Kurds in the Region of Västra Nyland (Länsi-Uusimaa)]*. SSKH Meddelanden 47 [Reports from the Swedish School of Social Science]. Helsingfors: Universitetstryckeriet [Helsinki: University Press].

Takala, S. (1993) Language policy and language teaching policy in Finland. In K. Sajavaara, R.D. Lambert, S. Takala and C.A. Morfit (eds) *National Foreign Language Planning: Practices and Prospects* (pp. 54–71). Institute for Educational Research. Jyväskylä: University of Jyväskylä.

Takala, S. (2000) Some questions and issues in content-based language teaching. In K. Sjöholm and A. Østern (eds) *Perspectives on Language and Communication in Multilingual*

Education (pp. 41–54). Reports from the Faculty of Education 6. Vasa: Åbo Akademi University.

Takala, S. and Sajavaara, K. (2000) Language policy and planning. In W. Grabe *et al.* (eds) *Annual Review of Applied Linguistics* 20. *Applied Linguistics as an Emerging Discipline* (pp. 129–46). New York: Cambridge University Press.

Takkinen, R. (2002) *Käsimuotojen salat. Viittomakielisten lasten käsimuotojen omaksuminen 2–7 vuoden iässä* [*The Secrets of Handshapes: The Acquisition of Handshapes by Native Signers Aged between 2 and 7*]. Helsinki: Kuurojen Liitto [Finnish Association of the Deaf].

Tandefelt, M. (1988) *Mellan två språk. En fallstudie om språkbevarande och språkbyte i Finland* [*Between Two Languages: A Case Study of Language Maintenance and Language Shift in Finland*]. Acta Universitatis Upsaliensis. Studia Multiethnica Upsaliensia 3.

Tandefelt, M. (1992) The Finland-Swedes – the most privileged minority in Europe? In G. Blom, P. Graves, A. Kruse and B.T. Thomsen (eds) *Minority Languages. The Scandinavian Experience* (pp. 21–72). Nordic Language Secretariat. Report 17. Oslo: Nordic Language Secretariat.

Thesleff, A. (1901) *Wörterbuch des Dialekts der finnländischen Zigeuner* [*Dictionary of the Dialects of the Finnish Roma*]. Acta Societatis Scientiarum Fennicae 29 (6). Helsinki: Suomalaisen Kirjallisuuden Seura [Finnish Literature Society].

Tilastokeskus (2000) *Joukkoviestimet 2000* [*Mass Media 2000*]. Kulttuuri ja viestintä [Culture and Communication] 2000 (1). Helsinki: Tilastokeskus [Statistics Finland].

Tilastokeskus (2001) *Oppilaitostilastot* [*Statistics on Educational Institutions*]. Koulutus [Education] 2001 (4). Helsinki: Tilastokeskus [Statistics Finland].

Tommila, P. (ed.) (1989) *Herää Suomi. Suomalaisuusliikkeen historia* [*Wake up Finland: The History of the Finnish Nationalist Movement*]. Kuopio: Kustannuskiila Oy [Publishing Quoin].

Tommila, P. and Salokangas, R. (1998) *Sanomia kaikille. Suomen lehdistön historia* [*Messages for All: The History of the Finnish Press*]. Helsinki: Edita.

Tommola, H. (forthcoming) What happens to our languages? In H. Metslang and M. Rannut (eds) *Languages in Development* (pp. 31–42). Tallinn: Tallinna Pedagoogikaülikool [Tallinn Pedagogical University].

Torvinen, T. (1989) *Kadimah. Suomen juutalaisten historia* [*Kadimah: The History of the Jews in Finland*]. Helsinki: Otava.

Tuokko, E. (2000) *Peruskoulun 9. Vuosiluokan englannin (A1) oppimistulosten kansallinen Arviointi 1999* [*National Evaluation of the Learning Results in English (A1) in the 9th Grade, 1999*]. Helsinki: Opetushallitus [National Board of Education].

Turunen, A. (1988) The Balto-Finnic languages. In D. Sinor (ed.) *The Uralic Languages: Description, History and Foreign Influences* (pp. 58–83). Leiden: E.J. Brill.

Uusi kielilaki / Ny språklag [*The New Language Act*] (2001) Kielilakikomitean mietintö [The Report of the Language Law Commission] 2001 (3). Helsinki.

Valtonen, P. (1972) *Suomen mustalaiskielen etymologinen sanakirja* [*The Etymological Dictionary of Romani in Finland*]. Helsinki: Suomalaisen Kirjallisuuden Seura [Finnish Literature Society].

van Els, T.J.M. (2001) The European Union, its institutions and its languages. Some language political observations. *Current Issues in Language Planning* 2, 311–60.

Virtala, A-L. (2002) Vieraskielisestä opetuksesta käyty julkinen keskustelu Suomessa. Argumentointi vieraskielisen opetuksen puolesta ja sitä vastaan [The public debate about content and language integrated learning in Finland: Arguments for and against content and language integrated learning]. Unpublished licensiate thesis, Centre for Applied Language Studies, University of Jyväskylä, Jyväskylä.

Virtaranta, P., Jönsson-Korhola, H., Martin, M. and Kainulainen, M. (1993) *Amerikansuomi* [*American Finnish*]. Helsinki: Suomalaisen Kirjallisuuden Seura [Finnish Literature Society].

Vuolab, K. (2000) Saamen kielen ja saamenkielinen opetus Suomessa [Instruction of and in Saami in Finland]. In H. Sulkala (ed.) *Kieli- ja kulttuurikontaktit. Kielikontaktit – Kieli ja kulttuuri päiväkodissa, koulussa ja opettajankoulutuksessa -seminaari 6.–7.5.1999* [*Language and Culture Contacts: Language Contacts – A Seminar on Language and Culture in Daycare, School and Teacher Training*] (pp. 190–7). Jyväskylä: Gummerus.

Vuolasranta, M. (1995) *Romano tšimbako drom* [*The Road of Romani*]. Jyväskylä: Opetushallitus [National Board of Education].

Winsa, B. (1999) Language planning in Sweden. *Journal of Multilingual and Multicultural Development* 19, 376–473.

Yleisradio (YLE) (2001) *YLE* [*Finnish Broadcasting Company*] *Annual Report 2001*. Helsinki: Yleisradio [Finnish Broadcasting Company].

Yrjölä, J. (1998) Monikulttuurisuus paikallisseurakunnassa [Multiculturalism in a local parish]. In A. Tammi (ed.) *Vieraita ja muukalaisia. Kirkko monikulttuurisessa yhteiskunnassa* [*Guests and Aliens: The Church in a Multicultural Society*] (pp. 167–77). Helsinki: Kirjapaja [Printing Forge].

Zetterberg, S. (1999) Main outlines of Finnish history. On WWW at http://virtual.finland.fi. Accessed 14.11.01.

Østern, A. (2000) Research into future possibilities: Genre proficiency in Swedish as a mother tongue in Finnish immersion. In K. Sjöholm and A. Østern (eds) *Perspectives on Language and Communication in Multilingual Education* (pp. 145–65). Vasa: Åbo Akademi University.

Language Planning in Sweden

Birger Winsa
Department of Finnish, Stockholm University, S-106 91 Stockholm, Sweden

This monograph presents a detailed study of the language planning situation in Sweden with particular emphasis on minority languages. Swedish language policies towards minorities have been nationalistic, reluctant, and directed towards assimilation. High labour immigration, which began in the late 1950s, effected bilingual education. Sweden has five minority language groups: Sami spoken by 5–10,000 in the northernmost regions, and especially by reindeer herders; Meänkieli and Finnish, two Finno-Ugric languages spoken by 40–70,000 Tornedalians in the northernmost county, Norrbotten, and by 200–250,000 Swedish Finns throughout Sweden, but especially in the capital region and major cities; 5–15,000 Roma speaking various Romani varieties and a few thousand Jews with competence in Yiddish. In practice Sami has had minority status since the early 1970s. In the spring of 2000 new minority legislation will come into force acknowledging these five groups as Swedish minorities, and Sweden will ratify two Council of Europe minority conventions. However, these first steps towards a new minority policy lag some 20 years behind general developments in the European Union, and except for the Sami, economic expenditure to support minorities, their languages and cultures is limited.

Introduction

Language planning is often defined as deliberate implementation of a given language policy.[1] There is, however, hardly any language planning that is independent of a multidimensional socio-political discourse. At one end of the spectrum, language planning is a socio-political value-laden ideology, whereas at the other end it is a linguistic attempt to apply an instrumental and restricted perspective to language diversity, although in the final analysis, both perspectives are political, rather than purely linguistic. As a political discourse, it may also represent various interests that seek to maintain an official (high status) policy for some languages and an unofficial (low status) reality for others.

Socio-political and ideological motives, rather than pedagogic ideas or attempts to maintain linguistic diversity, have, up to the early 1960s, dominantly underpinned Swedish language policy towards its national minorities. The Socialistic bloc in Swedish politics, which has been in power for several decades, has conceptualised various communities by dividing them according to social and hence economic classes, rather than according to ethnicity or language. This instrumental, ignorant and reluctant ideology which formed the general discourse for language planning, has been the basic component of Swedish social politics applied by the left as well as by the right-wing parties. Under this perspective, terms such as 'ethnicity' (used by United Nations after the Second World War) and 'minority' were associated with racism, conflict and backwardness, and were overshadowed by ideas of the 19th century on equal human rights, independent mother tongue(s) or gender. The social context-bound values of minority language groups have been neglected. However, this neglect has been deliberate because the cultural values inherent in the majority language have always been important status raising qualities for that majority.

If we define a language policy as the outcome of conscious ideologies based on an underlying discourse carried out by the government, public authorities, religious institutions, and educational system in various forms, then we can conceptualise language planning as the practical implications of these explicit and implicit policies. A description of a given language policy involves setting out the network of conceptualised ideas on the practical implications of the prevailing social and political discourse within a given period(s). The discourse as such is firmly rooted in the long traditions of national policies, constituted by inherited attitudes and practices towards linguistic diversity and dialects. Therefore, the strategy of politicians is often, by definition, not explicitly stated in any policy, and is to varying degrees not fully conceptualised by the politicians, or even by those affected. In order to map a given language policy, one must also consider the underlying practical, political, economic and social circumstances that underlie a policy, and the extent of its practical applicability.

One major influential aspect on language policy development is the spatial and social position of Sweden and Swedes in Europe. At its heart, Swedes often consider Sweden in historical reviews as a culturally peripheral region with a cold climate that has received waves of culture from the Continent (Sörlin, 1994: 33f) (except during the Geatish period). Even today, it is common to speak about the 'Continent', i.e. the 'real' Europe. Therefore the high culture – defined as the metacultural, literate, official, educated and public society – was predominantly located on the Continent, and Swedish society was just an outgrowth of the Continental Tree.[2] On the other hand, the low cultures of Europe – defined as the often functionally illiterate communities, subordinated to the high culture – constituted heterogeneous vernacular Europe.

With these perspectives in mind, Swedish language policy is and has been primarily deliberate – although not necessarily overtly declared in all its aspects – and the result of a long tradition of international social and ideological influences, e.g. from scientific paradigms, theological speculations, educational structures or colonial politics. In general terms, language policy in Sweden was, up to the 19th century, based on access to international communication, control of communities speaking languages/vernaculars other than Swedish, the influence of theology and religious ideologies, the development of the society and the institutionalisation of education and knowledge. Even today this perspective has not radically changed and is visible in the form of an attitudinal legacy vis-à-vis Swedish, other native and immigrant languages of Sweden and the perception of mono- or multilingual cultures.

Part I: The Language Profile of Sweden

The official languages

Despite the fact that the maintenance of a monolingual society is not inscribed in the Swedish constitution, Swedish is *de facto* the only nation-wide official language.

Swedish belongs to the Indo-European language family and is closely related to Danish, Norwegian, and Icelandic. Danish, and especially Norwegian, are largely comprehensible languages (especially in their written forms), whereas

Icelandic, which has preserved more features of an older Nordic variety, is no longer comprehensible for Swedes.

The spoken official standard is the variety of well-educated people living in the capital region as well as the nation in general. Up until the 1980s, newscasters and journalists in radio and TV were the dominant role models of the spoken standard. This meant in practice that communities who had problems adapting to the standard were in general unable to hold public positions in the broadcast media (as well as in schools of drama). People on the periphery of central Sweden, Skåne and the Finnish-speaking region, speak a distinct variety, clearly audible even in the standard mode. In official domains in local communities, a local standard has emerged; i.e. a variety with preserved intonation and prosodic features of the vernacular reflecting the local substrate vernaculars.

However, during the 1980s a more tolerant attitude developed where regional standard varieties of Swedish were accepted in the media. Even a slight Finnish accent is currently sometimes acceptable. One effect of this changing status of dialects is that they, and occasionally even Finnish, are now used in public advertisements on TV. Despite this progressive change in status planning, a homogeneous spoken language within the educational system is still implicitly required. In the broadcasting media, most of those being interviewed try to adapt to the formal pronunciation. A marked variety may still be a disadvantage in interviews with an employer.

The other *de facto* official language is Sami within the Sami Parliament and its sub-bodies. However, these are the only official domains of Sami.

After the Second World War, English began to dominate the official domains of international communication, and it has been a mandatory subject in primary school for several decades. It replaced German as the most popular second language in education. In the 1990s, many Swedes have a fairly broad formal competence in English, though often only in the receptive skills.

Within higher education, Sweden has a number of official dissertation languages. English is the predominant second language of instruction, especially in the natural sciences, e.g. 92% of all research seminars and guest lectures at the faculty of technical and natural sciences at Uppsala University were presented in English (Gunnarsson & Öhman, 1997). Besides Swedish, the full-status languages for dissertations are: Danish, Norwegian, English, French and German. Especially within medicine and the technical and natural sciences, English is used nearly exclusively as the written language of dissertations, and the use of spoken or written French or German is relatively rare. Upon an application for exemption, Finnish and other languages represented in the departments of Stockholm University are allowed to be used for dissertations (Lainio & Wande, 1996). The position of English as the international language of instruction is rapidly growing since Sweden took up membership in the European Union (EU) (Hyltenstam, 1996).[3] The EU seeks to integrate research and higher education and has set up a number of programmes to achieve this for European universities. This funding has effects on international contacts, the use of English, the exchange of students and professors, and on joint research projects.

The major minority languages

There is no agreement in international law on the definition of a minority or on how to distinguish a variety from a language (e g. EC, 1994). However, a minority is often defined as a group that is settled in a defined territory and has not recently immigrated, nor holds foreign citizenship. An informal categorisation, mentioned by experts on international law, is that the term 'autochthonous minority' can be applied to a group which has been living in a given area for at least 80 to 100 years (Hannikainen, 1996); i.e. more than three generations with an intergenerational transmission of language. Swedes have adapted the weak definitions of minority languages given in international conventions, e.g. the European Charter for Regional or Minority Languages and the International Labour Organisation (ILO)-conventions. According to these conventions, the Swedish linguistic minorities can be divided into indigenous, territorial and non-territorial autochthonous minority languages and groups.

The only indigenous minority in Sweden is the Sami, living originally in the Sápmi for at least two millennia. Sápmi is predominantly a wasteland and, loosely defined, the Sami area constitutes the western part of the northern provinces of Sweden; i.e. Norrbotten, Västerbotten, and Jämtland. Various Sami groups are also settled in four different nations: Russia, Finland, Norway, and Sweden.

The only territorial autochthonous minority is the Tornedalians (i.e. a Finnish-speaking group) who have inhabited the five northernmost municipalities of Sweden: Kiruna, Gällivare, Pajala, Haparanda and Övertorneå since the 12th century (see Figure 1).

The non-territorial minorities of Sweden are the Roma (in Sweden since the 17th century), Jews (in Sweden since the 18th century) and perhaps Swedish Finns (with migration from Finland since the 16th century). The leading organisation of the Swedish Finns has, in the early 1990s, declared itself as representing a Swedish territorial minority. This statement is, however, ignored by Finnish experts on international law who define the Swedish Finns as an immigrant group (Hannikainen, 1996; some 100,000 of the Swedish Finns have Finnish citizenship). However, the 'minority position' has recently had immense support from Lainio (1999) at the Department of Finnish, Stockholm University, who argues that the Sweden Finns constitute a territorial minority, due to their long tradition of migration from Finland, and their self-categorisation. Sweden is considering legislatively adopting this particular Nordic concept of 'minority', and experts on international law may also adapt this Nordic perspective. In the near future this could lead to a new emerging political discourse of minorities.

In the Swedish tradition, the Swedish Finns and their representative organisations as well as their language have been issues for the Board of Immigration, and they have been treated as immigrants, perhaps with a special position, by public authorities (EP, 1997). The general public perceives them as immigrants speaking an immigrant language, but with a special position within Swedish society. Migrations from Finland and frequent political contacts between the Nordic countries have located the Swedish Finns within that particular political discourse.

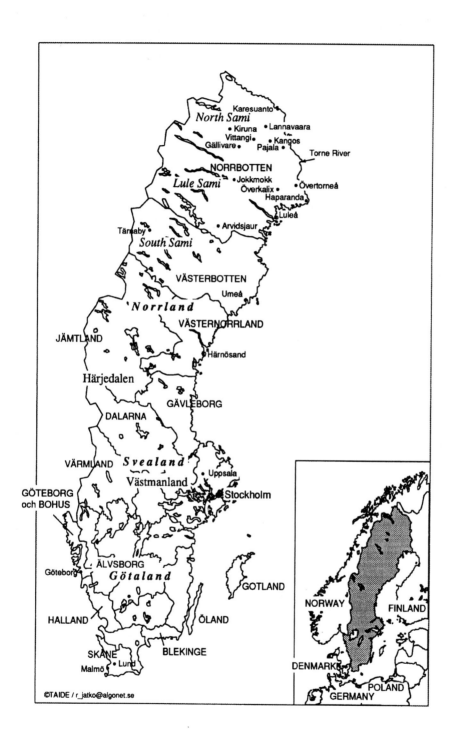

Figure 1 A map of Sweden listing the key locations and groups

The Swedish Finns have in general raised no arguments against their immigrant status, although the Swedish-Finnish movement made small attempts in the late 1970s to use the self-categorisation 'minority', even though this position gained little in-group support. However, a recent report of the Minority Commission defines the Swedish Finns as one of five Swedish minorities speaking a territorial language.[4] In addition, a Government bill introduced subsequent to the Minority Commission report proposes that Sami, Meänkieli and Finnish should be territorial minority languages in the northernmost region of Sweden, whereas Yiddish and Romani chib should be non-territorial minority languages (Prop., 1998/99: 143).

The Roma and the Jews are typical non-territorial minorities living mostly in urban areas. The Swedish Finns are scattered nation-wide, but in particular in the capital and the Gothenburg regions.

A small association in county Skåne claims that the group who speak that variety of Swedish actually constitutes a national minority, and that their vernacular is an East Danish variety. Linguists support the Danish roots of the Skåne dialect. However, few people in Skåne recognise the self-categorisation 'minority', and the association has not been acknowledged by official institutions as a representative minority language agency. Political strategies and economic motives are in this case decisive factors for this position.[5]

In addition, there are some 100–150 immigrant languages. All of them are spoken by first or second generation immigrants. In summary, the major minority languages are: Sami, Tornedalen Finnish (Meänkieli), Standard Finnish, and Romani Chib.

Tornedalen Finnish/Meänkieli

Tornedalen Finnish (henceforth Meänkieli) was originally based on East and West Finnish varieties, but has been strongly influenced by North Finnish, Swedish, Sami and some Norwegian. The morpho-phonological components and syntactical structure of Meänkieli have their strongest basis in West Finnish, though a great number of core lexical items as well as some morpho-phonological features can be traced to East Finnish varieties. Internal innovations – mainly in the vocabulary – often have a North Finnish spread. The rather few Sami loans occur mostly in terms for nature, cooking, clothing and reindeer herding. Norwegian loan words are rare. The strong influence of Swedish is predominantly found in loans for new terms, and in the frequent use of code switching (Winsa, 1991). However, some Swedish allophones are well integrated into Meänkieli. The fairly frequently occurring aspirated allophones /p'/, /t'/ or /k'/ in Meänkieli have no correspondence in standard Finnish (henceforth St Fi.) where only non-aspirated /p/, /t/ and /k/ occur. In addition, a few morphological differences can be traced to Swedish contacts, e.g. Meänkieli *mie häyn lähteä* 'I must go' has its correspondence in St Fi. *minun täytyy lähteä id.*[6]

Old well-integrated loan words from Nordic languages and German were common in spoken and written Finnish up to the 19th century, but were often replaced in modern Finnish through status planning during the nationalistic period in the late 19th century. These old loans are often preserved in Meänkieli due to the lack of influence from the Finnish purification process.

The Swedish loans began to enter Meänkieli in the 1930s, when access to radio broadcasting became common for most families, when education in Swedish improved and when Finnish was completely abandoned in school settings.

The main linguistic differences between Meänkieli and St Fi. can be summarised as follows:

(1) Lexicon: Where St Fi. has new Finnish terms in technology, modern occupations and administrative terminology, Meänkieli has borrowed corresponding terms from Swedish.
(2) Old Nordic loans in Finnish dialects were not integrated into St Fi. during the purification efforts in the latter part of the 19th century.
(3) The phonological gradation *t:0*, e.g. *lato* 'barn' in genitive case *laon* 'barn's', is a frequently occurring East Finnish feature preserved in Meänkieli (as well as in East Finnish and North Finnish varieties), but has its correspondence in the St Fi. as a *t:d* gradation, e.g. *lato: ladon*.
(4) The phoneme *h* occurs in a number of positions, but in particular in the illative case, e.g. *talo* 'house', *talhoon* 'to the house', *kello:kelhoon* 'clock: to the clock', and in particular genitive cases, e.g. *kirves* 'axe' and *kirhveen* 'axe's' (older forms *talohon, kellohon* and *kirvehen*); St Fi.: *talo:taloon, kello:kelloon* and *kirves:kirveen id.* The phoneme in this position is obsolete in many dialects, but preserved in the North Finnish dialects.
(5) The verb in the present tense third person pronoun has in Meänkieli a *-pi* ending in one syllable verbs, e.g. *hän saa-pi* 'he gets', in St Fi. *hän saa id.* This is an obsolete character in southern Finland, but frequent in North Finnish dialects.
(6) The vocabulary of Meänkieli is based on a mixture of various Finnish dialects, whereas St Fi. is based on the West Finnish lexicon. Hence, a fairly large number of Meänkieli words do not occur in St Fi.
(7) Meänkieli is a more analytical language than St Fi., e.g. *pöydällä* 'on the table' is the standard form and *pöyän päällä id.* the Meänkieli variant.
(8) St Fi. contains particular constructions which rarely occur in Meänkieli (e.g. temporal clauses and second infinitives), but which have to some extent been integrated into the Finnish dialects. These are without doubt comprehensible to all Finns, but hardly understood by the Swedish Tornedalians.

Despite these lexical and (a few) morpho-phonological differences, most linguists in Finland consider Meänkieli a variety of North Finnish, due to the fact that before 1809 there was no linguistic or cultural border between Swedish and Finnish Tornedalians.

The Swedish Tornedalians have, for more than a century, been subject to a Swedification policy which reduced all organised cross-border contacts and produced stigmatisation and alienation of Finnish and Finns. Some 50% of the Tornedalians argue that bilingualism is associated with that stigma and hence a Finnish identity is of low value. Only some 50 to 60% of the bilinguals claim to have a Finnish/Meänkieli or bilingual identity (Winsa, 1997). Most Swedes in southern Sweden categorise Swedish Tornedalians as immigrant Finns, although the in-group opinion marks a strong difference between Finns, Swedish Finns, and Tornedalians. In general, Finns, Swedish Finns and Finland are perceived as 'the other' by in-group members, whereas the Tornedalians are 'the other', the alien element, for the monolingual Swedes and most Swedish Finns (Winsa, 1997).

A cultural border was sensible when Swedish Tornedalians labelled the Finnish Tornedalians as Finland Finns (*suomen suomalaisia*). The language of the Finns was called Finland Finnish (*suomen suomea*), which in fact includes all Finnish varieties spoken in Finland, due to the fact that the Tornedalians are in functional terms illiterates in Finnish and cannot distinguish a variety from the standard form. Therefore, they perceive all varieties spoken in Finland as alien. The local language was called Finnish, or *meän kieli*, literally 'our language'.

Language shift began on a massive scale in the 1950s, and today people up to 30 to 35 years – where both parents are from Sweden – are predominantly Swedish in their informal and formal language use. Finnish is the language used among older people and immigrants and in interlingual-marriage families, though revival efforts have produced an awareness of bilingualism with the result that a small but increasing number of people have begun to speak Meänkieli/Finnish with their children. Interlingual marriages have had a major impact on the maintenance of bilingualism. In some villages up to 40% of all marriages have one spouse from Finland. There is a long tradition that the female should come from Finland, which has had a weaker economy. It has been suggested that this indicates that females tend to perceive marriage as a form of social positioning. Hence, higher socio-economic status predicts the structure in interlingual marriages (including linguistic status). Furthermore, Swedish Tornedalian females are over represented in interlingual marriages with mono-lingual Swedish males, despite the fact that hardly any socio-economic differ-ences can be discerned (Winsa, 1998; forthcoming b). Comparable gender differences in interlingual-marriages can be found in Canada and Finland, though a reverse situation is evident in Finland due to the dominant position of Swedish in traditional society. Figure 2 lists the number and birthplace of wife/husband in interlingual marriages in the bilingual region. Thus, the empir-ical evidence supports the assumption that linguistic status is a major factor determining direction in interlingual marriages.

Meänkieli is mostly spoken in the family domains and among closest friends, but rarely with strangers, or in public settings. In mixed marriages, the language of the woman most often predicts the home language of communication. A Swedish-speaking mother will usually lead to Swedish as the exclusive home language.

The idea of Meänkieli as a language is one part of the new self-categorisation of ethnic identity that distinguishes Swedish Tornedalians from Finnish Tornedalians. Language as a label of social identity is perceived as one of the most important instruments to improve the status of Meänkieli and indirectly Finnish. However, Tornedalians are divided into two groups over this hotly debated issue. Perhaps the majority considers Meänkieli to be a dialect, although contempt and emotional attitudes often direct the debate. Without doubt, most Finnish immigrants in Sweden and in the region perceive Tornedalen Finnish as a dialect. Many Tornedalians fear that Finns and the general public would ridi-cule an acknowledgement of Meänkieli and, therefore, any status planning and standardisation of Meänkieli would fail. There is, however, great ignorance of the distinctions between Meänkieli and Finland Finnish and the effects that

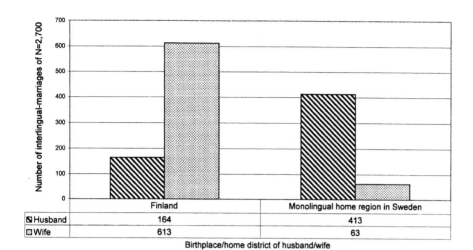

	Finland	Monolingual home region in Sweden
Husband	164	413
Wife	613	63

Birthplace/home district of husband/wife

Figure 2 Interlingual marriages in the Swedish Torne valley, 1946–1991

status planning has on attitudes (Winsa, 1998). It is, for example, not unusual to label all spoken forms in which frequent code switching and Swedish borrowing are common as Meänkieli, whereas all purified formal Meänkieli is called Finland Finnish, despite the fact that the formal language just has fewer 'unnecessary' loans. Another problem with the label 'language' is its political implications among the Swedish-Finnish organisations and other institutions.

The Church of Sweden takes a somewhat equivocal position with regard to Meänkieli, whereas Laestadianism, the religion specific to the Torne valley, opposes most attempts to support the local language, although this is beginning to change.

However, it is not possible to take a neutral position about 'language'. Each particular social position in the many other fields of social endeavour creates power and influence that predict language outcomes. (See discussion on language and dialect in Mühlhäusler, 1996.)

The development of written Meänkieli

Written Meänkieli has been slow to develop. During the 19th century, a tragi-comic oral poem from the 17th century was written down in Meänkieli. Between 1940–1960 two books appeared in Meänkieli. Rather than being attempts to develop a literary language, these books reflected oral traditions and had little significance for literacy development. In secondary schooling, only St Fi. was allowed as the normative language of literacy development. The Meänkieli movement began in the late 1970s, when the County Board of Education noticed that native Tornedalians with Finnish as a first language had lower marks in Finnish subjects than comparable Finnish immigrants, and that the pupils often complained that the subjects in school differed from their home language. The rather weak interest in mother tongue[7] instruction was interpreted to mean that St Fi. was too alien, instrumental and distanced from the familiar spoken variety, and that the teachers ought to begin with a write-as-you-speak pedagogy. The County Board of Education worked out simple text-books in Meänkieli and started to promote the vernacular in mother tongue instruction (henceforth MTI).[8] Meänkieli was perceived as a bridge between Swedish and St Fi.

The Swedish Tornedalians' Association (STA) was founded in 1981, and it adopted this new perspective on the vernacular and claimed that Meänkieli was a language in its own right. The lack of affinity shown to Finland or Finns is probably a legacy of the former language policy of the Swedish State and the nationalistic movement in Finland. The trilingual magazine of STA, *Met* 'We', points in the same direction.

For many years, migration from Finland to northern Sweden has been an everyday occurrence. Traditional Meänkieli is also spoken on the Finnish side of the border, though with a number of well-integrated St Fi. features, and it functions with different social dimensions. North Finnish varieties in general are perceived as having low prestige. St Fi. is the prestigious language among the immigrant Finns, and fairly often in interlingual-marriage families.

STA demands include such things as: bilingual education, more radio broadcasting, TV-programmes in Meänkieli, bilingual signs, support for bilingual culture, and minority status. Today, the STA, acting as an umbrella organisation, has some 5000 members (1500 direct members).

In 1987, Academia Tornedaliensis (Meän akateemi) was founded. Its original aim was to offer courses in Meänkieli, but it is currently working to have the new minority legislation adopted (see Part III).

In the 1990s, the decontextualised label, *Meänkieli* (literally 'Our Language'), began to be used for Tornedalen Finnish (*tornedalsfinska* in Swedish). While this is a label of self-identity, it is an older term used to differentiate Finland Finnish varieties from the local vernacular. The use of the term is somewhat disputed.

The promotion of Meänkieli has had a positive effect on cultural activities, such as amateur theatre, music, and literature. Since the early 1980s, some 35 books have been published in Meänkieli, local groups have produced some 200 different bilingual amateur theatre performances, and music is written in Meänkieli. Parts of the Bible have been translated, and all the gospels are scheduled to appear in Meänkieli by the year 2000. Today, there are some 10 to 15 active writers in Meänkieli, of whom half a dozen have published novels. The unifying principle in these artistic activities is the use of the local language, code switching and Swedish loans in the performance. This work has changed attitudes, and now as compared to the 1960s more people favour a Finnish/Meänkieli identity. Despite these influences on identity and cultural activity, some former activists argue that the STA has not achieved a dominant role in the cultural life of the Torne valley.

Without doubt, the majority of the population considers St Fi. to be the high-prestigious variety. Nevertheless, some 40% argue that Meänkieli should be defined as a language with its own institutional support, whereas some 40% claim that all instruction in school ought to be in St Fi. (Winsa, 1998).

With regard to schooling, some 20% oppose any form of voluntary or obligatory education in Finnish. Of those who advocate bilingualism, some 50% argue that Meänkieli should be the target language in MTI, whereas the rest favour St Fi. Less than 20% support mandatory Finnish (Winsa, 1998).

Clearly, those who are positive towards Meänkieli are also in practice more active in speaking Meänkieli with their children, which helps to institutionalise the language. Those disagreeing are divided between those who oppose all Finnish and those who truly favour St Fi. due to its higher instrumental and social value (although they do not necessarily actively promote it). Apart from the Meänkieli-activist Bengt Pohjanen, there is not one Tornedalian author who writes in St Fi.; no regular amateur theatre performances or local music occur in the standard form, simply because no one masters a context-bound St Fi. A context-reduced language is emotionally repelling for an audience, especially if the public is illiterate. Immediacy and emotions are best mirrored in a local vernacular (see discussion in D'souza, 1996). Based on the artistic progress in the region, one can argue that officialisation of the vernacular promotes creativity and artistic performance, produces cultural awareness and links the vernacular to a broad social dimension far beyond instrumental values. Consequently, there is hardly any bottom-up process favouring St Fi. for cultural activities except for the active support for the bilingual school in Haparanda, and other instrumental uses.

Standard Finnish (Finland Finnish)

In terms of number of speakers, Finnish is, after Hungarian, the largest language in the Finno-Ugric language family having some six million speakers. Standardisation of Finnish began on a large scale during the mid-19th century and therefore Finnish orthography still corresponds fairly well with its phonemes. Finnish differs distinctly from Swedish due to its fourteen cases and, hence, its synthetic structure. As a rough simplification, one can describe parts of Finnish grammar in the following way. One great challenge for a second language learner is the gradations, e.g. *t:d, sota:sodan* 'war:war's, *pp:p nappi:napin* 'button:button's, *tt:t, hattu:hatun* 'hat:hat's and *kk:k kukka:kukan* 'flower:flower's'. Furthermore, where Swedish uses a preposition, Finnish normally adds a case ending to the noun (except for the genitive case), e.g. Swedish *på bordet* 'on the table' is *pöydällä id*, where *pöytä* is the noun and *-llä* the adessive case.

The fourteen cases have singular and plural forms and may also have sub-forms. Possessive pronouns are marked in the word-ending: *hattu-ni* 'my hat', *kissa-si* 'your cat', *juusto-nsa* 'his cheese', *talo-mme* 'our house', *pöytä-nne* 'your table', *kirja-nsa* 'their book'. The most common cases are the following:

(1) Nominative: *auto* 'car', plural (pl.) *auto-t*.
(2) Partitive ('indefinite' number): *kala-a* 'fishes', pl. *kalo-ja*.
(3) Genitive: *puu-n* 'tree's', pl. *pu/i/-tten*.
(4) Accusative: *Kalle kirjottaa kirjee-n* 'Carl writes a letter', pl. *kirjee-t*.
(5) Inessive: *talo-ssa* 'in the house', pl. *talo/i/-ssa*.
(6) Elative: *talo-sta* 'from the house', pl. *talo/i/-sta*.
(7) Illative: *talo-on* 'to the house', pl. *talo/i/-hin*.
(8) Adessive: *pöydä-llä* 'at the table', pl. *pöyd/i/-llä*.
(9) Ablative: *pöydä-ltä* 'from the table', pl. *pöyd/i/-ltä*.
(10) Allative: *pöydä-lle* 'to the table', pl. *pöyd/i/-lle*.
(11) Essive: *(toimii) auto-na* '(functions) as a car', pl. *(toimivat) auto/i/-na*.

(12) Translative 'a quality in transformation': *tulee vanha-ksi* 'become old', pl. *tulevat vanho/i/-ksi.*
(13) Abessive: 'without': *raha-tta* 'without money', pl. *raho/i/-tta.*
(14) Instructive 'the way in which something is done': *kaksi-n käsi-n* 'with both hands'.

Some case endings have variations. Various forms of other less regular meanings cannot be covered with simple rules.

The verb has four tenses, four moods, and three infinitive forms, which are marked in a fashion similar to the cases, particular endings for person and participles. Therefore, verbs have a rather complicated structure of conjugations. In addition, the passive form is marked in the verb with a particular ending.

Apart from the status aspect to be found in borrowing, the great differences in structure and origin of Swedish and Finnish are probably reasons why majority loan words have a low acceptance in public domains. On the contrary, loan words from the majority language in the informal setting are frequent in all Swedish minority communities, but rarely vice versa.

St Fi. is favoured by the dominant group of Swedish Finns, and has, in terms of status in the Torne valley region, a strong position in the public debate, although it is not accepted as an official language of the region.

Sami

Sami probably belongs to the Finno-Ugric language family. There has been a long ongoing discussion on the relationship between Sami and Finno-Ugric languages, i.e. whether a substrate of Sami is independent of the Finno-Ugric languages, and whether the long-term contacts with Finnish may have transformed Sami to a surface relationship with Finno-Ugric languages. However, most Finnish linguists probably would still favour a common proto-language perspective, though the new perspective is being widely considered. It is thought that proto Sami developed around 1000 BC, and began to diverge into varieties after AD 800. One typical feature in Sami that deviates from Finnish is the dual case; i.e. 'two persons' is marked with a particular case. Otherwise, Sami has a structure similar to Finnish, although with fewer cases. However, it is not comprehensible to Finns. Every noun is inflected for case and number. North Sami has seven cases: nominative, genitive, accusative, illative, locative, komitative and essive. The verbs are declined for person, number, tense, and mood (Hyltenstam & Svonni, 1990). Sami has borrowed a great number of words from Finnish, but there has been much less borrowing in the other direction, according to Finnish etymologists.

Status and group size are predictive for the direction of loan words and for which group acquires bi- or trilingual competence. Sami have most often learned Finnish, Swedish and Norwegian, and borrowed words from these same sources, whereas Tornedalians have acquired Swedish as a second language, but rarely Sami (other than some competence in terms of a trading language), and have borrowed most terms from Swedish. Swedish-speaking monolingual Tornedalians have not borrowed from either language and hence, in general, have been reluctant to learn either minority language. Females, in particular, avoid acquiring Finnish or Sami, more often denying competence in the minority languages (up to the 1980s). Socioeconomic conditions and degree of institutionalisation of the languages predict their status.

In general, older people in family domains and among closest friends speak Sami. In mixed marriages, the language of the mother is the best predictor of the language of everyday communication. For example, if the mother is Finnish speaking, and the father Sami speaking, Finnish is likely to become the single home language. On the other hand, if the mother is Sami speaking and the father Finnish speaking, Sami is more often the everyday language. A small but perhaps increasing number of pupils acquire competence in Sami, especially in Karesuando where 94% of children enrolled in the Sami school use Sami as the everyday language compared with 70% in Kiruna, and 33% in Gällivare (Svonni, 1996).

Sami in official settings

The Swedish Sami Parliament was founded 1993. The main tasks of the parliament are:

- To foster a living Sami culture;
- To monitor the Sami language;
- To distribute state and EU funds for Sami culture;
- To appoint the boards of Sami schools;
- To advise the Swedish authorities on Sami affairs.

There are nine civil servant members of the parliament (in 1997) (www.sametinget.se). The Swedish State has adapted the Sami policies of the other Nordic countries. Norway founded its Sami parliament 1989 and Finland 1973. The three parliaments have a fairly tight network of organised contacts, and in 1994 the parliaments were granted observer status in the Nordic Council, as well as formal representation in various sub-committees of the Council of Barents Region.9 In 1996 a Sami Parliamentary Council, where all three parliaments are represented, was established (Eriksson, 1997: 107, 150).

All plenary sessions within the Sami parliament are translated into South Sami, Lule Sami, North Sami, and Swedish, though Swedish and North Sami dominate the proceedings. Those who have the competence use Sami. All three Sami languages must be interpreted by three, or more, interpreters.

A translator is employed to write up all minutes as well as some official documents of the plenary sessions in North Sami and Swedish. Given the problems with the technical and administrative terms, the task often demands that the translator develops new terms, or reformulate the Swedish version. To meet the demands made for new terminology, a Sami database is under development at the Department of Sami, Umeå University (A.K. Stenberg, 1998, personal correspondence). However, most written documents are in Swedish, the web site of the Sami parliament is in Swedish and English, and Swedish is the working language within the parliament whenever some members are not fluent in Sami (26% have no knowledge of Sami) (Labba, 1997). All sub-bodies of the Sami parliament use Swedish predominantly as their working language. The exceptions are the Sami Language Board (which holds all meetings in Sami (South, Lule and Ume) and Swedish, but without simultaneous interpretation services), a few pre-schools (which use Sami in meetings), and the Kiruna Sami School (which writes some documents in Sami). Finally, North Sami, along with Swedish, is one of the everyday working languages within the parliament.

Obstacles to maintaining official Sami are the lack of educated and authorised interpreters, the existence of three Sami varieties/languages, the small size of Sami linguistic communities and the lack of literacy in Sami among many of the representatives in the Sami parliament and its sub-bodies. One example of the problems that the Sami varieties cause is that the term for the Sami parliament has three official Sami names: *Sámediggi, Sámedigge* and *Saemiedigkie.*

The Sami argue that they are an indigenous people living in Sápmi. The Swedish Sami adopted a Sami flag in 1986, and their aim is probably to gain some loose kind of cultural autonomy within the Sápmi. The European Union has allocated substantial ear-marked funds to develop the Sami culture and enterprise.

State support to the three parliaments varies. The parliament in Norway provides some 6.9 million euro annually (of which some 2.3 million euro goes to administration; 1994).[10] The parliament in Finland provides approximately 384,000 Euro annually (all for internal administration; 1995) and applies extra funding for particular projects. The Sami parliament in Sweden provides about 1.7 million euro annually (of which 33% goes to administration, 35% to cultural projects, less than 10% to research and education and 20% to Sami handicraft 1995/1996) (SOU, 1997b, 184). The Sami parliaments are continuously developing their transborder polities (Eriksson, 1997), and therefore they collaborate increasingly on a number of issues.

The major language varieties

The varieties of Swedish

Sweden has a population of some 8.9 million. All native Swedes have Swedish as their first or second language. Swedish is also spoken in Finland by some 300,000 Finland Swedes. Sweden is more densely populated in the urban areas of southern Sweden, whereas settlement in the northern part of Sweden always has been sparse.

Until the 20th century, Swedish had a number of linguistic varieties, where the most distant linguistic communities lacked complete mutual comprehensibility. The Swedish varieties are often roughly divided into six groups, following geographic spread:

(1) South Swedish
(2) Götaland Swedish
(3) Svealand Swedish
(4) Northern Swedish
(5) East Swedish
(6) Gotland Swedish.

General schooling, mass media and the development of communication has homogenised the varieties. Today one can only find a few speakers of some major varieties among older generations of Swedes. The varieties spoken on the island of Gotland (south east of the mainland), the Överkalix variety (spoken in the south part of the linguistic border with Finnish), and the Älvdalen variety (spoken in the central west part of Sweden) are often considered to be the only remaining distinct varieties. Additionally, the variety spoken in the southern part of Sweden, Skåne, is not always mutually intelligible to Swedes living in the northern part of Sweden. However, these Swedish varieties have never been acknowledged as independent languages, basically due to the absence of organisations representing language communities. A common public perception, even within each particular linguistic community, has been that these Swedish varieties are subordinated dialects of standard Swedish

The Sami varieties

The Sami have populated northern parts of Sweden for many millennia. The first written information about their existence is from the first century AD. The original Sami reindeer herding required the use of waste pasturelands, with seasonal migration from winter to summer areas. Stable settlements were not possible under this nomadic life style, and thus the Sami culture remained dispersed and segmented throughout history. The long distances between the various Sami communities resulted in the different varieties/languages remaining extant into the 20th century.

Sami speakers may have a passive understanding of a neighbouring variety, but Sami language bilingualism is uncommon. Furthermore, because during summertime the pasturelands were in the mountains along the borders between Sweden, Finland and Norway, each particular Sami community developed a distinct geographical variety in an east–west direction crossing the border between Norway and Sweden. When the borders between Sweden/Finland and Denmark/Norway were drawn in 1751, a special agreement – the Lap Codicil (*Lappkodicillen*) – gave the Sami rights to maintain their traditional transborder nomadic lifestyle. This has resulted in three major Sami varieties/languages in the four countries: South Sami, Central Sami and East Sami. In Sweden it is common to distinguish five different Sami languages/varieties: South Sami, Ume Sami, Pite Sami, Lule Sami and North Sami (Norwegian Sami). However, in practice North Sami dominates in Sweden. One of the reasons for its dominance is that many Sami families were forcibly relocated, with their reindeer herds, from the northernmost areas to the more southern regions after 1889 when the Swedish Sami lost their traditional rights to use pasturelands in Finland. This transfer of Sami families continued into the early decades of the 20th century (See, e.g. www.sametinget.se). The North Sami speakers had a more solid Sami identity and language and began to dominate the smaller Sami language/variety communities.

Meänkieli varieties

The southern parts of the Torne valley had already been settled in the 12th century by Karelians and West Finns (Vahtola, 1980). They spoke at least two different varieties of Finnish (later termed Karelian, East, and West Finnish). In the 16th century, settlers from Savolax (i.e. Finns from eastern Finland) arrived in the Torne valley. Finns (from, e.g. Savolax and internal migration within the area) settled the municipalities of Pajala, Kiruna, and Gällivare in the 16th and 17th centuries. A strong in-migration of monolingual Swedes started during the late 19th century when mining began in the ore-fields of Kiruna and Gällivare.

During the centuries which followed, the language groups assimilated into one fairly homogeneous language, later termed Tornedalen Finnish/Meänkieli (formerly called Norrbotten Finnish and Finnish). Meänkieli is an amalgam of Karelian, East Finnish, West Finnish, North Finnish, Swedish, Sami and Norwegian. The variety has three sub-varieties: Gällivare Finnish (spoken/understood mainly in the Gällivare municipality by some 5–10,000 people), Vittangi Finnish (spoken/understood in parts of the Kiruna municipality by some 5–10,000) and the dominant Torne valley Finnish (spoken/understood along the border between Sweden and Finland by some 7–15,000). In addition, Finnish immigration has always been prevalent in the border region, and interlingual-marriages are frequent. Finland Finnish, therefore, has become a fourth variety, which is specifically spoken in those few official domains where Finnish is required. The three traditional varieties are mutually comprehensible, whereas Finland Finnish tends to be somewhat alien and hard to understand.

Up to 1809, Sweden and Finland were one nation. In 1809, Sweden lost the war against Russia, and a border was drawn between the two high cultures along the Torne river, which increasingly spoke two different languages, whereas, at the community level, language, culture, customs and traditions remained homogeneous until the latter part of the 19th century.[11] For a long time Swedish had been the language of society, but its position was strengthened after the loss of Finland, especially from the late 19th century onwards when Finnish was prohibited in Folk schools funded by the state (Slunga, 1965).

One result of these language policy developments has been contempt for the vernacular. Apart from the religious domain, where Finnish had a solid position, the vernacular was excluded from the public domain. Gällivare Finnish had the lowest status, followed by Vittangi Finnish and above them Torne valley Finnish, which was/is subordinated to Finland Finnish and Swedish. The number of Swedish and Sami loan words, group size, socioeconomic status, degree of institutionalisation, existence of a written form and closeness to the Finnish border are the main factors influencing language status. Thus, Gällivare Finnish has the highest percentage of Swedish and Sami lexical items, and the farmers in Gällivare were in general more poverty-stricken compared with other groups in the Torne valley region.

In the Torne valley region, there are two varieties of written Finnish: Meänkieli (including three sub-varieties) and St Fi.

Sweden Finnish varieties

Swedish Finns have centuries of tradition in Sweden, and being Nordic citizens have a special legal position in Swedish society. Their spoken varieties reflect their heterogeneous linguistic background in Finland. Hence, there is hardly any commonality in general spoken Finnish, apart from the increasing percentage of Swedish lexical loans. The dominant group of Swedish Finns, who support Finnish, favours St Fi. as their written form. However, there are some limited attempts to develop Swedish-Finnish, supported by an active teacher of Finnish and backed up by sociolinguistic research at the Department of Finnish, Stockholm University. Lack of resources and interest to develop a Swedish-Finnish standard variety hampers its further development.

Yiddish[12]

The first information about Jews in Sweden dates from the 17th century, e.g. a regulation in church law that required that all Jews in Sweden be baptised and converted to the Lutheran Church (Gluck *et al.*, 1997: 17ff). In 1815 fewer than 800 Jews lived in Sweden. In 1859 the Swedish school for Jews was established. In 1870 the Jews were given full constitutional civil rights. Today there are about 15 to 20,000 Jews in Sweden, mostly in urban areas, i.e. less than 0.2% of the total population. According to oral information, about 3 to 6000 have active / receptive competence in Yiddish, which, in general, has a weak position even within family domains, and is rapidly declining as it was the language of refugees who arrived in Sweden after the Second World War. In general, Jews are perceived to be highly educated.

Two Jewish schools exist in Stockholm. The Hillel school (*Hillelskolan*, grades 1–7), founded in the late 1950s, teaches Hebrew as a subject. Hebrew is, as well, a subject in the Religious school (grades 1–12, *Judiska församlingen*, brochure). In addition, in connection with the Hillel school there is a kindergarten for children from 1 to 6 years of age. The Hillel school and the Religious school stress Jewish culture, customs, history and traditions, but not the teaching of Yiddish. The Jewish parish (*Judiska församlingen*) has claimed to have some 5000 members in Stockholm; it has a Jewish library, a museum, radio, newspapers, etc. The number of members of Jewish associations and participants in activities of Jewish associations in Sweden were 10,378 in 1994/95 according to Boyd and Gadelii (1999).

A Jewish café exists to maintain Yiddish music, magazines, and newspapers. One course in Yiddish is available (spring 1999 in Stockholm). There has been no request to teach Yiddish as part of Mother Tongue Instruction (SOU, 1997b). Yiddish is claimed to be used in some orthodox ceremonies, in some musical performances and in lectures and presentations to older Jews, especially in the Malmö region (Boyd & Gadelii, 1999), though this statement is mostly based on interviews, rather than on observations of activities. It appears that Yiddish is rarely transferred to the younger generation. Yiddish is close to extinction, and very little is known of its present structure, or of how and where it is used. There is no modern literature on the Yiddish spoken in Sweden.

Romany

Romany Chib developed from the languages spoken in northern India and is split into a number of languages and varieties (about 60), which are not always mutually comprehensible (Fraurud & Hyltenstam, 1999). There is no unifying elaborated written language.

The first Roma arrived in Sweden in the 16th century. This ethnic group is very heterogenous, including Kelderasha, Kalé, Lovara, Sinti and travellers ('*tattare*') (SIV, 1996a). The entire group is often categorised by the authorities into three entities: Swedish, Finnish and non-Nordic Roma. Rough estimates of the number of travellers, who call themselves 'Romano', varies between 5 and 20,000, including assimilated people (Hazell, 1997). This group is considered distinct from the other Roma and has its roots in the 17th and 18th centuries. Kelderasha Roma consists of some 2500 individuals in total, all having Swedish citizenship, including some Roma families with other group solidarity, who have been in Sweden since the 19th century. Some 3000 Kalé Roma migrated from Finland in the 1960s.

Some 10,000 Roma have immigrated from non-nordic countries since the

1950s. This group is heterogeneous with, for example, Lovara, Sinti, and Xoraxane (Muslim Roma) identities. Most of them are, or have been, Czech, Polish, Romanian, Hungarian, or former Yugoslavian citizens, but many of them now have no citizenship.

With regard to their language, the International Romani Union uses the term *Romany Chib* which includes all Romany varieties and languages. In Sweden, there are some nine varieties of Romany Chib (SOU, 1997b: 141). Thus one of the many problems in communication is that the majority languages of their former home countries have left a major impact, especially on their lexicon. Each particular group has borrowed a great number of loan words from various majority languages. One study in Finland indicates that the Finnish Romany Chib has a limited morpheme stock, amounting to about 2200 words, and the percentage of Swedish loans is as much as 45% of the total vocabulary (Valtonen, 1979). However, variations in competence are great. One Swedish form of Romany Chib has earlier been termed 'Vagrant language' (*tattar-språket*); it uses mostly Swedish inflections, with a few hundred Romani words (Valtonen, 1979). Others claim that the Vagrant language is differentiated from Romany Chib and is termed, in Swedish, '*Rommani*' (Hazell, 1997). It is generally claimed that the intertwined varieties of Romany Chib are often based on Romany lexicon, whereas the grammar and phonology are borrowed from the majority language of the particular environment (Fraurud & Hyltenstam, 1999).

Romany Chib is an oral language acquired in the home environment. Internal closed mores and codes direct acquisition. A Roma is given continuous instruction in Romany Chib according to maturity and awareness of the social mores and codes within the particular community. The linguistic diversity, deviating customs, and resistance towards integration into the Swedish society create great challenges for formal education and instruction in the Romany languages (SIV, 1996a).

A new progressive policy towards the Roma may reinforce the maintenance of Romany Chib. The former language and society policy aimed to integrate and assimilate the Roma by abolishing all forms of social discrimination including particular forms of MTI, etc. This integration–assimilation policy meant that ethnic Roma were excluded from participation in the administrative structures of their own culture, i.e. there was no Roma society. The Roma were treated as a group of disorganised individuals, families, and clans constituting communities, but with hardly any official representation in society. In economic and social terms, this policy was a failure. The new progressive policy in some regions with relatively high percentages of Roma aims to integrate the Roma through organised segregation. Roma in the pilot projects are encouraged to take responsibility for their own education, culture and integration. Local authorities support their organisation, and transfer responsibility to their networks and weakly organised structures.

At the European level, the Roma receive some special funds from the EU for education in high school (grades 10 to 12) (henceforth *gymnasium*), teaching material and the like. The European Union supports a quarterly magazine, *Interface*, published by the Gypsy Research Center in Paris, which deals with the education of Roma. The Council of Europe has recommended that member states support Romany culture, e.g. in the form of music schools, translation agencies, studies in Romany Chib, establishment of cultural centres, etc. (CE, 1993: 1203).

The Finnish Roma constituted the first Romany Association in Sweden in 1971. One year later, the International Romani Union was established. The Roma in Sweden are to some extent organised into a Nordic Romany Council (founded in 1973), with 16 member associations, of which 12 are in Sweden. In total, 1200 Roma in Sweden are members of the Nordic Romani Council, though its economic base is rather weak. In general, their participation in public affairs is limited. The Swedish State has recently organised at least two Commissions to study problems of the Roma. One frequently mentioned cause for many of the policy failures, well intentioned as they were, is that the Roma have been seen as objects, instead of participating subjects in the attempts to improve their poor social and economic standard (SIV, 1996a).

The major religious languages

During the reformation in the 16th century, the Bible was translated into vernacular languages. Sweden, during one period in the 17th century, was a great power and had by the late 17th century six religious languages: Swedish, Finnish, German, Estonian, Latvian and Church Slavonic (Huovinen, 1986), and later on Sami. However, the Swedish Empire declined rapidly in the early 18th century and only Swedish, Sami and Finnish remained languages of religious ceremony.

Hebrew is the language of Judaism. Immigrants favour their religious languages in many ceremonies, especially Arabic.

However, there is one exception to the general rule that Swedish dominates all religious ceremonies. Finnish has a fairly strong position amongst the Swedish Finns and especially in the Laestadian movement in the northern part of Sweden.[13] Up to the 1960s, Finnish dominated all local prayer meetings in the five Finnish-speaking municipalities. One typical quality of the Laestadians is a strong resistance to any adaptation of their religious language to modern forms.

Swedish was introduced as a second (third) language in Laestadian meetings. Today, Swedish increasingly dominates religion for most Laestadians. All regional Laestadian prayer meetings are, however, interpreted into Finnish and Swedish. These languages have equal footing in larger prayer meetings, which gather believers from Norway, Finland, and Sweden, along with a few former North Scandinavian immigrants to the United States. The Laestadian movement is presently strongest in Finland, which has the effect of preserving Finnish in regional prayer meetings. In local prayer meetings, Finnish is rapidly losing its position and being replaced by Swedish. The religious community has at least one magazine written in St Fi. and Swedish. Swedish Laestadians and Tornedalians also arrange Laestadian prayer meetings in southern Sweden.

The Church of Sweden provides ceremonies in St Fi. in the Finnish-speaking region. The church used to require the local clergy to be bilingual, but this requirement has recently been relaxed. Currently, Swedish dominates religious ceremonies within the church (Winsa, 1998). Two of the gospels have been translated to Meänkieli, although they are hardly used in religious services; this despite the fact that Meänkieli in its oral mode is common in religious gatherings.

Finnish in religious ceremonies among the Swedish Finns

The oldest Finnish congregation was established 1533 in Stockholm. The so-called Forest Finns (*svedjefinnar*) who inhabited the northwestern parts of Värmland from 1570 onwards, for a long time had their own congregation and a clergy with competence in Finnish, but were completely assimilated in the 20th century. Attempts were made to support Finnish in the region during the 19th century, but these efforts gained little support from the state. Finns and Finnish began to be perceived merely as a problem in the 19th century.

Today's Swedish Finns who use Finnish as a religious language are either first or second generation immigrants. Besides the dominant Lutheran group – as well as some Swedish-Finnish Laestadians and a few nonconformists – there are some 6000 Orthodox Finns in Sweden with two churches linked to the Orthodox Church (Tarkiainen, 1996). The Bible used is the general Finnish Bible, but the complete Swedish hymnal will appear in a Finnish translation in 2000. The order of service book has recently been translated. Nevertheless, the Swedish church has for centuries provided services in Sami and Finnish; the new directive requests that the parishes in the near future describe their services for linguistic minorities (1999, oral communication, Bishop of Stockholm diocese).

Swedish Finns have maintained some religious periodicals. The monthly Finnish religious magazine is *Ankkuri* ('The Anchor'; circulation, *c.* 5000). The Finnish congregation in Stockholm has its own magazine, *Elävät kivet* ('Living Stones'), published five times per year. Both magazines are written in Finnish. Finnish ceremonies are given in 12 of 13 dioceses, which in 1991 employed 110 persons. However, besides the clergy working in the Finnish-speaking municipalities in northern Sweden, there are only ten clergymen with competence in Finnish serving more than 200,000 Swedish Finns (Tarkiainen, 1996).

Sami in religious services

The oldest written text in Sami is a small dictionary from the Kola Peninsula (1557). The first attempts to educate the Sami began in 1606, when 16 Sami boys were forced to go to Uppsala for training as priests. However, many of them fled during the journey and none of them appears ever to have completed his education (Wingstedt, 1998:37f). In 1619, the catechism and other religious literature were ordered to be translated into Sami, and the first school for Sami was established 1632, though it had little significance for secular education. The aim was to educate priests.

A number of primers appeared in the 18th and 19th centuries. The New Testament was published 1755 in South Sami, becoming the first normative version of the written Sami language. Other primers, simple school materials, and religious literature appeared early. In 1811, the complete Bible was made available in Sami (Forsgren, 1988). Thus, the Sami gained literacy in their mother tongue from the efforts of the Lutheran Church to convert the Sami from alleged paganism to Christianity. Using the vernacular was perceived as one of the most important instruments to effect this change. However, in practice Finnish dominated religious ceremonies, due to lack of competence in Sami among the clergy and also because the Sami were often bilinguals. Sami was used in some parishes with Sami inhabitants, but today it has little significance as a religious language.

However, language revival efforts are being made even in this domain. In 1996, international interest in indigenous people resulted in the Church of Sweden founding a Sami Council (*Sámi Girkoraddi-Same Girkkoráde-Saemien Gärhkoeraerie*), having nine members: The Sami parliament nominates five, and the church nominates four. According to the statutes of the Council, it is charged with promoting Sami culture and the particular lifestyle of these indigenous people. In particular, the Sami language is to be given greater recognition within the Church (Wikström, 1998). A new translation of the New Testament appeared in North Sami in 1998, and the Church of Norway will translate the Old Testament. The service book and hymnal are being translated into Lule Sami.

Languages of literacy

Literacy in Meänkieli

Up to 1888, the language of instruction in elementary school was Finnish. Since 1888 (in practice universally since about 1905), Swedish has been the only medium of instruction, and up to 1970 it was not possible to gain literacy in Finnish within the public primary schools. This means that between about 1900 and 1960, a high percentage of the Tornedalians had weak literacy in Finnish as well as in their second language, Swedish. Those who were involved in Laestadianism or in the Church of Sweden often achieved literacy, because religious services were often provided in Finnish. Others learned to read and write through private study. Nevertheless, one can assume that most Tornedalians had weak literacy in both languages up to the 1960s.

Probably more than 95% of Tornedalians (i.e. those who are born in Sweden) are functionally illiterate in Finnish and Meänkieli. Literacy in Swedish is, however, currently well developed. In the 1970s, the last generation of Tornedalians who were monolinguals in Finnish died. Since the 1980s, an increasing number of people write in Meänkieli. However, in actuality, there are perhaps only 20–30 people who have extensive and active literacy in Meänkieli, and less than ten Tornedalians who are literate in St Fi. Among the younger generations attending MTI and Finnish studies, literacy is better developed, though little practised.

Furthermore, immigrants make up 30 to 40% of the population in Haparanda, and 5 to 20% in the region. Many of them have weak literacy in Swedish or do not have a complete understanding of spoken Swedish, e.g. about 15% of all cases in the court of Haparanda district are interpreted into Finnish.

Literacy in Sami

The Church of Sweden planned literacy programmes for the Sami as early as the 17th century by producing bilingual (Swedish-Sami) religious texts. However, one of the main problems with the various Sami languages/varieties is that the orthographies have varied widely over the last few centuries. A number of spelling systems have been devised, often by well-meaning linguists whose aim has been to mark every deviation from spoken standard Swedish or Finnish with particular diacritical markers. Thus, the normative orthographies of Sami have been developed in relation to the majority languages (Swedish and Finnish), and not as independent systems. This approach has been a great obstacle for all literacy efforts in Sami. Two seminars (1743, 1744) failed to unite these various orthographies under one structure. By 1850, the various literacy campaigns had resulted in seven written Sami languages: South and Ume Sami, South Sami, Ume Sami, South Sami church language, Pite Sami, Lule Sami, and North Sami. In total, 115 publications, but only one book, were written in North Sami (Forsgren, 1988). Until the middle of 19th century instruction in Sami was frequent for religious purposes, but after that the nationalistic period began and Sami was excluded from the curriculum.

The Sami are now predominantly functionally illiterate in their mother tongue as well as in their second language/mother tongue, Meänkieli. For instance, it is claimed that there are less than half a dozen Sami with well-developed literacy in South Sam. However, Sami now have average literacy in Swedish.

North Sami is increasingly becoming the language of literacy. Because the Norwegian Sami constitute the largest group and have the best-developed educational system, North Sami dominates the infrastructure. Modern orthographies have been developed for North Sami, Lule Sami and South Sami. South Sami and Lule Sami are defined as local languages (Korhonen, 1997), though South and Lule Sami are traditionally the languages of literacy. Apart from the Sami Parliament, hardly any interpretation services are provided in Sami.

Literacy in Finnish

All first generation Finnish immigrants are literate in St Fi., but often have weak literacy in Swedish. Apart from those who are enrolled in the Finnish 'free' schools or home language classes, the second generation has, in general terms, better literacy in Swedish, although they often have Finnish as an oral home language. The third generation is, in general terms, monolingual, with some residual receptive knowledge of Finnish.

Literacy in Romany Chib

A high percentage of first and second generation Roma immigrants are functionally illiterate in Swedish and Romany Chib, as well as other mother tongues.

Numbers of minority language speakers

The numbers of minority language speakers in Sweden has been estimated as follows:

- Sami 5000–10,000;
- Tornedalians 25,000–70,000;
- Swedish Finns 200,000–250,000;
- Roma 5000–15,000 and
- Jews about 3000.

Figure 1 provides a map of Sweden listing the key locations and groups of minority language speakers.

The Finnish-speaking region

Swedish is spoken throughout the country, and dominates in almost every municipality. The only region that has a high percentage of Finnish speakers, especially among the older generations in the home environment, is the five originally Finnish-speaking municipalities: Gällivare, Haparanda, Övertorneå, Pajala, and Kiruna. All three border municipalities – Haparanda, Övertorneå, and Pajala – and the eastern parts of Kiruna have a high percentage of Finnish speakers. However, even in the Finnish-speaking region, Swedish is virtually the only language used for official purposes.

The status of Swedish and the social stratification of the majority members means that Swedish dominates in cities and central villages, especially amongst the well-educated class. Haparanda was earlier dominantly Swedish speaking, and bilingualism was often seen as a social handicap. Monolingual in-migrating Swedes rarely acquired full competence in Finnish, whereas Tornedalians rarely acquired competence in Sami. The Sami, however, were often tri- or sometimes even quatra-linguals: Sami, Finnish, Swedish, and Norwegian.

The Finnish-speaking municipalities have, in general, a weak socioeconomic position; the three border municipalities have particularly high unemployment, high out-migration (especially for females), and a higher percentage of illnesses and shorter life expectancy (males) than comparable interior municipalities in northern Sweden. Gällivare and Kiruna are in a more favourable position due to the mining industry. Economic diversification is limited in the whole region. The public sector is the main employer, involving some 50% of the work force. The computer industry is perhaps replacing farming and forestry as the main employer in Pajala.

A common assumption is that many minority regions are associated with a weak economy and low economic diversification. It can be argued that a major cause for the assumed poor socio-economic status of European territorial minorities until the 1970s was that they had little instruction in their first language resulting in weak school performance. It is, furthermore, well known that literacy in a monolingual's first language and second language competence among immigrants corresponds with better income, health, and employment (e.g. Saha, 1996; Mazumdar, 1996). However, second language competence in the host language of immigrants often corresponds with literacy in their first language. Hence, functional illiteracy in one's first language may have a general effect on socio-economic status (Winsa, forthcoming a).

Tornedalians

Table 1 lists the population and the percentage born in Finland in the five Finnish-speaking municipalities (1997; SK, 1994). Apart from Haparanda with 11.9 inhabitants per km^2, the Finnish-speaking region is sparsely populated. The other municipalities have between 1.1 and 2.6 inhabitants per km^2. Norrbotten is, in geographical terms, about twice the size of Denmark. The area has two major cities: Gällivare and Kiruna. The development of the mining industry in the 19th century caused high in-migration and thus a high percentage of Swedish-speaking people. Since the post-war period, out-migration from the region has been prevalent, whereas in-migration has only had a significant impact on major cities. In particular, females tend to migrate and, hence, the countryside of Sweden has a general imbalance of the sexes. The Tornedalians, and the people living in the ore-fields of Kiruna and Gällivare, constitute about 27% of the population in Norrbotten. Of them, approximately 20 to 35,000 speak Meänkieli/Finnish in everyday life, especially people over 30–35. (No reliable statistics are available; the numbers include Finnish immigrants living in the region.)

Table 1 Selected population figures and numbers of individuals born in Finland

Municipalities	Population	Born in Finland (%)
Haparanda	10,613	35.5
Övertorneå	5,959	19.4
Pajala	7,847	10.9
Gällivare	21,366	4.4
Kiruna	25,271	8.1
Total	71,059	6.8
Jokkmokk	6,305	4.2
Arjeplog	3,517	4.3
County Norrbotten	264,320	4.0

Moreover, many Finnish-speaking Tornedalians and Swedish Finns live in Luleå and other major cities of Norrbotten; perhaps 35–50,000 in Norrbotten speak and/or understand Meänkieli/Finnish. According to statistics (1996) 4.0% of the population in Norrbotten was born in Finland, and it is estimated that some 20% have knowledge of Finnish. In addition, several thousand have moved to southern Sweden, predominantly to urban areas, especially to the capital region and the south-western coastal city of Göteborg. The highest estimate of the total number of Finnish-speaking Tornedalians is between 70–80,000, or less than 1% of the total population having active or receptive competence in Meänkieli.

Sami

The total number of Sami in the North Calotte region is about 60,000: about 40,000 in Norway, about 4000 in Finland and some 2000 in Russia. The number of Sami in Sweden has been estimated by Svonni (1996) to be between 15 and 20,000, with those living in the municipalities estimated at:

- Kiruna (2500);
- Gällivare (1800);
- Jokkmokk (900) and
- Arvidsjaur (700).

Some 1500 Sami, including all family members, have reindeer herding as their occupation (Korhonen, 1997). It is in this setting that Sami language is at its strongest.

As reindeer herding demands movement across extensive areas, the geographic distribution of the Sami is essentially rural. Less than 10,000 speak Sami as an everyday language, or have some form of receptive competence in Sami, although estimates vary. The Sami constitute less than 10% of the inhabitants in the municipalities of Kiruna, Gällivare and Jokkmokk (about 55,000 inhabitants in total). The South Sami are in the weakest position with only a handful of speakers; Lule Sami is spoken by a few hundred, whereas North Sami is in the strongest position with perhaps more than 5000 speakers (Svonni, 1996).

Because of unemployment and out-migration, some 1200 Sami live in the capital region. Norrbotten county has some 6000 Sami out of a total of about 265,000 inhabitants (less than 2.5%), whereas neighbouring Västerbotten county has some 2200 Sami out of a total of 255,000 people (less than 1%). There is no municipality in Sweden where the Sami are in the majority (Korhonen, 1997). In northern Norway, two small municipalities are dominated by Sami (Karasjok and Kautokeino), as is the northernmost municipality in Finland (Utsjoki). Sami is the official language, along with Norwegian, in six of the northernmost municipalities of Norway, as well as in a few municipalities of northern Finland.

Their ongoing language shift follows the status of the vernaculars/languages in the region. Earlier, Finnish had a higher status than Sami, and hence many Sami first acquired Finnish, and only later Swedish. Perhaps more Sami speak Meänkieli than Sami? The Sami are one of the most multilingual groups in Sweden.

Swedish Finns

Migration from Finland to Sweden has been prevalent during the past several centuries, especially to the capital region. The existence of small and dispersed Finnish communities have, however, always ended with complete assimilation. After the Second World War, immigration from Finland began to meet labour needs, and was at its height during the 1960s and 1970s, with a peak in 1969–70 when 80 to 85,000 Finns arrived (Reinans, 1996). The number of Swedish Finns with active/receptive competence in Finnish is estimated at between 200 and 250,000 speakers, including second and third generations of people with Finnish ancestry (Reinans, 1996). Thus, they represent less than 3% of the total population. They live predominantly in urban areas all over Sweden, but especially in the capital region and Göteborg. They speak dominantly Finnish in the first generation and Swedish in the second generation while Finnish is weak in the third generation. In 1990, the counties with the highest number of Finns born in Finland were:

- County Stockholm 76,734;
- County Göteborg and Bohus 15,594;
- County Västmanland 15,309;
- County Älvsborg 12,581.

Roma

Today, approximately 20,000 Roma live in Sweden, predominantly in the urban areas in southern Sweden. Thus, less than 0.3% of the total population are Roma. There are no precise statistics because ethnicity is not an acceptable question in Swedish statistical collection. Approximately 12,000 Roma speak/understand/have some competence in Romany Chib varieties.

Part II: Language Spread

Languages in the educational system

Apart from Swedish for immigrants, English is the most important second language in the Swedish educational system. In the 1990s, 31% of all pupils had already begun to study English as a foreign language in the first grade and were reading it a few hours per week throughout primary school (Skolverket, 1996b: 17). English, French and German are the dominant languages of the European Union, and the latter two languages are increasingly attracting pupils in primary schools. Increasing numbers of pupils choose the linguistic option from among four options in the curriculum by the sixth grade. Pupils studying this option can study a B-language[14] (a home language, Swedish as a second language, Swedish, English, or Sign Language). Up to 80% of the eighth grade who have selected the language option study a B-language (Skolverket, 1997).

In 1997, a number of primary schools and *gymnasiums* used English as a medium of instruction. English-medium schools will probably increase in importance, especially for those in higher studies in professions that have frequent contacts with European Union institutions. In addition, the ERASMUS programme of the European Union, which promotes the exchange of students between universities, already has influenced instruction, i.e. English is the language of instruction in all courses enrolling foreign students. This programme is likely to increase in significance. Swedish may, in the future, become the local and semi-official language for the educational system, and English the official, context-reduced, international language (Thelander, 1996). Within universities, English is increasingly the language of instruction, especially in the natural sciences where reference books are predominantly in English.

In 1998/99, 3% (30,600) of all primary school pupils were enrolled in 331 'free' schools (www.artisan.se/skolverket/jmftal/), i.e. private schools in which funding of between 70 to 80% is provided by the municipality. Some 15 'free' schools have an Arabic–Muslim profile, and an additional 27 have applied for Muslim 'free' school status (Skolverket, 1997). The Sweden Finnish 'free' schools are the only 'free' schools that have programmes based on balanced bilingualism guidelines. Arabic is rarely a medium of instruction nor is it the target language in the Muslim 'free' schools.

In 1991, there were 313 home language classes (i.e. consisting of one fairly homogeneous group speaking one foreign language), of which 209 (67%) had Finnish as the medium of instruction. The other MTI languages include Arabic, Assyrian, Greek, Yugoslavian languages, Spanish and Turkish. Swedish is used as the medium of instruction in home language classes in about 10 to 20% of classes in grade one, and about 50% in the final grade, six. Slightly more than 10% of all entitled students were enrolled in home language classes in the mid 1980s. It is estimated that the participation rate has now declined to 5%. Since 1992, no statistics for those classes have been available, but it appears that the number of home language classes is rapidly declining.

There are no national statistics on the number of composed classes, i.e. classes with students who speak at least one foreign language together with pupils who speak Swedish as a mother tongue. Estimates based on statistics from particular years indicate that less than 5% of all pupils entitled to enrol in MTI are enrolled in composed classes (survey in Hyltenstam & Tuomela, 1996). Swedish is introduced successively into composed classes and dominates by grades five or six.

In 1995/96, the number of pupils eligible for MTI was 110,000 (12.7%) in primary school and 19,530 in *gymnasium*, speaking 143 different languages. In primary school about 60,000 participated in MTI while 7160 participated in MTI

Table 2 Summary information for the six largest mother-tongue instruction groups

Language	Number of pupils in MTI	Per cent of pupils eligible in MTI	Swedish L2
1. Arabic	7,980	66.6	8,365
2. Finnish	7,767	46.4	6,004
3. Yugoslavian l.	6,307	50.2	9,155
4. Spanish	5,703	61.4	4,819
5. Persian	5,694	69.8	4,441
6. Turkish	2,779	58.3	3,546
Other languages	24,500	61.0	21,800

in *gymnasium*. In general the participation rate in MTI is declining from a peak of 68% (1986) to 55% in primary school and 37% in *gymnasium* 1995/96 (Beijer, 1996). A list of the six largest languages, the number of pupils enrolled in MTI and the percentage of the eligible pupils enrolled is given in Table 2.

Of the ten largest immigrant languages in Sweden, interest in attending MTI is the weakest among Swedish Finns. About 46%, or 7767 Swedish Finn pupils, with Finnish as a home language, attended MTI in 1995 (the number includes Tornedalians and Meänkieli). The numbers had declined to 6960 in 1997. Arabic is the largest home language in terms of number of participating pupils, with 7980 pupils. The groups speaking Arabic are far smaller than the Finnish-speaking group, but they compensate for this with a higher rate of interest in acquiring Arabic (nearly 67%, which is the highest participation rate of all immigrant groups in Sweden; Beijer, 1996).[15] Hence, the religious function of Arabic is a strong element in language preservation, together with the birthplace of the parent. The minor home languages number 133 (Beijer, 1996). Sixty per cent of all MTI is chosen as a subject outside the normal school schedule (Skolverket, 1996b:19).

In 1995/96, 61,600 immigrants were enrolled in Swedish L2 programmes. Bosnian/Croatian/Serbian, Arabic, and Finnish constitute the largest first language groups in Swedish second language programmes. The average percentage enrolled in the Swedish second language programme ranges between 30 and 82.3% (Skolverket, 1996b).

Sami schools

The Sami have had five different forms of schooling during the early 20th century: Lapp Folk schools (*Lappfolkskola*), a Catechism school (*Kateketskola*), winter courses, General Folk schools and Separate schools (*Missionärskola*) (Johansson & Johansson, 1968).

With the establishment of Lapp schools in 1732, education took a more structured form. Sami was explicitly made the medium of instruction in a decree in 1723. In 1895, an itinerant schooling system for the Sami was set up which delivered ten weeks of education per year. The itinerant programme was provided during wintertime. This was the beginning of the Nomad school reform (Nomadskolereformen) of 1913. The reform was based on the idea that 'Lapp should be Lapp'; that is, reindeer herders must be segregated from modern society, because they were perceived as not able to adapt to the modern life style and must 'not have too much of civilisation' (see www.sametinget.se). Living in Lapp cotts was one part of the proposal to preserve Sami culture and lifestyle. Although Sami was probably used as an auxiliary language during the first years of schooling, Swedish was explicitly mentioned in the decrees from 1898 to 1925 as the language of instruction. A study, which reported on the success of this education, indicated that, after a short period, a Sami pupil did not use a word of Sami or Finnish (Henrysson & Flodin, 1992), though this may be an exaggeration.

The majority of Sami did not practise reindeer herding and were integrated into the general educational system, where Sami was never a medium of instruction nor a target language. In 1942/43, some 630 pupils were enrolled in the itinerant schools (Svonni, 1996). During the post-war period, the itinerant schools ceased operation and were replaced by permanent schools and boarding houses for the pupils. In the 1950s, the stationary schools began to accept Sami as a subject, although not for more than one or two hours per week. This pattern persisted until the home language reform was implemented in the late 1970s, and the amount of Sami instruction increased to 6 to 8 hours per week in a few schools. The primary school reform of the 1960s also included the Sami pupils, and the selective segregation policy came to an end in 1971 (Eriksson, 1997: 89).

In 1981, the Sami were given responsibility for their own educational system. A Sami School Board was established, drawing representatives from five Sami organisations (Hyltenstam & Svonni, 1990). In 1996, there were Sami schools (grades 1–6) in six communities: Karesuando, Lannavaara, Kiruna, Gällivare, Jokkmokk and Tärnaby. The school plans adapted the general National Curriculum, but included a particular Sami profile. In 1998/99, 171 pupils in total were enrolled in these schools (www.artisan.se/skolverket/jmftal). Hence, only a minority of Sami pupils is enrolled in the Sami school system. The medium of instruction must be Swedish and Sami, according to the Sami school regulation. Instruction in Sami was first introduced in Karesuando, the northern-most parish in Sweden, in the late 1970s. In 1991/92, the Karesuando school provided Sami-medium instruction in several subjects for 14 hours a week; in addition, Sami was taught six to seven hours a week as a subject. The Sami school in Kiruna offered nine hours a week of Sami medium instruction, and five hours a week of Sami as a subject. The other schools almost exclusively used Swedish as the medium of instruction, and had three to four hours a week of Sami as a subject. In addition, in 1994 there were nine schools in the Sami area with a Sami profile in language, community orientation, and handicraft. These schools enrolled about 160 Sami pupils.[16] However, Sami medium of instruction does not exist in the integrated type of schools.

In 1994/95, a bilingual project was launched in the Sami schools in Karesuando, Kiruna and Gällivare, aiming to develop a high level of bilingualism among all Sami pupils, as well as independent social background and language competence for every pupil (Svonni, 1996). The increased attention to instruction in Sami has resulted in the development of two pre-schools using Sami in Kiruna and Jokkmokk. Furthermore, each school uses the local variety of Sami, and as the varieties differ greatly, a Sami pupil from a more distant community must speak Swedish in order to be understood when visiting a pupil from another area (EUROMOSAIC, 1999).[17]

Participation in MTI has slowly increased from some 170 to 304 pupils enrolled in 1997 (SCB, 1997). The average participation rate in the municipalities concerned was 65% in 1997. However, the number of all the Sami pupils in primary school has been estimated to be 2500 (cf. Svonni, 1996). That number includes all Sami pupils in Sweden, whereas those who are entitled to MTI, according to the regulations, are pupils living in the Sami region – although all Sami pupils have the right to MTI irrespective of their place of residence. Sami MTI in *gymnasium* attracts fewer students, with only about 25 pupils of the 75 entitled attending, although the number is slowly increasing as well.

In addition, there are a number of institutions in Sweden and the northern-most region promoting education and research in Sami:

(1) Jokkmokk has one *gymnasium* with a Sami profile enrolling some twenty students (EUROMOSAIC, 1999). The Sami Folk High School (*Samij Almmukallaskåvllå*, or Adult College), established 1942, provides courses in Sami handicraft, ecology, reindeer herding, Sami language and culture. The state support for this school was 0.59 million euro in 1997 (SOU, 1997b: 168).

(2) The Sami High School (*Sámi Allaskuvla*, founded 1989) is located in Guovdageaidnu/Kautokeinio, Norway. It focuses on Sami teacher training and research. It is a state-operated college, fully funded by the Norwegian Ministry of Education and, according to its directives, it serves the entire Sami population in the Nordic countries.

(3) The Nordic Sami Institute (*Sámi Instituhtta*) was established in 1973 also in Guovdageaidnu/Kautokeino. It is a research and cultural institute, funded by the Council of Nordic Ministers having three sections: a section devoted to language and culture, a section on education and information and a section on livelihood, environment, and law. Both institutions in Guovdageaidnu strive to attract, involve, and employ Sami students and researchers. The language of instruction is Sami.

(4) Umeå University has been allocated special funds for a Sami department (founded 1975) for research and studies in Sami language and culture.

(5) Uppsala University has a department for Fenno-Ugric languages, where research and study in Sami is supported.

(6) Teacher training is provided at Luleå Technical University that has, as part of its profile, the responsibility to train teachers to work with Sami, Meänkieli, and Finnish pupils (SOU, 1997b: 155). However, there is only limited interest in the programme (EUROMOSAIC, 1999). Thus, one common problem is the lack of Sami-qualified teachers, as most have limited education in Sami.

Instruction in Meänkieli/Finnish in the Torne valley

Until 1888, most instruction was in Finnish, but since then (other than some auxiliary instruction in Finnish) Finnish has not been used in the educational system. After the Second World War, Finnish was included in the curriculum as a voluntary extra subject in *gymnasium*, formally from 1944 but in practice from 1955 (Wande, 1984b).

From 1957, all libraries were allowed to keep books in Finnish, and the pupils were allowed to speak Finnish during breaks in school. In practice, the local prohibition against speaking Finnish on the playground existed in some villages until 1967 (Hansegård, 1968). However, by 1961/62, economic support by the state for purchasing Finnish literature for libraries had been abolished (Tenerz, 1966: 73); in practice this meant that libraries had the option to buy Finnish books, but had no funding to do so. However, in the late 1980s a special North Calotte Library was established, which aimed to cover, e.g. Finnish literature in the region.

In 1962, Finnish could be studied in grades 7–8 as an optional subject. However, if this option was chosen, one was excluded from entrance to *gymnasium*. From 1970 onwards, Finnish could be studied at all levels in primary school, and Finnish as a subject attracted some 300 pupils. When the home language reform was adopted (1976), St Fi. could be studied in primary school and *gymnasium*, according to need, though in practice it turned out to be one or two hours a week. In the late 1970s, the first attempts to promote Meänkieli were undertaken by the County Board of Education, when it was revealed that pupils experienced alienation in St Fi. and Tornedalians with Finnish as a home language scored lower in tests than Finnish immigrant pupils. The slightly declining participation rates were interpreted to be consequences of these factors. The promotion of Meänkieli was based on pedagogic motives, but it turned out to be an ethnic movement favouring Meänkieli as a language in its own right.

Meänkieli medium of instruction is used in a few pre-schools and kindergartens in the Torne valley, especially in Kangos. The pedagogic idea for this is based on the principle that a context-bound language is best developed among children, and therefore a pre-school teacher should speak only one language and act as a role model for children. According to the idea, a child associates Finnish with a particular person, s/he responds only in that language to that person and acquires fluent bilingualism with equal input. However, there is probably no pre-school where Meänkieli is the only medium of instruction; the Swedish language dominates in most cases. The most common situation involves instruction solely in Swedish. Perhaps only in a few pre-schools in Haparanda is Finnish the medium of instruction. There are no data on how Meänkieli/Finnish is utilised by the pre-school teachers in the minority region.

Since the early 1990s, Meänkieli has been a mandatory subject in one 'free' school in the region (Kangos), but only for a few hours a week in grades 1 through 9. Only 62 pupils are enrolled. The first bilingual school (grades 1 through 9) was established in Haparanda in 1988; half the class comes from Finland and the other half is selected from monolingual pupils from Haparanda.[18] However, quite a few of the 'monolingual' pupils are children of immigrant Finns, and hence are already competent in Finnish. Only a few of the Haparanda pupils are true monolinguals; interest in the language school is greater on the Finnish side of the border (Waltari, 1998, personal communication). Hence, it is not an immersion school. This is, nevertheless, the first bilingual school in the region where the pupils acquire fairly fluent bilingual competence. Finnish and Swedish are the languages of instruction, although Swedish has higher status and dominates on the playground and during breaks, whereas Finnish is seemingly favoured among the staff. The Language school, however, in general terms, displays a hostile attitude towards Meänkieli (Lundh *et al.*, 1997). In 1998, the *'Eurogymnasium'* started in Haparanda-Tornio with pupils from Finland and

Sweden. The languages of instruction are Swedish, Finnish, and English (Lundh *et al.*, 1997).

Meänkieli is a defined subject in MTI, but it is not distinguished from St Fi. in the educational statistics. There are 1025 pupils, or 12% of all pupils (25% of those eligible) in primary school in the Finnish-speaking region, enrolled in MTI for one or two hours a week (1996/97). Females are slightly over-represented in MTI (516/458 in 1997). However, Finnish/Meänkieli is almost exclusively a target language for non-immigrant pupils. The medium of instruction is Swedish.

In 1991, the responsibility for primary school education was transferred from the former County Board of Education to the local authorities. During the same period, Sweden faced a general recession, and budget cuts in the public sector became common. One effect of this localisation of educational responsibility was that the expenditure for MTI was severely reduced (see Table 3).

Table 3 Percentage of all pupils in primary school in the Finnish-speaking region enrolled in 'mother tongue instruction'

Year	Gällivare	Kiruna	Pajala	Övertorneå	Haparanda
1992	13.7	22.2	38.1	15.7	26.3
1997	3.3	8.3	48.1	4.8	1 8.3*

* Inclusive of the language school

The statistics from Haparanda include the pupils in the Language school (Waltari, 1998, personal communication). Pajala municipality has the highest interest in stressing the local language, Meänkieli. The general conclusion is that the region has faced a massive decrease in the number of pupils enrolled in MTI. One way for the authorities to reduce interest in MTI is to put the MTI subject in competition with English and other foreign languages, and/or not to inform pupils and parents of the possibilities of MTI. The general lack of competent teachers in Finnish, and especially in Meänkieli, may also have negative effects on interest in MTI. It is otherwise difficult to explain the massive decline in MTI. There must be factors involved other than those specified. The obvious conclusion is that municipalities which support the local language have positive development programmes and much higher participation rates in MTI compared with municipalities with a high percentage of Finnish immigrants, or with resistance towards the local language. Haparanda should have the highest participation rate in MTI (about 40% Finnish immigrants), but is actually experiencing a decline in interest.

The interest in Finnish in *gymnasium* is clearly weaker; only 128 students (5.2%) were enrolled in 1993/94, and numbers seem to be declining even here. Due to the different way those who are entitled to MTI are assessed, the percentage enrolled in MTI in the Torne valley is lower than it is among Swedish Finns. In practice, as a consequence of the special regulations for Sami, Tornedalians and Roma, all Tornedalian pupils can request MTI. However, only the Pajala municipality claims that all pupils have a right to MTI. The four other bilingual municipalities maintain that only 37 to 57% of their pupils in primary schools are eligible for MTI (www.skolverket.se).

One major problem with MTI in the Torne valley lies in the variation in linguistic competencies. A class may contain pupils with hardly any knowledge of Finnish grouped with pupils who are fairly fluent speakers. Another problem lies in the attitudes towards Meänkieli and St Fi. Some parents (especially among Finnish immigrants), home language teachers and pupils are hostile towards Meänkieli, whereas many Tornedalians feel alienated from St Fi. In the 1980s, one solution was to keep the pupils in separate groups and try to group students according to linguistic competence. However, this is often not economically feasible. Another approach that has been used involves speaking Meänkieli, but writing St Fi.

In 1995–96, the first university courses in Meänkieli were offered in the Department of Finnish at Stockholm University. However, as the varying levels of competence of the students in Meänkieli/Finnish affects the ability to use Meänkieli, nearly all instruction was delivered in Swedish. (Some 10 to 15 students have passed the course.) In addition, the Universities of Stockholm and Luleå provide a few courses in Torne valley culture and language, and Luleå Technical University is obliged to offer teacher training for Meänkieli teachers (though it attracts few students). However, there is only one postdoctoral fellow and two professors (in Finnish and Pedagogy) with a dedicated interest in Meänkieli issues.

Education in Finnish

There are a number of pre-schools / kindergartens in major urban areas where Finnish is one of the languages of instruction.

About 6960 pupils (1997), including Tornedalians, in primary school were enrolled in Finnish MTI, usually for one to two hours a week. The home language pupils in Norrbotten constitute approximately 20% of this total group. Of these 6960 pupils, some 725 were enrolled in seven or eight bilingual Sweden Finnish 'free' schools (grades 1 to 9) in 1997. The language of instruction there is dominantly Finnish during the first grades (SCB 1997).

Four Folk High Schools have Finnish in their curricula as an option, though few students request these courses. The Folk High School in Haparanda (founded 1973) has no instruction in Finnish, despite the fact that it is, according to its guidelines, a bilingual institution.

Teacher training is provided at Luleå Technical University. Training for Finnish as a subject for home language teachers is provided at Uppsala and Stockholm Universities (EUROMOSAIC, 1999).

St Fi. is the medium of instruction in the Department of Finnish or Finno-Ugric languages at Luleå Technical University, Umeå, Uppsala, Stockholm and Lund Universities whenever possible, and for particular forms of instruction. In 1999, Stockholm University had some 200 students enrolled in Finnish studies. In addition, the Swedish officers' training programme provides courses in Finnish for bilingual and monolingual cadets. However, even within the Finnish departments, there has been a significant decline in the use of Finnish as an instructional language, because students are increasingly drawn from second or third generation Swedish Finnish backgrounds and have only limited competence in Finnish.

Only a few Tornedalians are enrolled in the postgraduate programmes of the Finnish departments.

The types of instruction in Finnish can be categorised into three groups:

(1) Finnish courses for beginners;
(2) Mother tongue instruction;
(3) Finnish for teachers (EUROMOSAIC, 1999).

In addition, Stockholm and Uppsala Universities provide courses in Swedish-Finnish and Finnish culture, and literature.

Education of Roma and instruction in Romany Chib

One of the main challenges in the education of the Roma lies in their lack of a tradition of formal education. The Kelderasha Roma achieved rights to formal education in the 1960s (SIV, 1996a). A survey from the late 1980s, revealed that only 4.4% of pupils attended MTI in the Stockholm region (Rapport, 1990). Recent statistics indicate that 190 (22%) of the officially registered 856 Roma pupils in all of Sweden participate in MTI (SCB, 1997). Training of home language teachers in Romany Chib has been arranged in Stockholm and Malmö and, since the 1980s, there have been a few home language teachers with this competence.

The objectives of language education

After the Protestant Reformation, the use of the 'vernacular' Bible began to spread, laying the foundation for the differentiation between a high status standard and low status dialects. The Lutheran Church initiated the process, not as a deliberate attempt to abolish dialects / vernaculars, but to spread the word of God to the illiterate and ignorant people. The Bible in the community language spread literacy as well as religious enlightenment, and hence metacultural awareness associated with and perceived through religious discourse and the native language. The well-developed literacy stimulated the growth of education, administrative bureaucracy, urbanisation and commerce. Hence, Martin Luther sparked modernisation through the development of literacy following the introduction of 'vernacular' Bibles.

Latin was the language of elite society, whereas the vernacular Bible unified the people. A normative Swedish evolved subsequent to the vernacular Bible. In the school curriculum of 1649, it was ordered that pupils should write and speak 'beautiful and pure' Swedish, in accordance with the standard norms for writing and pronunciation (Johansson, 1983: 38).[19] The standardisation of the 'vernacular' raised awareness of literacy as a mean for the creation of a single linguistic norm, which could unify the peoples and the various communities. By the end of the 17th century, the Lutheran Church in Sweden had launched a literacy campaign which, within a few generations, turned Sweden (and seemingly Finland) into one of the most literate nations in the world. Reading competence in religious discourse was first developed, because from 1686 a Church Law decreed that no illiterate was allowed to take Holy Communion, and a person who was not confirmed was not allowed to marry. In the countryside this literacy campaign was implemented almost completely without the aid of a proper school system. The responsibility for teaching children to read was ultimately placed on parents and godfathers. Thus the Church Law put enormous social pressure on communities (Johansson, 1998: 90f), which probably explains why Sweden was more literate than most European nations at that time.

The secondary effect of such literacy was the social stratification of vernaculars and an emerging diglossia. This change was reinforced during the Geatish period when deliberate attempts to raise the status of the standard form was an attribute of the first nationalistic period of Sweden. The promotion of an H standard[20] form was one of the achievements of a great power, and the development of an H standard occurred as status planning through the purification of a 'true' and particular Swedish language. After the establishment of the Swedish Academy, and its initiation of long-term deliberate status planning and elaboration of the standard, the H status form achieved its final position.

However, although the elite of society integrated this new social discourse into their language practice, the H standard was still relatively unknown among the less literate public. With the establishment of public schools, language planning efforts acquired a national instrument, far more efficient than the literacy programmes of the Lutheran Church. The official objective of language planning, in relation to the majority language varieties, has, in practice, been directed towards the establishment and reinforcement of a status relationship between the H standard and local varieties. As a result of this stratification of language practice, the dialects were designated as low status and as languages associated with identity, a process which initiated a movement to eradicate all dialects. Dialects had already been successively excluded from official society in the 16th century, but, after the public school reform, a general awareness of the stigma associated with dialects was spread nationwide. As the official policy was to train all pupils to be fluent in standard Swedish, the Swedish dialect varieties were, and continue to be, neglected, devalued and marginalised.

With respect to Sami, the state aimed to preserve the culture and perhaps even the language. In practice, little was done to spread literacy in Sami or to give it any sort of official status. Since the late 19th century, the Sami and the Tornedalians were forced into a process of language shift through a complete exclusion of the regional languages from all public institutions (except religion, where the state partly failed in its attempts). Nevertheless, in political and official policy terms, the state claimed that the policy was directed towards the establishment of bilingualism in the region (Slunga, 1965). This claim was, however, basically just rhetorical, and also a reflection of the existing conflict between Finland and Sweden, and later between academic research and political opinion.

Since the 1970s, the state has reconfirmed its official language policy that national language planning promotes active bilingualism for immigrants as well as minorities. The methods applied to achieve this 'new' objective include MTI (one or two hours per week); politically correct phrases inscribed in the constitution; Swedish L2 programmes; some subsidies for cultural activities, books, newspapers and magazines in the immigrant and minority languages, as well some radio and TV broadcasting in the native minority languages. Under these policies Sweden-Finnish organisations have achieved rather good support for the media.

Only the Finnish 'free' schools, some Sami schools and the Language school and *Eurogymnasium* in Haparanda have an active bilingual programme as one of their objectives, e.g. to foster internationalism, peace and friendship, tolerance, and cultural awareness, to develop border contacts and to foster ethnic identity. The programme's guidelines are liberal.

In the ethnic-religious 'free' schools, maintenance of bilingualism is of less importance, aside from the Muslim 'free' schools, which stress literacy in Arabic (Skolverket, 1997). (The language of the Koran is said to be complete in form and content.) The guidelines, instead, stress particular ethnic-religious identities, e.g. in the Jewish Hillel school, the Muslim schools, and the Catholic and noncon-formist schools. As a consequence, many evaluations of the 'free' schools, of MTI and of home language classes have often considered not only bilingual compe-tence and school success in general, but also more abstract and non-empirical concepts such as ethnic identity, self-esteem and ethnic tolerance.

Methods of assessment and results of MTI

Sweden has a long tradition of assessing language competence. In order to measure the results of the first literacy campaign, in 1686, a church law mandated that the parishes keep examination registers of reading and religious knowledge. The Scandinavian registers are as close as one is likely to come to a systematic assessment of reading ability over an historical time frame (Houston, 1988: 129, 199).

The agency responsible for the evaluation and assessment of Swedish L2 and MTI is the National Agency for Education (*Skolverket*). Up to the 1990s, there were few reports that summarised the research conducted, although a large number of projects had been carried out (i.e. survey in Paulston, 1983). From a general perspective, four areas of interest have been investigated:

(1) To what extent have the objectives of home language reform been imple-mented?
(2) How is MTI organised and conducted in the classroom?
(3) What factors influence immigrant pupils to choose MTI?
(4) How do pupils' linguistic, cognitive and emotional aspects correlate with received instruction? (Hyltenstam & Tuomela, 1996: 60)

Mother tongue, or to use an earlier term 'home language', as a subject, is taught through a set curriculum in primary school, and guidelines for compari-sons to be used by the teachers in marking are worked out. The methods used to collect data related to questions 1 through 3 above include: questionnaires, inter-views, observations, and statistical data. These questions have basically been answered through descriptive studies: models of organisation, group size, instructional hours in the home language in various grades, teacher qualifica-tions, teaching materials, etc. With respect to the fourth question, quantitative data dominate the research, although interviews and questionnaires are also used. Local teachers, research departments, the National Agency for Education, and the Board of Immigration (on Swedish L2) have essentially carried out these evaluation projects. Other methods employed include the measurement of linguistic skills through interviews with pupils, parents and teachers, as well as through the use of self-assessment. School performance has been measured by school grades. A number of other methods are used in studies of various aspects of MTI, Swedish L2 acquisition, etc.

In the late 1970s and early 1980s, L2 literacy programmes directed at immigrants and minorities attracted the attention of researchers and the media. The media interest sparked some research as well as an extensive and emotionally laden public debate that took two different directions:

- one recommended the use of composite classes, because MTI could affect L2 acquisition negatively, while
- the other favoured home language classes.

Tornedalians were used as the negative examples of L2 instruction. Both sides of the debate relied on research reports but, in the media, the discussion was popularised and was often perceived dichotomously as either in favour or against MTI (Hyltenstam & Tuomela, 1996). However, despite intensive debates on MTI, and a number of school strikes initiated by Swedish Finnish parents and sparked off by the lack of sufficient instruction in the mother tongue, a study conducted by a political scientist in the late 1980s concluded that the MTI reform was never fully implemented (Municio, 1987).

According to one study, there is frequent variation in the content in MTI. Some teachers stress realia instruction, whereas others focus attention on aspects of the home language as a subject. In an evaluation of the way in which teachers organise MTI, the most prevalent topics were ranked in the following order:

(1) Grammar
(2) Oral training;
(3) Vocabulary development:
(4) Reading literature;
(5) Realia;
(6) Writing;
(7) Text analysis;
(8) Reading aloud and pronunciation;
(9) Translation;
(10) Awareness of Swedish culture.

It became evident that the relationship between curriculum guidance and the practice of MTI was not strong (Hyltenstam & Tuomela, 1996: 67). Since the early 1990s, MTI has increasingly been provided outside of the normal school schedule. Parents seemingly favour this, whereas teachers as well as pupils seem to be much less satisfied with this change.

As the bulk of the 'free' schools were established after the early 1990s, few evaluations of them exist. Currently, there are 'free' schools using Finnish, English, German, French, Estonian, and Hebrew as instructional languages (Beijer, 1996). However, in the Muslim 'free' schools, Swedish is the only language of instruction in most subjects, and Arabic is studied both as a subject and in Koranic studies. One evaluation of Muslim religious schools concludes that 'free' schools may promote integration, but the focus on education and instruction is somewhat underdeveloped. The Muslim 'free' schools often place less stress on fundamentalist religious studies than does the Jewish Hillel school and some of the Swedish nonconformist schools. Evaluations of bilingual 'free' schools indicate 'very good' and 'impressive' results (Skolverket, 1997).

One study of the teachers' pedagogic methods revealed how MTI is carried out in actual practice. The study included three types of classes: home language classes, composite classes, and classes where a Finnish group formed a working sub unit within a Swedish class. In the independent classes one of the following models was applied:

(1) Monolingual instruction by class; each lesson is monolingual, either in Finnish or in Swedish and each language was frequently spoken only in particular subjects and with particular teachers.
(2) Language switching; one teacher uses both languages interchangeably.
(3) Language separation by person; instruction is dominantly in Swedish, and team teacher gives auxiliary instruction in Finnish.

The most common model, applied in nearly half of the 21 lessons observed, was that of monolingual instruction by class given by one Finnish and one Swedish teacher. This language switching may create an imbalance in status relation between the two teachers. Language separation was the model least used. A clear finding of this study was that actual instruction is often based on random intuitive awareness of strategies and lacks a well-defined set of guidelines for instruction.

A study of teaching material in Greek MTI revealed that the texts often stress nationalistic, moral and family values and admiration for the Greek culture. The teachers are often mouthpieces for the culture of the homeland. The teaching material, the didactic tradition of the teacher, and the way the family perceives how home language should be taught often guide instruction. A somewhat comparable study concludes that results in MTI are influenced by:

- Sociocultural factors;
- Organisation of the schedule;
- Individual motivation based on identification with and attitudes towards the mother tongue and the Swedish culture and language; and
- Level of education.

A survey of research within the field of MTI concludes that home language reform is, in its present form, a political tool where the existence of the reform is more important than its implementation. In spite of the fact that the regulation clearly states that MTI should be given according to need, in practice it has consisted of one or two hours a week, providing more symbolic value than would a programme aimed at developing balanced bilingualism (Hyltenstam & Tuomela, 1996). There are a number of practical problems, which the state and the responsible municipalities concerned have avoided, e.g.

- the limited time of instruction;
- the unclear models of instruction;
- inappropriate teaching material;
- a lack of local educational planning;
- low status due to lack of competent teachers;
- classes placed outside the normal school schedule;
- the mobile character of home language teachers; and
- the negative impact of the media.

The education of home language teachers has been held to a minimum, and funds for MTI have suffered extensive cuts (Beijer, 1996); the number of home language teachers has declined from a high of 4700 in 1989 to 2200 in 1994, and of these only 374 have certification for MTI (Hyltenstam & Tuomela, 1996). Some of the positive outcomes of MTI are:

- reinforced identity;
- a bridge to integration;
- often better school marks in Swedish, English and a better average grade than those who have discontinued MTI; and
- better marks in mathematics and some other subjects (Hyltenstam & Tuomela, 1996; Kostoulas-Makrakis, 1995).

These evaluations have, however, been carried out predominantly among immigrants and Swedish Finns. Little recent research has been carried out in the northernmost minority region; this hiatus will be discussed in the following section.

Sami
    In the former Nomadic schools, pupils were in continuous contact with other Sami-speaking pupils; hence Sami was acquired and developed in an informal setting. Those Sami pupils who were enrolled in general folk schools frequently lost their home language due to the stigmatisation of the minority language and the lack of natural everyday contacts with Sami-speaking pupils and adults.
    Today, competence in Sami varies among pupils, and teachers have problems in meeting this challenge. By the end of the 1980s, it was evident that pupils without any competence in Sami at the beginning of school had only achieved receptive competence after six years of Sami instruction. It has been concluded that the present form of MTI is not sufficient for those Sami who have Swedish as the dominant home language.
    It is suggested that instruction in parts of one subject ought to be taught solely in Sami (or in other home languages), thereby involving, in principle, the whole school, or even the whole municipality. Using this method, Sami pupils would not loose the subject MTI replaces in schools, and the acquisition of Sami would be interwoven with other knowledge. This approach would simplify teacher training, as well as the organisation of MTI, and it would transmit context-bound Sami knowledge (Svonni, 1993; 1996). However, this strategy has not been possible to implement due to the often indifferent attitudes among the Sami and resistance among the majority population in Sami regions.

Tornedalians
    The most assessed group until the late 1970s was the Tornedalians. In the 1960s, a study concluded that bilingual Tornedalians achieved lower scores than average monolingual Swedes in mathematics, Swedish, reading, writing and English (Björkquist & Henrysson, 1963). Even after comparisons with comparable social groups, they scored significantly lower in, for example, mathematics (Henrysson & Ljung, 1967). Bilingual Tornedalians, in general, scored lower than monolingual Tornedalians. The political reaction to this finding resulted in reinforced instruction in Swedish as the target language and as the medium of instruction, despite the fact that research reports indicated that lack of literacy in Finnish was probably the cause of the negative results (Winsa, 1998).

In an evaluation of IQ test performance by 18-year-old Swedish boys who were being inducted for military service, it was found that, between 1987 and 1988, Norrbotten had the third lowest scores of all counties in Sweden. Tornedalians, in general, scored lower than the average rural population, and also lower than populations in monolingual neighbouring municipalities such as Överkalix and Kalix (Idberger, 1989). This well-known generally weak school performance among bilingual pupils in the 1960s, and earlier, may have been due to a lack of metalinguistic awareness in the context-bound mother tongue. The lack of well-developed pragmatic qualities in the most literate language may also have influenced their analytical skills (Winsa, 1998). It may be suggested that successful bilinguals within the educational system have well-developed literacy skills in both languages.

In 1985, pupils in grade 3 in Pajala and Kiruna municipalities were tested in mathematics and Swedish. In both subjects the pupils' average scores were below the national average (Hansegård, 1990). When instruction included emphasis on the local environment, the school marks improved, significantly exceeding the average for the municipality (Hansegård, 1990: 48).

Contrary to the results found in the general education of bilingual pupils, the language school in Haparanda showed positive results. The pupils in the language school achieved better marks than the national average for Finland and Sweden. However, in their L2 tests, they received lower marks than the average pupils did in their L1 in the neighbouring country, and the Finnish pupils tend to be better in Swedish than their counterparts were in Finnish (Skolverket, 1996a; Lundh *et al.*, 1997). Swedish has higher status and is the dominant language on the playground and during breaks. This imbalance in status is claimed to be one reason why the Swedish pupils in general have a diminished interest in Finnish. A sociological evaluation concluded that if the school does not meet the intent of the guideline, it will result in the Swedish pupils not acquiring sufficient competence and gaining only weak literacy in Finnish (Lundh *et al.*, 1997: 27).

There has been no evaluation of the Tornedalians who are enrolled in MTI, nor have the Tornedalians' achievements been compared with those of other groups. However, one or two periods per week of instruction are unlikely to make any difference in the objective measures of language proficiency. MTI in the Torne valley region functions more as a transmitter of ethnic identity than as a developer of bilingualism.

Finnish in Sweden

Between 1986 and 1989 Swedish Finnish teachers in 14 municipalities were involved in the PUFF-project (Pedagogic development of Finnish) using various approaches to develop efficient pedagogical methods for bilingual pupils, and providing opportunities to discuss problems in Finnish instruction (Johansson, 1989).[21] There has, however, been little evaluation of the long-term effects of the PUFF-project, although particular schools involved have carried out various forms of evaluation (e.g. Sjölund, 1995; Janulf, 1997).

A few studies indicate negative results from MTI. However, the main research projects carried out by university departments in Finland and Sweden, as well as by the National Agency for Education, indicate that pupils enrolled in MTI, home language classes or in 'free' schools achieve comparable average marks in most subjects, better in some and weaker in others. Especially positive results have been derived from the existing Finnish 'free' schools (Skolverket, 1997; Janulf, 1997).

One survey of MTI concludes that attitudes in the environment and among the majority towards immigrant and minority languages are decisive for the outcome of MTI. The status of Finnish is low in Sweden; hence, a few studies indicate that self-esteem corresponds positively with Swedish identity and negatively with Finnish identity. One interpretation of these results maintains that Swedish-Finnish pupils in Swedish classes are anxious to avoid association with Finnish and to try to respond to an ideal image of Swedishness, whereas the Swedish-Finnish pupils in MTI had a more realistic self-image (Virta, 1994). Another interpretation is, of course, that MTI effects self-esteem and identity negatively as long as the home language possesses low status in society. These conclusions on the abstract association between language and social identity are predominantly based on small-scale qualitative research, rather than on more broadly-based statistical evidence (e.g. Liebkind, 1989). A low status language influences collective identity as well as self-esteem, but 'free' schools may reinforce minority identity.

Roma

Since the early 1990s, little statistical information on the school situation of the Roma has been provided. The dropout rate in primary school is high, especially among girls. Only 1% of Roma pupils in Stockholm have had a complete primary education. Since the 1970s, no Roma pupils in Uppsala have achieved complete primary education (Ds, 1997: 49, 33). Very few Roma adults have completed *gymnasium* (SIV, 1996b). The illiteracy rate is high, especially in the mother tongue, if not in Swedish. During the period between 1976 and 1985, Roma adults were given opportunities to enrol in special school programmes. However, there are no longer any earmarked funds for the education of Roma, due to the cuts in the public sector budget. Cultural and educational support varies among different municipalities, and that has had an effect on participation in primary schools. One municipality, Lund, has achieved good results in education after the establishment (in 1990) of a leisure centre for Roma between the ages of 7 and 12. Today, it is a rule rather than an exception that Roma in Lund complete their primary education (Ds, 1997: 49, 52). Another municipality has employed a Roma as a consultant working with the Roma. Teachers in Romany Chib experience low status, and the school plans of local authorities are short-range. If MTI is requested, many authorities reject the request on the grounds of lack of competent teachers. Another problem is that many Roma families do not accept the competence of the home language teacher if s/he does not speak the variety of Romany Chib spoken within the family, or if s/he is not perceived as trustworthy (SIV, 1996b: 14). Romany Chib is often perceived as a language of secrecy. The desire to preserve the secrecy of the home language, during the 1970s in Finland, prevented an edited basal reader in Romany Chib from being published (Valtonen, 1979). However, basic teaching material now exists in Finland as well as in Sweden.

In addition, the general lack of teaching material in Romany Chib and in the Roma culture is the result of the low interest in the language and insufficient teacher competence. One reason – among many others – for this situation is that the Roma themselves seem opposed to adapting a common written orthography.[22]

Evaluations of Swedish L2 programmes

The results of the Swedish second language literacy programmes for adult immigrants seem to be discouraging. In 1997, 22,252 participated in L2 programmes. Only 37% of those who took the examination passed it during the school year, or the subsequent year (1995). Thirty-five per cent leave the course, and high absenteeism is the general rule (SIV, 1996b). These statistics have been criticised for being based on rather weak empirical methods, leaving possibilities for misinterpretations to occur. Nevertheless, some possible reasons for this appalling result lie in organisational problems, the low status of L2 instruction, and hence the lack of competent teachers. Accordingly, the problems are similar to those found in MTI. Swedish L2 training for immigrants has slowly changed direction so that communicative competence is now stressed in research and in policy (Lindberg, 1996b). In 1997 the expenditure for the Swedish L2 programme was about 1200 euro per participating pupil.

The historical development of Swedish language policy

For centuries language planning in Sweden has had a political foundation the aim of which was to gain political control of various language groups. This colonialisation policy was especially evident during the 17th century when Sweden became a great power and a multilingual nation. During this period Sweden controlled Finland, the Baltic states, coastal parts of western Russia, parts of northern Germany, some former provinces of Denmark (Skåne, Blekinge, Halland, Bohuslän), and some Danish-Norwegian provinces (Jämtland and Härjedalen). The province Skåne had been, since the early Middle Ages, a wealthy Danish province. By the late 17th century, the Swedish empire included 14 community languages plus a great number of varieties: Swedish, Finnish, German, Sami, Danish, Norwegian, Karelian, Votian, Estonian, Livian, Latvian, Russian, Yiddish and Roma languages. In addition, French, Latin, and Izjorian – among other languages – were used in liturgy, in official institutions, and in diplomacy. At least seven languages had sanctioned status as written languages: Swedish, Finnish, German, Estonian, Latvian, French and Latin (Huovinen, 1986).

The political and military plans to maintain control of this multilingual empire were important issues for the nobility and the King of Sweden. During the Geatish period, the existence of diverse linguistic identities probably had a major impact on the strong interest in a standardised and noble Swedish. Sweden had already been a multilingual nation for centuries. The Swedish kings seemed to have acquired an awareness of the fact that an exclusion of the local vernaculars from official domains and public institutions constituted one of the most efficient non-violent instruments to subjugate the various language communities.

Sweden implemented this socio-political diglossia at least in Finland, in the Torne valley, in Finnish-speaking parts of Värmland and in other Finnish communities in Sweden, as well as in the Danish-speaking Skåne region. In border regions, where mutually intelligible varieties are spoken on both sides of the border, the Swedish strategy seems to have been to settle the Swedish border region with language groups speaking entirely different languages; it also supported a general exclusion of the community vernacular language from the high culture. Borders were established between two high cultures speaking two different languages. This top-down process slowly developed a linguistic and cultural border that, through language practice, developed attitudes and feelings of ethnic identity. When the community had integrated the ideologies, a true national border developed.

Literacy campaigns as a spark for economic development

After the Reformation, it was in the interest of the Lutheran Church to improve literacy. The main interest of the clergy was to convert Catholics to the Lutheran faith. Schooling and 'instruction' in the local vernacular were instruments in this process. Literacy, developed through religious scripts, formed the core, or the context-bound competence, of the new religious ideas, and therefore the Lutheran Church provided the impetus towards mass literacy in Sweden and demolished the Catholic libraries. Having all Europeans read the same Bible in various 'vernaculars' was an attempt to establish an earthly Kingdom of God in Europe.

Pupils had to memorise the catechism, the Ten Commandments, and the Creed. Rote learning was in the interest of the church in order to develop a unifying and collective imagination. However, schools in the rural areas were rare; often the homes of the parents functioned as schoolhouses with teaching by an itinerant cleric. In 1814, 92% of the people in the diocese of Lund in southern Sweden had access to schools, whereas there were hardly any schools in the thinly populated northern diocese of Härnösand (Barton, 1977: 536). In practice, the northernmost provinces only got regular schooling decades later, after the folk school system was implemented.

Through church literacy campaigns and the use of the vernacular Bible, Lutherans achieved a higher proportion of literacy than Catholics (Houston, 1988), although even some Catholic regions were influenced by the Reformation (Cipolla, 1969). The secondary effect of vernacular literacy was that Protestants (at least in Germany during the 19th century) were over-represented in modern language studies, technical and economic subjects, whereas Catholics were in general under-represented in most subjects, except in preparation for theology and studies in classical subjects. This, in turn, resulted in a dominance of Protestants in business and management (Weber, 1958: 35–45). Hence, increased literacy often corresponded with economic progress. It is claimed that those parts of Europe which had low levels of commercialisation and urbanisation were generally less literate (Houston, 1988: 99). Thus, according to the sociologist, Max Weber, Protestants showed better economic performance as a group than Catholics. On the other hand, if literacy is discourse-bound and linked to ideologies (Street, 1995), then the restricted and religious discourse of literacy developed in Catholicism also standardised negative reasoning in economic matters, as well as in other discourses. Weber argued that particular forms of religion reinforce economic progress. The individual calling he found in Protestantism, but especially in the stronger commitment and calling fostered by the Calvinist movement, created, as a byproduct, greater economic progress (Weber,

1958). However, Weber never perceived the influence of a new, broader and more popular literate discourse as one of the reinforcing qualities of the 'new' calling.[23]

Literacy corresponds with urbanisation and commerce, and with some exceptions (e.g. Sweden and perhaps lower Scotland) with economic progress (Cipolla, 1969; Gee, 1996:32f). However, literacy is by no means an absolute predictor of development; it must be supported and managed by a number of other factors. Social and economic progress may be prevented by a variety of social circumstances, e.g. war, political ignorance, forms of religion, or natural catastrophes. The Swedish literacy campaign was initiated at the height of Sweden's status as a Great Power and was sparked off by the church law that made literacy a prerequisite to marriage within the Lutheran church. It resulted in an expansion of the universities where new disciplines were established (e.g. economics); Swedish became the language of the elite and increasingly the language of imaginative literature, poetry and music (Tengström, 1973:54).

The literacy campaign also had a significant effect on education. In the 1740s, the number of students increased to 1000 at Uppsala University, book production developed enormously and about 150,000 publications were produced during the 18th century compared to 4600 publications during the previous century. However, interest in education declined after the 1740s, and the number of students fell to about 300 at Uppsala at the turn of the 18th century (Gunnarsson & Skolander, 1991:27). Correspondingly, interest in economics fell, and the number of economic journals rapidly declined from the 1760s onward (Gunnarsson, 1997). Sweden's period of greatness ended in Poltava, in 1712, when Sweden lost its entire army in a battle against Russia. A subsequent economic recession hampered the results that might have been expected from widespread and well-developed literacy. During the 18th century, Sweden could not defend its borders and lost several wars until the borders were finally fixed 1809. If Swedish foreign policy had been less aggressive, Sweden might have been in the forefront of industrial development.

Swedish high culture policy

Sweden took control of the western parts of Finland during the 12th century, and some centuries later of the remaining major Finnish-speaking areas. The developing administrative apparatus in Finland soon established high and low cultures, i.e. the distinction between Latin and Swedish as spoken and written by the clergy and the authorities and Finnish as the vernacular of the farmers. During the 16th century, Finnish gained a fairly strong position within the Lutheran Church, but in other public fields rarely was accepted by learned society. Language planning in Finland is therefore based on the typical relation between a dominating upper class society speaking a foreign language and the dominated lower class society excluded from the high culture.

The central western part of Sweden along the border with Norway was hardly populated, and Sweden has a long history of wars with Denmark, which from the 14th century until 1814 maintained control over Norway. The many wars between Denmark-Norway and Sweden created desolation in border areas (Tarkiainen, 1990: 142ff). Forest Finns (i.e. Finns from eastern Finland) were encouraged to settle these border regions through the use of tax incentives. The densest Finnish communities grew up in the border regions of the provinces Värmland and Dalarna (Tarkiainen, 1990: 172). This settlement pattern in the border region distinguished the 'Swedes' from the Norwegians by language. Without this strategy, Sweden would probably have had difficulty in establishing a recognisable border because Norwegians and Swedes in these border regions spoke mutually comprehensible languages, and the populations shared the same religion, and had generally similar cultures. These factors favoured social cross-border interaction that could hamper the nationalisation processes. Furthermore, if the newcomers were not allowed to set up any form of administrative structures in Finnish, the Swedish central government would have complete control of the group and the border regions. If the Finns had been allowed to develop a Finnish-speaking civil society, it would have been perceived as a threat, and their loyalty to the Swedish crown could have been questioned. Consequently, as early as 1647, a decree required the Forest Finns to learn Swedish, and in 1692 King Carl XI published a new decree requiring that Forest Finns return to Finland if they did not learn Swedish.

In eastern Finland, a number of wars between Sweden-Finland and Russia had emptied the eastern border regions. A report from the Board of Immigration (SIV, 1996a: 17) argues that these abandoned areas were to some extent, resettled by Roma in the late 17th century. According to the report,[24] Swedish officials forcibly relocated Roma families to the border regions of Finland-Russia (Karelia). This relocation was based on a 1636 law that promoted deportation of the Roma and even permitted genocide (Arnstberg, 1989).

A comparable concept of language planning was implemented in other border regions. In the former Danish-Norwegian provinces, Jämtland and Härjedalen, many of the inhabitants identified themselves with Norwegians, and therefore the Swedish authorities Swedified the high culture; the Church played a significant role in this process. Loyal Swedes replaced the Danish-Norwegian clergy during the early 17th century (Bromé, 1945).

In Halland, Swedification efforts began after 1645 when Denmark lost the province after several wars. The official policy, maintained in the beginning, was to support Danish language, customs, and law, but the underlying motives turned out to be directed towards complete assimilation. The Church also played an active role in this process. Education in Danish schools hampered social mobility, especially if the pupil aimed to become a cleric. Nearly all new appointments within the public administration were given to Swedes, and clerics in particular were recruited from a Swedish educational background. However, the cautious methods of language planning did not achieve the anticipated results, and a more radical form of Swedification took place when bishops were requested to replace the Danish primer, catechism and hymn book with Swedish ones. Accordingly, religious services had to be performed in the Swedish language and according to Swedish customs. The underlying intent was disguised through promises that Danish language, culture, customs and law would remain. In practice, they were gradually excluded. Finally, the economic base of the Danish nobility was diminished through the confiscation of their possessions. With a powerless nobility, Swedish language could penetrate the official domains, and the people of Halland were transformed to good Swedes by the year 1700 (Montell, 1978: 127ff, 138).

The southernmost province of Sweden, Skåne, was the object of the most extreme Swedification. After the incorporation of the region under the Swedish crown as a result of the Peace of Lund in 1679, a harsh and violent Swedification began. Swedish replaced Danish in all official domains. All civil officers in the administrative apparatus were recruited from Sweden, and not from the 'Skåne nation', as the province was labelled by Swedish authorities. Lund University – located in Skåne – proved to be an excellent instrument in this effort, although even here the official policy was more cautious and seemed to favour traditional Skåne values. The re-established Lund University had an entirely new staff recruited from Sweden, or from northern Germany (Fehrman & Westling, 1995: 36ff). The Church, as an institution with authority, with a dense network in all provinces, and with direct contact with nearly the entire population, was perceived as the most efficient instrument in socio-political language planning. All laws, customs, books, liturgies, etc., were required to be in Swedish. Contacts with Denmark were prohibited. The majority of the Skåne could hardly read Swedish, but were forced to listen to Swedish religious ceremonies and to acquire Swedish language and manners. An ethnic cleansing took place, leading to migration to Denmark. Resistance to this language plan caused extremely violent reactions; many villages were completely burned down, and hundreds of local farmers were executed (Lindqvist, 1995: 177ff).

The use of Danish shrunk to only the most intimate family domains, where it acquired the status of a vernacular. Through functional literacy acquired in the religious setting, Swedish penetrated the home domains, and Danish was slowly intermingled with Swedish. The language variety currently spoken in Skåne is perceived to be a Swedish dialect, despite the fact that it has similarities with East Danish dialects. It is possible that the massive Swedification efforts created a pidgin resulting from insufficient knowledge of Swedish, the only official language. In subsequent generations, the mixture of Swedish and Danish was transformed into a Creole, i.e. into contemporary Skanish. A similar process took place in Norway, where Danish was mixed with the local vernaculars. One form of the contemporary written standard for Norwegian (*bokmål*) is considered to be a Creole (Haugen, 1987).

Language planning in the Swedish Torne valley

Language planning in the northernmost region began much later, compared with other Swedish regions, simply because it was a peripheral bilingual Sami- and Finnish-speaking region. The Torne River municipalities belonged to the Härnösand diocese and the administrative structure was fully integrated into the Swedish system, where Swedish was the language of the administrative authorities. Since the 17th century, the only elementary education that was available was in Torneå. It is not known what languages were used for instruction, but presumably they were Swedish, Finnish and some Latin.

After 1809, the Swedish Tornedalians constituted a linguistic minority controlled by Swedish-speaking authorities. A new administrative structure was set up, and all the municipalities along the river were divided. The area was remote and thinly populated, and the Swedish authorities had little interest in the region, being fully occupied with the devastating consequences of the Sweden-Russia war of 1808–9. However, the Swedification efforts had already begun when the new regional city, Haparanda, was founded 1845. From the very beginning, the city council recruited solely Swedish-speakers (according to family names; Hederyd, 1992), and all street signs were written in Swedish. In sum, the minority language was generally excluded from all official domains. A border was created between the two high cultures, increasingly speaking two different languages, whereas the low cultures remained homogeneous for a long time. The cultural border developed slowly as the normative structures of the society penetrated the community.

In 1833, a 'lower apologist school' (*lägre apologistskola*) was founded, aimed at providing practical skills in the commercial professions. Finnish seems to have been the language of instruction. In the 1860s, when it was perceived that Russia was a threat and could use the Finnish language as an instrument to produce ethnic conflict, nationalism became more evident in the region. This reinforced the Swedification process. The first folk school was founded in 1854, and an elementary school teacher-training college was founded 1875 in Haparanda (SOU, 1921: 49). Applicants to the college were recruited largely from the region and, during the first ten years or so of its existence, instruction was offered mainly in Finnish (Slunga, 1965). After that, Swedish became the only language of instruction. The absence of a common lingua franca, however, resulted in some laws being translated into Finnish in the late 19th century (Tornedalica, 1989).

The municipalities had difficulties in establishing folk schools due to lack of resources, and the state began to subsidise folk schools in 1888, but only on the condition that all instruction was offered in Swedish. This precondition for economic support provided an incentive for all municipalities rapidly to replace Finnish with Swedish. In order to strengthen language planning efforts, a Folk High School was started 1899 in Matarenki-Övertorneå, with the aim of being 'a bulwark for Swedish cultivation and culture' and 'a seat of Swedishness for Sweden's outermost border to the east' (Tenerz, 1963: 35). The official policy of Sweden was to promote bilingualism (Slunga, 1965), but nationalistic, social-Darwinist and political ideologies influenced language planning (Eriksen, 1991). Finally, a State Commission concluded, in 1921, that there was no need for instruction in Finnish, not even as an auxiliary language (SOU, 1921). It was claimed that the local people supported this approach.

At the national level, a positive image towards Finnish was upheld by introducing Finnish as a university subject in 1894; the first professor in Finno-Ugric languages was appointed in 1905 at Uppsala University (Ds, 1994: 97). Hence there was not only a diglossia in language behaviour, but also in language policies: the officially declared (high status) ornamental policy and the (low status) implemented plan.

In every instance, Finnish speakers were precluded from having any formal linguistic rights. The first 'boarding house' (*arbetsstuga*) for rural pupils was founded in Matarenki in 1915. It was intended to serve pupils whose parents had insufficient economic resources. The *arbetsstuga* was in fact a reformatory, and its aim was to 'promote Swedish cultivation' in the Finn-districts. The everyday language was Swedish (SOU, 1921: 304, 310, 326). This institution had a long-term influence on attitudes towards Finnish and Torne valley culture.

The State Commission of 1921 took the first important steps to abolish Finnish literature by its support of a proposal from the County Administrative Board, which wanted to establish travelling libraries in the region. The aim was to 'maintain interest in Swedish language and Swedish literature' and to 'strengthen the knowledge of Swedish language and to spur the love of reading'. The idea was supported by local teachers who wanted to have library books available only in Swedish; a state forest keeper feared that it would be a 'great danger for the younger generations … if Finnish literature would be available'. One local newspaper argued that the majority supported a prohibition of Finnish literature (SOU, 1921: 391f). Ten travelling libraries and four minor libraries were established with aid from the government and were administered by the public library in Luleå (SOU, 1921: 302). There is no empirical evidence whether Finnish books were circulated, or whether the libraries adopted the proposals of the Commission. It was argued that even this action favoured bilingualism.

The first steps to ban Finnish from the playgrounds were taken at public meetings where many teachers, and perhaps some farmers as well, demanded that Swedish should be the only language on the playground (SOU, 1921: 392). A few years later, this became a rule supported by local authorities, but it had been locally applied as early as the turn of the century (Tenerz, 1966). It was in the interest of parents to encourage the use of Swedish. This was argued to be an efficient pedagogical idea.

In order to prevent any institutionalisation of relations with Finns, all organised cross-border contacts were opposed by the state, and those who held positive views towards Finnish were labelled as Finnish nationalists. The only official domain in which the state did not gain control was Laestadianism and the Church of Sweden. Despite many attempts, the religious services remained Finnish-speaking, and consequently the regional religious movement was perceived as a threat to the Swedish State.

The result of this policy was that the Swedish Tornedalians began to perceive Finnish Tornedalians as an alien element in Swedish society. The Finnish language was designated 'Finland Finnish' and their stigmatised vernacular called *Meänkieli*, literally 'Our Language'. A cultural border developed slowly between Finnish and Swedish Tornedalians (Winsa, 1998).

The exclusion of Finnish and Sami from education and the public sector in general has had the effect that a stranger travelling in the region would hardly notice that the area is trilingual. The symbolic value of Sami culture and language are accepted as a means of attracting tourists as almost any promotional brochure will attest, but it seems probable that the majority of the local people and politicians are hostile towards a true officialisation of the two minority languages in everyday life. In tourist areas, Sami culture is generally visible in museums, and in gift and handicraft shops, but would hardly be noticed in the everyday local environment. The Finnish culture is almost completely ignored, even in general information, tourist shops and sites. All street signs, with less than ten exceptions, in the whole Finnish-speaking region are in Swedish. The Sami have attempted to reintroduce the original Sami village and city names, but bilingual signs are quickly destroyed by local people, e.g. the modern name of the northernmost mining town is Kiruna, whereas the original Sami name is *Giron*. The authorities have tried to set up a bilingual road sign (Kiruna-Giron), but without success. However, the place names of the mountain regions in the northernmost municipalities are marked on current maps with Sami orthography, although even this has been resisted by local hunters and hunting associations. Nevertheless, the place names in mountain regions are in the process of 'Samification', that is, the original place names in the regional Sami variety are being reintroduced on maps. Furthermore, in the near future, a number of village names in the municipalities Kiruna and Gällivare will appear with bilingual signs.

Major media languages

TV and radio

Swedish dominates radio and TV broadcasting. Swedish is used for some 60% of the total TV broadcasting time, whereas English dominates in all foreign produced movies. There is no dubbing; all programmes produced abroad are subtitled in Swedish. Based on their number of speakers, the fourteen biggest immigrant languages are allocated 254 hours of TV broadcast time, of which 95 are in Finnish. The national radio broadcasts 5200 hours in foreign languages in 1995, of which 3700 hours were in Finnish (Prop. 1995/96: 161). In addition, local cable-TV channels provide programmes in immigrant languages, and immigrants are the subject of one programme broadcast in Swedish (*Mosaik*) for one hour a week. This programme has no equivalent for the national minorities.[25]

Compared to immigrant and minority languages, Meänkieli, Finnish and Sami have a special position in TV and radio. The regulations for the Swedish Radio Broadcasting Corporation state that these languages, and especially Meänkieli and Sami (plus Romany Chib as suggested in the minority reports), are to be given special consideration in the media (SOU, 1997b: 180). Finnish TV can be seen all over the Finnish-speaking area and in the Stockholm region, as well as in 25 other cable-TV regions. Since 1986, segments of Finnish TV have been screened on a special Finnish channel, administered, and funded by the Swedish state in cooperation with the Finnish national TV company. The same cooperative arrangement also works in the other direction, i.e. Swedish is broadcast in Finland. Finland and Sweden share the costs for this service. The Swedish expenditure for this service was 3.4 million euro in 1997 (SOU, 1997b: 180). The total broadcasting time for this Finnish channel, showing programmes from Finland, is approximately 105 hours per week. Since 1968, a few hours of programmes produced in Finland have also been broadcast on Swedish TV. In 1998, Finnish television programmes produced in Sweden consisted of 1.05 hours a week: news five minutes five days a week, debate and actual events 15 minutes a week and children's programmes 25 minutes a week (Vipåtv, 1998). There are no TV programmes in Meänkieli, although broadcasting in Meänkieli seems likely to be established in the near future.

In the Torne valley region, radio broadcasting in Finnish began in 1957 with one to two hours a week. St Fi., or Finland Finnish, was used most of the time, although whenever possible the vernacular spoken by local people was used. Since the late 1980s, journalists have begun to speak deliberately in Meänkieli. Nationwide radio broadcasting in Finnish began in 1969. In 1994, Finnish had 646 hours a year of nationwide broadcast time, whereas Meänkieli is broadcast only

26 hours a year nationwide (Jokinen, 1996). In addition, regional and local radio stations annually broadcast about 3000 hours in Finnish, employing some sixty or seventy staff. However, there is an unequal distribution of broadcasting time between the Swedish Finns and the Tornedalians. In the Torne valley region, the local radio station broadcasts about seven hours a week and employs three or four people (including about three hours/week in Meänkieli). If Tornedalians had, based on population, a comparable number of employees, twelve journalists would need to be employed.

In 1998, a new Finnish digital radio channel began broadcasting nationwide for 15 hours a day. At least 5% of the total time is planned for broadcasts in Meänkieli, although this is well below the percentage of Tornedalians in the Finnish-speaking population. Some 20 to 30% would be appropriate. This service is available on the world-wide web.

Sami radio has been active since the early 1970s and has successively extended its broadcasting time to four hours a week, of which three hours per week are in North Sami (200 hours a year in total). It employs about ten journalists and reaches some 20,000 Sami in Sweden. Some of the broadcasting time is only local in the Sami region. Lule and South Sami have no regular broadcast time on Sami radio, though the Sami radio in Norway broadcasts a few hours a week in Lule Sami as well (Media Sápmi, 1999). By comparison, Sami radio in Norway and Finland provide some 2000 broadcast hours a year. Sami TV started in the early 1990s, and employs six staff who produce ten hours a year, covering children's programmes, and educational and cultural matters (www.sametinget.se). Digital radio will, in the near future, be established; it has been suggested that the Sami radio should collaborate with the Sami radio in Norway and Finland. Eventually, this transborder Sami radio will extend broadcast hours in all three nations to 24-hour-a-day service.

Newspapers and magazines

Sami associations published the magazine, *Muittaleagje*, in Norway from 1873 to 1875, but it was replaced by *Naortunaste* in 1898; the latter is still published. In Norway, two weekly magazines are published in North Sami, *Áššu* and *Min áigi*. The Swedish monthly Sami magazine, *Samefolket*, founded 1918, is largely written in Swedish (budget 155,000 euro a year). The Finnish Sami produce a magazine in Sami, *Sápmelas*, founded in 1934 and still being published (www.sametinget.se). The youth associations use Swedish in their publications (EUROMOSAIC, 1999). The northernmost libraries keep a few thousand literature titles in Sami.

In the Torne valley, a bilingual daily newspaper, *Haaparannanlehti-Haparandabladet*, has appeared since 1872; it receives some direct support from the state. It is distributed along the border region in the Torne valley and has a circulation of 4000 to 5000 copies. Recently, it has ceased daily publication and now appears twice a week, printed in Finnish and Swedish (with half a page in Meänkieli since the 1980s). However, the Meänkieli corner is mostly devoted to folkloric material and the like. Since 1982, the interest organisation STA publishes a trilingual magazine (*Met-avisi*) four times a year, with a nationwide circulation of 1500. It is written in Swedish, Meänkieli and Finnish. The library in Matarenki-Övertorneå has funding to hold books from the northernmost region, and especially Finnish/Meänkieli literature (library leaflets are written in Meänkieli). Since 1980 about 35 books have been published in Meänkieli.

The Swedish Finns have no daily newspaper, but do have two weekly magazines, mainly administered by their cultural organisations. A weekly newspaper, *Viikkoviesti*, was founded by the state in 1967; it has a circulation of 2700 (Lainio, 1997). A magazine edited in Finland, *RSKL-lehti*, is published six times a year by *Suomen Silta*, and, a weekly *Ruotsinsuomalainen*, founded in 1964 has a circulation of about 3000. In addition, a few local and regional magazines and information brochures are regularly published in Finnish. The numbers of subscriptions are, however, declining rapidly from their peak in the 1970s and early 1980s. Earlier, a number of daily Swedish newspapers had a column written in Finnish, but editors abandoned this practice after the 1980s.

Only two Sweden Finnish newspapers have retained national coverage: *Ruotsinsuomalainen*, and *Viikkoviesti*. The state support to *Viikkoviesti* ended 1998, and the newspaper is now continuing with funding from private interests.

As the Swedish Finns have some literary activities, a magazine (*Liekki*) is published four times per year with a circulation of some 1500 copies. There are, furthermore, some religious magazines, of about 25,000 copies, often published four to eight times/year. Some 91 municipalities out of 288 have more than 1000 books in Finnish in their respective local libraries. Since the 1970s, a few hundred novels written in Finnish by Swedish Finns have been published (Jokinen, 1996).

There are no regular publications or broadcasting in Romany Chib or Yiddish.

Swedish L2 and mother tongue instruction for immigrants

Important dates for education of immigrants

Between 1951 and 1965, Sweden had a net immigration of 198,000 (SIF, 1988). The largest group came from Finland. In 1992, Sweden had 835,000 residents holding foreign citizenship and about 13% of the total population is of foreign descent (SK, 1994; Hyltenstam & Tuomela, 1996).

Before the 1960s there was no discernible policy for immigrant education, aside from schooling for Estonian immigrants who arrived after the Second World War, and the Hillel school (the Jewish school in Stockholm) founded in 1955 (Fris, 1982: 53). Both groups have had state support. In addition, French, English and German private schools have existed for several decades. A State Commission on education for Swedish citizens abroad, convened in the 1960s, resulted in a discussion of the educational problems of immigrants. During this period, a few linguists referred to the Tornedalians as semi-linguals, and the subsequent hot debate influenced the state to set up a Commission on Immigrants. Guidelines for a structured immigrant policy were developed by the Commission, which submitted its report in 1974 (Winsa, 1998).

Landmarks in Swedish immigration policy, mother tongue and L2 instruction

In the 1950s, Swedish public schools had some remedial instruction in Swedish. The large influx of immigrants began in the late 1950s and forced the politicians to plan for Swedish L2. The bilingual 'problem' in the north became a major issue in the Swedish Parliament. This debate affected Swedish language policy when school authorities faced similar problems with instruction for large immigrant groups. Nevertheless, the bilingual 'problem' in the Torne valley was essentially still neglected.

In 1965, teaching of Swedish was provided as a right for all immigrants, and was carried out by adult educational associations (*Studieförbund*). Immigrant pupils, and Swedish pupils abroad, received state subsidies for instruction. However, the instruction was often delivered by teachers who were employed part-time for only a few hours a week (Tingbjörn, 1988). In the late 1960s, education of immigrant children was included in the curriculum for the primary school. During the 1970s, foreign employees received the right to participate in 240 hours of education in Swedish (SIF, 1988: 108) on full pay from their employer. However, this generous regulation was modified in 1986. Teacher training for primary school teachers with Finnish and Swedish as instructional languages was introduced in 1974 (Fris, 1982: 65). The seemingly radical change in Swedish immigration policy began in 1975, when Sweden adopted an immigrant and minority policy. A general politically correct guideline for immigrant and minority policy was declared to be 'equality, freedom of choice and cooperation'. The constitution was amended to include a paragraph stating that the cultures of linguistic, religious and ethnic minorities should be promoted. The term 'minority', however, covered primarily immigrant groups. Since 1984, the Tornedalians have officially been excluded from this category, because they were not defined as a minority in the official policy of the Swedish Parliament. Before 1984, the Tornedalians were neglected by the state, because there was no local voluntary organisation interested in promoting bilingualism.

Home language reform adopted by the Swedish Parliament (1 July 1977)

The official language policy of Sweden is to promote active bilingualism. The 1970s policy statement echoes the official bilingual policy in the Torne valley region, but now covers immigrants and minorities in the whole of Sweden.

The immigrants receive special support: e.g.

- a newspaper in a number of immigrant languages;
- the activities of the immigrant associations are subsidised by the state;
- immigrant literature and amateur theatrical activities are supported;
- The state authorises the use of translators and interpreters in the immigrant languages.

Teaching of Swedish was provided through vocational training courses for unemployed people in 1977 (*AMU*) (Lindberg, 1996a). A two-year course for mother-tongue teachers was established. In the late 1970s, the Swedish Board of Education (SÖ) adopted a plan of action for immigrant education, and a seven-week training course for teachers of Swedish L2 was introduced (Fris, 1982: 65). Up to the late 1970s, all immigrant pupils were put into composite classes, but soon many of the parents discovered that MTI for a few hours a week, or pupils in composite classes, was far from sufficient to develop balanced bilingual competence. A strong demand from the Swedish Finnish movement resulted in the establishment of the first home language classes. Finnish pupils in Finnish classes became role models for other immigrant groups. This process was, however, met by strong resistance from local authorities and responsible government bodies. During the 1980s, the Swedish Finnish movement staged nine school strikes in support of their demands for sufficient Finnish-medium education. The strikes sparked nationalistic feelings and hostility towards the Sweden Finns, sentiments supported by the Minister of Immigration who declared that 'Sweden will remain Swedish' (Jaakkola, 1989a, 1989b: 155). Nevertheless, the strikes resulted in improved possibilities for instruction in Finnish and other immigrant languages.

Due to the more restrictive definition of the term 'minority' in international discourse, Swedish politicians adopted an immigrant and refugee policy in 1984/85. The term *minority* was excluded from the new guidelines (Winsa, 1998). All recently arrived immigrants (in the 1980s), having a lack of proficiency in Swedish, have the right to some 700 hours of instruction in Swedish (SIF, 1988: 108).

The Nordic countries adopted a Nordic language convention (*Den nordiska språkkonventionen*) which states that all Nordic citizens have, without any charge, a special right to interpretation and translation services in some official institutions, e.g. health care centres and in court (SIF, 1988). However, this right to interpretation services does not apply for Tornedalians, Swedish Roma, or Sami; it only applies to Nordic immigrants with non-Swedish citizenship.

The 'Free school' reform (*Friskolereformen*) was adopted in 1989/90, i.e. the right to start private schools funded by local authorities. This new more liberal school policy was followed by a decentralisation of responsibility for primary school education, which was transferred to local authorities, and the regional County Boards of Education were abolished. The National Agency for Education was established as the new institution responsible for the implementation, surveillance, and evaluation of the educational system. A new school curriculum was adopted (see next section).

The major economic recession of the early 1990s had an effect on education for immigrants and minorities, as former earmarked grants for MTI were transferred to a general pool, for which local municipalities were responsible. The state initiated cuts of some 30% from a roughly estimated annual expenditure of 109 million euro for MTI and Swedish L2. In practice, this meant severe cuts in, for example, teacher training and home language instruction (Hyltenstam & Tuomela, 1996: 19f).

In the 1990s, adult immigrants (age 16 and up) were entitled to receive training in Swedish L2 for an average 525 hours, and municipalities were made responsible for the provision of that training (Skolverket, 1996b). For pupils without competence in Swedish, short-term intensive instruction in their home language and Swedish L2 were already provided in preparatory classes.

Sweden gained membership of the EU in 1995, appointed two Commissions on minorities (1995, 1996) and has adopted an integration policy for immigrants, under which the Board of Integration is the responsible authority. However, there is little distinction made between integration and assimilation. Some 30 to 82% of all immigrant pupils in primary school participate in Swedish L2 programmes, and all immigrants have the right to MTI as a target language, as a medium of instruction, or for guidance purposes. There are a number of other L2 training programmes provided by the municipalities and the state (Lindberg, 1996a). Since 1997, the term *mother tongue* has replaced *home language*. On 1 April

2000, new minority legislation for Sami, Tornedalians, Swedish Finns, Roma and Jews comes into effect.

Institutions for assessment of objectives in language planning

Swedish L2 and L2 acquisition were introduced as university subjects in the 1980s. The Centre for Research on Bilingualism was established at Stockholm University in 1988. The Centre carries out research on bilingualism on commission or in the form of research projects. Since 1997, the Rinkeby Language Research Institute has carried out research on bilingualism and applied linguistics. The Institute is located in a Stockholm suburb, which is densely populated by immigrants.

In the 1970s, a research fund for immigrant studies was set up. In 1983, the Centre for Research in International Migration and Ethnic Relations (CEIFO), an inter-disciplinary research unit, was established at the Faculty of Social Sciences, Stockholm University. CEIFO has done some research on language planning for immigrants. Several departments of General Linguistics, Nordic languages, Finnish, Sami, Psychology, Sociology and Pedagogy have carried out various forms of research on bilingualism and literacy development. The National Agency for Education and the national research councils often fund these research projects. The Board of Immigration, as well as other authorities, carry out evaluations of Swedish L2 acquisition, including the way administration works, the results, comparisons between schools, and the way municipalities comply with regulations.

Part III Language Policy and Planning

Language planning legislation, policy, implementation

Language planning for immigrants and minorities in Sweden is directly linked to the legal status of each particular ethnic identity. The label 'minority' is of crucial importance to the way language planning legislation is adapted for the needs of particular groups.

Since 1976, Swedish language policy has been more favourable towards immigrants and their needs than towards the Tornedalians. The Sami are in the best minority position, but that is far from sufficient. In this regard, Sweden is not living up to international standards in the treatment of its national minorities, and it has not ratified the 1989 ILO-convention No. 169 on indigenous people (Hannikainen, 1996), the European Charter for Regional or Minority languages or the Framework Convention for the Protection of National Minorities (see next section). Nevertheless, in practice Sami have had national minority status since the early 1970s, although they are not defined as an indigenous people in the constitution (Eriksson, 1997). One of the greatest challenges for the state is whether the Sami have collective or individual rights. This distinction is important in determining whether the Sami have collective rights to maintain Sápmi, the Sami region, although one needs to distinguish collective linguistic rights from collective land rights. Nevertheless, a Commission authorised by the state suggests that Sweden should and may well ratify the ILO-convention No. 169 (SOU, 1999:25). However, ratification may cause conflicts between the majority population living in mountain regions and the Sami, and this is perhaps the major challenge for the state.

The Tornedalians, Sami, and Roma have special minor rights in MTI, whereas, since the early 1980s, Swedish Finns and the Finnish have had an undefined position within Swedish society (Winsa, 1998). This was reinforced in a government resolution of 1994 and is promoted in areas such as the media, education, cultural activities and care of the elderly. However, municipality school plans for the most part neglect this special status of Finnish with only Haparanda stressing its special position. In addition, the Finnish language is mentioned in the municipality school plans of the Finnish-speaking region as well as in a few other municipalities. Bilingualism is mentioned in 24 school plans, whereas interculturalism, internationalism and immigrant issues are mentioned in more than 150 school plans (of 288 municipalities; Skolverket, 1996a). These references are more often decorative than an indication of actual practice. Nevertheless, in many respects Swedish Finns have a more favourable position than do the Tornedalians.

Furthermore, there are several laws (*Förvaltningslagen, Rättegångsbalken*) that prescribe interpreting services that should be available for those who cannot speak Swedish, and authorities may not find a request or evidence inadmissible solely because it is not submitted in Swedish. However, in practice Swedish has been the only language possible for all non-immigrants to use since the 1960-70s. In the Torne valley region, Finnish is allowed in contact with authorities, but only by immigrants, in accordance with the Nordic language agreement. However, the courts in Gällivare and Haparanda must employ a public interpreter, according to a 1984 law (SFS, 1984: 140).

The Swedish Parliament has, in general terms, defined the rights of minority languages in the public media. Sami, Finnish and Meänkieli are languages with special status in the agreement between the state and the Swedish Radio Broadcasting Corporation (*SR*) (Prop. 1995/96: 161), though *SR* has not yet complied with the agreement with regard to Meänkieli in TV, and discriminates against Tornedalians in radio broadcasting.

However, traditional Swedish 'minority' policy (both official and semi–official) is confusing and contradictory. From the 1970s up to 1985, the term 'minority' included immigrants as well as the Sami. Between 1984 and the early 1990s, the Tornedalians have been defined a number of times by the Swedish Parliament as an 'original native population', rather than as a minority. Thus, according to this definition, the constitutional rights for minorities do not apply to Tornedalians. Nevertheless, in 1995 the Swedish State reported to the Council of Europe that Sweden had two minorities: Tornedalians and Sami (CE, 1995). This is still the position of the Swedish State (August 1999; see next section).

One major reason for this confusing 'minority' policy is that the Swedish Finns and the Tornedalians were treated as one social and ethnic group from the late 1960s to 1995 (Winsa, 1998). This was probably the reason why Sweden adopted an immigrant and minority policy, since an immigrant could not be distinguished from a minority. Furthermore, this is presumably the reason that the state argued, as late as 1994, that it would never ratify the European Charter for Minority Languages (Spiliopoulou, 1995). Since 1995, the Swedish Government has 'discovered' that nearly all Tornedalians and Swedish Finns perceive themselves as having two distinct socio-ethnic identities. This new awareness resulted in the appointment of two Minority Commissions with the aim of determining whether Sweden could ratify the international conventions for the protection of national minorities and minority languages (Winsa, 1998; see next section). In 1995, Tornedalians officially became accepted as one ethnic group represented by the STA.

Regulation of mother tongue instruction

Since 1977, all pupils with a foreign home language have had the right to request MTI in primary school and *gymnasium* according to need. All children with a home language other than Swedish have the right to receive training in the home language in preschool.

Since 1987, the definition of a home language states that the language must be spoken in the home of the pupil. Roma, Tornedalian, and Sami can, however, request MTI if their languages are living languages in the home environment, but not necessarily spoken in the home of the pupil. Adopted children are another exception. Roma pupils can occasionally request language instruction for two foreign languages.

Participation in MTI is voluntary. Decisions about enrolment in MTI are taken after consultation with the pupil and their parents.

The local authorities are responsible for MTI and provide four options for MTI:

(1) As a language option (replaces studies in a foreign B-language; in general French, Spanish, and/or German). The language option may also include the subjects: Swedish L2, Swedish, English, or Sign Language. A restriction demands that the home language group must consist of at least five pupils from the same language background before the local educational authorities must arrange education within the language option (on the condition that there is a qualified mother-tongue teacher). This restriction does not apply to the three minorities. (New regulations have been suggested; see the next section.)
(2) As a pupil's choice (continuation course).
(3) Within the framework of the school plan. (Every school has space for a local profile subject, which may include home languages.)
(4) Outside the normal schedule (as an additional subject) (Skolverket, 1996b: 17). In addition, a home language class is still an option. However, in practice option four is usually the only one available in many municipalities. Home language and composite classes are being reduced, but are still available in grades 1 through 6 (grades 1 through 9 Finnish pupils) (Hyltenstam & Tuomela, 1996).

In *gymnasium*, MTI can be chosen as an extended programme, by individual choice or by replacing a second, third or fourth language (SOU, 1996). The total instructional time in the home language should not exceed seven years within the public school system. (New regulations have been suggested; see next chapter.) The rule does not apply for Tornedalian, Sami or Roma pupils. Even at *gymnasium*, the instructional time depends on need, and home language/mother tongue may – if needed – be given as an instruction language. Finnish has a special position in the regulations for *gymnasium* where it can be the language of instruction in a whole programme (SOU, 1997b: 166).

Mother tongue instruction in practice

In implementing the home language reform, many municipalities have organised three types of classes: (1) Swedish classes; (2) home language classes and (3) composite classes, primarily in Finnish, but also in Turkish and other immigrant languages. This direction was taken because it soon became obvious that two to four hours a week of MTI was woefully insufficient to achieve active bilingualism (Tingbjörn, 1988).

During the initial period, immigrant pupils begin in a preparatory class where Swedish is the language of instruction. In a home language class (in practice a bilingual class), which can only be arranged in grades one through six (with the exception of Finnish pupils), the home language is used extensively as the medium of instruction and as the target language. Swedish is spoken from the first grade, and it successively replaces an increasing proportion of the home language as the medium of instruction. In composite classes, about 50% of the pupils have Swedish as a mother tongue, and the immigrant group shares a common mother tongue. In these composite classes, Swedish is used about 50% of the instructional time in grade four, but it dominates slightly in grades five and six. However, variations are frequent, and notions of 'home language class' and 'composite class' vary considerably (Hyltenstam & Tuomela, 1996). At present, at least 50% of instructional time must be in Swedish, and this share must increase progressively (SOU, 1997b: 164). Home language and composite classes are only provided for the largest immigrant groups and are in practice not actively promoted by the local authorities.

Detailed regulations on how classes are formed within MTI have been abandoned since the early 1990s, and each municipality may define its own policy for language teaching of immigrants (SOU, 1996: 157). In practice, this means that the municipalities undermine home language reform for economic reasons. Failing to provide funds for home language instruction constitutes one possible way to reduce budget expenditure in the municipalities.

Since 1990, parents have been able to start 'free' schools. Local authorities fund up to 75% of the cost of these 'free' schools, if the schools adopt the general National Curriculum (Lainio & Wande, 1996). This reform gives the immigrant organisations the specific opportunity to take responsibility for education. A number of such 'free schools' have been funded, often replacing home language classes.

New suggested language legislation and policy

A State Commission on Education has suggested that the 'new' term 'mother tongue' replace 'home language' (1997–), but the term has a more restrictive definition. Thus, a child cannot – according to the State Commission – have more than one 'mother tongue' (SOU, 1997a: 304, 306). If a pupil speaks several languages, the school decides, after consultation with the parents, what the 'mother tongue' of the pupil is. (This will, in practice, mean that Swedish will be favoured whenever possible.) The importance of acquiring Swedish L2 is stressed; it is an obligation for all immigrant pupils, whereas 'mother tongue' instruction should be provided and supported.

The Commission has proposed that the existing provision of seven years of MTI should be abolished, and instead 'mother tongue instruction' should be provided during the entire school period. Pre-schools should promote the development of 'mother tongue' competence, as well as Swedish L2. In addition, the Commission proposes that the requirement of at least five pupils in one class for MTI may be abolished. A specific curriculum for 'mother tongue instruction' has to be worked out and will be comparable with the curriculum for English instruction, i.e. a few hours a week throughout primary school. Hence, the time spent on 'mother tongue' instruction is to be on a par with that given to the acquisition of English L2. In order to reduce expenditure, the Commission suggests that 'mother tongue instruction' be given within the normal school schedule (SOU, 1997a: 318).

Furthermore, B- and C-language options are to include all major immigrant languages. All larger immigrant languages (e.g. Arabic, Turkish, and Spanish) should be available within the 'language option' of the curriculum. In cooperation with the parents, headmaster, and teachers concerned, every immigrant pupil should work out an individual development plan. To make this work successfully, the National Agency for Education should provide extra attention to evaluating this reinforced language instruction, and it should evaluate the cost of 'mother tongue instruction'. Research and pedagogic development projects as well as teacher training should be given extra support. Hence, the Commission has adopted a 'modern' approach to the UNESCO proposal of the early 1950s, which claimed that the best way to transmit majority L2 is to promote 'mother tongue instruction'.

Expenditure for MTI is less than 1% of the total expenditure for primary schools, or about 650 euro/year/pupil participating in MTI (SOU, 1997a: 304–305, 317).

The Reports of two Minority Commissions

In January 1998, two State Commissions recommended that Sweden should ratify the *European Charter for Regional or Minority Languages* and the *Framework Convention for the Protection of National Minorities*. Both reports conclude that all Sami varieties, all Finnish varieties, and all Romany Chib varieties are historical regional or minority languages in Sweden (SOU, 1997b, 1997c). The Swedish minorities listed are Sami, Tornedalians, Swedish Finns, Roma, and Jews. The reports did not suggest that Yiddish be given the status of a minority language, due to the small number of speakers and the rather weak interest among Jews in maintaining the language. (No MTI in Yiddish exists; Hebrew is preferred.) Furthermore, a professional report argues that Yiddish has perhaps not been intergenerationally transmitted for about 100 to 150 years in Sweden. In addition, the report excludes Sign Language from the possible minority languages, arguing that the Sign Language is an instrumental language rather than a cultural one.[26] The Convention is in principle based on the maintenance of historical territorial languages.

The minority language report suggests that all Finnish varieties spoken in Sweden have status equal with St Fi. and Meänkieli. Nevertheless, one expert consulted (Professor Hyltenstam) claimed that the definitions of language/dialect used are political rather than linguistic, but that Meänkieli fulfils the sociolinguistic criteria of a language. By ignoring the ideas put forward by this language expert, the Commissions avoid the problem of how to deal with the two Finnish languages in Sweden. Throughout the language report, varieties (including dialects and standard forms) are discussed and the term *language* is avoided, though the report is not always consistent and sometimes speaks of Finnish including Meänkieli, while excluding other varieties.

Romany Chib is cited as the only non-territorial language. In the northern-most region, Sami and Finnish languages have a historical geographic base. This means that the Swedish Finns and the Tornedalians have the same region as their 'home' territory.

It is recommended that the municipalities of Kiruna, Gällivare, Jokkmokk, and Arjeplog provide public services in Sami (and Swedish). The municipalities of Haparanda, Övertorneå, Pajala, Kiruna, and Gällivare are expected to provide public services in Meänkieli, Finnish (and Swedish). For these municipalities, the language report suggests new legislation under which individuals, by virtue of independent citizenship or home address, will have the right to use their own languages *vis-à-vis* administrative authorities and courts, irrespective of their knowledge of Swedish. The individual may write in one of the minority languages, but the authority can respond in Swedish, with a note written in the minority language indicating that an oral version of the content can be provided in the home language of the individual. However, it is suggested that the authorities should try to respond to minority language speakers in their own language / variety. If interpretation services are requested, the authorities must pay for these. Furthermore, none of the authorities are required to provide written services in the minority languages. Very few of the employees in the public sector have sufficient literacy in the respective minority languages. (Some 50% of civil servants have sufficient oral proficiency in Finnish / Meänkieli; fewer in Sami).[27]

The local and regional authorities claim that they do not have sufficient numbers of civil servants who can write formal letters in Sami or Finnish. (Haparanda might be one exception.) Therefore, the cost for providing transla-tion and information in Finnish and Sami was estimated to be too high. (Haparanda estimated its costs to be about 270,000 euro a year.) Thus, in practice this means that the existing weak literacy in Finnish is used as an excuse to avoid providing written services in Finnish / Meänkieli. Oral services ought to be avail-able in these three minority languages; civil servants should be provided further education; but not to exceed one month (SOU, 1997b: 236). Bi- and trilingualism is defined as an extra qualification in all public employment in the territories where Sami and Finnish are spoken. All language rights are considered indi-vidual matters, despite the fact that in practice they are collective rights that can only be exercised among groups of individuals (see discussion in Coulombe, 1993).

Meänkieli is explicitly mentioned a number of times as a minority language in the northernmost region, but is not given full recognition as a language, for polit-ical and economic reasons. It is easier to comply with the demands of the Charter by subordinating Meänkieli to St Fi., despite the fact that Meänkieli is a territorial language, whereas St Fi. is primarily a non-territorial variety, or at least not a community language.

The languages and their associated cultures should be part of the school curriculum, and at least one university or college should be assigned the task of arranging for education and research on the respective language, as well as for Jewish culture. This is already the case for Finnish, but there is no guarantee that Finnish will be provided for in the future. Sami is the only minority language that is the object of particular regulations for research and education. Furthermore, the existing Sweden Finnish Language Board is erroneously charged to work with Meänkieli; therefore, the report suggests that no other language board need be supported by the state. In practice, this suggests that the state wants to abolish Meänkieli by eschewing support for the codification and elaboration of Meänkieli.

The report also suggests support for these languages in the media, in literature, and in culture. Sami and Tornedalian cultures are particularly mentioned as fields of importance. It is suggested that public archives give particular attention to the minorities and their associated cultures. In pre-schools and in the care of the elderly in the northernmost region, parents or children should have a legal right to demand instruction, or care, in minority languages. However, the state should strive to make the same measures available nationwide, although not through legislative measures, according to the reports. Nordic networking is improved if the languages are supported.

The Sami Parliament is responsible for the implementation of the proposals concerning Sami. It is suggested that the County Administrative Board of Norrbotten set up a supervising committee with the aim of studying what other measures can be taken. Representative organisations of the minorities should have the status of reference bodies, as well as being involved in the supervising committee. The recommendations of the reports are described as first steps towards a minority policy.

However, the measures taken must not increase official expenditure – this was a basic guideline given to the Commissions. It is suggested that a number of measures be funded through re-allocations from existing sources (e.g. the National Council of Cultural Affairs).

In comparison with Norway, Finland, Hungary and the Netherlands, the suggested institutionalisation of Finnish/Meänkieli language is the weakest provided for minority languages, whereas the support for Sami in the report is more favourable. The report supports its position by maintaining that several of the proposed recommendations are already implemented nationwide. Thus, Finnish in Sweden has good support as a non-territorial language, whereas Finnish/Meänkieli in the region is in a less favourable position. However, in the implementation of the legislation, variations can seemingly be great. In order to fulfil the demands of the Charter, the language Commission continuously shifts its perspective in relation to the two Finnish-speaking groups. Whenever it is an advantage for the Commission to distinguish between the two groups, it does so, but it brings them together whenever there are political and economical benefits. The estimated expenditure for the reforms described in 500 pages making up the report is extremely small.

The Government bill on Swedish minorities

In 1999, the Ministry of Integration was given responsibility for national minority issues (except for Sami culture and reindeer issues). Under these arrangements it appears that the Tornedalians and the Sami, after living more than 1000 years in Sweden, will be treated on a par with immigrants as a problem of integration. In early June 1999, the Minister of Integration presented the Government bill, which followed from the reports of the Minority Commissions (Prop. 1998/99:143). The bill overrules some suggestions in the reports of the Commissions by proposing that Meänkieli, Sami, and Finnish are the territorial languages of Sweden. The territories for Finnish and Meänkieli coincide; that is, in the five northernmost municipalities in Sweden. Thus, Kiruna and Gällivare have three official minority languages designated for use by local, regional or national authorities in the region. In addition, the bill suggests that Yiddish also be given non-territorial status. The measures to promote and institutionalise the minority languages are estimated to cost some 1.1 million euro annually. Besides these deviations, the bill appears to adopt most of the Minority Commissions' recommendations, and proposes ratification of both Minority conventions. The overall outcome seems likely to bring few changes to the status of Swedish Finns compared to their existing position. The existing support for Sami will not be significantly different, whereas Tornedalians have achieved improvements. Romany Chib and Yiddish will receive significant support. The subsequent legislation should come into force from 1 April 2000.

Literacy planning legislation and implementation

Sweden has a nine-year compulsory state school system (funded 100% by municipalities) wherein pupils start at the age of six or seven. Virtually all children are enrolled in the nine-year system. Few private schools existed up to the early 1990s. After compulsory schooling there is a voluntary *gymnasium* (normally two–three years) which the municipalities are obliged to offer all youths between 16–20 years of age. More than 98% of pupils continue to *gymnasium*. About 13% of the pupils in *gymnasium* have an immigrant background (1995/95) (Beijer, 1996).

The National Agency for Education is responsible for the National Curriculum for the primary school and *gymnasium* which every private and state school must adopt as part of its educational plan (Beijer, 1996). The National Agency for Education is responsible for the central administration of all parts of the educational system (except universities): evaluation, development, supervision, research, follows ups, the 'free' schools and Swedish education abroad. The National Agency for Education has a field organisation in eleven communities, in direct contact with the local authorities. The National Agency for Education is also responsible for a system of special schools for handicapped and disabled pupils, schools for mentally retarded children, adult education (*Komvux, SSV* and for retarded adults *Särvux*), Sami schools, and Swedish instruction for immigrants (Skolverket, 1996b).

Traditionally Sweden has had a centralised educational administration, where the Ministry of Education and the parliament are the highest authorities, though minority issues – other than reindeer herding – are transferred to the Ministry of Integration. The government prepares legislation for the parliament by appointing a State Commission, which may be constituted solely of politicians, members of parliament, experts or a mixed group of politicians, representatives of the organisations concerned and experts. The report of the Commission is presented to the Minister of Education, who sends the report out to all concerned agencies for comment. Based on the report and the opinions expressed by those consulted, the Ministry of Education writes a government bill which is then presented to the parliament. This consultation process prior to the final decision is considered an important part of Swedish democracy.

The parliament defines the objectives and gives guidelines for political and ideological values and mores for education in Sweden. This political and ideological basis is integrated into the curriculum, school law and school regulations; these give the framework for the educational system. The National Curriculum contains two parts: one part contains plans for the primary school, Sami schools, special schools and the mandatory school for retarded children; the other part contains guidelines for the voluntary schools, i.e. *gymnasium*, special *gymnasium*, adult education administered by local authorities, special schools for adults, and the state schools for adults (Beijer, 1996).

Since 1991, the predominantly political boards of municipalities, 288 in total, have been responsible for the administration of the schools and the implementation of the curriculum and school law (Skolverket, 1996b: 6). Recently, the local authorities have been given a framework which allows greater freedom for planning. The municipalities must have a school plan for the organisation of education (showing how the objectives will be accomplished), as well as a plan for further education of the school staff. Schools must have responsible head teachers that work out plans for each particular school.

The Sami have a Sami School Board, which provides education for people with a Sami background. The Sami School Board defines who can attend a Sami school and where. In addition, local authorities can, in cooperation with the Sami School Board, arrange so-called 'integrated education' for Sami (in Sami and on Sami culture). The National Curriculum of 1994 reinforces the aim for the Sami schools as regards bilingualism. It states that, after enrolment in a Sami school, every pupil ought to be able to speak, read and write in Sami, as well as have thorough knowledge of the Sami culture (Lpo, 1994). However, these and similar guidelines are often mere rhetoric, as they fail to reflect realistic plans for implementing or achieving policy goals.

The historical development of language planning policies

The standardisation of Swedish

The development of a standard Swedish went through rapid changes during some periods with slow stabilisation processes occurring in between. The historical development of standard Swedish has often been roughly divided into three different periods:

(1) Old Swedish (800–1526);
     Runic Swedish (800–1225);
     Classic Old Swedish (1225–1375);
     Younger Old Swedish (1375–1526)

(2)   Modern Swedish (1526–1900);
       Older Modern Swedish (1526–1732);
       Younger Modern Swedish (1732–*c.* 1900)
(3)   Contemporary Swedish (1900–).

Changes in orthography are often based on historical circumstances influencing writing, e.g. the 'Black Death', innovations, or religious movements.

The oldest 'texts' in Nordic are found in the rune stones. These fragmentary pieces of written 'texts' are the first attempts to standardise the various vernaculars. The Vikings had a runic alphabet, but there are no other signs of a developed literacy. For the most part, rune stones pay tribute to heroic individuals or groups, who died or conquered enemies in battles.

The first institutionalised efforts to create a written language came with the introduction of Catholicism in the middle of the 12th century. The first preserved texts in Latin written in Sweden date from 1160s (Lindroth, 1975: 22ff). The schools of cathedral chapters (*domskolor*), established in the 13th century, pursued some elementary education for priests. Johansson *et al.* (1979: 167) mentions 1225 as the date the Latin alphabet replaced the runic alphabet. The first written texts in Swedish are from the middle of 13th century. The oldest law-rolls (*landskapslagarna*) of the Swedish Provinces are from the 1280s (*Äldre Västgötalagen*), written in Swedish with the Latin alphabet (Wollin, 1996), but using various written norms reflecting the variety of each particular province. These law-rolls were probably prominent status-raising instruments for Swedish.

The monks and nuns diligently copied Latin scripts. The Vadstena monastery had about 1400 volumes in the 15th century. The monastery was located in the province of Götaland, and it is for this reason that the Götaland variety greatly influenced the standardisation process of Swedish (Johansson *et al.*, 1979: 195). In fact, during the latter part of the 15th century preaching was done in Swedish; parts of the Bible had already been translated into Swedish (Lindroth, 1975: 178). The work of the nuns and monks raised the status of Swedish, especially the work of the internationally famous St Bridget (–1373) who wrote about 700 revelations (translated) in Old Swedish (Lindroth, 1975: 92, 107). The nuns and monks often had weak competence in Latin; therefore, they had to read and write in Old Swedish. Prescriptive books from the highest earthly authority, the King, had a major influence on the personal writing style of the nobility and theologians, and was adapted for use by literate society as a basis for early attempts to write in Swedish. The first national law (*landslag*) dates from the middle of 14th century (Johansson *et al.*, 1979: 195), and prescribed that contracts of sale and other specific public documents must be written in Swedish (Enc. 1995). This was probably the first book in Swedish which was used nationally by all authorities.

During the Middle Ages the Hanseatic League dominated and controlled trading around the Baltic Sea. The trading language was Low German. Its influence on the Nordic languages was enormous.[28] Low German was the source of a high percentage of loan words – especially terms for new technology, administration, trading and handicraft – and made structural changes in medieval Swedish. Rough estimates of the percentage of German loan words suggest that they constituted between 50 and 75% of the word stock. However, Low German was otherwise little used within learned society. During this period, learned society was a closed group, a fraternity, dominated by theologians who could read the sacred lingua franca, Latin, as well as some Greek and Hebrew (Lindroth, 1975: 213).

With the invention of printing in the 15th century, a new era began. Printed books laid an indisputable foundation for the standardisation of the vernaculars and established a powerful instrument for the expansion of administration. However, books printed in Latin had a small market. In the early 17th century, Sweden still had only one printing company, located in Stockholm (Lindroth, 1989: 69).

With the advent of printing, high culture society began to expand beyond its theologically based discourse, and universal knowledge became available to the public. The impact on the community-society of the growing gap between particular and general knowledge is of crucial importance in understanding the development of language planning in the late Middle Ages. Most farmers were illiterate and hence had, in general terms, only access to context-bound knowledge, whereas universal knowledge was filtered through the religious Latin paradigm.[29]

A secondary outcome of printing and literacy was an increasing metalinguistic awareness, and thereby metacultural knowledge. It can be argued that those who were literate could conceptualise the community and more efficiently structure their thoughts as well as develop societal planning. The Catholic Church and the clergy lost influence and dominance with emerging new literate discourses competing with and challenging general knowledge of the religious discourse. Therefore, books and literacy were perceived as threats by the church and the nobility. Censorship was common. By 1500, at least 20,000,000 books had been printed in Europe (Anderson, 1991: 37). However, the learned layer of the society in Sweden was thin.

In many regions of Europe, the vernaculars attracted interest in the 16th century, primarily among patriotic poets and literary men (Lindroth, 1989: 241). Martin Luther's interest in Biblical language was probably part of this discourse, and it sparked off the process of writing in the national vernaculars. Luther was ahead of his time in using the varieties spoken by the public as a basis for literacy development. Earlier translations into the vernacular existed, but gained little attention. Despite the fact that Martin Luther fought to throw off traces of his own Low German (Houston, 1988: 206), he argued that the spoken form of the ignorant people – e.g. peasants, craftsmen, beggars and illiterates in general – must be the normative form for the national Bible. By doing this, he transformed the context-bound 'language of the heart' to a religious style comprehensible to the common people (Stolt, 1994: 72). His success was evident. Luther became the first famous 'author' and the German Bible sold in large numbers. Between 1522 and 1546, a total of 430 editions (whole or partial) of his biblical translations appeared (Anderson, 1991: 39).

Old Swedish was heavily influenced by translations from the Latin with a complex syntax and grammar, and hence it was distant from spoken forms. The New Testament was translated into Swedish 1526 (in 2000 copies), and the complete Bible appeared in 1541 (Lindroth, 1975: 199, 230). The language used for the Bible translation adapted the norms of the German Bible and was simpler and closer to the vernaculars; a new era of the written language had begun (Enc., 1995). However, the cost of a copy made it nearly impossible for ordinary people to own one (Houston, 1988).

The Swedish Bible was the first book that left a major impact on the nationalisation process and the development of linguistic norms, because the written form was used in ceremonies all over the nation. The clergy and learned society began to use the text of the Bible as a normative structure for their own letters, and as the standard for formal speeches. The impact of the Lutheran movement on the homogenisation of vernaculars and mainstreaming the various communities into one nation can hardly be overestimated. The vernacular Bible homogenised and stratified the vernaculars and unified the nation into what has been called an 'imagined community' (Anderson, 1991: 442ff). The Swedish Bible laid the foundation for the coming nationalistic delirium and speculative madness.

The translators of the Bible lived in the capital region – which already was the economic, political and administrative centre of Sweden – and laid the foundation for a standardised norm (Johansson *et al.*, 1979: 195). The orthography of the vernacular was obviously not a deliberate choice but was preceded by earlier printings in Swedish and by the accidental awareness of Swedish by a particular editor. The spoken language of learned society in the capital region was widely adapted to the written form by the 17th and 18th centuries (Allén *et al.* 1967: 89). Hence, standard Swedish and the style of formal oral Swedish were effects of the concentration of public institutions in the capital region. Formal Swedish replaced disappearing Latin, and learned society increasingly used it to reflect high culture. The pure and noble form of Swedish was said to be given by God, whereas deviations and language changes were, according to one duke, punishments for sins and signs of linguistic poverty. The nobility was repeatedly, as early as 1587, ordered to use pure Swedish and avoid foreign elements. Loan words from German, Danish and Latin were discovered and labelled as impurities (Hernlund, 1883: 4). At the end of 16th century a royal censor was appointed with the task of cultivating and monitoring all Swedish publications (Enc., 1995).

Nationalism flourished for the first time in the 17th century, and Sweden improved its image as a great power with its first non-religious language planning efforts. However, in order to improve Sweden's image, Latin was reintroduced in parallel with the inflated interest of Swedish. The number of universities increased: Uppsala (1477–1515, re-established in late 16th century), Lund (1668), Dorpat, Estonia (1632) (where the students studied Latin, Latvian, Estonian, French and a Finno-Ugric language spoken in the capital region of Russia), Åbo Academy, Finland (1640) (Klinge *et al.*, 1988: 52). The University of Greifsvald, in northern Germany, was incorporated into the Swedish educational system after successful wars. Through these universities, the position of Latin was reinforced as the literate language of Sweden. In the 17th century, it was still the case that more texts were printed in Latin than in Swedish (Lindberg, 1984: 20),[30] and of the Swedish texts that were published, the religious literature dominated (Svensson, 1981: 11f). Although the general literacy level was raised during this period, it seems that Sweden lagged behind the linguistic development of other leading nations in Europe.

One of the most absurd products of this nationalistic self-centredness is exemplified in four large volumes in Swedish in which Rudbeck, the President of

Uppsala University, claimed that the Swedes were direct descendants from the first humans in the Bible. Swedish was also said to be closely related to Hebrew or even the first language of human race, and the first literal language of the world. He claimed Sweden was the centre of the spiritual world as well as one of the original locations of the human race, the vanished Atlantis of Plato. Accordingly, the president of Uppsala University was one of the first to hold lectures in Swedish (Tengström, 1973: 62). His son, Olof Rudbeck, argued that Sami and Finns were the lost tribes of the Israelites (Lindroth, 1989: 285ff, 303). The Rudbecks, and their compatriots, were the extreme products of the epoch, and reflected the tremendous change in national ideology. Their theses were received positively and sanctioned by influential parts of society, not just in Sweden (Lindroth, 1989: 297).

Latin was the language of international society, but also an instrument in raising status within the universities, which in the 17th century were still not acknowledged as influential parts of society. If the professors could be identified with learned society by their language behaviour, that action in itself would reinforce their status in learned society (Lindberg, 1984: 24).

In practice, it is not clear how much Latin was used within the educational system. Swedish grew in importance as a medium of instruction during the 17th century, at least in natural history, mathematics, and history. Latin was best preserved in theology where it was used even into the 19th century. Within universities, Latin was supposed to be the only language of instruction, according to the university constitution of 1655. However, in the 17th century, Swedish was already spoken in lectures and especially in private instruction.

The first scientific attempts at status planning, codification, standardisation, and elaboration of Swedish began during the Geatish period, in the 17th century, when bishops and learned individuals debated the correct spelling structure, and standard norm for writing and pronunciation were established. The first catalogue of Swedish literature and texts appeared in 1680 (Lindroth, 1989: 316). The code of laws was printed, wordbooks and popular literary works were sold, and almanacs and other light reading as well as the first newspaper appeared (Svensson, 1981: 12). Up to the middle of the 17th century, Swedish had been mainly used in religious literature and in documents within Government offices. The 17th century was an amazingly innovative period with new disciplines and new progress in many fields of literature. The first book for children appeared 1591, followed by some 200 books in the 17th century (Hedenborg, 1997: 158). From this time onwards, Swedish began to penetrate and expand into the official domains.

Aesthetic values and the search for the purity of Swedish, for example, in the form of etymological and comparative studies, became important instruments in the first deliberate and structured efforts at language planning. The cultivation of the written language aimed to replace loan words with 'authentic' Swedish ones, although the massive influence of Low German in Old Swedish was not yet understood. Nationalistic speculations continued to influence linguistic studies.

History and the search for the roots of Swedish became the main scientific interest of the Geatish period. Language was a major interest for the first philologists, especially in the studies and mappings of the rune stones and the runic alphabet. However, besides detailed collection of rune scripts, and an unpublished Swedish wordbook by Johannes Bureaus (1568–1652), the results were often tremendously speculative in the areas of etymology and comparative linguistics (Lindroth, 1989: 239ff). Nevertheless, Bureaus was one of the most prominent academics to argue that Swedish ought to be used in scientific literature. He wrote the first Swedish grammar (published much later), designed an explicit programme for Swedish orthography, and got support from the King Gustav II Adolf who, in 1626, tried to persuade the professors at Uppsala University to write in Swedish (Enc., 1995; Hernlund, 1883: 6; Fries, 1996).

Swedish grammar, comparative linguistics, lexicography, and etymology achieved positions as new fields of studies. The superiority of Latin was questioned, and the national vernaculars gained in status as reflectors of history and traditional culture. They were considered to be purer, and hence were closer to the superior form, which was maintained to be derived from the language of the Old Testament. Pure Swedish was the original language of the world. These language planning efforts justified the perception of Swedes as a self-sufficient people living in a great power. Vernaculars were no longer elementary spoken forms of illiterate peasants but were associated with national identity and pride and a new discourse for high culture. The development of a refined language mirroring that high culture was seemingly a product of the new nationalistic ideology. Social identity of learned society was slowly transferred from international Latin to standardised national Swedish. The forerunners were eminent patriots of the period, and the Geatish period produced the first novels in Swedish (Svensson, 1981: 54ff).

As learning Latin was a necessity for scholars, a consequent need, going back to the Middle Ages, was to compile structured wordbooks. Studies in theology and translations of religious scripts were the main interests of early scholars, and therefore the wordbooks had to reflect the order of this social discourse. Language planning mirrored the social, and later scientific, discourses/paradigms of society, where the rank order of the discourses/paradigms was given by the leading authority of the particular epoch. The Pope, and later the Lutheran Church, represented the highest worldly social authority, to which even the Swedish kings were subordinate. Hence, in the beginning codification of Swedish proceeded from the traditions developed in education and in studies of Latin. Twenty-four Latin-Swedish wordbooks were produced from 1538 onwards. The function of these wordbooks was primarily that of a database for particular terms used in translations. The source language in the wordbooks was Latin, and they were structured according to a rank order of subject fields, where the religious domains were perceived as the most important. With the progressive interest in Swedish, a need to compile monolingual dictionaries emerged and alphabetical order was perceived as a more rational structure as seen from a scientific and 'neutral' perspective.[31] The first printed grammar and noteworthy dictionary in Swedish appeared in 1696 and 1712 respectively (Lindroth, 1989: 304). The official Swedish psalm book – which went through more than 250 editions and 1.5 million copies before 1819 – had 413 psalms (Houston, 1988: 58f). Its impact on the standardisation of spelling and on the development of a religious language style can hardly be overestimated. A weekly magazine in Swedish (*Then Swänska Argus*) appeared 1732. The first Swedish newspaper in Finland appeared in 1771 (Huovinen, 1986). However, variations in spelling occurred frequently up to the early 19th century by which time normalised spelling had stabilised (Lange, 1996: 173).

The foundation of the National Board of Antiquities (1630) was a direct result of the nationalistic efforts (Lindroth, 1989: 245, 338). Along with the already existing National Archives, which in 1618 was given a more structured form, these institutions laid the foundations for gathering linguistic information from the whole nation. Archives of the nation were institutions of nationality. For the first time, the high culture of Sweden changed its perspective from reflecting the ideas of the Continent and maintaining its subordinated position to a search for the popular culture of Sweden to unite the nation. Language was one of the most important means to this end. By the end of the 18th century, only theologians maintained Latin in instruction and lectures.

Competence in Latin reflected social identity

Latin in Sweden can not solely be understood in terms of its being an international and instrumental language as it also brought with it social identification and status. Competence in Latin distinguished the learned from the ignorant and the illiterate peasant, and had prestige solely for this reason (Lindberg, 1984: 16ff). Latin provided social mobility and had the function of ornament, ceremony, and ritual to mirror social class distinctions. The great numbers of vernaculars were associated with the various individual communities, whereas members of the international learned society were associated through their shared language. During the 18th century, when political ideology shifted from stressing studies predominantly in classical humanism towards science as a tool for practical purposes, one of the first sociolinguistic debates emerged in Sweden: was Latin inseparable from knowledge or could one be a learned member of society without competence in Latin? Some feared that the use of national vernaculars in science could lead back to the Tower of Babel. The enlightenment, initiated by Rousseau, Diderot and Condorcet, argued that education should be available for all people and be about practical subjects in society, and in principle should be taught through local languages. By the 1750s, the first discussion on language, power, control, and gender had emerged. As women were more often excluded from education, they were more often illiterate and, consequently, less likely to read transactions and texts written in Latin. A woman in Sweden argued in a debate that women, desiring learning, were deliberately excluded from knowledge by men who feared competition and a critical evaluation of their maintained elaborated knowledge, which she believed was mere everyday knowledge covered by a façade of Latin (Tengström, 1973:77, 101ff). In the 19th century, those in favour of Latin in higher education were the universities, the Swedish king, and the courtiers in general. The feminists as well as the nonconformists of the late 19th century were in general opposed to Latin, seemingly due to the fact that they were not accepted as participants in society by traditional education authorities or by the Church. The new emerging upper class of business people had a practical approach to Latin and had little interest in classical education and ideals. Finally, the socialist movement broke all the remaining ties to Latin. The socially highly valued discourse of Latin was lost, and languages were labelled, according to their status, as reflectors of high or low cultures. There were hardly any socially neutral languages.

Swedish replaces Latin

Despite the fact that the Geatish period focused attention on the local vernacular, and the Lutheran church ordered preaching to be conducted in 'proper Swedish', Latin was nevertheless the language of the nobility, as well as the language of education. Latin was, in 1611, prescribed for 20 hours a week in school. It was the language of instruction from the second grade, and was always to be spoken in the presence of the teacher. However, the Swedish State needed to maintain the image of a Great Power in all international contacts by using Swedish. Until the 1660s letters to the Swedish State written in languages other than Latin, were responded to in Swedish. Latin was the language of the Swedish King in communication with regents and nobilities in Europe, until French replaced Latin, although Latin was used in diplomacy even during the 18th century (Tengström, 1973:56ff).

The pedagogical idea (e.g. inscribed in the school curriculum of 1724) prescribed Latin because learning Latin grammar and vocabulary were considered part of the mental training provided by education. It was argued that Latin developed cognitive skills due to its precise and well-described grammar and semantics. This acquired cognitive competence would be an advantage in other subjects as well, not only language studies (Lindberg, 1984: 16). One reason for this position was that grammars and dictionaries in the vernaculars had not been developed. Classical studies had been performed in Latin for a long time, and thus there were developed metacultural skills in Latin that laid the basis for and structured an image of a scientific discourse associated with logic, precise meaning and social status. Although this discourse information was derived, it seemed obvious that only those who had access to this discourse could acquire universal knowledge.

The debate over the role of Latin resulted in an increasing number of dissertations being written in Swedish – 281 of 6996 between 1719–1772 (4%) (Lindberg, 1984: 100). The Academy of Science – founded in 1739 – favoured transactions in Swedish (Lindberg, 1984: 87), and published annual almanacs in Swedish. A special language cultivator checked the style, grammar, and the spelling of the written form; his ideas of a written language probably left an important impact on the creation of a scientific style in Swedish. German Gothic script dominated during the early years in which the Academy published transactions,[32] though Roman script was gaining ground and became the only type of orthography used from 1743 onward. It was held that German type provincialised the culture for wider markets. Other Scandinavian countries followed, adopting the new type (Houston, 1988: 211). However, the German type was used for a long time in religious scripts and popular literature (Johansson, 1998: 90). Hence, for a long period elite culture identified itself with modern Roman typography.[33]

In comparison with other international Academies of Sciences, the idea of popular enlightenment was unique in the Swedish Academy of Science (Fries, 1996). The secondary function of the Academy of Science was to institutionalise and cultivate Swedish and form national identity. Its predecessor was the Academic Society of Uppsala, which published transactions in Latin, and which, around 1730, wanted to compile rules for spelling and a wordbook, but the result was meagre (Lindroth, 1989: 597). The main task in the cultivation of Swedish was to develop a language for eloquence, i.e. a high status variety that could replace Latin and provide a new high standard for learned and noble society. Formal standard Swedish entered the public stage in the middle of the 18th century. In 1753, a script discussed the distinction between the official fairly homogeneous language and the various informal dialects, and the language spoken by well-situated people in the capital which had already gained the highest prestige (Fries, 1996). Orthography and style were discussed, and in the 1750s the number of orthographies increased. Many learned experts, all of whom had their particular ideas about spelling, hotly debated this issue.

From Latin to Swedish to German to English

The prominent nationalism of the 19th century favoured the national vernaculars, which were believed to reflect the true spirit of the people. Swedish grew to a dominant position as the language of instruction within universities around the 1750s, and in regular schooling after the reform of 1807, when Swedish grammar became a subject in secondary grammar school, and when Latin was no longer used as a language of instruction. However, Swedish language and literature were officially declared subjects in mother tongue instruction only in 1856. From 1878 onward, Latin was an obligatory subject in the classical stream within *gymnasium*; this ended in 1965 (Tengström, 1973: 81, 99ff). Thus, the language reform began as an international top-down process in Germany that was first implemented within the Lutheran church for religious purposes. The reform reached the nobility some 150 years later, then reached the students of universities, and finally about 250 years later, reached the pupils in elementary schools who were instructed in the national language. Latin remained, however, as the language of dissertations until the middle of 19th century (Lindroth, 1981: 207). German replaced Latin in Sweden as a major foreign language. French was of minor importance within the sciences, but remained influential in diplomacy and political affairs. In the 1930s, English began to dominate the academic fields in Sweden as the language of scholars and professors (Sörlin, 1994: 208), although Swedish was and is used frequently in dissertations, especially within the humanities.

The language chosen for science was and is strongly predicted and influenced by the learned networks and traditional contacts between individual scientists, departments, faculties, and universities. Germany and Great Britain, in particular, and to some extent France, have for centuries been influential in Swedish university policies' perception of ideas and paradigms. However, even before the Second World War research institutions in America and Anglo-American research in general, began to attract interest among Swedish scholars, especially in the natural and social sciences, whereas studies in the humanities had more communication with the Continent (Sörlin, 1994).

Apart from economic power, possessed by the speakers of a particular language, and political ideologies as guidelines for a scientific language, another normative element for the Swedish language policy for universities is the working language of international institutions. For a long time, French was the language of diplomacy and political matters (and is still within the European

Union). After 1924, the League of Nations and other international institutions started to use English, and to some extent French, as their working languages. The scientific community adapted the new language policy. After the First World War, use of English as a lingua franca began to spread within international society. From the very beginning English was the primary language within the United Nations, even though French is one of the six official working languages (Coulmas, 1992: 115). The process was supported by the tremendous increase of scientific journals and periodicals – by 1972 eight periodicals each day were founded in natural sciences; in 1986 the cumulative number exceeded 82,000 periodicals in natural sciences and technology (Sörlin, 1994: 172; see also Ammon, 1998). The international linguistic movement was guided by the economic strength of language societies. The United States flourished after 1945, and challenged all other nations in terms of economic power and scientific strength.

In order to counterbalance the Anglification of Swedish society, in 1997 the state requested that the Swedish Language Council work out directives for the protection of Swedish. The Council suggests a number of measures for the promotion of Swedish within education, public life, computer technology, administration, and legislation. In line with the international tendency (e.g. in the United States), the Council claims that the status of Swedish should perhaps be inscribed in legislation, and that measures should be taken to guarantee the official position of Swedish in the European Union. In addition, the Council wants to promote Swedish in education and argues that Swedish should in general be the official language in education. The Council fears that a loss of linguistic domains for Swedish creates weakened competence in Swedish in science, education, and information access. Furthermore, the Council proposes to reinforce education in another foreign language, at the expense of English. Competence in two official European Union languages, besides the national language, is in accord with the directives given by the European Union commission. Therefore, the suggestions of the Council directly contradict the general opinion that education ought to be more internationalised. The Council defends its position by arguing that the Swedish public in general lacks awareness of the consequences of Anglification and that the general public has a naive confidence in the absolute status of Swedish. Therefore, the public is not able to anticipate the effects of using English as a language of instruction in *gymnasium* and even in primary school. According to the Council, a good mastery of Swedish, in as many domains as possible, is a prerequisite for the acquisition of foreign languages (www.spraknamnden.se). With regard to the treatment of immigrants in Sweden, this statement is contradictory, because acquisition of the mother tongue is argued by politicians to hamper acquisition of Swedish. It remains, however, to be seen how these proposals will be treated by the Swedish Parliament. Furthermore, it is also evident that if Swedish researchers and scholars want to keep up with the competition, being future citizens of the European Union they must acquire well-developed competence in at least one foreign international language. It is not enough to acquire general literacy in English, but this must be developed through extensive practice in various academic discourses.

The development of Finnish until 1809

In the historical discourse of language policy, Finland was a part of Sweden until 1809. In Finland, Swedish and Latin were the spoken languages of the nobility. In fact, three languages were used in Finland in three socially stratified discourses within the society. Latin was the formal and official language, whereas the vernacular of the nobility (Swedish) was the prestigious language for the ordinary people. Finnish had the lowest status, with little official significance. For Finns access to social mobility demanded competence in two foreign languages. (The Sami were marginalised and lived in poverty in the northernmost region.)

The New Testament appeared in the vernacular 1543 (*Se Wsi Testamentti*). Four decades later (in 1583) Finland got its first hymnal in the vernacular. The Finnish Bible appeared 1642. From 1562, the Lutheran Church met the demand to impart elementary biblical knowledge to the ordinary people in Finnish.

Latin and Swedish were used exclusively within higher education, universities, and public administration. The only official domain of Finnish was within the church. In total, 174 'books' were published in Finnish before 1809, mainly hymnals, and the like. However, in the 1580s, the Swedish national law (*landslag*) was translated into Finnish. Swedish law appeared in Finnish in 1759, but never gained any official status. Church law was translated in 1688 (*Kircko-Laki ja Ordningi*). In addition, some official documents were published in Finnish, e.g. the form of government (*Regeringsformen*) (Huovinen, 1986).

Schooling was haphazard and limited until the 19th century. During the late 18th century, one *gymnasium*, eight casual schools (*trivialskolor*), ten pedagogic schools (*pedagogier*) and one university, constituted the total educational institutions of Finland. The medium of instruction in these schools was always Latin, which was replaced by Swedish in the 18th century. Latin was used in the Latin schools up to the early 19th century (Klinge *et al.*, 1988: 36). Finnish was sometimes used as an auxiliary language in lower education, and when reading from the Bible. A Finnish almanac appeared 1705, and found a good market. A Finnish newspaper was founded in 1775 but was discontinued one year later.

The first small Latin–Swedish–German–Finnish dictionary appeared in 1637 (*Lexicon Latino-scondicum*), but the first comprehensive Finnish–Latin–Swedish wordbook appeared in 1745 (*Suomalaisen Sana-Lugun Coetus*). The first wordbook where Finnish was the source language appeared in 1745. In 1880, wordbook subject fields as the basis for categorisation were completely replaced by the alphabetical order, though alphabetical order occurred already in wordbooks of the 17th century (B. Romppanen, personal communication). The first comprehensive and prescriptive dictionary appeared in 1874–1880. Along with the interest in lexicon, the first grammar of Finnish appeared in 1649, written in Latin (*Linguae Finnicae brevis institutio*). This grammar was, however, inadequate, as it relied heavily on Latin grammar applied to Finnish. The first basis for the development of a comprehensive Finnish grammar came with the *Grammatica fennica* in 1733 (Huovinen, 1986).

Language planning agencies within the polity

The most eminent institution for the maintenance of the Swedish language is The Swedish Academy (*Svenska Akademien*) founded 1786. This was the very first institution that worked solely for the promotion of Swedish. The Academy was given the motto 'genius and style' by its founder King Gustav III. One of its primary tasks was to 'work for the purity, strength and loftiness of Swedish language' within science, poetry and eloquence in speech (Allén *et al.*, 1986). Another main task was to compile a Swedish dictionary and grammar as well as dissertations and contributions to the development of good style and manners. The programme and regulation of the Swedish Academy was basically copied from the statutes of the French Academy. There have been eighteen members of the Academy ever since it was founded.

One way that was used to promote a normative style was by giving rewards for eloquence in speech and poetry. These rewards were given between 1786 and 1839 when they were abandoned, but they undoubtedly had an impact on the formation of an academic prose. The first attempt by the Academy to normalise Swedish orthography can be found in a dissertation on Swedish spelling (*Afhandling om svenska stafsättet*) published 1801. In 1836 the Academy published a massive volume, containing close to 500 pages, on orthography and grammar (*Svensk språklära ugifven af Svenska Akademien*). In addition, the first monumental work on the structure of Swedish (*Svenska språkets lagar*) appeared in six volumes between 1850 and 1883 (Allén *et al.*, 1986: 59, 89), and laid the basis for a simplified elementary grammar that was used extensively in schools in the late 19th century.

The first word list in contemporary Swedish for public use appeared 1874. It gave directives on, e.g. spelling, word gender, grammatical category, and inflection. In 1892, the Academy published the first volume of the continuously updated 'complete' description of Swedish vocabulary, including comprehensive descriptions and analysis of, e.g. spelling, meaning, inflection, and etymology. Volume 31 – ending with '*sulky*' – appeared in 1997, running to more than 28,000 pages. Government guidelines state that the Academy's word list must be the basis for the orthography used in all schools from 1890 onwards. All textbooks and teaching aids ought to adapt this orthography. Under these guidelines, the word list of the Academy achieved a monopoly in Swedish schools that it has kept during the 20th century. The popular contemporary word list, eleventh revised edition, appeared 1986. The intention of the Swedish orthography was that phonemes in general should correspond with graphemes, but also that the modern written form should not deviate too much from older orthographies. These guidelines are more an ideal than a reality. The Academy has been rather conservative in spelling reforms, and was once overruled by the government, which in 1906 provided its own guidelines for a reformed orthography.

In 1939, the Academy authorised a prescriptive grammar (*Riktig Svenska*). This book has had a major impact on the standardisation of Swedish. The grammar is based on the spoken forms of its author who had lived in the capital region, Uppsala, and Nyköping (Allén *et al.*, 1986: 217). Furthermore, the Academy has supported the Centre for Technical Terminology (*Tekniska Nomenklaturcentralen, TNC*) since its foundation 1941 (Allén *et al.*, 1986: 224). TNC employs sixteen staff, has a board representing public and private institutions, and is 50% funded by the state. Other income is derived from commissioned work ordered by private and public companies, and institutions.

More than 30 books in various technical fields are available from the TNC. Another important task of the TNC is to provide all users with a database of technological terms on CD-ROM. The database TERMDOK has some 500,000 entries, and includes a number of databases, e.g. from Denmark, Finland, Norway, Iceland, Canada, and smaller Swedish databases (TNC, 1997). With Sweden's membership of the European Union (since 1995), the TNC has been commissioned by the EU to transfer Swedish technical terminology to an EU database, *Eurodicautom*. In 1998, it is anticipated that the database will have some 110,000 Swedish entries. This database serves the needs of translators and interpreters of the EU. Standardisation of terminology is also carried out by the Swedish Standards Institution (*Standardiseringskommissionen, SIS*).

Three years after the establishment of TNC (1944), the Swedish Academy founded the Swedish Language Council (*Svenska språknämnden*). The board of the Swedish Language Council is constituted of representatives from various organisations with interest in Swedish, e.g. National Agency for Education, Swedish Radio Broadcasting Corporation and TNC. The resources available include nine regular staff plus several others working on a project basis. It publishes a quarterly publication, *Språkvård*, 'Language Cultivation' (6000 subscriptions) and brochures, booklets and books of rules on writing, spelling rules, pronunciation, place names, etymology, etc.

The directives on standard norms given by the Swedish Academy are implemented by a number of other boards, maintained by a number of public institutions, e.g. the government employs a Plain Language Group to promote the use of plain everyday language. The Swedish Broadcasting Corporation, the Post, the National Tax Board, the Swedish Federation of County Councils, and other public institutions currently have language consultants. The consultants are organised in an association, which is represented by a special language group made up of representatives from the Academy, Language Committee, TNC and SIS (Allén *et al.*, 1986: 238). Since 1975, this Language group has worked to implement the standardisation of Swedish through meetings, seminars, and articles published in *Språkvård*.

Other language planning institutions independent of the Swedish Academy include, for example, the Commission of Place Names (1902–). Departments of Swedish and Nordic languages in Swedish universities are often involved in the normalisation of Swedish. Swedish is also one of the national languages of Finland, where a number of institutions carry out research, promote, and standardise Swedish, e.g. The Swedish Language Board (1942–) (Allén *et al.* 1967: 95). In Uppsala there is a specific association which works for the cultivation of Swedish (*Språkvårdssamfundet*).

There is also the Nordic Language Board (consisting of ten members representing all Nordic Language Boards) which, according to its statutes, works to promote common Nordic terminology and advises on linguistic issues related to and for the comprehension of Nordic languages (Lindgren, 1997). Among its publications are an annual booklet – Languages in the Nordic Countries (*Språk i Norden*) – as well as a number of reports (*Nordisk språksekretariat*).

Since 1987, Latin terms in medicine have been cultivated by a Language Board of Medical Terms funded by the Swedish Society of Medicine; it has one employee. The major newspapers have language consultants who write articles on language cultivation for their respective newspapers. Recently, a Swedish board on computer terminology (*Svenska datatermgruppen*) was established with representatives from language cultivators, media and the computer industry (www.spraknamnden.se).

The main agency for the spread of Swedish abroad is the Swedish Institute (SI, 1997, 1998), with a budget of 1.09 million euro a year, which employs some 70 teachers/lecturers working in 42 countries – especially in the United States, Germany and the Baltic states – where Swedish L2 (and L1) is taught. In total, some 900 teachers/lecturers/professors teach Swedish and Swedish society in 200 universities, although all are not employed by SI. Bilingual Finland has a high percentage of these teachers, but apart from Finland, Swedish has no official position in other countries. The number of high school students enrolled abroad is estimated at 50,000 (SI, 1997/98). (Finland obviously contributes most to this total.) Furthermore, SI arranges about ten summer courses in Swedish annually.

To promote literacy in immigrant and minority languages the Swedish National Council for Cultural Affairs (*Statens Kulturråd*) has had a special fund for library purchases and for the publication of literature in foreign languages since 1975. In 1997, the Council distributed more than 218,000 euro to some 30 small publishing companies for the translation of children's books in Swedish into foreign languages (INV rapport, 1997). In addition, the National Agency for Education supports publications in lesser-used languages.

Since 1977, The Board of Immigration has subsidised immigrant associations and the publication of newspapers and magazines in immigrant and minority languages. This particular fund is, however, facing a radical change in 1998 because of the new integration policy. The Swedish Radio Broadcasting Corporation has an agreement with the state to broadcast major immigrant and minority languages, and to provide language courses.

The Immigrant Institute was founded by immigrants and immigrant associations in 1973 and receives state subsidisation (INV rapport, 1997). Its aim is to serve as an office and publishing company for immigrant authors and artists, as well as to collect information on immigrant issues.

To promote efficiency in Finnish education, there is a Finnish-Swedish Council of Education, and a Nordic Association (*Föreningen Norden*) which provides language courses in Nordic languages, e.g. by arranging language courses during summer time at least in Sweden and Finland.

With regard to language acquisition and language services, there are a number of private and public associations that arrange language courses in Swedish and foreign languages, and especially in the Nordic languages. There are eleven Educational Associations (*Studiecirkelförbund*) (32% funded by the state, 17% by the local authorities) and most of them provide language courses for adults. The state funds 147 Folk High Schools (*Folkhögskolor*) which provide a number of language courses for adults, especially in Swedish, English, German, and French.

The Department of Scandinavian Languages at Stockholm University provides a five-semester course for language consultants working as editors, language cultivators, journalists etc. Today, some 120 language consultants are employed in public administration, the media and by various organisations. The training of interpreters and translators in different languages has been provided for at Stockholm University since 1986 by the Institute for Interpretation and Translation Studies (IITS) (*Tolk- och översättarinstitutet*) as well as by a few other university departments. The Swedish Judicial Board for Public Lands and Funds (*Kammarkollegiet*) authorises translators and interpreters. The Nordic Language Convention (*Den Nordiska språkkonventionen*) is administered by the Swedish Immigration Board (*Invandrarverket*) (DNS, 1994). However, civil servants in official institutions are often unaware of the regulations on interpreting and translating and neglect to provide this service when it is requested.

To conclude, perhaps the most internationally influential agency for the promotion of Sweden, Swedish culture, science, language and enterprise is the Nobel Foundation. Its impact on the image of Sweden abroad can hardly be over-estimated. The Swedish Academy awards annually the Nobel Prize in literature to one carefully selected author, although Swedish authors are greatly over-represented.

The Sweden-Finnish Language Board

The Sweden-Finnish Language Board (*Ruotsinsuomalainen kielilautakunta*) was founded in 1975 and employs 2–3 staff. It is partly funded by the Finnish State and promotes St Fi. in Sweden. It is an advisory body on language cultivation issues. The Board has developed new administrative terminology for Swedish conditions, published three dictionaries covering different social fields (i.e. school, social welfare, and labour market terminology), a Swedish–Finnish dictionary for immigrants, four booklets on vocabulary and a booklet on language cultivation (circulation 1200 quarterly; *Kieliviesti*). Its main task is to develop terminology and to inform Finnish-speakers and the media on linguistic issues. It arranges seminars and courses, advises, gives lectures, and works on commission. The Board has representatives from 15 associations and institutions working with Finnish (two from Finland), and is represented on the Nordic Language Board. One of the greatest challenges for the Language Board is the implementation of its proposals (Lainio, 1997).

Editors for newspapers and newscasters in TV and radio broadcasting show a keen interest in adopting new terminology and often request information on cultivation issues. However, Finnish-speaking communities have a rather weak interest in integrating the new terms into their everyday language and have a strong tendency to use Swedish loan words whenever an appropriate and common Finnish term is lacking. The main problems are, of course, the overwhelming dominance of Swedish, the limited broadcasting hours for TV and radio and the rather weak interest among the Swedish Finns in Finnish newspapers. Hence linguistic information provided by the Language Board is to some extent integrated by the well educated but has lesser impact on the speech of the blue-collar workers, who are the very foundation of the maintenance of Finnish in Sweden. In this respect, language planning efforts are often in vain, and have merely a symbolic effect on Finnish in Sweden. The spoken language deteriorates slowly and is reduced to the inner circles of family life and closest friends where frequent code switching and Swedish loan words are well accepted. The gap between official Swedish-Finnish and informal spoken Finnish is growing rapidly and language planning efforts produce an increasing distinction between the Standard and the vernaculars. Alienation from the Standard is an increasing reality rather than a mere possibility.

However, The Sweden-Finnish Language Board has not made any explicit attempt to promote Finnish in the Finnish-speaking region. Its linguistic border has, from the very start, been drawn outside the region where Finnish is traditionally spoken, although its publications are to some extent promoted in the minority region. The Board has been rather reluctant to adapt to sociolinguistic reality, but applies a model of language planning devised for a majority language to this subordinated language.

Cultivation of Meänkieli

There is no language board funded by public authorities to promote Meänkieli; only a few voluntary activists work on the standardisation of the language. The author Bengt Pohjanen, former teacher Matti Kenttä and teacher Kerstin Johansson, have been the most active cultivators. Kenttä, Johansson and Pohjanen standardise text material submitted to the magazine *Met-avisi*, written in Swedish, Meänkieli and Finnish, as well as the 35 or so books published by *Kaamos*, a publishing firm owned by STA. In practice, they constitute a language board, which works in close collaboration with STA. The editors and journalists of *Met-avisi* now have fairly well-developed literacy in Meänkieli, and thereby function as language cultivators. The local trilingual newspaper *Haaparannanlehti* has about five active writers in Meänkieli. In addition, Bengt Pohjanen is working on a translation of the New Testament. Two parts have appeared: the gospels according to St Mark (1988) and St John (1995). By the year 2000 he expects to publish a translation of all four gospels. Kenttä and Pohjanen (1996) have produced, among other publications, a grammar (*Meänkielen kramatiikki*), and have been the initiators of an educational radio programme in Meänkieli (1997, 1998) which, since 1999, has been available on the web: http://www.ur.se/sprak/finska/n&m.htm. Professor Erling Wande and Matti Kenttä (1992) have compiled a wordbook in Meänkieli (*Meänkielen sanakirja*).

Professor Wande and Assistant Professor Winsa, at the Department of Finnish, Stockholm University, have been actively involved with the compilation of dictionaries in Meänkieli, as well as with the production of textual role models for written Meänkieli through written articles. In 1998, a trilingual discussion network on the World Wide Web was started for Tornedalians and the people in the northern region. The aim of the network is to promote and strengthen linguistic and cultural diversity. Meänkieli and Finnish are used rather extensively in the new medium, thus including people who have rarely been exposed to written Meänkieli/Finnish. Code switching and grammatical errors are frequent. It seems as if this lack of a normative style encourages individuals to acquire literacy in their mother tongue. Some 30 to 50% of all email is written in Meänkieli/Finnish.

No other university Finnish department actively supports Meänkieli (other than some support from Finland). On the contrary, a patronising attitude towards Meänkieli is often evident among representatives of the various Finnish departments and Swedish Finnish organisations.

Another activity that influences language cultivation and status raising is the bilingual amateur theatre movement, local musicians, and authors playing, writing and acting in Meänkieli.

However, dissemination of formal Meänkieli into everyday life faces great challenges due to the insufficient institutional support and rather weak interest among local people in cultivating the vernacular. One may argue that there are only about ten to twenty persons who are able to write an elaborated Meänkieli, and less than ten non-immigrant Tornedalians have well-developed literacy in St Fi.

By comparison with the Swedish-Finnish broadcasting media, the local radio station in Pajala in the Torne valley has fewer resources. The station adapts purified Meänkieli to meet listener needs, recognising their lack of practical competence, and using a different pedagogical approach and a more relaxed relationship to the implicit demand for St Fi. (or Finland Finnish) in the formal setting. The local radio station in the region broadcasts news in Finland Finnish. Other programmes are broadcast basically in formal Meänkieli, the journalists avoiding frequent code switching, and common but unnecessary loan words, i.e. words that have an equivalent term in Meänkieli. The lack of competence in St Fi. has meant that few people know modern technological terms. Hence, it would have a disastrous effect on comprehension and on the number of listeners if all new terminology were borrowed from Finland Finnish. The radio journalists frequently use Swedish loan words, often followed directly by the equivalent Finland Finnish term. In the long run, this form of cultivation transfers awareness and familiarity with the most common modern vocabulary in St Fi. terms as well as an idea of cultivated Meänkieli. Illiteracy in Finnish as well as in Meänkieli creates a greater distance between spoken Meänkieli and St Fi. and weak social identification with St Fi. The local radio station works in practice as a role model of standardised and formal Meänkieli in public domains. Of minority language broadcasters, the radio station in Pajala is one of the most popular in Sweden, with, in relative terms, a high number of listeners. Its popularity is probably an effect of its use of the local vernacular/language in a cultivated form. A similar popularity was experienced by a local radio station in Texas in the United States when it began to broadcast in the local Spanish ('Spanglish'); even advertisements were produced using the local vernacular (Jarman, 1994).

Sami Language Board

In Sweden the Sami Language Board (*Samisk språknämnd*) was founded 1974. Today it has two employees (a third person was employed in 1998) and works mainly with South Sami and Ume Sami by collecting Sami nature-names. It has been said that the Board is very conservative, purist and tradition-oriented regarding language planning (EUROMOSAIC, 1999). All three Nordic Sami parliaments have language boards, and as North Sami dominates the work of the three language boards it affects all three Nordic Sami communities, although technical and administrative terms are often developed independently in each community. This lack of an integrated Nordic Sami language policy reinforces the problems of the divergent varieties.

The Sami Council (*Sámi Raddi*) is a trans-border agency that works with some form of language cultivation. Since 1971, there has been a Sami Language

Committee having the goal of coordinating language planning efforts on a Nordic basis (EUROMOSAIC, 1999). However, this does not seem to be an efficient committee, and at present the development of a Nordic Sami Language Board is being considered (NSD, 1997-11-02); the aim is to establish a more independent and efficient language planning body. With one language board, all Sami varieties would be elaborated by one institution, which in the end would unify the Sami people and standardise the North Sami language/variety. This approach to language planning provides some impetus to the overall aim of establishing a Sápmi for all Sami people speaking one official language.

Sami radio and TV broadcast what seems to be a more cultivated language than the Meänkieli radio station, though language activists often criticise the use of loan words. Interviews are often in Swedish. A marked diglossia may result in a declining number of listeners, though its function, as a role model and language cultivator for Sami speakers is indisputable. Public media and role models are probably more efficient for the codification, elaboration and standardisation of minority languages than the work of language boards which have great problems in implementing new lexical material in everyday practice.

Among the Nordic countries language planning for Sami is best developed and supported by the Norwegian State. The lack of resources and well-educated language planners, as well as the number of varieties, logistical problems, small groups, and a rather weak interest in acquiring Sami hampers the elaboration of the Sami language.

Informal language planners

A major influence on the maintenance of Finnish/Meänkieli in the Torne valley is the continued existence of frequent so called crossborder- and interlingual-marriages (*poikkinainti* 'cross-marriage' in local Finnish). This continuous contact with Finland Finnish is the main reason that Meänkieli has survived Swedification efforts. Finnish immigrants have the highest prestige varieties of Finnish and hence act as role models for the Tornedalians in all informal and formal meetings and gatherings.

The development of high and low Meänkieli varieties is a consequence of the local radio station, language-based activities, and the promotion of Meänkieli in MTI. Since the 1960s, the status of Meänkieli has risen because of this small degree of institutionalisation. This has caused minor but progressive attempts to speak 'proper' Meänkieli and a more tolerant approach to St Fi. words, e.g. 'car' is expressed as *'biili'* in Meänkieli, but one can now hear the St Fi. term *'auto'* replacing the Swedish loan word, even in informal settings. Previously, Tornedalians refused to use common and well-known St Fi. terms, preferring to use relatively old Swedish loan words to integrating St Fi. terms. It was often perceived as snobbish to use a large number of St Fi. terms.

Bilingual amateur theatre, language courses on radio, in novels, and children's books, and in popular music in Meänkieli are all examples of the practical outcomes of the work of STA. When language attitudes change, linguistic practice is slowly redirected. This ethnic mobilisation is a markedly bottom-up process that reinforces ethnic identity and thus encourages a stronger will to cultivate the 'proper' vernacular, or a will to acquire oral competence in Finland Finnish. The mere existence of public institutions favouring Meänkieli/Finnish positively influences prevalent and widespread negative attitudes. The most recent initiative in support of Meänkieli is a training course for radio journalists able to speak Meänkieli arranged by Radio Norrbotten (NSD, 1998-03-03), and there is a plan to establish multimedia journalism training in the minority languages Meänkieli and Sami.

Labour unions can demand salary increases for bilingual employees if and when the proposed new legislation favouring bilingual employees in the public sector comes into force. Thus, competence in Meänkieli will constitute an additional qualification for the labour market. This is in marked contrast with the 1960s when bilinguals were more frequently unemployed than monolinguals, even in the Finnish-speaking region.

Authors writing articles and novels in Sami promote cultivated Sami. There are a growing number of authors, musicians, and researchers writing in Sami, especially in Norway. According to databases, of the several hundred monographs published in Sami, approximately 80% of them are published in Norway. The bulk of the publications probably represent material from previous decades.

Informal Sami within the Sami parliament, Sami TV and radio reflect diglossia and serve to mark the social stratification of speakers acting as role models. Another body that promotes language is the Sami theatre, which will be institutionalised in the near future.

The Swedish Finns, due to the size of their population, have a number of associations, which informally promote Finnish. One example of a method used to promote their language is a literacy project in which parents had their children read aloud every day. The activity was supported by teachers making appropriate books available and by helping to transfer their awareness of the links between literature and everyday culture. The books were read and discussed with parents, teachers and pupils working as teams, e.g. fairy tales were mapped for structure, content, story-line and details (Ewerlöf, 1987). Swedish Finnish communities have few official institutions that use Finnish, and hence few meeting points in everyday public life where the minority language has a normative position. Instead, a number of local organisations arrange festivities to bring Swedish Finns together in situations where Finnish is the language spoken. Furthermore, the Sami and the Swedish Finns attempt to establish ethnic-based sports associations, and other public organisations, e.g. the Sami parliament wants to be a fully recognised member of the Nordic Council and Council of Barents (Eriksson, 1997).

Globalisation of the economy has merged a number of Swedish and Finnish companies into Swedish-Finnish corporations, which by their very existence have influenced attitudes and associated Finnish with social mobility. These economic changes may, in the long run, have an impact of the maintenance of Finnish.

Some 200 novels in Finnish have been published in Sweden. In general, Finnish immigrants take the Finnish spoken in Finland as their role model and have, through their extensive contacts with their former home country, rather good contacts with Finland Finnish.

The Roma have made few attempts to develop Romany Chib. Yiddish is hardly promoted in Sweden, although recently it has become a symbol of cultural identity.

International influences affecting language planning and policy

While the colonial tradition of language planning has a long history in Sweden, dating back to the 13th century, in general, Swedish language planning has followed the pattern of language planning in other major European nations, although lagging behind mainstream developments. The Swedish Academy (1739) was an effect of the Geatish period, but had several international antecedents: *Academia della Crusca* (1582), the *Académie Française* (1635) and the *Real Academia de la Lengua* (1713) (Cobarrubias, 1983: 10).

The structure of wordbooks and dictionaries reflected those aspects of society that were given highest priority. Alphabetical organisation was well known before the Middle Ages, but had little significance in the structure of wordbooks until the invention of printing; rather, the theological influence on wordbooks meant that words were ordered according to themes, or conventional topics. Religious domains were given the highest position, and in one form of ordering, all general terms were placed at the end. Lexicons in alphabetical order were firmly established in about 1600 (France and England), although religious ranking of subject fields was sometimes replaced by the scientific order of subject fields in the 17th century (McArthur, 1986: 75, 77, 114). This process seems to have been delayed in Sweden.

In the late 16th century, at least 18 languages had developed grammars (Cobarrubias, 1983: 10), and accordingly Latin began to lose its position since the Bible was translated into many vernaculars, its use expanding into new language domains all over Europe during the 16th and 17th centuries (Burke, 1991). The first noteworthy Swedish grammar appeared in 1696, and a Swedish wordbook some decades later. After the codification of the language around one standard, domestic literature began to expand and became available for the well-educated, as well as in the form of books for children (Hedenborg, 1997: 158).

European nationalistic movements, originating in Germany during the late 18th century, reached Sweden in the 19th century. The practical implications of nationalism were visible in the minority areas only after 1888.

In the late 19th century, the social-Darwinist paradigm was implemented in the Finnish/Sami-speaking regions. It coincided with the first Swedification efforts, and the ideology of language planning could for the very first time, refer to 'scientific' ideas of racial differences (Eriksen, 1991). The Sami were perceived as a subordinate race, to be preserved in their traditional culture, whereas the agricultural Tornedalians had somewhat better status. Fear of ethnic conflicts and the idea of the homogeneous nation were intertwined with the pedagogic notion that minority members should be instructed in the majority language.

When the positivistic paradigm was applied to linguistics during the first part of the 20th century, the language of the elite became a priori a logically superior language, and the standard form was the only form promoted through the educational system. It was believed that the elite spoke a more elaborated language because they had better cognitive access to a cultivated form of the language. By definition, the blue-collar workers spoke a 'distorted' variety of the underlying superior structure. Hence, there was no need to support or to encourage the maintenance of the vernacular varieties. Progress was to be achieved through the use of a homogeneous and superior standard.

However, after the Second World War the social-Darwinist paradigm rapidly lost its position in a modernising discourse for new ideas on language planning in the international context.[34] Now the varieties spoken in the communities were not taken to be worse than the language of the elite, but rather were less elaborated than the standard form due to social circumstances (Bernstein, 1971). This line was followed by William Labov (1974) who showed that non-standard English was as complex and structured as that of any standard. One major influence on ideas and research on language acquisition for minorities and subsequently for immigrants was the UNESCO declaration of 1951, which argued that first language instruction promotes second language learning. Another line of reasoning claimed that bilingualism as such has negative effects on cognitive development and linguistic competence. This idea was held as a general principle in the Western world up to the early 1960s (Virta, 1994). A Swedish researcher from Norrbotten made one of the first attempts to alter this attitude. In the early 1960s, he maintained that local varieties are in fact languages, and that Sweden still had a great number of bilinguals (Österberg, 1961). Thus, 'bilingual' pupils faced greater challenges in education. This could be resolved by promoting the vernacular during the early grades in primary school.

The reconstruction of Europe, and the industrial development that formed the basis for the urbanisation process, began in the 1950s in Sweden; as a consequence, little attention was given to the situation of national minorities before the 1960s. Although Sweden was a member of the League of Nations, and often up to the time of the Second World War championed the cause of minorities in this forum, the Swedish State did not admit to having any minorities in its territory (Eriksen, 1991). In fact, in the 1950s Sweden still claimed, in international fora, that it had no minorities (Ekenberg, 1994). This may have been because a mutual social advantage was perceived for the state and for people who were willing to migrate and to adapt to a modern industrial lifestyle. Competence in Swedish corresponded with employment and migration, and Finnish was stigmatised (Winsa, 1998). This political attitude was probably built on the premiss that any support for minority languages could hamper the urbanisation process. Many politicians apparently argued that it was in the national interest to build a homogeneous and equal society, without particular ethnic identities. Sweden maintained its image as one of the most equal nations in the world. However, the debate on semilingualism in the Torne valley left a profound impact on the immigrant and minority policy of the 1970s.

Another important influence on language planning has been the ILO-conventions on human rights for indigenous peoples. The Sami gained status as a national minority, in practice by the early 1970s (Winsa, 1998). With that exception, Swedish policy was based on completely 'equal' treatment of every social group. The socialistic bloc based its language policy on the Marxist ideology of social groups as the primary constituent in social policies. There was no need to distinguish any particular group, except in relation to economic class. In principle, the political right also adopted the ideas of social categories (Eriksen, 1991), although maintaining the general left–right distinction in perception of the concepts 'collective' versus 'individual'. Thus, Sweden was resistant towards the concept of ethnic identity. Negative discrimination did not exist, according to the ideology of the state. Despite the fact that the famous

Swedish 'art' of social engineering was at its height in the 1950s and 1960s, few were aware that the social exclusion of the minority languages from use in public affected social identity, competitiveness, and education as well as economic performance. These top-down 'equality' processes were in accord with the beliefs of the community, and there were almost no bottom-up in-group organisations advocating bilingualism, although the Sami already had begun to mobilise in the 1950s.

In the early 20th century, the only problems with the national language policy were to be found in the minority regions. But given the weakness of these minorities in social and numerical terms, they could be ignored, although Finnish authorities, activists and linguists on a number of occasions called for public debate of minority language policy and alleged that the Swedish government was involved in linguistic oppression. Finnish society was, however, strongly influenced by the nationalistic movement, and the political and social 'support' received from Finland was mostly harmful for the Tornedalians, who feared that any collaboration with Finns or Finnish would be taken as a reflection of Finnish nationalism. The minority region was, in political terms, a sensitive issue, and the state feared that the loyalty of the Tornedalians would be questioned if Finnish gained official status. The ideology of the time was that 'language' was strongly associated with 'nation' (Winsa, 1998).

With the development of socio- and psycholinguistics, the cognitive qualities of language were given new, more abstract dimensions. Language was an expression of cultural and personal identity, rather than of national identity. A particular language was the means for interpretation of the local environment. Language and culture were intertwined. Contextual meaning was argued to be non-translatable, and the dichotomy of context-bound–context-reduced meaning was given a social dimension in the Torne valley. These new and challenging ideas reached Sweden in the early 1960s, together with a great number of Finnish immigrants, and this focused attention on the debate on language policies.

A strong impetus for changing the new language policy and language planning was put forward by the umbrella organisation for Swedish Finns, the National Association of Swedish Finns (NAFS), established in 1957 (*Sverigefinska Riksförbundet-Ruotsinsuomalaisten Keskusliitto*). In the early 1970s, NAFS already was associated with the Social Democrat Party and the Swedish Confederation of Trade Unions (*LO*) (Tarkiainen, 1996). NAFS had its strongest following in 1980 with 56,000 members (Jaakkola 1989b), but has declined to some 20 to 25,000 members in the late 1990s. The Board of Immigration, as well as local and regional sources, subsidise its activities.[35] NAFS also has close ties with Finland.

NAFS, as well as Jewish and Estonian associations, were directly involved as representative ethnic/immigrant organisations in the preparation of the Swedish Immigrant and Minority Policy. Since the early 1990s, NAFS has argued that the Swedish Finns represent a Swedish minority. However, until recently, and to some extent even now, NAFS has avoided supporting the Meänkieli movement for political reasons. This exclusion and deliberate opposition has created an obstacle for the Tornedalians' language efforts and has been a source of antagonism.

In 1995, Sweden and Finland became members of the European Union, which favours cross-border contacts, integration of regions and regionalisation of Europe. This policy is based on economic ideas of how to improve the wealth of weaker regions and strengthen the status of successful regions. This process of European integration means, in practice, that the national and cultural border between Sweden and Finland will lessen in significance, and bilingualism will be perceived as a social advantage.

This top-down process, initiated by the States, has created cross-border cooperation and a transnational Torne Valley Council, and has positively affected former often hostile attitudes towards Finns living on the eastern side of the border. Nevertheless, integration policy has forced the Tornedalians to expand their use of oral Meänkieli into official domains. Although not deliberate, that expansion is a natural effect of ongoing regionalisation. The two border cities, Haparanda and Tornio, are merging to create a single set of public institutions, which means that bilingualism will be necessary for most of the civil servants working in these cities.

After the breakdown of the political structures in Eastern Europe, the Council of Europe focused a lot of attention on minority issues and adopted two international conventions on minority rights, which came into force in 1997. Since the 1980s, the European Parliament has supported linguistic diversity in the European Union by funding The European Bureau for Lesser Used Languages (EBLUL). EBLUL took the Swedish minorities – the Sami, Tornedalians, Swedish Finns, Jews, and Roma – into their network 1996. The European Union supports lesser-used languages with a budget of about 4 million euro annually. This lobbying organisation had a profound impact on the appointment of the two Swedish Minority Commissions and their respective reports.

Recently, Finland has once again raised questions about Swedish minority policy. Especially in 1995–1997, the Finnish government had an influence on the position of Finnish in Sweden, and has strongly supported the Swedish-Finnish movement. In this political context, Tornedalians and Meänkieli have seemingly been neglected. Methods for practical and effective language planning have been of less importance than political strategies, and the minority reports were more concerned with the political and direct economic aspects, rather than with the development of ways to improve efficient language planning and indirect long-term economic benefits in the Torne valley region. However, the government bill on minority issues has overruled these political influences and acknowledges Meänkieli as a distinct language.

Part IV Language Maintenance and Prospects

Intergenerational transmission of the major languages

In general, Swedish minorities are facing serious obstacles in reproduction of the minority languages. The general trend in all five linguistic communities reflects a rapid decline in the number of bilingual people. In the Torne valley, especially in the Gällivare municipality, there is rapid movement towards becoming a Swedish-speaking community. Second and third generation Swedish Finns in general have Swedish as their dominant or only language.

The border region will, most likely, remain bilingual due to membership of the European Union, interlingual-marriage, progressively organised cross-border contact, and an increasing demand for bilingualism in public institutions. The attitudes in favour of bilingualism have, without doubt, become more positive since the 1960s, when bilingualism was associated with semilingualism and poverty.

A few thousand people, approximately 40 years of age or older, are bilingual in two minority languages, and speak Swedish as their third language, whereas Tornedalians are often monolinguals in Swedish up to the age of 30 to 35. The traditional domains where the local languages were acquired have changed or disappeared. The strongest Sami language domain is reindeer herding but, with the mechanisation of the occupation, there are fewer face-to-face contacts between reindeer herders. Snowmobiles and small tractors are the everyday transport vehicles for Sami, and everyday linguistic interaction has declined.[36] Another problem is that Sami females, who traditionally have been the transmitters of language, migrate to urban areas, and are often 'replaced' by monolingual Swedes (EUROMOSAIC, 1999). Hence, despite revival efforts, the use of Sami varieties/languages is rapidly declining, especially with respect to South and Lule Sami.

There are, however, some encouraging signs. The Sami schools, the bilingual school in Haparanda, bilingual pre-schools and kindergartens and MTI in the region have changed minority language status. For example, a small but increasing number of parents have begun to speak Finnish/Meänkieli with their children. In addition, Finnish immigrants and interlingual-marriage families are becoming more aware of the social advantage of bilingualism. The upcoming new minority policy should positively affect the status and reproduction of minority languages.

Swedish Finns are without doubt the most dominant minority group in Sweden, but participation rates in MTI are, in general, rapidly declining. In the Torne valley region, the decline in MTI is most marked in Gällivare, Övertorneå and Kiruna, but even Haparanda has declining figures (Winsa, 1998). Hence, even among the Swedish Finns, the promotion of St Fi. in the Torne valley is meagre. Pajala is the only municipality showing a positive development in terms of participation rates in MTI. Pajala also reflects the most positive attitude towards Meänkieli.

The general decline in the acquisition of Finnish is especially apparent in the number of pre-school children with Finnish as a home language. A major obstacle for Swedish Finns maintaining Finnish lies in the fact that they have no particular territory of their own where Finnish can be used in the local public and official community, and in that a fairly high percentage of immigrants perceive themselves as permanent, although they often hold Finnish citizenship. The only natural communication in Finnish is performed within the family, with closest friends and within the local Finnish associations (*Suomi seura*). In these circumstances, Swedish Finns find it hard to develop communities where Finnish has official functions (aside from media and newspapers), e.g. in shops, post offices or banks. This reality hampers the bilingual efforts of this community.

With regard to Romany Chib in Sweden, there are few statistics available on the inclination of Roma towards acquiring Romany Chib. However, in general, the Roma have little interest in participating in MTI (SIV, 1996a), or in developing a homogeneous and elaborated Romany Chib. There are several reasons for this lack of interest. One is the lack of competent teachers, teaching aids and text-books. The Roma group/s is/are small and diverse, scattered all around Sweden, speaking several varieties/languages. Therefore, a textbook in a different variety can be rejected due to the deviation from the spoken form. Another general problem for the society is that a high percentage of Roma pupils, especially females, frequently drop out and never complete primary school. An obvious consequence is reflected in high levels of illiteracy, i.e. both in the home and in the second/third languages. Even MTI may be interpreted as intruding on cultural values in the Roma community (SIV, 1996a).

Language death

Most of the mutually non-intelligible Swedish varieties/languages are extinct, and only a few thousand older people speak the remaining varieties. In the 1960s, a small revival effort took place to promote the Swedish vari-eties/languages. However, this effort did not gain wide acceptance,[37] perhaps because the national Swedish Radio Broadcasting Corporation, up to the 1970–1980s, did not accept journalists and newscasters who spoke a variety other than the commonly acknowledged 'neutral' standard. During the last decade a more tolerant approach has been taken and some Swedish varieties are allowed if the dialects are not too marked. Even a few journalists with a slight Finnish 'accent' have been hired to work on radio and TV. Nevertheless, in general, a marked 'foreign' accent or variety is a social handicap, especially in the case of Tornedalen Swedish with a Finnish/Sami intonation. A common implicit assumption is that all public performances should be presented in the standard form. The resistance to the penetration of varieties into the public sphere is prob-ably a legacy of normative language policy.

Local varieties are stressed in local school plans in a few regions. However, these efforts for the most part are not aimed at re-introducing the local varieties, but rather are mostly directed at strengthening the identity of the community. The regionalisation of Europe also means the territorialisation of language vari-eties.

At present there is no strong motivation for maintaining bilingualism among the Swedish Finns. It is probable that the number of Finnish-speakers will decline steeply within 30 years (Janulf, 1998). Finnish in southern Sweden will probably not survive – except perhaps in Stockholm – unless there are new waves of Finnish immigrants who revive the language. The new minority policy, as well as the mergers of Nordic companies and transnational cooperation, counter the assimilation process, but it is doubtful if these positive top-down processes are sufficient to maintain Finnish as an everyday language in local communities.

The Sami languages in Sweden are the most seriously endangered, despite revival efforts. South Sami is spoken by not more than a few hundred persons, perhaps fewer. North Sami has the best opportunity for survival because the Sami community in Norway also has North Sami as its normative variety and the language has a more established position. Few people in Sweden master Sami in official settings, and it seems that the Sami parliament of Sweden has not given the language issue high priority, though it supports bilingual publications and officially holds quatra-lingual sessions. If a major change does not occur, the only variety that may have a future is North Sami. The status of Sami is, in a number of domains, moving towards becoming a relic with strong symbolic value for the Sami culture. Identification with the Sami language reinforces the symbolic value of language through language-based activities in theatre, literature, traditional Sami songs (*jojk*), music, radio, TV, a few hours a week in MTI, and other public activities.

The Finnish spoken in northern Sweden is unlikely to disappear, but it will probably shrink in domains and in numbers of speakers. People living along the border with Finland will continue to speak Meänkieli/Finnish. The general opinion in the region regarding Meänkieli/Finnish is, however, divergent and confused. Meänkieli is often socially stigmatised and perceived as a low-status vernacular language, whereas St Fi. is associated with something alien but more prestigious. A local association supports Meänkieli (and Finnish), whereas the Swedish-Finnish association (NAFS), which has weak support in the Torne valley region, supports St Fi.

In general, those who acknowledge the local vernacular/language more actively promote bilingualism, whereas those favouring St Fi. often have a hostile attitude towards bilingualism, or favour it only as a symbol without any practical significance or implication. Those opposed to Meänkieli fear isolation, stronger stigmatisation and, in general, greater obstacles to the maintenance of a local language with few speakers. Very few native Tornedalians favour St Fi. in practice. Thus, the low-culture community is divided into three opinions: those in favour of Meänkieli, those in favour of St Fi. or those in favour of monolingualism. Officially, about 40% support Meänkieli, some 40% support St Fi. and some 20% want to abolish all voluntary and mandatory instruction in Finnish (Winsa, 1998). Monolingualism is still sometimes considered to carry social advantage in the region (Lundh *et al.*, 1997).

Pidginisation of minority languages

Meänkieli and Swedish-Finnish in their informal spoken form are strongly influenced by Swedish lexical items, but the syntax and morpho-phonological structure remain and are based on the original Finnish dialectal forms. Meänkieli has retained its North Finnish grammatical structure and therefore cannot be seen as a creole or pidginised language.[38] (For definitions, see Mühlhäusler, 1974.) Meänkieli has preserved linguistic features which are lost in other Finnish varieties, and is therefore often perceived by Finns as an archaic form of Finnish.

Romany Chib is strongly influenced by lexical and grammatical items from the various majority languages of the immigrant Roma. Little linguistic research has, however, been carried out, and pidgins, amalgamations, and Creole may be evident.

Influences on language planning

Based on the discussion about language and minorities in this monograph, the main principles influencing language planning can be summarised in the following scheme (see Figure 3) (Winsa, 1997, 1998):

- in social life there are no equal languages/varieties;

- the status of a language/variety equals its instrumental value for social mobility;
- language is associated with individual and collective identity;
- speaking a high status variety reinforces self-esteem;
- success in education, enterprise and creativity is associated with self-esteem;
- linguistic role models are the spoken forms in formal and official society;
- wherever a spoken form is excluded from society, the public labels it as a 'dialect', or stigmatises the lesser-used community language.
- a group speaking a minority language, which is excluded from society life develops negative attitudes towards the vernacular and weakens self-esteem.

Gesellschaft	Formal High culture	Public	High status 'Languages'/varieties	
				Economic class
Gemeinschaft	Low culture Private	Informal	Low status Varieties/'dialects'	

Figure 3 The main principles influencing language planning

Hence, the state defines the collective identity of the group through language planning by bringing the language of the low culture into the higher domains. Complete success in such planning is obviously impossible, because once such a plan 'succeeds' a new low culture variety/language must result in order to maintain the distinction between society-community.

This scheme is illustrated in the Torne valley region by St Fi. which belongs to the high culture of Finland, and hence has strong support among Swedish Finns and the high culture of Sweden, and by the low culture language, Meänkieli, which by definition must be rejected – as long as it belongs to the domain of low culture. The most efficient way to change this underlying covert language planning is to support the weak but persistent bottom-up processes of language development in the region. The positive treatment of Meänkieli in the Government bill on minority issues is hopefully based on the local demand and a will to implement an efficient language policy. The ratification of the European Charter will have a profound impact on the border municipalities, the status of Meänkieli/Finnish, reproduction, and cross-border contacts.

The future of minority languages in Sweden

The old saying that one should not listen to the words of the politicians, but to their deeds is useful in order to understand language planning in Sweden. The official policy has often been supportive, but this in practice has frequently been merely rhetoric. In the Torne valley region, the state has maintained the position that it promotes bilingualism, whereas the practice has been directed towards assimilation. In the 1960s, the weak school performance of the Tornedalian children was defined by linguists as being a consequence of illiteracy in the mother tongue. The linguists wanted to introduce voluntary/mandatory study of Finnish, but were overruled by the politicians who wanted to strengthen instruction in Swedish. From the 1960s through to the 1990s, the approach to immigrant and minority languages was once again supportive, even inscribed in the constitution and backed up by research on language acquisition, but in practice the traditional assimilationist policy has dominated by consensus.

In general, the public debate has an ethnocentric perspective. Expenditure for education of immigrant groups is questioned (e.g. second language and mother tongue instruction), but hardly any discussion occurs on how the costs of language instruction for the majority population affects the economy (Hyltenstam & Tuomela, 1996: 13) or what the costs in economic and social terms are of illiteracy in L1 and L2. Home language reform from the very beginning has been in practice mainly ideological rhetoric. Despite the fact that nearly all first and second language researchers have supported the idea of instruction in the mother tongue, public opinion has nevertheless been reluctant to support MTI.

Apart from some minor attempts to introduce a truly integrated policy where minorities and immigrants have possibilities to develop their own civil societies, an assimilation policy is the generally applied ideology in language planning in Sweden. The lack of competence in Swedish as well as in the mother tongue among immigrants is once again perceived as being a result of deficient instruction in Swedish.

In the jargon of modern political discourse, it is fashionable to speak of 'integration', when in practice this often means assimilation. Without the pressure from international minority rights conventions, the Swedish language policy would probably be explicitly termed as assimilationist. Politicians reflect the general opinion, and that opinion favours the image of a homogeneous nation.

This nationalistic attitude is not one that is reflected upon; rather it is felt to be a natural part of the Swedish monolingual identity, not one derived from a long tradition of language planning. There is little will to discuss efficient language planning in terms of socioeconomic development and the symbolic value immigrant and minority languages have for collective identity. As long as this general attitude prevails, immigrants and minorities will be perceived as a threat to Swedish nationalism, with subsequent lesser representation in politics and public institutions.

Role models for a true integration policy are the Jews and the Estonians. They are well integrated and still have been able to maintain their particular cultures. Both groups are well organised as distinct communities within Sweden and are probably in general socioeconomic terms in a more favourable position than the average Swede and certainly better off than the immigrant and minority groups.

The future of minority languages in the European context

For many centuries, Latin represented the elite culture of Europe. There was little awareness of the possibility of using a standardised vernacular as the basis for an imagined nation-state.

The institutionalisation of European culture and languages is today the basis for the development of a new citizenship, which includes all the officially recognised languages of Europe. European discourse will – once again – be the elite culture of Europe. This time, however, the aim is to preserve linguistic and cultural diversity. With the enlargement of the European Union, the official languages will grow in number to at least 17 (and more within two decades), and a complete translation and interpretation service would demand 272 translation and interpretation combinations. The enormous expenditure needed to maintain these services for all languages will be questioned whenever the European Union faces a period of recession. There is an ongoing informal process whereby English is slowly becoming the international lingua franca, where the smaller officially recognised languages of Europe are informally being deleted from the public high culture of Europe. Small official languages of the European Union will be defended strongly by the member states using those languages, but eventually the European Union will be forced to realise the economic benefits of fewer official languages.

The instrumental approach of Swedish language planning promotes expansion of English language domains. This ongoing process of Anglification may progressively displace and shrink the use of Swedish in official domains. Teachers and students will acquire an analytical but not a fully adequate English. Researchers and professionals will, on the other hand, seemingly not acquire proficient Swedish in their professional field and incomplete English in other fields, i.e. they will not acquire full literacy in Swedish in every domain of their occupations. The discrepancy between a context-reduced English and a context-bound Swedish may widen the gap between analytic rational reasoning and emotions and empathy (cf. Teleman & Westman, 1997). Some 18% of all schools of adult education and *gymnasiums* already offer subjects with English as the medium of instruction, while a few schools are entirely English medium (Hyltenstam, 1996). The leading and normative institutions in this process are universities, and the diglossia already visible within faculties of medicine and technical sciences will most likely increase and widen the gap between informal Swedish and formal English. This is perceived as a threat to Swedish democracy (Gunnarsson & Öhman, 1997:79f). Major Swedish companies already often have English as their internal working language, although smaller enterprises often lack sufficient competence in foreign languages (Expr, 1979), but public research in this field is rare. Nevertheless, the increasing influence of English has affected occupational titles. Even in entirely Swedish-speaking companies, these titles are increasingly expressed in English. Occupational titles in English are perceived as one means of promoting an image of a highly skilled international company. The Swedish Air Force, as well as other institutions, is preparing for European cooperation by replacing Swedish with English in all official communication. This ongoing process of Anglification has also been taken up by the advertising business. TV advertisements in English are more frequent because such advertising raises the image of company products. The loss of domains for Swedish is only just beginning.

Correspondence

All correspondence should be directed to Dr Birger Winsa, Department of Finnish, Stockholm University, S-106 91 Stockholm, Sweden (birger.winsa@finska.su.se).

Notes

1. For definitions, see e.g. Baldauf (1990, 1994).
2. For the use of the terms high–low cultures, see Gellner (1994). Another common dichotomy is elite and popular cultures, see Burke (1994).
3. Professor Hyltenstam at Stockholm University has provided valuable comments regarding bilingual education. I am grateful for his assistance.
4. A probably decisive influence on Swedish minority policy will be the position of the minority survey conducted by the EU-commission DG XXII, which has already mapped all autochthonous minorities of the EU (Nelde *et al.*, 1996). In 1997, the new member states, Sweden, Finland and Austria, were included in the report. In the Swedish report only Sami and Tornedalians are termed as territorial minorities, whereas the Swedish Finns are termed as immigrants (EUROMOSAIC 1999; http://www.uoc.es/euromosaic/).
5. There is an increasing European and Swedish tendency for 'dialect' groups to claim to speak minority languages, e.g. Bavarian and English in Scotland are claimed to be autochthonous languages. 'Scots' is represented in the European Bureau for Lesser Used Languages.
6. The St Fi. pronoun (*minun*) has a genitive case, whereas the Meänkieli pronoun (*mie*) stands in nominative, like the corresponding sentence in Swedish: *Jag måste gå.*
7. The term 'mother tongue' is used in a variety of ways in the literature and for this reason is not a very useful term. In Swedish, the term 'mother tongue instruction' is used for vernacular teaching, and the term is used in that sense in this monograph.
8. The term 'home language' refers to languages other than Swedish.
9. The Barents region incorporates the following: northern Sweden, northern Norway and northern Finland, as well as north-west parts of Russia.
10. The European currency unit (the euro) was worth about US$ 0.85 in September 1998.
11. Up to 1917, Finland was part of Russia, but the Russian language never had any significance in the border region.
12. As there is limited information about Yiddish and the Jewish community due to its small size and the declining number of Yiddish speakers, most information about this minority is summarised in this section.
13 Lars Levi Laestadius (1800–1861) initiated the Laestadian religious movement in the early 19th century. He had Sami and Swedish as mother tongues, and acquired Finnish in the northernmost municipalities. Finnish became the first language of the Laestadians (along with some Sami). Lars Levi Laestadius wrote books of sermons in Finnish, printed in the German Gothic type. These sermons form the basis of the Laestadian movement, and are sometimes still read from the German script. This old Finnish has been preserved due to a resistance to any linguistic change, and is considered an archaic form by most Finns.
14. The B-language level means that the learner has some previous knowledge in a language. The C-language is the beginners' level.
15. Obviously, recency of immigration partly determines interest in MTI. Finns arrived in the 1960–1970s, whereas Arabic-speakers immigrated primarily in the 1980s. However, Spanish speakers emigrated for the most part from Chile in the 1970s; nevertheless their interest in MTI is fairly high. Relations between Sweden and Finland structured by tradition may contain factors influencing present use of MTI.
16. Compared with Norway the difference is revealing. Some 1700 pupils in primary school study Sami, of whom some 50% have Sami as a first language (Svonni, 1996).
17. By comparison, three municipalities in northern Norway have mandatory Sami for all pupils in primary school.
18. In 1997/98 126 pupils from Haparanda of 1365 in the municipality, and 137 from Tornio.
19. The process of language standardisation had already begun in the early 16th century, e.g. in a decree in France 1539. Sweden was an early participant in this process. In Germany treatises on pronunciation and spelling were disseminated in the later 17th century. Newspaper advertisements in England and Scotland, which promised to eradicate the dialects, were popular in the 18th century (Houston, 1988: 206ff).

20. H standard 'high standard', and L status 'low status'.
21. However, the pedagogical projects in Finnish continue. In 1997, 0.36 million euro was allocated by the state to the bilingual school in Haparanda, and to pedagogical projects (SOU, 1997b: 164).
22. Standardisation and the use of written language for schooling for Roma is a problem that has only recently begun to be examined. Hübschmannová and Neustupný (1996) have discussed this issue for the Slovak and Czech dialect of Romani.
23. Weber's ideas in relation to literacy development could be discussed further. Current research shows an inconsistent correspondence between economic development and literacy, although current functional illiteracy in many western countries corresponds with unemployment and low income (OECD, 1995). 'The literature on development economics evidences that the research on the relationship between social development and economic growth has taken at least four different strands: (i) that social development is a product of economic growth; (ii) that economic growth and social development are two unrelated events; (iii) that neither social development nor economic growth is a primary cause of the other, but they are interdependent; (iv) that social development precedes economic growth' (Mazumdar 1996: I). [However,] 'adult literacy can be considered the most excellent overall quality-of-life indicator' (Mazumdar, 1996: III). Mazumdar (1996: VIII) concludes that 'observation has been drawn that there is no uniform causal relation between economic growth and social development'. (See also Saha, 1996; Temple & Johnson, 1998.)
24. It is well known that Roma families were moved to Finland, but earlier reports had not been able to track Roma resettlement to any particular region in Finland. This report is not based on scientific evidence, and may therefore be misleading.
25. However, through satellite TV, many foreign-produced programmes are available.
26. This is not an argument accepted by the Deaf Community; it reflects profound ignorance of the linguistics of Sign Language, and is based on political strategies, rather than general linguistic rights. One major reason why Sign Language is excluded from the report, and from the European Charter for Regional or Minority Languages, is that the Council of Europe has focused a lot of attention on European territorial minority languages and groups after 1989, i.e. after the break down of the political structures in Eastern Europe (cf. EC, 1994). The new rapidly emerging geo-political discourse suggested that minority groups were perceived as possible sources of ethnic conflicts; by supporting their linguistic rights, the risk of future conflicts could be reduced. Sign Language speakers are not generally recognised as a particular ethnic group, nor perceived as being a spark to ignite social tensions.
27. The first motion written in Finnish, presented to the municipal council in Haparanda, caused irritation among bilingual politicians. One delegate argued that he could not read St Fi. and therefore motions in Finnish were unacceptable (NSD, 1998-03-21). Thus, the prevalence of illiteracy is one means of maintaining a monolingual society.
28. Germans were not allowed to constitute more than half of the members of the city councils (*rådman*).
29. In analogy with, e.g. the written language bias in linguistic theory building (Linell, 1982).
30. Latin had already begun to lose its dominant position in the 17th century, especially within natural sciences (Sörlin, 1994:171).
31. With the advent of electronic dictionaries, alphabetical order has lost its function. Instead, we may anticipate databases for all written words in any form, tense or case ending. The improvement means that a foreigner can translate texts written in, say Finnish. At present it is nearly impossible to find the nominative case for many nouns, or the first infinitive for many verbs if one does not have a well-developed awareness of the grammatical structure of Finnish. (Oral information on categorisation, interpreter B. Romppanen)
32. See Atkinson's (1999) book on the transactions of the Royal Society of London for a comparison of developments in England.
33. Scandinavia, parts of Eastern Europe and Germany kept Gothic type until the 18th

century. In other parts of Europe, Roman type already dominated by the end of the 16th century (Houston, 1988: 211f).

34. The positivistic paradigm continued, though, in a 'modern' form in the work of Chomsky where a 'true' and 'pure' language was to be found in innate structures, and through difficult to grasp transformational parameters.

35. The total budget of NAFS is claimed to be about 32.6 million euro. In comparison, STA has a budget of some 0.11 million euro a year.

36. A pilot project in Kiruna aims to monitor reindeer via satellite linked to computers.

37. Some representatives of 'dialect' communities have, however, complained that their 'languages' were excluded from the recent Minority reports, e.g. Skanish and Älvdalen varieties spoken in Skåne and central west parts of Sweden.

38. One could perhaps describe Meänkieli in terms of amalgamation, but that runs the risk of developing a new stigmatising term which associates the language with backwardness and linguistic confusion.

References

Allén, S., Dahlstedt, K-K., Fant, G., Marc-Wogau, K. and Teleman, U. (1967) *Språk, språkvård och kommunikation*. Stockholm: Prisma.

Allén, S., Loman, B. and Sigurd, S. (1986) *Svenska Akademien och svenska språket*. Stockholm: Norstedts.

Ammon, U. (1998) *Ist Deutsch noch internationale Wissenschaftssprache? Englisch auch für die Lehre an den deutschsprachigen Hochschulen*. Berlin/New York: Walter de Gruyter.

Anderson, B. (1991) *Imagined Communities*. London/New York: Verso.

Arnstberg, K-O. (1989) Zigenare. In I. Svanberg and H. Runblom (eds) *Det mångkulturella Sverige* (pp. 484–490). Stockholm: Gidlunds bokförlag.

Atkinson, D. (1999) *Scientific Discourse in Sociohistorical Context: The Philosophical Transactions of the Royal Society of London, 1675–1975*. Mahwah, NJ: Lawrence Erlbaum.

Baldauf, R.B., Jr (1990) Language planning: Corpus planning. In W. Grabe *et al.* (eds) *Annual Review of Applied Linguistics*, 10 (pp. 3–12). Cambridge: Cambridge University Press.

Baldauf, R.B., Jr (1994) 'Unplanned' language policy and planning. In W. Grabe *et al.* (eds) *Annual Review of Applied Linguistics* 14 (pp. 82–89). Cambridge: Cambridge University Press.

Barton, H.A. (1977) Popular education in Sweden: Theory and practice. In J.A. Leith (ed.) *Facets of Education in the Eighteenth Century. Studies on Voltaire and the Eighteenth Century 167* (pp. 523–541). Oxford: Oxford University Press.

Beijer, M. (1996) *Undervisningen av minoritetselever med flykting- och invandrarbakgrund i Sverige* [How to Help Minority Children to Become Multilingual] (pp. 159–164). Helsingfors: Hakapaino OY.

Bernstein, B. (1971) *Class, Codes and Control. Volume 1. Theoretical Studies Towards a Sociology of Language*. London: Routledge.

Björkquist, L-M. and Henrysson, S. (1963) *Standardprovsresultat för tvåspråkiga elever i norra Sverige*. Stockholm: Rapport nr 6. Pedagogisk- psykologiska institutionen Lärarhögskolan i Stockholm.

Boyd, S. and Gadelii, K.E. (1999) Vem tillhör talgemenskapen? Om jiddisch i Sverige. In K. Hyltenstam (ed.) *Sveriges sju inhemska språk* (pp 299–328). Lund: Studentlitteratur.

Bromé, J. (1945) *Jämtlands och Härjedalens Historia. Andra delen*. Stockholm: Norsteds.

Burke, P. (1991) *Heu domine, adsunt Turcae*: A sketch for a social history of post-medieval Latin. In P. Burke and R. Burke (eds) *Language, Self, and Society* (pp. 23–50). Cambridge: Polity Press.

Burke, P. (1994) *Popular Culture in Early Modern Europe*. Aldershot: Scolar Press.

CE (1993) *Recommendation 1203. On Roma in Europe*. Strasbourg: Council of Europe.

CE (1995) *The Situation of Regional or Minority Languages in Europe. Contributions Submitted by National Delegations*. Strasbourg: Council of Europe.

Cipolla, C.M. (1969) *Literacy and Development in the West*. Harmondsworth: Penguin Books.

Cobarrubias, J. (1983) Language planning: The state of the art. In J. Cobarrubias and J.A. Fishman (eds) *Progress in Language Planning. International Perspectives* (pp. 3–26). Berlin: Walter de Gruyter.

Coulmas, F. (1992) *Language and Economy*. Oxford: Blackwell Publishers.

Coulombe, P.A. (1993) Language rights, individual and communal. *Language Problems and Language Planning* 17, 140–52.

Den Nordiska Språkkonventionen (DNS) (1994). *Den Nordiska Språkkonventionen*. Helsingfors: Nordiska språk- och informationscentret.

Ds (1994) *Finska i Sverige. Ett inhemskt språk. Regeringskansliet Utbildningsdepartementet*. Ds 1994:97. Stockholm.

Ds (1997) *Romer i Sverige - tillsammans i förändring*. Regeringskansliet. Inrikesdepartementet. 1997:49. Stockholm.

D'souza, J. (1996) Creativity and language planning: The case of Indian English and Singapore English. *Language Problems and Language Planning* 20, 244–262.

EC [Thornberry, P. and Estebanez, M.A.M. authors] (1994) *The Council of Europe and Minorities*. Strasbourg: Council of Europe.

Ekenberg, S. (1994) Nationalism in the Swedish welfare state. *Migration* 3/4, 43–62.

Enc. (1995) *Nationalencyklopedin*. Höganäs: Bokförlaget Bra Böcker.

EP (1997) *Lesser Used Languages in Austria, Finland and Sweden*. Working Document. Directorate-General for Research. Education and Culture Series. W-5. European Parliament. Luxemburg.

Eriksen, K. (1991) Norwegian and Swedish educational policies vis-à-vis non-dominant ethnic groups, 1850–1940. In J. Tomiak, K.E. Eriksen, A. Kazamias and R. Okey (eds) *Schooling, Educational Policy and Ethnic Identity* (pp. 63–86). New York: New York University Press.

Eriksson, J. (1997) *Partition and Redemption. A Machiavellian Analysis of Sami and Basque Patriotism*. Umeå: Umeå universitet.

EUROMOSAIC (1999) *Report on the Swedish Minorities*. Brussels: EU-Commission. http://www.uoc.es/euromosaic/

Ewerlöf, S. (1987) *Finska genom skönlitteraturen*. PUFF. Södertälje kommun. Skolförvaltningen. Stencil.

Expr 1979. *Språk i små och medelstora företag*. Stockholm: Sveriges Exportråd.

Fehrman, C. and Westling, H. (1995) *Lund and Learning*. Lund: Studentlitteratur.

Forsgren, T. (1988) *Samisk kyrko- och undervisningslitteratur i Sverige 1619–1850*. Forskningsarkivet. Umeå: Umeå universitet.

Fraurud, K. and Hyltenstam, K. (1999) Språkkontakt och språkbevarande: Romani i Sverige. In K. Hyltenstam (ed.) *Sveriges sju inhemska språk* (pp. 241–298). Lund: Studentlitteratur.

Fries, S. (1996) Lärdomsspråket under frihetstiden. In L. Moberg and M.Westman (eds) *Svenskan i tusen år* (pp. 88–103). Stockholm: Norstedts.

Fris, A-M. (1982) *Policies for Minority Education : A Comparative Study of Britain and Sweden* [Studies in Comparative and International Education 7]. Stockholm: Institution of international education.

Gee, J.P. (1996) *Social Linguistics and Literacies*. Great Britain: Taylor and Francis.

Gellner, E. (1994) *Nations and Nationalism*. Oxford: Blackwell.

Gluck, D., Neuman, A. and Stare, J. (1997) *Sveriges judar. Deras historia tro och traditioner*. Stockholm: Judiska museet i Stockholm.

Gunnarsson, B-L. (1997). On the sociohistorical construction of scientific discourse. In B.L. Gunnarsson,. P. Linell, and B. Nordberg (eds) *The Construction of Professional Discourse* (pp. 99–126). London/New York: Longman.

Gunnarsson, B-L. and Öhman, K. (1997) *Det internationaliserade universitetet*. Uppsala: Uppsala universitet.

Gunnarsson, B-L. and Skolander, B. (1991) *Fackspråkens framväxt*. Terminologi och ordförråd från tre sekler. Institutionen för Nordiska språk. Uppsala: Uppsala universitet.

Hannikainen, L. (1996) The status of minorities, indigenous peoples and immigrant and refugee groups in four Nordic states. *Nordic Journal of International Law* 65, 1–71.

Hansegård, N-E. (1968) *Tvåspråkighet eller halvspråkighet*. Stockholm: Aldus/Bonnier.

Hansegård, N-E. (1990) *Den norrbottensfinska språkfrågan. En återblick i halv-språkighetsdebatten*. Uppsala Multiethnic Papers 9. Uppsala: Centre for Multiethnic Research.

Haugen, E. (1987) *Blessings of Babel. Bilingualism and Language Planning*. Berlin: Mouton de Gruyter.

Hazell, B. (1997) Folket som försvann. *Invandrare & Minoriteter* 6,17–20. [Stockholm]

Hedenborg, S. (1997) *Det gåtfulla folket*. Barns villkor och uppfattningar av barnet i 1700-talets Stockholm. Stockholm: Almqvist & Wiksell International.

Hederyd, O. (1992) *Haparanda efter 1809*. Tornedalens historia III. Haparanda: Birkkarlens Förlag.

Henrysson, S. and Flodin, J. (1992) *Samernas skolgång till 1956*. Umeå: Umeå Universitet.

Henrysson, S. and Ljung, B-O. (1967) *Tvåspråkigheten i Tornedalen*. En studie av standardprovresultat i årskurserna 3 och 6. Rapport nr 26 från Pedagogisk-psykologiska institutionen. Lärarhögskolan i Stockholm.

Hernlund, H. (1883) *Svenska skriftspråkets reglerande 1691–1739*. Stockholm: Norstedt.

Houston, R.A. (1988) *Literacy in Early Modern Europe*. London/New York: Longman.

Hübschmannová, M. and Neustupný, J.V. (1996) The Slovak-and-Czech dialect of Romani and its standardization. *International Journal of the Sociology of Language* 120, 85–109.

Huovinen, S. (ed.) (1986) *Finland i det svenska riket*. Stockholm: Kulturfonden för Sverige och Finland.

Hyltenstam, K. (1996) Svenskan, ett minoritetsspråk i Europaoch i världen? In A.-M. Ivars, A.-M Londen, L. Nyholm, M. Saari, and M. Tandefelt (eds) *Svenskans beskrivning* 21 (pp 9–33). Lund: Lund University Press.

Hyltenstam, K. and Svonni, M. (1990) *Forskning om tvåspråksbehärskning hos samiska barn*. Stockholm: Stockholms Universitet.

Hyltenstam, K. and Tuomela, V. (1996) Hemspråksundervisningen. In K. Hyltenstam (ed.) *Tvåspråkighet med förhinder? Invandrar- och tvåspråkighetsundervisning i Sverige* (pp. 9–109). Lund: Studentlitteratur.

Idberger, Gunnar (1989) *Allmänbegåvning inom Milo ON 1987 och 1988*. Värnpliktsverket Ovre Norrlands Värnpliktskontor. Boden. Stencil.

INV rapport (1997) *Invandrar rapport*. Argång 25, nr 1. Borås.

Jaakkola, M. (1989a) *Skolstrejken i Rinkeby: en undersökning om Sverigefinnarnas etniska mobilisering i en Stockholmsförort*. Centrum för invandringsforskning. Stockholm University.

Jaakkola, M. (1989b) *Den etniska mobiliseringen av sverigefinnarna*. Centrum för invandringsforskning. Stockholm University.

Janulf, P. (1997) *Utvärdering av utvecklingsprojekten för finskspråkiga elever läsåret 1996/97*. Botkyrka Kommun.

Janulf, P. (1998) *En jämförande undersökning av tvåspråkighet bland sverigefinska och finlandssvenska grundskoleelever år 1980*. Finska institutionen. Stockholms Universitet.

Jarman, R. (1994) The popularity of the Tejano radio station format as evidence of regional South Texas 'Tejano' identity. Paper presented at Hispanic Language and Social Identity, February 10–12, 1994, Albuquerque.

Johansson, E. (1998) *Alphabeta Varia Orality, Reading and Writing in the History of Literacy*. Album Religionum Umense 1. Umeå: Umeå University.

Johansson, H. (1983) Läroverket i Haparanda - en resurs med dubbel kulturförankring. In K. Pekkari (ed.) *Tornedalens skola 150 år* (pp 37–46). Tornedalica nr 40. Luleå.

Johansson, H. (1989) *Har kaosforskning och undervisning av finsktalande elever i svensk grundskola något med varandra att göra*. Utvärdering av pedagogisk utvecklingsverksamhet i fjorton kommuner. Arbetsrapport 4. Högskolan i Luleå.

Johansson, H. and Johansson, S. (1968) *Nomadskolan. En historisk översikt*. Umeå: Umeå Universitet.

Johansson, L., Lindvall, P., Ljungmark, E. and Melchior, A. (1979) *Svensk blandning*. Stockholm: Fakta & Färdigheter. Akademiförlaget.

Jokinen, M-L. (1996) Sverigefinska kultursträvanden. *Finnarnas historia i Sverige 3. Tiden efter 1945* (pp. 379–424). Helsingfors.

Judiska församlingen i Stockholm. Brochure. Stockholm.

Kaplan, R.B. and Baldauf, R.B., Jr (1997) *Language Planning from Practice to Theory.* Clevedon: Multilingual Matters.

Klinge, M., Knapas, R., Leikola, A. and Stormberg, J. (1988) *Kungliga Akademien i Åbo 1640–1808.* Helsinki: Otava.

Korhonen, O. (1997) Hur samiskan blev samiska. I Westergren, E. and Ahl, H. (eds) *Mer än ett språk* (pp. 79–115). Stockholm: Norstedts.

Kostoulas-Makrakis, N. (1995) *Language Maintenance or Shift? A Study of Greek Background Students in Sweden* [Studies in Comparative and International Education]. Stockholm: Institute of International Education. Stockholm University.

Labba, P. S. (1997) *Samiska språket inom samiska institutioner.* Samiskt språkråd. Sametinget. Kiruna: Stencil.

Labov, W. (1974) Logiken i 'Nonstandard English'. In Loman, B. (ed.) *Barnspråk i klassamhälle* (pp. 188–215). Lund: Liber Läromedel.

Lainio, J. (1997) Swedish-Finnish. In H. Goebl, P.H. Nelde and Z. Stary (eds) *Kontaktlinguistik Contact Linguistics Linguistique de contact* (pp. 982–992). Berlin, New York: Walter de Gruyter.

Lainio, J. (1999). Språk, genetik och geografi - om kontinuitetsproblematiken och debatten om finska som minoritetsspråk. In K. Hyltenstam (ed.) *Sveriges sju inhemska språk* (pp. 138–204). Lund: Studentlitteratur.

Lainio, J. and Wande, E. (1996) Finskan i utbildningsväsendet och sverigefinnarnas utbildning i Sverige. In J. Lainio (ed.) *Finnarnas historia i Sverige 3. Tiden efter 1945* (pp. 311–378). Helsingfors.

Lange, S. (1996) Prästrannsakningarna på 1600-talet och det svenska riksskriftspråkets framväxt. In *Språket lever* (pp. 173–180). Utgiven av Svenska språknämnden. Stockholm.

Liebkind, K. (1989) Conceptual approaches to ethnic identity. In K. Liebkind (ed.) *New Identities in Europe* (pp. 13–40). Aldershot: Gower in association with European Science Foundation.

Lindberg, B. (1984) *De lärdes modersmål. Latin, humanism och vetenskap i 1700–talets Sverige.* Acta universitatis Gothoburgensis. Göteborgs Universitet.

Lindberg, I. (1996a) Svenskundervisning för vuxna invandrare (sfi). In K. Hyltenstam (ed.) *Tvåspråkighet med förhinder? Invandrar- och tvåspråkighetsundervisning i Sverige* (pp. 224–284). Lund: Studentlitteratur.

Lindberg, I. (1996b) *Språka samman.* Stockholm: Natur och Kultur.

Lindgren, B. (1997) *Stadgar för Nordiska språkrådet* [Statutes for the Nordic Language Board]. Svenska språknämnden. Stockholm. Stencil.

Lindqvist, H. (1995) *Historien om Sverige.* Stockholm: Norstedts.

Lindroth, S. (1975) *Svensk lärdomshistoria. Medeltiden Reformationstiden.* Stockholm: Norstedt & Söner.

Lindroth, S. (1981) *Svensk lärdomshistoria. Gustavianska tiden. Utgiven av Gunnar Eriksson.* Stockholm: Norstedt & Söner.

Lindroth, S. (1989) *Svensk lärdomshistoria. Stormaktstiden.* Stockholm: Norstedts.

Linell, P. (1982) *The Written Language Bias in Linguistics.* Linköping University. http://english-server.hss.cmu.edu/langs/linell/

Lpo (1994) *Läroplaner för det Obligatoriska Skolväsendet och de Frivilliga Skolformerna.* (National Curriculum) Utbildningsdepartementet. Stockholm.

Lundh, A., Ramsby, F. and Waara, P. (1997) *Språkskola och kulturell identitet - utvärdering av ett försök med integrerade skolklasser inom grundskolan i Haparanda.* Umeå. Stencil.

Mazumdar, K. (1996) An analysis of causal flow between social development and economic growth. *American Journal of Economics & Sociology* 55 (3), 361–384.

McArthur, T. (1986) *Worlds of Reference.* Cambridge: Cambridge University Press.

Media Sápmi (1999) *Etablerandet av radiostudio och samisk mediautbildning i Jokkmokk Projektplan. John E Utsi.* Jokkmokk. Stencil.

Montell, E. (1978) *Halländsk historia.* Halmstad: Spektra Förlag.

Mühlhäusler, P. (1974) *Pidginization and Simplification of Language*. Pacific Linguistics. Series B, No. 26. Canberra: Australian National University.

Mühlhäusler, P. (1996) *Linguistic Ecology*. London: Routledge.

Municio, I. (1987) *Från lag till bruk. Hemspråksreformens genomförande*. Centrum för invandrarforskning. Stockholm Studies in Politics No. 31. Stockholm University.

Nelde, P., Strubell, M, and Williams, G. (1996) *Euromosaic. The Production and Reproduction of the Minority Language Groups in the European Union*. Luxembourg, Brussels: European Commission Document.

NSD 97-11-02, 1998-03-03, 03-21. *Norrländska Social Demokraten*. Luleå. (local newsp.)

OECD 1995. *Literacy, Economy and Society*. Organization for Economic Cooperation and Development. OECD, Paris. Statistics Canada, Ottawa.

Österberg, T. (1961) *Bilingualism. And the First School Language - An Educational Problem Illustrated by Results from a Swedish Dialect Area*. Umeå.

Paulston, C. B. (1983) *Forskning om tvåspråkighet*. Stockholm: Skolöverstyrelsen.

Prop. 1995/96:161. En radio och TV i allmänhetens tjänst 1997–2001. Proposition. Riksdagen. Stockholm. (Government Bill).

Prop. 1998/99:143. Nationella minoriteter i Sverige. Proposition. Riksdagen. Stockholm. (Government Bill).

Rapport (1990) *Zigenska elevers skolsituation. Rapporter från Stockholms skolor*. 1990: 2. Stockholm.

Reinans, S. E. (1996) Den finländska befolkningen i Sverige - en statistisk- demografisk beskrivning. *Finnarnas historia i Sverige 3. Tiden efter 1945* (pp. 63–104). Helsingfors.

Saha, S. K. (1996) Literacy and development in South Asia. *Contemporary South Asia* 5 (3), 263–288.

SCB (1997) *Statistics of Sweden*. Stockholm.

SFS (1984) *Svensk författningssamling*. Stockholm: Fritzes.

SIF (1988) *Svensk Invandrar och Flyktingpolitik*. Arbetsmarknadsdepartementet. Stockholm.

SIV (1996a) = *Romer i Sverige. Situationsbeskrivning. Arbetsgruppen SIV- Nordiska Zigenarrådet*. Statens Invandrarverk. Nordiska Zigenarrådet.

SIV (1996b) *Situationsbeskrivning. Vuxna invandrares kunskaper i svenska och svenskundervisning för invandrare*. Statens invandrarverk.

Sjölund, J. (ed.) (1995) *Från skogsfinnar till datafreaks!* Utvärderingsrapport. PUFF-projektet 1986–1995. Hallstahammar.

SK (1994) *Levnadsförhållanden i Sveriges kommuner*. Svenska Kommunförbundet. Stockholm.

Skolverket (1996a) *Pedagogisk utvecklingsverksamhet för finskspråkiga elever*. Skolverkets rapport 111. Stockholm: National Agency for Education.

Skolverket (1996b) *Beskrivande data om skolverksamheten*. Skolverkets rapport nr 107. Stockholm: National Agency for Education.

Skolverket (1997) *Barn mellan arv och framtid*. Skolverket. Dnr 97:810. Stockholm: National Agency for Education.

Slunga, N. (1965) *Staten och den finskspråkiga befolkningen i Norrbotten*. Tornedalica 3. Luleå.

Sörlin, S. (1994) *De lärdas republik. Om vetenskapens internationella tendenser*. Malmö: Liber-Hermods.

SOU (1921) *Betänkande och förslag rörande folkskoleväsendet i de finsktalande delarna av Norrbottens län*. Avg. den 25/11 1921. Stockholm.

SOU (1996) *Krock eller möte. Om den mångkulturella skolan. Delbetänkande av Skolkommittén*. 1996: 143. Utbildningsdepartementet. Stockholm.

SOU (1997a) *Skolfrågor - Om skola i en ny tid. Slutbetänkande av Skolkommittén*. 1997: 121. Utbildningsdepartementet. Stockholm.

SOU (1997b) *Steg mot en minoritetspolitik. Europarådets konvention om historiska minoritetsspråk. Betänkande av Minoritetsspråkkommittén*. 1997: 192. Jordbruksdepartementet. Stockholm.

SOU (1997c) *Steg mot en minoritetspolitik. Europarådets konvention för skydd av nationella minoriteter. Betänkande av Minoritetsspråkkommittén*. 1997: 193. Jordbruksdepartementet. Stockholm.

SOU (1999) *Samerna - ett ursprungsfolk i Sverige - Frågan om Sveriges anslutning till ILO:s konvention nr 169. Betänkande av utredningen om ILO- konvention nr 169.* 1999: 25. Jordbruksdepartementet. Stockholm.

Spiliopoulou, A. (1995) De nordiska ländernas behandling av den europeiska språkstadgan. *Minoritetsspråk i Norden. En rapport från seminariet Tala eller tiga i Norden* (pp. 28–41). Mariehamn.

Stolt, B. (1994) *Martin Luther Människohjärtat och Bibeln.* Stockholm: Verbum.

Street, B.V. (ed.) (1995) *Cross-cultural Approaches to Literacy.* Cambridge: Cambridge University Press.

Svenska Institutet (SI) (1997/98) *Lärarförteckning. Svenskundervisning vid universitet och högskolor i utlandet.* Stockholm: Swedish Institute.

Svensson, L. (1981) *Ett fall av språkvård under 1600-talet.* Lundastudier i nordisk språkvetenskap. Lund.

Svonni, M. (1993) *Samiska skolbarns samiska.* Umeå: Umeå University.

Svonni, M. (1996) Skolor och undervisning för en inhemsk minoritet. In K. Hyltenstam (ed.) *Tvåspråkighet med förhinder? Invandrar- och tvåspråkighetsundervisning i Sverige* (pp. 148–186). Lund: Studentlitteratur.

Tarkiainen, K. (1990) *Finnarnas historia i Sverige 1.* SHS: Helsinki.

Tarkiainen, K. (1996) *Sverigefinska infrastrukturer. Finnarnas historia i Sverige 3. Tiden efter 1945* (pp. 143–184). Helsingfors.

Teleman, U. and Westman, M. (1997) Behöver Sverige en nationell språkpolitik? In S. Löland (ed.) *Språk i Norden. Sprog i Norden* (pp.5–22). Utgiven av nordiskt språkråd. Oslo: Novus Förlag.

Temple, J. and Johnson, P.A. (1998) Social capability and economic growth. *Quarterly Journal of Economics* 113 (3), 965–991.

Tenerz, H. (1963) *Folkupplysningsarbetet i Norrbottens finnbygd under förra hälften av 1900-talet jämte språkdebatten.* Stockholm: Seelig.

Tenerz, H. (1966) *Språkundervisningsproblemen i de finsktalande delarna av Norrbottens län.* Lund: CWK Gleerup.

Tengström, E. (1973) *Latinet i Sverige.* Stockholm: Bonniers.

Thelander, M. (1996) Från dialekt till sociolekt. In L. Moberg and M. Westman (eds) *Svenskan i tusen år* (pp. 163–181). Stockholm: Norstedts.

Tingbjörn, G. (1988) Active bilingualism – the Swedish goal for immigrant children's language instruction. In T. Skutnabb-Kangas and J. Cummins (eds) *Minority Education: From Shame to Struggle* (pp. 103–126). Clevedon: Multilingual Matters.

Tornedalica (1989) *Svensk lag och rätt i finskspråkig bygd.* Luleå: Tornedalica 46.

TNC Publikationsförteckning (1997) Stockholm: TNC.

Vahtola, J. (1980) Tornionjoki- ja Kemijokilaakson asutuksen synty. Nimistötieteellinen ja historiallinen tutkimus. *Studia historica septentrionalia 3.* Rovaniemi.

Valtonen, P. (1979) Trends in Romani Finnish. *International Journal of the Sociology of Language* 19, 121–124.

Vipåtv (1998) *Interntidning för Sveriges Television.* No 4. Stockholm.

Virta, E. (1994) *Tvåspråkighet, tänkande och identitet.* Studier av finska barn i Sverige och Finland. Del 1 Sammanfattning. Psykologiska institutionen. Stockholms universitet.

Wande, E. (1984) Two Finnish minorities in Sweden. *Journal of Multilingual and Multicultural Development* 5, 225–242.

Weber, M. (1958) *The Protestant Ethic and the Spirit of Capitalism.* New York: Charles Scribner.

Wikström, L. (1998) Rapport till SFRV-styrelsen 98 01 29 om Svenska Kyrkans Samiska Råd (Unpublished report). Svenska Kyrkans Samiska Råd. Uppsala.

Wingstedt, M. (1998) *Language Ideologies and Minority Language Policies in Sweden.* Stockholm: Center for Research on Bilingualism, Stockholm University.

Winsa, B. (1997) Från ett Vi till ett Vi och Dom Torne älv som kulturgräns. In B. Winsa and O. Korhonen (eds) *Språkliga och kulturella gränser i Nordskandinavien. Två uppsatser. Kulturens frontlinjer* (pp. 5–52). Skrifter från 'Kulturgräns Norr' 7. Umeå Universitet.

Winsa, B. (1998) *Language Attitudes and Social Identity. Oppression and Revival of a Minority Language in Sweden.* Canberra: Applied Linguistics Association of Australia.

Winsa, B. (forthcoming a) The socioeconomic status of the Tornedalians. In F. Grin and A. Price (eds) *Minority Languages and Regional Economics*. Stockholm: Stockholm University.

Winsa, B. (forthcoming b). *Giftermål över språk- och kulturgränser* [Interlingual Marriages in the Torne Valley]. Umeå University.

Wollin, L. (1996) Munklatin och riddarsvenskan. In L. Moberg and M. Westman (eds) *Svenskan i tusen år* (pp. 11–30). Stockholm: Norstedts.

Biographical Notes on Contributors

Sirkku Latomaa is Senior Lecturer in the School of Modern Languages and Translation Studies at the University of Tampere. Since 1990, she has taught Finnish as a second language (FSL) in several educational institutions in Finland. She has also worked as a visiting lecturer in Finnish language and culture at the University of Washington, Seattle, (1996–1998) and at the Moscow State University (2003–2004). Her research focuses on multilingualism among language minorities in Finland: language maintenance, second language learning, language attitudes, and language proficiency assessment. At the beginning of the 1990s, she worked in a Nordic research project intended to register the present language situation of new linguistic minorities and to investigate the future possibilities for continued usage and survival of minority languages in the Nordic region. Later, commissioned by the National Board of Education, she studied the effects of one year of language training on the proficiency level in Finnish among adult immigrants. In addition, she has contributed to an overview and a bibliography of the research on FSL. During the past decade, she has been involved with the development of teacher training programmes of FSL, and in 2001–2003 she was a member of two working groups (immigrant minority languages, Finnish as a second language) in the Finnish National Board of Education revising the national curricula for basic education (grades 1–9) and upper secondary education. Currently, she is a member of the ECML funded project VALEUR (Valuing All Languages in Europe), investigating provision for community languages across member states of the Council of Europe. Since 2002, she has worked as an editor of *Virittäjä*, the journal of the Society for the Study of Finnish (Kotikielen Seura).

Péter Medgyes has had a varied career as a school teacher, teacher trainer, textbook writer, researcher, and educational policy maker. He was founding Director of the Centre for English Teacher Training at Eötvös Loránd University, Budapest, and Vice Rector of his university. As a visiting fellow, he spent long periods of time at the University of Southern California and Lancaster University. Professor Medgyes has written numerous professional books and articles, including *Changing Perspectives in Teacher Education* (Heinemann 1996; co-edited with Angi Malderez), *The Language Teacher* (Corvina, 1997), *The Non-native Teacher* (Hueber Verlag, 1999; Second Edition), and *Laughing Matters* (Cambridge University Press, 2002). He is a regular keynote speaker at international conferences, and is on the editorial board of *ELT Journal* (Oxford University Press), *Language Teaching* (Cambridge University Press), and *Language and Education* (Multilingual Matters). Professor Medgyes has been awarded several titles, including the *Duke of Edinburgh Book Prize* (1995), the *Gold Medal of the President of Hungary* (1998), *Honorary Doctor of the State University of New York* (1998), and *Honorary Commander of the Order of the British Empire* (1999). At present, he is Deputy State Secretary responsible for international relations in the Hungarian Ministry of Education.

Katalin Miklósy teaches ELT methodology at the Centre for English Teacher Training of Eötvös Loránd University, Budapest. Since 1989, she has been a part-time lecturer in the California-Wisconsin Education Abroad Program in

Hungary, where her duties include teaching Hungarian as a foreign language and Hungarian cultural studies, as well as designing curricula for the program. Between 1995 and 1997 she worked at the Center for Hungarian Studies of Rutgers University, New Jersey. Her primary research interest lies in language shift and the language use of Hungarian minorities.

Pirkko Nuolijärvi is professor and director of the Research Institute for the Languages of Finland in Helsinki where she has been since 1998. She obtained her PhD in Finnish at the University of Helsinki in 1986. From 1986 to 1987 she worked as a lecturer in Finnish at the University of Uppsala in Sweden and, from 1987 to 1988, as a professor of Finnish at the University of Helsinki. Between 1989 and 1998 she was professor of Finnish and communication at the Helsinki School of Economics and Business Administration. Her research focuses on Finnish variation, institutional interaction and language policy. She has studied the language of those persons who have moved from the countryside to Helsinki, the immigrant language situation in Finland as well as Finnish language variation in the public sphere in several Finnish and Nordic projects. She has published several books and numerous articles in sociolinguistics; she has also written about language policy and language planning. She has been a member of many scientific committees of experts in Finland and outside the country as well. From 1999 to 2001 she was a member of the committee working toward a new Language Act for Finland. She has visited many universities and institutes outside Finland. In 2000, she was awarded the Finnish Cultural Foundation prize for her studies of spoken language.

John Birger Winsa (b. 1955), is Associate Professor at Department of Finnish, Stockholm University, Sweden. He has published more than 30 articles in refereed journals and chapters in books and 4 monographs on language sociology, social capital and cultural development, interlingual marriages, cultural borders, language and policy planning and a lexicon of Meänkieli (Tornedalen Finnish). As the President of the Swedish Bureau for Lesser Used Languages (2002-) he represents the five national minority languages in Sweden: Saami, Meänkieli, Finnish, Romany Chib and Yiddish in international fora for minority languages. He is currently doing research on social representativity of minority language speakers as elected representatives in labour unions and political parties. Winsa is also editing a volume on *Language Emancipation and Cultural Development* – the outcome of the ICML-IX conference he organised in Kiruna in 2003.